THE WORKS OF
HENRY VAUGHAN

EDITED BY

L. C. MARTIN

SECOND EDITION

OXFORD
AT THE CLARENDON PRESS

Oxford University Press, Ely House, London W.1

GLASGOW   NEW YORK   TORONTO   MELBOURNE   WELLINGTON
CAPE TOWN   SALISBURY   IBADAN   NAIROBI   LUSAKA   ADDIS ABABA
BOMBAY   CALCUTTA   MADRAS   KARACHI   LAHORE   DACCA
KUALA LUMPUR   HONG KONG   TOKYO

5 8 - 1 1 9 8

FIRST EDITION 1914
SECOND EDITION 1957

REPRINTED LITHOGRAPHICALLY IN GREAT BRITAIN
AT THE UNIVERSITY PRESS, OXFORD
BY VIVIAN RIDLER
PRINTER TO THE UNIVERSITY

PREFACE.

HENRY VAUGHAN'S works were first included in the Oxford English Texts in 1915, with date of the previous year. As now revised and expanded, the edition owes much to the many scholars who have since added to what was known about the poet and his writings. It is specially indebted to the late Canon F. E. Hutchinson for his careful biography of Vaughan published by the Clarendon Press in 1947, and through him to the two ladies, Louisa Imogen Guiney and Gwenllian E. F. Morgan, on whose combined investigations the biography largely depends, and who did not live to write their own projected volume. The outline of Vaughan's life given for convenience in the present introduction is based on Canon Hutchinson's book, which is also frequently referred to in the Commentary.

Besides their collections for a life of Vaughan Miss Guiney and Miss Morgan left a number of notes on the poems, textual, illustrative, and explanatory, some of them throwing fresh light on the poet's reading and literary relationships. The notes were in disorder but were arranged by Canon Hutchinson, who transcribed those which seemed to be of most value, sometimes adding his own observations. The resulting 'Commentary on the Poems of Henry Vaughan' was not printed, but a copy of the typescript can be seen in the National Library of Wales, where the notes themselves were also deposited. A second copy, which has come to me through the kindness of Mrs. Hutchinson and Miss Lucy Hutchinson, is with their permission being presented to the Bodleian Library. A selection from this material has been utilized in the present Commentary, together with some notes derived from Canon Hutchinson's copy of the 1914 edition, now in the English Library at the Examination Schools, Oxford. Information from these sources is acknowledged at the relevant places, but it must be added that some of the points have been made independently by other scholars, e.g. by Miss Elizabeth Holmes, author of *Henry Vaughan and the Hermetic Philosophy* (1932). The work of Vaughan scholars down to the end of 1945 is listed in *A Comprehensive Bibliography of Henry Vaughan*, by A. Marilla (University of Alabama Press, 1948).

The Commentary of 1914 has been a good deal enlarged. Errors have been corrected and many of the notes recast. Others remain as before, especially those which illustrate the poet's echoings of other writers or the freedom of his translations. It is often of great interest to know when he leaves his originals altogether to write what his own impulses dictate. The notes do not claim to be complete in this respect, but as a rule only record longer or more revealing departures from less accessible originals. In general, no attempt is made, where Vaughan is translating, to explain the allusions or identify quotations in the original texts. It also seemed unnecessary to give chapter and verse for all Vaughan's citations and reminiscences of the Bible. Some of the less obvious ones, however, have been pointed out, as well as some which might be missed through their close welding into the poet's own creative thought. Several of the obscurities in the poems have had to be left unexplained.

The text is based on the early editions. Long 'ſ' and such purely typographical devices as 'VV' for 'W' have been discarded ; errors of spacing, wrong founts, and turned letters have been silently corrected ; other departures from the early texts are recorded in the footnotes. The text as it was presented in 1914 has been amended in a few places and some additional footnotes have been supplied. The outstanding improvement, however, is that all Vaughan's known published works are now brought together for the first time, through the recovery of *The Chymists Key*. This brief treatise, translated from the Latin of Heinrich Nolle, was printed in 1657 but has had no second edition until

now. Under its original title, *De Generatione*, it was claimed
by Vaughan in his letter to Aubrey of 15 June 1673 (see
p. 688), but as this letter was not in print until 1915 and
as Vaughan's name does not appear on the title-page of
the translation, or anywhere else in the book, his authorship was long unrecognized. Moreover, until recently it was
even questionable whether any copies had survived into the
twentieth century. On this subject see pp. xxv and 753.

The order in which Vaughan's works are printed is that
of the 1914 edition as far as p. 592. *The Chymists Key* is
then inserted and runs from p. 593 to p. 612. References
to pp. 593–674 of the 1914 edition, e.g. in Hutchinson's
Life, can be adapted to the present edition by adding 20 to
the page-number. The letters in Appendix II are increased
in number from six to nine, the additions being Nos. VI,
VIII, and IX.

I wish again to record my obligations to all those who
gave me the benefit of their personal advice and help when
the earlier edition was taking shape, especially Professors
E. Bensly, G. S. Gordon, and D. Nichol Smith, Sir John
Ballinger, Sir James Murray, and Dr. Percy Simpson; and
I now add the names of Canon F. E. Hutchinson, Miss
Elizabeth Holmes, Mr. R. F. Hill, Mr. J. B. Leishman, and
Dorothy Martin, who have helped me more recently. I am
under a special debt also to the staff of the British Museum,
the Bodleian Library, the Libraries of Birmingham University, Edinburgh University, Christ Church, Oxford, and
the Royal Society of Medicine, the National Library of
Wales, and the English Library, Examination Schools,
Oxford; and I gratefully acknowledge the care and skill
with which the members of the Clarendon Press staff have
checked and improved my work.

L. C. M.

CONTENTS.

Contents. ix

Contents.

SILEX SCINTILLANS

Contents. xi

xii *Contents.*

Contents.

INTRODUCTION.

I. LIFE AND STANDING.

HENRY VAUGHAN and his twin brother Thomas were born in 1621 or early in 1622. Henry was the elder. They were the sons of Thomas and Denise Vaughan of Trenewydd or Newton, a small house and estate in the parish of Llansantffread, Breconshire, inherited by Denise from her father, David Morgan. Thomas Vaughan senior, whose home was at Tretower Court, a few miles away, moved to Newton on his marriage in 1611. The fact that Henry Vaughan, of wholly Welsh extraction, was to live at Newton for much the greater part of his life was not without effects upon his poetry, which was clearly influenced not only by the impressive scenery of his birthplace but by some distinctively Welsh habits of thought, sentiment, and expression. He liked to call himself 'Silurist', after the local British tribe whom Tacitus called 'Silures'.

The two boys received their early formal education from a neighbouring clergyman, Matthew Herbert, incumbent of Llangattock (see pp. 32 and 93); and both, it seems, went to Jesus College, Oxford, though there is record only of Thomas's admission (4 May 1638), matriculation (14 Dec. 1638), and residence. Henry's own statement on this, sent to Aubrey in 1673 (see p. 687), was that 'I stayed not at Oxford to take any degree, butt was sent to London, beinge then designed by my father for the study of the Law, wch the sudden eruption of our late civil warres wholie frustrated. my brother continued there for ten or 12 yeares'. According to *Athenae Oxonienses* (1721) Henry spent 'two Years or more in Logicals under a noted Tutor' at Oxford, so

B

that presumably he went to London in the latter part of 1640, remaining there until the outbreak of the war in 1642. Aubrey records that 'he was a clarke sometime to Judge Sir Marmaduke Lloyd', Chief Justice of the Brecon circuit; and this must have been before the end of 1645, when Lloyd, as a Royalist combatant, was taken prisoner at Hereford and dismissed from his office.

From allusions in Vaughan's poems (e.g. pp. 50–51) it appears that he too was for a time on military service for the king, probably not after 1646, when the Puritan régime was established in South Wales. It was presumably about this time that he married Catherine Wise, of Coleshill, Warwickshire, and settled at Newton, where his father lived on until 1658. Henry's first book, *Poems, With the tenth Satyre of Iuvenal Englished*, is dated 1646.

He soon had another volume ready, for at the end of 1647 he wrote the Dedication subsequently prefixed to *Olor Iscanus*, 1651; but the material first prepared was withdrawn, and it can be guessed that the reason for this was in part political, some of the pieces having probably shown too clearly, in a worsening situation, where the writer's sympathies lay. A stronger motive may have been his growing seriousness of mind, which later (in the Preface to *Silex Scintillans*, the second edition, 1655) led him to reprobate all 'idle books'. He there connected this development with his reading of George Herbert. It is likely, however, that the political upheavals of the later 1640's had much to do with it. He was also greatly affected by the death, in July 1648, of his younger and much beloved brother, William. But the poems which in 1647 he intended to publish were apparently not all lost; for *Olor Iscanus* contains some that were written before, as well as some written after, that year. It was 'Published by a Friend', ostensibly, though perhaps not entirely, without the poet's consent (see p. 36). It also contains four prose-translations serious in character. Meanwhile *Silex Scintillans* in its earlier and shorter form had appeared in 1650.

Thomas Vaughan, who was ordained and held the living

of Llansantffread for a short time until he was evicted from it in 1650, produced his theosophical and quasi-scientific works between 1650 and 1655 (the preface to the earliest is dated 1648). These were considerably indebted to the Hermetic traditions, and Henry evidently shared this kind of interest, for some of his ideas and images are derived directly or indirectly from the Hermetic writings. Henry also translated two short treatises in which Hermetic doctrine, in its medical aspects, was expounded. These were published as *Hermetical Physick*, 1655, and *The Chymists Key*, 1657. Other works of the 1650's were (1) *The Mount of Olives: Or, Solitary Devotions*, 1652 ; (2) *Flores Solitudinis*, consisting of three prose-translations and a biography of St. Paulinus of Nola, 1654 ; and (3) *Silex Scintillans* (enlarged), 1655. *Thalia Rediviva* was still to come, in 1678, having been mentioned as a forthcoming work by Vaughan himself five years before (see p. 688). This collection of poems, early and later, was not manifestly published with the poet's approval, as his name does not appear on the title-page. The volume includes ' Some Learned Remains of the Eminent Eugenius Philalethes ', i.e. Thomas Vaughan. One of Henry's pieces, the elegy ' Daphnis ', plainly refers to Thomas Vaughan's death, which took place in 1666 ; but the poem is likely to have been first written for a previous occasion, probably the death of William Vaughan in 1648.

When Henry began to practise as a doctor is unknown. The addition of ' M.D.' to his name is not found in references earlier than 1677, but already in 1673 he told Aubrey that he had been in practice for many years (see p. 688). The title may have been complimentary, as no evidence has yet come to light that he obtained the degree from a British or foreign University or from the Archbishop of Canterbury.

At some time in or near to 1653 his wife Catherine died ; and he married her sister Elizabeth about 1655. There were four children by each marriage. The last few years of Henry's life were much beclouded by lawsuits, two of which were brought against him by children of the first marriage. One of the claims had the effect in January 1688/9 of inducing him to make over his tenure of the Newton property to his elder son Thomas, who on his side was to make provision for his father and stepmother and their children. Henry and his wife were to remove to a cottage at Scethrog, which like Newton itself has since been demolished. Henry Vaughan died on April 23rd, St. George's Day, in 1695, and was buried in Llansantffread Churchyard, where the gravestone is still to be seen with the inscription: HENRICUS | VAUGHAN · SILURIS | M · D · OBIIT · AP · 23 · AÑO | SAL · 1695 · ÆTAT · SUÆ · 73 | [Arms] | QUOD IN SEPULCHRUM | VOLUIT | SERVUS INUTILIS: | PECCATOR MAXIMUS | HIC IACEO | + | GLORIA MISERERE · |

Little notice appears to have been taken of Vaughan's works during his lifetime. None of them reached a genuine second edition. He was briefly mentioned in Edward Phillips's *Theatrum Poetarum* (1675). Wood's *Historia et Antiquitates Universitatis Oxoniensis* (1674) has a short description of Henry and Thomas together. There was no fuller account of Henry until the second edition of *Athenae Oxonienses* (1721). In the eighteenth century the only reference to him after 1721 is incidental to Headley's account of Davenant in *Select Beauties of Ancient English Poetry* (1787); and none of his works was reprinted. In 1801 stanzas 1, 2, and 4 of the verses 'To the best, and most accomplish'd Couple' (see p. 57) were included in Ellis's *Specimens of the Early English Poets* (iii, pp. 304–5). Campbell's *Specimens* (1819), iv, pp. 347–51, gave stanzas from 'Rules and Lessons' and 'The Timber', and lines from 'The Rainbow' and 'The Wreath', with the remark that 'He is one of the harshest even of the inferior order of conceit ; but he has some few scattered thoughts that meet our eye amidst his harsh pages like wild flowers on a barren heath'. The *Retrospective Review*, iii, 1821, pp. 336–54, has an article on *Olor Iscanus*. Vaughan is noticed in R. A. Willmott's *Lives of the Sacred Poets*, First Series

(1834); and seven lyrics are printed in Edward Farr's *Gems of Sacred Poetry* (? 1841). In 1847 *Silex Scintillans* with the religious verse in *Thalia Rediviva* was published under the editorship of the Reverend H. F. Lyte, and Vaughan's *Complete Works*, edited by the Reverend A. B. Grosart, appeared in 1871.

Vaughan gained a good deal of ground in the latter part of the nineteenth century, being variously admired as a Royalist Anglo-Catholic, a writer of devotional or 'mystical' verse, and a precursor of Wordsworth, who, it was supposed, might have had 'The Retreat' in mind when writing his Immortality Ode. It was never proved, however, that Wordsworth was acquainted with Vaughan's poetry, and the peculiar phase of Neoplatonic doctrine incorporated in the Ode could undoubtedly have reached Wordsworth through other channels. In the last fifty years more attention has been paid to the differences than to the resemblances between the two poets, to the qualities and interests which Vaughan shared, more or less, with his contemporaries, and to the circumstances which may have encouraged him to write as he did. 'I honour the truth where ever I find it', he once remarked (p. 548), 'whether in an old, or new Booke'; and scholars have shown how this impartiality appears on the one hand in his indebtedness to various kinds of theological and philosophical tradition and on the other in his willingness to learn by imitation from such recent writers as Donne, George Herbert, Habington, Randolph, and Owen Felltham. But nothing that he inherited or borrowed was as important as his own gift of fresh creativeness, the vein of authentic poetry which could assert itself even when he was translating Latin prose and which at its best shone out in some of the most arresting lyrical verse in the English language. The value of Vaughan's contribution to English literature has yet to be fully assessed. He has gained most credit by the quiet intensity of his feeling, by his gift of spiritual vision, and by his subtle employment of imagery and symbolism. Less notice has been taken of his verbal artistry, the flexible rhythms, the memorable phrasing, the effective use of speech idioms. But his merits no longer need to be underlined. A century of recognition has sufficiently answered two centuries of neglect; and Vaughan now stands securely among the more eminent writers of his day.

II. THE EARLY EDITIONS.

(The original title-pages are reproduced literatim without correction of misprints. The copy-text for each work is that which is given first in the mention of copies used.)

1. *Poems, with the tenth Satyre of Iuvenal*, 1646.

Registered 15 September 1646. Roxburghe Club, i, 245.
Title-pages. See pp. 1 and 17.
Collation. 8°: $\S^4$ ($-\S1$) A^8 ($-$A1) B–E^8 F^4. $\$1$–4. $\S4$, F4 not signed.
Pages. [6] [2] 3–87.
Contents. $\S1$ missing (blank?), $\S2^r$ title, $\S2^v$ blank, $\S3^r$–$\S4^v$ Preface, A1 missing (blank?), A2^r–C6^v Poems, C7^r Juvenal title, C7^v blank, C8^r–F4^r Juvenal translation.
Running-titles. To all Ingenious (on $\S3^v$) | Lovers of Poœsie (on $\S4^r$). To all Ingenious Lovers, &c. (on $\S4^v$). No other running titles.
Copies used. British Museum C. 56. b. 16; two other British Museum copies.
Note. Manuscript alterations in an early hand are found in the B.M. copy C. 56. b. 16, and are given in the footnotes.

2. *Silex Scintillans*, 1650.

Registered 28 March 1650. Roxburghe Club, i, 341.
Title-page. See plate facing p. 386.
Collation. 8°: A–G^8 ($-$G8). $\$1$–4. A4 not signed.
Pages. [6] 7–110.
Contents. A1^r blank, A1^v *Authoris* (*de se*) *Emblema*, A2^r title A2^v blank, A3^r dedication, A3^v blank, A4^r–G7^v poems, G8 missing, (blank?).
Running-titles. *Silex Scintillans* (on versos A4–G7) | *Or Sacred Poems.* (on rectos A5–G7). A8^v has *Or Sacred Poems.*
Copies used. British Museum 238. b. 8; Bodleian Library; National Library of Wales; also copies of *Silex Scintillans*, 1655, in which, save for two cancelled leaves, the unsold sheets of 1650 were incorporated as 'Part I'. The two parts are again printed together in the present edition.
Note. In Bodleian copy 'A2' precedes 'A1'.

3. *Olor Iscanus*, 1651.

Registered 28 April 1651. Roxburghe Club, i, 365.

Title-pages. (Engraved) facing p. 32 ; (printed) pp. 33, 95, 109, 115, 123.

Collation. 8ᵘ : A–L⁸. Separate leaf of Errata. $1–4. A1, A2, A3 not signed.

Pages. [*16*] 1–158. 65-67, 96-98, 107-108, 124-126 not paged.

Contents. A1ʳ blank, A1ᵛ *Ad Posteros*, A2ʳ engraved title, A2ᵛ blank, A3ʳ printed title, A3ᵛ two lines of Virgil, A4ʳ–A5ᵛ dedication, A6ʳ–A6ᵛ Publisher to Reader, A7ʳ–A8ᵛ commendatory verse, B1ʳ– E8ᵛ *Olor Iscanus*, F1ʳ title of *Of the Benefit, &c.*, F1ᵛ blank, F2ʳ–G8ʳ translation, G8ᵛ blank, H1ʳ title of *Of the Diseases, &c.* (Plutarch), H1ᵛ blank, H2ʳ–H5ᵛ translation, H6ʳ title of *Of the Diseases, &c.* (Maximus Tyrius), H6ᵛ blank, H7ʳ–I6ʳ translation, I6ᵛ blank, I7ʳ title of *The Praise, &c.*, I7ᵛ blank, I8ʳ–L7ᵛ translation, L8ʳ missing (blank ?), Errata on additional leaf.

Running-titles. *The Epistle* (on A4ᵛ) | *Dedicatory.* (on A5ʳ) *The Epistle, &c.* (on A5ᵛ) The Publisher to the Reader. (on A6ᵛ) *Olor Iscanus.* (B1ʳ–E8ᵛ). No other running-titles.

Copies used. Bodleian Library Art. 8° M. 5. BS and Antiq. f. E. 4 ; British Museum ; Dyce Collection, South Kensington ; National Library of Wales.

Notes. 'A2' sometimes precedes 'A1'. The errata-list is not found in all copies. One of the errors ('faith' for 'fate', p. 76, l. 5 below) is corrected in the text of the Dyce copy, which contains the list, and the British Museum copy, which omits it.

4. *The Mount of Olives*, 1652.

Registered 16 December 1651. Roxburghe Club, i, 386.

Title-pages. See pp. 137 and 191.

Collation. 12° : A¹²(–A1) B–I¹²(–I12). $1–5. A5, E5 not signed, B5 missigned R5.

Pages. [*22*] 1–189. 132, 134 not paged. 72 paged 48.

Contents. A1 missing (blank ?), A2ʳ title, A2ᵛ blank, A3ʳ–A6ʳ dedication, A6ᵛ blank, A7ʳ–A10ʳ To the Reader, A10ᵛ blank, A11ʳ– A12ʳ Table, A12ᵛ crown ornament, B1ʳ–G6ʳ Devotions, G6ᵛ blank, G7ʳ title of *Man in Glory*, G7ᵛ blank, G8ʳ–G9ʳ *To the Reader*, G9ᵛ poem, G10ʳ–G10ᵛ preliminary texts, G11ʳ–I10ʳ translation, I10ᵛ–I11ʳ publisher's list, I12 missing (blank ?).

Running-titles. *The Epistle* (on versos A3–5) | *Dedicatory.* (on rectos A4–6) To the Reader. (A7ᵛ–10ʳ) and the TABLE. (A11ᵛ–A12ʳ) *The Mount of Olives,* (on versos B–G5) | *or Solitary Devotions.* (on rectos B2–G6) *To the Reader.* (G8ʳ–G9ʳ) *Man in Glory.* (G10ʳ–I10ʳ).

Copies used. Bodleian Library I. g. 124 ; British Museum.

5. *Flores Solitudinis*, 1654.

Registered 15 September 1653. Roxburghe Club, i, 430.

Title-pages. See pp 211, 219, 311, and 337.

Collation. 12° : π² A⁴ 2π⁴ B–I¹² ²A–²G¹²(–G12). $1–5. A1 signed.

A2, 3, 4 C5 D5 F3 H5 ^{2}A1, 3, 4, 5 ^{2}C4, 5 ^{2}E5 not signed. C4
missigned B4. The order $\pi^2 A^4 2\pi^4$ is that of the Bodleian copy. See
Note.

Pages. [*20*] 1–191 [*2*] 3–165.

Contents. $\pi 1^r$ general title, $\pi 1^v$ blank, $\pi 2^r$ Nieremberg title, $\pi 2^v$
blank, A1^r–A4^r dedication to Sir Charles Egerton, A4^v blank, $2\pi 1$ recto
and verso 'To the onely true, &c.', $2\pi 2^r$–$2\pi 4^v$ To the Reader: B1^r–G1^r
Of Temperance, G1^v–I12^r *Of Life and Death*, I12^v blank, ^{2}A1^r title of
The World Contemned, ^{2}A1^v blank, ^{2}A2^r–^{2}A2^v Advertisement, ^{2}A3^r–
^{2}C4^r text of *The World Contemned*, ^{2}C4^v blank, ^{2}C5^r title of *Primitive
Holiness*, ^{2}C5^v blank, ^{2}C6^r–^{2}C6^v To the Reader, ^{2}C7^r–^{2}G8^r text of
Primitive Holiness, ^{2}G8^v blank, ^{2}G9^r–^{2}G11^r poem, ^{2}G12 missing
(blank ?).

Running-titles. The Epistle Dedicatory. (A1^v–A4^r) To the Reader.
($2\pi 2^v$–$2\pi 4^v$). No other running-titles.

Copies used. Bodleian Library Th. 8° F. 2. BS; British Museum;
National Library of Wales; Christ Church, Oxford; New York
Public Library.

Note. The order of the preliminary sections—Nieremberg title,
Egerton dedication, 'To the onely true', To the Reader—varies in
different copies. The Nieremberg title is correctly placed at the end
of the preliminaries as a wrap-around A^4, $2\pi^4$.

6. *Silex Scintillans*, 1655.

Registered 20 March 1654/5. Roxburghe Club, i, 463.

Title-page. See p. 387.

Collation. 8°: A^4 (–A1) B^8 ^{X}A^8 (–^{X}A1, 2, 3) ^{X}B^8 ($\pm$ ^{X}B2, 3) ^{X}C–^{X}G^8
(–^{X}G8) C–G^8 H^4. $1–4. A4 not signed.

Pages. [*6*] 7–110, 1–84.

Contents. A1 missing (blank ?), A2^r title, A2^v blank, A3^r–B4^r Preface, B4^v blank, B5^r–B8^r prefatory texts and dedication, B8^v prefatory
poem, ^{X}A4^r–^{X}G7^v Part I (unsold sheets from 1650 edition, except B2
and B3), C1^r–H2^v Part II, H3^r–H4^v Table.

Running-titles. The Preface. (A3^v–B4^r) The Dedication (B7^r–B8^r)
Silex Scintillans (on versos ^{X}A4–^{X}G7) | *Or Sacred Poems.* (on rectos
^{X}A5–^{X}G7). A8^v has *Or Sacred Poems.* *Silex Scintillans,* (on versos
C1–H1) *Or Sacred Poems.* (on rectos C2–H2) *Silex Scintillans, or
Sacred Poems.* (on H2^v). B3^r misprints *Of* for *Or.*

Copies used. British Museum 11626. b. 52; National Library of
Wales.

Notes. This volume comprises a reissue of the edition of 1650, save
for the cancels B2 and B3, together with new introductory matter and
a second part (beginning on p. 481 below). The cancel leaves, represented by p. 407, l. 75–p. 410, l. 22 in the present edition, introduce
alterations of sense and phrase as well as of spelling and punctuation.
The edition of 1655 is the basis of the present text; but as the two
leaves in question were reprinted somewhat carelessly, the readings of
1650 have been preferred in a few places. The two parts are printed
together in the present edition, as in 1655.

Silex Scintillans, 1655, was registered two months later than *Hermetical Physick*, 1655. *Silex Scintillans*, however, more appropriately
follows *Flores Solitudinis*, and *Hermetical Physick* more appropriately
precedes *The Chymists Key.*

Introduction.

7. *Hermetical Physick,* 1655.

Registered 16 January 1654/5. Roxburghe Club, i, 468.
Title-page. See p. 547.
Collation. 12°: A⁴ B–F¹² G⁶ (− G6). \$1–5. A4 D3 G5 not signed.
A3 missigned A5. B4 missigned B7.
Pages. [*8*] 1–130.
Contents. A1ʳ title, A1ᵛ blank, A2ʳ–A4ʳ To the Reader, A4ᵛ ' Plautus ', B1ʳ–G5ᵛ translation.
Running-titles. *To the Reader.* (A2ᵛ–A4ʳ) *Hermetical Physick.* (D1ᵛ–G5ᵛ).
Copies used. British Museum E. 1714. (1); National Library of Wales.

8. *The Chymists Key,* 1657.

Not registered.
Title-page. See p. 593.
Collation. 24°: A⁶ B–C¹² D⁶ E². \$1–5. A4 E2 not signed.
Pages. [*12*] 1–63.
Contents. A1ʳ title, A1ᵛ blank, A2ʳ–A6ᵛ To the Reader, B1ʳ–B10ʳ The *Authour's* Epistle; B10ᵛ–C1ʳ *The Authour's Preface,* C1ʳ–D6ᵛ *Of the Generation, &c.,* E1ʳ–E2ʳ The Authour's Postscript, E2ᵛ blank.
Running-titles. To the READER. (A2ᵛ–A6ᵛ) *The Chymists Key.* (B1ᵛ–E2ʳ).
Copies used. Edinburgh University Library Dd. 10. 107, formerly *I. 33. 52; Christ Church, Oxford. The only other copy at present known is in the University Library at Harvard.

9. *Thalia Rediviva,* 1678.

'Licensed, *Roger L'Estrange.*' (On title-page.)
Title-page. See p. 613.
Collation. 8°: A–C⁸. \$1–4.
Pages. [*16*] 1–93.
Contents. A1ʳ title, A1ᵛ blank, A2ʳ–A3ᵛ dedication, A4ʳ To the Reader, A4ᵛ–A8ᵛ commendatory verses and 'To his Learned Friend', B1ʳ–F5ʳ other poems by H. V., F5ᵛ blank, F6ʳ title: Eugenii Philalethis . . . Vertumnus Et Cynthia, &c., F6ᵛ blank, F7ʳ–G7ʳ poems by Thomas V., G7ᵛ–G8ᵛ publisher's advertisement.
Running-titles. *The Epistle Dedicatory.* (A2ᵛ–A3ᵛ) *Choice Poems,* &c. (A8ᵛ) *Choice Poems* (on versos B1–G6) | *On several Occasions.* (on rectos B2–G7).
Copies used. Bodleian Library Antiq. f. E. 4; British Museum.
Note. Two or three manuscript alterations in an early hand are found in the Bodleian copy, and are given in the footnotes.

10. *Olor Iscanus,* 1679.

A reissue (not a reprint) of the edition of 1651. See No. 3. Copies seen (National Library of Wales; Cardiff Public Library) contain all the original misprints as well as the list of errata. The new title-page is reproduced on p. xxvi. Its verso does not carry the two lines from Virgil on A3ᵛ in *1651.*

OLOR ISCANVS.

A COLLECTION
Of fome SELECT
POEMS,

Together with thefe Tranflations following, *viz.*

1. Of the benefit wee may get by our *Enemies,*
2. Of the difeafes of the mind, and of the body. Both
written in *Greek*, by that great *Philofopher Plutarch.*
3. Of the difeafes of the mind, and of the body, and
which of them is most pernicious, written in *Greek* by
Maximus Tyrius.
4. Of the praife and happinefs of a Country Life;
written in *Spanifh* by *Antonio de Guevara* : Bifhop of
Carthagena.

All Englifhed by *H. Vaughan, Silurift.*

LONDON:

Printed, and are to be fold by *Peter Parker,*
at the *Leg* and *Star* in *Cornhil,* againft the
Royal Exchange, 1679.

III. SOME MODERN REPRINTS.

1. *The Sacred Poems and Private Ejaculations of Henry Vaughan with a Memoir by the Rev. H. F. Lyte* (William Pickering, 1847).

   This was the first edition of a complete work by Henry Vaughan to be published since the seventeenth century. It was reprinted in 1856 (Boston, U.S.A.), 1858, and 1883 (the last is the Aldine edition), and contains *Silex Scintillans* with the Pious Thoughts and Ejaculations from *Thalia Rediviva*. The text of 1847 is generally faithful to the original editions, but it embodies several unacknowledged attempts to improve Vaughan's work, and in the subsequent 'corrected' versions these were not all removed.

2. *The Works in Verse and Prose Complete of Henry Vaughan, Silurist, for the first time collected and edited . . . by the Rev. Alexander B. Grosart . . . in four volumes . . . 1871.* [The Fuller Worthies Library.]

   The usefulness of this edition is marred by a number of unnecessary emendations and by inadvertent mistakes, including the omission of several lines. The text is partially modernized.

3. *The Poems of Henry Vaughan, Silurist, edited by E. K. Chambers, with an introduction by H. C. Beeching . . . London: Lawrence & Bullen . . . 1896 &c.* [Two volumes.]

   The text is based on the original editions, but modernized. It contains a few unintentional departures from what Vaughan wrote, notably in *Olor Iscanus*, where the list of errata was not used.

4. *The Mount of Olives and Primitive Holiness set forth in the Life of Paulinus Bishop of Nola. By Henry Vaughan, Silurist. Edited by L. I. Guiney. London: Henry Frowde . . . 1902.*

   Many of the mistakes in Grosart's text were corrected in this modernized edition.

5. *Silex Scintillans by Henry Vaughan Silurist. With an introduction by W. A. Lewis Bettany. London: Blackie. 1905.*

IV. LIST OF ABBREVIATIONS.

A. *In the footnotes.*

The original editions are referred to by their dates; the above-mentioned reprints by the letters *L*, *G*, *C*, *Gu*, *B*, respectively. *M* indicates the present editor. Other sigla, in the separate volumes, are as follows:

In *Poems*, 1646, *MS.* = the alterations mentioned in the bibliographical note above.

In *Olor Iscanus*, *Er* = the list of errata. (See note above.)

In *Olor Iscanus*, *Ct* = *The Plays and Poems of William Cartwright*, 1651. (See note to p. 55 in Commentary, p. 709.)

In *Olor Iscanus*, *El. Opt.* = *Elementa Opticae*, by Thomas Powell. (See note to p. 93 in Commentary, p. 713.)

In *Flores Solitudinis*, *Vita* = *Vita Divi Paulini*. (See note to p. 337 in Commentary, p. 723.)

In *Silex Scintillans*, *WR* = *Witt's Recreations*. (See note to p. 434 in Commentary, p. 735.)

In *Thalia Rediviva*, *KP* = *The Poems of Katherine Philips*. (See note to pp. 617–18 in Commentary, p. 756.)

B. *In the Commentary.*

EB = notes by Edward Bensly.

GM = notes by Miss L. I. Guiney and Miss G. E. F. Morgan. (See p. iii.)

H = notes by F. E. Hutchinson. (See pp. iii–iv.)

Life = *Henry Vaughan, a Life and an Interpretation*, by F. E. Hutchinson, 1947.

In references to George Herbert *Works* = the edition by F. E. Hutchinson, *O.E.T.*, 1941.

POEMS,

WITH

The tenth SATYRE of

IUVENAL

ENGLISHED.

By *Henry Vaughan*, Gent.

——— *Tam nil, nullâ tibi vendo*
Illiade ——————

LONDON,
Printed for *G. Badger*, and are to be fold at his
fhop under Saint *Dunftans* Church in
Fleet-ftreet. 1 6 4 6.

To all Ingenious Lovers

OF

POESIE.

Gentlemen,

To you alone, whose more refined Spirits *out-wing these dull Times, and soare above the drudgerie of durty* Intelligence, *have I made sacred these* Fancies : *I know the yeares, and what course entertainment they affoord* Poetry. *If any shall question that* Courage *that durst send me abroad so late, and revell it thus in the* Dregs *of an Age, they have my silence : only,*

Languescente seculo, liceat ægrotari ;

My more calme Ambition, *amidst the common noise, hath thus exposed me to the World : You have here a* Flame, *bright only in its* 10 *owne* Innocence, *that kindles nothing but a generous* Thought ; *which though it may warme the Bloud, the fire at highest is but* Platonick, *and the* Commotion, *within these limits, excludes* Danger : *For the* Satyre, *it was of purpose borrowed, to feather some slower Houres ; And what you see here, is but the* Interest : *It is one of his, whose* Roman *Pen had as much true* Passion, *for the infirmities of that state, as we should have* Pitty, *to the distractions of our owne : Honest (I am sure) it is, and offensive cannot be, except it meet with such* Spirits *that will quarrell with* Antiquitie, *or purposely* Arraigne *themselves ; These indeed may thinke, that they have slept out so* 20 *many* Centuries *in this* Satyre, *and are now awaked ; which, had it been still* Latine, *perhaps their Nap had been Everlasting : But enough of these,—It is for you only that I have adventured thus far, and invaded the Presse with* Verse ; *to whose more noble* Indulgence, *I shall now leave it ; and so am gone.* ——

H. V.

To my Ingenuous
Friend, *R. W.*

When we are dead, and now, no more
Our harmles mirth, our wit, and score
Distracts the Towne; when all is spent
That the base niggard world hath lent
Thy purse, or mine; when the loath'd noise
Of Drawers, Prentises, and boyes
Hath left us, and the clam'rous barre
Items no pints i'th' Moone, or Starre;
When no calme whisp'rers wait the doores,
To fright us with forgotten scores;   10
And such aged, long bils carry,
As might start an Antiquary;
When the sad tumults of the Maze,
Arrests, suites, and the dreadfull face
Of Seargeants are not seene, and wee
No Lawyers Ruffes, or Gownes must fee:
When all these Mulcts are paid, and I
From thee, deare wit, must part, and dye;
Wee'le beg the world would be so kinde,
To give's one grave, as wee'de one minde;   20
There (as the wiser few suspect,
That spirits after death affect)
Our soules shall meet, and thence will they
(Freed from the tyranny of clay)
With equall wings, and ancient love
Into the Elysian fields remove,
Where in those blessed walkes they'le find,
More of thy Genius, and my mind:
    First, in the shade of his owne bayes,
Great *B E N* they'le see, whose sacred Layes,   30
The learned Ghosts admire, and throng,
To catch the subject of his Song.
Then *Randolph* in those holy Meades,
His Lovers, and *Amyntas* reads,

34 Lovers] Looers *1646*

Whilst his Nightingall close by,
Sings his, and her owne Elegie ;
From thence dismiss'd by subtill roades,
Through airie paths, and sad aboads ;
They'le come into the drowsie fields
Of Lethe, which such vertue yeelds,   40
That (if what Poets sing be true)
The streames all sorrow can subdue.
Here on a silent, shady greene,
The soules of Lovers oft are seene,
Who in their lifes unhappy space,
Were murther'd by some perjur'd face.
All these th' inchanted streames frequent,
To drowne their Cares, and discontent,
That th' inconstant, cruell sex
Might not in death their spirits vex :   50
   And here our soules bigge with delight
Of their new state will cease their flight :
And now the last thoughts will appeare,
They'le have of us, or any here ;
But on those flowry banks will stay,
And drinke all sense, and cares away.
   So they that did of these discusse,
Shall find their fables true in us.

Les Amours.

Tyrant farewell : This heart, the prize
And triumph of thy scornfull eyes,
I sacrifice to Heaven, and give
To quit my sinnes, that durst believe
A Womans easie faith, and place
True joyes in a changing face.
   Yet e're I goe ; by all those teares,
And sighs I spent 'twixt hopes, and feares ;
By thy owne glories, and that houre
Which first inslav'd me to thy power ;   10
I beg, faire One, by this last breath,
This tribute from thee after death.
If when I'm gone, you chance to see
That cold bed where I lodged bee :

Let not your hate in death appeare,
But blesse my ashes with a teare :
This influxe from that quickning eye,
By secret pow'r, which none can spie,
The cold dust shall informe, and make
Those flames (though dead) new life partake.   20
Whose warmth help'd by your tears shall bring,
O're all the tombe a sudden spring
Of Crimson flowers, whose drooping heads
Shall curtaine o're their mournfull beds :
And on each leafe by Heavens command,
These Emblemes to the life shall stand :
   Two Hearts, the first a shaft withstood ;
The second, shot, and washt in bloud ;
And on this heart a dew shall stay,
Which no heate can court away ;   30
But fixt for ever witnesse beares,
That hearty sorrow feeds on teares.
   Thus Heaven can make it knowne, and true,
That you kill'd me, 'cause I lov'd you.

To Amoret.
The Sigh.

Nimble Sigh on thy warme wings,
   Take this Message, and depart,
Tell *Amoret*, that smiles, and sings,
At what thy airie voyage brings,
   That thou cam'st lately from my heart.

Tell my lovely foe, that I
Have no more such spies to send,
   But one or two that I intend
Some few minutes ere I dye,
   To her white bosome to commend.   10

Then whisper by that holy Spring
   Where for her sake I would have dyed,

Whilst those water Nymphs did bring
    Flowers to cure what she had tryed;
And of my faith, and love did sing.

That if my *Amoret*, if she
    In after-times would have it read,
How her beauty murther'd mee,
With all my heart I will agree,
    If shee'le but love me, being dead.   20

To his Friend
Being in Love.

Aske Lover, ere thou dyest; let one poor breath
Steale from thy lips, to tell her of thy Death;
Doating Idolater! can silence bring
Thy Saint propitious? or will *Cupid* fling
One arrow for thy palenes? leave to trye
This silent Courtship of a sickly eye;
Witty to tyranny: She too well knowes
This but the incense of thy private vowes,
That breaks forth at thine eyes, and doth betray
The sacrifice thy wounded heart would pay;   10
Aske her, foole, aske her, if words cannot move,
The language of thy teares may make her love:
    Flow nimbly from me then; and when you fall
On her breasts warmer snow, O may you all,
By some strange Fate fixt there, distinctly lye
The much lov'd Volume of my Tragedy.
    Where if you win her not, may this be read,
The cold that freez'd you so, did strike me dead.

Song.

Amyntas *goe, thou art undone,*
    Thy faithfull heart is crost by fate;
That Love is better not begunne,
    Where Love is come to love too late;
Had she professed hidden fires,
    Or shew'd one knot that tyed her heart:
I could have quench'd my first desires,
    And we had only met to part;

4 *Where Love is come to love*] Whose pure offering comes *MS.*
5 *professed*] profess'd her *MS.*   6 *one*] yᵗ *MS.*

But Tyrant, thus to murther men,
    And shed a Lovers harmles bloud,   10
And burne him in those flames agen,
      Which he at first might have withstood :
Yet, who that saw faire Chloris *weep*
      Such sacred dew, with such pure grace ;
Durst thinke them fained teares, or seeke
      For Treason in an Angels face :
This is her Art, though this be true,
      Mens joyes are kil'd with griefes and feares ;
Yet she like flowers opprest with dew,
      Doth thrive and flourish in her teares :   20
This Cruell thou hast done, and thus,
      That Face hath many servants slaine.
Though th' end be not to ruine us,
      But to seeke glory by our paine.

To Amoret,
Walking in a Starry Evening.

If *Amoret,* that glorious Eye,
    In the first birth of light,
    And death of Night,
Had with those elder fires you spye
    Scatter'd so high
    Received forme, and sight ;

We might suspect in the vast Ring,
    Amidst these golden glories,
    And fierie stories ;
Whether the Sunne had been the King,   10
    And guide of Day,
    Or your brighter eye should sway ;

But, *Amoret,* such is my fate,
    That if thy face a Starre
    Had shin'd from farre,
I am perswaded in that state
    'Twixt thee, and me,
    Of some predestin'd sympathie.

14 *such pure*] such a *MS.*   18 *kil'd with*] kill'd by *MS.*   23 *Though th' end be not*] Your aim is sure *MS.*   24 *But to seeke glory*] seeking your glory *MS.*   7 might] may *MS.*   8 Amidst these golden glories] wʰ rolls those fie'ry Spheres *MS.*   9. And fierie stories] Thro' years & years *MS.*   18 Of some predestin'd] There wᵈ be perfect *MS.*

For sure such two conspiring minds,
 Which no accident, or sight,   20
  Did thus unite ;
Whom no distance can confine,
  Start, or decline,
One, for another, were design'd.

To Amoret gone from him.

Fancy, and I, last Evening walkt,
And, *Amoret*, of thee we talkt ;
The West just then had stolne the Sun,
And his last blushes were begun :
We sate, and markt how every thing
Did mourne his absence ; How the Spring
That smil'd, and curl'd about his beames,
Whilst he was here, now check'd her streames :
The wanton Eddies of her face
Were taught lesse noise, and smoother grace ; 10
And in a slow, sad channell went,
Whisp'ring the banks their discontent :
The carelesse ranks of flowers that spread
Their perfum'd bosomes to his head,
And with an open, free Embrace,
Did entertaine his beamy face ;
Like absent friends point to the West,
And on that weake reflection feast.
If Creatures then that have no sence,
But the loose tye of influence,   20
(Though fate, and time each day remove
Those things that element their love)
At such vast distance can agree,
 Why, *Amoret*, why should not wee.

A Song to *Amoret.*

If I were dead, and in my place,
 Some fresher youth design'd,
To warme thee with new fires, and grace
 Those Armes I left behind ;

8 streames : *GC* : streames *1646* 24 wee.] wee ? *GC*

Were he as faithfull as the Sunne,
    That's wedded to the Sphere;
His bloud as chaste, and temp'rate runne,
    As Aprils mildest teare;

Or were he rich, and with his heapes,
    And spacious share of Earth,   10
Could make divine affection cheape,
    And court his golden birth:

For all these Arts I'de not believe,
    (No though he should be thine)
The mighty Amorist could give
    So rich a heart as mine.

Fortune and beauty thou mightst finde,
    And greater men then I:
But my true resolved minde,
    They never shall come nigh.   20

For I not for an houre did love,
    Or for a day desire,
But with my soule had from above,
    This endles holy fire.

An Elegy.

'Tis true, I am undone; Yet e're I dye,
I'le leave these sighes, and teares a legacye
To after-Lovers; that remembring me,
Those sickly flames which now benighted be,
Fann'd by their warmer sighs may love; and prove
In them the Metempsuchosis of Love.
'Twas I (when others scorn'd) vow'd you were fair,
And sware that breath enrich'd the courser aire,
Lent Roses to your cheekes, made *Flora* bring
Her Nymphs with all the glories of the Spring   10
To waite upon thy face, and gave my heart
A pledge to *Cupid* for a quicker dart,
To arme those eyes against my selfe; to me
Thou owest that tongues bewitching harmonye:
I courted Angels from those upper joyes,
And made them leave their spheres to heare thy voice:

19 But my true resolved] But with my true steadfast *MS.*   20 They never
shall come nigh.] None can pretend to vie. *MS.*

I made the Indian curse the houres he spent
To seeke his pearles, and wisely to repent
His former folly, and confesse a sinne
Charm'd by the brighter lustre of thy skinne.   20
I borrow'd from the winds, the gentler wing
Of *Zephirus*, and soft soules of the Spring :
And made (to ayre those cheeks wth fresher grace)
The warme Inspirers dwell upon thy face.

Oh ! jam satis ———

A Rhapsodie.

Occasionally written upon a meeting with some of his
friends at the Globe Taverne, in a Chamber painted
over head with a Cloudy Skie, and some few dispersed
Starres, and on the sides with Land-scapes, Hills,
Shepheards, and Sheep.

Darknes, & Stars i' th' mid day ! they invite
Our active fancies to beleeve it night :
For Tavernes need no Sunne, but for a Signe,
Where rich Tobacco, and quick tapers shine ;
And royall, witty Sacke, the Poets soule,
With brighter Suns then he doth guild the bowl ;
As though the Pot, and Poet did agree,
Sack should to both Illuminator be.
That artificiall Cloud with it's curl'd brow,
Tels us 'tis late ; and that blew space below   10
Is fir'd with many Stars ; Marke, how they breake
In silent glaunces o're the hills, and speake
The Evening to the Plaines ; where shot from far,
They meet in dumbe salutes, as one great Star.
    The roome (me thinks) growes darker ; & the aire
Contracts a sadder colour, and lesse faire :
Or is't the Drawers skill, hath he no Arts
To blind us so, we cann't know pints from quarts ?
No, no, 'tis night ; looke where the jolly Clowne
Musters his bleating heard, and quits the Downe.   20
Harke ! how his rude pipe frets the quiet aire,
Whilst ev'ry Hill proclaimes *Lycoris* faire.
Rich, happy man ! that canst thus watch, and sleep,
Free from all cares ; but thy wench, pipe & sheep.
          Title Rhapsodie *M:* Rhapsodis *1646*

But see the Moone is up; view where she stands
Centinell o're the doore, drawn by the hands
Of some base Painter, that for gaine hath made
Her face the Landmarke to the tipling trade.
This Cup to her, that to *Endymion* give;
'Twas wit at first, and wine that made them live: 30
Choake may the Painter! and his Boxe disclose
No other Colours then his fiery Nose;
And may we no more of his pencill see,
Then two Churchwardens, and Mortalitie.
    Should we goe now a wandring, we should meet
With Catchpoles, whores, & Carts in ev'ry street:
Now when each narrow lane, each nooke & Cave,
Signe-posts, & shop-doors, pimp for ev'ry knave,
When riotous sinfull plush, and tell-tale spurs
Walk Fleet street, & the Strand, when the soft stirs   40
Of bawdy, ruffled Silks, turne night to day;
And the lowd whip, and Coach scolds all the way;
When lust of all sorts, and each itchie bloud
From the Tower-wharfe to Cymbelyne, and Lud,
Hunts for a Mate, and the tyr'd footman reeles
'Twixt chaire-men, torches, & the hackny wheels:
    Come, take the other dish; it is to him
That made his horse a Senatour: Each brim
Looke big as mine; The gallant, jolly Beast
Of all the Herd (you'le say) was not the least.   50
    Now crown the second bowle, rich as his worth,
I'le drinke it to; he! that like fire broke forth
Into the Senates face, crost Rubicon,
And the States pillars, with their Lawes thereon:
And made the dull gray beards, & furr'd gowns fly
Into *Brundusium* to consult, and lye:
    This to brave *Sylla*! why should it be sed,
We drinke more to the living, then the dead?
Flatt'rers, and fooles doe use it: Let us laugh
At our owne honest mirth; for they that quaffe   60
To honour others, doe like those that sent
Their gold and plate to strangers to be spent:
    Drink deep; this Cup be pregnant; & the wine
Spirit of wit, to make us all divine,

That big with Sack, and mirth we may retyre
Possessours of more soules, and nobler fire ;
And by the influxe of this painted Skie,
And labour'd formes, to higher matters flye ;
So, if a Nap shall take us, we shall all,
    After full Cups have dreames Poeticall. 70

Lets laugh now, and the prest grape drinke,
Till the drowsie Day-Starre winke ;
And in our merry, mad mirth run
Faster, and further then the Sun :
And let none his Cup forsake,
Till that Starre againe doth wake ;
So we men below shall move
    Equally with the gods above.

To Amoret, *of the difference 'twixt him, and other Lovers, and what true Love is.*

Marke, when the Evenings cooler wings
    Fanne the afflicted ayre, how the faint Sunne,
        Leaving undone,
        What he begunne,
Those spurious flames suckt up from slime, and earth
        To their first, low birth,
        Resignes, and brings.

They shoot their tinsill beames, and vanities,
    Thredding with those false fires their way ;
        But as you stay 10
        And see them stray,
You loose the flaming track, and subt'ly they
        Languish away,
        And cheate your Eyes.

Just so base, Sublunarie Lovers hearts
    Fed on loose prophane desires,
        May for an Eye,
        Or face comply :
But those removed, they will as soone depart,
        And shew their Art,
        And painted fires. 20

Whil'st I by pow'rfull Love, so much refin'd,
 That my absent soule the same is,
   Carelesse to misse,
   A glaunce, or kisse,
Can with those Elements of lust and sence,
   Freely dispence,
   And court the mind.

Thus to the North the Loadstones move,
 And thus to them th' enamour'd steel aspires :
   Thus, *Amoret,*
   I doe affect ;
And thus by winged beames, and mutuall fire,
   Spirits and Stars conspire,
   And this is L O V E.

To Amoret Weeping.

Leave, *Amoret,* melt not away so fast
Thy Eyes faire treasure, Fortunes wealthiest Cast
Deserves not one such pearle ; for these well spent,
Can purchase Starres, and buy a Tenement
For us in Heaven ; though here the pious streames
Availe us not ; who from that Clue of Sun-beams
Could ever steale one thread ? or with a kinde
Perswasive Accent charme the wild, lowd winde ?
 Fate cuts us all in Marble, and the Booke
Forestalls our glasse of minutes ; we may looke,   10
But seldome meet a change ; thinke you a teare
Can blot the flinty Volume ? shall our feare,
Or griefe adde to their triumphes ? and must wee
Give an advantage to adversitie ?
Deare, idle Prodigall ! is it not just
We beare our Stars ? What though I had not dust
Enough to cabinett a worme ? nor stand
Enslav'd unto a little durt, or sand ?
I boast a better purchase, and can shew
The glories of a soule that's simply true.   20
 But grant some richer Planet at my birth
Had spyed me out, and measur'd so much earth
Or gold unto my share ; I should have been
Slave to these lower Elements, and seen

My high borne soul flagge with their drosse, & lye
A pris'ner to base mud, and Alchymie ;
I should perhaps eate Orphans, and sucke up
A dozen distrest widowes in one Cup ;
Nay further, I should by that lawfull stealth,
(Damn'd Usurie) undoe the Common-wealth ;   30
Or Patent it in Soape, and Coales, and so
Have the Smiths curse me, and my Laundres too ;
Geld wine, or his friend Tobacco ; and so bring
The incens'd subject Rebell to his King ;
And after all (as those first sinners fell)
Sinke lower then my gold ; and lye in Hell.
   Thanks then for this deliv'rance ! blessed pow'rs,
You that dispence mans fortune, and his houres,
How am I to you all engag'd ! that thus
By such strange means, almost miraculous,   40
You should preserve me ; you have gone the way
To make me rich by taking all away.
For I (had I been rich) as sure as fate,
Would have bin medling with the King, or State,
Or something to undoe me ; and 'tis fit
(We know) that who hath wealth, should have no wit.
But above all, thanks to that providence,
That arm'd me with a gallant soule, and sence
'Gainst all misfortunes ; that hath breath'd so much
Of Heav'n into me, that I scorne the touch   50
Of these low things ; and can with courage dare
What ever fate, or malice can prepare :
I envy no mans purse, or mines ; I know,
That loosing them, I've lost their curses too ;
And, *Amoret,* (although our share in these
Is not contemptible, nor doth much please)
Yet whilst Content, and Love we joyntly vye,
   We have a blessing which no gold can buye.

UPON THE PRIORIE GROVE,

His usuall Retyrement.

Haile sacred shades ! coole, leavie House !
Chaste Treasurer of all my vowes,
And wealth ! on whose soft bosome layd
My loves faire steps I first betrayd :
   Henceforth no melancholy flight,
No sad wing, or hoarse bird of Night,
Disturbe this Aire, no fatall throate
Of Raven, or Owle, awake the Note
Of our laid Eccho, no voice dwell
Within these leaves, but *Philomel.*   10
The poisonous Ivie here no more
His false twists on the Oke shall score,
Only the Woodbine here may twine,
As th' Embleme of her Love, and mine ;
The Amorous Sunne shall here convey
His best beames, in thy shades to play ;
The active ayre, the gentlest show'rs,
Shall from his wings raine on thy flowers ;
And the Moone from her dewie lockes
Shall decke thee with her brightest drops :   20
What ever can a fancie move,
Or feed the eye ; Be on this Grove ;
   And when at last the Winds, and Teares
Of Heaven, with the consuming yeares,
Shall these greene curles bring to decay,
And cloathe thee in an aged Gray :
(If ought a Lover can foresee ;
Or if we Poets, Prophets be)
From hence transplanted, thou shalt stand
A fresh Grove in th' Elysian Land ;   30

Where (most blest paire !) as here on Earth
Thou first didst eye our growth, and birth ;
So there againe, thou 'lt see us move
In our first Innocence, and Love :
And in thy shades, as now, so then,
Wee'le kisse, and smile, and walke agen.

FINIS.

IVVENALS
TENTH
SATYRE
TRANSLATED.

Nèc verbum verbo curabit reddere fidus
Interpres ————————

LONDON,
Printed for **G. B.** and are to be fold at his Shop
under Saint *Dunſtans* Church. 1646.

JVVENALS tenth Satyre
TRANSLATED.

In all the parts of Earth, from farthest West,
And the Atlanticke Isles, unto the East
And famous Ganges ; Few there be that know
What's truly good, and what is good in show
Without mistake : For what is't we desire,
Or feare discreetly ? to what e're aspire,
So throughly blest ; but ever as we speed,
Repentance seales the very Act, and deed.
The easie gods mov'd by no other Fate,
Then our owne pray'rs whole Kingdomes ruinate,   10
And undoe Families, thus strife, and warre
Are the swords prize, and a litigious barre
The Gownes prime wish ; vain confidence to share
In empty honours, and a bloudy care,
To be the first in mischiefe, makes him dye
Fool'd 'twixt ambition, and credulitie ;
An oilie tongue with fatall, cunning sence,
And that sad vertue ever, Eloquence,
Are th' others ruine ; but the common curse,
And each dayes ill waits on the rich mans purse :   20
He, whose large acres, and imprison'd gold
So far exceeds his Fathers store of old,
As Brittish Whales the Dolphins doe surpasse.
    In sadder times therefore, and when the Lawes
Of *Nero's fiat* raign'd ; an armed band
Ceas'd on *Longinus*, and the spacious Land
Of wealthy *Seneca*, besieg'd the gates
Of *Lateranus*, and his faire estate
Divided as a spoile ; In such sad Feasts,
Souldiers (though not invited) are the guests.   30
    Though thou small peeces of the blessed Mine
Hast lodg'd about thee ; travelling in the shine
Of a pale Moone, if but a Reed doth shake,
Mov'd by the wind, the shadow makes thee quake.
Wealth hath its cares, and want hath this reliefe,
It neither feares the Souldier, nor the Thiefe ;

2 unto] unro *1646*

Thy first choyce vowes, and to the Gods best knowne,
Are for thy stores encrease, that in all towne
Thy stocke be greatest, but no poyson lyes
I'th' poore mans dish, he tasts of no such spice :   40
Be that thy care, when with a Kingly gust,
Thou suck'st whole Bowles clad in the guilded dust
Of some rich minerall ; whilst the false Wine
Sparkles aloft, and makes the draught Divine.
   Blam'st thou the Sages then ? because the one
Would still be laughing, when he would be gone
From his owne doore, the other cryed to see
His times addicted to such vanity ?
Smiles are an easie purchase, but to weep
Is a hard act, for teares are fetch'd more deep ;   50
Democritus his nimble Lungs would tyre
With constant laughter, and yet keep entire
His stocke of mirth, for ev'ry object was
Addition to his store ; though then (Alas !)
Sedans, and Litters, and our Senat Gownes,
With Robes of honour, fasces, and the frownes
Of unbrib'd Tribunes were not seene ; but had
He lived to see our *Roman Prætor* clad
In *Ioves* owne mantle, seated on his high
Embroyder'd Chariot 'midst the dust and Crie   60
Of the large Theatre, loaden with a Crowne
Which scarse he could support, (for it would downe,
But that his servant props it) and close by
His page a witnes to his vanitie :
To these his Scepter, and his Eagle adde
His Trumpets, Officers, and servants clad
In white, and purple ; with the rest that day,
He hir'd to triumph for his bread, and pay ;
Had he these studied, sumptuous follies seene,
'Tis thought his wanton, and effusive spleene   70
Had kill'd the Abderite, though in that age
(When pride & greatnes had not swell'd the stage
So high as ours) his harmles, and just mirth
From ev'ry object had a suddaine birth ;
Nor wast alone their avarice, or pride,
Their triumphs, or their cares he did deride ;

62 (for *GC* : for *1646*

Their vaine contentions, or ridiculous feares ;
But even their very poverty, and teares.
He would at fortunes threats as freely smile
As others mourne ; nor was it to beguile   80
His crafty passions ; but this habit he
By nature had, and grave Philosophie.
He knew their idle and superfluous vowes,
And sacrifice, which such wrong zeale bestowes,
Were meere Incendiaries ; and that the gods
Not pleas'd therewith, would ever be at ods ;
Yet to no other aire, nor better place
Ow'd he his birth, then the cold, homely *Thrace* ;
Which shewes a man may be both wise, & good,
Without the brags of fortune, or his bloud.   90
    But envy ruines all : What mighty names
Of fortune, spirit, action, bloud, and fame,
Hath this destroy'd ? yea, for no other cause
Then being such ; their honour, worth, and place,
Was crime enough ; their statues, arms & crowns ;
Their ornaments of Triumph, Chariots, Gowns,
And what the Herauld with a learned care,
Had long preserv'd, this madnes will not spare.
    So once *Sejanus* Statue Rome allow'd
Her Demi-god, and ev'ry Roman bow'd   100
To pay his safeties vowes ; but when that face
Had lost *Tyberius* once, it's former grace
Was soone eclips'd ; no diff'rence made (Alas !)
Betwixt his Statue then, and common Brasse ;
They melt alike, and in the Workmans hand
For equall, servile use, like others stand.
    Goe now fetch home fresh Bayes, and pay new vowes
To thy dumbe Capitoll gods ! thy life, thy house,
And state are now secur'd ; *Sejanus* lyes
I'th' Lictors hands ; ye gods ! what hearts, & eyes   110
Can one dayes fortune change ? the solemne crye
Of all the world is, Let *Sejanus* dye :
They never lov'd the man they sweare, they know
Nothing of all the matter ; when, or how,
By what accuser, for what cause, or why,
By whose command, or sentence he must dye.
But what needs this ? the least pretence will hit,
When Princes feare, or hate a Favourite.

A large Epistle stuff'd with idle feare,
Vaine dreames, and jealousies, directed here   120
From *Caprea* does it ; And thus ever dye
Subjects, when once they grow prodigious high.
   'Tis well, I seeke no more ; but tell me how
This tooke his friends ? no private murmurs now ?
No teares ? no solemne mourner seene ? must all
His Glory perish in one funerall ?
O still true Romans ! State-wit bids them praise
The Moone by night ; but court the warmer rayes
O' th' Sun by day ; they follow fortune still,
And hate, or love discreetly, as their will   130
And the time leades them ; This tumultuous fate
Puts all their painted favours out of date :
   And yet this people that now spurne, & tread
This mighty Favourites once honour'd head,
Had but the Tuscaine goddesse, or his Stars
Destin'd him for an Empire, or had wars,
Treason, or policie, or some higher pow'r
Opprest secure *Tyberius* ; that same houre
That he receiv'd the sad Gemonian doome,
Had crown'd him Emp'ror of the world, & Rome.   140
   But Rome is now growne wise, & since that she
Her Suffrages, and ancient Libertie,
Lost in a Monarchs name ; she takes no care
For Favourite, or Prince ; nor will she share
Their fickle glories, though in *Cato's* dayes
She rul'd whole States, & Armies with her voice,
Of all the honours now within her walls,
She only doats on Playes, and Festivalls :
Nor is it strange ; for when these Meteors fall,
They draw an ample ruine with them ; All   150
Share in the storm ; each beame sets with the Sun,
And equall hazard friends, and flatt'rers run.
This makes, that circled with distractive feare
The livelesse, pale Sejanus limbes they teare,
And least the action might a witnesse need,
They bring their servants to confirme the deed,
Nor is it done for any other end,
Then to avoid the title of his friend.
So fals ambitious man, and such are still
All floating States built on the peoples will :   160

Hearken all you ! whom this bewitching lust
Of an houres glory, and a little dust
Swels to such deare repentance ! you that can
Measure whole kingdoms with a thought or span
Would you be as *Sejanus*? would you have
So you might sway as he did, such a grave ?
Would you be rich as he ? command, dispose,
All Acts, and Offices ? All friends, and foes ?
Be Generalls of Armies, and Colleague
Unto an Emperour ? breake, or make a league ?   170
No doubt you would ; for both the good, and bad,
An equall itch of honour ever had :
But O what State can be so great, or good,
As to be bought with so much shame, and bloud !
Alas ! *Sejanus* will too late confesse
'Twas only pride, and greatnes made him lesse :
For he that moveth with the lofty wind
Of Fortune, and ambition, unconfin'd
In act, or thought ; doth but increase his height,
That he may loose it with more force, & weight ;   180
Scorning a base, low ruine, as if he
Would of misfortune, make a Prodigie.
    Tell mighty *Pompey*, *Crassus*, and O thou
That mad'st Rome kneele to thy victorious brow,
What but the weight of honours, and large fame
After your worthy Acts, and height of name,
Destroy'd you in the end ? the envious Fates
Easie to further your aspiring States,
Us'd them to quell you too ; pride, and excesse
In ev'ry Act did make you thrive the lesse :   190
Few Kings are guiltie of gray haires, or dye
Without a stab, a draught, or trecherie :
And yet to see him, that but yesterday
Saw letters first, how he will scrape, and pray ;
And all her Feast-time tyre *Minervaes* eares
For Fame, for Eloquence, and store of yeares
To thrive and live in ; and then lest he doates,
His boy assists him with his boxe, and notes ;
Foole that thou art ! not to discerne the ill
These vows include ; what, did Rom's Consull kill   200
Her *Cicero*? what, him whose very dust
Greece celebrates as yet ; whose cause though just,

172 equall] eqnall *1646*

Scarse banishment could end; nor poyson save
His free borne person from a forraigne grave:
All this from Eloquence! both head, and hand,
The tongue doth forfeit; pettie wits may stand
Secure from danger, but the nobler veine,
With losse of bloud the barre doth often staine.

     *   *   *   *   *   } *Carmen*
O fortunatam natam me Consule Romam. } *Ciceroni-*
     *   *   *   *   *   } *anum.*

Had all been thus, thou might'st have scorn'd the sword   210
Of fierce *Antonius*, here is not one word
Doth pinch, I like such stuffe; 'tis safer far
Then thy Philippicks, or Pharsalia's war:
What sadder end then his, whom Athens saw
At once her Patriot, Oracle, and Law?
Unhappy then is he, and curs'd in Stars,
Whom his poore Father, blind with soot, & scars
Sends from the Anviles harmles chime, to weare
The factious gowne, and tyre his Clients eare,
And purse with endles noise; Trophies of war   220
Old rusty armour, with an honour'd scar;
And wheeles of captiv'd Chariots, with a peece
Of some torne Brittish Galley, and to these
The Ensigne too, and last of all the traine
The pensive pris'ner loaden with his Chaine,
Are thought true Roman honors; these the Greek
And rude Barbarians equally doe seeke.
Thus aire, and empty fame, are held a prize
Beyond faire vertue; for all vertue dyes
Without reward; And yet by this fierce lust   230
Of Fame, and titles to ovtlive our dust,
And Monuments; (though all these things must dye
And perish like our selves) whole Kingdomes lye
Ruin'd, and spoil'd: Put *Hannibal* i'th' scale,
What weight affords the mighty Generall?
This is the man, whom Africks spacious Land
Bounded by th' Indian Sea, and Niles hot sand,
Could not containe; (Ye gods! that give to men
Such boundles appetites, why state you them
So short a time? either the one deny,   240
Or give their acts, and them Eternitie)

218 chime *M*: chine *1646*   227 seeke. *GC*: seeke *1646*

All Æthiopia, to the utmost bound
Of *Titans* course, (then which no Land is found
Lesse distant from the Sun) with him that ploughs
That fertile soile where fam'd Iberus flowes,
Are not enough to conquer ; past now o're
The Pyrene hills, The Alps with all its store
Of Ice, and Rocks clad in eternall snow
(As if that Nature meant to give the blow)
Denyes him passage ; straight on ev'ry side   250
He wounds the Hill, and by strong hand divides
The monstrous pile, nought can ambition stay,
The world, and nature yeeld to give him way :
And now past o're the Alps, that mighty bar
'Twixt France, and Rome, feare of the future war
Strikes Italy; successe, and hope doth fire
His lofty spirits with a fresh desire.
All is undone as yet (saith he) unlesse
Our Pænish forces we advance, and presse
Upon Rome's selfe ; break downe her gates, & wall,   260
And plant our Colours in *Suburra's* Vale.
O the rare sight ! if this great souldier wee
Arm'd on his Getick Elephant might see !
But what's the event ? O glory ! how the itch
Of thy short wonders doth mankinde bewitch !
He that but now all Italy, and Spaine,
Had conquer'd o're, is beaten out againe ;
And in the heart of Africk, and the sight
Of his owne Carthage, forc'd to open flight.
Banish'd from thence, a fugitive he posts   270
To Syria first, then to Bythinia's Coasts ;
Both places by his sword secur'd ; though he
In this distresse must not acknowledg'd be ;
Where once a Generall he triumphed, now
To shew what Fortune can, he begs as low.
   And thus that soule, which through all nations hurl'd
Conquest, and warre, and did amaze the world ;
Of all those glories rob'd at his last breath,
Fortune would not vouchsafe a souldiers death,
For all that bloud the field of Cannæ boasts,   280
And sad Apulia fill'd with Roman ghoasts :

245 fam'd *GC* : fram'd *1646*   252 stay, *M* : stay *1646* : stay : *G* : stay. *C*
262 sight *GC* : slight *1646*

No other end (freed from the pile, and sword)
Then a poore Ring would Fortune him afford.
  Goe now ambitious man ! new plots designe,
March o're the snowie Alps, and Apennine ;
That after all, at best thou mayst but be
A pleasing story to posteritie !
  The *Macedon* one world could not containe,
We heare him of the narrow Earth complaine,
And sweat for roome, as if Seryphus Ile,   290
Or Gyara had held him in Exile :
But Babylon this madnes can allay,
And give the great man but his length of clay ;
The highest thoughts, and actions under Heaven,
Death only with the lowest dust layes even.
It is believed (if what Greece writes be true)
That *Xerxes* with his Persian Fleet did hewe
Their waies throgh mountains, that their sails full blowne,
Like clouds hung over Athos, and did drowne
The spacious Continent, and by plaine force   3c0
Betwixt the Mount, and it made a divorce ;
That Seas exhausted were, and made firme land,
And Sestos joyned unto Abidos Strand ;
That on their march, his Meades but passing by,
Dranke thee Scamander, and Melenus dry ;
With what soe're incredible designe
Sostratus sings inspired with pregnant Wine :
But what's the end ? He that the other day
Divided Hellespont, and forc'd his way
Through all her angry billowes ; that assigned   310
New punishments unto the waves, and wind :
No sooner saw the Salaminian Seas,
But he was driven out by *Themistocles,*
And of that Fleet (suppos'd to be so great,
That all mankinde shar'd in the sad defeate)
Not one Sayle sav'd, in a poore Fishers boat,
Chas'd o're the working surge, was glad to float,
Cutting his desp'rate course through the tyr'd floud,
And fought againe with Carkasses, and bloud.
O foolish mad ambition ! these are still   3a0
The famous dangers that attend thy will.

    305 thee Scamander,] the Scamander ! *G* : thee, Scamander, *C*
    316 sav'd, *C* : sav'd *1646*

Give store of dayes, good *Iove*, give length of yeares,
Are the next vowes ; these with religious feares,
And Constancie we pay ; but what's so bad,
As a long, sinfull age ? what crosse more sad
Then misery of yeares ? how great an Ill
Is that, which doth but nurse more sorrow still ?
It blacks the face, corrupts, and duls the bloud,
Benights the quickest eye, distasts the food,
And such deep furrowes cuts i'th' Checker'd skin   330
As in th'old Okes of Tabraca are seene.
Youth varies in most things ; strength, beauty, wit,
Are severall graces ; but where age doth hit,
It makes no diff'rence ; the same weake voice,
And trembling ague in each member lyes :
A generall, hatefull baldnes, with a curst
Perpetuall pettishnes ; and which is worst,
A foule, strong fluxe of humors, and more paine
To feed, then if he were to nurse again.
So tedious to himselfe, his wife, and friends,   340
That his owne sonnes, and servants, wish his end,
His tast, and feeling dyes ; and of that fire
The am'rous Lover burnes in, no desire :
Or if there were, what pleasure could it be,
Where lust doth raigne without abilitie ?
Nor is this all, what matters it, where he
Sits in the spacious Stage ? who can nor see,
Nor heare what's acted, whom the stiller voice
Of spirited, wanton ayres, or the loud noise
Of Trumpets cannot pierce ; whom thunder can   350
But scarse informe who enters, or what man
He personates, what 'tis they act, or say ?
How many Scænes are done ? what time of day ?
Besides that little bloud, his carkasse holds,
Hath lost its native warmth, & fraught wth colds,
Catarrhs, and rheumes, to thick, black jelly turns,
And never but in fits, and feavers burns ;
Such vast infirmities, so huge a stock
Of sicknes, and diseases to him flock,
That *Hyppia* ne're so many Lovers knew,   360
Nor wanton *Maura* ; Phisick never slew

334 diff'rence] difference *C*   355 lost *GC* : low *1646*

So many Patients, nor rich Lawyers spoile
More Wards, and Widowes; it were lesser toile
To number out what Mannors, and Demaines,
Licinius razer purchas'd : One complaines
Of weaknes in the back, another pants
For lack of breath, the third his eyesight wants ;
Nay some so feeble are, and full of paine,
That Infant like they must be fed againe.
These faint too at their meales ; their wine they spill,   370
And like young birds, that wait the Mothers Bill
They gape for meat ; but sadder far then this
Their senslesse ignorance, and dotage is ;
For neither they, their friends, nor servants know,
Nay those themselves begot, and bred up too
No longer now they'le owne ; for madly they
Proscribe them all, and what on the last day,
The Misers cannot carry to the Grave
For their past sinnes, their prostitutes must have.
But grant age lack'd these plagues ; yet must they see   380
As great, as many : Fraile Mortalitie
In such a length of yeares, hath many falls,
And deads a life with frequent funerals.
The nimblest houre in all the span, can steale
A friend, or brother from's ; there's no Repeale
In death, or time ; this day a wife we mourne,
To morrowes teares a sonne, and the next Urne
A Sister fills ; Long-livers have assign'd
These curses still : That with a restles mind,
An age of fresh renewing cares they buye,   390
And in a tide of teares grow old and dye.
Nestor, (if we great *Homer* may believe)
In his full strength three hundred yeares did live :
Happy (thou'lt say) that for so long a time
Enjoy'd free nature, with the grape, and Wine
Of many Autumnes ; but I prethee, heare
What *Nestor* sayes himselfe, when he his deare
Antilochus had lost, how he complaines
Of life's too large Extent, and copious paines ?
Of all he meets, he askes what is the cause   400
He lived thus long ; for what breach of their Laws

The gods thus punish'd him? what sinne had he
Done worthy of a long lifes miserie?
Thus *Peleus* his *Achilles* mourned, and he
Thus wept that his *Vlysses* lost at Sea.
Had *Priam* dyed, before *Phereclus* Fleet
Was built, or *Paris* stole the fatall Greeke,
Troy had yet stood, and he perhaps had gone
In peace unto the lower shades ; His sonne
Saved with his plenteous offspring, and the rest   410
In solemne pompe bearing his fun'rall Chest ;
But long life hinder'd this : Unhappy he,
Kept for a publick ruine ; lived to see
All Asia lost, and e're he could expire,
In his owne house saw both the sword, and fire ;
All white with age, and cares, his feeble arme
Had now forgot the warre ; but this Allarme
Gathers his dying spirits ; and as wee
An aged Oxe worne out with labour, see,
By his ungratefull Master, after all   420
His yeares of toyle, a thankles victime fall :
So he by *Ioves* owne Altar ; which shewes, wee
Are no where safe from Heaven, and destinie :
Yet dyed a man ; but his surviving Queene,
Freed from the Greekish sword was barking seen.
    I haste to Rome, and Pontus King let passe,
With Lydian *Crœsus*, whom in vaine (Alas !)
Just *Solons* grave advice bad to attend,
That happines came not before the end.
    What man more blest in any age to come   430
Or past, could Nature shew the world, or Rome,
Then *Marius* was? if 'midst the pompe of war,
And triumphs fetch'd with Roman bloud from far
His soule had fled ; Exile, and fetters then,
He ne're had seen, nor known *Mynturna's* fenne ;
Nor had it, after Carthage got, been sed,
A Roman Generall had beg'd his bread.
    Thus *Pompey* th' envious gods, & Romes ill stars
(Freed from *Campania's* feavers, and the Wars)
Doom'd to *Achilles* sword : Our publick vowes   440
Made *Cæsar* guiltles ; but sent him to loose
His head at Nile ; This curse *Cethegus* mist ;
This *Lentulus*, and this made him resist

That mangled by no Lictors axe, fell dead
Entirely *Catiline*, and saved his head.
  The anxious Matrons, with their foolish zeale,
Are the last Votaries, and their Appeale
Is all for beauty ; with soft speech, and slow,
They pray for sons, but with a louder vow
Commend a female feature : All that can   450
Make woman pleasing now they shift, and scan :
And why reprov'd they say, *Latona's* paire
The Mother never thinks can be too faire.
  But sad *Lucretia* warnes to wish no face
Like hers ; *Virginia* would bequeath her grace
To Crooke-backe *Rutila* in exchange ; for still
The fairest children do their Parents fill
With greatest cares ; so seldome Chastitie
Is found with beauty ; though some few there be
That with a strict, religious care contend   460
Th' old, modest, Sabine Customes to defend :
Besides, wise nature to some faces grants
An easie blush, and where shee freely plants,
A lesse Instruction serves ; but both these joyn'd,
At *Rome* would both be forc'd or else purloyn'd.
  So steel'd a forehead vice hath, that dares win,
And bribe the Father to the Childrens sin ;
But whom have gifts defiled not ? what good face
Did ever want these tempters ? pleasing grace
Betraies it selfe ; what time did *Nero* mind   470
A course, maim'd shape ? what blemish'd youth confin'd
His goatish Pathick ? whence then flow these joies
Of a faire issue ? whom these sad annoies
Waite, and grow up with ; whom perhaps thou'lt see
Publick Adulterers, and must be
Subject to all the Curses, Plagues, and awe
Of jealous mad men, and the *Iulian* Law ;
Nor canst thou hope they'le find a milder Starre,
Or more escapes then did the God of Warre ;
But worse then all, a jealous braine confines   480
His furie to no Law ; what rage assignes,
Is present justice : Thus the rash Sword spils
This Lechers bloud, the scourge another kils.

452 why] when *GC*

But thy spruce boy must touch no other face
Then a *Patrician*? Is of any race
So they be rich ; *Servilia* is as good
With wealth, as shee that boasts *Iulus* blood :
To please a servant all is cheape ; what thing
In all their stocke to the last suite, and Ring
But lust exacts? the poorest whore in this,   490
As generous as the *Patrician* is.
   But thou wilt say what hurt's a beauteous skin
With a chaste soule ? aske *Theseus* sonne, and him
That *Stenobœa* murther'd ; for both these
Can tell how fatall 'twas in them to please ;
A womans spleene then carries most of fate,
When shame and sorrow aggravate her hate :
Resolve me now, had *Silius* been thy sonne,
In such a hazzard what should he have done?
Of all *Romes* youth, this was the only best,   500
In whom alone beauty, and worth did rest :
This *Messalina* saw, and needs he must
Be ruin'd by the Emp'rour, or her lust,
All in the face of *Rome*, and the worlds eye,
Though *Cesars* wife, a publicke Bigamie
Shee dares attempt ; and that the act might beare
More prodigie, the notaries appeare,
And Augures to't ; and to compleat the sin
In solemne forme, a dowrie is brought in ;
All this (thou'lt say) in private might have past,   510
But shee'le not have it so ; what course at last?
What should he doe ? If *Messaline* be crost
Without redresse thy *Silius* will be lost ;
If not, some two daies length is all he can
Keep from the grave ; just so much as will span
This newes to *Hostia*, to whose fate he owes
That *Claudius* last his owne dishonour knowes.
   But he obeyes, and for a few houres lust,
Forfeits that glory should outlive his dust,
Nor was it much a fault ; for, whether he   520
Obey'd, or not ; 'twas equall destinie :
So fatall beauty is, and full of wast,
That neither wanton can be safe, nor chast.

489 Ring *M* : King *1646*   503 lust,] lust ; *G* : lust. *C*

What then should man pray for? what is't that he
Can beg of Heaven, without Impiety?
Take my advice: first to the Gods commit
All cares; for they things competent, and fit
For us foresee; besides man is more deare
To them, then to himselfe: we blindly here
Led by the world, and lust, in vaine assay   530
To get us portions, wives, and sonnes; but they
Already know all that we can intend,
And of our Childrens Children see the end.
　　Yet that thou may'st have something to commend
With thankes unto the Gods for what they send;
Pray for a wise, and knowing soule; a sad
Discreet, true valour, that will scorne to adde
A needlesse horrour to thy death; that knowes
'Tis but a debt which man to nature owes;
That starts not at misfortunes, that can sway,   540
And keep all passions under locke and key;
That couets nothing, wrongs none, and preferres
An honest want before rich injurers;
All this thou hast within thy selfe, and may
Be made thy owne, if thou wilt take the way;
What boots the worlds wild, loose applause? what can
Fraile, perillous honours adde unto a man?
What length of years, wealth, or a rich faire wife?
Vertue alone can make a happy life.
To a wise man nought comes amisse: but we   550
Fortune adore, and make our Deity.

　　　546 what can *GC* : what *1646*

FINIS

Ad Posteros.

Diminuat ne sera *dies* præsentis *honorem,*
  Quis, qualisq; *fui, percipe* Posteritas.
CAMBRIA *me genuit,* patulis *ubi* vallibus *errans*
  Subjacet aeriis montibus ISCA pater.
Inde sinu placido *suscepit maximus arte*
  HERBERTUS, Latiæ *gloria prima* Scholæ,
Bis ternos, *illo me Conducente, per* annos
  Profeci, & geminam *Contulit unus opem,*
Ars *&* amor, mens *atǫ* manus *certare solebant,*
  Nec lassata Illi mensve, manusve *fuit.*   10
Hinc qualem cernis crevisse: Sed ut mea Certus
  Tempora Cognoscas, dura *fuere, scias.*
Vixi, divisos cum fregerat *hæresis Anglos*
  Intèr Tysiphonas *presbyteri & populi.*
His *primùm* miseris *per* amæna *furentibus* arva
  Prostravit sanctam *vilis avena* rosam,
Turbârunt fontes, *& fusis* pax *perit undis,*
  Mæstaǫ Cœlestes *obruit umbra* dies.
Duret ut Integritas *tamen, &* pia gloria, *partem*
  Me nullam in tantâ strage *fuisse, scias ;*   20
Credidimus nempè insonti vocem *esse Cruori,*
  Et vires *quæ post funera* flere *docent.*
Hinc Castæ, fidæq; *pati me more* parentis
  Commonui, & Lachrymis fata *levare meis ;*
Hinc nusquàm horrendis violavi Sacra *procellis,*
  Nec mihi mens *unquàm, nec* manus *atra fuit.*
Si pius *es, ne plura petas ;* Satur-*Ille recedat*
  Qui sapit, *& nos non Scripsimus* Insipidis.

OLOR ISCANUS.

SELECT
Poems, and translations
by
Hen: Vaughan Silurist.

Flumina amo Silvasq́, inglorius

Engraved title-page of *Olor Iscanus* (1651)

OLOR ISCANUS.

A COLLECTION

OF SOME SELECT

POEMS,

AND

TRANSLATIONS,

Formerly written by

Mr. Henry Vaughan *Silurist.*

Publifhed by a Friend.

Virg. Georg.
Flumina amo, Sylvafᶇ Inglorius——

LONDON,
Printed by *T.W.* for *Humphrey Mofeley,*
and are to be fold at his fhop, at the
Signe of the Prince's Arms in St. *Pauls*
Church-yard, 1651.

——O quis me gelidis in vallibus ISCÆ
Sistat, & Ingenti ramorum protegat umbrâ !

TO

The truly Noble, and most
Excellently accomplish'd, the
Lord KILDARE DIGBY.

MY LORD,

It is a Position *anciently* known, and *modern Experience* hath allowed it for a *sad truth*, that *Absence* and *time*, (like *Cold weather*, and an *unnaturall dormition*) will *blast* and *wear* out of memorie the most *Endearing obligations*; And hence it was that some *Politicians* in *Love* have lookt upon the *former* of these *two* as a main remedy against the *fondness* of that *Passion*. But for my own part (my Lord) I shall deny this *Aphorisme* of the *people*, and beg leave to assure your *Lordship*, that, though these *reputed obstacles* have lain long in my way, yet neither of them could *work* 10 upon me : for I am now (without adulation) as *warm* and *sensible* of those *numerous* favours, and *kind Influences* receiv'd sometimes from your Lordship, as I really was at the *Instant* of *fruition.* I have no *plott* by *preambling* thus, to set any *rate* upon this present *addresse*, as if I should presume to value a *Return* of this nature equall with your Lordships *Deserts*, but the *designe* is, to let you see that this *habit* I have got of being *troublesome* flowes from two *excusable principles*, Gratitude, and Love. These inward *Counsellours* (I know not how discreetly) perswaded me to this *Attempt* and *Intrusion* upon your *name*, which if your Lordship 20 will vouchsafe to own as the *Genius* to these *papers*, you will *perfect* my *hopes*, and place me at my full *height.* This was the *Ayme*, my Lord, and is the *End* of this work, which though but a *Pazzarello* to the *voluminosè Insani*, yet as *Jezamin* and the *Violet* find room in the *bank* as well as *Roses* and *Lillies*, so happily may this, and (if *shin'd* upon by your *Lordship*) please as much. To whose *Protection*, Sacred as your *Name*, and those eminent *Honours* which have alwayes attended upon't through so many *generations*, I humbly offer it, and remain in all *numbers* of *gratitude,* 30

Newton by Usk
this 17. of *De-cemb.* 1647.

My honour'd Lord,

Your most affectionate,
humblest Servant

VAUGHAN.

The Publisher to the Reader.

It was the glorious Maro, *that referr'd his* Legacies *to the* Fire, *and though* Princes *are seldome* Executors, *yet there came a* Cæsar *to his* Testament, *as if the* Act *of a* Poet *could not be* repeal'd *but by a* King. *I am not Reader* Augustus vindex : *Here is no* Royall Rescue, *but here is a* Muse *that* deserves *it. The* Author *had long agoe condemn'd these* Poems *to* Obscuritie, *and the* Consumption *of that* Further Fate, *which* attends *it. This* Censure *gave them a* Gust *of* Death, *and they have* partly *known that* Oblivion, *which our* Best Labours *must* come to *at* Last. *I present thee then not onely with a* Book, *but with a* Prey, *and in* 10 *this kind the first* Recoveries *from* Corruption. *Here is a* Flame *hath been sometimes* extinguished : *Thoughts that have been* lost *and* forgot, *but now they* break out *again like the* Platonic Reminiscencie. *I have not the Author's* Approbation *to the* Fact, *but I have* Law *on my* Side, *though never a* Sword : *I hold it no man's* Prærogative *to* fire *his* own House. *Thou seest how* Saucie *I am* grown, *and if thou doest expect I should* Commend *what is* published, *I must tell thee,* I crie no Sivill Oranges. *I will not say, Here is* Fine *or* Cheap : *that were an* Injurie *to the* Verse *it selfe, and to the* Effects *it can* produce. *Read on, and thou wilt find thy* Spirit 20 ingag'd : *not by the* Deserts *of what wee call* Tolerable, *but by the* Commands *of a* Pen, *that is* Above it.

Vpon the most Ingenious
pair of Twins, *Eugenius Philalethes,*
and the *Authour* of these
Poems.

What *Planet* rul'd your *birth* ? what *wittie star* ?
That you so like in *Souls* as *Bodies* are !
So like in *both*, that you seem *born* to free
The *starrie art* from *vulgar* Calumnie.
My *doubts* are solv'd, from hence my *faith* begins,
Not only your *faces*, but your *wits* are *Twins*.

When this bright *Gemini* shall from earth ascend,
They will *new light* to dull-ey'd mankind lend,
Teach the *Star-gazers*, and delight their *Eyes*,
Being fixt a *Constellation* in the Skyes. 10
T. Powell Oxoniensis.

To my friend the Authour
upon these his *Poems.*

I call'd it once my *sloth*: In such an age
So many *Volumes deep*, I not a *page*?
But I recant, and vow 'twas thriftie Care
That kept my *Pen* from spending on *slight ware*,
And breath'd it for a *Prise*, whose pow'rfull *shine*
Doth both *reward* the striver, and *refine*;
Such are thy *Poems*, friend: for since th'hast writ,
I cann't reply to any *name*, but *wit*;
And lest amidst the *throng* that make us *grone*,
Mine prove a groundless *Heresie* alone,   10
Thus I dispute, Hath there not rev'rence bin
Pay'd to the *Beard* at doore, for *Lord* within?
Who notes the *spindle-leg*, or *hollow eye*
Of the *thinne Usher*, the *faire Lady* by?
Thus I *sinne* freely, *neighbour* to a *hand*
Which while I aime to *strengthen*, gives *Command*
For my *protection*, and thou art to me
At once my *Subject* and *Securitie*.

I. Rowlandson Oxoniensis.

Vpon the following
Poems.

I write not here, as if thy *last* in store
Of learned *friends*, 'tis known that thou hast *more*;
Who, were they told of this, would find a way
To rise a guard of *Poets* without *pay*,
And bring as many *hands* to thy *Edition*,
As th'*City* should unto their *May'rs* Petition,
But thou wouldst none of this, lest it should be
Thy *Muster* rather, than our *Courtesie*,
Thou wouldst not beg as *Knights* do, and appeare
Poet by *Voice*, and *suffrage* of the *Shire*,   10
That were enough to make thy *Muse* advance
Amongst the *Crutches*, nay it might enhance
Our *Charity*, and we should think it fit
The *State* should build an *Hospital* for wit.

11 thy *Er*: my *1651*

E

But here needs no *reliefe* : Thy richer *Verse*
Creates all *Poets*, that can but *reherse*,
And they, like *Tenants* better'd by their *land*,
Should pay thee *Rent* for what they understand,
Thou art not of that *lamentable Nation*,
Who make a blessed *Alms* of *approbation*,   20
Whose *fardel-notes* are *Briefes* in ev'ry thing,
But, that they are not licens'd *By the King*.
Without such *scrape-requests* thou dost come forth
Arm'd (though I speak it) with thy *proper worth*,
And needest not this *noise* of friends, for wee
Write out of *love*, not thy *necessitie* ;
And though this *sullen age* possessed be
With some strange *Desamour* to Poetrie,
Yet I suspect (thy fancy so delights)
The *Puritans* will turn thy *Proselytes*,   30
And that thy *flame* when once abroad it *shines*,
Will bring thee as many *friends*, as thou hast *lines*.

> Eugenius Philalethes *Oxoniensis.*

Olor Iscanus.

To the River *Isca.*

When *Daphne*'s Lover here first wore the *Bayes*,
Eurotas secret streams heard all his *Layes.*
And holy *Orpheus*, Natures *busie* Child
By headlong *Hebrus* his deep *Hymns* Compil'd.
Soft *Petrarch* (thaw'd by *Laura*'s flames) did weep
On *Tybers* banks, when she (*proud fair!*) cou'd sleep;
Mosella boasts *Ausonius*, and the *Thames*
Doth murmure *SIDNEYS Stella* to her *streams*,
While *Severn* swoln with *Joy* and *sorrow*, wears
Castara's smiles mixt with fair *Sabrin*'s tears.   10
Thus *Poets* (like the *Nymphs*, their *pleasing themes*)
Haunted the *bubling Springs* and *gliding streams*,
And *happy banks*! whence such *fair flowres* have sprung,
But happier those where they have *sate* and *sung*!
Poets (like *Angels*) where they once appear
Hallow the *place*, and each succeeding year
Adds *rev'rence* to't, such as at length doth give
This aged faith, *That there their Genii live.*
Hence th'*Auncients* say, That, from this *sickly aire*
They passe to *Regions* more *refin'd* and *faire*,   20
To *Meadows* strow'd with *Lillies* and the *Rose*,
And *shades* whose *youthfull green* no *old age* knowes,
Where all in *white* they walk, discourse, and Sing
Like Bees *soft murmurs*, or a *Chiding Spring.*
   But *Isca*, whensoe'r those *shades* I see,
And thy *lov'd Arbours* must no more *know* me,
When I am layd to *rest* hard by thy *streams*,
And my *Sun sets*, where first it *sprang* in beams,
I'le leave behind me such a *large, kind light*,
As shall *redeem* thee from *oblivious night*,   30
And in these *vowes* which (living yet) I pay
Shed such a *Previous* and *Enduring Ray*,
As shall from age to age thy *fair name* lead
'Till *Rivers* leave to *run*, and *men* to *read.*

6 *proud C* : *prou'd 1651*   9 *swoln Er* : sworn *1651*

First, may all *Bards* born after me
(When I am *ashes*) sing of thee !
May thy *green banks* and *streams* (or none)
Be both their *Hill* and *Helicon* ;
May *Vocall Groves* grow there, and all
The *shades* in them *Propheticall*,   40
Where (laid) men shall more *faire truths* see
Than *fictions* were of *Thessalie*.
May thy gentle *Swains* (like *flowres*)
Sweetly spend their *Youthfull houres*,
And thy *beauteous Nymphs* (like *Doves*)
Be *kind* and *faithfull* to their *Loves* ;
Garlands, and *Songs*, and *Roundelayes*,
Mild, dewie *nights*, and Sun-shine *dayes*,
The *Turtles voyce*, *Joy* without *fear*,
Dwell on thy *bosome* all the year !   50
May the *Evet* and the *Tode*
Within thy Banks have no abode,
Nor the *wilie*, *winding Snake*
Her *voyage* through thy *waters* make.
In all thy *Journey* to the *Main*
No *nitrous Clay*, nor *Brimstone-vein*
Mixe with thy *streams*, but may they passe
Fresh as the *aire*, and cleer as *Glasse*,
And where the *wandring Chrystal* treads
Roses shall *kisse*, and *Couple* heads.   60
The *factour-wind* from far shall bring
The *Odours* of the *Scatter'd* Spring,
And *loaden* with the rich *Arreare*,
Spend it in *Spicie whispers* there.
No *sullen heats*, nor *flames* that are
Offensive, and *Canicular*,
Shine on thy *Sands*, nor *pry* to see
Thy *Scalie*, *shading familie*,
But *Noones* as mild as *Hesper's* rayes,
Or the first *blushes* of fair dayes.   70
What *gifts* more *Heav'n* or *Earth* can adde
With all those *blessings* be thou *Clad* !
  Honour, *Beautie*,
  Faith and *Dutie*,
  Delight and *Truth*,
  With *Love*, and *Youth*

Crown all about thee ! And what ever *Fate*
Impose else-where, whether the graver state,
Or some toye else, may those *lowd, anxious Cares*
For *dead* and *dying things* (the Common *Wares*　　　　80
And *showes* of time) ne'r break thy *Peace*, nor make
Thy *repos'd Armes* to a new warre *awake* !
　　　But *Freedome, safety, Joy and blisse*
　　　United in one loving *kisse*
　　　Surround thee quite, and *stile* thy borders
　　　The Land redeem'd from all disorders !

The Charnel-house.

Blesse me ! what damps are here ? how stiffe an aire ?
Kelder of mists, a second *Fiats* care,
Frontspeece o'th' grave and darkness, a Display
Of ruin'd man, and the disease of day ;
Leane, bloudless shamble, where I can descrie
Fragments of men, Rags of Anatomie ;
Corruptions ward-robe, the transplantive bed
Of mankind, and th'Exchequer of the dead.
How thou arrests my sense ? how with the sight
My *Winter'd* bloud growes stiffe to all delight ?　　　　10
Torpedo to the Eye ! whose least glance can
Freeze our wild lusts, and rescue head-long man ;
Eloquent silence ! able to Immure
An *Atheists* thoughts, and blast an *Epicure.*
Were I a *Lucian*, Nature in this dresse
Would make me wish a Saviour, and Confesse.
　　Where are you shoreless thoughts, vast tenter'd hope,
Ambitious dreams, *Aymes* of an Endless scope,
Whose stretch'd Excesse runs on a string too high
And on the rack of self-extension dye ?　　　　20
Chameleons of state, Aire-monging band,
Whose breath (like Gun-powder) blowes up a land,
Come see your dissolution, and weigh
What a loath'd nothing you shall be one day,
As th' Elements by Circulation passe
From one to th'other, and that which first was
Is so again, so 'tis with you ; The grave
And Nature but Complott, what the one gave,

The other takes ; Think then, that in this bed
There sleep the Reliques of as proud a head   30
As stern and subtill as your own, that hath
Perform'd, or forc'd as much, whose tempest-wrath
Hath levell'd Kings with slaves, and wisely then
Calme these high furies, and descend to men ;
Thus *Cyrus* tam'd the *Macedon*, a tombe
Checkt him, who thought the world too straight a Room.
    Have I obey'd the *Powers* of a face,
A beauty able to undoe the Race
Of easie man ? I look but here, and strait
I am Inform'd, the lovely Counterfeit   40
Was but a smoother Clay.   That famish'd slave
Begger'd by wealth, who starves that he may save,
Brings hither but his sheet ; Nay, th'*Ostrich-man*
That feeds on *steele* and *bullet*, he that can
Outswear his *Lordship*, and reply as tough
To a kind word, as if his tongue were *Buffe*,
Is *Chap*-faln here, wormes without wit, or fear
Defie him now, death hath disarm'd the *Bear*.
Thus could I run o'r all the pitteous score
Of erring men, and having done meet more,   50
Their shuffled *Wills*, abortive, vain *Intents*,
Phantastick *humours*, perillous *Ascents*,
False, empty *honours*, traiterous *delights*,
And whatsoe'r a blind Conceit Invites ;
But these and more which the weak vermins swell,
Are Couch'd in this Accumulative Cell
Which I could scatter ; But the grudging Sun
Calls home his beams, and warns me to be gone,
Day leaves me in a double night, and I
Must bid farewell to my sad library.   60
Yet with these notes.   Henceforth with thought of thee
I'le season all succeeding Jollitie,
Yet damn not mirth, nor think too much is fit,
Excesse hath no *Religion*, nor *Wit*,
But should wild bloud swell to a lawless strain
One Check from thee shall *Channel* it again.

    37 of a face *Er* : of face *1651*   52 Phantastick] Phautastick *1651*
66 One *Er* : On *1651*

In Amicum fœneratorem.

Thanks mighty *Silver*! I rejoyce to see
How I have spoyl'd his thrift, by spending thee.
Now thou art gone, he courts my wants with more,
His *Decoy* gold, and bribes me to restore.
As lesser lode-stones with the *North* consent
Naturally moving to their Element,
As bodyes swarm to th' Center, and that fire
Man stole from heaven, to heav'n doth still aspire,
So this vast crying summe drawes in a lesse,
And hence this bag more Northward layd I guesse,   10
For 'tis of *Pole-star* force, and in this sphere
Though th'least of many rules the master-bear.
Prerogative of debts! how he doth dresse
His messages in *Chink*? not an Expresse
Without a fee for reading, and 'tis fit,
For gold's the best restorative of wit,
O how he gilds them o'r! with what delight
I read those lines, where Angels doe Indite?
  But wilt have money *Og*? must I dispurse?
Will nothing serve thee but a *Poets* curse?   20
Wilt rob an Altar thus? and sweep at once
What *Orpheus*-like I forc'd from stocks and stones?
'Twill never swell thy *Bag*, nor ring one peale
In thy dark *Chest*. Talk not of *Shreeves*, or gaole,
I fear them not. I have no land to glutt
Thy durty appetite, and make thee strutt
Nimrod of acres; I'le no Speech prepare
To court the *Hopefull Cormorant*, thine heire.
Yet there's a Kingdome, at thy beck, if thou
But kick this drosse, *Parnassus* flowrie brow   30
I'le give thee with my *Tempe*, and to boot
That horse which struck a fountain with his foot.
A Bed of Roses I'le provide for thee,
And Chrystal Springs shall drop thee melodie;
The breathing shades wee'l haunt, where ev'ry leafe
Shall *Whisper* us asleep, though thou art deafe;
Those waggish *Nymphs* too which none ever yet
Durst make love to, wee'l teach the Loving fit,

18 where] which *GC*   21 thus] thu *1651*

Wee'l suck the *Corall* of their lips, and feed
Upon their spicie breath, a meale at need,   40
Rove in their *Amber-tresses*, and unfold
That glist'ring grove, the Curled wood of gold,
Then peep for babies, a new Puppet-play,
And riddle what their *pratling Eyes* would say.
But here thou must remember to dispurse,
For without money all this is a Curse,
Thou must for more bags call, and so restore
This Iron-age to gold, as once before ;
This thou must doe, and yet this is not all,
For thus the Poet would be still in thrall,   50
Thou must then (if live thus) my neast of honey,
Cancell old bonds, and beg to lend more money.

To his friend——.

I wonder, *James*, through the whole Historie
Of ages, such *Entailes* of povertie
Are layd on Poets ; Lawyers (they say) have found
A trick to cut them, would they were but bound
To practise on us, though for this thing wee
Should pay (if possible) their bribes and fee.
Search (as thou canst) the old and moderne store
Of *Rome* and ours, in all the wittie score
Thou shalt not find a rich one ; Take each Clime
And run o'r all the pilgrimage of time   10
Thou'lt meet them poor, and ev'ry where descrie
A thredbare, goldless genealogie.
Nature (it seems) when she meant us for Earth
Spent so much of her treasure in the birth
As ever after niggards her, and Shee,
Thus stor'd within, beggers us outwardly.
Wofull profusion ! at how dear a rate
Are wee made up ? all hope of thrift and state
Lost for a verse : When I by thoughts look back
Into the wombe of time, and see the Rack   20
Stand useless there, untill we are produc'd
Unto the torture, and our soules infus'd
To learn afflictions, I begin to doubt
That as some tyrants use from their chain'd rout
Of slaves to pick out one whom for their sport
They keep afflicted by some lingring art,

So wee are meerly thrown upon the stage
The mirth of fooles, and Legend of the age.
When I see in the ruines of a sute
Some nobler brest, and his tongue sadly mute   30
Feed on the *Vocall silence* of his Eye,
And knowing cannot reach the remedie,
When soules of baser stamp shine in their store,
And he of all the throng is only poore,
When *French* apes for forraign fashions pay,
And *English* legs are drest th'outlandish way,
So fine too, that they their own shadows wooe,
While he walks in the *sad* and *Pilgrim-shooe*,
I'm mad at Fate, and angry ev'n to sinne,
To see deserts and learning clad so thinne :   40
To think how th'earthly Usurer can brood
Upon his bags, and weigh the pretious food
With palsied hands, as if his soul did feare
The Scales could rob him of what he layd there ;
Like Divels that on hid Treasures sit, or those
Whose jealous Eyes trust not beyond their nose
They guard the durt, and the bright Idol hold
Close, and Commit adultery with gold.
A Curse upon their drosse ! how have we sued
For a few scatter'd *Chips?* how oft pursu'd   50
Petitions with a blush, in hope to squeeze
For their souls health, more than our wants a peece ?
Their steel-rib'd Chests and Purse (rust eat them both !)
Have cost us with much paper many an oath,
And Protestations of such solemn sense,
As if our soules were sureties for the Pence.
Should we a full nights learned cares present,
They'l scarce return us one short houres Content,
'Las ! they're but quibbles, things we Poets feign,
The short-liv'd Squibs and Crackers of the brain.   60
    But wee'l be wiser, knowing 'tis not they
That must redeem the hardship of our way,
Whether a Higher Power, or that starre
Which neerest heav'n, is from the earth most far
Oppresse us thus, or angel'd from that Sphere
By our strict Guardians are kept luckless here,
It matters not, wee shall one day obtain
Our native and Celestiall scope again.

To his retired friend, an Invitation to *Brecknock.*

Since last wee met, thou and thy horse (my dear,)
Have not so much as drunk, or litter'd here,
I wonder, though thy self be thus deceast,
Thou hast the spite to Coffin up thy beast ;
Or is the *Palfrey* sick, and his rough hide
With the penance of *One Spur* mortifide ?
Or taught by thee (like *Pythagoras's Oxe*)
Is then his master grown more *Orthodox* ?
What ever 'tis, a sober cause't must be
That thus long bars us of thy Companie.   10
The Town believes thee lost, and didst thou see
But half her suffrings, now distrest for thee,
Thou'ldst swear (like *Rome*) her foule, polluted walls
Were sackt by *Brennus*, and the salvage *Gaules.*
Abominable face of things ! here's noise
Of bang'd Mortars, blew Aprons, and Boyes,
Pigs, Dogs, and Drums, with the hoarse hellish notes
Of politickly-deafe Usurers throats,
With new fine *Worships*, and the old cast *teame*
Of Justices vext with the *Cough*, and *flegme.*   20
Midst these the *Crosse* looks sad, and in the *Shire-*
-Hall furs of an old *Saxon Fox* appear,
With brotherly Ruffs and Beards, and a strange sight
Of high Monumentall Hats ta'ne at the fight
Of *Eighty eight*; while ev'ry *Burgesse* foots
The mortall *Pavement* in eternall boots.
    Hadst thou been batc'lour, I had soon divin'd
Thy Close retirements, and Monastick mind,
Perhaps some Nymph had been to visit, or
The beauteous Churle was to be waited for,   30
And like the *Greek*, e'r you the sport would misse
You stai'd, and stroak'd the *Distaffe* for a kisse.
But in this age, when thy coole, settled bloud
Is ty'd t'one flesh, and thou almost grown good,
I know not how to reach the strange device,
Except (*Domitian* like) thou murther'st flyes ;
Or is't thy pietie ? for who can tell
But thou may'st prove devout, and love a Cell,

24 ta'ne] t'ane *1651*

And (like a Badger) with attentive looks
In the dark hole sit rooting up of books.   40
Quick Hermit! what a peacefull Change hadst thou
Without the noise of *haire-cloth*, *Whip*, or *Vow*?
But is there no redemption? must there be
No other penance but of liberty?
Why two months hence, if thou continue thus
Thy memory will scarce remain with us,
The Drawers have forgot thee, and exclaim
They have not seen thee here since *Charles* his raign,
Or if they mention thee, like some old man
That at each word inserts—Sir, *as I can*   50
Remember—So the *Cyph'rers* puzzle mee
With a dark, cloudie character of thee.
That (certs!) I fear thou wilt be lost, and wee
Must ask the *Fathers* e'r 't be long for thee.
    Come! leave this sullen state, and let not Wine
And precious Witt lye dead for want of thine,
Shall the dull *Market-land-lord* with his *Rout*
Of sneaking Tenants durtily swill out
This harmlesse liquor? shall they knock and beat
For Sack, only to talk of *Rye*, and *Wheat*?   60
O let not such prepost'rous tipling be
In our *Metropolis*, may I ne'r see
Such *Tavern-sacrilege*, nor lend a line
To weep the *Rapes* and *Tragedy* of wine!
Here lives that *Chimick*, quick fire which betrayes
Fresh Spirits to the bloud, and warms our layes,
I have reserv'd 'gainst thy approach a Cup
That were thy Muse stark dead, shall raise her up,
And teach her yet more Charming words and skill
Than ever *Cælia*, *Chloris*, *Astrophil*,   70
Or any of the Thredbare names Inspir'd
Poore riming lovers with a *Mistris* fir'd.
Come then! and while the slow Isicle hangs
At the stiffe thatch, and Winters frosty pangs
Benumme the year, blith (as of old) let us
'Midst noise and War, of Peace, and mirth discusse.
This portion thou wert born for: why should wee
Vex at the times ridiculous miserie?
An age that thus hath fool'd it selfe, and will
(Spite of thy teeth and mine) persist so still.   80

Let's sit then at this *fire*, and while wee steal
A Revell in the Town, let others seal,
Purchase or Cheat, and who can, let them pay,
Till those black deeds bring on the darksome day ;
Innocent spenders wee ! a better use
Shall wear out our short Lease, and leave th'obtuse
Rout to their *husks* ; They and their bags at best
Have cares in *earnest*, wee care for a *Jest.*

Monsieur Gombauld.

I 'ave read thy Souls fair night-peece, and have seen
Th'*Amours* and Courtship of the *silent Queen,*
Her stoln descents to Earth, and what did move her
To Juggle first with *Heav'n*, then with a *Lover,*
With *Latmos* lowder rescue, and (alas !)
To find her out a *Hue and Crie* in Brasse,
Thy Journall of deep Mysteries, and sad
Nocturnall Pilgrimage, with thy dreams clad
In fancies darker than thy *Cave*, Thy *Glasse*
Of sleepie draughts, and as thy soul did passe   10
In her calm voyage what discourse she heard
Of Spirits, what dark Groves and ill-shap'd guard
Ismena lead thee through, with thy proud flight
O'r *Periardes*, and deep, musing night
Neere fair *Eurotas* banks, what solemn *green*
The neighbour shades weare, and what forms are seen
In their large Bowers, with that sad path and seat
Which none but light-heeld *Nymphs* and *Fairies* beat ;
Their solitary life, and how exempt
From Common frailtie, the severe contempt   20
They have of Man, their priviledge to live
A *Tree*, or *Fountain*, and in that *Reprieve*
What ages they consume, with the sad *Vale*
Of *Diophania*, and the mournfull tale,
Of th' bleeding vocall *Myrtle* ; These and more
Thy richer thoughts we are upon the score
To thy rare fancy for, nor doest thou fall
From thy first Majesty, or ought at all
Betray Consumption, thy full vig'rous *Bayes*
Wear the same *green*, and scorn the lene decayes   30

18 beat *GC* : heat *1651*

Of *stile*, or *matter* ; Just so have I known
Some *Chrystal* spring, that from the neighbour down
Deriv'd her birth, in gentle murmurs steal
To their next Vale, and proudly there reveal
Her streams in lowder accents, adding still
More noise and waters to her Channell, till
At last swoln with Increase she glides along
The Lawnes and Meadows in a wanton throng
Of frothy billows, and in one great name
Swallows the tributary brooks drown'd fame.   40
   Nor are they meere Inventions, for we
In th' same peece find scatter'd *Philosophie*
And hidden, disperst truths that folded lye
In the dark shades of deep *Allegorie,*
So neatly weav'd, like *Arras,* they descrie
Fables with *Truth, Fancy* with *Historie.*
So that thou hast in this thy curious mould
Cast that commended mixture wish'd of old,
Which shall these Contemplations render far
Lesse mutable, and lasting as their star,   50
And while there is a *People,* or a *Sunne,*
Endymions storie with the *Moon* shall runne.

An Elegie on the death of Mr. *R. W.* slain in the late unfortunate differences at *Rou-ton* Heath, neer *Chester,* 1645.

I am Confirm'd, and so much wing is given
To my wild thoughts, that they dare strike at heav'n.
A full years griefe I struggled with, and stood
Still on my sandy hopes uncertain good,
So loth was I to yeeld, to all those fears
I still oppos'd thee, and denyed my tears.
But thou art gone ! and the untimely losse
Like that one day, hath made all others Crosse.
Have you seen on some Rivers flowrie brow
A well-built *Elme,* or stately *Cedar* grow,   10
Whose Curled tops gilt with the Morning-ray
Becken'd the Sun, and whisperd to the day,
When unexpected from the angry *North*
A fatall sullen whirle-wind sallies forth,
And with a full-mouth'd blast rends from the ground
The *Shady twins,* which rushing scatter round

Their sighing leafes, whilst overborn with strength,
Their trembling heads bow to a prostrate length;
So forc'd fell he; So Immaturely Death
Stifled his able heart and active breath.   20
The world scarce knew him yet, his early Soule
Had but new-broke her day, and rather stole
A sight, than gave one; as if subt'ly she
Would learn our stock, but hide his treasurie.
His years (should time lay both his *Wings* and *glasse*
Unto his charge) could not be summ'd (alas!)
To a full *score*; Though in so short a span
His riper thoughts had purchas'd more of man
Than all those worthless livers, which yet quick,
Have quite outgone their own *Arithmetick.*   30
He seiz'd perfections, and without a dull
And mossie *gray* possess'd a solid skull,
No Crooked knowledge neither, nor did he
Wear the friends name for Ends and policie,
And then lay't by; As those *lost Youths* of th'stage
Who only flourish'd for the *Play's* short age
And then retir'd, like *Jewels* in each part
He wore his friends, but chiefly at his heart.
      Nor was it only in this he did excell,
His equall valour could as much, as well.   40
He knew no *fear* but of his *God*; yet durst
No injurie, nor (as some have) e'r purs't
The sweat and tears of others, yet would be
More forward in a royall gallantrie
Than all those vast pretenders, which of late
Swell'd in the ruines of their King and State.
He weav'd not *Self-ends*, and the *Publick* good
Into one piece, nor with the peoples bloud
Fill'd his own veins; In all the doubtfull way
Conscience and *Honour* rul'd him. O that day   50
When like the *Fathers* in the *Fire* and *Cloud*
I mist thy face! I might in ev'ry *Crowd*
See Armes like thine, and men advance, but none
So neer to lightning mov'd, nor so fell on.
Have you observ'd how soon the nimble *Eye*
Brings th' *Object* to *Conceit*, and doth so vie
Performance with the *Soul*, that you would swear
The *Act* and *apprehension* both lodg'd there,

42 purs't *M*: pur'st *1651*

Just so mov'd he : like *shott* his active hand
Drew bloud, e'r well the foe could understand.   60
But here I lost him. Whether the last turn
Of thy few sands call'd on thy hastie urn,
Or some fierce rapid fate (hid from the Eye)
Hath hurl'd thee Pris'ner to some distant skye
I cannot tell, but that I doe believe
Thy Courage such as scorn'd a base Reprieve.
What ever 'twas, whether that day thy breath
Suffer'd a *Civill* or the *Common* death,
Which I doe most suspect, and that I have
Fail'd in the *glories* of so known a grave,   70
Though thy lov'd ashes misse me, and mine Eyes
Had no acquaintance with thy Exequies,
Nor at the last farewell, torn from thy sight
On the *Cold sheet* have fix'd a *sad delight*,
Yet what e'r pious hand (in stead of mine)
Hath done this office to that dust of thine,
And till thou rise again from thy low bed
Lent a Cheap pillow to thy quiet head,
Though but a private *turffe*, it can do more
To keep thy name and memory in store   80
Than all those *Lordly fooles* which lock their bones
In the dumb piles of Chested brasse, and stones.
Th'art rich in thy own fame, and needest not
These *Marble-frailties*, nor the *gilded blot*
Of posthume honours ; There is not one sand
Sleeps o'r thy grave, but can outbid that hand
And pencill too, so that of force wee must
Confesse their *heaps* shew lesser than thy *dust*.
      And (blessed soule !) though this my sorrow can
Adde nought to thy perfections, yet as man   90
Subject to Envy, and the common fate
It may redeem thee to a fairer date ;
As some blind Dial, when the day is done,
Can tell us at mid-night, *There was a Sun*,
So these perhaps, though much beneath thy fame,
May keep some weak remembrance of thy name,
And to the faith of better times Commend
Thy loyall upright life, and gallant End.

   Nomen & arma locum servant, te, amice, nequivi
   Conspicere,——   100

Upon a Cloke lent him by Mr. *J. Ridsley.*

Here, take again thy *Sack-cloth*! and thank heav'n
Thy Courtship hath not kill'd me; Is't not Even
Whether wee dye by peecemeale, or at once
Since both but ruine, why then for the nonce
Didst husband my afflictions, and cast o're
Me this forc'd *Hurdle* to inflame the score?
Had I neer *London* in this *Rug* been seen
Without doubt I had executed been
For some bold *Irish* spy, and crosse a sledge
Had layn mess'd up for their *foure gates* and *bridge*.   10
When first I bore it, my oppressed feet
Would needs perswade me, 'twas some *Leaden sheet*;
Such deep Impressions, and such dangerous holes
Were made, that I began to doubt my soals,
And ev'ry step (so neer necessity)
Devoutly wish'd some honest Cobler by,
Besides it was so short, the *Jewish* rag
Seem'd Circumcis'd, but had a *Gentile* shag.
Hadst thou been with me on that day, when wee
Left craggie *Biston*, and the fatall *Dee*,   20
When beaten with fresh storms, and late mishap
It shar'd the office of a *Cloke*, and *Cap*,
To see how 'bout my clouded head it stood
Like a thick *Turband*, or some Lawyers *Hood*,
While the stiffe, hollow pletes on ev'ry side
Like *Conduit-pipes* rain'd from the *Bearded hide*,
I know thou wouldst in spite of that day's fate
Let loose thy mirth at my new shape and state,
And with a shallow smile or two professe
Some *Sarazin* had lost the *Clowted Dresse*.   30
Didst ever see the *good wife* (as they say)
March in her short cloke on the *Christning* day,
With what soft motions she salutes the Church,
And leaves the Bedrid Mother in the lurch;
Just so Jogg'd I, while my dull horse did trudge
Like a Circuit-beast plagu'd with a goutie Judge.
  But this was Civill. I have since known more
And worser pranks: One night (as heretofore
Th' hast known) for want of change (a thing which I
And *Bias* us'd before me) I did lye   40

Pure *Adamite*, and simply for that end
Resolv'd, and made this for my bosome-*friend*.
O that thou hadst been there next morn, that I
Might teach thee new *Micro-cosmo-graphie* !
Thou wouldst have ta'ne me, as I naked stood,
For one of th' *seven pillars* before the floud,
Such *Characters* and *Hierogliphicks* were
In one night worn, that thou mightst justly swear
I'd slept in *Cere-cloth*, or at *Bedlam* where
The mad men lodge in straw, I'le not forbear   50
To tell thee all, his wild *Impress* and *tricks*
Like *Speeds* old *Britans* made me look, or *Picts* ;
His villanous, biting, *Wire-embraces*
Had seal'd in me more strange formes and faces
Than *Children* see in dreams, or thou hast read
In *Arras*, *Puppet-playes*, and *Ginger-bread*,
With *angled Schemes*, and *Crosses* that bred fear
Of being handled by some *Conjurer*,
And neerer thou wouldst think (such *strokes* were drawn)
I'd been some rough statue of *Fetter-lane*,   60
Nay, I believe, had I that instant been
By *Surgeons* or *Apothecaries* seen,
They had Condemned my raz'd skin to be
Some walking *Herball*, or *Anatomie*.
    But (thanks to th'day !) 'tis off. I'd now advise
Thee friend to put this peece to Merchandize ;
The *Pedlars* of our age have business yet,
And gladly would against the *Fayr-day* fit
Themselves with such a *Roofe*, that can secure
Their *Wares* from *Dogs and Cats* rain'd in showre,   70
It shall performe ; or if this will not doe
'Twill take the *Ale-wives* sure ; 'Twill make them *two*
Fine Roomes of *One*, and spread upon a stick
Is a partition without Lime or Brick.
Horn'd obstinacie ! how my heart doth fret
To think what *Mouthes* and *Elbowes* it would set
In a wet day ? have you for two pence e're
Seen King *Harryes* Chappell at *Westminster*,
Where in their dustie gowns of *Brasse* and *Stone*
The Judges lye, and markt you how each one   80

70 rain'd] rained *C*

F

In sturdie Marble-plets about the knee
Bears up to shew his legs and symmetrie?
Just so would this; That I think't weav'd upon
Some stiffneckt *Brownists* exercising loome.
O that thou hadst it when this Jugling fate
Of Souldierie first seiz'd me! at what rate
Would I have bought it then, what was there but
I would have giv'n for the *Compendious hutt?*
I doe not doubt but (if the weight could please,)
'Twould guard me better than a *Lapland-lease,*   90
Or a *German* shirt with Inchanted lint
Stuff'd through, and th'devils *beard* and *face* weav'd in't.
   But I have done.   And think not, friend, that I
This freedome took to Jeere thy Courtesie,
I thank thee for't, and I believe my Muse
So known to thee, thou'lt not suspect abuse;
She did this, 'cause (perhaps) thy *love* paid thus
Might with my *thanks* out-live thy *Cloke,* and *Us.*

Upon Mr. *Fletchers* Playes, published, 1647.

I knew thee not, nor durst *attendance* strive
Labell to *wit, Verser remonstrative,*
And in some *Suburb-page* (scandal to thine)
Like *Lent* before a *Christmasse* scatter mine.
This speaks thee not, since at the utmost rate
Such *remnants* from thy *peece* Intreat their date;
Nor can I *dub* the *Coppy,* or afford
Titles to *swell* the *reare* of *Verse* with Lord,
Nor politickly big to *Inch* low fame
Stretch in the *glories* of a strangers name,   10
And Clip those *Bayes* I Court, weak *striver* I,
But a faint *Echo* unto *Poetrie.*
I have not *Clothes* t'adopt me, nor must sit
For *Plush* and *Velvets* sake *Esquire* of wit,
Yet *Modestie* these *Crosses* would improve,
And *Rags* neer thee, some *Reverence* may move.
   I did believe (great *Beaumont* being dead,)
Thy *Widow'd Muse* slept on his *flowrie bed*;
But I am *richly* Cosen'd, and can see
Wit *transmigrates,* his *Spirit* stayd with thee,   20
Which *doubly* advantag'd by thy *single* pen
In *life* and *death* now treads the *Stage* agen;

And thus are wee freed from that *dearth* of wit
Which *starv'd* the Land since into *Schismes* split,
Wherein th'hast done so much, wee must needs guesse
Wits last *Edition* is now i'th' *Presse*,
For thou hast *drain'd* Invention, and he
That writes hereafter, doth but *pillage* thee.
But thou hast *plotts*; and will not the *Kirk* strain
At the *Designes* of such a *Tragick brain*?   30
Will they themselves think safe, when they shall see
Thy most *abominable policie*?
Will not the *Eares* assemble, and think't fit
Their *Synod fast*, and *pray*, against thy wit?
But they'le not *tyre* in such an *idle Quest*,
Thou doest but *kill*, and *Circumvent* in *Jest*,
And when thy anger'd Muse *swells* to a blow
'Tis but for *Field*'s, or *Swansteed*'s overthrow.
Yet shall these *Conquests* of thy *Bayes* outlive
Their *Scotish zeale*, and *Compacts* made to grieve   40
The *Peace* of *Spirits*, and when such deeds fayle
Of their foule Ends, a *faire name* is thy *Bayle*.
   But (happy thou!) ne'r saw'st these *stormes*, our *aire*
Teem'd with even in thy time, though *seeming faire*;
Thy gentle *Soule* meant for the *shade*, and *ease*
Withdrew betimes into the *Land* of *Peace*;
So *neasted* in some Hospitable shore
The *Hermit-angler*, when the *mid-Seas* roare
Packs up his *lines*, and (ere the tempest *raves*,)
Retyres, and leaves his *station* to the *waves*.   50
Thus thou diedst almost with our *peace*, and wee
This *breathing time* thy last fair *Issue* see,
Which I think such (if *needless Ink* not soyle
So *Choice a Muse*,) others are but thy *foile*;
This, or that *age* may write, but never see
A *Wit* that dares run *Paralell* with thee.
True, *B E N* must live! but bate *him*, and thou hast
Undone all *future wits*, and match'd the *past*.

Upon the *Poems* and *Playes* of the ever memorable Mr. *William Cartwright.*

I did but *see* thee! and how *vain* it is
To *vex* thee for it with *Remonstrances*,
Though *things* in fashion, let those *Judge*, who sit

Their *twelve-pence* out, to *clap* their *hands* at *wit*;
I fear to *Sinne* thus *neer* thee; for (*great Saint!*)
'Tis known, *true beauty* hath no need of *paint.*
   Yet, since a *Labell* fixt to thy fair *Hearse*
Is all the *Mode*, and *tears* put into *Verse*
Can teach *Posterity* our present *griefe*
And their own *losse*, but never give *reliefe* ;   10
I'le tell them (and a *truth* which needs no *passe*,)
That *wit* in *Cartwright* at her *Zenith* was,
Arts, Fancy, Language, all *Conven'd* in thee,
With those *grand Miracles* which *deifie*
The old worlds *Writings*, kept yet from the *fire*,
Because they *force* these worst times to *admire.*
Thy matchless *Genius*, in all thou didst write,
Like the *Sun*, wrought with such *stayd heat*, and *light*,
That not a *line* (to the most *Critick* he)
Offends with *flashes*, or *obscuritie.*   20
   When thou the *wild* of *humours* trackst, thy *pen*
So Imitates that *Motley stock* in men,
As if thou hadst in all their *bosomes* been,
And seen those *Leopards* that lurk within.
The am'rous *Youth* steals from thy *Courtly page*
His *vow'd Addresse*, the *Souldier* his *brave rage* ;
And those *soft beauteous Readers* whose *looks* can
Make some men *Poets*, and make any man
A *Lover*, when thy *Slave* but *seems* to dye,
Turn all his *Mourners*, and melt at the *Eye.*   30
Thus, thou thy *thoughts* hast *drest* in such a *strain*
As doth not only *speak*, but *rule* and *raign*,   .
Nor are those *bodyes* they assum'd, *dark Clouds*,
Or a *thick bark*, but *clear, transparent shrouds*,
Which who *lookes* on, the *Rayes* so strongly beat
They'l *brushe* and *warm* him with a *quickning heat*,
So *Souls* shine at the *Eyes*, and *Pearls* display
Through the *loose-Chrystal-streams* a *glaunce of day.*
But what's all this unto a *Royall Test*?
Thou art the *Man*, whom great *Charles* so exprest !   40
Then let the *Crowd* refrain their *needless humme*,
When *Thunder* speaks, then *Squibs* and *Winds* are *dumb.*

   9 *griefe*] grief, *Ct*   12 was,] *was. Ct*   32 *raign*,] raign; *Ct* .

To the best, and most accomplish'd
Couple——

Blessings as rich and fragrant crown your heads
  As the mild heav'n on *Roses* sheds,
    When at their Cheeks (like Pearls) they weare
    The Clouds that court them in a teare,
  And may they be fed from above
  By him which first ordain'd your love !

Fresh as the *houres* may all your pleasures be,
  And healthfull as *Eternitie* !
    Sweet as the flowres *first breath*, and Close
    As th'*unseen spreadings* of the Rose,
  When he unfolds his Curtain'd head,
  And makes his bosome the *Suns bed.*

Soft as *your selves* run your whole lifes, and cleare
  As your own *glasse*, or *what shines* there ;
    Smooth as heav'ns *face*, and bright as he
    When without *Mask*, or *Tiffanie*,
  In all your time not one *Jarre* meet
  But peace as silent as his *feet.*

Like the dayes *Warmth* may all your Comforts be,
  Untoil'd for, and *Serene* as he,
    Yet free and full as is that *sheafe*
    Of Sun-beams gilding ev'ry leafe,
  When now the *tyrant-heat* expires
  And his Cool'd locks breath milder fires.

And as those *parcell'd glories* he doth shed
  Are the *faire Issues* of his head,
    Which ne'r so distant are soon known
    By th' *heat* and *lustre* for his own,
  So may each branch of yours wee see
  Your *Coppyes*, and our *Wonders* be !

And when no more on Earth you must remain
  Invited hence to heav'n again,
    Then may your vertuous, virgin-flames
    Shine in those *Heires* of your fair names,
  And teach the world that mysterie
  Your selves in your Posteritie !

So you to both worlds shall *rich presents* bring,
And *gather'd* up to heav'n, leave here a *Spring.*

An Elegie on the death of Mr. *R. Hall,*
slain at *Pontefract,* 1648.

I knew it would be thus! and my Just fears
Of thy great spirit are Improv'd to tears.
Yet flow these not from any base distrust
Of a fair name, or that thy honour must
Confin'd to those cold reliques sadly sit
In the same Cell an obscure Anchorite.
Such low distempers *Murther,* they that must
Abuse thee so, *weep* not, but *wound* thy dust.
But I past such dimme Mourners can descrie
Thy fame above all Clouds of obloquie,   10
And like the Sun with his victorious rayes
Charge through that darkness to the last of dayes.
'Tis true, fair *Manhood* hath a *female* Eye,
And tears are beauteous in a Victorie,
Nor are wee so high-proofe, but griefe will find
Through all our guards a way to wound the mind;
But in thy fall what addes the brackish summe
More than a blott unto thy *Martyrdome,*
Which scorns such wretched suffrages, and stands
More by thy single worth, than our whole bands.   20
Yet could the puling tribute rescue ought
In this sad losse, or wert thou to be brought
Back here by tears, I would in any wise
Pay down the summe, or quite Consume my Eyes.
Thou fell'st our double ruine, and this rent
Forc'd in thy life shak'd both the *Church and tent,*
Learning in others steales them from the *Van,*
And basely wise *Emasculates* the man,
But lodged in thy brave soul the *bookish feat*
Serve'd only as the light unto thy *heat;*   30
Thus when some quitted action, to their shame,
And only got a *discreet Cowards* name,
Thou with thy bloud mad'st purchase of renown,
And diedst the glory of the *Sword* and *Gown,*
Thy bloud hath hallow'd *Pomfret,* and this blow
(Prophan'd before) hath Church'd the Castle now.

34 *Gown, M* : *Gown 1651* : gown : *G* : gown. *C*

Nor is't a Common valour we deplore,
But such as with *fifteen* a *hundred* bore,
And lightning like (not coopt within a wall)
In stormes of *fire* and *steele* fell on them all.   40
Thou wert no *Wool-sack* souldier, nor of those
Whose Courage lies in *winking* at their foes,
That live at *loop-holes*, and consume their breath
On *Match* or *Pipes*, and sometimes *peepe* at death ;
No, it were sinne to number these with thee,
But that (thus poiz'd) our losse wee better see.
The fair and open valour was thy *shield*,
And thy known station, the *defying field*.
    Yet these in thee I would not *Vertues* call,
But that this age must know, that thou hadst all.   50
Those richer graces that adorn'd thy mind
Like stars of the *first magnitude*, so shin'd,
That if oppos'd unto these lesser lights
All we can say, is this, *They were fair nights.*
Thy *Piety* and *Learning* did unite,
And though with *Sev'rall beames* made up *one light*,
And such thy Judgement was, that I dare swear
Whole *Counsels* might as soon, and *Synods* erre.
    But all these now are out ! and as some *Star*
Hurl'd in Diurnall motions from far,   60
And seen to droop at night, is vainly sed
To fall, and find an *Occidentall bed*,
Though in that other world what wee Judge *West*
Proves *Elevation*, and a new, fresh *East.*
So though our weaker sense denies us sight
And bodies cannot trace the *Spirits* flight,
Wee know those graces to be still in thee,
But wing'd above us to eternitie.
Since then (thus flown) thou art so much refin'd,
That we can only reach thee with the mind,   70
    will not in this *dark* and *narrow glasse*
Let thy scant *shadow* for *Perfections* passe,
But leave thee to be read more high, more queint,
In thy own bloud a *Souldier* and a *Saint.*

    —— *Salve æternum mihi maxime Palla !*
Æternumq̃ vale ! ——

To my learned friend, Mr. *T. Powell*, upon His Translation of *Malvezzi's Christian Politician.*

Wee thank you, worthy Sir, that now we see
Malvezzi languag'd like our Infancie,
And can without suspition entertain
This forraign States-man to our brest or brain,
You have enlarg'd his praise, and from your store
By this Edition made his worth the more.
Thus by your learned hand (amidst the *Coile*)
Outlandish plants thrive in our thankless soile,
And wise men after death, by a strange fate,
Lye *Leiguer* here, and beg to serve our *State.*   10
Italy now, though *Mistris* of the *Bayes,*
Waits on this *Wreath,* proud of a forraign praise,
For, wise *Malvezzi,* thou didst lye before
Confin'd within the language of one shore,
And like those *Stars* which neer the *Poles* doe steer
Wer't but in one part of the *Globe* seen cleer,
Provence and *Naples* were the best and most
Thou couldst shine in, fixt to that single Coast,
Perhaps some *Cardinal* to be thought wise
And honest too, would ask, *what was thy price?*   20
Then thou must pack to *Rome,* where thou mightst lye
E'r thou shouldst have new cloathes eternally,
For though so neer the *seav'n hills,* ne'rthelesse
Thou cam'st to *Antwerp* for thy *Roman* dresse ;
But now thou art come hither, thou mayst run
Through any Clime as well known as the *Sun,*
And in thy *sev'rall dresses* like the *year*
Challenge acquaintance with each peopled Sphere.
  Come then rare Politicians of the time,
Brains of some standing, Elders in our Clime,   30
See here the method : A wise, solid state
Is quick in acting, friendly in debate,
Ioynt in advice, in resolutions just,
Mild in successe, true to the Common trust.
It cements ruptures, and by gentle hand
Allayes the heat and burnings of a land,
Religion guides it, and in all the Tract
Designes so twist, that heav'n confirms the act ;

If from these lists you wander as you steere,
Look back, and *Catechise* your actions here,   40
These are the *Marks* to which true States-men tend,
And *greatness* here with *goodness* hath one End.

To my worthy friend Master *T. Lewes.*

Sees not my friend, what a deep snow
Candies our Countries wooddy brow?
The yeelding branch his load scarse bears
Opprest with snow, and *frozen tears,*
While the *dumb* rivers slowly float,
All bound up in an *Icie Coat.*
   Let us meet then! and while this world
In wild *Excentricks* now is hurld,
Keep wee, like nature, the same *Key,*
And walk in our forefathers way;   10
Why any more cast wee an Eye
On what *may come,* not what is *nigh?*
Why vex our selves with *feare,* or *hope*
And cares beyond our *Horoscope?*
Who into future times would peere
Looks oft beyond his terme set here,
And cannot goe into those grounds
Bnt through a *Church-yard* which them bounds;
Sorrows and sighes and searches spend
And draw our bottome to an end,   20
But discreet Joyes lengthen the lease
Without which life were a disease,
And who this age a Mourner goes,
Doth with his tears but feed his foes.

To the most Excellently accomplish'd,
Mrs. *K. Philips.*

Say wittie fair one, from what Sphere
Flow these rich numbers you shed here?
For sure such *Incantations* come
From thence, which strike your Readers dumbe.
A strain, whose measures gently meet
Like *Virgin-lovers,* or times *feet,*

Where language *Smiles,* and accents rise
As quick, and pleasing as your *Eyes,*
The *Poem* smooth, and in each line
Soft as *your selfe,* yet *Masculine ;*   10
Where no Coorse trifles blot the page
With matter borrow'd from the age,
But thoughts as Innocent, and high
As *Angels* have, or *Saints* that dye.
These Raptures when I first did see
New miracles in Poetrie,
And by a hand, their God would misse
His *Bayes* and *Fountaines* but to kisse,
My weaker *Genius* (crosse to fashion)
Slept in a silent admiration,   20
A Rescue, by whose grave disguise
Pretenders oft have past for wise,
And yet as *Pilgrims* humbly touch
Those *Shrines* to which they bow so much,
And Clouds in Courtship flock, and run
To be the Mask unto the Sun,
So I concluded, It was true
I might at distance worship you
A *Persian* Votarie, and say
It was your light shew'd me the way.   30
So *Lodestones* guide the duller *Steele,*
And high perfections are the *Wheele*
Which moves the lesse, for gifts divine
Are strung upon a *Vital line*
Which touch'd by you, Excites in all
Affections *Epidemicall.*
And this made me (a truth most fit)
Adde my weak *Eccho* to your wit,
Which pardon, Lady, for Assayes
Obscure as these might blast your Bayes,   40
As Common hands soyle *Flowres,* and make
That dew they wear, *weepe* the mistake.
But I'le wash off the *staine,* and vow
No *Lawrel* growes, but for your *Brow.*

11 no *Er*: not *1651*   17 God *Er*: good *1651*

An Epitaph upon the Lady *Elizabeth*, Second Daughter to his late Majestie.

Youth, Beauty, Vertue, Innocence
Heav'ns royall, and select Expence,
With Virgin-tears, and sighs divine,
Sit here the *Genii* of this shrine,
Where now (thy fair soule wing'd away,)
They guard the *Casket* where she lay.

Thou hadst, e'r thou the light couldst see,
Sorrowes layd up, and stor'd for thee,
Thou suck'dst in woes, and the *brests* lent
Their *Milk* to thee, but to lament ; 10
Thy portion here was *griefe*, thy years
Distilld no other rain, but tears,
Tears without noise, but (understood)
As lowd, and shrill as any bloud ;
Thou seem'st a *Rose-bud* born in *Snow*,
A flowre of purpose sprung to bow
To headless tempests, and the rage
Of an Incensed, stormie Age.
Others, e're their afflictions grow,
Are tim'd, and season'd for the blow, 20
But thine, as *Rhumes* the tend'rest part,
Fell on a *young* and *harmless* heart.
And yet as *Balm-trees* gently spend
Their tears for those, that doe them rend,
So mild and pious thou wert seen,
Though full of *Suffrings*, free from *spleen*,
Thou didst nor murmure, nor revile,
But drank'st thy *Wormwood* with a *smile.*

As envious Eyes blast, and Infect
And cause misfortunes by aspect, 30
So thy sad stars dispens'd to thee
No Influxe, but Calamitie,
They view'd thee with *Ecclypsed* rayes,
And but the *back-side* of bright dayes.

      *   *   *

These were the Comforts she had here,
As by an unseen hand 'tis cleer,
Which now she reads, and smiling wears
A Crown with him, who wipes off tears.

To Sir *William D'avenant,* upon
his *Gondibert.*

Well, wee are rescued! and by thy rare Pen
Poets shall live, when *Princes* dye like men.
Th'hast cleer'd the prospect to our harmless *Hill,*
Of late years clouded with imputed Ill,
And the *Soft, youthfull Couples* there may move
As chast as *Stars* converse and smile above.
Th'hast taught their *Language,* and their *love* to flow
Calme as *Rose-leafes,* and coole as *Virgin-snow,*
Which doubly feasts us, being so refin'd
They both *delight,* and *dignifie* the mind,   10
Like to the watrie Musick of some Spring,
Whose pleasant flowings at once *wash* and *sing.*
   And where before *Heroick Poems* were
Made up of *Spirits, Prodigies,* and *fear,*
And shew'd (through all the *Melancholy flight,*)
Like some dark Region overcast with night,
As if the Poet had been quite dismay'd,
While only *Giants* and *Inchantments* sway'd,
Thou like the *Sun,* whose Eye brooks no disguise
Hast Chas'd them hence, and with Discoveries   20
So rare and learned fill'd the place, that wee
Those fam'd *Grandeza's* find out-done by thee,
And under-foot see all those *Vizards* hurl'd,
Which bred the wonder of the former world.
'Twas dull to sit, as our fore-fathers did,
At *Crums* and *Voyders,* and because unbid
Refrain wise appetite.   This made thy *fire*
Break through the *ashes* of thy aged *Sire*
To lend the world such a Convincing light
As shewes his *fancy* darker than his sight.   30
Nor was't alone the *bars* and *length* of dayes
(Though those gave *strength* and *stature* to his *bayes,*)
Encounter'd thee, but what's an old Complaint
And kills the fancy, a *forlorn Restraint;*
How couldst thou mur'd in solitarie stones
Dresse *BIRTHA'S smiles,* though well thou might'st her *grones?*
And, strangely Eloquent, thy self divide
'Twixt *Sad misfortunes,* and a *Bloomie Bride?*

36 *smiles* GC : *similes 1651*

Through all the tenour of thy ample Song
Spun from thy own rich store, and shar'd among   40
Those fair *Adventurers*, we plainly see
Th' *Imputed* gifts, *Inherent* are in thee.
Then live for ever (and by high desert)
In thy own *mirrour*, matchless *Gondibert*,
And in *bright Birtha* leave thy *love* Inshrin'd
Fresh as her *Emrauld*, and *fair* as her *mind*,
While all Confesse thee (as they ought to doe)
The Prince of *Poets*, and of *Lovers* too.

Tristium Lib. 5⁰. *Eleg.* 3ᵃ.
To his fellow Poets at *Rome*, upon the birth-day of *Bacchus*.

This is the day (blith god of *Sack*) which wee
If I mistake not, Consecrate to thee,
When the soft *Rose* wee marry to the *Bayes*,
And warm'd with thy own wine reherse thy praise,
'Mongst whom (while to thy *Poet* fate gave way)
I have been held no small part of the day,
But now, dull'd with the Cold *Bears* frozen seat,
Sarmatia holds me, and the warlike *Gete*.
My former life, unlike to this my last,
With *Romes* best wits of thy full Cup did tast,   10
Who since have seen the savage *Pontick* band,
And all the *Choler* of the Sea and Land:
Whether sad Chance, or heav'n hath this design'd,
And at my birth some fatall Planet shin'd,
Of right thou shouldst the *Sisters* knots undoe,
And free thy *Votarie* and *Poet* too.
Or are you Gods (like us) in such a state
As cannot alter the decrees of fate?
I know with much adoe thou didst obtain
Thy *Jovial godhead*, and on earth thy pain   20
Was no whit lesse, for wandring thou didst run
To the *Getes* too, and Snow-weeping *Strymon*,
With *Persia*, *Ganges*, and what ever streams
The thirsty *Moore* drinks in the mid-day beames.
But thou wert twice-born, and the Fates to thee
(To make all sure) doubled thy miserie,

43 desert] defert *1651*

My suffrings too are many : if it be
Held safe for me to boast adversitie,
Nor was't a Common blow, but from above
Like his, that died for Imitating *Jove*,   30
Which when thou heardst, a ruine so divine
And *Mother*-like, should make thee pitty mine.
And on this day, which *Poets* unto thee
Crown with full bowles, ask, *What's become of me ?*
    Help bucksome God then ! so may thy lov'd *Vine*
Swarm with the num'rous grape, and *big* with Wine
Load the kind *Elm*, and so thy *Orgyes* be
With priests lowd showtes, and *Satyrs* kept to thee !
So may in death *Lycurgus* ne'r be blest,
Nor *Pentheus* wandring ghost find any rest !   40
And so for ever bright (thy Chiefe desires,)
May thy *Wifes Crown* outshine the lesser fires !
If but now, mindfull of my love to thee,
Thou wilt, in what thou canst, my helper be.
You *Gods* have Commerce with your selves, try then
If *Cæsar* will restore me *Rome* agen.
    And you my trusty friends (the Jollie Crew
Of careless *Poets* !) when, without me, you
Perform this dayes glad Myst'ries, let it be
Your first Appeal unto his Deitie,   50
And let one of you (touch'd with my sad name)
Mixing his wine with tears, lay down the same,
And (sighing) to the rest this thought Commend,
O ! Where is Ovid *now our banish'd friend ?*
This doe, if in your brests I e'r deserv'd
So large a share, nor spitefully reserv'd,
Nor basely sold applause, or with a brow
Condemning others, did my selfe allow.
And may your happier wits grow lowd with fame
As you (my best of friends !) preserve my name.   60

De Ponto, Lib. 3⁰.
To his friends (after his many sollicitations) refusing to petition *Cæsar* for his releasement.

You have Consum'd my language, and my pen
Incens'd with begging scorns to write agen.
You grant, you knew my sute : My Muse, and I
Had taught it you in frequent Elegie,

That I believe (yet seal'd) you have divin'd
Our *Repetitions*, and *forestal'd* my mind,
So that my thronging Elegies, and I
Have made you (more then *Poets*) prophesie.
  But I am now awak'd ; forgive my dream
Which made me Crosse the *Proverb* and the *Stream*,   10
And pardon, friends, that I so long have had
Such good thoughts of you, I am not so mad
As to continue them. You shall no more
Complain of troublesome *Verse*, or write o're
How I endanger you, and vex my *Wife*
With the sad legends of a banish'd life.
I'le bear these plagues my selfe : for I have past
Through greater ones, and can as well at last
These pettie Crosses. 'Tis for some young beast
To kick his bands, or wish his neck release   20
From the sad Yoke. Know then, That as for me
Whom Fate hath us'd to such calamitie,
I scorn her spite and yours, and freely dare
The highest ills your malice can prepare.
  'Twas Fortune threw me hither, where I now
Rude *Getes* and *Thrace* see, with the snowie brow
Of Cloudie *Æmus*, and if she decree
Her sportive pilgrims *last bed* here must be
I am content ; nay more, she cannot doe
That Act which I would not consent unto.   30
I can delight in vain hopes, and desire
That state more then her *Change* and *Smiles*, then high'r
I hugge a strong *despaire*, and think it brave
To *baffle* faith, and give those hopes a *grave*.
Have you not seen cur'd wounds enlarg'd, and he
That with the first wave sinks, yielding to th'free
Waters, without th'Expence of armes or breath
Hath still the easiest, and the quickest death.
Why nurse I sorrows then ? why these desires
Of Changing *Scythia* for the *Sun* and *fires*   40
Of some calm kinder aire ? what did bewitch
My frantick hopes to flye so vain a pitch,
And thus out-run my self ? Mad-man ! could I
Suspect fate had for me a Courtesie ?
These errours grieve : And now I must forget
Those pleas'd *Idæa's* I did frame and set

Unto my selfe, with many fancyed *Springs*
And *Groves*, whose only losse new sorrow brings.
And yet I would the worst of fate endure,
E're you should be repuls'd, or lesse secure,   50
But (base, low soules!) you left me not for this,
But 'cause you durst not.   *Cæsar* could not misse
Of such a trifle, for I know that he
Scorns the *Cheap triumphs* of my miserie.
    Then since (degen'rate friends) not he, but you
Cancell my hopes, and make afflictions new,
You shall Confesse, and fame shall tell you, I
At *Ister* dare as well as *Tyber* dye.

De Ponto, lib. 4º. *Eleg.* 3ª.
**To his Inconstant friend, translated for
the use of all the *Judases* of this
touch-stone-Age.**

Shall I complain, or not? Or shall I mask
Thy hatefull name, and in this bitter task
Master my just Impatience, and write down
Thy crime alone, and leave the rest unknown?
Or wilt thou the succeeding years should see
And teach thy person to posteritie?
No, hope it not; for know, most wretched man,
'Tis not thy base and weak detraction can
Buy thee a *Poem*, nor move me to give
Thy name the honour in my Verse to live.   10
    Whilst yet my *Ship* did with no stormes dispute
And temp'rate winds *fed* with a calme salute
My prosp'rous sailes, thou wert the only man
That with me then an equall fortune ran,
But now since angry heav'n with Clouds and night
Stifled those *Sun*-beams, thou hast ta'ne thy flight,
Thou know'st I want thee, and art meerly gone
To shun that rescue, I rely'd upon;
Nay, thou dissemblest too, and doest disclame
Not only my *Acquaintance*, but my name;   20
Yet know (though deafe to this) that I am he
Whose *years* and *love* had the same *Infancie*
With thine, Thy *deep familiar*, that did share
Soules with thee, and partake thy *Joyes* or *Care*,

Whom the same *Roofe* lodg'd, and my *Muse* those nights
So solemnly endear'd to her delights ;
But now, perfidious traitour, I am grown
The *Abject* of thy brest, not to be known
In that *false Closet* more ; Nay, thou wilt not
So much as let me know, I am forgot.   30
If thou wilt say, thou didst not love me, then
Thou didst dissemble : or, if love agen,
Why now Inconstant ? came the Crime from me
That wrought this Change ?   Sure, if no Justice be
Of my side, thine must have it.   Why dost hide
Thy reasons then ? for me, I did so guide
My selfe and actions, that I cannot see
What could offend thee, but my miserie.
'Las ! if thou wouldst not from thy store allow
Some rescue to my wants, at least I know   40
Thou couldst have writ, and with a line or two
Reliev'd my *famish'd Eye*, and eas'd me so.
I know not what to think ! and yet I hear,
Not pleas'd with this, th'art *Witty*, and dost Jeare ;
Bad man ! thou hast in this those tears kept back
I could have shed for thee, shouldst thou but lack.
Know'st not that *Fortune* on a *Globe* doth stand,
Whose *upper* slipprie part without command
Turns *lowest* still ? the sportive leafes and wind
Are but dull *Emblems* of her fickle mind,   50
In the whole world there's nothing I can see
Will throughly parallel her wayes, but thee.
All that we hold, hangs on a slender twine
And our best states by sudden chance decline ;
Who hath not heard of *Cræsus* proverb'd gold
Yet knowes his foe did him a pris'ner hold ?
He that once aw'd *Sicilia's* proud Extent
By a poor art could famine scarce prevent ;
And mighty *Pompey* e'r he made an end
Was glad to beg his slave to be his friend ;   60
Nay, he that had so oft *Romes* Consull bin,
And forc'd *Jugurtha*, and the *Cimbrians* in,
Great *Marius* ! with much want, and more disgrace
In a foul Marsh was glad to hide his face.
A divine hand swayes all mankind, and wee
Of one short houre have not the certaintie ;

G

Hadst thou one day told me, the time should be
When the *Getes* bowes, and th'*Euxine* I should see,
I should have check'd thy madness, and have thought
Th' hadst need of all *Anticira* in a draught;   70
And yet 'tis come to passe! nor though I might
Some things foresee, could I procure a sight
Of my whole destinie, and free my state
From those eternall, higher *tyes* of fate.
Leave then thy pride, and though now *brave* and *high*,
Think thou mayst be as *poore* and *low* as *I.*

Tristium Lib. 3º. *Eleg.* 3ª.
To his Wife at *Rome*, when he was sick.

Dearest! if you those fair Eyes (wondring) stick
On this strange Character, know, *I am sick.*
Sick in the *skirts* of the lost world, where I
Breath hopeless of all Comforts, but to dye.
What heart (think'st thou?) have I in this sad seat
Tormented 'twixt the *Sauromate* and *Gete*?
Nor *aire* nor *water* please; their very *skie*
Looks strange and unaccustom'd to my Eye,
I scarse dare breath it, and I know not how
The Earth that bears me shewes unpleasant now.   10
Nor *Diet* here's, nor *lodging* for my Ease,
Nor any one that *studies* a disease;
No friend to comfort me, none to defray
With smooth discourse the Charges of the day.
All tir'd alone I lye, and (thus) what e're
Is absent, and at *Rome* I fancy here,
But when thou com'st, I blot the *Airie Scrowle*,
And give thee full possession of my soule,
Thee (absent) I embrace, thee only *voice*,
And night and day *bely* a Husbands Joyes;   20
Nay, of thy name so oft I mention make
That I am thought distracted for thy sake;
When my tir'd Spirits faile, and my sick heart
Drawes in that *fire* which actuates each part,
If any say, th'art come! I force my pain,
And hope to see thee, gives me life again.
Thus I for thee, whilst thou (perhaps) more blest
Careless of me doest breath all peace and rest,

Which yet I think not, for (*Deare Soule!*) too well
Know I thy griefe, since my first woes befell.   30
But if strict heav'n my stock of dayes hath spun
And with my life my errour wilbe gone,
How easie then (*O Cæsar!*) wer't for thee
To pardon one, that now doth cease to be?
That I might yeeld my native aire this breath,
And banish not my ashes after death ;
Would thou hadst either spar'd me untill dead,
Or with my bloud redeem'd my absent head,
Thou shouldst have had both freely, but O! thou
Wouldst have me live to dye an *Exile* now.   40
And must I then from *Rome* so far meet death,
And double by the place my losse of breath?
Nor in my last of houres on my own bed
(In the sad Conflict) rest my dying head?
Nor my soules *Whispers* (the last pledge of life,)
Mix with the tears and kisses of a wife?
My last words none must treasure, none will rise
And (with a teare) seal up my vanquish'd Eyes,
Without these *Rites* I dye, distrest in all
The *splendid sorrowes* of a Funerall,·   50
Unpittied, and unmourn'd for, my sad head
In a strange Land goes friendless to the dead.
When thou hear'st this, O how thy faithfull soule
Will sink, whilst griefe doth ev'ry part controule!
How often wilt thou look this way, and Crie,
O where is't yonder that my love doth lye!
Yet spare these tears, and mourn not now for me,
Long since (*dear heart!*) have I been dead to thee,
Think then I dyed, when *Thee* and *Rome* I lost
That death to me more griefe then this hath Cost ;   60
Now, if thou canst (but thou canst not) *best wife*
Rejoyce, my Cares are ended with my life,
At least, yeeld not to sorrowes, frequent use
Should make these miseries to thee no newes.
And here I wish my Soul died with my breath
And that no part of me were free from death,
For, if it be Immortall, and outlives
The body, as *Pythagoras* believes,
Betwixt these *Sarmates ghosts*, a *Roman* I
Shall wander, vext to all Eternitie.   70

But thou (for after death I shall be free,)
Fetch home these bones, and what is left of me,
A few *Flowres* give them, with some *Balme*, and lay
Them in some *Suburb-grave* hard by the way,
And to Informe posterity, who's there,
This sad Inscription let my marble weare,
  „ *Here lyes the soft-soul'd Lecturer of Love,*
  „ *Whose envy'd wit did his own ruine prove.*
But thou, (who e'r thou beest, that passing by
Lendst to this *sudden stone* a *hastie* Eye,)   80
If e'r thou knew'st of *Love* the sweet disease,
Grudge not to say, *May* Ovid *rest in peace !*
This for my tombe : but in my books they'l see
More strong and lasting Monuments of mee,
Which I believe (though fatall) will afford
An Endless name unto their ruin'd Lord.
    And now thus gone, It rests for love of me
Thou shewst some sorrow to my memory ;
Thy Funerall offrings to my ashes beare
With Wreathes of *Cypresse* bath'd in many a teare,   90
Though nothing there but dust of me remain,
Yet shall that *Dust* perceive thy pious pain.
But I have done, and my tyr'd sickly head
Though I would fain write more, desires the bed ;
Take then this word (perhaps my last to tell)
Which though I want, I wish it thee, *Fare-well.*

Ausonii Cupido, Edyl. 6.

In those blest fields of *Everlasting aire*
(Where to a *Myrtle*-grove the soules repaire
Of deceas'd *Lovers*,) the sad, thoughtfull ghosts
Of *Injur'd Ladyes* meet, where each accoasts
The other with a sigh, whose very breath
Would break a heart, and (*kind Soules !*) love in death.
A thick wood clouds their *walks*, where day scarse peeps,
And on each hand Cypresse and Poppey *sleepes*,
The drowsie Rivers *slumber*, and *Springs* there
Blab not, but softly melt into a teare,   10
A sickly dull aire *fans* them, which can have
When most in force scarce breath to *build* a wave.

80 Eye,) *GC* : Eye, *1651*

On either bank through the still shades appear
A *Scene* of pensive flowres, whose bosomes wear
Drops of a *Lover's* bloud, the *Emblem'd* truths
Of deep despair, and Love-slain *Kings* and *Youths.*
The *Hyacinth,* and self-enamour'd Boy
Narcissus flourish there, with *Venus* Joy
The spruce *Adonis,* and that *Prince* whose flowre
Hath sorrow languag'd on him to this houre ;   20
All sad with love they hang their heads, and grieve
As if their passions in each leafe did *live ;*
And here (*alas !*) these soft-soul'd Ladies stray,
And (oh ! too late !) treason in love betray.
　　Her blasted birth sad *Semele* repeats,
And with her *tears* would quench the thund'rers *heats*
Then shakes her bosome, as if fir'd again,
And fears another lightnings *flaming train.*
The lovely *Procris* (here) bleeds, sighes, and swounds
Then wakes, and kisses him that gave her wounds.   30
Sad *Hero* holds a torch forth, and doth light
Her lost *Leander* through the waves and night.
Her *Boateman* desp'rate *Sapho* still admires,
And nothing but the *Sea* can quench her *fires.*
Distracted *Phœdra* with a restless Eye
Her disdain'd Letters reads, then casts them by.
Rare, faithfull *Thysbe* (sequestred from these)
A silent, unseen sorrow doth best please,
For her *Loves* sake, and last *good-night,* poor she
Walks in the shadow of a *Mulberrie.*   40
Neer her young *Canace* with *Dido* sits
A lovely Couple, but of desp'rate wits,
Both dy'd alike, both pierc'd their tender brests,
This with her *Fathers* Sword, that with her *Guests.*
Within the thickest *textures* of the Grove
Diana in her *Silver-beams* doth rove,
Her Crown of stars the *pitchie aire* Invades,
And with a faint light *gilds* the silent shades,
Whilst her sad thoughts fixt on her *sleepie Lover*
To *Latmos*-hill, and his retirements move her.   50
A thousand more through the wide, darksome wood
Feast on their cares, the *Maudlin-Lovers* food,

29 *Procris*] *Pocris 1651*

For *griefe* and *absence* doe but *Edge* desire,
And Death is *fuell* to a Lovers *fire.*

   To see these *Trophies* of his wanton bow
Cupid comes in, and all in triumph now
(Rash, unadvised Boy!) disperseth round
The sleepie Mists, his *Wings* and *quiver* wound
With noise the quiet aire. This sudden stirre
Betrayes his *godship*, and as we from far   60
A clouded, sickly *Moon* observe, so they
Through the *false Mists* his *Ecclyps'd torch* betray.
A hot pursute they make, and though with care,
And a slow wing he softly *stems* the aire,
Yet they (as subtill now as he) surround
His silenc'd course, and with the thick night bound
Surprize the *Wag.* As in a dream we strive
To voyce our thoughts, & vainly would revive
Our Entraunc'd tongues, but can not speech enlarge
'Till the Soule wakes and reassumes her Charge,   70
So joyous of their *Prize*, they flock about
And vainly *Swell* with an *Imagin'd* shout.

   Far in these shades, and melancholy Coasts
A *Myrtle* growes, well known to all the ghosts,
Whose stretch'd top (like a *great man* rais'd by Fate)
Looks big, and scorns his neighbours low estate ;
His *leavy arms* into a *green Cloud* twist,
And on each Branch doth *sit* a lazie mist.
A fatall tree, and luckless to the gods,
Where for *disdain* in life (loves *worst* of *Ods*,)   80
The *Queen* of shades, fair *Proserpine* did rack
The sad *Adonis*, hither now they pack
This little *God*, where, first disarm'd, they *bind*
His skittish wings, then both his hands behind
His back they tye, and thus secur'd at last
The *peevish wanton* to the tree make fast.
Here at adventure without *Judge* or Jurie
He is condemn'd, while with united furie
They all assaile him ; As a thiefe at Bar
Left to the Law, and mercy of his Star,   90
Hath *Bills* heap'd on him, and is question'd there
By all the men that have been rob'd that year,

So now what ever *Fate*, or their own *Will*
Scor'd up in life, *Cupid* must pay the bill.
Their *Servants* falshood, Jealousie, disdain,
And all the plagues that *abus'd Maids* can feign,
Are layd on him, and then to heighten spleen
Their own deaths crown the summe.   Prest thus between
His faire accusers, 'tis at last decreed,
He by those weapons, that they died, should bleed.   100
One grasps an *airie Sword*, a second holds
Illusive *fire*, and in *vain*, wanton folds
Belyes a flame ; Others lesse kind appear
To let him bloud, and from the purple tear
Create a *Rose.*   But *Sapho* all this while
Harvests the aire, and from a thicken'd pile
Of Clouds like *Leucas-top*, spreads underneath
A *Sea* of *Mists*, the peacefull billowes breath
Without all noise, yet so exactly move
They seem to *Chide*, but distant from above   110
Reach not the eare, and (thus prepar'd) at once
She doth o'rwhelm him with the *airie Sconce.*
Amidst these tumults, and as fierce as they
Venus steps in, and without thought, or stay
Invades her *Son ;* her old disgrace is cast
Into the *Bill*, when *Mars* and *Shee* made *fast*
In their Embraces were expos'd to all
The *Scene* of gods stark naked in their *fall.*
Nor serves a *verball* penance, but with hast
From her fair brow (O happy flowres so plac'd !)   120
She tears a *Rosie garland*, and with this
Whips the *untoward Boy*, they gently kisse
His *snowie skin*, but she with angry hast
Doubles her strength, untill bedew'd at last
With a thin bloudie sweat, their *Innate Red*,
(As if griev'd with the Act) grew pale and dead.
This *layd* their spleen : And now (*kind soules !*) no more
They'l punish him, the torture that he bore,
Seems greater then his crime ; with joynt Consent
Fate is made guilty, and *he* Innocent.   130
As in a dream with dangers we contest,
And *fictious pains* seem to afflict our rest,
So frighted only in these shades of night
Cupid (got loose) stole to the upper light,

Where ever since (for malice unto these)
The *spitefull Ape* doth either *Sex* displease.
But O that had these *Ladyes* been so wise
To keep his *Arms*, and give him but his *Eyes*!

Boet. Lib. 1. *Metrum* 1.

I whose first year flourish'd with youthfull verse,
In slow, sad numbers now my griefe reherse ;
A broken stile my sickly lines afford,
And only tears give weight unto my words ;
Yet neither fate nor force my Muse cou'd fright
The only faithfull Consort of my flight ;
Thus what was once my green years greatest glorie,
Is now my Comfort, grown decay'd and hoarie,
For killing Cares th'Effects of age spurr'd on
That griefe might find a fitting Mansion ;   10
O'r my young head runs an untimely gray,
And my loose skin shrinks at my blouds decay.
Happy the man ! whose death in prosp'rous years
Strikes not, nor shuns him in his age and tears.
But O how deafe is she to hear the Crie
Of th' opprest Soule, or shut the weeping Eye !
While treacherous Fortune with slight honours fed
My first estate, she almost drown'd my head,
But now since (clouded thus) she hides those rayes,
Life adds unwelcom'd length unto my dayes ;   20
Why then, my friends, Judg'd you my state so good?
He that may fall once, never firmly stood.

Metrum 2.

O in what haste with Clouds and Night
Ecclyps'd, and having lost her light,
The dull Soule whom distraction rends
Into outward Darkness tends !
How often (by these mists made blind,)
Have earthly cares opprest the mind !
    This Soule sometimes wont to survey
The spangled *Zodiacks firie way*
Saw th'early Sun in Roses drest
With the Coole Moons unstable Crest,   10

Met. 1.   5 fate *Er and some copies of 1651*: faith *other copies of 1651*

And whatsoever wanton Star
In various Courses neer or far
Pierc'd through the orbs, he cou'd full well
Track all her Journey, and would tell
Her Mansions, turnings, Rise and fall,
By Curious Calculation all.
Of sudden winds the hidden Cause,
And why the Calm Seas quiet face
With Impetuous waves is Curld,
What spirit wheeles th'harmonious world,   20
Or why a Star dropt in the *West*
Is seen to rise again by *East*,
Who gives the warm Spring temp'rate houres
Decking the Earth with spicie flowres,
Or how it Comes (for mans recruit)
That Autumne yeelds both Grape and fruit,
With many other Secrets, he
Could shew the Cause and Mysterie.
   But now that light is almost out,
And the brave Soule lyes Chain'd about   30
With outward Cares, whose pensive weight
Sinks down her Eyes from their first height,
And clean Contrary to her birth
Poares on this vile and foolish Earth.

Metrum 4.

Whose calme soule in a settled state
Kicks under foot the frowns of Fate,
And in his fortunes bad or good
Keeps the same temper in his bloud,
Not him the flaming Clouds above,
Nor *Ætna's* fierie tempests move,
No fretting seas from shore to shore
Boyling with Indignation o're
Nor burning thunderbolt that can
A mountain shake, can stirre this man.   10
Dull Cowards then ! why should we start
To see these tyrants act their part ?
Nor hope, nor fear what may befall
And you disarm their malice all.

28 Mysterie. *C* : Mysterie, *1651*

But who doth faintly fear, or wish
And sets no law to what is his,
Hath lost the buckler, and (poor Elfe !)
Makes up a Chain to bind himselfe.

Metrum 5.

O thou great builder of this starrie frame
Who fixt in thy eternall throne dost tame
The rapid Spheres, and lest they jarre
Hast giv'n a law to ev'ry starre !
Thou art the Cause that now the Moon
With full orbe dulls the starres, and soon
Again growes dark, her light being done,
The neerer still she's to the Sun.
Thou in the early hours of night
Mak'st the coole Evening-star shine bright,   10
And at Sun-rising ('cause the least)
Look pale and sleepie in the East.
Thou, when the leafes in Winter stray,
Appointst the Sun a shorter way,
And in the pleasant Summer-light
With nimble houres doest wing the night.
Thy hand the various year quite through
Discreetly tempers, that what now
The North-wind tears from ev'ry tree
In Spring again restor'd we see.   20
Then what the *winter-starrs* between
The furrowes in meer seed have seen
The Dog-star since (grown up and born)
Hath burnt in stately, full-ear'd Corn.
    Thus by Creations law controll'd
All things their proper stations hold
Observing (as thou didst intend)
Why they were made, and for what end.
Only humane actions thou
Hast no Care of, but to the flow   30
And Ebbe of Fortune leav'st them all,
Hence th' Innocent endures that thrall
Due to the wicked, whilst alone
They sit possessours of his throne,

The Just are kill'd, and Vertue lyes
Buried in obscurities,
And (which of all things is most sad)
The good man suffers by the bad.
No perjuries, nor damn'd pretence
Colour'd with holy, lying sense   40
Can them annoy, but when they mind
To try their force, which most men find,
They from the highest sway of things
Can pull down great, and pious Kings.
   O then at length, thus loosely hurl'd
Look on this miserable world
Who e'r thou art, that from above
Doest in such order all things move !
And let not man (of divine art
Not the least, nor vilest part)   50
By Casuall evills thus bandied, be
The sport of fates obliquitie.
But with that faith thou guid'st the heaven,
Settle this Earth, and make them even.

Metrum 6.

When the Crabs fierce Constellation
Burns with the beams of the bright Sun,
Then he that will goe out to sowe,
Shall never reap where he did plough,
But in stead of Corn may rather
The old worlds diet, Accorns gather.
Who the Violet doth love
Must seek her in the flowrie grove,
But never when the *Norths* cold wind
The *Russet* fields with frost doth bind.   10
If in the Spring-time (to no end)
The tender Vine for Grapes we bend,
Wee shall find none, for only (still)
Autumne doth the Wine-presse fill.
   Thus for all things (in the worlds prime)
The wise God seal'd their proper time,
Nor will permit those seasons he
Ordain'd by turns, should mingled be

Then whose wild actions out of season
Crosse to nature, and her reason,   20
Would by new wayes old orders rend,
Shall never find a happy End.

Metrum 7.

Curtain'd with Clouds in a dark night
The Stars cannot send forth their light.
And if a sudden Southern blast
The Sea in rolling waves doth cast,
That angrie Element doth boile,
And from the deep with stormy Coile
Spues up the Sands, which in short space
Scatter, and puddle his Curl'd face;
Then those Calme waters, which but now
Stood clear as heavens unclouded brow,   10
And like transparent glasse did lye
Open to ev'ry searchers Eye,
Look foulely stirr'd, and (though desir'd)
Resist the sight, because bemir'd,
So often from a high hills brow
Some Pilgrim-spring is seen to flow,
And in a straight line keep her Course
'Till from a Rock with headlong force
Some broken peece blocks up her way
And forceth all her streams astray.   20
   Then thou that with inlightned Rayes,
Wouldst see the truth, and in her wayes
Keep without *Errour*; neither fear
The future, nor too much give ear
To present Joyes; And give no scope
To griefe, nor much to flatt'ring hope.
For when these Rebels raign, the mind
Is both a Pris'ner, and stark blind.

Lib. 2. *Metrum* 1.

Fortune (when with rash hands she quite turmoiles
The state of things, and in tempestuous foiles
Comes whirling like *Euripus*,) beats quite down
With headlong force the highest Monarchs crown
And in his place unto the throne doth fetch
The despis'd looks of some mechanick wretch.

So Jests at tears and miseries, is proud,
And laughs to hear her vassals grone aloud.
These are her sports, thus she her wheele doth drive
And plagues man with her blind prerogative ;   10
Nor is't a favour of Inferiour strain,
If once kickt down, she lets him rise again.

Metrum 2.

If with an open, bounteous hand
(Wholly left at Mans Command)
Fortune should in one rich flow
As many heaps on him bestow
Of massie gold, as there be sands
Tost by the waves and winds rude bands,
Or bright stars in a Winter-night
Decking their silent Orbs with light,
Yet would his lust know no restraints,
Nor cease to weep in sad Complaints.   10
Though heaven should his vowes reguard,
And in a prodigall reward
Return him all he could implore,
Adding new honours to his store,
Yet all were nothing.   Goods in sight
Are scorn'd, and lust in greedy flight
Layes out for more ; What measure then
Can tame these wild desires of men ?
Since all wee give both last and first
Doth but inflame, and feed their thirst ;   20
For how can he be rich, who 'midst his store
Sits sadly pining, and believes he's poore.

Metrum 3.

When the Sun from his Rosie bed
The dawning light begins to shed,
The drowsie sky uncurtains round,
And the (but now bright) stars all drown'd
In one great light, look dull and tame,
And homage his victorious flame.
Thus, when the warm *Etesian* wind
The Earth's seald bosome doth unbind,

Straight she her various store discloses,
And purples every Grove with Roses ;   10
But if the Souths tempestuous breath
Breaks forth, those blushes pine to death.
Oft in a quiet sky the deep
With unmov'd waves seems fast asleep,
And oft again the blustring North
In angrie heaps provokes them forth.
  If then this world, which holds all Nations,
Suffers it selfe such alterations,
That not this mighty, massie frame,
Nor any part of it can Claime   20
One certain course, why should man prate,
Or Censure the designs of Fate ?
Why from fraile honours, and goods lent
Should he expect things permanent ?
Since 'tis enacted by divine decree
That nothing mortall shall eternall be.

Metrum 4.

Who wisely would for his retreat
Build a secure and lasting seat,
Where stov'd in silence he may sleep
Beneath the *Wind*, above the *Deep* ;
Let him th' high hils leave on one hand,
And on the other the false sand ;
The first to winds lyes plain and even
From all the blustring points of heaven ;
The other hollow and unsure,
No weight of building will endure.   10
Avoyding then the envied state
Of buildings bravely situate,
Remember thou thy selfe to lock
Within some low neglected Rock ;
There when fierce heaven in thunder Chides,
And winds and waves rage on all sides,
Thou happy in the quiet fense
Of thy poor Cell with small Expence
Shall lead a life serene and faire,
And scorn the anger of the aire.   20

Met. 4.   17 fense] sense *GC*

Metrum 5.

Happy that first white age! when wee
Lived by the Earths meere Charitie,
No soft luxurious Diet then
Had Effeminated men,
No other meat, nor wine had any
Then the Course Mast, or simple honey,
And by the Parents care layd up
Cheap *Berries* did the Children sup.
No pompous weare was in those dayes
Of gummie Silks, or Skarlet bayes,   10
Their beds were on some flowrie brink
And clear Spring-water was their drink.
The shadie Pine in the Suns heat
Was their Coole and known Retreat,
For then 'twas not cut down, but stood
The youth and glory of the wood.
The daring Sailer with his slaves
Then had not cut the swelling waves,
Nor for desire of forraign store
Seen any but his native shore.   20
No stirring Drum had scarr'd that age,
Nor the shrill Trumpets active rage,
No wounds by bitter hatred made
With warm bloud soil'd the shining blade;
For how could hostile madness arm
An age of love to publick harm?
When Common Justice none withstood,
Nor sought rewards for spilling bloud.
    O that at length our age would raise
Into the temper of those dayes!   30
But (worse then *Ætna's* fires!) debate
And Avarice inflame our state.
Alas! who was it that first found
Gold hid of purpose under ground,
That sought out Pearles, and div'd to find
Such pretious perils for mankind!

31 worse] worst *1651*

Metrum 6.

He that thirsts for glories prize,
　　Thinking that the top of all
Let him view th'Expansed skies,
　　And the Earths Contracted ball,
'Twill shame him then, the name he wan
Fils not the short *walk* of one man.

2.

O why vainly strive you then
　　To shake off the bands of Fate,
Though fame through the world of men
　　Should in all tongues your names relate,　　　10
And with proud titles swell that storie
The Darke grave scorns your brightest glorie.

3.

There with Nobles beggers sway,
　　And Kings with Commons share one dust,
What newes of *Brutus* at this day,
　　Or *Fabricius* the Just?
Some rude *Verse* Cut in stone, or led
　　Keeps up the names, but they are dead.

4.

So shall you, one day (past reprieve)
　　Lye (perhaps) without a name,　　　20
But if dead you think to live
　　By this aire of humane fame,
Know, when time stops that posthume breath,
You must endure a second death.

Metrum 7.

That the world in constant *force*
Varies her *Concordant course*;
That *seeds* jarring *hot* and *cold*
Doe the *breed* perpetuall hold;
That in his golden Coach the *Sun*
Brings the *Rosie day* still on;
That the *Moon* swayes all those *lights*
Which *Hesper* ushers to *dark nights*

19 shall you, *M*: shall, you *1651*: shall you *GC*

That *alternate tydes* be found
The Seas *ambitious* waves to bound, 10
Lest o'r the wide Earth without End
Their *fluid Empire* should extend ;
All this frame of *things* that *be*, ⎫
Love which rules *Heaven, Land,* and *Sea,* ⎬
Chains, keeps, orders as we see. ⎭
This, if the raines he once cast by,
All things that now by turns comply,
Would fall to discord, and this frame
Which now by sociall faith they tame,
And comely orders in that fight 20
And jarre of things would perish quite.
This in a holy league of peace
Keeps King and People with Increase ;
And in the sacred nuptiall bands
Tyes up chast hearts with willing hands,
And this keeps firm without all doubt
Friends by his bright Instinct found out.
    O happy Nation then were you
If love which doth all things subdue,
That rules the spacious heav'n, and brings 30
Plenty and Peace upon his wings,
Might rule you too ! and without guile
Settle once more this floting Ile !

Casimirus, Lib. 4. *Ode* 28.

All-mighty *Spirit* ! thou that by
Set *turns* and *changes* from thy high
And glorious *throne*, dost here below
Rule all, and all things dost *foreknow* ;
Can those *blind plots* woo here discusse
Please thee, as thy *wise Counsels* us ?
When thou thy *blessings* here dost strow,
And poure on *Earth,* we flock and flow
With *Joyous strife*, and *eager care*
Strugling which shall have the best share 10
In thy *rich gifts*, just as we see
Children about *Nuts* disagree.
Some that a *Crown* have got and foyl'd
Break it ; Another sees it *spoil'd*

H

E're it is *gotten* : Thus the *world*
Is all to *peece-meals* cut, and hurl'd
By *factious hands,* It is a *ball*
Which *Fate* and *force* divide 'twixt all
The *Sons* of *men.* But ô good God !
While these for *dust* fight, and a *Clod*,   20
Grant that poore I may *smile*, and be
At rest, and *perfect peace* with thee.

Casimirus, Lib. 2. Ode 8.

It would lesse vex *distressed man*
If *Fortune* in the same *pace* ran
To *ruine* him, as he did *rise* ;
But highest *states* fall in a trice.
No *great Successe* held ever *long* :
A restless *fate* afflicts the throng
Of *Kings* and *Commons*, and lesse dayes
Serve to *destroy* them, then to *raise.*
Good luck *smiles* once an age, but *bad*
Makes *Kingdomes* in a *minute* sad,   10
And ev'ry *houre* of *life* wee drive,
Hath o're us a *Prerogative.*
   Then leave (by *wild Impatience* driv'n,
And *rash resents*,) to rayle at *heav'n*,
Leave an *unmanly, weak complaint*
That *Death* and *Fate* have no restraint.
In the same *houre* that gave thee *breath*,
Thou hadst ordain'd thy houre of *death*,
But *he* lives *most*, who here will *buy*
With a few tears, *Eternitie.*   20

Casimirus, Lib. 3 Ode 22.

Let not thy *youth* and *false delights*
Cheat thee of *life* ; Those *headdy flights*
But wast thy *time*, which posts away
Like *winds* unseen, and swift as they.
Beauty is but meer *paint*, whose *die*
With times *breath* will *dissolve* and *flye*,
'Tis *wax*, 'tis *water*, 'tis a *glasse*
It *melts, breaks,* and *away* doth *passe*

'Tis like a *Rose* which in the *dawne*
The *aire* with gentle breath doth *fawne*   10
And *whisper* too, but in the houres
Of *night* is sullied with smart showres.
Life spent, is wish'd for but in vain,
Nor can past *years* come back again.
  Happy the *Man* ! who in this *vale*
Redeems his time, shutting out all
Thoughts of the *world,* whose *longing Eyes*
Are ever *Pilgrims* in the *skyes,*
That views his *bright home,* and desires
To *shine* amongst those *glorious fires.*   20

Casimirus Lyric. Lib. 3. *Ode* 23.

'Tis not *rich furniture* and *gems*
With *Cedar-roofes,* and ancient *stems,*
Nor yet a *plenteous, lasting floud*
Of *gold,* that makes man *truly good.*
Leave to Inquire in what *faire fields*
A *River* runs which *much gold* yeelds,
Vertue alone is the *rich prize*
Can purchase *stars,* and buy the *skies.*
Let others build with *Adamant,*
Or pillars of *carv'd Marble* plant,   10
Which *rude* and *rough* sometimes did dwell
Far under *earth,* and neer to *hell.*
But *richer* much (from *death* release)
Shines in the *fresh groves* of the *East*
The *Phœnix,* or those *fish* that dwell
With *silver'd scales* in *Hiddekel.*
Let others with rare, various *Pearls*
Their *garments* dresse, and in *forc'd Curls*
Bind up their *locks,* look *big* and *high,*
And shine in *robes* of *Scarlet-die.*   20
But in my thoughts more *glorious* far
Those *native stars,* and *speckles* are
Which *birds* wear, or the *spots* which wee
In *Leopards* dispersed see.
The harmless *sheep* with her warm *fleece*
Cloathes *man,* but who his *dark heart* sees
Shall find a *Wolfe* or *Fox* within
That kills the *Castor* for his *skin.*

Vertue alone, and nought else can
A diffrence make 'twixt *beasts* and *man*,　　30
And on her *wings* above the *Spheres*
To the *true light* his *spirit* bears.

Casimirus, Lib. 4. *Ode* 15.

Nothing on *Earth*, nothing at all
Can be exempted from the *thrall*
Of peevish *weariness*! The *Sun*
Which our *fore-fathers* Judg'd to run
Clear and *unspotted*, in our dayes
Is tax'd with *sullen, Ecclips'd rayes.*
What ever in the *glorious skie*
Man sees, his rash, *audacious Eye*
Dares Censure it, and in meer *spite*
At *distance* will condemn the *light.*　　10
The *wholsome mornings*, whose *beams* cleer
Those *hills* our *fathers* walkt on here
Wee fancy not, nor the *Moons* light
Which through their *windows* shin'd at *night,*
Wee change the *Aire* each year, and scorn
Those *Seates*, in which we first were *borne.*
Some nice, affected *wand'rers* love
Belgia's mild winters, others remove
For want of *health* and *honestie*
To *Summer* it in *Italie* ;　　20
But to no end : The *disease* still
Sticks to his *Lord*, and kindly will
To *Venice* in a *Barge* repaire,
Or *Coach* it to *Vienna's* aire,
And then (too late with *home* Content,)
They leave this *wilfull banishment.*
　　But he, whose *Constancie* makes sure
His *mind* and *mansion*, lives secure
From such *vain tasks*, can *dine* and *sup*
Where his *old parents* bred him up.　　30
Content (no doubt !) most times doth dwell
In *Countrey-shades*, or to some *Cell*
Confines it selfe, and can alone
Make simple *straw*, a Royall *Throne.*

11 cleer] cheer *G*

Casimirus, Lib. 4. *Ode* 13.

If *weeping Eyes* could wash away
Those *Evills* they mourn for *night and day,*
Then gladly I to *cure* my *fears*
With my best *Jewells* would buy *tears.*
But as *dew* feeds the growing *Corn,*
So *Crosses* that are grown *forlorn*
Increase with *griefe, teares* make *teares* way,
And *cares* kept up, keep *cares* in *pay.*
That *wretch* whom *Fortune* finds to *feare,*
And *melting* still into a *teare,*   10
She *strikes* more *boldly,* but a *face*
Silent and *drie* doth her *amaze.*
Then leave thy *teares,* and tedious *tale*
Of what thou doest *misfortunes* call,
What thou by *weeping* think'st to *ease,*
Doth by that *Passion* but *Increase*;
Hard things to *Soft* will never yield,
'Tis the *drie Eye* that wins the field;
A noble *patience* quells the *spite*
Of *Fortune,* and *disarms* her quite.   20

The Praise of a Religious life by *Mathias Casimirus.*
In Answer to that Ode of *Horace,*
Beatus Ille qui procul negotiis, &c.

Flaccus not so: That worldly *He*
Whom in the Countreys *shade* we see
Ploughing his own *fields,* seldome can
Be justly stil'd, *The Blessed man.*
    That title only fits a *Saint,*
Whose free thoughts far above restraint
And weighty Cares, can gladly part
With *house* and *lands,* and leave the smart
Litigious troubles, and lowd strife
Of this world for a better life.   10
He fears no *Cold,* nor *heat* to blast
His *Corn,* for his *Accounts* are cast,

He *sues* no man, nor stands in Awe
Of the *devouring Courts* of Law ;
But all his time he spends in *tears*
For the *Sins* of his youthfull years,
Or having tasted those *rich Joyes*
Of a Conscience without *noyse*
Sits in some fair *shade*, and doth give
To his *wild thoughts* rules how to live.   20
He in the *Evening*, when on high
The *Stars* shine in the *silent skye*
Beholds th'*eternall flames* with mirth,
And *globes* of *light* more large then *Earth*,
Then weeps for *Joy*, and through his tears
Looks on the *fire-enamel'd* Spheres,
Where with his *Saviour* he would be
Lifted above mortalitie.
Mean while the *golden stars* doe set,
And the *slow-Pilgrim* leave all wet   30
With his own tears, which flow so fast
They make his *sleeps* light, and soon past.
By this, the *Sun* o're night *deceast*
Breaks in *fresh Blushes* from the *East*,
When mindfull of his former *falls*
With *strong Cries* to his *God* he calls,
And with such *deep-drawn sighes* doth move
That he turns *anger* into *love*.
In the Calme *Spring*, when the Earth *bears*,
And feeds on *Aprils breath*, and *tears*,   40
His Eyes accustom'd to the *skyes*
Find here *fresh objects*, and like *spyes*
Or busie *Bees* search the soft *flowres*
Contemplate the *green fields*, and *Bowres*,
Where he in *Veyles*, and *shades* doth see
The *back Parts* of the *Deitye*.
Then sadly sighing sayes, ,, *O how*
,, *These flowres With hasty, stretch'd heads grow*
,, *And strive for heav'n, but rooted here*
,, *Lament the distance with a teare!*   50
,, *The Honey-suckles Clad in white,*
,, *The Rose in Red point to the light,*
,, *And the Lillies hollow and bleak*
,, *Look, as if they would something speak,*

„ *They sigh at night to each soft gale,*
„ *And at the day-spring weep it all.*
„ *Shall I then only (wretched I !)*
„ *Opprest with Earth, on Earth still lye ?*
Thus speaks he to the neighbour trees
And many sad *Soliloquies*   60
To *Springs*, and *Fountaines* doth impart,
Seeking God with a longing heart.
   But if to ease his busie breast
He thinks of *home*, and taking rest,
A *Rurall Cott*, and *Common fare*
Are all his *Cordials* against *Care.*
There at the *doore* of his low *Cell*
Under some *shade*, or neer some *Well*
Where the *Coole Poplar* growes, his *Plate*
Of Common *Earth*, without more *state*   70
Expect their *Lord.* *Salt* in a *shell*,
Green *Cheese*, thin *beere*, *Draughts* that will *tell*
No *Tales*, a *hospitable Cup*,
With some *fresh berries* doe make up
His healthfull feast, nor doth he wish
For the fatt *Carp*, or a rare dish
Of *Lucrine Oysters* ; The swift *Quist*
Or *Pigeon* sometimes (if he list)
With the *slow Goose* that loves the *stream*,
Fresh, various *Sallads*, and the *Bean*   80
By Curious *Pallats* never sought,
And to Close with, some Cheap unbought
Dish for *digestion*, are the most
And Choicest *dainties* he can *boast.*
   Thus feasted, to the *flowrie Groves*,
Or pleasant *Rivers* he removes,
Where neer some *fair Oke* hung with Mast
He shuns the *Souths* Infectious blast.
On shadie *banks* sometimes he lyes,
Sometimes the open *Current tryes*,   90
Where with his *line* and *feather'd flye*
He sports, and takes the *Scaly frie.*
Mean-while each *hollow wood* and *hill*
Doth ring with *lowings* long and shrill,

64 rest, *GC* : rest *1651*

And shadie *Lakes* with *Rivers* deep,
Eccho the *bleating* of the *Sheep*.
The *Black-bird* with the pleasant *Thrush*
And *Nightingale* in ev'ry Bush
Choice *Musick* give, and *Shepherds* play
Unto their *flocks* some loving *Lay* ;   100
The thirsty *Reapers* in thick throngs
Return home from the *field* with Songs,
And the *Carts* loden with ripe *Corn*
Come groning to the well-stor'd *Barn*.
Nor passe wee by as the least good,
A *peacefull, loving neighbourhood*,
Whose *honest Wit*, and *Chast discourse*
Make none (by hearing it) the *worse*,
But *Innocent* and *merry* may
Help (without *Sin*) to spend the day.   110
Could now the *Tyrant-usurer*
Who *plots* to be a *Purchaser*
Of his poor neighbours *seat*, but taste
These *true delights*, ô with what haste
And hatred of his wayes would he
Renounce his *Jewish Crueltie*,
And those *Curs'd summes* which poor men borrow
On *use* to day, *remit* to morrow !

Ad fluvium Iscam.

Isca *parens florum, placido qui spumeus ore*
    Lambis lapillos aureos,
Qui mæstos hyacinthos, & picti ἄνθεα *tophi*
    Mulces susurris humidis,
Dumꝗ novas *pergunt* menses *Consumere* Lunas
    Cœlumꝗ mortales *terit,*
Accumulas cum Sole *dies, ævumꝗ per omne*
    Fidelis *Induras* latex,
O quis Inaccessos & quali murmure lucos
    Mutumq; *Solaris* nemus *!*   10
Per te discerpti credo Thracis *ire querelas*
    Plectrumꝗ divini senis.

Venerabili viro, præceptori suo olim
& semper Colendissimo M^{ro}.
Mathæo Herbert.

Quod vixi, Mathæe, *dedit* Pater, *hæc tamen olim*
Vita fluet, *nec erit fas meminisse datam.*
Ultrà Curâsti Solers, perituraſ, mecum
Nomina post Cineres *das resonare* meos.
Divide discipulum : brevis hæc &° lubrica nostri
Pars vertat Patri, *Posthuma vita* tibi.

Præstantissimo viro, Thomæ Poëllo *in*
suum de Elementis opticæ libellum.

Vivaces *oculorum* Ignes &° lumina dia
Fixit in angusto *maximus* orbe *Deus,*
Ille Explorantes radios *dedit*, &° vaga lustra
In quibus Intuitûs *lexſ, modusſ, latent.*
Hos tacitos Jactus, lususq; volubilis orbis
Pingis in Exiguo, *magne Poëlle*, libro,
Excursusq; situsq;, *ut* Lynceus opticus, *edis*
Quotſ, modis fallunt, *qʋotſ, adhibenda* fides.
Æmula naturæ manus ! &° mens *Conscia cœli !*
Illa videre dedit, *vestra videre* docet.   10

Ad Echum.

O Quæ frondosæ per amœna Cubilia *sylvæ*
Nympha volas, *lucoſ,* loquax *spatiaris in alto,*
Annosi numen *nemoris, saltusſ, verendi*
Effatum, *cui sola placent* postrema *relatu !*
Te per Narcissi *morientis verba, precesſ,*
Per pueri Lassatam animam, &° Conamina *vitæ*
Ultima, *palantisſ, precor* suspiria *linguæ.*
Da quo secretæ hæc Incædua devia *sylvæ,*
Anfractusq; *loci dubios*, &° lustra *repandam.*
Sic tibi perpetuâ (*meritoſ,*) *hæc regna* Juventâ   10
Luxurient, dabiturſ, tuis, sinè fine, viretis

Venerabili viro.   2 *fluet*] *fluat 1651*
   Præstantissimo viro.   1 Ignes] *Ignes, El. Opt.*   2 *Deus,*] *Deus ; El. Opt.*
6 *magne*] docte *El. Opt.*   7 *Excursusq; situsq;* (ut *Lynceus opticus*) edis,
El. Opt.
   Ad Echum.   4 *relatu Er* : *relatûs 1651.*   5 *Te per Er* : *Per te 1651.*

Intactas *Lunæ* lachrymas, *&° lambere* rorem
Virgineum, *Cæliɫ* animas *haurire tepentis.*
Nec cedant ævo stellis, *sed* lucida *sempèr*
Et satiata sacro *æterni* medicamine *veris*
Ostendant longè vegetos, *ut Sydera,* vultus *!*
Sic spiret Muscata Comas, *&°* Cynnama *passim !*
Diffundat levis umbra, in funere qualia spargit
Phœnicis rogus *aut Pancheæ* nubila *flammæ !*

OF THE

BENEFIT

Wee may get by our

ENEMIES.

A DISCOURSE

Written originally in the
Greek by *Plutarchus Chæronensis*,
tranflated in to Latin by *I. Reynolds* Dr.
of Divinitie and lecturer of the Greeke Tongue
in *Corpus Chrifti* College In *Oxford.*

Englifhed By H : V : *Silurift.*

——*Dolus , an virtus quis in hofte requirat.*
——*fas eft, et ab hofte doceri.*

LONDON.
Printed for *Humphry Mofeley* and are to
be fold at his fhop at the figne of the
Princes Armes in St. Pauls
Church-yard, 1651.

Of the Benefit we may get by our Enemies.

I observe thee ; O *Cornelius Pulcher* ; though wholly given to
a quiet and calme course of life, Sequestred from all Publique imployments : yet out of that stillnesse, and most private Recession
to afford much fruit and satisfaction to the Publique ; while with
so much sweetnes of carriage, and a kind of Native complacency
thou entertainest all comers, whose hazardous affairs cast them of
necessity upon thy most tender Retirements.   And (indeed) true
it is, that such a Region, not pestered with Salvages, or Venomous beasts (as the report is of *Crete*) may be easily found ; But a
Common-wealth not distempered with Envy, Emulation, Ambitious 10
heates, and Contentions (out of which, Enmity and Warres at last
breake forth) could never yet be found.   For if nothing else, yet
in proces of time (which corrupts all things) our very Friendship
and Sociablenes would bring us into Distastes and Enmity.   And
this it was that *Chilo* the wise thought upon, when hearing one
affirme That he had not an Enemy in the World, he return'd upon
him this Quere, *If he had ever a Friend ?*   But in my opinion (as
to the use now to be made of Enemies) there are in that point
many other *Secrets* which more concerne a *Prince*, and (as he is
to sway a Common-wealth burthen'd with a various and vicious 20
multitude) of more advantage and necessity to be considered.
And amongst those, I think that not the least, which *Xenophon*
hath left us recorded in this saying ; *That it is the part of a Wise
man, to derive Profit from his very Enemies.*   Upon this very Consideration (coming but of late into my mind) I resolved to make
some search and discussion, which now finished, in as few words
as the matter would permit, I have sent you to peruse ; wherin
also, you shall find this care taken, that (as far as it might be) I
have avoided to touch upon any Observations formerly given you
in my Civill precepts, because I have already found you a very 30
familiar Student in those papers.

24 this *catchword 1651* : his *text 1651*   25 into *G* : nto *1651*

Mankind in that first age of the world thought it well enough
with them, if they could but so keep, as not to be hurt by those
many fierce, and divers kinds of wild beasts, with which the earth
was then replenished; and this was the period of their atchievements, *To defend themselves.* But one day teaching another, and
Posterity growing more wary than their Fathers, It was found out,
that those very Creatures which their Ancestors deemed noysome
and hurtfull, were of speciall use and comodiousnes unto man; so
that afterwards they were not only not hurt by them, but very
10 much helpt. They fed upon their flesh, made Garments of their
hair, preservatives of their blood, milk, and gaule, and defensive
Arms of their skins. So that it is now much to be feared, that if
Man were deprived of those Creatures, he would be driven to a
subsistance more sordid and rude than the beasts themselves.
Seeing then it is sufficient to some, to receive no damage from
their Enemies, but the wise (as *Zenophon* affirms) will also derive
profit from them; we must not now turn Infidels to his position,
or crie it down for a *Paradox*, but rather make diligent Inquirie
for that secret, whereby those may acquire some benefit from
20 their Enemies, who (as long as they live) shall not live without them.

The husband-man cannot make every tree fruitfull, nor the
hunts-man tame every wild beast; they must therefore assay other
remedies, whereby the one may deduce some furtherance from
fruitles things, and the other from things untractable. Sea-
water is neither good to drink, nor pleasant to the tast; notwithstanding it breeds fish, and feeds them; It serves commodiously
to transport men, and maintaines with generall advantage, a rich
Commerce, and Exchange of wares. When the *Satyre* upon the
first *shine*, and noveltie of the fire would have entertaind it with
30 kisses and embracements, *Take heed goate* (said *Prometheus*) *or it
will make thy Chin smart.* If wee kisse fire, it will burn our lips,
and yet, it affords us both light and heate, and to (those that can
rightly skill it) is the prime Instrument in all learned and reserved arts. I would have thee therefore to think so of thine
enemie, and to consider whether his person, which otherwise wilbe
ever hurtfull, and (viper-like) cannot be touched without evident
danger, may not by some secret meanes be made tractable, and to
afford some notable use of himselfe to thy speciall advantage.
There are in nature many things unmeete for use, and altogether
40 Inconsistent and repugnant to those very ends for which they may
be politickly imployed; so hast thou seene some effeminate,

32 to (those] —to those *G*

voluptuous constitutions to pretend sicknes, or some other infirmitie, that they might only live at more ease, and deliciousnes.
Others to procure themselves a more hardie health, have volun-
teer'd it in all maner of Drudgerie, and made their bodies subject
to the most slavish and toilesome Imploiments. Some again, as
Diogenes and *Crates*, have made Poverty and Banishment the
meanes to acquire knowledge and retirement. So *Zeno*, when it
was told him, that the ship he had sent to sea with his goods was
cast away, replies presently, *Thou hast done very well Fortune, for
now thou hast taught me to make use again of my thredbare, cast* 10
Coate. For as those living creatures which have the hardiest
stomacks, and the healthiest bodies, feed on Serpents and Scor-
pions, and concoct them, others upon Shells and Stones which by
reason of the vehemencie and heate of their spirits they turn presently into a *Chylus*, and nutriment, while the more infirme and
sickly surfeit on wines, and the best diet ; so Weak understandings
corrupt the sincerest Friendship, while the Wise and solid make a
precious use of the most deadly Enmities. And truly in the first
place, that seemes unto me to be most advantagious, than which
(if rightly considered) nothing can be more grievous to our 20
Enemies ; and what that is I will shew thee presently. An
Enemy is alwaies watchfull, lying *perdue* (as it were) to all thy
actions, and (seeking an occasion to mischiefe thee) runns over all
thy life with a most curious eye. He doth not only see through
Timber, Stone-walls, and Curtaines as *Lynceus* did, but perhaps
through the Bosomes and inward parts of thy Friend, thy Servant,
and thy Familiar ; There (as far as he can see) he apprehends
and reads all thy Actions, dives and screws into thy most hidden
and future Intentions. Our Friends oftentimes while we linger
from them, or neglect them, fall sick, and dye unknowne to us ; 30
But our Enemies cannot so much as dream, but most commonly
we inquire into it. Our inward defects, our debts, and domestick
discontents may be sooner hidden from our selves than from our
Enemies, they are the first that prie and search into those maladies.
As Vultures take from far the sent of corrupt carkasses, and
flock to them, but passe by the sound and untainted bodies ;
so the diseased and vitious parts of our lives and affections
are alwaies resented by our enemies, they fly upon those soares,
handle them continually, and love to see them bleed afresh.
Let this benefit therefore redound to thee, that thou have a care 40
to live circumspectly, to be attentive to thy selfe, neither speak,
nor act any thing negligently or unadvisedly, but keep thy tongue

and thy hands within the *Lists*, and let thy maners be (as in a strict prescription of diet) uncorrupt, that thy very enemy may find no place for a just Reprehension. For such a caution as this, which bridles the affections of the mind, and drives her home into her selfe, creates in us a kind of virtuous ardour, and a stedfast resolution to lead a life blameles, and incalumniable. As those Cities which are oft-times visited, somtimes chastised by a warlike neighbour and ly subject to incursions and velitations of Armes, retain most commonly the wholesomest lawes, and strict-
10 est form of Government, so those that have their enemies for *Censours*, and are compelled (as it were) to a sober and vartuous vigilancy; though Reason in this point should be dumb, yet Necessity will tell them, that they must avoid all dissolutnes and neglect, do all things seasonably, not suffering themselves to be insensibly led away with custom, but compose and regulate their manners, least at any time they fall into some irrecoverable and destructive delinquency; for where that festivall but fatall verse is alwaies at hand

Sure Priam *will to mirth incline,*
20 *And all that are of.*Priam's *line.*

Hom:
Illia:

It lulls asleep all Cautelousnes, and blinds their reason untill at last (*Priam*-like) by their own ruin they procure the mirth, and triumph of their Enemies. Wee see Stage-players in Common assemblies, and their own private assayes, remisse and negligent, not acting so accuratly and to the life, as when the Theater is throng'd with judicious spectatours. But when they strive for some prize, or the masterie, they doe not only refine themselves, their habits, and gestures, but with exactest care key all their Instruments, trye every string, and with most nimble and arted
30 motions strik up their most delicious and pleasing strain; so he that knowes himselfe to have an Enemie Competitour both of his life and fame, must be very intentive, weigh all his actions, and make his steps sure and orderly; Especially he is bound to doe it, because vice hath in it this one abominable property, *That those things, wherein wee offend, make our Enemies reverend, and our friends Contemptible.* And therefore it was that *Scipio Nasica*, when some told him that the State of *Rome* was then in saftie, the *Carthaginians*, being quell'd, and *Greece* reduced, gave this answer, *I* (said he) *now is all our daunger, when wee have left us*

21 Cautelousnes] Cauteloutnes *1651*
31 Enemie Competitour] enemie, competitour *G*

no Enemy to feare, nor any to reverence. To the same purpose was that speech of *Diogenes*, most becomming a *Philosopher*, and worthy the practise of all Common-wealthes, *By what meanes* (said he) *shall I be avenged of mine Enemie? If thou Diogenes, will be a good man.* Cowardly, sordid persons if they see us but well horsed, or sworded, or a faire dog following us, are instantly cut to the heart; If they see our fields well husbanded, our mansion-houses, and gardens flowrishing, they break presently into sighes ; But what thinkest thou, will they doe, if thou shew thy selfe an honest, prudent, just man, grave in thy words, sincere in thy actions, and temperate in thy diet,

> *Feeding on fruits which in the heavens dœ grow,*
> *Whence all divine and holy Counsells flow.*

Those, who are overcome (saith *Pindarus*) have their mouthes so bung'd up, that they dare not speak ; he saith not this *simply*, nor of all men, but of those only who are overcome by their Enemies, either in point of action, honestie, magnanimitie, humanitie, or good turnes. These are the vertues, which (as *Demosthenes* saith of them) put the tongue into a traunce, damme up the mouth, choake the whole man, compell and commaund our silence.

> *Excell then if thou canst, be not withstood,*
> *But strive, and overcome the evill with good.*

If thou would'st vex thine Enemie, cal him not by way of reproch an impudent, loose, or intemperate Companion, a knave, or a base fellow ; but shew thy selfe a man, keepe to moderation, embrace truth civilitie, and equitie, and in what company soever thou art, bring those with thee for thy associates. But if at any time thou art compell'd to rebuke him, have a care that thy own beauty be not soiled with the same blemishes thou layest to his charge, look well into thy own bosome, consider the ruins, and dilapidations there, lest happily another more bitter then he, whisper in thy eare that verse of the Tragedian,

> *You minister to others wounds a Cure,*
> *But leave your own all rotten and impure.*

If he calls thee an ignorant, unlearned, emptie fellow, ply thy study; if a Coward, stirre up those seeds of valour, and fortitude which lye asleep in thee ; if wanton, or incontinent, raze out of thy breast all secret Impressions of lust. For nothing can be more dishonourable, or bitter, than to have those arrowes wee shoot at our enemies, to wound our own bosomes. It is commonly

known, that the repercussion of light is most grievously offensive to sore eys, and those reprehensions which truth casts back
into our own faces give the deepest check, for as the *north-west*
wind gathers clouds, so a dissolute life attracts infamie; wherefore *Plato*, if at any time he lighted upon disorderly Companions,
used always when he was rid of them, to question with himselfe,
have I bin ever as mad as these? And yet the most busie back-
biter, whose only dialect is slander, did he but consider, and reform
his own life, would from that very office (otherwise the most odi-
10 ous, and basest of all) derive some benefit. Wee see them commonly derided, who being bald, or crooked themselves, laugh at
those defects in others, And is it not altogether as ridiculous to
charge our Enemies with those very vices, that are most rife in
our selves? When *Leo Byzantinus* the Philosopher was twitted by
a bunch-backt fellow with the infirmity of his eye-sight, *Thou doest
taxe me* (said he) *with a Common misfortune, but wilt not see that
brand of divine vengeance upon thy own back.* Wherefore never
object to another his Adulterie, if thou thy selfe burnst with unlawfull Lust; nor his Prodigalitie, or loosenes, if thou beest a
20 Covetous, sordid wretch. Said *Alcmæon to Adrastus, A kins-
woman of thine hath killed her husband.* But what did he replie?
He taxed him not with anothers villanie, but his own; *And thou*
(said he) *with thy own hands hast killed thy own mother.* It was
a question of *Domitius* to *Crassus, Whether upon the death of the
lamprey fed in his fish-ponds he had not mourn'd?* Yea, (said
Crassus,) *But thou hast buried three wifes without shedding one
teare.* It is an easie matter to be wittie, lowd, and bitter in our
revilinges, but to be the man upon whom those taunts cannot
justly fasten, there lyes the difficulty. And truly it seemes that
30 god by that divine Iniunction *Nosce teipsum,* warnes none so much
as those, who are the revilers and rebukers of others, lest happily,
while they take the liberty to speak what they will, they may heare
what they will not; for it happens oft-times to such Companions
according to that saying of *Sophocles, while they give the raines to
their own tongues, they heare from themselves, what they would not
willingly heare from others*; and in this point the reviled and the
reviler have equall advantage. It was a true saying of *Antisthenes,
That those who would live uprightly, had need either of very honest
friends, or very harsh enemies,* because the one by exhortation, the

other by defamation, will be sure to keep them from offending. But
seeing the tongues of friends (as the times now runne) are too short
to speak home, too long when they smooth us, and quite dumb to
admonish ; it followes that wee can only heare the truth from our
Enemies, for as *Telephus* when he could not find a friend to cure
him, was glad to have it done with the weapon of his foe, so
where our wellwishers will give us no Councell, wee must make
use of our Enemies words, and by a discreet application advantage
our selves. And in this case wee ought not to consider the
malice of the reviler, but the benefit of the reviled. For as that 10
enemie of *Prometheus* by running at him with his sword to have
killed him, broke only the Imposthume in his body and so cured
him ; In like manner an evill word spoken sometimes out of anger,
or enmitie, may cure some ulcer in our manners, which either wee
knew not of before, or else neglected. But most men, when
they are thus publickly reproach'd, weigh not so much whether
they be guiltie, as they doe cast about to learne the vices, and
lewd life of their reproacher, and (after the maner of wrestlers)
wipe not off those aspersions, which (like dust) they throw one
upon the other, but strugling more and more, remain both 20
equally defiled. Whereas (in truth) it concerns him that is so
branded, to clear all objections, and that much more then to take
a spot of his garment, when 'tis once shewed him. But suppose
an Enemy should lay that to our charge, which wee are not guiltie
of ? yet must wee examine our selves well, whether wee ever gave
any cause for it, or heedlesly let slip our selves into any errour of
the like nature, or that had any the least relation or similitude to
what wee are taxed with. This was the very *Case* of *Lacides* King
of the *Argives*, who for some effeminate Curiositie about his haire,
and softnes of apparell was thought wanton, and lascivious. The 30
same thing happened to *Pompey*, * for being ac-   * *This was held by*
custom'd to scratch his head with one finger only *the Romans for a*
(as if he had bin afeard to disorder his locks) he *sure mark of lasci-*
was termed effeminate, a vice (in truth) he was *viousnes.* Iuvenal
furthest from, of any. But *Crassus* for being a *toucheth upon't.*—
great observer of a vestal virgin, and using often- huc venient car-
times to give her the meeting about some parcell pento, et navibus
of land, he would have bought of her, was omnes Qui digito
publickly charged to have deflowred her. So *Posthumia*
another *Vestall* for her freedome of speech with men, and a 40
jovial, merry nature was accused of incest, And though she
was afterwards found Innocent, yet upon her absolution *Spurius*

Minucius then Regent of the *Vestals*, gave her strict charge that in her after-course of life she should have equall care of her deportment, as of her chastitie. But what shall wee say of *Themistocles*, that faithful Patriot ? who upon a bare point of civilitie for shewing some kindnes and humanitie to *Pausanias*, and vouchsafing him a few letters was suspected of treason. If at any time therefore thou art falsly accused, slight not, nor neglect the accusation because it is false, but calling thy selfe to an account, inquire diligently, if there ever happen'd any thing in thy *words*,
10 *actions*, or *Councells*, amongst thy familiars, or elsewhere that might give a just cause for that calumnie. And if so, be warie and avoid it. For if others by suddaine and unexpected accidents have bin taught to know what is best for them, as *Merope* tells of her selfe.

Chance taking from me things of highest price
At a deare rate hath taught me to be wise,

What hinders but that wee may learne that lesson from an Enemie, as from a kind of cheap school-master, whose reprehensions may shew us what wee want, and put us in mind of what wee
20 have forgotten ? for an Enemy will sooner see our defects, than a friend ; because the lover (as *Plato* saith) is, in that which he loves, stark blind, but in hatred there is not only curiositie of observation, but freedome of speech also. When *Hjero* was twitted by his enemie for having an offensive breath, being come home to his wife, *What is this* (said he) *couldst not thou tell me, that my breath was not sweet ?* but she (a chast and modest woman) replies, *Indeed I thought that all mens breaths had the like smell:* So those things which are subject to sense, visible as our bodies and open to every eye, wee shall sooner know from our
30 enemies and ill-willers, than from our friends and familiars. Moreover although it is not the least part of vertue to bridle the tongue, to keep it conformable, and alwayes obedient to reason, yet without a primarie subduing of thy worst affections, anger, and the rest, which must be done by a constant practise, premeditation, and perseverance thou canst never get the masterie over it. For this vitious unfolding of our selves, extenuated with an Apologie of *a word escaped from me*, or, *I slipt a word unawares*, never happens but to lavish, irresolute persons who by reason of their infirmitie of judgment, or loose Custome of life, stick alwaies in the same errours.
40 Besides Speech though the vainest and emptiest thing under the Sun, yet (according to the sentiment of divine *Plato*) is usually

punished with the heaviest judgments both by *God* and *Man*. But silence on the Contrary is alwayes safe, and hath no accusers ; neither doth it only (as *Hippocrates* saith) keep us not thirstie, but in the presence of a rayling Enemie is full of majesty, wisedome, and fortitude ; And a man so qualified

> *Knaves tongues, and calumnies no more doth price*
> *Then the vaine buzzing of so many flies.*

Certainly there is nothing in the world hath more of worth and gallantrie in it, than to beare the *big browes* of a base, upstart foe with a calme and smiling carriage ; wee should passe by a tongue 10 given to detraction, as by a rock used to the froth and scumme of the waves ; The benefit will sweeten the practise : for if thou canst beare quietly the affronts of an Enemie, thou mayest easily beare with a sharp wife, or any bitter passages from a friend or brother, and if thy parents chance to strike thee, thou art so season'd as not to be angrie with them. Thus *Socrates* made it his frequent practise to beare the stormes of his lowd wife (a *Gentlewoman* that for peevishnes and furie out did all her sex) for said he, If I can *beare* with *Xantippe*, *I make no question but I shall bear with all others.* Now, the main end is (after wee have 20 bin thus exercised by the frequent scoffes, reproaches, excessive anger, and sauciness of our enemies) to accustome our selves to such a solid temper, and magnanimous patience, as never to be moved at their weake noise, and detractions. By this means wee shall shew towards our enemies mansuetude, and a kind of virtuous Contempt ; to our friends simplicitie, magnanimitie, and sinceritie. Neither is it so praise-worthy to doe good turnes to our friends, as it is base to deny them to those that want ; But to forbeare revenge upon an Enemie, when wee opportunely may, is the highest glory in all humanity ; And if any man mourn for the 30 misfortunes of his foe, succour him in his wants, be a support to his Children, and domestick decayes, who doth not with thanks accept of such a benevolence, acknowledge such a miracle,

> *His deepe, dark heart (bent to supplant)*
> *Is Iron, or else Adamant.*

Said *Cicero* to *Cæsar* (when he commanded the statues of *Pompey*, that had fallen down, to be erected) *hast thou set up the statues of Pompey ? thou hast established thy own.* This intimates that wee should keep back no praise, nor any point of honour from a noble Enemie that may justly claime it ; for by bearing testimonie to 40

27 turnes *text 1651* : turns *catchword 1651*

the truth, and fastening Commendations where desert is, wee doe commend our selves.   Nay wee shall have this advantage, that if wee chance afterwards to blame them, wee shalbe believed of all men as disliking their actions, not hating their persons ; and which is most laudable of all, they that use to speak well of their Enemies, without repining at their successe, will hardly envie the prosperity of their friends, or the good parts of their associates.   What better exercise then, or more virtuously fruitfull, or leaving nobler impressions in the soul can wee pitch upon ?   It takes away from us all
10 perverse emulations, and puts quite out all fomentations of envie. As in a Common-wealth many things necessarie, (otherwise bad enough) when they are once confirm'd by Custome, or power of law, are not easily forgotten of those whom they have once annoyed ; so hostilitie and variance bringing in with them envie and hatred, leave planted in the mind obtrectation, malevolence, with an Implacable and endles resentment of Injuries.   Adde to this that Couzenage, trecherie, breach of oath, private wiles, and policies which by perverse and bloudie Enemies are held lawfull, where they once begin to be practised, will by a habituation be so per-
20 fectly naturalized, that they can hardly ever be removed, and may afterwards (grown masters by Custome) if not refused against our Enemies, prove hurtfull to our nearest friends.   For this very cause (if I judge right) *Pythagoras* used to abstaine from flesh, and the slaughter of harmles creatures, intreating and sometimes hiring fowlers, not to kill their birds, and Anglers to let goe their fish, and publickly forbad the killing of any tame beast.   Without doubt a generous, just, and solid Enemie will in all Contentions think it the best victorie to bridle an irreligious, insatiable malice, that by teaching his stubbournes to submit to vertue, he may ever after
30 be master of himself.   When *Domitius* was accused by *Scaurus* his Enemie, a servant of his, stept to the barre where *Scaurus* pleaded, about to informe him of some heynous offence done by his master, which *Scaurus* knew not of, but he not suffering him to speak, sent him with a guard back to his master.   So *Cato* when he was drawing up certain heads of an accusation against *Muræna*, had alwaies following him a knot of busie fellows, who of set purpose pryed into his actions ; These oftentimes asked him, if he had yet finished the Charge, or had any more Articles to insert, or witnesses to examine ? if he answered, no ; They would instantly
40 believe him, and depart ; a great argument of the good opinion they had of *Cato*.   And indeed that which excells all, and is (in truth) most justly preheminent, is the equall administration of

justice to our very Enemies ; for who useth to doe so, can hardly use any fraud, or injustice against his friends. But seeing it is so (as *Simonides* saith) that every lark must have a Crest, and worth, in whomsoever it is, breeds contention, obtrectation, and the envie of fools ; wee shall find no small advantage, if wee put quite from us all sillie and weak ways of revenge even against our most bitter Enemies, and remove them as durt and drosse far enough from our friends. Which very point (in my opinion) *Onomademus* (a very skilfull states-man) made speciall use of ; for living in *Chios*, and happening to be (upon a sudden Insurrection) of that side which then prevailed, he advised his Confederates, that they should not banish all of the adverse partie, but leave some to live amongst them *Lest* (said he) *being rid of our Enemies*, wee *begin to fall out with our friends*. For as long as wee have an Enemy to consume, and weare out our ill affections upon, wee shall give the lesse distast to our friends. It is not convenient (saith *Hesiodus*) that one *Potter* should envie the other, nor ought wee to be troubled at the prosperitie of our brother, or a good neighbour. But if thou canst not otherwise than by doing so, free thy selfe from strif, envy, and Contention, then suffer thy self to fret at the good successe of thine Enemie, and cut him with the edge and keeness of thy anger. For as skilful gardiners think *roses* and *violets* will thrive the better, if *Onions and garlick* be sowed neare them, (because these later attract all harsh qualities that may be in the Compost,) so an Enemie by drawing on himself all the perversnes and morositie in thee, will render thy disposition more mild and pleasing to thy friend. Therefore when wee have any thing to doe with an Enemie either in point of honour, popularitie, or a just benefit, wee must so contend, as not only to be blindly vext because he excells us, but to observe also in what particulars, and by what means he doth so excel. Nor must wee stay there, but with all diligence, industrious sobrietie, and watchfullnes labour to overtake him, after the example of *Themistocles*, whom the victorie of *Miltiades* upon the plaines of *Marathon* would not suffer to sleep. For such a spirit that thinks his Enemie better than himselfe because he hath great offices, patronage, numerous friends, or the favour of Princes, and therefore gives him over and despaires, when he ought rather to be stirring and emulous, doth but pine away with most sordid and cowardly envie. But he that hath a strict eye over him, not blinded with hatred, and stands in the light a discerning spectatour of his life and actions, shall at last find it true, that all those prosperous passages he envied him for,

were brought about by a Judicious care, eminent diligence, and sincere dealings ; and having got these virtues for his presidents, he instantly cuts of all dulness and delayes, and treads in the same steps to arrive at the same height. But if it so happens to any that their Enemies by unlawfull and irreligious means grow powerfull, as by flattery, exactions, perverting of justice, briberie, perjurie or bloud-shed, they ought not so much to mourne, as to rejoyce, considering that they have to oppose to all that rottenness, a sound conscience, unpolluted pietie, and innocent hands. For (as *Plato*
10 saith) All *the gold above the earth, and under the earth is by no meanes to be compared with a religious Integritie.* Neither must wee leave them untwitted with that of *Solon,*

> *What though they boast their riches unto us ?*
> *Those cannot say, That they are virtuous.*

Let us then neither labour for bribed suffrages, nor bought honours, nor for the chief place with Eunuchs, and Concubines of Kings, or pandars of state ; for nothing is amiable, nothing honourable, that is acquird by baseness. But (as *Plato* saith) *The lover, in that which he loveth is stark blind,* but quick-sighted enough to
20 see the failings of his Enemies ; It will become us then, neither to rejoyce at their sins, nor to mourn for what they doe well, but wisely to weigh both, that by avoyding the one we may grow *better,* and by imitating the other not grow *worser* then they themselves are.

1 Judicious] *text 1651* : Iuditious *catchword 1651*

FINIS.

OF THE
DISEASES
OF THE
MIND

And the

BODY.

A DISCOURSE

Written originally in the
Greek by *Plutarchus Chæronensis,*
put into latine by *I. Reynolds D.D.*

Englifhed by *H* : *V* : Silurift.

Omnia perverfæ poterunt Corrumpere mentes.

LONDON.
Printed foi *Humphry Mofeley* and are to
be fold at his fhop at the figne of the
Princes Armes in St. Pauls
Church yard, 1 6 5 1.

Of the Diseases of the Mind and the Body.

When *Homer* had diligently considered the severall kinds of living Creatures, and compared the various dispositions, and provident subsisting of the one with the other, he cryed out,

> *That man for misery excell'd*
> *All creatures which the wide world held.*

A very wretched Prerogative! that excels in nothing, but a calamitous superiority of evils. Seeing then, that by this sentence we are eminent for nothing, but unhappinesse, and in that also more miserable than other creatures, we shall in this discourse (by way of comparison) bring man to a combate with himself about his own calamities ; taking the *mind* asunder from the *body* (not vainly, but to a good purpose) that by a distinct examination of both we may come to know from which of these two his miseries flow.

Bodily diseases happen alwaies by a depravation of temperament; but the vitiositie, and taint of the mind, is first the free act of the mind it self, and afterwards its disease. But it would not a little conduce to the ease of the mind, if either that which is infected might be restored ; or that which cannot be wholly taken away might be partly mitigated. When *Æsops* fox contended with the *Panther* for variety, after the *Leopard* had bragg'd of the beauteous spots and speckles in his skin, vilifying the other for his sordid, reddish, and ill-sented Coate, *But couldst thou* (said the Fox) *discerne that which is within me, thou wouldst confesse thy selfe lesse various than I am ;* Meaning thereby the many fetches and subtilties he had there, and could commodiously use when he pleased. So may we say of our selves. Many diseases truly (O man!) and many infirmities attend on thy Body, some casually and from without, others naturally out of the Body it self: But if thou wouldst but search thy self within, where no eys shine but thy own, what variety of distempers shouldst thou find there? giddie distractions, blind conceits, crooked affections, shuffled wils, and phantastick humours, which lying there as in a Box, or Cabinet, flow not from without, but are Natives and Inhabitants of the place, springing there like so many Wels. Now

33 phantastick] phanstastick *1651*

the diseases of the Body are ordinarily known by the *Pulse*, or beating of the vitall spirits, and a high colour; and those againe are manifested by other *Symptoms*, as excessive heat, wearinesse, and a dangerous aptnesse to faint; But the diseases of the Mind so delude most men, that they are not suspected for maladies, and the case of the patient is then most desperate, when he hath no sense of his paine. But in bodily diseases the judgement remaines sound, and there is still in the patient a very quick and clear perception both of his *time of ease*, and of *accessions*; whereas
10 those that are sick in Mind can find no difference between sicknesse, and health, and indeed how should they, seeing that wherewith they Judge, is the part affected? It is therefore very just that we adjudge this *senslesnesse* to be the most pernicious, and principall of all the diseases of the mind, for by this it comes to passe that many men converse, live, and dye in an uncurable madnesse : for as in ordinary diseases the first step to health is to have a feeling of the disease, for that sets on the patient to inquire for help; so in mentall distempers (wherein men state themselves sound, that are indeed sick,) though they knew a remedy for
20 their disease, yet will they not use it, because they believe, they have no need of it. Of bodily diseases those are most dangerous, which render men senselesse, as *Lethargies*, *head-akes*, the *falling sicknesse*, *dead Palsies*, and *Feavers* also, whose vehement Inflammations breed an alienation of mind, and (like unskilfull *Musicians*) put the whole inward harmony out of tune. Therefore honest *Physicians* first wish, that men were not sick at all; Secondly, that if they happen to sicken, they may be sensible of their disease : but in mentall maladies this deliration is so prevalent that it is impossible to remove it; for neither those that
30 rave with some mad conceit, or burne with lasciviousnesse, or delight in doing injuries seeme to themselves to offend, nay, they are so far from it, that they glory in such actions; And yet, who ever gave the name of health to a Feaver, of soundnesse to corruption, of activitie to the Goute, or of Blushes to Palenesse? but to call *anger* fortitude, *love* friendship, *envie* emulation, and *Cowardice* discretion is frequent. Besides, those who have their *Bodies* ill-affected send presently for the *Physician*, because they find themselves to have need of him; but those who have their *minds* so, flye from the *Philosopher*, and will not endure any
40 Precepts of virtue. Moved then with these reasons, I hold an *Outward blindnesse* more tollerable than an *Inward*, and the paine of the *Gout*, than the Dotage of the *mind*; for he that is

diseas'd in his eys, useth his best diligence to have them cured, provides waters, and ointments, breaths a veine, and purgeth his head; but come to mad *Agave*, and you shall heare her singing, having killed her son,

> *A tender Kid (see, where 'tis put,)*
> *I on the Hils did slay,*
> *Now drest, and into quarters cut,*
> *A pleasant, daintie prey.*

Adde to this, that a Patient in the Body takes present notice of his disease, gets him to bed, and while he is in cure, is quiet and 10 tractable, or if he chance to be something wayward and offer to rise thence by reason of wearinesse or a Feaverish heat, yet if a friend say to him, *Lye still*, or *keep in thy Bed*, he will instantly refraine; whereas those that are diseas'd in Mind, are then most restlesse and tumultuous; for from the Commotions of the mind all actions take their beginning, but mentall diseases are the most vehement Commotions, and therefore will not suffer the mind to be in quiet, yea, when a man hath most need to shew patience, silence, and submission of mind, then will these inward maladies most annoy him, giving the rains to anger, contention, lust, and 20 tumults, which dissect and lay him open to his enemies, while he strives to doe many things repugnant to reason, and spits out unseasonable, and dangerous speeches. Therefore, as that tempest at Sea, which keeps us from putting into the Harbour, is more dangerous than that which hinders us to put forth; so those tempests of the mind, which will not suffer us to containe and pacifie our selves, are the most pernicious, for they hurry us away without Pilot or Saile through Gulfs and Quicksands, untill at last upon some rock or other we cast away both our lifes and estates; wherefore in my opinion were there no other Inconvenience but 30 that, it is enough to prove that the disease of the *mind* is far more perillous than the disease of the *body*; though this we shall adde, that the *one* offends only the patient, but the *other* offends all that come neare it.

But to what purpose shall we multiply arguments? seeing the events of the present time sufficiently demonstrate it. You see this numerous and promiscuous multitude here met, justling and shouldring one another from the streets to the Court, from the Court to the Bar, and so out againe; These are come together not to celebrate any works of piety, as sacrifice, or prayer; but a certaine 40 *Epidemicall fit* which once a year all *Asia* shakes of, hath hurryed them hither about some vaine controversies and matters of Law, which upon a prescript day are here to be heard and determined; for at this one Bar (like the breaking in of so many Rivers) all the Contestations in *Asia* meet, here they are canvased, decided, and grow up into mortall dissentions, betwixt the *undoer* and the *undone*. What Feavers, what Agues, Malignant heats, or Superfluous humours ever so troubled mankind? If aswell as the men, you examine the grounds of their sutes and contentions in Law, you shall find some of them to proceed from a slight word spoken, 10 some from malice, some from anger, others from a mad desire to be contentious, and all of them from *Covetousnesse*.

FINIS

OF THE
DISEASES
OF THE
MIND,
AND THE
BODY,
And which of them is
moſt pernicious.

The Queſtion ſtated, and decided
by *Maximus Tirius* a Platonick Phi-
loſopher, written originally in
the Greek, put into Latine by
John Reynolds D.D.

Engliſhed by Henry Vaughan *Siluriſt.*

LONDON,
Printed for *Humphry Moſeley*, and are to be
Sold at his Shop at the Sign of the
Prince's Arms in St. *Pauls*
Church-yard, 1651.

Of the Diseases of the Mind, &c.

There is sung from all antiquity by some unknowne Poet this following *Hymne* in the stile of a prayer,

> *O Cælestium princeps Sanitas !*
> *Utinam tecum degere possim*
> *Quod mihi tempus superest vitæ !*

> O health the chief of gifts divine !
> I would I might with thee and thine
> Live all those days appointed mine !

I would gladly be resolved by the Authour of this verse, what kind of health it was, which in those preceding lines he begg'd to have for his Companion in life ; for verily I suspect it was some divine thing worthy the devotion and fervency of prayer ; for sure he could not rashly and upon a suddaine find matter worthy of verse, or being put into verse, it could hardly have past with such generall applause from one age unto another. If it be then such a thing as I suspect, reason it self (instead of the *Poet,*) will give us an answer. For seeing there are but *two things* of which *man* consists, the *Soule,* and the *Body,* if the *Soule* be free from the nature of diseases, it follows of necessity, that, what is petitiond for in this *Hymne* belongs to the *Body,* which naturally useth to fall sick, and to recover againe. But if it be so that both *Soule* and *Body* have from discreet nature a like temperament, which is never disturbed but by a petulant perversitie of parts, when excesse in the one (like a tyrant and his people in a Common-wealth) is destructive to the other, and confounds the genuine harmony, (which excesse wheresoever it is, whether in the soule, or else in the body, we define to be *an impotent Cupidity,* both which as they make up one whole man share equall power, though taken by themselves they bear no proportion at all,) the question now is, to which of these two shall this Celestiall temperament, or Princesse mentioned in the Hymne, be adjudged most necessary ? To resolve this *Quære* with safety, we must compare the diseases of the *one,* with the diseases of the *other,* that by so doing we may see which of them is most pernicious to the whole man, and then like indifferent Arbiters settle to a righteous judgement.

K

Man then (as we have said before) is made up of *Soule* and *Body*, in which Composure the *Soule* is regent, and the *Body* obeys, as in a Common-wealth the *Prince*, and his *Subjects*; and worthily too, for as in this of the *Body*, so in all other Governments the *Prince* is not only the head, or Superiour part of the Commonwealth, but by a kind of *Sacred affinitie* part also of the Subject. The question then is, *Whether in a languishing Commonwealth the Prince, or the People, the Soule, or the Body, are the destroying party?* I decide it thus: The Common people are
10 sick, but *Pericles* the good Prince is in health, apprehends the disease, and cures the people: contrariwise, *Dionysius* the *Siracusian* hath the *Kings evill*, but the people, though healthfull themselves, want strength to restore him. Will you therefore, that henceforth we substitute for the *Soule*, the *Prince*; and for the *Body* the *People*? If so, weigh the example, aswell as the thing.

The People for number exceed the Prince, and the Body the Soul. The People without a Prince are dead, and heartless; so is the Body without the Soul. The People consist of many
20 degrees, many voices, and many affections; so hath the Body diverse, and different parts. The people are in their anger *Merciless*, in their desires *vehement*, in their pleasures *dissolute*, in their troubles *abject,* and in their furie *Mad*; The same vices attend the Body, for now 'tis lustfull, now winie, anon dejected, and sometimes hurried away with most impetuous, excessive madnes. Let us see now what Comparatives wee can make between the *Prince*, and the *Soul*. A *Prince* in a Commonwealth is the fittest person to govern, as most honourable, and most able; so is the *Soul* in the *Body*. A *Prince* is by nature provident in his affaires, and
30 prudent in advice; the very same faculties are usually in the Soul. The *Prince* hath a freedome royall, and is above the Censure of the people; so is the Soul above the Body. Seeing then that these Comparisons are true in both, which of these parts (when diseas'd) shall wee judge the worst, as well in the Commonwealth, as in Man? surely the best; because the Corruption of things that are excellent is the most pernicious: For the People though sick, if the Prince be well, shall have their liberties preserved; but the disease of the Prince (though the People be in health) brings inevitable bondage. And that I may in one word summe up all,
40 the Soul is far more excellent than the Body, and the Prince than the People: Now that *good* which is most excellent, is by somuch the greater; and that which is repugnant to the *greater good*, must

needs be the *greater Evill*;—But the health of the *Soul* is a greater good than the health of the *Body*; therefore the disease of the Soule is a greater Evill than the disease of the Body. The health of the body is restored by Art, but the health of the soul by virtuous Industrie. The disease of the soul is wickednes, that of the body is but sorrow: Wickednes comes by a voluntarie sinning, but calamitie against our wills. If any body hurt us against their will, they deserve our Charitie; if of set purpose, they deserve our Hatred. Where wee are charitable, there wee relieve; where revengefull, there wee punish. Those wee relieve are commonly good; those wee punish, notoriously bad. Again, The health of the soul is full of Chearfullnesse, the body may be in health, and yet want it. The health of the soul leads us to blisse, the other to miserie. The health of the soul hath no iniquitie, the other is wholly vitious. The health of the soule is celestiall, the other earthly; the one is durable, the other transitorie; the one eternal, the other mortall. And so much touching their dispositions in that state, let us now consider their diseases. Bodily diseases if not wholly taken off, yet by the help of art may be very much mitigated; but the mind once infected contemnes the correction of severest Laws. The first (after a few days paine) by making the patient desirous of health, makes him also fitter for cure; the last by bewitching the mind so hinders the Cure, that it will not somuch as heare of health. The divine mercy may succour the one, but from the other it is alwaies averse. The disease of the body hath never yet occasion'd wars, but that of the mind hath occasion'd many. No man sick in body burns with lust, robs Churches, steales from his neighbour, or doth any other villanie, that disease offends only the patient, the other offends all men. But let us now render this truth more evident by a similitude taken from Civill Government.

When *Pericles* was Duke of *Athens*, a Citie govern'd by *Democracie*, and burthend with a great & populous multitude, large in Jurisdiction, powerfull for riches, and stored with many and eminent Commanders, the plague then rife in *Æthiopia* (where it first began) past thence into *Persia*, and afterwards to *Athens*, where having (as it were) taken footing, it increased daily and afflicted the Citie. To augment this miserie, it happend at the same time that they had open war with the *Peloponnesians*; In this state therefore when the Countrey lay wasted by the Enemie, the Inhabitants tortured, their houses rifled, their armies defeated, and the whole body of the Commonwealth exposed to pillage and

destruction, *Pericles* the good *Prince* being then in health, himselfe
rebuilds the Citie, recruits their armies, restores their Courages,
and dividing himselfe betwixt the Sword and the Pest-house with
the one hand subdued the Infection, and with the other the
Enemie. Thus much for the Soul, let us now find a similitude
for the Body. When the Infection ceased, and the Commonwealth
again took breath, and recovered, those persons in the Citie, who
had the charge of the Republick (as Popular government hath
ever too many) so burnt with hatred, ambition, and Covetousnes
10 one towards another, that they seemed rather to be out of their
witts, than rightly in them. These mentall diseases in a short time
so increased, and dispersed, that all *Athens* was infected, and so
prevalent was the Contagion that it took also the Common people ;
And why not ? for here they had not one *Cleon* to rave with, or one
Alcibiades to burn with, but (as the nature of *Democracie* is) a hundred, or more ; and these (every man as his disease moved him)
plyed severall interests, one this way, another that way, *Alcibiades*
shewed them *Sicilia, Cleon Sphacteria,* another some other territorie,
or *Ocean,* like so many springs to one sick of a feaver. O blessed
20 Statesmen ! this was your Reformation ! Ruine, Confusion,
prodigious Changes, nationall Miseries, and civill Inflammations
were the religion, and liberty they had from you ! so woefully
pernicious is the Maladie of the Soul, if compared with the disease
of the Body. For though the Body lye sick, languishing, and
afflicted, yet if a resolute, immoveable spirit hath the guidance of
it, diseases, Convulsions, and death it selfe can prevail nothing ;
Thus *Pherecides* (though he was * laid quick in
A philosopher, and the grave, and saw Corruption while he lived)
Master to Pythago- the grave, and saw Corruption while he lived)
ras, he died of the slighted both the loathsomnes and pain of the
Phthiriasis.
30   disease, wishing only that he might be freed
from that unprofitable body wherewith he was then cloath'd upon.
Nay, I shall not doubt to say, that a soul thus gifted lives in the
body by meere compulsion, for I look upon such a one, as upon
some captive or slave, who seeing the walls of his prison decayed,
and grown ruinous, expects every moment to be set at liberty, that
freed from the darknes and horrour of that dungeon, which
formerly opprest him, he may at last enjoy a cleare aire, and the
comforts of light. Canst thou believe that a hired labourer
accustomed to the hardest, and most toilesome imployments, wilbe
40 any thing astonished to see a suddaine rent, or hole in his

apparell ? or will he not rather cut off that which hangs about him, and leave his body naked to the aire, that he may with more ease and nimblenes prosecute his task ? And doest thou think the soul esteemes otherwise of flesh and bones than of a Coat which cndures but for a day, or some thred-bare, cheap rags, which sometimes the sword, sometimes the fagot, but most times diseases devoure ? Wherefore a generous, and sustaining spirit, when he finds the body begining to undresse, and the bolts of his prison loosed, makes no more account of that Change than a snail doth of her cast shel, or *Vlysses* of the ten yeares suit he wandered in. 10 But the fearefull, and Cowardly soul, stoved in the body, like some lazie beast in his den, will by no meanes be released thence, no, nor somuch as take the aire, but delighting in the passions and miseries of that burthen, is now torn, now burnt, by and by grieves, and alwaies groanes with it. Wee heare *Philoctetes* crying out, *O my foot, I must lose thee !* why, good man, if thou must, lose it willingly, and doe not crie so ; Doth it any thing ease thee to raile at thy friends, and make the *Echo* in *Lemnos* mock at thy Complaints ? *O Death my only Cure !* well said *Philoctetes*; but if by so saying thou meanest only an Exchange of one Evill for 20 the other, then cannot I approve of thy wish : But if by that Exclamation thou doest acknowledge death the only soveraign remedie, and revenger of a loathsome disease, thou hast spoken right ; call, and crie for thy Cure. And now seeing wee have mentioned *Philoctetes* most opportunely will he afford us a very pregnant example. There was heretofore at the siege of *Troy* (for valour and number) an Army of *Grecians* altogether incredible, as many as there be leafes or flowers in the spring, all of them able, hardie, and healthfull bodies lying about the walls and trenches of their Enemies for ten whole yeares, and prevailed 30 nothing ; not *Achilles* the pursuer, *Aiax* the defyer, *Diomedes* the slaughterer, *Teucer* the Archer, *Agamemnon* the Counsellour, *Nestor* the Oratour, *Chalcas* the Soothsayer, nor *Vlisses* the Deceiver. But what saies the *Oracle* ? *In vain* (*O noble youths and souldiers of Greece !*) *in vain I say doe you skirmish, batter, assault, and advize ; for never shall you be able to take those walls, before you have to your aid, a mind indeed prudent and healthy, but a body infected, languishing, lame and allmost consumed ;* They obey the oracle, and fetch him from *Lemnos*, him (I say) sick in body, but sound in mind. And thus wee see what the Soul can 40 doe in health, let us now consider it when diseased. The mind is infected with sensualitie, it burnes, melts, and pines away.

What will you doe to the patient? what benefit, or advantage can the Body (in this Case) minister to the Soul? *Sardanapalus* lies sick of this disease; Doe not you see, how like an Insatiable *ulcer* it hath taken hold of all the parts of his body? his Colour is gone, his Beauty spent, his Eyes dull'd, and his whole frame burnes with most obscene Impatiencie. *Alcibiades* is in the same case. An outragious, restles fire feedes upon him, overthrowes his reason,
* Aristotles *School* hurries him up and down, from *Lycæum* to the
in Athens. multitude, from the multitude to the sea, from
10 the sea to *Sicilia*, from *Sicilia* to *Lacedemon*, from *Lacedemon* to *Persia*, from *Persia* to *Samos*, from *Samos* to *Athens*, from *Athens*
* *One of the* 30 *ty-* to *Hellespont*, and from *Hellespont* I know not
rants in Athens. whither. *Critias* lyes sick, taken with a most grievous, desperate, intolerable disease, and burthensome to a whole Commonwealth. But all these had very healthfull, proper, and handsome bodies; spruce *Sardanapalus*, beautifull *Alcibiades*, and portly *Critias*. But in men of such dispositions I never loved health. Let *Critias* then be sick, untill he may play the tyrant; *Alcibiades* because he cannot bring *Athens* into *Sicilie*; And for
20 *Sardanapalus* let him be sick to death, for it is more manly for him to perish by a disease, than an excessive obscenitie. Yea, and may every one perish, who is only fertill in Continuall evills! for as running ulcers where they once seize, spread further still, and corrupt those parts which are sincerest, dispersing and prevailing against all medicines, untill the very seat and hold of the disease be cut out; So those minds which are used to rotteness, Corruption, and dishonest Intentions will (like infected people) endanger all that have Commerce with them; And therefore in such persons the *strength* and *spring* of the disease should be taken off, as the
30 *hand* of a thiefe, the *Eye* of a leacher, and the *belly* of a glutton. For though against these enormities thou shouldst constitute Iudges, prisons, and tortures, yet would the Evill increase, prevaile, and overflow; for the headines of vice where it finds a predisposition, and growes once habituall, is altogether Incredible, and attended with most desperate licentiousnes, and a frontles audacitie.

FINIS.

THE
PRAISE
AND
HAPPINESSE
OF THE
COUNTRIE-LIFE;

Written Originally in
Spanish by *Don Antonio de Guevara*,
Bishop of *Carthagena*, and
Counsellour of Estate to
Charls the Fifth Emperour
of *Germany*.

Put into Englifh by H. Vaughan *Silurift.*

Virgil. Georg.
O fortunatos nimiùm, bona fi fua nôrint,
Agricolas !——

LONDON,
Printed for *Humphry Moseley*, and are to be
Sold at his Shop at the Sign of the
Prince's Arms in St. *Pauls*
Church-yard, 1651.

The Praise and Happinesse of the Country-Life, &c.

The First CHAPTER.

Whoever Loves the *Country*, and Lives in it upon his owne Estate, whether *Hereditarie* or *Purchased*, and lends not his Ears to any flatt'ring *allurements* perswading to ambition and greatnesse, but carefully avoids those dangerous *Precipices* and *Quicksands*, I shall not feare to affirme, That such a liver is the *wisest of men* ; for he living upon his own, is no mans debtour, and is offensive to none but either a *Courtier*, or a *Citizen* ; and therefore is much more happy than if he had Ingrost to himself all *Court favours*, 10 or had bin expert in the *subtiltie* and *Politicks* of all forraign Nations.

He fears no *discontents* to disturbe his *Peace*, but lives well-pleased with what *providence* gives him though never so little. He is free from all fretting *cares*, and is fed with no mans *provision* but his *own*. The *Crop* of his *Land* comes in certainly once a *yeare*, it is got with a *good conscience*, and is ever ready upon any necessity. These are *returns* which he needs not *complement* for, nor be thought troublesome, or rudely *importunate*. A pompous and splendid *fortune* hath seldome *better blessings* ; but instead of 20 those lavish and sumptuous *Excesses* she is sometimes accustom'd to, she frequently deceives our hopes with the worst kind of *Exigencies*. A *Nobleman* or *Citizen* living upon the Revenues and accommodations of his Country estate finds more of honour, reputation and authority amongst his Neighbours, than all those *Sycophants* (though outwardly more rich and sumptuous) whom either an antient *descent*, a large *retinue*, or the beauty and sprucenesse of their *wifes*, hath preferr'd at *Court*. There the lustre of *greater persons* makes theirs to be of no notice ; but in his Country-house he is *Lord* alone, and his Wife is *Lady*, there he is 30 really honour'd and admir'd of all. Wherefore it was well said of *Julius Cæsar, That he had rather be the prime Freeholder in a Country Village, than the second Magistrate in the City of Rome.*

Pietie and Religion may be better Cherish'd and preserved in the Country than any where else.   While the Husbandman with a *cheerfull* and *holy hope* expects the fruit and recompense of his pains, out of the earth, the Inhabitants of great *Cities* (yea those that have no more than one *garrish suit* of Cloaths, and a very *mean subsistance*) will be reproaching and envying one the other. Hence very many of them are suddenly undone, and by some ambitious attempt of *precedency*, come to lose that little they had gotten, in which ruins their friends also are sometimes involved, whom they had drawn in for greater undertakings than their 10 abilities could bear out.   The *Countryman* living private, repines at no man, is alwaies contented, and contributes something towards the relief of the *poor*.   But he that seeks after places of Eminency will be sure to find *Envy* and *Competitors*, and these last will be still watching to reduce him to such a condition as shall be far beneath their Envy.   To keep a *School*, to be a hir'd *labourer*, or to live by Compounding of *Salves* and *Plaisters*, is a far more blessed and a securer life.

He that lives in his own *fields* and *habitation*, which God hath given him, enjoys true Peace ; for no Phantastick, Impudent 20 *Companion* turns in thither to disturbe him, and to seek after a sumptuous entertainment, or to corrupt his family in his absence ; the very occasion of *ill-doing* is by his presence taken away.   He busieth not himself in a *search* of pleasures, but in regulating, and disposing of his family ; in the education of his Children, and Domestick Discipline.   No violent tempestuous motions distract his *rest*, but soft gales, and a silent aire refresh and breath upon him.   He doth all things commodiously, ordereth his life discreetly, not after the opinion of the people, but by the rules of his own certain experience ; he knows he must not live here for ever, and 30 therefore thinks frequently of *dissolution* and the day of *death.* He knows his resting place at night, and is not like *travellours* and *runagates*, sollicitous and uncertaine of his *lodging*, or the manners of *those* that are to entertaine him ; he wants no furniture, his *bed* is ready at the time of rest, and his *Horses* and *Sadles* when he rides abroad.   He fears not the violence of *Judges*, nor their perverse judgements, which to others is a frequent trouble ; And which is a blessing above all, he meets not in the recesse of his fields with any *Impostor, busie-body*, or *lewd-woman*, whose temptations sometimes turne men into beasts, and hurry them into divers 40 lusts, which oftentimes have bin so sadly effectuall as to cause *discord* and *bloudshed.*

He that lives in the Country, hath *time* for his servant, and whatsoever occasions offer themselves (if he be but a *discreet observer* of his *hours*) he can have no cause to complaine that they are unseasonable. Nothing will hinder him from the pleasure of *books*, from *devotion*, or the fruition of his *friends*. If he finds himself remisse and voyd of businesse, there is nothing hinders but he may take either the pleasure of *hunting*, or of visiting some well accomplish'd, pleasing *Companion*; Whereas those that are *tyed* to businesse, whose *profession* makes their *life* a meer *slaverie*, 10 are alwaies imprison'd (as it were) and barr'd from *recreation*. Sometimes they are driven upon far Journeys against their will, and spend their time of life (which to *Christians* should be most pretious) in the negotiations of others, in *complementing, scraping, intreating, petitioning*, feigned *sighing*, and a ridiculous *humbling* of themselves. Insomuch that the saying of *Augustus Cæsar* to a laborious Citizen of *Rome*, may very well be applyed to them. *I wonder* (said he) *thou doest not leave off, thou art so constant in imployment, thou wilt have no time to dye.*

A *Nobleman* or *Citizen* retyr'd into the Country, may without 20 prejudice to his *honour* walk alone, without the noyse and trouble of *Attendants*, he needs there no *Couches* to stretch upon, nor his *Gentleman* at his back ; and his *Lady* may take the aire without her *Gentlewoman* ; but in *Courts* and great assemblies these *formalities* (with excessive charge and pride) must be kept up to carry the eys of the *multitude*, which are alwaies taken with such vaine *shows* and *Pageantrie*.

We may in the Country, when we please and without offence take the *aire*, walk to the next *neighbourhood*, or *village*, and with an untainted *repute* return home at what houre we shall set to our 30 selves, having no troublesome occasions to entangle and delay us. The Countryman is *slave* to no body, he walks not loaded with *boots* and *spurs*, ready at all *Commands*, as *Souldiers* at the *sound* of the trumpet.

In the Country the *Gentleman* aswell as the *Ploughman* may live, to please himself, and is not bound to a chargeable Imitation of the *fashions* and *foppery* of others. There is no necessity of any thing but a *Cloak* for feare of raine, and a *warme garment* more for health than ostentation. A *bill* to walk his grounds with, a *fish-basket*, an *angling-rod*, or *birding-piece* are his chiefest 40 accoutrements. Yea, the Nobleman in the Country is as much honour'd in his coarsest habit, as he can be elsewhere in his richest and most pompous ornaments.

Of what degree soever he be, that lives in the Country, whether a *Gentleman* or a *Plebeian*, he is not therefore held the more despicable, or unfortunate, because he rides to the market upon his own *working beast*, than the most Lordly *gallant* upon his *great horse*; Yea, more *blessed* is he, that living honestly in the *sweat of his face*, rides his own simple *Asse*, than a rich unconscionable *Tyrant* that furnisheth his great *stable* or *dairie* with the *Cattel* and *Horses* of an innocent, honest *man*.

The Second C H A P T E R.

THE Husband-man never wants *good Corne*, and which in great 10 *Towns* and *Courts* is very rare, he' is alwaies furnished with welrellishing *bread* and well baked; for in populous *Cities* their *Corne* is either mouldie, or not wel grinded, or their *water* with which they knead it, is brackish and unwholesome, which oftentimes is the cause of divers diseases and mortalitie amongst the Inhabitants. But that which is most worthy our observation in this Chapter, is, that in the Country there are more healthfull exercises, and better opportunities and means to spend our time than can possibly be had in Cities and Courts. Frequent *dissimulation*, dangerous *reservednesse*, an evill *eye*, ridiculous *affectation*, *policie*, 20 *revenge*, supercilious *scorns*, a phantastick *gate*, affected *motions*, *Chambering*, splendid and swelling *words*, grosse *calumnie*, *defamation*, *cursing*, *swearing*, (which would make a good *Christian* wish himself deafe) with *ambition* the most poysonous *weed* of the mind are the *plants* which grow in those *Gardens*.

More happy then, yea by much more happy than any *King*, if not nearer to a *divine felicitie* is that person who lives and dwels in the Country upon the Rents and profits of his own grounds. There without danger he may act and speake as it becomes *simplicity* and naked *truth*; he hath liberty and choice in all his 30 imployments; there is no place for flattery, which drives headlong the *bad*, entiseth the *good*, and *Proteus*-like transforms it self into all shapes, and yet at last purchaseth nothing but the hatred of all, especially when it is busied in *tale-bearing* and *back-biting*. In the Country we can have a harmelesse and cheerfull conversation with our familiar friends, either in our *houses* or under some *shade*, not troubling or endangering our selves with the *secret mischiefs* and *designs* of *States-men*. Whereas in publick Company there are many things spoken at randome, which bring more of *wearinesse*, than *pleasure* to the hearers. But the quiet retyr'd *liver*, in 40 that calme silence, reads over some profitable histories or books

17 healthfull] healtfull *1651*　　　41 profitable] prositable *1651*

of devotion, and very often (stird up by an inward and holy joy) breaks out into divine praises and the singing of *Hymnes* and *Psalms*; with these sacred recreations (more delightfull than *Romances*, and the lascivious Musick of *Fidlers* which only Cloy and weary the ears) doth he feed his *soule* and refresh his *body*. Besides by this recesse from places of eminent Confluence, we avoid the clamours and officious *morning salutations* of such chargeable *Parasites*, which *strike it up* under every lodging, and disturbe our rest, that they may have wherewith to be *drunk* and
10 *disorderly*.

Those that live in the Country are much more healthfull, and are not subject to so many diseases as *Citizens* and *Courtiers*, for in Cities the *buildings* are high, the *lanes* narrow and durtie, the *aire* dull and for want of *rarification* and *motion* breeds many diseases. But in the Country the *Villages* are built at a great distance, the *Inhabitants* are more carefull of their healths, the *aire* is quick and fresh, the *Sun* unclowded and cheerfull, the *earth* lesse subject to vapours and noysome Exhalations, and whatsoever *accident* happens either publick or private it is put up,
20 or reconciled without noise and fury. Severall recreations call the Countryman abroad, now his *Orchard* and *Gardens*, now his *fallow*, now his *meadows*, another time his *corne fields*, and when all these are lookt to, there remains something to be done at *home*; hence commeth he to be so *vigorous* and *strong*, so *secure* and *cheerfull*, and is alwaies accompanied with more *pleasure* than *paine*. This *Privilege* also the Country hath above other places, That there are in it neither *young Physicians*, nor *old diseases*. But the *Courtier* hath his *substance* alwaies divided into *foure parts*; The first he gives to his *flatterers*, the second to his *Sollicitour* and the *devour-*
30 *ing irreligious Lawyer*, the third to his *Apothecary*, and the fourth to the *Physician*. O how happy then in comparison of these *wretches* is the contented, peacefull Countryman, who never heard of the *Neopolitan* disease, nor any other *bodily disorders*, the rewards of an unlimited *lust*! He knows not what is meant by the *Canker*, the *Apoplexie*, or the *Gout*, never saw a *Juleb*, a *Purge*,
* *A decoction made* or an * *Apozeme*. The peacefull *Country-Life*
of severall herbs.   is seldome broken with so many and so weighty cares and molestations as may hasten an untimely end, and make the soule and body part by a forced and painfull dissolution.
40 Briefly so far are the Country people from a pompous Curiositie and ostentation, that they had not known what *brick* or *lime* is, but for the necessary use of it to build Stables and Out-houses for

their Cattell. Their own *Cots* are for the most part built with *Tymber* which they cover over with *Clay*, and Thatch with *Straw*. And those few more costly buildings which are to be seen there, for sweetnesse of *situation* and *contrivance*, exceed all regal Palaces, or other sumptuous structures built by Citizens.

The day it self (in my opinion) seems of more *length* and *beauty* in the Country, and can be better enjoyed than any where else. There the *years* passe away calmly, and one *day* gently drives on the other, insomuch that a man may be sensible of a certaine *satietie* and *pleasure* from every *houre*, and may be said to feed 10 upon *time* it self, which devours all other things. And although those that are imployed in the mannaging and ordering of their own estates in the Country, have otherwise, namely by that very imployment, much more pleasure and delights than a *Citizen* can possibly have, yet verily so it is, that one *day* spent in the recesse and privacie of the *Country*, seems more pleasant and lasting than a whole year at *Court*. Justly then and most deservingly shall we account them most happy with whom the Sun stays longest, and lends a larger day. The Husbandman is alwaies up and drest with the morning, whose dawning light at the same instant of time 20 breaks over all the Fields and chaseth away the darknesse (which would hinder his early labours) from every *valley*. If his days task keep him late in the *fields*, yet *night* comes not so suddenly upon him, but he can returne home with the *Evening-star*. Whereas in *Towns* and populous *Cities* neither the *Day*, nor the *Sun*, nor a *Star*, nor the *Season* of the *Year* can be well perceived. All which in the Country are manifestly seen, and occasion a more exact care and observation of *Seasons*, that their *labours* may be in their appointed time, and their *rewards* accordingly.

Another most profitable Prerogative also the Husband-man 30 hath, and that is the cheapnesse of all necessary commodities, as *Wood* for fuell, *Hay*, and *Straw*, which in the *Cities* cannot be had but at a most dear rate. Besides he *Dines* and *Sups* both when and where, and with whom he pleaseth, though not delicately, yet so as to satisfie nature, and not offend his health ; but in Cities and Courts the long *preparation* and *Cookery* makes their meals alwaies *unseasonable* ; and their meat is most commonly either raw, or with long stay lukewarme, and ill-relishing ; which notwithstanding they devoure with so much eagernesse, as if they were half starved. And which is worst of all, they are oftentimes 40 driven to sit at the same Table with their enemies and persecutors, which makes their most dainty morsels relish no better than *gaul*

and *wormewood*.   This intemperate manner of feeding is too too
often the cause of sudden deaths, or a forward decrepitnesse, with
lingring and obstinate diseases.   But the Husbandman all this while
hath *life* and *health* at will, he keeps good hours, Dines and Sups
seasonably, eats cheerfully without *suspition* and a *taster* in the Company of his faithfull friends, which at *Court*, and in *Cities*, are meere
prodigies and *miracles*.   Or if he Dines privately, yet hath he the
comfort and *societie* of a modest, vertuous *wife*, sweet and healthfull
Children, a religious and quiet *family*, whose very sight is the best
10 *sauce*, and gives most *content*.   And though none of all these feed
high & daintily, yet by *Gods* goodnesse they have both healthfull
bodies and cheerfull *complexions*, and never complaine of *famine*
or *scarcitie*.   A Messe of *Milk* and a piece of *Cheese* rellish better
with them in their own *homes*, than the most sumptuous provisions and banquets in the house of a *stranger* ; Yea the coarsest
dish their table affords is as welcome to them, as if it were drest
with rich *Oils*, rare *Sallads*, and the most costly *Spices*.

This Privilege also (above others) makes the Country-man
happy, that he hath alwaies something at hand which is both
20 usefull and pleasant.   A blessing which hath never bin granted
either to a *Courtier*, or a *Citizen*.   They have *enemies* enough,
but few *friends* that deserve their love, or that they dare trust to
either for *Counsell* or *action*.   O who can ever fully expresse the
pleasures and happinesse of the Country-life ! with the various and
delightfull sports of *fishing, hunting* and *fowling*, with *guns, Greyhounds, Spaniels,* and severall sorts of *Nets* ! what oblectation and
refreshment it is, to behold the *green shades*, the beauty and
Majestie of the tall and antient *groves*, to be skill'd in *planting* and
dressing of *Orchards, Flowres* and *Pot-Herbs*, to temper and allay
30 these harmlesse *imployments* with some innocent merry *song*, to
ascend sometimes to the *fresh* and *healthfull hils*, to descend into
the *bosome* of the *valleys*, and the fragrant, deawy *meadows*, to
heare the *musick* of *birds*, the *murmurs* of *Bees*, the *falling* of
springs, and the pleasant discourses of the *Old Plough-men*, where
without any impediment or trouble a man may walk, and (as *Cato
Censorius* us'd to say) discourse with the *dead*, that is read the
pious works of learned men who departing this life left behind
them their *noble thoughts* for the benefit of *posterity*, and the
preservation of their own worthy *names*.   Where the Christian
40 pious *Countryman* may walk with the learned Religious *Minister*
of his *Parish*, or converse with his familiar faithfull *friends*, avoyding

28 Majestie *text 1651* : Majesty *catchword 1651*

the dissimulation and windinesse of those that are *blown* up with the *spirit,* and under the pretence of *Religion* commit all *villanies.* These are the blessings which only a *Countryman* is ordain'd to, and are in vaine wish'd for by *Citizens* and *Courtiers.*

The third CHAPTER.

The Inhabitants of the Country meet with nothing all the *week* that can make them miserable, and when the *Sabbath day* comes, or other *festivall solemnities,* they enjoy a more sincere and heavenly comfort, than those that live in *Cities* and *Courts ;* for such a troop of intricate and numerous *negotiations* take up the *thoughts* 10 and *souls* of those people, that they never make any difference betwixt *working* and *holy* days. O what a pious and beautifull work it is, when *holy* and *solemne days* are observ'd in the Country, according to the *sacred rules* and *Ordinances* of *Religion* ! The *doore-keepers* of the *house* of *God* set wide open their *beautifull gates,* The *Church-bels* Ring, and every pious Soule is ravish'd with the *Musick,* and is sick of *love* untill he come into the *Courts* of the *Lord.* The *Temples* and *Communion tables* are drest, and the *beauty of holinesse* shines every where. The poorest *Country-labourer* honours that day with his best *habit ;* their *families,* their 20 *beasts,* and their *cattell* rest on that day, and every one in a decent and Christian *dresse* walks Religiously towards his *Parish Church,* where they heare Divine *Service,* performe all *holy duties,* and after Dinner releast from all their labours *rest* in the *practice* of true *piety.* But in *Cities* there are no other signs of *holy days* than to sleep them out, or to see their *Wifes* and their *Daughters* richly cloath'd, with their *haire* artificially combed and curiously tyed up ; The men walk out into the *Suburbs,* where they fall to drinking and disorder. And if you enter into their *Churches* you shall find a very thin Company, and most of them either *strangers,* or some 30 inferiour *Trades-men.* The chiefest *Citizens* aswell as the *Courtiers* spend those blessed days in pampering themselves, and obeying their own lusts and devices.

But let us return from this *vitious place* into the *harmles Country :* What dainties are there at Court (omiting the pleasure of taking them) which are not first had from the *Countrey* ? The *Courtier* pleaseth his palat with a peece of *stale venison,* but the *Countreyman* by the help of his *bow,* his *nets,* or his *gun,* can have it *fresh,* and consequently more *pleasant* and more *healthie.* He hath not a familie whose necessities must be alwaies furnished out 40

27 curiously] cuririously *1651*

of the *shop*, nor their table out of the *market*, but a provident and gainfull familie ; His provision is alwaies out of his own *store*, and agreeable with the season of the Yeare ; *Pigeons, Partridges, Capons, Quists, Hares*, with severall sorts of *fish* and *fowle* he hath in abundance, and is ever ready to pleasure a friend if call'd upon. His *sheepe* furnish him and his familie with *wooll* for clothing. His fat *weathers* and *goates* are numerous and alwaies at hand. He hath his *Oxen* to plough with, his *kine* and *heifers* yeeld him *milk, butter*,and *Cheese*; His *Kitchin* is alwaies well stor'd with *Bacon* and
10 *Beefe*, nor wants he any thing that is necessary towards the *breeding* or the *maintaining* of a familie.   If wee look abroad into his *fields*, wee shall find him well furnished with young *Cattell* and *Colts*, some ready for the *Yoke*, and *Sadle*, others fit for the *Market* and *Sale*. Thus by Gods blessing upon his labours he thrives by an honest Industrie without supplanting his neighbour, while others out of an unsatiable madnes and a devlish avarice by meere rapine and a tyrannicall power, maintaine their abominable greatnes with the *bloud* and *teares* of poore Innocents and Orphans, and like *Harpyes* and *heathens* take the *bread* out of the *mouths* of the helples and
20 harmles *Children*.

In the *Countrey* every *one* finds reverence proportionable to his worth, and those that have none are accordingly esteemed of. But in *Citties* and *Courts* it is otherwise, for there, no man is honour'd for his *worth*, but for his *riches*, nor for his *deserts*, but for his outward *port* and *greatnes*.   And to such *Swoln outsides* (though never so *hollow* and *rotten* within) all *Parasites* and *suters* run like rivers to the sea.   But the honest, plaine Husbandmen, if there lives amongst them a discreet, learned, and upright Patriot, faithfull and able to give them advise, can never think themselves
30 thankfull enough, for the good offices, fidelitie, and kindnes they receive from him ; what ever in their fields, gardens and orchards is most rare, that they present him with, and all of them from the lowest to the highest make frequent profession of their love and duty unto him.   But at Court and in great Cities all honour is conferred upon subtile dissembling *favorites*, while the wise, honest, and constant *man* is neglected and past by like a *fruitles tree*, none but *knaves* and *parasites* being admitted to preferment. The wicked men there carry all the *rewards*, and the righteous grone under those *punishments* which are due to the bad.

40 The *Countrey-gentleman* and the *husbandman* breed up and accustome their *sons* and *daughters* to modest, and virtuous Courses, lest by any remissnes or Loose Carriage, they might incurre the

danger of an ill name. Equall *matches*, and unforc'd *Affections*
make them live *happily*, and the *tyes* of Kinred and marriage so
unite all neighbourhoods there, that their affections and Courtesies
to one another last equally with their lives, which in greater
fortunes use to end with the *marriage-day*. This is a happines
which *Cittizens* and *Courtiers* seldome enjoy ; for they looking
after great fortunes, match their Children far off, and are oftner
Troubled with their *absence*, than Comforted with their *presence*.

O too too fortunate, and in every Circumstance most blessed
and happy Husband-men ! who marry their Children to their 10
neighbours, and live alwaies within the *breath* of their Sons in Law,
their grand Children, and their families. Who *reverence*, *love*, and
willingly performe all kind and honest offices for their *superiours*,
and which is a speciall Comfort to their soules in their old age, visit,
relieve, and cherish the *sick* and the *poore*. Such peacefull private
livers as these feare no *fines*, nor *forfeitures*, which many times
bring in a *Stranger* or an *Enemie* to be the heire of all our labours
under the *Sun*.

It is a singular privilege also which the Countrey hath, that the
Inhabitants there are not troubled with any *Importunate Visits*, 20
and yet have no Cause to complaine of *Solitude*. This fashion of
visiting is in great *townes* and *Courts* grown up to a kind of a
politick *vocation* ; when their *purses* are emptied of money, then
their *heads* are full of gadding thoughts, and they are casting about
what acquaintance or friend they shalbe troublesome to, under a
pretence of Courtesie ; so that they can neither sleep well at *nights*,
nor suffer their friends to be quiet in the *day-time*.

How happy then is the Countrey-man which moves only in the
Circuite of his own grounds, that is absolute master of his time,
and is not compelled to waite at the litigious *bars*, and *Courts* of 30
Law by a set houre ! that goes not *capping* from Lawier to Lawier
for their opinion, and then payes for it, before he hath it. That
Supplicates not to *door keepers*, *Clarks*, and *officers*, nor with much
sorrow and more amazement is forced to heare a great deale
of invented *barbarisme*, and strange *terms*. That is not driven to
make humble requests to ev'ry rotten *Sycophant* and *favourite*,
which yet in vaine he often solliciteth, and prostrates himselfe to
the *Corrupt Magistrates*, for feare of being devoured by such
Cyclops and harpyes. Happy I say is the Husband-man, who lives
a stranger to all these miseries, and in the shadow of some faire 40
wood with unspeakable delight contemplates the beauty of the
fields, *meadows*, *fountaines*, and *rivers* of *water*. He admires and

adores the only wise, and almightie god, who first *created*, and still *preserves* all things in a flourishing and fruitfull condition. With this Consideration of *gods* infinite goodnes he mightily comforts himselfe, and is daily delighted to heare the *bleating* of his *sheepe* and *lambs,* the *lowing* of his *Oxen*, and the *neighing* of his *horses*. Towards *sun setting*, the *nightingale* and other pleasant *birds* caroll to him out of the *wood*, his *dogs* like faithfull attendants walk about him ; The *Rams* leap, the *kids* skip, and his *Yard* abounds with *Pigeons, Turkeys, Capons, ducks* and all sorts of *Poultrie*. In-
10 numerable other pleasing objects greet his Eyes, as the leaping of fish, the flying of *fowles*, and the casuall meeting of wild *beasts*, which steale through the *woods* and pleasant *pastures* to some *green banke*, where they may quench their thirst with the *coole streames*. Happy therefore I say, yea, truly happy is the Husbandman who is every day *feasted* (as it were) with so many and such various delights ; who in a certaine and silent tranquillitie enjoys all these blessings with a thankfull heart. Though he should rest no where else, but on *straw*, or the bare *Earth*, yet are his sleeps unbroken, and far more sweet, than those *naps* which are taken upon *silks*,
20 and *beds* of *down*.

Another advantage which the Husband-man hath is this, That in the Country there is more emulation and striving to be good, and lesse occasion of malice than in *Courts* and places of eminence, where sin and wickednesse find alwaies an open entrance. The Confluence there is at all times populous, few or none exhorting to a virtuous life, and many, yea most of them inciting to vice ; but the most dangerous are those, who doe not so much allure with words as with examples, teaching us to esteeme of every man according to his outside, not considering what he may be within,
30 or how qualified towards *God* and his *neighbour*. These kind of people the wise *Seneca* judged to be the most miserable, compar-ing them to *whited wals* and *painted tables*, whose outward show might deceive a very good judgement ; so easily may an honest man be over-reach'd, though never so wise.

But let us proceed to another consideration. There is not in the Country such frequent miscarriage, and occasion of offence, as in *Cities* and *Courts* ; they justle not, nor overtop one another ; They seek all for a subsistence by manuring their lands, and look-ing to their cattell ; there is no *eminencie* amongst them, and con-
40 sequently no *envy*. There are no *Wine-taverns* nor *Cook-shops* for riotous, lewd livers to frequent ; no *night-wanderers* to sit up, drink, and vomit in every corner, making the rooms loathsome, and their

Company lesse tollerable than that of *Swine*. There are no nice, curious *Dames*, that never come abroad without a Guard of Hand-mayds ; no quarrels, no bloodshed, nor provocations to them. There are no voluptuous, lascivious *shows*, no *Arts* to egge men on to impietie and *Epicurisme*. All that can be said to offend there, are a few *gnats* and *flies* ; which notwithstanding are not so troublesome, as that they need to *keep up a troop of horse* to drive them out : But there are *Hornets* elsewhere which sting worse, and a Company of *Drones* whose robbery and greedinesse will admit of no cure at all. 10

We are now come to the last *Prerogative*, which in this short discourse we shall reckon for the Country-Inhabitants, and that is this ; They can with lesse charge maintaine their families, and better their estates, than it can be done in *Cities* and *Courts* ; for it is well known at what vast, and unreasonable expences they live at Court, especially in this age, wherein the excessive charge of *rich habits* and a *luxurious diet* is grown to such a height both in *Courts* and *Cities*, that it seems to call for not only the *censure* of the earthly Magistrate, but the *Divine judgement* it self.

O what *Peace*, what *privacy*, and *securitie* is to be found in the 20 *Country* ! No silken *Curtains*, no costly *Arras*, no *Gold* or *Silver* Plate, no sumptuous *Jewels*, no Embroyderd *Garments*, no *Coaches*, nor *Sedans*, with an unprofitable and troublesome *traine* of atten-dants are there in request. The *expenses* we must be at there, are both *frugall* and *necessary*, there is nothing to incite us to a lavish imitation of every ridiculous *Prodigall*, that claps his Revenues upon his back, and by the way of *bravery* comes at last to *beggery*. The Countrymans *Household-stuffe* is but ordinary, his *Tables* and *Chairs* are of plaine Timber, his *Beds* neither carv'd, nor gilded. The *Cups* he drinks in, are in the *Winter* of wholesome *earth*, or 30 the season *Oke*, and in the *Summer* of *glasse*. His richest habit is a plaine *coate*, or *cloke* worne first by his own *sheep*, afterwards *shorne* and *spun* for himself ; an able *horse*, a *man-servant* and a *maid* are all his *retinnue*. And truly this plaine *Husband-man* both in reguard of the *Utensils* of his house, his *provision* and *course* of life, is and ever shalbe in my opinion far more happy than either the *Nobleman*, the *Courtier*, or the *Citizen* ; And if we con-sider him for *uprightnesse*, and *purity* of *conscience*, I believe there is no *man* so *Irrationall*, but will confesse him to exceed them all. As for the *Courtier*, all that ever he gets, comes either by some 40 base, servile *prostitution* of his person, or by *flatterie* and *insinua-tion* ; sometime the rich *donatives* of *Princes* and *Noblemen*,

wearied with their importunate begging and sollicitations, conduce much to their advancement. But *vultures* and *harpies* are more tollerable in a *Common-wealth* than this kind of creatures ; for those feed only upon *Carkasses* & the *dead* ; but these prey upon and devoure the *living*. That *God* in whose hand the hearts of Princes are, root out of the earth all such *Caterpillers*, which have occasion'd the ruine of many pious *Kings*, and most flourishing *Kingdomes*. There would be something commendable in them, if they would at last in their *old age* leave off their odious *practices* ;
10 but as the Proverb goes, *they are never asham'd to swallow the Oxe and his tayle too.* Good *stomacks* they have, and can convert any thing into *bloud* and *nutriment*. Such, and so fatall is the misery of man, that though he plainly sees the *errours* of his life, yet he neither will *Reforme*, nor use the *means* for *Reformation*. May this *ambition* once perish, and *humilitie* take place, such an *happy* change would (no doubt) have an *holy* end.

FINIS.

THE
MOUNT of OLIVES:
OR,
SOLITARY DEVOTIONS.

By

HENRY VAVGHAN *Silurift.*

With

An excellent Difcourfe of the
bleffed ftate of MAN in GLORY,
written by the moft Reverend and
holy Father ANSELM Arch-
Bifhop of *Canterbury,* and now
done into Englifh.

LUKE 21. V. 39, 37.

*Watch ye therefore, and pray always, that ye may
be accompted worthy to efcape all thefe things
that fhall come to paffe, and to ftand before the
Sonne of Man.
And in the day time he was teaching in the
Temple, and at night he went out, and abode in
the Mount that is called the Mount of Olives.*

LONDON, Printed for WILLIAM LEAKE at the
Crown in Fleet-ftreet between the two
Temple-Gates 1652.

TO THE
Truly Noble and Religious
Sr. CHARLES EGERTON
KNIGHT.

SIR,

Though I should have no other *defence*, that near *relation* by
which my *dearest friend* laies claime to your *person*, might in some
measure excuse this otherwise *unhansome adventure* of publishing
these *weake productions* under the *shelter* of your *name*.   But
I was not so much induced to *it* by that *Tye*, though very deare
unto me, as by your *love* to *Religion* and *Learning*, and the
respects due from my selfe to your *person*, and those *reverend years*,
which by a *faire* and *virtuous disposal* of your *time* you have
10 happily attained to, and wherein you *safely* are,

> ——*Cælo dignus canente senectâ*
> *Consilioque deûm*, ——

I know, *Sir*, you will be pleased to accept of this poore *Olive-leafe*
presented to you, so that I shall not be driven to put forth my
hand to take in my *Dove* againe.   And indeed (considering how
fast and how *soone* men degenerate), It must be counted for
a great *blessing*, that there is yet any left which dares *look* upon,
and *commiserate* distressed Religion.   *Good men* in *bad times* are
very scarce ; They are like the *standing eares of Corne escaped out*
20 *of the Reapers hands*, or the *Vine-dressers last gleanings after the*
first ripe fruits have been gathered.   Such a *precious generation are*
the Just in the *day of trouble*, and their *names* are like to *afflicted*
truth, like the *shadow of a great rock in a weary land*, or a *way-*
faring mans lodge in the waste and howling Wildernesse.   The
Sonne of *God* himselfe (when *he* was *here*,) had no place to put his
head in ; And his *Servants* must not think the *present measure* too
hard, seeing their *Master* himself took up his *nights-lodging* in the
cold *Mount* of *Olives*.

By this time, *Sir*, you may see the *reason* which moved me to
30 take *Sanctuary* at your *name*, and now I will acquaint you with
my *designe*.   To be short, *Sir*, It is no other, but that your *name*
(like the *royall stamp*) may make *current* and commend this *poore*

mite to posterity : And that the unfained *lover* of your *Person* may in these few and *transitory sheets* waite upon your memory in the ages to come ; when your immortal and precious *soule* shall be bound up in the bundle of the living, in the *ever-lasting book* of life ; which is devoutly desired by

SIR,

Newton by *Usk*
this first of
October.
1651.

Your very affectionate

and faithful Servant

VAVGHAN.

TO THE

Peaceful, humble, and pious READER.

I know the world abounds with these Manuals, and triumphs over them. It is not then their scarsity that call'd this forth, nor yet a desire to crosse the age, nor any in it. I envie not their frequent Extasies, *and raptures to the third heaven ; I onely wish them real, and that their actions did not tell the world, they are rapt into some other place. Nor should they, who assume to themselves the glorious stile of Saints, be uncharitably moved, if we that are yet in the body, and carry our treasure in earthen vessels, have need of these helps.*

10   *It is for thy good, and for his glory, who in the dayes of his flesh prayed here himselfe, and both taught and commanded us to pray, that I have published this. Thou hast here sound directions and wholsome words, and if thou wilt enquire of the Lord and say,* If the Lord will, I shall live, and do this or that, *thou mayest. Here are* Morning *and* Evening *sacrifices, with holy and apposite* Ejaculations *for most times and occasions. And lastly, here are very faithful and necessary Precepts and Meditations before we come to the Lords Table. To which last part I have added a short and plaine Discourse of Death, with a Prayer in the houre thereof. And*
20 *for thy comfort after thou hast past through that* Golgotha, *I have annexed a Dissertation of the blessed state of the righteous after this life, written originally by holy* Anselme *sometimes Arch-Bishop of* Canterbury.

I *have purposely avoided to leade thee into this little Book with a large discourse of Devotion, what it is, with the severall Heads, Divisions, and sub-divisions of it, all these being but so many fruitlesse curiosities of Schoole-Divinity,* Cui fumus est pro fundamento. *Neither did I thinke it necessary that the ordinary Instructions for a regular life (of which theere are infinite Volumes already extant)*
30 *should be inserted into this small Manuall, lest instead of Devotion, I should trouble thee with a peece of Ethics. Besides, thou hast them already as briefly delivered as possibly I could, in my* Sacred Poems.

And thus, Christian Reader, do I commend it to thy practise, and

the benefit thou shalt finde thereby. Onely I shall adde this short
Exhortation: That thou wouldest not be discouraged in this way,
because very many are gone out of it. Think not that thou art alone
*upon this Hill, there is an innumerable company both before and
belinde thee.* Those with their Palms in their hands, and these
expecting them. If therefore the dust of this world chance to prick
thine eyes, suffer it not to blinde them ; but running thy race with
patience, look to J E S U S the Authour and finisher of thy faith,
who when he was reviled, reviled not againe.   Presse thou towards
the mark, *and let the people and their Seducers rage ;* be faithful 10
unto the death, and he will give thee a Crowne of life.   *Look not
upon transitorie, visible things, but upon him that is eternal, and
invisible.*   Choose the better part, yea, that part with *Saint* Hierome,
who preferred the poore Coate of Paul *the Hermite to the purple and
pride of the world.*   Thus with my simple Advise unto thee, I bid
thee farewel.

Thy Christian friend

Henry Vaughan.

7 running] runniug *1652*   12 *eternal*] etern l *1652*

The Table.

FINIS.

27 *Enemies.*] *Enemies 1652*

ADMONITIONS

FOR

Morning-Prayer.

The night (saith *Chrysostome*) was not therefore made, that either we should sleep it out, or passe it away idly ; and Chiefly because we see many worldly persons to watch out whole nights for the Commodities of this life. In the *Primitive* Church also the *Saints* of God used to rise at midnight to praise the *Rock of their salvation* with *Hymns and Spiritual Songs.* In the same manner shouldst thou do now, and Contemplate the *Order* of the Stars, and how they all in their several stations praise their Creator. When all the world is asleep, thou shouldst watch, weep and pray and propose unto thy self that *Practise* of the 10 Psalmist, *I am weary of my groaning, every night wash I my bed, and water my Couch with my tears ;* for as the *Dew* which falls by night is most fructifying, and tempers the heat of the *Sun ;* so the tears we shed in the night, make the soul fruitful, quench all Concupiscence, and supple the hardnesse we got in the day. *Christ* himself in the day-time taught and preach'd, but continued all night in prayer, sometimes in a Mountain apart, sometimes amongst the wild beasts, and sometimes in solitary places.

They, whose Age or Infirmity will not give them way to do thus, should use all Convenient means to be up before the Sun- 20 rising, for *we must prevent the Sunne to give God thanks, and at the day-spring pray unto him,* Wisd. 16. It was in the morning that the Children of *Israel* gathered the *Manna ;* and of the Just man it is said, *That He will give his heart to resort early to the Lord that made him, and will pray before the most high,* Eccl. 39. So soon therefore as thou dost awake, shut thy door against all prophane and worldly thoughts, and before all things let thy God be first admitted, offer unto him thy first fruits for that day, and commune with him after this manner.

When thou dost awake. 30

O God the Father ! who saidst in the beginning, *Let there be light,* and it was so ; *Inlighten my Eyes that I never sleepe in death :* lest at any time my Enemy should say, *I have prevailed against him* COSMIC
O God the Sonne ! light of light ; the most true and perfect light, from whom this light of the Sun, and the day had their

beginning; thou, that art the light shining in darknesse, Inlightning every one that cometh into this world, expell from me all Clouds of Ignorance, and give me true understanding, that in thee, and by thee I may know the *Father*; whom to know is to live, and to serve is to reigne.

O God the Holy Ghost! the fire that inlightens, and warms our hearts, shed into me thy most sacred light, that I may know the true Joyes of Heaven, and see to escape the illusions of this world.   Ray thy selfe into my soul that I may see what an
10 Exceeding weight of glory my Enemy would bereave me of for the meer shadowes and painting of this world.   Grant that I may know those things which belong unto thee, and nothing else; Inflame me with thy divine love that with a true Christian Contempt I may tread upon all transitory Pleasures, and seek only those things which are eternal.

Most blessed Trinity! and one eternal God! as thou hast this day awaked me from this bodily sleep, so awake my soule from the sleep of sin, and as thou hast given me strength after sleep, now again to watch, so after death give me life, for what is death
20 to me, is but sleep with thee, to whom be ascribed all glory, wisdome, majesty, dominion and praise now and for Ever, Amen.

When thou dost arise.

Arise O my soul that sleepest, arise from the dead, and Christ shall give thee light.   Arise O daughter of *Sion*, O my soul redeemed with the blood of Christ! sit no more in the dust of thy sins, but arise, and rest in that peace which is purchas'd by thy Saviours merits.

Christ Jesus! my most merciful and dear Redeemer! as it is thy meer goodness that lifts up this mortal and burthensome body,
30 so let thy grace lift up my soul to the true knowledge and love of thee; grant also that my body may this day be a helper and servant to my soul in all good works, that both *body* and *soul* may be partakers of those Endlesse Joyes, where thou livest and reignest with the Father and the Holy Ghost, one true God world without End, *Amen.*

As soone as thou art drest, before thou comest forth from thy Chamber, kneel down in some convenient place, and in this, or the like Prayer commend thy self for that day unto thy Creator's Protection.

40   Almighty, eternal God, the Father of our Lord *Jesus Christ,*

34 Father] Faher *1652*

I blesse and praise thy holy name, and with my whole heart give thee all possible thanks, that out of thine infinite goodness thou wert pleased to watch over me this night, to resist my adversary, and to keep me from all perils of body and soul; O thou! that never slumbrest nor sleepest, how careful hast thou been of me! how hast thou protected me, and with thy holy angels, thy ministring spirits sent forth to minister for the heirs of salvation, incompast me about! yea, with what unmeasurable love hast thou restored unto me the light of the day, and rais'd me from sleep and the shadow of death, to look up to thy holy hill; Justly 10 mightst thou, O God, have shut the gates of death upon me, and laid me for ever under the barres of the Earth, but thou hast redeemed me from Corruption, and with thy *Everlasting armes* enlarged my time of Repentance.

And now O Father of mercies, and God of all Consolation, hear the voyce of thy Supplicant, and let my cry be heard in thy highest heavens: As I do sincerely love thee, and beg for thy Protection, so receive thou me under the shadow of thy wings, watch over me with the Eyes of thy mercy, direct me in the wayes of thy Law, and enrich me with the gifts of thy Spirit, that I may passe 20 through this day, to the glory of thy great name, the good of others, and the comfort of my own soul. Keep me, O my God, from the great offence; quench in me all vain Imaginations, and sensual desires; sanctifie and supple my heart with the dew of thy divine Spirit, refresh it with the streams of thy grace, that I may bring forth fruit in due season, and not cumber the ground, nor be cut off in thy anger. And to this end I do here resigne my body and my soul, with all the faculties thou hast bestowed upon both, into thy Almighty hands; Guide thou them in the works of thy Law, turne my eyes from all transitory objects, to the things 30 which are eternal, and from the *Cares* and *Pride* of this world to the *fowles of the aire* and the *Lillies of the field*; And now, O my God, seeing I am but Dust and Ashes, and my Righteousnesse a filthy Rag, having no deserts in my self but what should draw Everlasting vengeance, and the Vials of thy bitter wrath upon my body and soul; behold, I have brought with me thy first-born and onely begotten, the propitiation for my sins, the *Incense* I offer up with my prayers, *Rev.* 8. 3. my Redeemer and Mediatour in whom thou art well-pleased, hear thou him. O look not upon my Leprosie, but on his beauty and perfection! and for the righteous- 40

11 mightst] mighst *1652*
32 *aire G Gu*   *aire*; *1652*   *field*; *M*: *field 1652* : *field. G Gu*

nesse of thy *Son*, forgive the sins of thy *Servant.* Grant this for his sake, to whom with thee and the Holy Ghost, be all glory and majesty, Dominion and power now and for ever. Amen.

Admonitions when we prepare for any farre Journey.

When thou art to go from home, remember that thou art to come forth into the *World*, and to Converse with an Enemy; And what else is the World but a Wildernesse? A darksome, intricate wood full of *Ambushes* and dangers; A Forrest where spiritual hunters, principalities and powers spread their nets, and
10 compasse it about; wouldst thou then escape these ghostly snares; this *wickednes in high places*, and return home if not better and holier, yet not worse then at thy setting out? Wouldst thou with *Jacob* passe over these *Waters* with thy staffe onely, and in thy return become two bands? *Gen.* **32. 10.** Why then, do as he did, begin thy Journey with prayer, and say, *If God will be with me, and keep me in this way that I go, and will give me bread to eate, and raiment to put on, so that I come again to my fathers house in peace: then shall the Lord be my God,* Gen. 28. 20, 21. This was his practise, and the practise of his fathers; *The Lord God of*
20 *heaven* (saith *Abraham*) *who took me from my fathers house, and from the land of my kindred, &c. he shall send his Angel before thee.* Nor must thou pray only at thy setting forth, but all the way, and at all times; Thus *Eliezer* prayed at the Well, *Isaac* in the field, and *Elias* (in his journey to *Mount Horeb*) under a *Juniper* tree in the Wildernesse. This also (if thou wilt imitate these holy men) thou may'st do, and for that pious purpose thou hast here these following Prayers.

When we go from home.

Almighty and everlasting God, who art the *Way*, the *Life* and
30 the *Truth*; look down from heaven, and behold me now betwixt the Assaults of the Devil, the allurements of the World, and my own inclinations; I cannot look abroad, but these flock about me; But O thou that leadest *Joseph* like a sheep, thou most faithful and Almighty guide, lend me thy hand, open mine Eyes, direct my steps, and cause me to walk in thy fear; Thou that didst go out with *Jacob* from *Beer-she-ba* unto *Padan-aran*, guiding him in the *waste plaines*, and watching over him on his *Pillow of stones*, be not now farre from me; Leade me, O Lord, in thy righteousnesse, make my paths straight, and strengthen my goings, that
40 having finished my Course here, I may sit down in thy Kingdome, an Inheritance undefiled, purchased for me with the blood of my Saviour, and thy beloved Son *Jesus Christ*, Amen.

II.

O thou, that art every where ! *Thou that sittest upon the Circle of the Earth, and all the Inhabitants thereof are as Grashoppers before thee ! Whose Eyes discover the deep things of the night, before whom Hell is naked, and all the Devices of my spirituall Enemies !* Thou that didst leade *Abraham* thy chosen from *Ur* of the *Chaldees* into a land flowing with milk and honey, favour I beseech thee the present harmlesse Enterprise and innocent purpose of thy servant, be unto me in my Journey a Comfort, in the heate a shadow, in stormes a shelter, and in adversity my 10 protection ; That having finished my intended course, I may return in peace full of thy praises, who art near to all those that call upon thee ; Grant this for *Christ Jesus* his sake, *Amen.*

Meditate in the way upon the sojournings and travels of the Patriarchs and Prophets, the many weary journeys of *Jesus Christ* in the flesh, the travels of his Apostles by sea and land, with the pilgrimage and peregrinations of many other precious Saints that wandred in Deserts and Mountains, of whom the world was not worthy.

Admonitions how to carry thy self in the Church. 20

Holinesse (saith the Royall Prophet) *becometh thy house for ever.* When thou art going thither then, carry not the world with thee.

Let vain or busie thoughts have there no part,
Bring not thy *Plough*, thy *Plots*, thy *Pleasures* thither,
Christ purg'd his Temple ; so must thou thy heart.
All worldly thoughts are but Theeves met together
To Cousin thee.   Look to thy actions well,
For *Churches* are either our Heav'n or Hell.

These reverend and sacred buildings (however now vilified and shut up) have ever been, and amongst true Christians still are the 30 solemne and publike places of meeting for Divine Worship : There the *flocks feed at noon-day*, there the great *Shepherd* and *Bishop* of their souls is *in the midst of them*, and where he is, that *Ground is holy* ; Put off thy shoes then, thy worldly and carnall affections, and when thou beginnest to enter in, say with *Jacob, How dreadful is this place ! sure this is none other then the house of God, and this is the gate of heaven !*   Such reverence and religious affection hath in all ages been shew'd towards these places, that the holy men of God detain'd either by Captivity, or other neces- sary occasions, when they could not remedy the distance, yet to 40 testifie their *desire and longing for the Courts of the Lord*, Psal. 84. they would always worship towards them.   Thus *Daniel* upon the

Idolatrous Decree signed by *Darius, goes into his house, and his windows being open in his Chamber towards Jerusalem, he kneeled upon his knees, and prayed and gave thanks before his God as he did afore-time,* Dan. 6. 10. which fully proves it to have been his Constant manner of Devotion.   And of *Judith* we read *that about the time that the Incense of that Evening was offered up in* Hierusalem, *she cried unto the Lord,* Iud. 9. 1.   But above all, most pathetical and earnest is that crie of King *David* in the 85. *Psalm.*

How amiable are thy Tabernacles O Lord of Hosts!

10   *My soul longeth, yea even fainteth for the Lord, my heart and my flesh cryeth out for the living God.*

Yea the Sparrow hath found an house, and the Swallow a nest for her selfe, where she may lay her young, even thine Altars, O Lord of Hosts, my God and my King!

Blessed are they that dwell in thy house, they will be still praising thee.

For one day in thy Courts is better than a thousand; I had rather be a doore-keeper in the House of my God, than to dwell in the tents of wickednesse.

20   Let it be thy Care then, when thou art there present to carry thy self like a true worshipper; Give none offence, neither outwardly to thy *Brethren,* nor the *Angels,* 1 Cor. 11. 10.   Nor inwardly to thy God, whose Eyes shine within thee, and discern thy reins and thy heart.   Look seriously about thee, and Consider with thy self how many beauteous, wittie, and hopeful personages in their time lie now under thy feet ; thou canst not tell but thy turn may be next.   Humble thy self in this dust, and all vain Imaginations will flie from thee.   Consider that thou art now in the *Cave of Macpelah,* in a sacred *Repositorie* where the Bodies of
30 Saints are asleep, expecting that hour, *when those that are in the grave shall hear his voyce.*   Do not then stop thy eares against the *Charmer,* but give diligent attention, and hear him while it is yet to day, that in the day of thy death thou mayst rest there in the same hope.   When thy vessell is fill'd with this *Manna,* and thy soul satisfied, go not off without Thanksgiving ; Be not like those nine *Leapers* who never returned to give glory to God ; but come back with the thankfull *Samaritane,* and receive another blessing, *Go in peace.*   Saint *Luke* in the *Acts* of the Apostles making mention of the *Ethiopian Eunuch,* who came up to *Jerusalem* for to wor-
40 ship, tells us, that in his returne he was reading in *Isaiah* the

Prophet ; This blessed *Convert* I would have thee to imitate : When thou hast fill'd thy *Hin* with this living water, leave it not behinde thee at the Fountain ; spill not thy *Milk* and thy *Wine*, because thou hast it without *money and without price*, but carry it home and use it. Thou mayest have need of it in six dayes, and perhaps shalt not come to draw again, untill thou drinkest it anew with thy Saviour in *his Fathers Kingdom.*

A Prayer before thou goest to Church.

Lord *Jesus Christ*, who out of thy Fathers bosome wert sent into this world to reveal his will unto sinners, and to instruct them 10 in the way of salvation ; behold, I am now going to hear thy blessed word, and these many yeers have so done, expecting still thy good pleasure and the Consummation of thy sacred will in me. I have come unto the bread of life, and yet am hungry ; into the light, and yet am blind ; unto the great Physician, and yet my Issue runs : The former and the later rain of thy heavenly Doctrine falls still without intermission upon my heart, but this bad ground yeelds nothing but Thornes and Briers. Many dayes, many moneths, and many yeers hast thou expected fruit, and found nothing but leaves. It is thy Infinite mercy, O Lord, that 20 thou hast left unto us the seed of thy word, and sendest into thy harvest such upright and faithful labourers ; but in vain, O Lord, shall they cry in our Ears, unlesse thou openest and renewest our hearts. Open then, I beseech thee (O blessed Jesu !) the eares of my heart, that not onely the outward hearing, but the inward also may be stirr'd up in me, and what I hear with the eare, I may understand with the spirit. O thou most mild and merciful *Lamb of God !* the onely, and the Almighty sower ! grant, I beseech thee, that the seed which falls this day upon my heart, may never be choak'd with the Cares of this world, nor be devoured by the 30 fowles of the aire, nor wither away in these times of persecution and triall : but so Cherish it with the Dew of thy divine spirit, that (as in a good and faithful ground) it may bring forth fruit unto eternal life, to the glory of thy great name, and the Comfort of my poor soul, which thou hast bought with thy most precious and saving blood. *Amen.*

Another when thou art come home, or in the way
if thou beest alone.

Lord *Jesus Christ*, my ever mercifull, and most loving Redeemer ! I give unto thee most hearty thanks for this thy heavenly, spiritual 40 provision wherewith thou hast fed and refreshed my soul. Grant

M

I beseech thee that this Celestial seed may take root in me, and be effectual to my salvation ; Watch over my heart, O Lord, and hedge it in with thy grace, that the fowles which descend in the shadows of the Evening may not pick it out ; But so prepare and fit me for thy love, that I may never forget thy gracious words, thy blessed and saving advice, but may know in *this my day what belongs unto my peace.* It is thy promise by thy holy Prophet, *That as the rain cometh down, and the snow from heaven, and returneth not thither, but watereth the earth, and maketh it bring*
10 *forth and bud, that it may give seed to the sower, and bread to the eater: So thy word that goeth forth out of thy mouth, shall not return unto thee void, but shall accomplish that which thou pleasest, and prosper in the thing whereto thou sendest it,* Isai. 55. 10, 11. Even so, Lord *Jesus*, let it be as thou hast promised. Let the words I have heard this day out of the mouth of thy servant, the *Dispenser*, and *Steward* of thy Mysteries prosper in me, and make my life answerable to his Doctrine ; that I may not onely know what thy blessed will is, but performe also and fulfill it ; so that at last by thy mediation and mercies I may attain to thy eternal and
20 most glorious Kingdom. *Amen.*

Admonitions for Evening-Prayer.

Remember that in the *Levitical* Law there is a frequent Commemoration and Charge given of the two daily Sacrifices, the one to be offer'd up in the morning and the other in the Evening, *Exod.* 30. 7, 8. These offerings by *Incense*, our holie, harmlesse and undefiled High-Priest hath taken away, and instead of them every devout *Christian* is at the appointed times to offer up a Spiritual Sacrifice, namely that of *Prayer* ; for *God is a Spirit, and they that worship him, must worship him in spirit and in truth,* John 4. 24.
30 At these prescribed times (if thou wilt have thy Prayers to ascend up before God) thou must with-draw from all outward occupations to prepare for the inward and divine. To which end thou hast here this following Meditation, that thou maiest therewith season and invite thy soul from thy worldlie imployments to her proper vocation, and so come not altogether undrest into the presence of the *King of glory.*

A Meditation at the setting of the Sun, or the Souls Elevation to the true light.

The path of the Just (O my God) is as the shining light,
40 that shineth more and more unto a perfect day of eternity,

Prov. 4. But the wicked neither know, nor understand, they walk in darknesse, and from the inward darknesse of their minds passe at last into the outward, eternal darknesse. O most miserable and undone soul! to whom thy *Sunne* is set; that everlasting glorious *Sun*! which in thy holy Elects never setteth, but is alwaies at the height, full of brightnesse and Consolation. A heavie night sits in the noone-day upon those souls that have forsaken thee; They look for light, and behold darknesse; for brightnesse, and they walk in obscurity. They grope for the wall like the blind, as if they had no Eyes; They stumble at noone-day as in the night, 10 they are in desolate places as dead men. But on those that walk with thee an everlasting day shines; This *Sun* of the firmament hath his Course; it riseth, setteth, comes up again, and again goes down: But thou Lord, knowest no vicissitudes, thou art the *Ancient of dayes*, thou art the *Rock of ages from Everlasting to Everlasting.* O thou, *the same to day and yesterday, and for evermore! Thou bright and morning Starre springing from on high,* illuminate me, who am now sitting in darknesse and in the shadow of death. *O light of light, the brightnesse of thy Fathers glory,* inlighten all inward obscurities in me, that after this life I 20 may never be cast into the outward darknesse. O most blessed, most merciful, and Almighty *Jesu*! abide I beseech thee with me, *for it is towards Evening, and the day is far spent, Luke* 24. As long as thou art present with me, I am in the light, but when thou art gone, I am in the shadows of death, and amongst the stones of emptinesse. When thou art present, all is brightnesse, all is sweetnesse, I am in my Gods bosome, I discourse with him, watch with him, walk with him, live with him, and lie down with him. All these most dear and unmeasurable blessings I have with thee, and want them without thee. Abide then with me, O thou whom my soul 30 loveth! Thou Sun of righteousnesse with healing under thy wings arise in my heart; refine, quicken, and cherish it; make thy light there to shine in darknesse, and a perfect day in the dead of night.

A Prayer for the Evening.

Most gracious, Almighty God! full of loving kindnesse, and long-suffering, whose mercy is above all thy works, and thy glory above the heavens; whose truth reacheth unto the Clouds, and whose words shall never passe away, forgive me, I beseech thee, my transgressions this day, my vain thoughts, idle words, and loose conversation; my exceeding neglect and forgetfulnesse of thee, my head- 40

long inclinations and lusting after the world, preferring this land of *Cabul* before the snow of *Lebanon,* and a broken Cistern before the Well of life. Justly, O Lord, might'st thou have shewed me thy back this day, and cut me off from amongst thy people, *Jer.* 18. 17. but thou hast had mercy, and not sacrifice ; thou hast shed upon me the light of thy Countenance, and removed my sins farre out of thy sight. I know, O my God, it is not in man to establish his own ways, it is thy Almighty arme must do it ; It is thou alone that hast led me through this day, and kept me both from doing and
10 from suffering evill. And now, O thou preserver of men ! What shall I do unto thee ? What shall I render unto my Lord for all the mercies and loving kindnesses shewed unto thy servant this day, and all the dayes of my life hitherto ? *I will offer unto thee the sacrifice of thanksgiving, and call upon the name of the Lord.* I will ever love thee, fear thee, praise thee, and trust in thee ; My song shall be of thee in the night season, and in the day time I will be speaking of thy wondrous works, thy most merciful and liberal arme ; I will make thee my *Delight* in the house of my pilgrimage, and I shall alwayes with all my strength, with all my heart, and
20 with all my soul ascribe unto thee, all glory, wisdome, majesty, dominion, and honour this day and for evermore. *Amen.*

A Prayer when thou art going into bed.

Most glorious, and onely wise God ! to whom the light and the darknes are the same, whose dwellings are eternal, and in whose Kingdome there is no need of Candles, nor of the light of the Sunne ; look, I beseech thee, upon thy servant, who tarries in this *place all night,* Gen. 28. 11. And forasmuch as thou (out of thy tender love and Compassion on thy Creatures) hast ordained this time for their repose and refreshing, that having past through the
30 Cares and dangers of the day, they might under the shadow of thy wings finde rest and security ; keep me, I most humbly beseech thee, from the hours and the powers of darknesse ; watch over me this night in thy Almighty providence, and scatter all the rebellions and devices of my Adversaries. Inlighten my soul, sanctifie my body, govern my affections, and guide my thoughts, that in the fastest closures of my eyelids my spirit may see thee, and in the depth of sleep be Conversant with thee. Suffer me not, O my God, to forget thee in the dark, or to say, *The Lord seeth me not, The Lord hath forsaken the earth,* Ezek. 8. 12. but so keep me in
40 thy fear, and sanctifie me with thy grace, that all the words of my mouth, and the meditations of my heart may be alwayes of thee.

Make my soul to thirst for thee, and my flesh also to long after thee. And at what time soever thou shalt awake me from this bodily sleep, awake also my soul in me, make thy morning-star to arise in my heart, and let thy spirit blow upon my garden, that the spices thereof may flow out. Quicken me O Lord, according to thy wonted kindnesse, so shall I seek thee early, and make my prayer unto thee with joyful lips. And now O my most loving and faithful Creatour, take me, I beseech thee, into thy Almighty protection, stretch over me the *Arme* of thy mercy, let thine Eye be towards the work of thine own hands, and the purchased pos- 10 session of thy onely begotten, and my most merciful Redeemer *Jesus Christ*, Amen.

¶ As often as thou dost awake in the night, be sure to lift up thy heart unto God in this or the like short *Ejaculation. Holy, holy, holy, Lord God of Sabbath ! heaven and earth are full of the majesty of thy glory.* By resorting thus unto God, thou shalt finde a great furtherance and cheerfulnesse in thy spiritual exercises, and besides it will keep always about thee the *savour of life.* And because thou shalt not be unfurnished upon any incident occasions, I have strowed here this handful of savoury 20 herbs, which thou mayest take up as thou findest them in thy way.

EJACULATIONS.

When the Clock strikes.

Blessed be the houre in which my Lord Jesus was borne, and the houre in which he died ! O Lord Remember me in the houre of death !

When thou intendest any businesse, or Journey.

O do well unto thy servant ! that I may live and keep thy Word.

When thou art persecuted. 30

Haste thee, O God, to deliver me, make haste to help me, O Lord!

Upon some suddaine fear.

O set me upon the Rock that is higher then I, for thou art my hope, and a strong tower for me against my enemy.

Upon any disorderly thoughts.

Make me a clean heart, O God, and renew a right spirit within me.

Upon any occasions of sadnesse.

Thy rebuke hath broken my heart, I am full of heavinesse, but thou, O Lord, shalt lift me up again.

Upon any Diffidence.

Thou art my hope, O Lord, even from my youth, through thee have I been holden up ever since I was borne ; though thou shouldst kill me, yet will I trust in thee.

When thou dost any good work.

Not unto me, O Lord, not unto me, but unto thy name give the 10 *praise.*

When thou art provoked to anger.

Give thy peace unto thy servant, O God, let no man take away my Crown ; In patience, O Lord, let me possesse my soul.

For thine Enemies.

Lord, lay not this sinne to their Charge ; they know not what they do.

Upon any gracious deliverance, or other mercies conferr'd upon thee.

The Lord is my Shepherd, I shall not want. He maketh me to 20 *lie down in green pastures, he leadeth me besides the still waters. He hath prevented me with the blessings of goodnesse, he hath granted me my hearts desire, and not with-holden the request of my lips. Surely goodnesse and mercy shall follow me all the dayes of my life : And I will dwell in the house of my God for ever.*

Upon any losses, or other adversities.

Shall we receive good at the hand of God, and shall we not receive evill? Naked came I out of my mothers womb, and naked shall I return thither ; the Lord gave, and the Lord hath taken away, blessed be the name of the Lord.

30 When thou hearest that any is dead.

Teach me, O Lord, to number my dayes, that I may apply my heart unto wisdome.

Upon thought of thy sins.

Turn away thy face from my sins, O Lord, and blot out all mine offences.

Praise the Lord, O my soul, and forget not all his benefits, who forgiveth all thy sins, and healeth all thine Infirmities.

When thou art weary of the cares and vanities of this world. *Like as the Hart brayeth for the water-brooks, so thirsteth my soul after thee O God.*

O who will give me the wings of a Dove, that I may flie, and be at rest.

¶ *Admonitions, with Meditations and Prayers to be used before we come to the Lords Supper.*

All the Sacraments of the New Testament, in those that come to participate them, require a most Exquisite and sincere preparation. But this Sacrament of the Lords Table, because in *Institu-* 10 *tion* and *Effect* it is the highest of all, requires the most perfect and purest Accomplishments. Our preparation to this Sacrament is not perfected by Contrition onely and Confession of sins, (both which are unavoidably requisite) but if we will be worthy receivers and partake of those graces which are exhibited unto us in this heavenly banquet, there are many other duties we must necessarily performe, for this Sacrament is of an infinite vertue, having in it the *Wel-spring* of all graces, even *Jesus Christ* with all the merits of his most bitter passion, which admit neither number nor measure. Wherefore such as our pre-disposition is, such also 20 shall our proportion be of this spiritual *Manna*; for as he that cometh to a Well to draw water, takes no more thence, then what his vessel contains; which yet he cannot impute unto the Well, but unto his Pitcher which could hold no more; so they that come unto this glorious Sacrament, receive onely so much grace as their preparation and holines makes them capable of. Now there are required of us, before we presume to lay hands upon this bread of life, three things.

1. Purity of Conscience.
2. Purity of Intention. 30
3. Fervent and effectual Devotion.

We must (as far as it lies in us) refrain from all actual sins in thought, word, and deed. Secondly, We must do it to a good end, not for any private benefit; not by compulsion, or for fear of Censure, or any other Ecclesiastical correction; not out of Custome, nor for any sensual devotion or joy because of the confluence and company at these love-feasts. Thirdly and lastly, we must watch over our owne souls, and take heed that no wind blows upon our garden but the spiritual and eternal; we must labour for an heavenly setlednesse, sanctified affections, holy hopes, new garments, a clean heart, and a right spirit. *Cant.* 2. The soul must be sick of love, she must long for the banqueting house, nothing now must appear but flowers, nothing must be heard but the singing of birds, and the voice of the Turtle. Lord God (saith S. *Ambrose*) with what contrition of heart, with what fountains of tears, with what reverence & fear, with what chastity of body and purity of mind should this divin mystery be celebrated! where thy flesh is the meat, where thy blood is the drink, where the creature feeds upon the Creatour, and the Creatour is united unto the creature, where Angels are spectators, and God himself both the Priest and the Sacrifice, what holinesse and humility should we bring thither?

O what pure things, most pure, must those hands be
which bring my God to me!

As therefore some rich, odoriferous water is distill'd out of many and several sorts of fragrant herbs and flowers, so our devotion at this soveraigne Sacrament should be composed of many spiritual, acceptable affections with God, as (amongst others) are profound humility, unmeasurable reverence, ardent love, firme faith, actuall charity, impatient hunger, and an intollerable longing after this heavenly banquet.

And because we may not touch these white robes with dirty hands, nor come neer the Rose of *Sharon* with ill sents and offensive fumes, it hath been ever the Custom of Gods Church to injoyn and set apart a certain limited time of purification before this mysterious solemnity, wherein all religious and worthy Communicants addressed and prepared themselves in some measure for this unmeasurable mercy. Such was in our Church, that more strict and holy season, called *Lent*, and such still are the preparation-dayes before this glorious Sabbath in all true Churches. Two dayes were given the *Israelites* to sanctifie themselves, and to wash their clothes, that they might be ready against the third day, upon which the Lord was to come downe (in the sight of all the people) upon Mount *Sinai*; And this onely at the reception of the Law which was given by Angels; much more then ought we to wash and cleanse our vessels from all vaine affections, idle words and actions, and to separate our selves from the world for three dayes at least, that we may be ready against that great and blessed day, wherein we are to come, not to a mountain that might not be touched, nor to the sound of a Trumpet, nor to the voice of words spoken to us out of the midst of fire, but to the general assembly, and Church of the first-borne, which are written in heaven, and to *Jesus the Mediatour of the new Covenant, and to the blood of sprinkling, that speaketh better things then that of Abel.* See then that thou refuse not to come to this great marriage of the Kings Son with thy soul, and see withall, that thou comest not without a wedding garment, that is to say, unprepared. *For, whosoever shall eate this bread, and drink this cup of the Lord unworthily, shall be guilty of the body and blood of the Lord; But let a man examine himselfe, and so let him eate of that bread, and* 10 *drink of that cup of the Lord, for he that eateth and drinketh un-worthily, eateth and drinketh damnation to himselfe, not discerning the Lords body,* 1 Cor. 11. 27, 28, 29. These are the words of a faithful witnesse, and thou maiest beleeve them.

When therefore thou doest intend to be a partaker of this merciful and mysterious Sacrament, be sure for three daies at least not to intermeddle with any worldly businesse, but all that time redeeme those many daies which were vainly spent by thee; enter into thine owne bosome, examine what thou hast there, and if thou findest any sons of darknesse lurking under those fig-leaves, 20 conceal them not, but turne them out of doors, and wash their Couch with thy teares; have a care that in the Bridegroomes bed, instead of myrrhe and flowers, thou strowest not thornes and thistles. The Evening before thou art to communicate, feed but moderately, and after supper use no corrupt communication, but converse inwardly with thine own heart, and meditate what an Almighty guest thou art to entertaine there next day. Consider seriously thine own unworthinesse, and desire of him that he would sanctifie and furnish the roome where he is to eate the Passeover with thee. Intreat him to defend thee that night from all sinful 30 Illusions and temptations, and to keep the house cleane and garnished for himself. When thou hast thus commended thy self into his hands, let thy sleep that night be shorter then usual, be up with the day, or rather with thy Saviour, who rose up early, while it was yet dark. Meditate with thy self what miracles of mercy he hath done for thee. Consider how he left his Fathers bosome to be lodged in a manger, and laid by his robes of glory to take upon him the seed of *Abraham,* that he might cloath thee with Immortality. Call to minde his wearisome journeys, con-tinual afflictions, the malice and scorne he underwent, the perse- 40 cutions and reproaches laid upon him, his strong cries and teares in the days of his flesh, his spiritual agony and sweating of blood,

4 *the] ehe 1652*

with the Implacable fury of his Enemies, and his own unspeakable
humility, humbling himself to the death of the Crosse, a death
accursed by Gods own mouth.   Consider againe (if thou canst) of
what unmeasurable love was he possessed, who having designed
and spent his time of life here for thy salvation, did not onely
leave thee those divine Oracles and Instructions to be guided by,
but to seale up the summe and make heaven sure unto thee, did
by his last Testament give himself with all the merits of his life and
death to be wholly thine, and instead of them took upon him all
10 thy transgressions, bore all thine iniquities, and to appease the anger,
and satisfie the Justice of his Father, became the holy, harmlesse,
and undefiled sacrifice and perfect satisfaction for the sins of the
world, reconciling all things unto his Father, whether they be
things in earth, or things in heaven.

When thou hast thus considered him in his acts of love and
humility, consider him again in his glory, take thine Eyes off from
Bethlehem and *Golgotha*, and look up to the mount of *Olives*, yea,
to heaven where he sits now upon the right hand of his Father,
Angels, principalities and powers being made subject unto him.
20 Call to minde his Joyful resurrection, his most accomplished
conquest, and triumph over the world, death and hell; his most
gracious and familiar conversation with his Apostles before his
Ascension, with his most loving and comfortable carriage towards
them at his departure, *leading them out as farre as* Bethanie, *and
lifting up his hands, and blessing them.*   Lastly, close up these
thoughts with a serious and awful meditation of that great and
joyful, though dreadful day of his second coming to judgement,
promised by himself, and affirmed at the time of his Ascension
by the two men in white apparel.   *Ye men of Galilee, why stand*
30 *ye gazing up into heaven? this same Jesus which is taken up from
you into heaven, shall so come in like manner as ye have seen him go
into heaven.*

*Behold! he cometh with clouds, and every eye shall see him, and they
also which pierced him, and all kindreds of the earth shall waile
because of him.   Amen! even so, come quickly, Lord Jesus!*

¶ These are the duties required of thee, and which thou must
faithfully and punctually performe, if thou wouldst be a worthy
Communicant, and receive those sacred and mystical Elements to
that blessed end for which they were ordained.   But when I speak
40 of three dayes preparation, I do not impose that proportion of
time, nor conclude it sufficient, as if it were enough for thee to

recede from thy corrupt inclinations, and the myre of thy sins for such a terme, with an intention to returne and wallow in it again, when that holy season is over, for our whole life (had we the purity of Angels, and the innocence of infants,) bears no proportion at all, nor can it (without an immediate sanctification from God himself) any way qualifie, or make us fit for the reception of this unmeasurable mercy. But when I spoke of such a proportion of time, I did onely propose it to my Readers for the performing of those holy and necessary duties, which have particular relation to this solemne Feast, and which (indeed) are required then from every Christian. And as for a regular, sober, and holy life ; we should in all places, and at all times labour for it, for *without holinesse no man shall see the face of God*, much lesse be partaker of his merits, and by this spiritual eating and drinking become a member of that body, whose life and head he is.

A Prayer for the grace of repentance, together with a Confession of sins.

O holy, blessed and glorious Trinity ! three persons, and one eternal God, have mercy upon me a miserable sinner.

O who will give mine head waters, and mine eyes a fountain of tears ! that I may weep night and day for my infinite transgressions, ingratitude and rebellion against my most milde and merciful Creatour ! O God my God be not farre from me ! hide not thy face from the work of thine hands, reject not my sighing and mournful spirit, nor the earnest endeavours and desires of mine undone and miserable soul ! O thou that breakest not the bruised Reede, nor quenchest the smoking Flax, quench not in me these weak sparks, this dawne and beginnings of the promised earnest. Take away, O my God ! this heart of stone, and give me a heart of flesh, renew a right spirit within me ; cloath me with white raiment, and anoint mine Eyes with Eye-salve, that I may know and see how wretched, and miserable, and poore, and blinde, and naked I am, and may be zealous therefore and repent ! O thou that didst cause the waters to flow out of the stonie rock, and gavest to *Magdalen* such store of teares that she washed thy feet with them, give to me true remorse, and such a measure of repentance as may become a most miserable sinner ! I confesse dear God, that I am not worthy of the least of thy mercies, much lesse to appear at this great and solemne Feast, this Feast of mercy and miracles, where none but with holy hands, pure intentions, crucified affections, and renewed spirits should presume to

enter. But as for me I am all uncleannesse, a polluted, vile creature, and nothing belongs unto me at this great day, but confusion of face, and an utter separation from this glorious and saving Communion. I have wasted thy stock, consumed thy talents, and destroyed thy goods. I was restlesse, and unquiet till I had found out wayes to offend thee. I have broken thy Commandments, laid open thine Inclosures, and most grievously trespassed against thy truth, and against the light of mine own Conscience. I have preferred rottennesse and dust to the treasure
10 of thy word, and mine own voluptuousnesse to thy revealed will. And now *O thou preserver of men ! What shall I do unto thee ? Against thee onely have I sinned, and my transgressions are ever in thy sight.* Lord God ! I lay me down at thy footstoole, *and if thou wilt be extreme to mark what is amisse*, I shall from my very heart acknowledge and adore thy Justice. But O my dear Creatour, for Christ Jesus his sake have mercy upon me ! look not on my deserts, but on thy glory ; O Lord do not refuse me, but reforme and restore me ! O Lord hearken, and do, and deferre not, but speak peace to my troubled soul, and send thy loving
20 spirit to strengthen and confirme me in the way of holinesse, bring me home, O Lord, and leade me now unto these living waters, incorporate me into the saving vine, and purge me, that I may bear more fruit. O cast me not away like an abominable and withered branch, but make me to flourish in the Courts of thy house, where thy Children are like Olive-branches round about thy table ! O Lord hear, and have mercy, and forgive me, and be reconciled unto me for *Christ Jesus* his sake ! To whom with thee and the holy Ghost be glory in the Church through all ages world without end, *Amen.*

30 *A Meditation before the receiving of the holy Communion.*

Holy, holy, holy, is the Lord God of Hosts, the whole earth is full of his glory ! Behold to the Moone, and it shineth not, and the Starres are darknesse in his sight. The Pillars of heaven do tremble, and are astonished at his reproof. O who then am I, that I should appear before thee, or *what is man that thou shouldest regard him ?* O light of light, the all-seeing light that shineth in darknesse, and the darknesse comprehendeth it not, what will be-come of me, when I shall appear before thy glorious and searching Eye ! What an habitation of darknesse and death wilt thou finde
40 within me ? What abominable desolations and emptinesse ?

3 glorious] glorions *1652*

What barrennesse and disorders wilt thou see there? Many a time hast thou knockt, and I have shut the doors against thee, thou hast often called, and I would not answer. Sleeping and waking, early and late, day and night have I refused instruction, and would not be healed. And now, O my God, after all this rebellion and uncleannesse, wilt thou come and lodge with me? O Lord, where shall I prepare, and make ready for thee? *What communion can there be betwixt light and darknesse,* purity and pollution, perfection and deformity? O Rose of *Sharon*! thou undefiled and everlasting flower, the glory of the fields, and the first fruits of the dead, shall the wilde Asses and the beasts of the wildernesse feed now upon thee? Wilt thou give the bread of life unto dogs, and cast thy pearls before swine? O *Jesus Christ,* the lover and the redeemer of all humble and penitent souls! Thou that feedest among the Lilies untill the day breaks and the shadows flee, what is there in my heart where onely tares and thistles grow, that thou canst feed upon? Thy blessed body was wrapt in fine and white linen, (which is the righteousnesse of the Saints.) It was laid in a new and undefiled grave, hewen out of a rock, wherein never man was laid before. But all my righteousnesse is a filthy rag, my heart neither new nor undefiled, but a nest of unclean birds, where they have not onely laine, but hatched and brought forth their viperous young ones.

I confesse, dear God, I confesse with all my heart mine own extrem unworthynes, my most shameful and deplorable condition. But with thee, O Lord, there is mercy and plenteous redemption. Thou dost not use to reject and cast off those that unfeignedly repent and return unto thee; the great design and end of thine Incarnation was to save sinners: Thou hadst never come into this world, but for thy love to thy lost sheep, and those thou didst then love, thou dost love still unto the end. Thou didst not come unto the whole, but to the sick. The first (had there been any such,) had no need of a *Physician,* and the last (hadst not thou come to restore them,) had perished for ever. It was thy gracious pleasure (while thou wert here in the world) to receive Publicans and sinners, and though thou art now ascended to thy Father, yet hast not thou changed thy nature. Thou art the same yesterday, to day, and for evermore. Thy life here was nothing else but a pilgrimage and laborious search after sinners, that thou mightst finde them out and make them whole. And how willingly (O blessed Jesus!) didst thou lay down thy robes of glory, and cloath thy self with flesh, that thou mightst afterwards

lay down thy life a propitiation for our sins ! How many scorching and wearisome journeys didst thou undergo for our sakes ! How many cold and tedious nights didst thou watch and spend abroad in prayer, when the birds of the aire lay warme in their nests, and thou hadst not a place to put thy head in ! In the day time I finde thee preaching in the Temple, and all night praying in the Mount of *Olives* ; a little after on thine own Sabbath travelling for me in the corne-field ; Another time (wearied with thy journey) sitting on the Well of *Jacob,* and begging a draught of that cold water from the
10 woman of *Samaria* ; Now again I meet thee on the Asse, made infinitely happy by so glorious a rider, by *the God of Jeshurun who rideth on the heavens, and in his excellencie on the skies.* Sure, it was his simplicity and ordinary contempt with man, that made him so acceptable in thy sight. But (Oh !) with what language shall I attempt thy passion ? thy bloody sweat, thy deep and bitter agony, thy lingring peece-mealed death, with all the lively anguishments, and afflictions of thy martyr'd Spirit? O my most loving and merciful Saviour ! It is onely thy own Spirit, that can fully character thy own sufferings.
20 These miracles of love and most comfortable circumstances encourage me (O my God) to draw neer unto thee : for it is not probable that thou wouldst have subjected thy self to such bitter reproaches, blasphemies, and torments, had not thy love to man (for whose redemption thou didst suffer them,) been as infinite as thy self ; *And greater love then this hath no man, that a man lay down his life for his friends.* And lay it down thou didst, for *no man could take it from thee.* Thou couldst have commanded twelve legions of Angels from thy Father, and when thou wentest forth to meet thy murtherers, they went backwards and fell to the
30 ground, and without thy permission (in whose hand their breath was) they could have done nothing. These merciful passages, together with thy own voice and frequent invitation much encourage me to draw neer unto thee.

Come unto me all ye that labour, and are heavy laden, and I will give you rest. Matth. 11. 28.

If any man thirst, let him come unto me, and drink, John 7. 37.

These, with many more, are thy loving Invitations : This is the voyce of the great Shepherd, and thy sheep hear thy voyce. Thus thou didst cry, and these were the words thou didst speak
40 while thou wert here upon earth, and shall I then turn away from thee, *that speakest now from heaven ? Thou art a Priest for ever*

24 redemption] redemprion *1652*

after the order of Melchisedech, and thy preaching and Intercession shall last untill the heavens be no more, and woe unto them that refuse to hear thee.

Wherefore, most holy *Jesus,* seeing thou dost invite sinners to thee, and didst die to redeem them, and *art able to save them to the uttermost, that come to God by thee, and dost live for ever to make intercession for them,* Heb. 7. 25, 26. I the most wretched and the worst of sinners in full assurance of thy mercies, and that *thou art touched with the feeling of mine infirmities,* Heb. 4. 15. and wilt have compassion upon my penitent soul, draw neer to 10 thy throne of grace, that I may obtaine mercy, and finde grace to help in time of need.

O Lord be merciful unto me, forgive all my sins, and heal all mine infirmities. Cleanse my heart, sanctifie my affections, renew my spirit, and strengthen my faith, that I may at this great Feast discerne thy blessed body, and eate and drink salvation to my self, to the glory of thy great name, and the comfort of my poor and sorrowful soul, *Amen.*

Now unto him that hath loved us, and washed us from our sins in his own blood, and hath made us Kings and Priests unto God 20 and his Father, to him be glory and dominion for ever, and ever. *Amen.*

A Prayer when thou art upon going to the Lords Table.

In the name of the Father, and of the Son, and of the holy Ghost, *Amen !*

Jesus Christ, the Lamb, the Branch, the bright and morning-Starre, the bread of life that came down from heaven, have mercy upon me ! It is thy promise, that whosoever eateth thy flesh, and drinketh thy blood, he shall have eternal life in him, and thou 30 wilt raise him up at the last day. Behold, O God, I am now coming to thee ; O thou fountain of purgation ! thou Well of living waters wash me cleane ! be unto me the bread of life to strengthen me in my pilgrimage towards heaven ! grant that I may suck salvation from thy * heart, that spring of the blood of God, which flowes into all believers. Thy flesh is meat indeed, and thy blood is drink Indeed. O give me grace to receive both worthily, that I may never incurre thy anger, and eternal condemnation ! Lord *Jesus Christ* ! I beleeve all that thou hast said, and all that thou hast promised, helpe thou

Cyprian de cænâ domini. Cruci hære-mus, sanguinem fugimus, & inter ipsa redemptoris nostri vulnera figimus linguam.

40

mine unbelief; thou art the Author, be thou the finisher of my
faith ; And for thy glories sake, for thine own names sake, leade
me in the right way to this great mercy and mystery, *Amen !*

Immediately before the receiving, say,

O Lord I am not worthy of the least of all the mercies, and
of all the truth which thou hast shewed unto thy servant, all my
life long unto this very day ; much lesse am I worthy thou shouldst
come now under my roof but seeing it is thy institution and free
10 mercy that will have it so, be jealous, O God, of the place of thine
honour, cause me to remember whose Temple I am, and suffer
not my last state to be worse then the first.   Even so, Lord Jesus,
come quickly, *Amen !*

¶ *Admonitions after receiving the holy Communion.*

When you have received the Sacred Elements, you should not
presently after spit, nor eate and drink, but refraine untill they are
perfectly digested and resolved.   You must lay aside all worldly
communication, and humane discourses, though never so serious ;
for judge of your self, what an uncivil part it will be in you, when
you have received so great a guest as *Jesus Christ* with all his
20 merits, to turne your back upon him presently, and neither to
meditate of him, nor to discourse with him, and keep him company.   Wherefore you should all that day be instant in prayer,
meditations, thanksgiving, and good works ; you should consider
and think upon the love of God, who so loved the world, that he
gave his onely begotten Son to redeeme it.   You should meditate
upon his birth, life, doctrine and passion, his death and buriall,
resurrection and ascension, and his second coming to judgement.
You should pray, that you may be found blamelesse and without
spot of him, and so much the more, because you see the day
30 approaching.   Tread not under foot the Son of God, and his
precious blood wherewith you are sanctified and saved, by
returning again to your former sins, like the dog to his vomit, but
be sure that you walk warily, and fall not wilfully into the myre.
Be not regular and holy for a day or two, but all the dayes of thy
life, and number thy dayes, that thou mayst apply thy heart unto
wisdome.   Cast thy bread upon the waters, (be merciful to the
poor) and remember thy Creator, for the dayes of darknesse are
many, but the outward darknesse is eternal, and from it there is
no redemption.

40   Instead of printed Meditations which are usually prescribed

after communicating, I would advise the pious receiver to read over all these following parcels of Scripture, *John* 6. 22. *to the end, John* 17. *Rom.* 8. 2 *Cor.* 5. *Ephes.* 1. *&* 4. *Heb.* 10. 1 *Pet.* 1. *Rev.* 5.

A Prayer after you have received.

Lord Jesus Christ, very God, and very man, made in all things like unto us, sin onely excepted ; I blesse and praise thy holy name, and with all my heart, with all my strength, and with all my soul give thee all possible thanks for thy infinite love and pity towards lost man. Blessed be the hour in which thou wert born, and the hour in which thou didst die ! Blessed and for ever hallowed be thy most comfortable and glorious name, the name J E S U S C H R I S T, *at which every knee shall bow, of things in heaven, and things in earth, and things under the earth ; for thy name is above every name, and there is no other name by which we can be saved.* O most holy, most humble and harmlesse Lamb ! how didst thou make thy self of no reputation, and becamest obedient to the death of the Crosse for my sake ! And when thou wert to drink the cup of thy Fathers anger due to my sins, didst instead of it ordain and bequeath to me the cup of life and everlasting salvation ! O Lord give me a heart to understand, and eyes to see what thou hast done for me ; O never suffer me to crucifie thee again by returning to my former iniquities and pollutions, but write thy sufferings and the price of my redemption in the tables of my heart, set them for a signet upon mine hand, and for a bracelet upon mine arme, that by a continual and careful remembrance of them, I may in the strength of this bread received to day at thy table travel to thy holy mountain, and that this drink which I drank out of the spiritual rock may become a Well of living waters, springing up in me to eternal life. Grant this, O God, for thy glories sake, and for that love and mercies sake which brought thee hither out of thy Fathers bosome to suffer so many things for his Elects sake, *Amen!*

Worthy is the Lamb that was slaine, to receive power, and riches, and wisdome, and strength, and honour, and glory, and blessing ; for he hath redeemed us to God by his blood out of every kindred, and tongue, and people, and nation, and hath made us unto our God Kings and Priests, and we shall reigne on the earth.

Now the God of peace that brought again from the dead my Lord Jesus, that great Shepherd of the sheep, through the blood of the everlasting Covenant,

10

20

30

40

23 pollutions] pollutious *1652*   30 O] G *1652*

*Make me perfect in every good work, to do his will, working in
me that which is well-pleasing in his sight through Jesus Christ, to
whom be glory for ever and ever, Amen!*

A Prayer in time of persecution and Heresie.

Most glorious and Immortall God, the Prince of peace, unity
and order, which makest men to be of one mind in a house, heale
I beseech thee these present sad breaches and distractions!
Consider, O Lord, the teares of thy Spouse which are daily upon
her cheeks, whose adversaries are grown mighty, and her enemies
10 prosper.   The wayes of *Zion* do mourne, our beautiful gates are
shut up, and the Comforter that should relieve our souls is gone
far from us.   Thy Service and thy Sabbaths, thy own sacred
Institutions and the pledges of thy love are denied unto us; Thy
Ministers are trodden down, and the basest of the people are set
up in thy holy place.   O Lord holy and just! behold and consider,
and have mercy upon us, for thy own names sake, for thy promise
sake suffer not the gates of hell to prevaile against us; but return
and restore us, that joy and gladnesse may be heard in our dwellings, and the voyce of the Turtle in all our land.   *Arise O God,*
20 *and let thine enemies be scattered, and let those that hate thee flee
before thee.   Behold, the robbers are come into thy Sanctuary, and
the persecuters are within thy walls.   We drink our own waters
for money, and our wood is sold unto us.   Our necks are under
persecution, we labour and have no rest.   Yea, thine own Inheritance
is given to strangers, and thine own portion unto aliens.   Wherefore
dost thou forget us for ever, and forsake us for so long a time?
Turne thou us unto thee, O Lord, and we shall be turned, renew our
dayes as of old.   Lord hear, and have mercy, and be jealous for the
beloved of thine own bosome, for thy truth, and for the words of thine*
30 *own mouth.   Help us, O God of our salvation, and for thine own
honours sake deal Comfortably with us,* Amen, Amen.

A Prayer in adversity, and troubles occa-
sioned by our Enemies.

O holy and almighty God, full of goodness and compassion,
look I beseech thee with thine Eye of mercy upon my present sad
sufferings and most bitter afflictions! Behold, O God, I put my
mouth in the dust, and confess I have deserv'd them.   I despise
not thy Chastenings, but begge grace of thee that I may not
faint, and that they may yeild the‧ fruits of righteousnesse unto

36 afflictions] afflctions *1652*

me, who am now exercised by them. Thou seest, O God, how furious and Implacable mine Enemies are, they have not only rob'd me of that portion and provision which thou hadst graciously given me, but they have also washed their hands in the blood of my friends, my dearest and nearest relatives. I know, O my God, and I am daily taught by that disciple whom thou did'st love, that no murderer hath eternal life abiding in him. Keep me therefore, O my God, from the guilt of blood, and suffer me not to stain my soul with the thoughts of recompense and vengeance, which is a branch of thy great prerogative, and belongs wholly unto thee. Though they persecute me unto death, and pant after the very dust upon the heads of thy poore, though they have taken the bread out of the childrens mouth, and have made me a desolation, yet Lord, give me thy grace, and such a measure of charity as may fully forgive them. Suffer me not to open my mouth in Curses, but give me the spirit of my Saviour, who reviled not again, but was dumb like a Lamb before his shearers. O Lord, sanctifie all these afflictions unto thy servant, and let no man take away my crown. Remember those that are in troubles for thy truth, and put their tears into thy bottle. Grant this, O merciful Father, for my dear Saviours sake, and bring me quickly into thy Kingdom, where I shall have all these tears wiped away from mine eyes, Amen, Amen !

M A N

I N

Darkneſs,

O R,

A DISCOURSE

O F

D E A T H.

Eccles. 11. 7, 8, 9, & 10.

Truly the light is sweet, and a pleasant thing it is to behold the Sun.

But if a man live many dayes and rejoyce in them all, yet, let him remember the dayes of darknesse, for they are many.

Rejoyce, O young man, in thy youth, and let thy heart cheere thee in the dayes of thy youth, and walk in the wayes of thy heart, and in the sight of thine eyes, but know thou, that for all these things God will bring thee into judgement.

10 *Therefore remove sorrow from thy heart, and put away evil from thy flesh, for childhood and youth are vanity.*

¶

Draw neer, fond man, and dresse thee by this glasse,
Mark how thy bravery and big looks must passe
Into corruption, rottennesse and dust;
The fraile Supporters which betray'd thy trust.
O weigh in time thy last and loathsome state,
To purchase heav'n for tears is no hard rate.
Our glory, greatnesse, wisdome, all we have,
If misimploy'd, but adde hell to the grave:
20 Onely a faire redemption of evill Times
Finds life in death, and buryes all our Crimes.

It is an observation of some *spirits*, that * *the night is the mother of thoughts*. And I shall adde, that those thoughts are *Stars*, the *Scintillations* and *lightnings* of the soul strugling with *darknesse*. This *Antipathy* in her is *radical*, for being descended from the *house of light*, she hates a contrary *principle,* and being at that time a prisoner in some measure to an enemy, she becomes pensive, and full of thoughts. Two great *extremes* there are, which she equally abhors, *Darkness* and *Death*. And 'tis observable, that in the *second death*, when she shall be wholly mancipated to her enemies, those [10] two are united. For those furious and unquenchable burnings of hell (which the *Scripture* calls *the lake of fire, &c.*) though they be of such an insuperable *intense heat*, as to work upon *spirits*, and the most subtile Essences, yet do they give no light at all, but burn blacker then *pitch, Cremationem habet, lumen verò non habet.* (Greg. Mor. c. 46.) The Contemplation of *death* is an obscure, melancholy *walk* an Expatiation in *shadows* & *solitude*, but it leads unto *life*, & he that sets forth at *midnight*, will sooner meet the *Sunne*, then he that sleeps it out betwixt his curtains. Truly, when I consider, how I came first into this world, and in what [20] condition I must once again go out of it, and compare my appointed time here with the *portion* preceding it, and the *eternity* to follow, I can conclude my present *being* or *state* (in respect of the *time*) to be nothing else but an *apparition*. The first man that appeared thus, came from the *East*, and the *breath* of *life* was received there. Though then we travel *Westward*, though we embrace *thornes* and swet for *thistles*, yet the businesse of a *Pilgrim* is to *seek his Countrey*. But the *land* of *darknesse* lies in our way, and how few are they that study this *region*, that like holy *Macarius* walk into the *wildernesse*, and discourse with the skull [30] of a dead man? We run all after the present world, and the Primitive Angelical life is quite lost.

It is a sad perversnesse of *man*, to preferre warre to peace, cares to rest, grief to joy, and the vanities of this narrow Stage to the true and solid comforts in heaven. *The friends of this world* (saith a holy father) *are so fearful to be separated from it, that nothing can be so grievous to them as to think of death. They put farre away the evill day, and cause the seate of violence to come neer; They lie upon beds of Jvory, and stretch themselves upon their Couches ; they eat the lambs* [40] *out of the flock, and the calves out of the midst of the stall; They chant to the sound of the viol, they drink wine in bowls, and anoint*

*A Proverb in *Italy*, La notte é madre de pensieri.

—Contempsit mori Qui non concupiscit—

24 *apparition.*] *apparition 1652*   39 *seate of*] *seate ef 1652*

themselves with the chief ointments; they account the life of the
righteous to be madnesse, and his end to be without honour, Amos 6.
In this desperate and senselesse state they cast away their precious
souls, and make their brightest dayes but *dayes of darknesse and*
gloominesse, dayes of clouds and of thick mists. They consider not
the day that *shall burne like an Oven, when the heavens being on fire*
shall be dissolved, and the Elements shall melt with a fervent heat;
when the wicked shall be stubble, and all the workers of iniquity shall
be burnt up. Miserable men! that knowing their masters pleasure,
10 will not do it, that refuse Oyle and balsame to make way for
poyson and corrasives. And why will they call him *Master,*
Master, whose precepts they trample on, and whose members
they crucifie? It is a sad observation for true Christians to see
these men who would seem to be Pillars, to prove but reeds and
specious dissemblers. For what manner of livers should such
professors be, seeing they expect and beleeve the dissolution of all
things? With what constant holinesse, humility and devotion
should they watch for it? How should they *passe the time of their*
sojourning here in fear, and be diligent that they may be found of him
20 *in peace, without spot, and blamelesse?* What preparation should
they make against the evill day? What comforts and treasures
should they lay up for that long voyage? For what a day of
terrors and indignation is the day of death to the unprepared?
How will they lie on their last beds, *like wilde Buls in a net, full*
of the fury of the Lord? When *their desolation shall come like*
a flood, and their destruction like a whirle-wind; How will they
say in the morning, would God it were Even, and at night, would God
it were Morning! for the fear of their heart wherwith they shal
fear, and for the sight of their Eyes wherewith they shall see? This
30 is a truth they will not believe, untill death tells it them, and then
it will be too late; It is therefore much to be wished, that they
would yet, while it is life-time with them, remember their last ends,
and seriously question with themselves, what is there under the
Sun, that can so justly challenge their thoughts as the contemplation of their own mortality? We could not have lived in an age
of more instruction, had we been left to our own choice. We
have seen such vicissitudes and examples of humane frailty, as the
former world (had they happened in those ages) would have
judged prodigies. We have seen Princes brought to their graves
40 by a new way, and the highest order of humane honours trampled
upon by the lowest. We have seene Judgement beginning at Gods
Church, and (what hath beene never heard of, since it was

redeem'd and established by his blessed Son,) * we have seen his Ministers cast out of the Sanctuary, & barbarous persons without *light* or *perfection*, usurping holy offices. A day, an hour, a minute (saith *Causabone*) is sufficient to over-turn and extirpate the most settled Governments, which seemed to have been founded and rooted in Adamant.

* There is extant a little book called *Speculum Visionis* printed at *Norimberge* 1508, wherein this fearful desolation and destruction of the Church by Lay-men is expressely foretold.

Suddenly do the high things of this world come to an end, and their delectable things passe away, for when they seem to be in their *flowers* and full strength, they perish to astonishment ; And sure the ruine of the most goodly peeces seems to tell, that the dissolution of the whole is not far off. It is the observation of a known Statesman, (Sir *Water Rawleigh*) *That to all dominions God hath set their periods, who though he hath given to man the knowledge of those wayes, by which Kingdoms rise and fall, yet he hath left him subject unto the * affections which draw on these fatal mutations in their appointed time.* Vain therefore and deceitful is all the pomp of this world, which though it flatters us with a seeming permanency,

* N. *Marcellus* de doctorum indagine. Potest fatum morum mutabilitate converti, ut ex iis celeriùs vel tardiùs aut bonum fiat, aut pessimum.

will be sure to leave us even then, when we are most in chase of it. And what comfort then, or what security can poor man promise to himself? whose breath is in the hand of another, and whose few dayes are most commonly out-lived by every creature, and sometimes by a *flower* of his own *setting*. Or what benefit can these * humane delights though blest with successe, and a large time of fruition, afford him at his death ? for satisfaction in this point, let us but have recourse to the ages that are past, let us aske the *Fathers*,

* Non est, falleris, hæc beata non est,
Quam vos creditis esse, vita non est.
Fulgentes manibus videre gemmas,
Aut auro bibere, & cubare cocco :
Qui vultus Acherontis atri,
Qui Styga tristem non tristis videt,
Audétque vitæ ponere finem,
Par ille regi, par superis erit.

& they will tell us. If we insist upon eminent persons, the rulers of this world, & the Counsellors of the earth who built *sumptuous Palaces for themselvs and filled their houses with silver*; we shall have no better account from them, then if we enquired of the *prisoners* & the oppressed. They are gone all the same way, *their pomp & the noise of their viols is brought down to the grave, the worms cover them, and the worms are spread under them. Riches* and *power* travel not beyond this life ; they are like *Jobs* friends, *deceitful as a brook, and as the stream of brooks they passe away, which*

16 *knowledge*] knowlededge *1652*

vanish when it is hot, and are consumed out of their place. Hast thou found riches (saith one) then, thou hast lost thy rest. Distractions & cares come along with them, and they are seldome gotten without the worme of conscience. It was an act of *Anacreon* becoming the royalty of a *Poets* spirit : *Policrates* rewards him with five talents ; but he, after he had been troubled with the keeping of them for two nights, carries them back to the owner, telling him, that, *if he had been accustomed to such companions he had never made any verses.* Certainly there is so much of *Mammon* and *darknesse* in them, as sufficeth to shew their *parentage* is low, and not very far from *hell.* Some such thing we may gather from that exclamation of S. *James* against the rich men ; *Your gold and your silver is canker'd, and the rust of them shall be a witnesse against you, and shall eate your flesh as it were fire, you have heaped treasure together for the last dayes.* But to return thither from whence we are digrest : What is become now of these great *Merchants of the earth,* and where is the fruit *of all their labours under the Sun?* Why, truly they are *taken out of the way as all others, and they are cut off as the tops of the eares of corn.* Their dwelling is in the dust, and as for their place here, it lies wast, & is not known : *Nettles and Brambles come up in it, and the Owle and the Raven dwell in it.* But if you will visit them at their *long homes,* and knock at those *desolate doors,* you shall find some remains of them, a heap of loathsomness and corruption. O miserable and sad mutations ! (*Petrarch. de otio Rel.*) Where is now their *pompous* & *shining train?* Where are their *triumphs, fire-works, and feasts,* with all the *ridiculous tumults* of a *popular, prodigious pride?* Where is their *purple* and *fine linen,* their chains of *massie gold,* and sparkling ornaments of *pearls?* Where are their *Cooks* and *Carvers,* their * *fowlers* and *fishers?* Where are their curious *Utensils,* their *Cups* of *Agate, Chrystal,* and *China-earth?* Where are their sumptuous *Chambers,* where they inclosed themselvs in *Cedar, Ivory,* and *Ebeny?* Where is their *Musick,* their *soft* and *delicate dressings, pleasing motions,* and *excellency of looks?* Where are their rich *perfumes,* costly *Conserves,* with their precious and various store of *forreign* and *domestick* wines ? Where

* Ingeniosa gula est : siculo scarus æquore mersus
Ad mensam vivus perducitur, inde lucrinis
Eruta littoribus vendunt conchylia cænas
Ut renovent per damna famem. Jam Phasidos unda,
Orbata est avibus ; mutoque in littore tantum
Solæ desertis aspirant frondibus auræ.

are their *sons* and their *daughters* fair as the *flowers*, strait as the *Palm-trees*, and *polish'd as the corners of the Temple*? O pittiful and astonishing transformations! all is gone, all is dust, deformity, and desolation. *Their bones are scatter'd* —mors sola fatetur *in the pit, and instead of well-set hair, there* Quantula sunt hominum *is baldnesse, and loathsomnesse instead of* corpuscula.—— *beauty.* This is the state of their *bodies,* and (O blessed *Jesus* !) who knowes the state of their *souls*? To have a sad guesse at this, it will not be much out of our way, if we step and visit a *Roman Emperour* upon his death-bed. If you desire his name, 10 it is *Hadrianus,* the most ingenious and learned that ever sate upon the throne of *Cæsar.* You may beleeve, he was royally accommodated, and wanted nothing which this world could afford ; but how farre he was from receiving any comfort in his death from that pompous and fruitlesse abundance, you shall learn from his own mouth, consider (I pray) what he speaks, for they are the words of a dying man, and spoken by him to his departing soul,

> Animula vagula, blandula,
> Hospes comésque corporis,
> Quæ nunc abibis in loca ?   20
> Pallidula, querula, nudula,
> Nec, ut soles, dabis jocos.

> *My soul, my pleasant soul and witty,*
> *The guest and consort of my body,*
> *Into what place now all alone*
> *Naked and sad wilt thou be gone ?*
> *No mirth, no wit, as heretofore,*
> *Nor Jests wilt thou afford me more.*

Certainly, this is the saddest *poetrie,* that ever I met with ; and what he thought of his soul in that last *agonie,* when the *pangs* of 30 *death* came *thick* upon him, is enough to draw tears and commiseration from a heart of flint. O happy then, yea Infinitly happy is that religious liver, who is ever meditating upon the houre of death before it comes, that when it is come, he may passe through it with joy, and speak to his   * Egredere, quid times? soul in the language of old *Hilarion,* * *Go* egredere anima mea ; Sep- *forth, O my soul, go forth ; what is it that* tuaginta propè annis Christo servisti, & mortem times? *thou art afraid of ? Seventy yeers almost Hieron.* in vitâ *Hilar.* *hast thou serv'd Christ, and art thou now afraid of death ?*

Alas ! what is *life* if truly and throughly considered, that we 40 should trust to it, and promise to our selves a multitude of years, as if we held *time* by the *wings,* and had the *spirit* of life in our

6 of their] of their of their *1652*

own *hands*? *Our present life* (saith *Chrysostome*) *is a meere apparition, and differs but very little from a dreame; therefore that minde which is proud of a shadow, and relies upon a dreame, is very idle and childish.* Natural histories tell us of a bird called *Hemerobios* by the river *Hypanis*, which receives his life in the *morning*, sings at *noon*, and dyes at *night*. This *bird* may very well signifie our *life*, and by the *river* we may understand *time*, upon whose brink we are always pearching. *Time* runs faster then any *streame*, and our *life* is swifter than any *bird*, and oft-times
10 all the pomp of it comes to an end in one *day*, yea sometimes in an *houre*. There is no *object* we can look upon, but will do us the kindnesse to put us in minde of our mortality, if we would be so wise as to make use of it. The *day* dyes into *night*, the *spring* into *winter*, *flowers* have their *rootes* ever in their *graves*, *leaves* loose their *greenenesse*, and drop under our feete where they *flye* about and *whisper* unto us. The *beasts* run the Common lott with *us* and when they dye by our hands to give us *nourishment*, they are so kinde as to give us *Instruction* also. And if from these *frailer objects* we turne our Eyes to things that are more *permanent*,
20 we may by the doctrine of *contrarieties* make them as useful as any of the former; And this is elegantly done by the *poet*, who was then *serious* and *stayed* enough, though somewhat *passionate*.

> Nam mihi quid prodest quod longo flumina cursu
> Semper inexhaustis prona feruntur aquis ?
> Ista manent : nostri sed non mansêre parentes,
> Exigui vitam temporis hospes ago.

> *What is't to me that spacious rivers run*
> *Whole ages, and their streams are never done ?*
> *Those still remain : but all my fathers di'd,*
30 *And I my self but for few dayes abide.*

Thus he of the *water-course*, which he saw would out-run him, and will do so with all that come after him. But the quick *tyde* of mans life, when it is once turned and begins to *ebbe*, will never *flow* again. The *Spring* comes constantly once a yeere, and *flowers*, when the *frosts* are past, keep *house* no longer under *ground*, but feel the *Sun*, and come *abroad*. The *leaves* come again to *whisper* over our heads, and are as *green* and as *gay* as ever, *but man dieth and wasteth away, yea man giveth up the ghost, and where is he?* In these sad contemplations was the *Brittish*
40 *Bard*, when he broke out into this Eloquent complaint

1 *Chrysostome*] *Chrystostome 1652*
5 *Hemerobios conj. G Gu* : *Hemerovios 1652*   receives] rceives *1652*
38 *man*] *mau 1652*   *wasteth*] *wastesh 1652*

Mis mawrddh rhyddhig Adar,
Pob peth y ddhaw trwz ddhayar,
Ond y marw maur by garthar.

In March birds couple, a new birth
Of herbs and flowers breaks through the earth,
But in the grave none stirs his head;
Long is th' Impris'ment of the dead.

The dayes of darknesse are many, and he that *goeth down to the grave shall not come up, his place shall not know him, nor shall he returne to his house; he shall not be awaked nor raised out of his* 10 *sleep, untill the heavens be no more.* These last words were put in for our *comfort,* and imply the *resurrection* or the time of restoring all things. This was manifested to *Ezekiel* by the vision of dry bones with a noise and a shaking amongst them, and they came together bone to bone, and were clothed with sinews, flesh and skin, and the breath of life entered into them, and they stood upon their feet an exceeding great army. We have it also confirmed out of the mouth of *Jesus Christ* himself, *John* 5. 28, 29. his words are these, *Marvel not at this, for the hour is coming, in the which all that are in the grave shall hear his voyce; And they* 20 *shall come forth that have done good unto the resurrection of life; but they that have done evill unto the resurrection of condemnation.* The *Scripture* is every where full of these *proofs*: But I shall insist only upon *three.*

1. *For I know that my Redeemer liveth, and that he shall stand at the later day upon the earth. And though after my skin worms destroy this body, yet in my flesh shall I see God. Whom I shall see for my self, and mine eyes shall behold and not another, though my reins be consumed within me.* Job. 19. 25, 26, 27.

2. *Thy dead men shall live, together with my dead body shall they* 30 *arise; Awake and sing ye that dwell in the dust, for thy dew is as the dew of herbs, and the earth shall cast out the dead.* Isa. 26 19.

3. *Behold (O my people) I will open your graves; and cause you to come up out of your graves; And ye shall know that I am the Lord when I have opened your graves, O my people, and brought you up out of your graves, and shall put my spirit in you, and yee shall live.* Ezek. 37. 12, 13, 14.

And thus have we most full and absolute promises from the *divine spirit,* and from *Jesus Christ,* who is *the life of the world,* for the redemption of our bodies. Nor are we left destitute of very clear 40 and inexcusable demonstrations of it in *nature.* We see mortal

29 19.] 19 *1652*   32 Isa.] Isa *1652*   41 inexcusable] inexcussable *Gu*

men when the *body* and *substance* of *vegetables* is consumed in the *fire*, out of their very *ashes* to make *glasse*, which is a very bright and noble *body*, how much more shall the Immortal and Almighty God (who created all things of nothing) out of dust and corruption, raise us up incorrupt and glorious bodies? *Thou fool*, (saith St. *Paul*) *that which thou sowest is not quickened, except it die first ; and that which thou sowest, thou sowest not that body which shall be, but bare grain ; but God giveth it a body as he pleaseth.* There are in *nature* many *creatures* which at certain *seasons*, that their
10 *spirit* is inconsistent with, fall into a *dormition*, or *dead sleep* which differs little from *death*, and convey themselves into *secret places*, as *hollow trees*, or some *desolate ruines*, where they may rest in safety during that *season*, as being taught by some *secret informant* that they shall *awake* again. Here have we a clear type of the *resurrection*, for what else is *death* but *sleep*, as the *Apostle* calls it? A great *Philosopher* and *Secretary* to *nature* discoursing of the *resurrection* of the *dead*, tells us, *that he oftentimes lighted upon some of those creatures in that dark state of dormition, and did dissect some of them, and cut off the limbs of others, and yet* (saith he) *could*
20 *I perceive no signe of life at all in them, their arteries and flesh being as hard and as dry as a stick, but casting them into a pot of seething water, they would soften by degrees, and shortly after stir about, and those very parts which were dissected, would give very clear and satisfactory Indications of life.* This is so strong a *Symboll* of the resurrection, that I think it needlesse to make any application. Onely this I shall adde, that the curious observers of nature reckon these creatures amongst those of the *lunar order* ; And indeed if we consider well the nature of that *planet* (whose *sphere* is the *veil* or *partition* drawn betwixt us and *Immortality*) and whose *relation* to this lower world is more intimate, and of a *greater tye* then any of the other *six*, we shall finde that she exactly typifies and demonstrates unto us those two famous *states* of terrestrial bodies, *viz.* their state of *darknesse* and their state of *glory*, their *dissolution* and *restoration* ; for she doth *agonizare*, and suffers a monethly *recession* of *light*, and in a short time becomes *full* again. And I pray, are

*Omne quod est suprà lunam
30 æternumque bonúmque
Esse scias nec triste aliquid cœlestia tangit.
Quippe ultra fines lunæ illætabile nil est ;
Cuncta mala in terris posuit Deus, illáque clausit
In medio, & vetuit sacrum contingere cœlum.
Supra autem lunam lucis sunt omnia plena
Nec non lætitiæ & pacis, non tempus & error
Et senium & mors est illîc, nec
40 inutile quicquam. *Mar. Pal.*

1 (*of Latin*) bonúmque] bonúmque. *1652*

not *light* and *life* compatriots? What else is *death* but the recession and absence of *life*? or *darknesse* but the absence of *light*?

> *Sic nostros casus solatur mundus in astris.*
> So our decays God comforts by
> The Stars concurrent state on high.

Do not we see divers birds of this *regiment* such as are commonly known to us, with other meaner Creatures as *silk-worms* and the *humble-bee*, which yet are not so contemptible, but they may serve us for noble instances in this point, seeing there is in 10 them a *living spirit*, and that creatures of the same *rank* with them are recorded in Gods own *word*, yea, and are own'd by him as *memorable* and *select Instruments* of his service, as Joshuah *Cap.* 24. *ver.* 12. *And I sent the hornet before you, which drove them out from before you, even the two kings of the Amorites, but not with thy sword, nor with thy bowe.* And Isaiah Chap. 6 ver. 18, 19. *And it shall come to passe in that day, that the Lord shall hisse for the flye that is in the uttermost parts of the river of Egypt, and for the Bee that is in the land of Assyria ; And they shall come, and shall rest all of them in the desolate valleys, and in the holes of the rocks, and upon* 20 *all thornes, and upon all bushes.* I say then, do not we see that these *birds* and inferiour *creatures* which in the *spring* and *summer* continue here very merry and *musical*, do on a sudden leave us, and all *winter*-long suffer a kind of *death*, and with the *Suns* warmth in the *youth* of the year *awake* again, and *refresh* the world with their *reviv'd notes?* For the singing of birds is *naturalis musica mundi*, to which all *arted strains* are but *discord* and *hardnesse*; How much more then shall *Jesus Christ* the *Sun of righteousnesse rising with healing under his wings*, awake those that sleep in him, and bring them again with a joyful 30 resurrection?

Having then these *prolusions* and strong *proofs* of our *restoration* laid out in *nature*, besides the promise of the *God* of nature, who cannot faile, let us so dispose of this short time of our sojourning here, that we may with joy and sure comforts expect that day of refreshing. Let us number our dayes, and apply our hearts unto wisdome. What ever happens here under our feet, let it not draw down our eyes from the *hill*, whence cometh our help. Let not these sudden and prodigious mutations (like violent *earth-quakes*) shake our foundation ; let us hold fast the *faith*, and presse 40 towards the *mark*, that whether absent or present we may be

7 divers] divets *1652*   9 *humble*] *humhle 1652*

accepted of him ; for many are already gone astray, and have slipt into the same damnable estate with those *wretches,* whom a very *Heathen* could reprove,

> Sunt qui in fortunæ jam casibus omnia ponunt,
> Et nullo credunt mundum rectore moveri,
> Naturâ volvente vices & lucis & anni.

> *There are that do believe all things succeed*
> *By chance or fortune, & that nought's decreed*
> *By a divine, wise will; but blindly call*
> *Old time and nature rulers over all.*

Let us consider him that is *invisible,* and *those that are righteous, let them be righteous still; let them have respect unto the recompence of the reward, for he comes quickly, and his reward is with him.* Let *us endure unto the end, and overcome, that we may have right unto the tree of life, and may enter in through the gates into the City:* for, *Ex hoc momento pendet æternitas.* Upon our little inch of time in this life, depends the length and breadth, the height and depth of Immortality in the world to come : even two eternities, the one infinitely accursed, the other infinitely blessed. I remember (saith a reverend Author) that I have read (and not without admiration) of some Primitive *Christian,* that considered with himself the eternity of the torments to be endured in hell, after this manner. " *What man living* (said he) *that were in his right minde and reason,* " *if he were offered the most spacious and flourishing Kingdoms of* " France, Spain *and* Polonia, *onely for lying continually upon any* " *one part of his body in a bed of roses for the space of forty yeers,* " *would accept of them upon that condition? And though perhaps* " *such a mad man could be found, as would accept of the offer, yet, it* " *is a thing most certain, that before three yeers would come about, he* " *would get him up, and beg to have the conditions cancell'd. And* " *what madnesse then is it, for the enjoying of one minutes pleasure,* " *for the satisfaction of our sensual, corrupt appetite, to lie for ever in* " *a bed of burning brasse, in the lake of eternal and unquenchable fire?* " *Suppose* (saith the same Writer) *that this whole Globe of earth* " *were nothing else but a huge masse, or mountain of sand, and that* " *a little Wren came but once in every thousand yeers to fetch away* " *but one grain of that huge heap; what an innumerable number of* " *yeers would be spent, before that world of sand could be so fetcht* " *away? And yet* (alas *!*) *when the damned have laine in that fiery* " *lake so many yeers as all those would amount to, they are no nearer* " *coming out, then the first houre they entered in.* To the same purpose is this *Hymne* of the *Ancients.*

8 *fortune*] *fortnne 1652*   14 *the*] *ehe 1652*

Ex quo poli sunt perfecti
Aude numero complecti
Stellas cœli, stillas roris,
Undas aquei fluoris,
Guttas imbris pluvialis,
Floccos velleris nivalis.
Quot sunt vere novo flores,
Quot odores, quot colores,
Quot vinacios Autumnus,
Poma legit & vertumnus ; 10
Quot jam grana tulit œstas,
Frondes hyemis tempestas,
Totus orbis animantes,
Aër atomos volantes,
Pilos ferœ, pecus villos,
Vertex hominum capillos ;
Adde littoris arenas,
Adde graminis verbenas,
Tot myriades Annorum,
Quot momenta sœculorum : 20
Heus adhuc œternitatis
Portus fugit à damnatis !
Æternum, æternum ! quanta hæc duratio, quanta !
Quàm speranda bonis, quámque tremenda malis !

From the first hour the heav'ns were made
Unto the last, when all shall fade,
Count (if thou canst) the drops of dew,
The stars of heav'n and streams that flow ;
The falling snow, the dropping showres,
And in the moneth of *May* the flowres, 30
Their sents and colours, and what store
Of grapes and apples Autumne bore ;
How many grains the Summer beares,
What leaves the wind in Winter tears ;
Count all the creatures in the world,
The motes which in the air are hurl'd,
The haires of beasts and mankind, and
The shores innumerable sand,
The blades of grasse, and to these last
Adde all the yeers which now are past, 40
With those whose course is yet to come,
And all their minutes in one summe.
When all is done, the damneds state
Out-runs them still, and knows no date.

O *Eternity, eternity* (saith a holy *Father*) *whose strength is able*
to bear out thy torments ! And the smoke of their torments ascendeth

2 *Aude M* : *Audet 1652*   25 heav'ns] heavn's *1652*

up for ever & ever! & they have no rest day nor night! O what is this same for ever and ever! Gladly would I speak something of it, but I know not what to speak. All that I know, is this ; That it is that, which onely the infinitenesse of the Almighty God doth compasse about and comprehend. Seeing then it is so, that eternal pleasures or eternal pains do inavoidably and immediately overtake us after our dissolution, with what unwearied care and watchfulnesse should we continue in well-doing, and *work out our salvation with fear and trembling?* How should we *as strangers*
10 *and pilgrims abstain from fleshly lusts, which warre against the soul? What manner of persons ought we to be in all holy conversation and godlinesse?* With what Christian thrift and diligence should we dispose of every minute of our time that we might make *our calling and election sure?* It is a fearful thing to die without reconciliation; And with what confusion of face and horrour of spirit (if we die in that state,) shall we appear before the *Judge of all the world?* when he shall come in the *Clouds of heaven* with his *holy Angels,* and all mankind from the *first* man created, unto the *last* that shall be borne upon the earth shall appear before his
20 Judgement-seate.   Me thinks I see the remisse, lukewarme *professour,* and the *hypocritical, factious pretender* of *sanctity* looking up to the *Clouds,* and crying out, *O that throne! that flaming, white, and glorious throne! and he that sits thereon, with the sharp sickle in his hand and the crown of pure gold upon his head!* Revel. 14. 14, *from whose face the heaven and the earth flye away, and the foundations of the world are brought to nothing.   Oh! is he the Lamb that was slain whose blood was poured out like water upon the earth to save his people from their sins? Is he the Prince of life that was crown'd with thornes, scourged, spit upon, crucified, pierced through,*
30 *and murthered, and comes he now to judge the world? Oh! It is he! It is he! miserable wretch that I am! What shall I do, or whither shall I go?*

Such will be the *dreadful agonies* and *concertations* in that *day* betwixt the *Hypocrite* and his *conscience,* betwixt the *enemies* of Gods truth and their *gasping undone souls.   When the people that forget God shall go down quick into hell, and the secrets of all hearts shall be disclosed and laid open before Angels and men ;* For in that day all their dark and private *lusts,* their *closet-sins, bosome-councels, specious pretences,* and *bloody machinations,* which now (like so many
40 *foul spirits*) lurk in their *gloomy breasts,* shall be forced out, and will appear as visible to all *mankind,* as if they were written with the *beams* of the *Sun* upon the pure and unclouded *firmament.*   In

the * mean while the very *fowles of the aire,* and their own *horrid guilt* either in time of *distraction* (which they are alwayes subject to) or in their *sleep* (which is alwayes fraught with *penal visions* and *spiritual tumults*) may make a *full discovery* of their most *secret villanies* before the appointed time.

* Est pœna præsens consciæ mentis pavor,
Animúsque culpâ plenus,
& semet timens.
Scelus aliquis tutum, nullus securum tulit.

It was a blessed and a glorious age the Primitive *Christians* lived in, *when the wildernesse and the solitary places were glad for them, and the desert rejoyced and blossom'd as the rose.* When the blood of 10 *Christ* was yet warme, and the memory of his *miracles* and *love* fresh and vigorous ; what *Zeale,* what powerful *faith,* what perfect *charity,* hearty *humility,* and true *holinesse* was then to be found upon the earth ? If we compare the *shining* and *fervent piety* of those Saints, with *the painted* and *illuding appearance* of it in *these of our times,* we shall have just cause to fear that our *Candlestick* (which hath been now of a long time under a Cloud) is at this very instant upon removing. But I had rather you should be informed of their true *holinesse* and *love* to *Christ,* by an *Eye-witnesse* that was conversant with them, *and went in and out amongst them,* then by a bare 20 relation from my pen. Heare therefore what he saith. *Vidi ego, & verè vidi thesaurum Christi in humanis absconditum vasculis, &c. vidi enim apud eos multos Patres in terra positos cœlestem vitam agentes, & novos quosdam Prophetas tam virtutibus animi, quàm vaticinandi officio imbutos, &c. Nonnullos namque eorum ità ab omni malitia, cogitatione & suspicione vidimus alienos, ut nec si aliquid mali adhuc in seculo gereretur, meminissent, tanta in eis erat tranquillitas animi, tantúsque in eis inoleverat bonitatis affectus, &c. Commanent autem per eremum dispersi & separati cellulis, sed charitatis vinculo connexi. Ob hoc* 30 *autem dirimuntur habitaculis, ut silentii sui quietem & intentionem mentis nec vox aliqua, nec occursus ullus, aut sermo aliquis otiosus obturbet. Intentis ergo in suo quisque loco animis velut fideles servi adventantem dominum expectant. Omnes hi nullam cibi, aut indumenti, aut ullius horum sollicitudinem gerunt. Justitiam & regnum Dei requirunt, armis orationum pugnant, & scuto fidei ab inimico insidiante protecti patriam sibi cœlestem conquirunt.* " I have seen " (saith he,) and I was not deceived, the treasure of Christ laid up " in earthen vessels ; for amongst those Christians in *Egypt* I have " seen many Fathers who had here upon earth already begun the 40 " heavenly life ; and regenerate Prophets who were indued not " onely with holy habits, but had received therewith the Spirit of

Hieron. in vit. Pat.

"promise : for I have known many of them that were so free from
"malice, perverse thoughtfulnesse and suspition, as if they had
"never known that there were such evill wayes to be followed in
"the world, Such a great tranquillity of mind, and such a powerful
"love or longing after goodnesse had wholly possessed them.
"They lived dispersed up and down the wildernesse, and separated
"from one another in several Cells or Cots, but knit all together
"in the perfect bond of Charity. The reason of their distinct and
"distant habitations, was, because they would not have the silence
10 "of their retirements disturbed, nor their minds diverted from the
"contemplation of heavenly things by any noyse, sudden occurrence,
"or idle discourse ; for this cause they have every one their par-
"ticular mansion, where with intentive or earnest minds they do
"(like faithful servants) expect and look for the coming of their
"Master. They take no thought for meat and drink and cloathing,
"nor for any such accommodations ; they seek onely the Kingdome
"of God and the righteousnesse thereof, they fight with the
"weapons of prayer, & being guarded with the shield of faith
"from the devices of their spiritual enemies, so travel on towards
20 "their heavenly countrey. This was the *old way,* and whether we
are *in it,* or *out* of it, is not hard to be decided. A pretended
sanctity from the teeth outward, with the frequent *mention* of the
Spirit, and a presumptuous assuming to our selves of the stile of
Saints, when we are within full of *subtilty, malice, oppression, lewd
opinions,* and *diverse lusts,* is (I am sure) a convincing argument
that we are not onely *out* of it, but that we have no mind to returne
into it. The *way* to heaven is *wet* and *slippery,* but it is made so with
teares and not with *blood ;* it is through the *vale of miseries, and the
raine filleth the pooles,* Psal. 85. There is no *voyce* in those *shades
30 of Palme,* but the *voyce* of the *Turtle,* which is alwayes *groning,* and
Naturalists say, *she hath no gall.* It is ill coming to the *Lamb* of
God in a *Wolfes* skin ; They that do so, must be taught that he
hath another *attribute,* and they shall finde him a *Lion.* It is strange
that (after the experience of almost *six thousand yeares*) men will
hazard so highly, as to purchase a few dayes false honours, with
the losse of eternal and true glory. In what a horrid darknesse
and agony will the pleasures of this world leave us, after we have
cast away our bodies and souls in the acquisition of them ? how
suddenly must the *rich man* leave his *barnes,* and the *oppressour*
40 his ill-gotten *power* ? how do they labour under the load of their
private guilt, and feele the flames of hell while they are yet alive ?
With what gloomy and despairing looks do they passe from hence,

as if that eternal darknesse they are going into, were already in their faces? It was a sad and a dark reply that *Henry* the *fourth* made to his *hasty son*, when he had taken away the *Crowne*; *God knowes* (said he and sighed) *what right I had unto it.* Tyrants and oppressors may very well be compared to the *Hyæna*; while they prosper, and devoure the *prey*, there is nothing to be seene amongst them but *mirth* and *triumphs*; but when they have drank *blood* enough, when they are full and cloyed, *then they *weepe.* The onely difference is this, that the Hyæna's teares are deceitful, but the teares of Tyrants springing from their inward guilt and horrour, are wofully true, though (like *storms* in *harvest*) they are unprofitable and prodigious.

* Sinnes are not felt, till they are acted.

The difference betwixt the *righteous* and the *wicked* is to be seene in their *death*. The good man goes hence like the *Sunne* in the *summers evening* chearful and unclouded, his memory is precious here with men, and his spirit is received into the *joy of his Master.* This Saint *Hierome* saw in the death of *Paul* the *Heremite*, whose *coate* of *Palm-leaves* he preferr'd to the *purple robes* of the proud. *Let me now* (saith he) *aske the great men of this world, whose possessions are numberlesse, and whose dwellings are of marble, what was it, that was ever wanting to this poor old man? They drink rich wines out of gold, and he drank clean water out of the fountains. They have silk and gold weav'd into their coates, and he had not so much as the coursest wooll. But then is he out of that simple habit carried into Paradise, and they out of their silk and gold into hell.* Paul *the Heremite hath no covering but the * common earth; Their karkasses are laid up in ¶ costly Sepulchres of marble and brasse; but Paul shall be raised to glory, and they to condemnation.* And presently after directing his speech to the Reader, he concludes thus: *Who ever thou art, that shalt reade this Book, I beseech thee to remember* Hieronymus the ** sinner, who (if God would grant him his desire) had rather be master of* Paul *the Heremites coate with his rewards then of the purple robes of Princes with their punishments.* A *dinner of herbes* with a *good conscience* is *heavenly fare*, and *godlinesse is great gaine, if we would be contented therewith.* I do not so

* Cœlo tegitur, qui non habet urnam.

¶ Jam ruet & bustum, titulúsque in marmore sectus, —tumulis autem morientibus, ipse Occumbes etiam, sic mors tibi tertia restat.

** Non sanctum dixit, sed peccatorem.

—O quantum bonum est obstare nulli, carpere securas dapes!

Humi ejacentem scelera non intrant casam.

35 and note: *one* asterisk in *1652*　　39 *herbes*] herbs catchword *1652*
39 (*Latin*) scelera] sclera *1652*

much admire *Apitius* his feasts, and *Cleopatra's* banquets of *dissolved pearles*, as I do the *Raven* of *Elias*, and *Hilarion's Crow*. Neither can I in this place passe by that *old Cilician* and Countreyman to Saint *Paul*, who (I verily beleeve,) for a reward of his contented and harmlesse life, had the *honor* and the *happinesse* to have it described and left for ever upon record to posterity, by that inimitable *Prince* and *Patriarch* of *Poets* ;

Virg. lib. 4. Georgic.

Namque sub Oebaliæ memini me turribus altis
10 Corycium vidisse senem : cui pauca relicti
Jugera ruris erant, nec fertilis illa juvencis,
Nec pecori opportuna seges, nec commoda Baccho.
Hic rarum tamen in dumis holus, albáque circum
Lilia, verbenásque premens, vescúmque papaver,
Regum æquabat opes animo, seráque revertens
Nocte domum, dapibus mensas onerabat inemptis.
Primus vere rosam, atque Autumno carpere poma :
Et cum tristis hyems etiamnum frigore saxa
Rumperet, & glacie cursus frænaret aquarum,
20 Ille comam mollis jam tum tondebat Acanthi
Æstatem increpitans seram, Zephirósque morantes.

Englished thus.

I saw beneath Tarentum's *stately towers*
An old Cilician *spend his peaceful houres :*
Some few bad acres *in a waste, wild* field,
Which neither Grasse, *nor* Corne, *nor* Vines *would yield,*
He did possesse ; There (amongst thorns *and* weeds)
Cheap Herbs and Coleworts, *with the common* Seeds
Of Chesboule *or* tame poppeys *he did sowe,*
30 *And* Verveyne *with* white Lilies *caus'd to grow.*
Content he was, as are successeful Kings,
And late at night come home (for long work brings
The night still home,) *with* unbought messes *layd*
On his low table, *he his* hunger *stayd.*
Roses *he gather'd in the* youthful Spring ;
And Apples *in the* Autumn *home did bring ;*
And when the sad, cold winter *burst with frost*
The stones, *and the* still streams *in* Ice *were lost,*
He would soft leaves of Beares-foot *crop, and chide*
40 *The slow West-winds, and lingring Summer tyde !*

Saint *Hierome* in the life of *Antonius*, (who was nobly borne and as tenderly bred) tells us, that about the age of *eighteen* (his parents being then dead,) he gave away all his possessions, & resolving upon a strict, religious life betook himself to the *wildernesse* ; where having erected for himself a poore narrow *Cottage*, he digg'd hard by it, and found a *well*, with whose streams he watered a small piece of *ground*, which he did sowe and set with some ordinary *herbs* for his own provision. To this place thus furnished by his industrie, the *wild asses* would in great numbers very often resort, and not contented to borrow of his *water*, they would some times trespasse upon his *garden*, and make bold with his *sallads*. But he upon a time comming amongst them, commanded the *leader* of them, which he had observed to *guide* the *rest*, to stand still, and beating him upon the sides with his hand, reproved him in these words, *What is the reason that thou com'st to eat that which* 10 *thou hast not sowen ? Et exinde* (saith my Author) *acceptis aquis ad quas potandas ventitabant, nec arbusculam, nec holera unquam contigebant.* We see by these Examples how safe it is to rely upon our *Masters* promise, and how needlesse and superfluous in the Christian state this worldly abundance is. This our Saviour himself hath admonished us of, and upraids our diffidence with the examples of the *birds* and the *lilies* of the *field*. Certainly it is dangerous medling with the *world* ; It is like the * *Torpedo*, he that catcheth it, comes to lose his life by   * *A fish that (as soon as* the bargain. *Love not the world* (saith *ever he is struck,) so be-* 20 St. *John) neither the things that are in the* *nums the Angler, that he* *dies.* *world, if any man love the world, the love*   Arcanas hyemes & cæca *of the Father is not in him.* We should papavera ponti Abdo sinu, therefore be very cautious how we deal necem. with it, or with the followers and favourites of it. *Condescend to men of low estate*, saith the *chosen vessel* ; This is good counsel, but it lies so low that most men tread upon it, & very few are they that will stoop to take it up. There is nothing can bring us sooner to it then the serious consideration of our own frailty. This is the *Catharma* that turns away the plague ; and as 30 *Physicians* say of *fasting*, that it cures almost all bodily diseases : So may I say of this, that it prevents (if timely applyed) all the *depravations and diseases* of the mind. It will bring down every *high thought* & set us upon even ground, Qui jacet in terra, non where we shall be in no danger of soul or habet undè cadat. body. Our Saviour was buried in a Rock, and he that builds upon his grave, he that mortifies his affections, and hides his life in him, needs feare no *stormes*. What beauty is there in a *deaths-head* crownd with *roses* ? If we carry the *one* about us, we shall be safe enough from the temptations of the *other*. Let sensual *natures* 40 judge as they please, but for my part, I shall hold it no *Paradoxe*

16 diffidence] dffidence *1652*

to affirme, *there are no pleasures in this world.* Some *coloured griefes* and *blushing woes* there are, which look so clear as if they were *true complexions*; but it is a very sad and a tryed truth that they are but *painted.* To draw then to an end, let us looke alwayes upon this *Day-Lilie* of life, as if the *Sun* were already *set.* Though we *blossome* and *open* many *mornings*, we shall not do so always, *Soles occidere & redire possunt*; but *man* cannot. *He hath his time appointed him upon earth, which he shall not passe, and his days are like the* 10 *days of an hireling.* Let us then so husband our time, that when the *flower* falls, the *seed* may be preserved. We have had many blessed Patterns of a holy life in the *Brittish Church*, though now trodden under foot, and branded with the title of *Antichristian.*

I shall propose but * one to you, the most obedient *Son* that ever his *Mother* had, and yet a most glorious true *Saint* and a *Seer.* Heark how like a *busie Bee* he hymns it to the *flowers*, while in a handful of *blossomes* gather'd by himself, he foresees his own *dissolution.*

Omnem crede diem tibi diluxisse supremum.

* Mr. *George Herbert* of blessed memory; See his incomparable prophetick Poems, and particularly these, *Church-musick, Church-rents, and schisms* 20 *The Church militant.*

> I made a Posie while the day ran by :
> Here will I smell my remnant out, and tye
> > My life within this band,
>
> But time did becken to the flowers, and they
> By noon most cunningly did steal away,
> > And wither'd in my hand.
>
> My hand was next to them, and then my heart :
> I took, without more thinking, in good part
> > Times gentle admonition ;
>
> 30   Who did so sweetly death's sad taste convey,
> Making my mind to smell my fatal day ;
> > Yet sugring the suspition.
>
> Farewel dear flowers ! sweetly your time ye spent,
> Fit, while ye liv'd, for smell or ornament,
> > And after death for cures.
>
> I follow strait without complaint or grief,
> Since if my sent be good, I care not if
> > It be as short as yours.

15 * Mr.] Mr. *1652*

As often therefore as thou seest the *full* and *ripe corne*, to succeed the *tender* and *flowery Spring*, the Autumne again to succeed the *Summer*, and the *cold* and *snowie Winter* to succeed the *Autumne*, say with thy self, *These seasons passe away, but will returne againe : but when I go, I shall returne no more.*

When thou seest the *Sun* to set, and the melancholy *shadowes* to prevaile and

Petrar. *de Contemp. mundi.*

Immortalia ne speres monet
annus, & almum
Quæ rapit hora diem.
Frigora mitescunt Zephyris,
ver proterit æstas
Interitura simul
Pomifer Autumnus fruges
effuderit, & mox
Bruma recurrit iners.

increase, meditate with thy selfe, *Thus when my life is done, will* 10 *the shadowes of death be stretched over me ; And yet this Sun which now leaves me, will be here againe to morrow : but when the Sun of my life sets, it shall not returne to me, until the heavens be no more.*

When the *night* is drawn over thee, and the whole world lies slumbring under it, do not thou sleep it out ; for as it is a *portion* of time much abused by wicked livers, so is it of all others the most powerful to excite thee to *devotion ;* be stirring therefore, and make special use of that *deepest* and *smoothest current* of *time,* like that vigilant *Pilot* who alwayes mistrusted the *greatest calms,*

Sydera cuncta notat   *And rising at midnight the Stars espi'd*   20
tacito labentia cœlo.   *All posting Westward in a silent glide.*

When thou also seest those *various, numberles, and beautiful luminaries* of the night to move on in their *watches,* and some of them to *vanish* and *set,* while all the rest do *follow after,* consider that *thou* art carried on with *them* in the *same motion,* and that there is no hope of subsisting for thee, but in *him who never moves, and never sets.*

Consider thy own *posterity* (if thou hast any) or those that are *younger then thy self,* and say, *These are travelling up the hill of life, but I am going head-long down.* Consider thy own *habitation,* how 30 many have been there before thy *time,* whom that place must never know again, and that there is no help, but *thou* must follow. Consider the *works of thine own hands,* the *flowers, trees* and *arbours* of thine own planting, for all those must survive thee ; Nay, who knows but thou mayst be gone, before thou canst enjoy those pleasures thou dost expect from them ; for the *Poet* in that point proves oftentimes a *Prophet,*

> *The trees, we set, grow slowly, and their shade*
> *Stays for our sons, while (we the Planters) fade.*
>   *Virg. Georg.*   40
> Tarda venit, serísque futura nepotibus umbra.

4 (*of Latin*) simul] simul. *1652*   22 *various,*] various *1652*
39 (*we*] we (*GC*

To be short, acquit thee *wisely* and *innocently* in all thy Actions, live a *Christian,* and die a *Saint.* Let not the *plurality* of *dayes,* with the numerous *distinctions* and *mincings* of thy *time* into *moneths, weeks, houres* and *minutes* deceive thee, nor be a means to make thee misspend the *smallest portion* of it ; let not the *empty honours* and *pompous nothing* of this world keep thee back from the *grapes* of the *brook* of *Eshcol.* Remember that we must account for every idle *word,* much more for our *actions.* If thou hast lost any *dear friends,* have them alwayes before thine eyes, visit their *graves*
10 often, and be not unkind to a *Jonathan* though in the *dust.* Give eare to *heaven,* and forget not what is spoken to thee from thence. *Behold, I come as a thief; blessed is he that watcheth and keepeth his garments, lest he walk naked, and they see his shame.* The time of life is short, and *God* (when he comes to see us) *comes without a bell. Let us therefore gird up the loynes of our minds, and be sober, and hope to the end. Let us keep our selves in the love of God as obedient children, not grieving his holy Spirit, by which we are sealed unto the day of redemption. And let us not give place to the devil, nor be weary of well-doing; but let us be renewed daily in the spirit of our*
20 *mind that when he comes (who will not tarry) we may be found faithful, and about our masters businesse.*

Let us feare God, and forgive men, blesse those that persecute us, and lay up treasure for our selves in heaven, that where our treasure is, there our hearts may be also, and this (if God permits) will we do, and then

> —*We can go die as sleep, and trust*
> *Half that we have*
> *Unto an honest, faithful grave*
> *Making our pillows either down or dust.*

30 Now unto him, who shall change our vile bodies, that they may be fashioned like unto his glorious body, according to the working whereby he is able to subdue all things unto himselfe, even unto *Jesus Christ* the Prince of the Kings of the earth, and the first begotten of the dead, be glory and dominion for ever and ever. *Amen.*

A Prayer when thou findest thy self sickly, or when thou art visited with any Disease.

Most merciful, and wise God, who *bringest light out of darknesse,* and true *comforts* out of the greatest *afflictions,* I do in all humility and with all my soule resigne my selfe unto thy divine pleasure,
40 and give thee most hearty and unfeined thanks for this thy present *visitation,* an infallible argument of thy fatherly love, and that

tender care which thou hast of my salvation. Thou gavest me
health, and I took no notice of thy *gift*, and but very little of the
Giver: Thou gavest me dayes of gladnesse and I *numberd them not.*
Wherefore with most true sorrow for my unthankfulnesse, and
with all the *sad Resentments* of a most penitent heart I do acknowledge thy *justice*, adore thy *providence*, and beg thy *mercy*. O
righteous Father! Though I have gone astray, do not thou cast
me off: though *I am no more worthy to be called thy son*, yet have
thou a minde to the work of thine own hands. Confirme my *faith*,
sanctifie my *affections*, give me a lively and enduring *hope*, with 10
an unwearied *patience*; And strengthen me in all my *Agonies*
with the *celestial assistance* and *inexpressible refreshments* of thy
overcoming spirit. Thou that didst give to thy blessed and faithful *Martyrs* such a glorious *measure* of thy Almighty *spirit*, as
encouraged them for thy sake to be *sawed* asunder, to be *burnt*,
stoned and beheaded, give unto me now such a gracious *portion* of
the same *Comforter* as may leade me through *death* unto *life*. Or
if thou wilt in mercy restore me again, and enlarge my time, give
me, I beseech thee, a thankful *heart*, holy *resolutions*, and a stedfast *spirit* to performe them; And for *Jesus Christ* his sake never 20
suffer me to forget thy *tender and fatherly compassion*, or to fall
again into my old sins, and *heap* up for my self thy eternal anger
and most just indignation.

For what end soever thou hast sent this present *sicknesse*,
whether for my *dissolution*, or for a temporal *correction* of my sinful life, grant I beseech thee, that both may be for thy *glory*, and
the salvation of my poore soule, purchased with the *precious blood*
of thine only *Sonne* and my dear *Redeemer*, to whom with thee
and the *holy Ghost* be ascribed by *Angels* and *men*, all wisdome,
dominion and majesty for ever and ever, *Amen!* 30

A Prayer in the hour of Death.

O my most blessed and glorious *Creatour* that *hast fed me all*
my life long, and *redeemed me from all evil*, seeing it is thy merciful pleasure to take me out of this fraile body, and to *wipe away*
all teares from mine eyes, and all sorrowes from my heart, I do
with all humility and willingnesse consent and submit my self
wholly unto thy sacred will. *I desire to be dissolved and to be with*
my Saviour. I blesse and praise thy holy name for all thy great
mercies conferred upon me, from the first day of my life unto this
present hour. I give thee all possible thanks for this gracious & 40
kind *visitation*, in which thou art mercifully pleased to order this

last act of thy *poor creature* to thy *glory*, and the *fruition* of those *heavenly comforts* which have already *swallowed* up my whole *spirit*. O let *all* that come after me speak of thy *wondrous mercies*, and the *generations* which are yet unborn give praise unto thy *name*.

Lord *Jesus Christ* my most loving Redeemer, into thy saving and *everlasting Armes* I commend my *spirit*, I am ready my *dear Lord*, and earnestly expect and long for thy good pleasure; *Come quickly*, and receive the soul of thy *servant* which trusteth in thee.

Blessing, and honour, and glory and power be unto him that sitteth upon the throne, and unto the Lamb and to the holy Ghost for ever and ever Amen.

10

Glory be to God on high, and on earth peace, good will towards men !

Blessed be God alone !
Thrice blessed three in one !

MAN

IN

Glory:

OR,

A Discourse of the blessed
state of the Saints in the
New JERUSALEM.

Written in Latin by the most
Reverend and holy Father

ANSELMUS

Archbishop of *Canterbury*, and now
done into English.

Printed *Anno Dom.*   1 6 5 2.

Reader,

Anselmus Archbishop of *Canterbury* lived here in *Britaine*, in the reigne of *Rufus*, and striving to keep entire the Immunities of the Church, (which the spirit of Covetousnesse and Sacriledge did then begin to encroach upon,) he was twice banished, first by *William* the second called *Rufus* or *red-hair'd*, and after by *Henry* the first his youngest brother and successor. Men of fierce and unmanagable spirits they were, and by so much the fitter for the throne. The first was such an infamous lover of money, that the
10 *Neophyte-Jews* were at a constant fee with him, for renouncing *Christianity*; and the later (like a true son of *Ottoman*,) caused
* *Robert* Duke of *Nor-*   his eldest * brothers eyes to be pull'd out,
mandy.   who was then his prisoner in the Castle of
Cardiffe. To avoid the fury of *Rufus* (who had thus banished him,) our Author here retired into *France*, and shelter'd himself in the Abbey of *Clunie*, where by way of discourse with that reverend family, he shed forth this Dissertation, which (at the same time it proceeded from him,) was exactly taken, and put into writing by *Eadinerus*, a Canon regular of the Church of *Canterbury*,
20 and his *Amanuensis* in his banishment. Some brokages and disorderly parcels of it, are to be found in his book *De Similitud*, but the entire and genuine discourse was first made publick at *Paris* 1639. where it took so well, that it was presently translated into French. This much I thought fit to acquaint thee with; and so I shall leave thee to thy owne affaires, which I wish to be such as may bring thee to the fruition of those joyes, which are showne thee here through a glasse darkly, and but in part; untill that which is perfect shall come, and this which is in part shall be done away.

30   *Thy Friend*

H EN. V AUGHAN.

Here holy *Anselme* lives in ev'ry page,
And sits Arch-bishop still, to vex the age.
Had he foreseen (and who knows but he did ?)
This fatal wrack, which deep in time lay hid,
'Tis but just to believe, that little hand
Which clouded him, but now benights our land,
Had never (like *Elias*) driv'n him hence,
A sad retirer for a slight offence.
For were he now, like the returning year,
Restor'd to view these desolations here,   10
He would do penance for his old complaint,
And (weeping) say, That *Rufus* was a Saint.

Revel. Chap. 7.

1. *And after this I beheld, and lo a great multitude which no man could number, of all nations and kindreds, and people, and tongues stood before the throne and before the Lamb, clothed with white robes, and palms in their hands.*

2. *And cried with a loud voice, saying, Salvation to our God, which sitteth upon the throne, and unto the Lamb.*

3. *And one of the Elders answered saying unto me, Who are these* 20 *which are arayed in white robes ? and whence came they ?*

4. *And I said unto him, Sir, thou knowest. And he said unto me, These are they which came out of great tribulation, and have washed their robes, and made them white in the blood of the Lamb.*

5. *Therefore are they before the throne of God, and serve him day and night in his Temple : and he that sitteth on the throne shall dwell among them.*

6. *They shall hunger no more, neither thirst any more, neither shall the Sun light on them, nor any heate.*

7. *For the Lamb which is in the midst of the throne, shall feed* 30 *them, and shall leade them unto living fountains of waters, and God shall wipe away all tears from their eyes.*

7, 8 *precede ll.* 5, 6 *in 1652*

Many men, when a holy conversation and good works are proposed unto them, and when they are advised to exercise themselves therein, and not to follow after the vanities of this world,
are wont to question for what end, reward, or retribution shall
they do so ? The answer to these men must be this : Because
it is written, *that Eye hath not seen, nor eare heard, neither have
entred into the heart of man, the things which God hath prepared
for them that love him,* 1 Cor. 2. Which words, because they
cannot plainly understand what is meant by them, must be
10 expounded to them by other circumstances, and it must be told
them, that the reward which in the life to come shall be given
unto those that serve God in this life, is, everlasting life, eternal
happinesse, never-ending pleasures, and a fulnesse and sufficiency
of all accommodations to their own desires without any scarcity, or
want at all. When these things are thus told them, they seeme
to be (as they are indeed) very great, and very good. But because,
that neither by this expression they do perfectly apprehend, what
those things are which they shall receive in the life to come ; nor
can they of a sudden rightly perceive what is meant by a sufficiency
20 of all accommodations without any want at all, they continue still
in a doubtful minde, and are not effectually drawn to take any
relish or delight in the things so told them. What course then
shall we take to render these eternal rewards more relishing and
delightful to them ? I hold that the best way is, to feed them as
Nurses feed their little children ; who, (if at any time they give
them a large faire apple, which for the tendernesse of their teeth,
and the narrownesse of their mouths they cannot feed upon) cut
it (according to the capacity of the child) into several bits or parts,
and so give it them to eate by peece-meales.
30   We shall therefore divide this great sufficiencie of all accommodations in the life to come, into several parts or portions, that (by so
doing) they may with those things we shall deliver be fed to eternal life. And because they may appear more plainly to them, we
shall consider what those things are, which the minde of man
most affects in this life ; and by those, (as farre as we may) we
shall make it evident that they shall enjoy them after a more
excellent manner in the life to come : if being placed here in the
midst of dangers and worldly temptations, they stick fast to the
precepts of Christ ; and when they have kept them, they will of
40 themselves quickly perceive, that by no meanes they shall lose,
nor be deceived of the utmost of their desires. This Course we

shall take in the Explication of this Doctrine, and beginning with the least, passe on to our desired end.

That we may then in the first place briefly summe up all those things which have reference to the body, I suppose them to be such things as are (indeed) desirable of themselves, and for whose service or use all other things are desired of men, and those are Beauty, Activity, Strength, Liberty, Health, Pleasure, & Long Life. But if amongst these we have reckoned, there are some things, which the servants of God have no respect to, but take special care to neglect and avoid them, as (for instance sake) beauty and pleasure are; yet do they not therefore despise them, because that naturally they affect them not, but because they would not offend God in them; for if they certainly knew that by caring for such things, they could not offend God, nor have their affections with-drawn from heavenly things, without doubt they would take more delight in the fruition of them, then in a contrary state. These things being now thus premised, I shall as briefly as I may treat of every one of them distinctly, or by it self, and labour to demonstrate unto you (as God shall enable me) after what manner they shall be enjoyed by us after the resurrection of the body.

To begin then, *Beauty* is a certaine good, which all men naturally desire to have. But in the life to come the beauty of the righteous shall shine equally with the Sunne, this the sacred Scripture testifies, *Matth.* 13. *Then shall the righteous shine forth as the Sun in the Kingdome of their Father.* Adde to this, that the body of our Lord Jesus Christ (which none I hope will deny) shall outshine the brightnesse of the Sun. But by the testimony of the Apostle *we shall be made like unto him*, for he saith, *He shall change our vile bodies, that they may be fashioned like unto his glorious body*, and this is the confession of that authority, which to contradict, is blasphemy. Now if any man would have this proved to him by reason, I beleeve it ought not to seeme incredible to any, that the righteous in that life which is to come, *when this mortality shall be swallowed up of life*, shall shine as bright as the Sun, seeing they are truly *called*, and truly *are* the temple and the seat of God himself, which (as I remember) is no where in sacred Scripture spoken of this visible Sun.

As for *Activity*, which is every way as desirable as *Beauty*, we shall be indued with such a measure of it, as shall render us equall for swiftnesse to the very Angels of God, which in a moment passe from the highest heaven unto the earth, and from the earth again into heaven; which swiftnesse, if it were necessary

to prove it so in the Angels, we might for instance produce that place of Scripture, where it is written, that the Angel of the Lord took *Habakkuk* the Prophet by the haire of the head, and carried him through the vehemency of his spirit (when he was yet in the flesh) from *Jury* into *Babylon*, and having delivered the dinner unto *Daniel*, brought him again immediately to his own place. Therefore I say again, that a swiftnesse every way equal to that which is in them, shall be given to those, who labour in their lives here to be like unto them. The Apostle also, who affirms
10 that our bodies shall in the twinkling of an eye be perfectly raised, notwithstanding that our limbs be separated or dispersed one from another, and the distance of place never so great, hath thereby sufficiently proved, that our very bodies which in that day shall be raised incorruptible, shall be gifted with the very same swiftnesse ; for he testifies that *this corruptible shall put on incorruption, and this mortal shall put on immortality,* 1 Cor. 15. An instance or demonstration of this swiftnesse we have in the beams of the Sunne, which as soone as ever the body of that Planet appears above the earth in the East, passe in a moment to the utmost
20 West. By this consideration we may conclude that what hath been spoken touching our velocity in the life to come, is not impossible, especially because that animated bodies have in them a greater agility, then those which are inanimate. To this instance of the Sun-beams we may adde another of the like nature, which we have in our selves ; for the beams or ray of the Eye, when we open our eye-lids passeth immediately to the utmost point of the Horizon or visible part of the sky, and when we shut them returnes wholly and unimpaired into it self. Again, it is a thing certainly known, that the souls of the Elect which are in
30 the hand of the Lord, have not yet enjoyed the fulnesse of felicity, untill their bodies shall be restored unto them incorruptible ; which when they shall enjoy, there will be nothing more left for them to wait for and desire. But these bodies whose redemption they long and grone for if they would retard or hinder their swiftnesse, they would rather abhorre their fellowship, then long for it ; therefore it is certain that such a swiftnesse or agility as we have spoken of shall be given us of God in the life to come.

The next thing we are to treat of is *Fortitude* or *Strength*, which most men affect, as it is opposite to imbecillity and faint-hearted-
40 nesse. But they who shall be worthy to walk with the Citizens of the new *Jerusalem*, shall excell so much in strength, that nothing can have power to resist them : whether their desire be to remove,

34 for] for, *G*

or over-turn any thing out of its station, or by any other way to
divert it, nothing can hinder them ; nor shall they in compassing
their desire be put to any more trouble or pains, then we are put
to at present when we move an Eye, or turne it towards any
object we desire to look upon. But let us not in this place forget
to instance in the Angels, to whom we labour in this life to
assimilate our selves ; for if in this branch, or in any of the rest
which we are to handle, we can finde no other example or
demonstration, we must apply to them. I suppose there is none
will deny, but that the Angels excel so much in strength, as to be 10
able to effect whatsoever shall be enjoyned them. But here some
body may ask, of what use shall this fortitude or strength be unto
us in that life, when all things shall be put in such perfect order,
that there cannot be a better ; when there shall be no need of
mutations, eversions, or reformation wherein this fortitude or
strength may be imployed? Whoever shall ask this question, let
him attend a little to me, and consider what use we make at
present of the faculties given us in this life ; and he shall finde
that we do not alwayes imploy some of those abilities with which
we are now gifted in the body ; as the faculty of seeing, our 20
utmost strength, and our knowledge of some select things, with
many more ; In the like manner shall it be then with this fortitude we are now speaking of, for the onely possession of it will be
an incredible pleasure and joy unto us, though we shall have no
use for it, all things being (as it is said before) in the state of
perfection. If this *objection* be made concerning *velocity*, or any
of the other *branches* which are to follow in this discourse ; I hold
this *solution* (if we finde not a better) satisfactory enough.

We are now come to the fourth branch, which is *Liberty*, and
is no lesse desired then any of the former. Whoever then shall 30
leade an Angelical life here upon earth, shall without doubt be
admitted into an equal liberty with the Angels in heaven. Therefore as nothing can resist, hinder, or confine the Angels, but that
they may passe freely through all things according to their own
desires ; so shall there be no obstacle or restraint of the Elects :
there shall be no inclosure that can hold us, nor any Element
which shall not be pervious or passable for us, when, and how we
please. An eminent and most certain example of this we have
left us in the body of our Lord Jesus Christ, to which blessed
body (Saint *Paul* affirms) *that our vile bodies shall be fashioned* 40
and made like, according to the working whereby he is able to subdue
all things unto himself. Now the Scripture beares record that he

P

rose from the dead after the Sepulchre was made sure and sealed, and that he came in to his Disciples, the doors being shut upon them, and at the same time caused *Thomas* to thrust his hand into his side ; all which (without doubt) was laid down for a strong and comfortable demonstration to us *of the glorious liberty of the children of God*, Rom. 8.

In this fifth place comes *Health*, which of all temporal blessings is the principal, and the most to be desired. And of this what can be better said, then that which hath been already spoken by
10 the Psalmist, *The salvation of the righteous cometh from the Lord*, Psal. 37. What infirmity then can lay hold upon those, whose health or salvation is from the Lord ? But what example or similitude to introduce, whereby you may perceive what manner of health that shall be which we are to enjoy in the world to come, I do not know ; for neither I in my own body, nor the holiest man that ever lived in the flesh, can finde in himself any state of health which may be compared or liken'd to this eternal and incorruptible health. For in this life (when we finde our bodies without any paine or disturbance) we conclude that we
20 are in health, and yet are we therein oftentimes deceived. For it happens very frequently that we are infirme or sickly in some particular member, which yet we can by no means discover, but by motion of the said member, or by touching the place affected. But to come to those that are not thus affected, but seeme to themselves to be in perfect health, what shall we judge of them, that they are in health, or that they are not ? Propose to thy self some one of a most healthful constitution, and that thou shouldst enquire of him concerning the state of his body : he will tell thee, that in his own judgement he finds himself in perfect health.
30 But let his body be examined and felt with a little rigidnesse more then ordinary, or wring him hard in any part of it, he will presently cry out, forbeare, you hurt me. What is this? Did not he a little before affirme himself sound, and being now but moderately touched, doth he cry out of paine ? Is this man thinkst thou in health ? Truly I think not. It is not then such a health as this (which is but a meere remission) that they shall receive in the life to come, whose salvation is expresly promised to proceed from the Lord, *Rev.* 21. *For God shall wipe away all teares from their eyes, and there shall be no more death, neither*
40 *sorrow nor crying, neither shall there be any more paine, for the former things are past away*, Rev. 7. *They shall hunger no more, neither thirst any more, nor shall the Sun light on them, nor any*

heate, for God shall cover them with his right hand, and with his holy arme shall he defend them. What then shall be able to hurt them whose covering and inclosure shall be the arme of God? But what manner of health that shall be, I know for a certain, that neither I, nor any man else, (either by my owne or anothers apprehension or experiment) can possibly expresse. If any man desires to know the qualities of Feavers and diverse other diseases, I can quickly satisfie him, as well by the experience I have had of them in my own body, as by relation from others, but that which neither by my own understanding nor sensation I have 10 never perceived, nor received any knowledge of it from another, how can I say any thing of it? Onely this I shall absolutely assert (and I do verily beleeve it) that this health of the life to come shall fill the whole man with such an immutable, inviolable, and inexpressible sweetnesse and solace, as shall utterly repel and for ever drive away all thoughts of infirmities, their accessions, or revolutions. And let this suffice to have been spoken of our health in the world to come.

The next branch that comes in order to be now spoken of, is *Pleasure*, which by another name, or definition rather, we shall 20 call the *Delectation* of the corporeal senses. And this (truly) most men are very much taken with, because the corporeal senses in every man delight in those things which are adjudged proper or peculiar to them, and withal beneficial or helpful. For (to instance in a few) the sense of smelling is much recreated or pleased with the variety of sweet and comfortable odours ; the sense of tasting with the different relishes or gust of several meats, confections, and drinks ; And all the rest (as every mans natural appetite carries him) have their several and different delights. But these delectations are not alwayes pleasing ; nay, they prove 30 oftentimes distastful and troublesome to their greatest lovers, for they are (indeed) but transitory and bestial. But those delectations or pleasures which in the world to come shall be poured out upon the righteous are everlasting and rational. And for this cause I do not see how it is possible to expresse them so, as to make them intelligible, or subject to our understanding in this life, especially because we cannot find in the pleasures of this life any example or similitude which hath in it any collation with them, or can give us the least light or manifestation of them ; for those heavenly delights, the more we enjoy them, will be the 40 more deare and acceptable to us, for the fulnesse of those joyes breeds no surfeit. And such delights as these are, I beleeve no

man ever in this world did so far perceive or taste, as to be able to describe unto others the true state or savour of them. Two blessed and two miserable states of man we know to be, the greater and the lesser. His great or perfect state of blisse is in the Kingdome of God; his lesser is that which *Adam* forfeited, the joy of Paradise. As for his states of misery, his great and endlesse one is in the lake of fire and brimstone; and his lesser in the continual travels and afflictions of this present life. Now it is clear, that no man in this life (after *Adam*) did ever taste of
10 either of those two states of blisse. But if we had tried or tasted of (onely) that lesser state of blisse which *Adam* enjoyed in Paradise, we might then perhaps by the mediation or means of the lesser conjecture or guesse at the greater. As now being borne and bred up in the lesser state of misery, we can give many plain and convincing demonstrations of our deplorable condition in the greater. Wherefore seeing the pleasure we speak of, is a branch or portion of that greater state of blisse, I cannot conceive of any possibility to expresse it, unlesse we may do it by some similitudes that are quite contrary to the greater state of
20 misery, and drawne from the lesser. For example, or instance, let us suppose that there stood before us a naked man with hot and flaming irons thrust into the very apples of his eyes, and into every part and member of his body, his veines, nerves and muscles, so that neither his marrow, nor his entrails, nor any the most inward and tender parts were free from the anguish and immanity of the torment, and that he were as sensible of the paine in every member, as he must needs be in the very balls of his eyes. What shall I say now of this man? is he not miserably tormented? And who amongst these dispersed and ubiquitary
30 paines thus inflicted will be so irrational as to think that he can have any ease or pleasure? In the same manner, but by a quite contrary consideration may we conjecture or guesse at the delectations and pleasures of the life to come; for as this man is filled and pained all over with torments, so shall ineffable and endlesse pleasures be poured upon, and over-flow the righteous. Their eyes, their eares, and their hearts, yea their very bones (as the Prophet *David* saith) *shall be glad and rejoyce*; every part and every member of them shall be crowned and replenished with the fulnesse and the life of pleasures. Yea their whole man shall be
40 truly and abundantly satisfied with the fatnesse of Gods house, and he shall make them drink of the river of his pleasures; *for with him is the fountain of life, and in his light shall we see light.*

Whosoever then is the happy man that shall be counted worthy to enjoy these heavenly pleasures, I cannot see (as to the comforts of the body) what more he can desire. The onely thing that (in order to what we are to treat of) shall be added to him, is long life. And this shall not be wanting there, for our Saviour testifies, that the wicked shall go into everlasting punishment, but the righteous into life eternal, *Matth.* 25.

Having done now with these blessings bestowed upon the body, there remaine other more excellent gifts, which are every way as desirable, but these belong to the soul as the former did to the body. We shall reduce them all into seven principal heads, and here they follow, 1. *Wisdome.* 2. *Friendship.* 3. *Peace.* 4. *Power.* 5. *Honour.* 6. *Security*, and 7. *Joy.* Our wisdome then, which in this life all men desire, and worthily too, shall be so great in the life to come, that nothing shall be hidden from us, that we have a minde to know ; for we shall know all things, which God ordained to be known of man, as well those things which are past, as those which (in this world) are yet to come. There all men shall be known by every man, and every man shall be known by all men. Neither shall any one there be ignorant of what Countrey, Nation, stock or linage every one is descended ; nay, he shall know all that ever we did in our life-time. Here some body perhaps may say, how is this ? shall all men know the secret sins that I have committed ? Is my confession of them come to this ? Is it thus that they are blotted out, forgotten, and never more discovered ? Well, this is thy objection. But when thou in that state of glory shalt stand in the presence of God, purged from all thy sins, canst thou be unthankful to him for that great mercy shewed thee in the remission of all thy offences ? And how canst thou be thankful, if none of those sins for whose forgivenesse thou doest owe those thanks unto him, will be left in thy memory ? That therefore thou mayest for ever take delight in the singing of his prayses, thou wilt (I beleeve) have alwayes in thy mind those great transgressions and eternal miseries from which he delivered thee. Seeing then that the consciences of all men shall (in that state) remaine entire to them, I dare affirme that those sinnes for whose remission thou doest then give thanks, shall likewise be openly known, not to thy confusion, but to the glory of God, and the mutual rejoycing of the Saints, for thou shalt be no more troubled then with the remembrance of thy sins, nor be any more ashamed of thy most secret transgressions, then any one is in this life with the memory of some dangerous wounds

or loathsome disease that he is perfectly cured of; or then we are
in the state of men of those inconveniences we were subject to when
we were little infants in our cradles and swadling-bands; for in
that life when we shall be blessed with inviolable health, perfect
purity, a full remission and most certain impunity of all our sins,
why should the memory or publike knowledge of them be any
more grievous to us then his denying of *Jesus Christ* is now to
Peter, or his persecution of him to *Paul*, or her sins which were
many to that blessed Convert *Mary Magdalen*, with diverse
10 others whose sins and infirmities are already in this world pub-
likely known of all men? And besides all this, by this publike
manifestation of sins, as of thy enormous and loathsome infirmities, the power and wisdome of the great Physician will by
all the Elect be so much the more admired, praised and magnified;
and the praise and magnificence of the divine glory (if rightly
considered by thee) is thy glory. But thou wilt say, I consent
indeed that the praise of God is my glory, but when from all
parts of the earth such an exceeding number of innocent and
righteous persons (if compared to me) shall appeare there, who
20 considering the odious obscenity of my life, will (as it is most fit)
abhorre me as a most abominable creature, what shall I say then,
seeing there is a reward as well for unrighteousnesse as for
righteousnesse? Thy feare in these circumstances is needlesse,
for it will be otherwise there with thee then thou dost suppose;
for thou shalt finde, that those Elects which (in comparison of
thee) thou dost hold righteous and innocent, will have no such
thoughts of thee, as thou at present dost suspect. For they upon
the first sight of thee, will presently know and consider, that by
committing those obscenities thou didst not sin against them, but
30 against God. And when they see that God hath freely and fully
forgiven thee, they will not so much as have a thought of abhor-
ring, or judging thee in the smallest matter; for they know, that
if they should any way contemne or censure thee in that state,
What God hath cleansed, wherein thou shalt be perfectly reconciled
call not thou common, to the Father and all thy transgressions
Acts 10. 15. blotted out, they would thereby sin grievously against the Lord. They will therefore be the more
thankful, and have in greater admiration the infinite mercy of
God both towards thee, and towards themselves. Towards thee,
40 because he brought thee up out of hell, and saved thee from thy
grievous and crying sins. Towards themselves, because it was his
free grace that saved and held them up from falling into the like

enormities. By praysing God thus they will magnifie and admire in thee after Gods goodnesse, his power and * sure mercies by relying on which

* Constantiam.

thou didst escape and get out of the pit of perdition ; into which pit (had they been left to themselves) they would have fallen as well as thou didst ; and here they will consider, that had they been in that dangerous state, they should (perhaps) have been utterly cast away, and not break the snare as thou didst. Thou seest now that a publike manifestation of thy sins will in the state of glory be no disgrace nor prejudice at all to thee, and how great a furtherance of divine praise and thanksgiving the knowne remission of them will prove. Yea, if the very Angels should reprove and censure thee (for the heynousnesse of thy sins) to be altogether unworthy of their society, yet hast thou left thee very just reasons wherewith to vindicate and defend thy self. And here perhaps thou wilt aske me, how this may be done? do but give attention, and I will tell thee. Suppose that any one of the Angels should rebuke, or upbraid thee in these words : * dost thou a fraile and mortal creature, made of the dust of the earth, and whose doome was to returne into dust again, after thou hast rebelled against thy Maker, and wallowed in all manner of sins and pollutions, seek now to be like one of us, who never in any thing resisted the divine will?

* This is onely proposed, not asserted, nor (indeed) can it be, for our Saviour himself tels us, That there is joy in the presence of the Angels of God over one sinner that repenteth, *Luke* 15. 10. and their song is, *good will towards men.*

To this Charge thou mayst answer thus. If I (as you say) have been formed out of the dust, it is no wonder then that (being driven up and down by every wind of temptation) I fell at last into the mire of sin ; but afterwards (having first acknowledged, and then believed in the mercies of *Jesus Christ,*) I did renounce and cast off all those courses which I knew to be contrary to his will, and exercised my self in all those wayes which I understood to be well-pleasing unto him. I fainted not, nor refused to under-go and suffer for his glory diverse tribulations and distresses, in hunger, in thirst, in watchings, persecutions, reproaches and manifold afflictions ; And having utterly cast off and contemned all the pleasures of the world, I strongly endeavoured, and earnestly desired to be perfectly reconciled unto my Saviour. But you never suffered any of these things for his sake, you dwelt alwayes in glory, and the joyes of heaven ; The arme of God alwayes sustained and defended you from being assaulted by any sinne, so that you were never stained

3 Constantiam] Constantiam *1652*

with the least spot of it. Wherefore it is his owne free gift, whose hand with-held you from it, that hath kept you from falling away from his will. But because this way of reasoning may be onely used by those who have forcibly resisted their owne damnation, and taken the kingdome of heaven by violence; they that shall enter into it upon other conditions, must finde another reason by which they may claime a parity, or equal degree of glory with the Angels. And if they desire to know what manner of reason that is, it may be this which followes : They may tell them that the
10 ground upon which they lay their just claime to an equality of blisse with them in the kingdome of God, is the free mercy and donation of *Jesus Christ*; who for that very end vouchsafed to be made man, and to suffer death upon the Crosse, that being saved from our sins, and justified through his blood, we might be with him where he is, and be partakers of his kingdome; consider you therefore, if the blood of *Jesus Christ* which was shed for us is not a sufficient price for our salvation, and for an equality of glory with you. What reply now can the Angels (who because they are good of themselves, will be therefore the sooner won with reason)
20 make unto this ? truly none at all, unlesse by way of Confession, that men redeemed with so high a price may justly claime and partake with them an equal glorification. When therefore both Angels and men, whom thou didst judge more righteous then thy self shall consent unto thy glory, and hold thee worthy in all things of those true and eternal honours conferred upon thee, consider (if thou canst) how acceptable and pleasing such a know-ledge will be to thee, which shall make thee known to all men, and all men to be known of thee.

And shall not consequently out of that mutual and perfect
30 knowledge arise a certaine inestimable and inviolable friendship ? which shall so warm the hearts of every one towards another, that the love which every one shall have for another, shall be evident and convincing in the knowledge of all. Neither do I see how it can be otherwise, seeing that all in that kingdome are but one body, and Christ himself (who is very peace,) the head thereof; neither will they with lesse affection imbrace one another, then the members of one natural body are united to one another. Thou wilt therefore in that state love all men as thy self, and every one will love thee as dearly as himself. O (now thinkest thou,) how
40 full of love shall I be towards all men, if I were in that happy

32, 33 evie | dent . . . . knowledg - | *1652*   36 another] anothtr *1652*
37 members] membets *1652*

state? But passe by that Meditation, and consider him, by whose mediation and grievous sufferings all these blessings were purchased for thee; and thou wilt then perceive that he will love thee incomparably more then any others; yea, more then thou canst love thy self; and so wilt thou with a certaine inward, inexpressible delight come to love him more then any others, yea infinitely more then thou canst love thy self.

But seeing it fals out very frequently amongst men, that those persons who continue in a reciprocal and unanimous love, do not in all circumstances accord and consist, but differ in opinion, and 10 sometimes also in their passions, while that which seems right to the one, appears clean contrary to the other, and the one may affect something which the other hath no appetite at all unto; It follows of necessity that to this perfect friendship in the state of glory, we must adde perfect concord or agreement. There will be therefore such perfect agreement and unity there betwixt all, that none shall dissent from that which another desires. As many as shall be counted worthy of that kingdome, shall be one body, one Church, and one Spouse of *Jesus Christ*; and there shall be no more discord betwixt them, then there is betwixt the members 20 now in the natural body. But as you see in the motion of the Eyes, that which way soever the one is turned, the other immediately followes, so whatsoever any one in that state shall delight in, he shall finde all the rest to consent to it. * Seeing then that God himself with all the Angels and *Saints will be propitious and favourable to thy desires, it is cleare that thou wilt desire nothing which thou mayst not obtaine.

> * Here the Translatour omitted some passages which he conceived not necessary, and perhaps they might be spurious.

So that in a modest sense it may be said, thou shalt be Almighty in respect of thy will, because the Almighty God will in 30 all things consent to it, for thy will shall be then his will, and his will shall be thine.

Seeing then that they shall excell so much in power, there is no doubt to be made, but that an honour proportionable to that power shall be given unto them. Now what manner of honour that shall be, we shall labour to demonstrate by this following similitude. Let us suppose there were laid before our eyes, some poore begger destitute of all comfort, and smitten in every part with ulcerous biles, corrupt sores, and all manner of infirmities, and having not so much as a rag to cover or defend him from the 40 cold: If some mighty and mercifull King passing by, should look upon this begger lying in so miserable a condition, and having

compassion on him, should give command to heale his infirmities, and being afterwards recovered, should give order to have him cloathed with his own royal apparel, and being brought before him in that habit, should adopt him for his son, and give strict command that he should be received and acknowledged by all men for his son, and that he should be contradicted in nothing by any of his subjects, he having adopted him for his son, and made him coheire with his onely begotten, and calling him after his own name : You would easily grant that this were a great honour to be
10 conferr'd upon so despicable and loathsome a begger.   But all this and more will the merciful God most certainly confer upon his faithful servants ; for of his own free mercy will he receive us, who being born of the corruption of the flesh are surrounded with many miseries ; in which we are estated as it were, and destitute of all comforts ; but alwayes subject to, & overcome by many noxious passions, which fill us up with foule and ulcerous sins, and most odious corruptions, from all which he will purge and heale us, and being restored to perfect health, he will cloath us with the ornaments of true righteousnesse and incorruption, and adopt us
20 for his sons, making us his Consorts in his own kingdome, and coheires with his only begotten Son who is in every thing coequal with himself, *changing our vile bodies, that they may be like unto his glorious body*, and commanding every creature to be subject unto us in all things, calling us also by his own name, and making us gods ; for he saith in the Scripture, *I have said you are all gods, and the sons of the most high.*   But he himself is the *God deifying*, and we are but *deified*, or *gods* made by him.   But perhaps thou wilt say, This reason of mine may stand good in the Apostles and other holy Martyrs, but with thee who art a wretched sinner, and
30 desirest onely to be the least in the kingdome of heaven, thou canst not see how it can consist.   Give eare and understand, for God in that recited Scripture, *I have said you are all gods, &c.* excepts none.   But that thou mayst more clearly perceive, Consider the nature of fire and of all things that are put therein ; if happily thou canst imagine with thy self after what manner, (in the degree appointed for thee) thou shalt be glorified.   The fire (thou seest) is but one, and of nature hot ; put into it either wood, or lead, or iron, or all these together ; when the wood is turn'd into embers, so that nothing appears unto thee but fire, & the lead so
40 melted, that it cannot admit of a greater degree of heat, yet can neither of them be equall to Iron for an intense burning heat, which perhaps hath not yet grown red with the fire.   Now although

every one of these doth exceed the other, & is of a more suparla-
tive heat, yet every one of them (as we commonly say) is fire.
So shall it be in that glorious society of the Elect, which we now
speak of; For as those, who are neerer to the *Divine Majesty*, and
therefore better then others, shall be called *gods*: So even those,
who are inferiour to them, because they participate according to
their capacity of the same *Deity* with those that are superiour,
shall be likewise honoured with the same title of *gods*.

When therefore together with so much happinesse, thou hast
attained to so much honour, I do not see with what reason thou 10
canst desire a greater Preferment. Whiles then thou art blessed
with the possession of those high Benefits, which we have mentioned, wilt thou not think thy selfe sufficiently happy? Yes verily,
thou wilt say, well then! but if thou couldst really injoy all those
things as we have described them, but for one short *day*, wouldst
thou not rejoice? No question, but thou wouldst. But if thou
shouldst injoy them for a *moneth*, or one whole *yeare* thou wouldst
rejoyce exceedingly: neither indeed do I thinke it possible to
expresse thy manner of joy. Suppose then if thou shouldst
possesse this happinesse all thy *life-time*, what thou wouldst do. 20
What price wouldst thou give for so great a Blessing? Even willingly all that ever thou hadst: nay, thy very owne selfe, if thou
couldst purchase it at no other Rate.

But if besides all this Fruition, thou wert certaine also of a
perpetuall security, and that all thy life long no accident whatsoever could rob thee of thy happinesse, I will not determine,
whether it were possible for thee to imagine, how great thy joy
would be. Seeing then that in the life to come, thou shalt live for
ever, and together with the possession of all these things, thou
shalt also be eternally secured from all danger of losing them, I 30
beseech thee, how dost thou thinke it will go with thee? I beleeve
truly, that at the very name of security, there springs in thee a
certaine joy of heart, and thou dost greedily desire to know,
whether thou mayst with safety, and for ever injoy such great
and extraordinary Blessings? I tell thee then, if thou art like to
lose these things, thou must either voluntarily, and of thy owne
accord relinquish them, or God must take them from thee whether
thou wilt or no; or else another, who is more powerful then God,
must rob thee of them in spite of God, and thy selfe. But certainly, neither wilt thou reject so great a Blessing, and relapse 40
into those miseries from which thou hast beene graciously
delivered; neither will God at any time take that away which his

large and mercifull goodnesse hath bestowed upon thee ; nor is there any stronger then God, who should be able to make thee miserable against thy will, as long as God is thy Protector. Thou shalt therefore securely, and for ever injoy all these Benefits, nor shalt thou feare the attempts of any, who would willingly deprive thee of them.

What dost thou thinke then will thy condition be, when thou shalt eternally injoy all these things ; namely, Beauty, Strength, Swiftnesse of motion, Liberty, Health, Pleasure, Length of life, 10 Wisedome, Love, Peace, Power, Honour, and a Security of all, as we have described them : nay, above all humane Description or Conception, in a more glorious, and a more stately manner, then we can possibly expresse. Will not thy condition be all Joy, which is the End and Effect of these Blessings ? Verily I cannot see how that man should not abound with inestimable Joy, who is compast about with all the riches of eternall happinesse. Thou shalt therefore most certainly attaine to such a Joy, because nothing can happen to thee, that should minister occasion of Grief. For if thou hadst any Friend, whom thou didst love as 20 well as thy selfe, and in whose good thou wouldst rejoyce as in thy owne, and shouldst see this friend admitted to the same Heaven, and happinesse with thy selfe ; wouldst thou not extremely rejoyce in his Felicity ? But if thou hadst two or three, or more such friends, and shouldest see them all glorified with a state equal to thy own, would not thy joyes also exceed, and increase together with their number ? And as formerly, when we discoursed of Love, we did there shew how all the Inhabitants of the world to come, should love thee as well as themselves, and thou on the contrary shouldst love them as thy owne soul : How is it there-30 fore possible for any man to apprehend the manner of that *mutual Joy*, seeing there are there above a thousand thousands and ten thousand times hundreds of thousands : nay, an innumerable company, and all of them injoying the same Beatitude ; nor is there any one of them, who doth not as much rejoyce in the happinesse of another, as he doth in his owne. Moreover, they seeing God love them in a more excellent way then they love themselves, and againe perceiving themselves (after some inexpressible manner) to love God better then themselves, they do infinitly triumph in his Glory, and in his wonderful and inex-40 pressible Joyes. They have Joy therefore within, and Joy without :

3 miserable] miserablee *1652*   27 Inhabitants] Inbabitants *1652*

Joy from above, and Joy beneath : In the Compasse, and Circuit of them there is Joy, and in a word every where.

And this (as we think, and as we have exprest our selves in the beginning of this Book) is that thing which God hath prepared for those that love him, namely *Joy.* Therefore in my opinion, eternal Beatitude, or eternal felicity is nothing else but a sufficiency, or fulnesse of all good things, according to our own desire, and without any indigency, which felicity all the friends of God shall fully injoy in the life which is to come. For when we speake of good things, we do not say but that life eternal is farre more great 10 and glorious then this temporal life, which we have mentioned onely by way of Manuduction. Seeing then that the Just shall be rewarded with so great a Felicity, it remaines on the contrary, that the unjust shall be visited with some extraordinary Infelicity. For as we have described the Elect according to those abilities which God gave us : namely that their Beauty, Swiftnesse, and Strength, their Liberty, Health and Pleasure should render them Cheerful and Triumphant : So on the other side a certaine horrible, inestimable deformity, a dulnesse of motion and spirit, together with their Impotencie, and Captivity in Chaines of Dark- 20 nesse, as also their Melancholy, and paine shall make the Reprobate to mourne and howle. Verily that *Length* of *Life*, which the just shall most joyfully embrace, because it conduceth to their fruition of eternal happinesse, will be very odious, and a meere Curse to the unjust, because it exposeth them to an endlesse sense of ever-lasting tortures. If I look on their *Wisdome*, I know not what to speak of it, unlesse I say, that as to the just it will be great joy and honour, so in the unjust knowledge shall be turned into sadnesse and distraction of spirit. As for Love, whereby the Saints of God shall be link'd together with joy unspeakable : 30 It shall be a meer Affliction to the Impious, for by how much the more they love one another, by so much will they be the more troubled one at anothers punishment. If it be question'd whether they may injoy any peace or concord ? It is answered, they will be at discord with every creature, and every creature with them. Hence in opposition to the power of the Saints, the wicked shall be deprived of all power : They shall never be able to attaine to any thing they would have, and what they can have, even that is it which they would not have. The wicked then instead of the honour and eternal happinesse of the Saints shall 40 receive to their portion eternal shame, and now what more shall we say for a Conclusion to these things ? Truly, that as the friends of God shall alwayes triumph in the security of their everlasting Beatitude, so the Enemies and Adversaries of God shall utterly despaire of any redemption from their endlesse Miseries : But in lieu of the eternal ineffable joyes of the Blessed, they shall inherit unspeakable everlasting woes ; especially such, who because of their impenitency for their sinnes, shall be condemned to passe into the society of Devils.

FINIS.

Soli Deo Gloria.

Flores Solitudinis.
Certaine Rare and Elegant
PIECES;
Viz.

Two Excellent Difcourfes
Of $\left\{\begin{array}{l} \text{1. } \textit{Temperance, and Patience;} \\ \text{2. } \textit{Life and Death.} \end{array}\right.$

B Y
I. E. NIEREMBERGIUS.

THE WORLD
CONTEMNED;
B Y
EUCHERIUS, Bp of LYONS.

And the Life of
PAULINUS,
Bp of *NOLA.*

Collected in his Sickneffe and Retirement
BY
HENRY VAUGHAN, Silurift.

Tantus Amor Florum, & generandi gloria Mellis.

London, Printed for *Humphrey Mofeley* at the
Princes Armes in St *Pauls* Church-yard. 1654.

TO
THE TRUELY NOBLE
And Religious
Sir *CHARLES EGERTON*
Knight.

Sir,

If, when you please to looke upon these Collections, *you will find them to lead you from the* Sun *into the* shade, *from the open* Terrace *into a private* grove, *& from the* noyse *and* pompe *of this world into a silent and solitary* Hermitage : *doe not you thinke then, that you have descended (like the* dead) in Occidentem & tenebras, *for in this* withdrawing-roome *(though secret and seldome frequented,) shines that happy* starre, *which will directly lead you to the* King *of* light. *You have long since quitted the* Publick, *& to present you now with some thing of solitude* and the contempt of the world, 10 *would looke like a* designe *to Flatter you, were not my* Name, *argument enough for the contrary. Those few that know me, will (I am sure) be my* Compurgators ; *and I my selfe dare assert this,* you have no cause to suspect it. *But what ever the thoughts of men will be, I am already sure of this advantage, that we live in an age, which hath made this very* Proposition *(though suspected of* Melancholie,) *mighty pleasing, and even* meane witts *begin to like it ; the* wiser sort *alwaies did, for what (I beseech you,) hath this world, that should make a wise man in love with it? I will take the boldnesse to describe it in the same character which* Bisselius *did the hansome* 20 *concubine of* Mahomet *the great :*

> Puella tota quanta, nil erat aliud
> Quàm Illecebra picta, delicatus harpago, &c.

The whole wench *(how compleat soe'r) was but
A specious* baite ; *a soft, sly, tempting* slut ;
A pleasing witch ; a living death ; *a faire,
Thriving* disease ; *a fresh,* infectious aire ;
A pretious plague ; *a furie sweetly drawne ;*
Wild fire *laid up and finely drest in* Lawne.

This delicate, admir'd Inchantresse (even to those who enjoy her 30 *after their owne lusts, and at their owne rate,) will prove but a very sad bargaine ; she is all deception and sorrow. This* world *and the* prince *of it are the* Canker-Rose *in the mouth of the* fox :

4 *into*] *nto 1654*

Q

Decipit, arefit, pungit. *But those future, supreme* fruitions *which* God *hath in store for those that love him are neither* Phantasmes, *nor* fallacies *; they are all substantiall and certaine, and in the Apostles phrase,* Καθ' ὑπερβολὴν εἰς ὑπερβολὴν αἰώνιον Βάρος δόξης, a far more exceeding and eternall weight of glory. *Nothing can give that, which it hath not, this transitory, changeable and corrupt world cannot afford permanent treasures. All it gives, and all it shewes us, is but* trash & illusion. *The true incorruptible riches dwell above the reach of rust and theeves.*

10 *Man himselfe in his* outward part, *which was taken out of the world, feeles the like passions with the world, he is worn, washed, dissolved and changed, he comes hither, he knowes not how, and goes from hence, he knowes not whither.* Nescio quò vado, valete posteri ! *was the* Roman's *Epitaph : One generation commeth, and another passeth away.* Properant & decurrunt in absconditum, *they hasten and drive on to their appointed place, untill the great day of accompt. All the severall* shapes *and* gestures *we see in this wild* Masque *of* time *are but so many* disguises *which the* Spirits *that first assumed them, cast off againe when they have acted their* 20 parts. *Most elegantly did* Augurellius *sing to* Peter Lipomanus *upon the death of his sister* Clara ;

Amæna, Petre, cum vides, &c.

Peter, *when thou this pleasant world dost see,*
Beleeve, thou seest meere Dreames *and* vanitie *;*
Not reall *things, but* false *: and through the* Aire
Each where, an empty, slipp'rie Scene, *though faire.*
The chirping birds, *the fresh* woods *shadie boughes,*
The leaves *shrill whispers, when the* west-wind *blowes.*
The swift, fierce Greyhounds *coursing on the plaines,*
30 *The flying* hare *distrest 'twixt feare and paines ;*
The bloomy Mayd *decking with* flowers *her head,*
The gladsome, easie youth *by light* love *lead ;*
And whatsoe'r heere with admiring eyes
Thou seem'st to see, 'tis but a fraile disguise
Worne by eternall things, *a passive* dresse
Put on by beings *that are passiveles.*

All the gay appearances in this life seeme to me but a swift succession of rising Clouds, *which neither abide in any certaine* forme, *nor continue for any* long time *; And this is that, which* 40 *makes the* sore travell of the sonnes of men *to be nothing else, but a meere chasing of shadowes.* All is vanity (*said the Royall Philosopher,*) and there is no new thing under the Sun.

I present you therefore with a discourse perswading to a contempt

& a desertion *of these* old things which (*our Saviour tells us*) shall passe away; *And with an historicall, faithfull relation of the life and happinesse of a devout, primitive* father, *who gave all that he had upon earth to the poore, that he* might have treasure in heaven. *Some other* Additions *you will finde, which meeting now in this volume under your name, will in their descent to posterity, carry with them this fairest Testimonie,* I loved you. *This* (*Sir*) *is my maine and my sole designe in this* Addresse, *without* reservation *and without* flattery, *for which respect, and for no other, I beleeve you will accept of what I have done, and looke upon my* 10 *suddaine and small* Presents, *as upon some forward* flowers *whose kinde hast hath brought them above ground* in cold weather. *The incertainty of life, and a peevish, inconstant state of health would not suffer me to stay for greater performances, or a better season; least loosing this, I should never againe have the opportunity to manifest how much and how sincerely I am*

Newton by
Uske neare
Sketh-Rock.
1653.

Sir

Your Servant and
well-wisher

Henry Vaughan. 20

To the Reader.

Candidus & medicans Ignis deus est. *So sings the* Poet, *and so must I affirme, who have been tryed by that* white *and* refining fire, with healing under his wings. *Quarrelling with his* light, *and wandring from that fresh and competent* gourd, *which he had shadowed me with, drew those* Sun-beames *upon my head, whose strong and fervent* vibrations *made me oftentimes beg of him,* that I might dye. *In those sad* Conflicts *I dedicated the* Remissions *to thy* use, Reader, *& now I offer them to thy* view. *If the* title *shall offend thee, because it was found in the* woods *and the* wilder-
10 nesse, *give mee leave to tell thee, that* Deserts *and* Mountaines *were the* Schooles *of the* Prophets, *and that* Wild-hony *was his* diet, *who by the testimony of the* Sonne *of* God, *was* the greatest amongst those that are borne of women. *It may be thy spirit is such a popular, phantastick* flye, *as loves to gad in the* shine *of this* world; *if so, this* light *I live by in the* shade, *is too great for thee. I send it abroad to bee a companion of those wise* Hermits, *who have withdrawne from the present generation, to confirme them in their* solitude, *and to make that* rigid *necessity their pleasant* Choyse. *To leave the* world, *when it leaves us, is both* sordid *and* sorrowfull;
20 *and to quitt our* station *upon discontents, is nothing else, but to be the* Apes *of those* Melancholy Schismaticks, *who having burnt off their owne hands in setting the world on fire, are now fallen out with it,* because they cannot rule it. *They are* Spirits *of a very poore, inferiour* order, *that have so much* Sympathy *with worldlie things, as to weepe at* Parting; *And of as low a* Parentage *are those, that will be sick of* Leap-yeares *&* Sublunarie mutations. *I honour that* temper, *which can lay by the* garland, *when he may keepe it* on: *which can passe by a* Rosebud, *and bid it* grow, *when he is invited to* crop *it,*

30 ———— Whose gentle measure
        Complyes and suits with all *estates*;
    Which can let loose to a *Crown*, and yet with pleasure
        Take up within a *Cloyster* gates.
    This Soule doth *Span* the world, and *hang* content
        From either *pole* unto the *center*,
    Where in each *Roome* of the well-furnished *tent*
        He lyes warme and without adventure.

Prince Lewes, *the eldest Son of* Charles *King of* Naples, *at the age of twenty one yeares, and just when he should have been married to*
40 *the youthfull Princesse of* Majorica, *did suddenly at* Barcellon *put on the rough and severe* habit *of the* Franciscans: *The* Queens *and* Princesses *there met to solemnize the marriage of his sister* Blanch

with James *King of* Aragon, *imployed all their* Rhetorick *to dis-swade him from it; but to no purpose, he loved his* Sackcloth *more then their* silks, *and (as* Mounsier Mathieu *(alluding to that* young Princesse,) *speakes of him,)* Left Roses to make Conserve of thornes. *Resolution,* Reader, *is the Sanctuary of Man, and Saint* Pauls *content is that famous* Elixir, *which turnes the* rudest mettall *into* smooth *and* ductible gold: *It is the Philosophers* secret fire, *that* stomack *of the* Ostrich *which digests* Iron, *and dissolves the hard flint into bloud and nutriment. It was an honest* Reply *that his* Cook *made unto the Duke of* Millain, *when worsted in a great* 10 *battell by the* Florentines, *the over passionate resentment of so unexpected a repulse, made him quarrell with his meate:* If the Florentines *(said he)* have spoyled your tast, that is no fault of mine ; the meate is pleasant, and well drest, but the good successe of your Enemies hath made your appetite ill.

I protest seriously unto thee, and without Scepticisme, *that there is no such thing in this world, as* misfortune *; the foolish* testinesse *of man arising out of his* misconstruction *and* ignorance *of the wise method of* Providence, *throwes him into many* troubles. *The* Spouse *tells us, that the fingers of the* Bride-groome *are deckt with* 20 Beryll *and* pretious stones: *what ever falls upon us from that* Almighty *hand, it is a* diamond *; It is celestiall* treasure, *and the matter of some new* blessing, *if we abuse it not.* God *(saith the wise King,)* created not Evill, but man (who was created upright) sought out many inventions : *these indeed beget that* monster *; his ill* digestion *of his* punishment *(which is a kinde of* divine diet,) *makes him to pine away in a sinfull discontent. If thou art sick of such an* Atrophie, *the precepts layd down in this little booke (if rightly* understood, *and faithfully* practised) *will perfectly cure thee.* 30

All that may bee objected is, that I write unto thee out of a land of darkenesse, out of that unfortunate region, where the Inhabitants sit in the shadow of death: where destruction passeth for propagation, and a thick black night for the glorious day-spring. If this discourage thee, be pleased to remember, that there are bright starrs under the most palpable clouds, and light is never so beautifull as in the presence of darknes. At least intreat God that the Sun may not goe down upon thy own dwelling, which is hartily desired and prayed for, by

Newton by Usk in
South-wales.
April. 17. 1652.   Hen : Vaughan. 40

To the onely true and glorious
God, the Sole disposer of
Life and Death.

O doe not goe, thou know'st I'le dye,
My *Spring* and *Fall* are in thy Booke !
Or if thou goest, doe not deny
To lend me, though from far, one looke !

My sinnes long since have made thee strange,
A very stranger unto me;
No *morning-meetings* (since this change)
Nor *Evening-walkes* have I with thee.

Why is my God thus hard and cold,
When I am most, most sick and sad ?
Well-fare those blessed dayes of old,
When thou did'st heare the *weeping Lad* !

O doe not thou doe as I did,
Doe not despise a love-sick heart !
What though some *Clouds* defiance bid,
Thy *Sun* must shine in every part.

Though I have spoyl'd, O spoyle not thou,
Hate not thine owne deere gift and token !
Poore *Birds* sing best, and prettiest show,
When their *neast* is fallen and broken.

Deare Lord ! restore thy Ancient peace,
Thy quickning friendship, mans bright wealth,
And if thou wilt not give *me* Ease
From sicknes, Give my *Spirit* health !

Two Excellent
DISCOURSES

Of $\left\{\begin{array}{l} \text{1. Temperance and Patience.} \\ \text{2. Life and Death.} \end{array}\right.$

Written in Latin by
Johan : Euseb : Nierembergius.

Englifhed by

HENRY VAUGHAN, Silurift.

—— *Mors Vitam temperet, & vita Mortem.*

LONDON:
Printed for *Humphrey Moseley*, and
are to be fold at the *Princes Armes*
in St *Paul's* Church-yard. 1654.

OF
TEMPERANCE
AND
PATIENCE.

The *Doctrine* of good living is short, but the *work* is long and hard to be perswaded, though easie to bee learnt: for to be good, is of all things the most easie, and the most ready, if wee could learne but one other *Art*, which *Antisthenes* termed the most necessary, I will add, the most difficult, and that is, *to forget to doe Evill*. I find that *peace* and *joy* have two *handles*, whereby we may take hold of them, *Patience*, and *Temperance*. Rule thy *Evil* with these, and then thy *will* may rule thee well. Horses are ruled with bridles and spurs. In prosperity use the first, that is,
10 restraine, or keepe in thy selfe. In adversity the last, that is, Incite, and use thy selfe to a gallant *Apathie*, and contempt of misfortunes. Generous and metlesome *Coursers* when they are breathed, or rid abroad, are compelled to trample upon those very things, whose first sight startled and terrified them; doe so with thy selfe: tread under thy feet thy most hideous adversities; so shalt thou forget the feare of fortune, which makes men unfit for vertue. Patience in adversity is temperance in prosperity. Nor can it be easily resolved, which of these two excells: This is most certaine, that noble sufferance is as necessary to man, as the
20 virtue of temperance. Some few Crosses thou canst beare well, but fortune can afflict thee with many, and thou by patience (the greatest of virtues) must afflict her with more; for

 —— *The naked man too getts the field,*
 And often makes the armed foe to yeeld.

It costs not much to live well, and it is as cheape to learne it. The whole Art is comprised in these two words, *Patience*, and *Temperance*. In these lies all the *Mysterie* of Peace: you would think it a *Secret* of the Priests of *Ceres*, it is so unknown to any, but sacred minds. These are the Domestick Gods of tranquility,
30 and the tutelar Angels of good men: beleeve with *Epictetus*, that the Quintessence of all Philosophie is squeezed into these two, Ἀνέχου, καὶ ἀπέχου, beare and forbeare. He neither obtaines, nor retaines his joy, that doth not abstain, and sustaine. These are the two

Poles upon which tranquility and vertue move. To obtain peace, you must bear; to retain it, you must forbeare. An odd way of fruition; By refusing you obtaine, and by suffering you preserve: by refusing the favours, and suffering the spite of fortune. By this very carriage did *Diogenes* beleeve that he had quite deposed and overthrown her: hee crowned his temples with branches of *Pine*, the old *Isthmian* ceremonie, and walked like an absolute victour in the Sacred Games. Being required by a crosse fellow, not to usurpe that honour till he had lawfully strived, he answered, that he had overcome two enemies, *Pleasure* and *Griefe*, the one by forbearing, the other by bearing. Make not thy self a Woman: thou hast (if thou wilt use them) both *Temperance* and *Patience*, the best Stratagems, and Countermines against the Wiles of Fortune. Her storms and suddaine furies (which are alwaies clean, and without dissimulation,) thou mayst break and overcome by bearing; Her Arts, her deep and cankerd hatred, by listning to Reason, and a warie, stayd Circumspection, while she spends and wasts with her owne malice. The wrath of furious and hasty persons is sincere, and without artifice; It hath no poyson, but what breakes out presently at the tongue, or the hand: Fortune too, when in this humour, is lesse Noxious, for She makes then an indifferent use of all Tooles, and disposeth of them without Study. But when She begins to hate, She becomes slow and weary, and not contented with open valour, addes to it Treachery. She pines with the Memory of her old favours, and that She may pull down what She built, adornes her most deadly Intentions, as Poverty and grievous Miseries, in the dresse of Felicity. All her projects, machinations and Engines to Torture and vex Man, amount to no more, then to give him what he would not have, and to deny him what he would have. He breaks her neck that abstaines from the *first*, and contemnes the *last*.

But here is our double Disease, by which *Virtue* Conceived for a great end, together with *Felicity*, become both abortive, that wee neither rightly wish, nor rightly abstain, loath, or love, but doe both most absurdly, most preposterously. We Covet most unseasonably, when even necessity is necessary, and this to him that wants, is no more then a wish. We covet, I say, such things as fortune hath not, and in a time when they may not be had. Wee would have *Cherries* in *January*: These wishes are their own Torments: Fortune too most Commonly gives them but cold Comfort. Why should we Covet extraneous Goods? It is better to serve the necessity of the time, then to be a slave to Fortune.

Wee are set upon longing like Woemen with Child, that labour with strange appetites and depraved stomacks ; that loath health-full Viands, and (which in them is very strange) abhorre sweet meats ; That affect raw, absurd compositions, that eat lime, Char-coles and Ashes, that in the dead of Winter long for Summer-fruits, and in Summer for Winter-fruits. What dost thou think is bearing and forbearing ? It is to be even with Fortune, discreetly to abstaine, discreetly to will, and to covet nothing. Abstain then : otherwise what wilt thou do by Coveting, but make way for Fortune, and
10 enlarge her Empire ? Though she would not, she must needs hit thee. Her being blind, hinders not but she may shoote well : When the mark is *have at all*, and *every where* : an Archer without Eyes cannot misse it. Though unwilling, her Arrowes cannot wander from him, whose lust wanders after all things. She will hit him without Ayming, whose hope aymes at every thing. No Weapon falls in vaine amongst a multitude. Her scope to hurt, is the same scope thou takest to wish.

Thou must know that the Command of Fortune over man about these outward things, lies in the midst of the will, as the hand in
20 the midst of a bended bow. If thou holdest thy will by the middle, then art thou master of both ends, and mayst doe any thing. If thou commandst the one halfe, I will not say, thou hast no hold at all. Liberty hath two Limbs, to *Will*, and to *refraine* : The one is a stronge *Arme*, the other a weak *Hand* : What thou hast not, thou mayst refraine from wishing to have, but no man can have what ever he would have. When you refrain from willing, then have you Power over all things ; when your will lusteth, then you are subject to all things. Outward goods are fleeting things, and the faithfull servants of unfaithfull chance. O how great a treasure, how
30 provident and infallible a supply against these sudden Ebbs and diminutions is a regular and resolute will ! Why are we troubled at them ! We are too hard for Fortune, and by much too hard, if wee command but the one halfe of our will ; that maimed and halting hand (if I may so speak) will overtake and bring back the most averse and winged Felicities. It will enrich us sooner and surer then all the Treasures of *Cræsus* : Those are but beggerie before thee if thou covet them not, if thy will be not a begger. Not to will, makes thee securely rich, even when thou wilt, that is, when thou doest will nothing. Thou makest Fortune poore by
40 leaving her no power over thee, and nothing in her self, wherewith to please thee ; I meane to deceive thee. Thou wilt be richer than *Attalus* by contemning his store, and of greater power than *Midas* ;

for his was placed in fruition and touching, but thine in absence and emptinesse. By wishing nothing thou hast all, yea those things which thou seest not : and what wonder then, if those things thou seekest not, being abundantly enriched by thy most pretious povertie? It was Divinely argued by *Eusebius, That he onely should be esteemed rich, who was perswaded that he had enough. For those that adde still to what they have already gotten, and never thinke that they can get enough, though richer than* Midas, *are most poor and miserable beggers ; because they are nothing rich in their own minds.* And in another place, *An unreasonable covetousnesse* (saith 10 he) *is sooner driven away with the losse of riches allready gotten, then by a plenteous and dayly accesse of more treasures.* Wherefore thou art then only rich, and possessest all things to thy mind, when to have nothing is in thy will : When ever thou sayest, *It is enough,* thou hast all. Yea, thou hast more then thou shouldst have. All that comes afterwards doth but load and overwhelme thee.

Of such an Immoderate use is Temperance, and I Judge Patience to be of no lesser. Happily it may be easier ; for having learnt to abstain, we may the better sustain. Impatience ariseth naturally out of Cupidity, and feare is the Daughter of hope. 20 Cast these away, and you will find, that an adverse Fortune may be entertained, not onely with Patience, but with much wellcome. *Crates,* or *Zeno* (a gallant man, if either of the two) being at Sea in a great storm, caus'd all his goods (wherewith the Ship was Loaden) to be thrown over board, and thanked Fortune for the kindnesse : doe thou the like, and approving of thy misfortunes, say, *It is well done, Fortune, thou hast read me a good lesson, thou hast had care of my Soul. I thank thee that thou art Come thy selfe to fetch these burthens, which I should have brought thee home. Thou hast dealt courteously to lend me their use, and to prevent their* 30 *Abuse. I like thy Method, and prefer thy advise to thy favours ; I know thy meaning. I must make a wise use of these crosses, I must have recourse to virtue, to my self, and to my God. Thou dost not onely Incite, but compell me to goodnesse. I am brought safe to shore, by the splitting of the Ship : hereafter I will be better provided. Behold, thou hast left yet behind thee some moveables, which thou shouldst have taken with thee, they are thine by right. Thou gavest me so many things, that thou canst not well remember them. I desire not to conceale them, take all thy Reliques and appendencies with thee, all that is here besides my selfe ; I hold thy leavings not* 40 *worthy of acceptance from the mind of man.* I wish that we would so deal with Fortune, as a certain old man did with theeves that

34 *goodnesse*] *gooduesse 1654*

came to rob his house. *Take with you* (said he) *all that you see here.* They did so, leaving nothing behind them but an empty purse ; which the old man tooke up, and following after, called to them ; *Take this also with you, which you forgot to put up.* Fortune perhaps amazed at such a Noble, Serene disposition, would restore all : It is most certaine the Theeves did. But let a Christian reject this figment of Fortune, and in all worldly mutations acknowledge and kisse the divine hand.

But if after all this, thou wilt not excuse the outward and
10 ravenous manners of Fortune ; there will be no Just cause for thee to accuse them, having received no damage by her. If thou wilt purge thy mind from wishes and hopes, thou mayst safely place thy selfe before her very Arrowes, and defie them. And truly I believe it will be thy most secure station. When *Stratonicus* saw an unskilfull fellow shooting at *Buts*, he got presently close to the *White*, as the onely place free from danger : and being asked his reason for that unusual Refuge, he answered ; *Least that fellow should hit me.* Fortune (we say) is blind ; stand then in her way : She hits that the least, which she most aimes at ; but if all her
20 shafts should fall upon thee, they can draw no blood from thee, as long as thou art not drawn by covetousnesse. If you break off the point of the Weapon, it cannot hurt you. Our own Covetousnesse is Fortunes edged toole ; take that away, and you disarme her, and secure your selfe : blunt weapons wound not to blood.

I suppose now that *Epictetus* his abridgement, or reduction of Philosophy into two words, *Abstain* and *Sustain*, will seeme prolix enough to you. The first we have past through ; the second and last, I meane *Sustain*, or the *Art of bearing well*, wee shall find tedious enough. Hee cannot be said to wish for nothing, that
30 finds fault with that which he hath. This bearing well is to desire nothing but what wee have. A Serene, bright Will then, not clouded with thick and muddy desires, will find the burdens of Fortune to be very light : For Fortune of her selfe is very light and easie, but she hath for *pannels* our own Lusts, which are heavier than her *packs*, and without these shee puts not one loade upon us. Nothing tires and weighs us down but our own wishes, which evills (being ignorant that our burthen proceedes from them,) we multiply with an Intent to ease our selves, but in the meane time the weight increaseth. A certain plain Countryman wearied with
40 ploughing, and returning home from the field after his daies task, tyed the Plough to his Asse, and afterwards mounted himself upon his back ; but the tyred Asse, and overloaden, could not stirre

from the place ; whereupon the Country-man lights, and with the Plough upon his backe remounting the Asse, tells him, *Now I hope thou canst goe well, for it is not thou, but I that carry the Plough.* Wee are every day as ridiculous, though not so harmlesse as this Country-man. Wee study with new cares and new desires to ease and diminish our old lusts ; which not onely keepes under, but choaks and presseth to death all the seeds of Joy and Content. This is nothing else, but to retain the former load undiminish'd, and to put another on the top of it. As long as we tolerate these burthens, we become intollerable to our selves, without any exaggeration of Fortune. Let us shake them off, let us cast off hope, that troublesome *Tympany*; so shall we find Fortune light, and be able to bear both her and our selves. All things may be born of him, that bears not future Evills; Those are grievous burthens, which miraculously oppresse us, and so strangly accommodate themselves to our hurt, that they exist in the heart, and vexe it, before they can exist in time. Not onely Evil, but Good, when it is hovering and uncertain, doth afflict us. Of Evills themselves there cannot come so many together upon us, as we can feare : fortune can throw at us but few darts at one time, and were she not still furnished by our lusts, we should quickly see her quiver empty. Abstinence then, or the restraining of our desires is the Nurserie of patience, by a like title as the toleration of evill and good.

But when I name Patience, I speake not of a *Simple* thing ; for there is not onely patience in *Evill*, but in *Good* also, and this later is sometimes the most difficult. There is one when we *suffer*, and another when we *act*. There be also other divisions of Patience. Holy *Ephrem* makes it threefold : the *first* towards *god*, the *second* towards the *tempter*, or wicked Angel, and the *third* towards *man*. I shall add a *fourth*, and the most difficult of all, towards our *selves* ; or I will make it onely *twofold*, *first* towards *those* that are *without us*, the *second* and last towards our *selves*, or those *commotions* which fight against us from *within*. This last is the greatest, because it teacheth us to beare those pressures which lean upon us, and bow us down. It is harder to resist those weights which come forcibly upon us from above, then those which come oppositly, or over against us. The beasts can draw more after them, then they can carry upon their backs. Man hath enough to beare within himselfe : but evills are a great familie, and keep aswell without doores as within. Every minute of our tranquility is purchased with patience ; It is the great Sacrament of peace, the Sanctuary of Security, the Herald and the badge of felicity. What will it availe us to be at peace with those that are without, while we suffer intestine warres and tumults within ? let us have peace in our selves, and having mastered the rebellion and disorders of the will, let us be the patients of our sadnesse, yea of our Impatience, and some times of our patience.

As nothing is more accidentall to man then to suffer, so should he conclude, that nothing is more necessary for him than patience.
10 It is the naturall medicine for all humane calamities, with which (as the *heart* with *Dittany*) wee pull out the heads and splinters of those arrowes which the *mighty hunters* of this world shoot at us. Nature dealt not more unkindly with man, than with other creatures : The *Boare* is cured with *Jvie*, the *Dragon* with *wild-lettice*, and the *Snake* with *Fennell.* Others have their cure nearer, in their owne members : his *tongue* is the *Balsom* to a wounded *dog*; and the *Catholicon* of man is silence and patience. But did I say that to suffer was accidentall to man ? I blot out that errour, and affirme, It is necessary : wherefore patience is most necessary ;
20 for by that we are freed from a slavish sufferance, as by a certaine gifted premunition and defensive faculty. By patiently enduring we become impassible. The minde is invulnerable, unlesse in the fits of impatience, as *Achilles* was in the heele. Think not the Art of patience to be any more, then not to suffer voluntarily ; at least, not in spight of thy will. Hee that gently endures, doth by a short cut free himself from the tedious labours and numerous punishments of life. Necessities should be chearefully borne. The hands, the feet, and the other limbs will sooner fail to execute their duties, then to be Insensible of paine. The sick, the
30 maimed, yea and the dismembred are not so mortified, but they are subject to sensation. It was an excellent saying of *Herod* the Sophist, when hee was pained with the gout in his hands and feet ; *When I would eat,* (said he) *I have no hands ; when I would goe I have no feet ; but when I must be pained, I have both hands and feet.* So entire and whole are we alwaies to griefe ; which sufficiently sheweth, that the soundnesse of man is best seene in his patience ; and such a strong necessity of suffering is laid upon us, that when our limbs faile us in their offices, they must not faile of sufferings. Thou wilt aske then what can they suffer, when without spirit and
40 motion ? I will tell thee ; Not to be apt to suffer, is their suffering. Nothing is lacking to the misery of man, though his limbs should be wanting, his griefe by that defect will abound the more.

Deeply, and into the Inmost Closets of our hearts should that saying of the *Temanite* descend, *Man* (said he) *is borne unto trouble, and the bird to flye.* Observe, if the birds be unfurnish'd of any thing for flight : they are all over arm'd for it ; Their Bills are keen and sharp-pointed, and serve like *foredecks* to cut their aire ; Their pinions are two swift *rowers,* and the feathers in both wings placed orderly every one longer then the other represent soe many *oares.* Their traines are the *Sternes,* with which they bend their whole bodies, and govern them in their flights, and with their feete and crooked clawes like *Anchors,* they stick and fasten themselves to the green branches, which are their *Havens,* and shady Harbours. Though thou hadst never seene them use their wings, yet by their very *Structure,* thou would'st Judge that those feathered *Sayles* were design'd for the aire, and flying. Man is every way as well accoutred for trouble. Observe him : Thou shalt find nothing wanting that may conduce to his passion, though he wants much of Patience. Man is every way most exactly trimmed and adorned for trouble ; He was made unfit for labour, that he might be fit for sufferings ; He hath no wings to fly from them, he is poor, infirme, naked, defencelesse ; and (which is worse than all) forsaken of himself : Betwixt nakednesse and poverty he is on all sides exposed and appointed for misery, as the bird is for the flight. Thou shalt observe all this in him ; for wanting all the necessaries which support life, he is surrounded onely with those sad necessities and intanglements which make life grievous and burthensome ; as a *Sparrow* is drest and cloathed all over with those soft habiliments which make his flights easie and pleasant. The onely difference betwixt them is this, that those Instruments of flying may faile the birds, but those of suffering cannot faile Man. So carefull was Nature of Mans condition, that she would not trust Fortune with his relatives. The *Eagle* may casually lose his sharpnesse of sight, the *Roe* her swiftnesse, and the *Lyon* his strength ; but Man while he lives cannot misse of afflictions. There is a greater care had of our affaires ; And to a glorious end are these Calamities made sure unto us, if wee can make them beneficiall.

The first token, and evidence of life is crying. The Prim-roses, or first blossoms of it are teares ; from these it takes its inauguration. Man is not borne before he suffers : Yea, he grones and complaines in his very passage into the World. The first homage he payes to life is sufferance, and from that minute to his last, he becomes (as *Blesensis* saith) *a constant tributary to misery.* I Judge him that murmurs at this payment, that kicks under this generall burthen, to wrong and disesteem the Noblest Nature, I mean Man; and to be worthy of this very punishment, *not to be at all.* He is a most vile abuser of Humane Nature, that thinks it not worth his patience, and values himselfe at a most sordid rate; let him beare in his manhood, what he bore in his Infancie, and not be ashamed of his Investiture, because he felt affliction, before he felt the light. It is the first lesson we are taught here, and the last that wee shall learn. All other Creatures, as soone as they are born, make some use of their strength; but Man knowes no use of any thing but teares: He must afterwards be taught the cause of them. We must teach him every thing, but weeping. All other things are given him for his labour, but teares he can have for nothing. This onely faculty was bestowed upon him *gratis*, all other concessions are the rewards of his paines; but teares were given him freely, because they ease and allay his sorrowes. This convenient *Salve* did nature ordain for some inevitable Sores. She prepared this *Oyle* to allay the aking of those stripes the World gives us, which without this *Native Oyntment* would have smarted more: for those wounds, whose anguish is not vented at the Eyes, lie heaviest upon the heart. And by this I am induced to believe, that it is naturall for man to Suffer, because he onely naturally weepes. Every extraneous felicity of this life is violent, or forced; and these constrained, though splendid *Adiuncts* of Fortune are therefore short, because noe violent thing can be perpetuall. To suffer is the naturall condition and manner of man, this is believed to be his misery; without patience, I confesse, it is. Nature never failes us in those things which are needful, much lesse divine providence and grace. Wee shall therefore never faile of Sufferings, because they are the great *Necessaries*, & *Medicines* of Humane Nature. Wee read of many men that never laught, but never heard of any that never wept. *Democritus* himself came weeping into the World; none ever came without labour, none without griefe.

Thou wilt ask, why man, the only creature addicted to beatitude should bee borne to trouble? why through the vale of teares travells he to the house of joy? why is he alone, being capeable of felicity made subject unto misery? Because he is borne for virtue, the next and readiest instrument to attaine beatitude. Now troubles or miserie are the masse, or first matter of virtue, and without this hard rudiment, without this *coyne* of sorrow he cannot purchase it

3 punishment] puishment *1654*   22 heart.] heart *1654*

Nor are the good offices which these calamities doe for us, either meane or few; for wherefore flowes, yea overflowes the divine mercy upon man, but because he is miserable? wherefore is Gods sure power and saving arme stretched out, but because he is fraile? wherefore are his comforts and refreshments so plentifully showred down, but because he is sorrowfull and helplesse? wherefore is his liberality and most faithful providence seen every minute, but because he is poore and constantly needy? yea wherefore is Immortality, everlasting pleasures, and a glorious resurrection secured unto us, but because our bodies are mortal, and subject to death 10 and putrefaction? By this time perhaps you see the appositnesse of that comparison which *Eliphaz* made betwixt *man* and a *bird*. The bird by nature lifts himself above the earth upon his wings, he passeth from hence into the cleare confines and neighbourhood of heaven, where he dwells for a time, and looks with contempt upon this inferiour darksome portion of the world : when hee descends towards the earth, he keepeth still above us, he lodgeth in the height and freshnesse of the trees, or pitcheth upon the spires or ridges of our houses, or upon some steepe rock, whose height & inaccessiblenesse promise him securitie ; something that 20 is eminent and high he alwaies affects to rest upon. Man likewise ordained for heaven, and the contempt of this spot of earth is by his very calamities borne up and carried above the world, yea into heaven, as an Eagle by the strength of his wings ascends above the clouds. O the depth of the riches of the wisedome of God ! O the mercifull designe, and device of his providence ! who knowing our corrupt nature, hath laid upon us a necessity of seeking those blessings, whose inestimable value ought to stirre us up to a most voluntary and diligent searching after them. To this *necessity* by the same chain of his providence hath 30 hee tyed *utility*. These are sufficient motives to perswade us to patience. It was wisely said by some *Arabian, that the hedge about patience was profit :* for he that thinks gaine to be necessary, must think labour so too. Allthough Fortune should be so prodigal as to poure all her Treasures into the bosome of one man, and not repent when she had done ; yet would this very man sometimes feele strong exigencies in indigencie. *Pompey,* and *Darius* were both hardly distrest with thirst ; they that were Lords of so many Rivers, did then wish for one drop of Water. *Alexander* the *Great,* in some of his expeditions was like to perish with cold, 40 though his Dominion did in a manner extend to the very Sun ; for in the *East* (which I may call the Suns House,) he was such an absolute Lord, that (bating the Power to forbid the Sun to rise) there was nothing more could be added to his conquests.

Seeing then that labour or troubles are a necessity imposed upon man, it followes, that there are other labours belonging unto him, which are also as necessary; and those I shall terme *Voluntarie Labours.* Of these the Elegant Philosopher *Eusebius* hath excellently spoken; *Voluntary Labours* (saith he) *are necessary, because of future Labours which hang over our heads: he will beare those with more ease when they fall upon him, who of his own* 10 *accord, and beforehand hath exercised himself in them:* But you see that in this course also the maine remedy is patience. He that suffers willingly, suffers not, even that which is necessary to be suffered. One wedge drives out another. Venemous bitings are allayd by Venemous Medecines; therefore in necessary troubles, there is a necessity of voluntary Labours, that *Violent Evills* meet not with *Obstinate Wills*: but the unavoydablenesse of suffering would not be grievous, nor the necessity or Law of Nature any way rigorous, did not we by our owne exaggerations adde to their weight, and our owne pain. Wee helpe to encrease our owne 20 Calamities *by reason of our Inerudition,* as *Diphilus* tells us, who adviseth even *the happy man to learn miseries.* What can wee doe more becomming our fraile condition, then to teach our Mortality the troubles of life, which are certain prolusions, or arguments of death? What is more beneficiall, then to learn great tryalls and dangers, that wee may leave that servile custome of fearing Fortune, whose burthens we ought to bear as willingly, as if wee desired to undergoe them?

It is a great rudiment of patience to suffer willingly, when we least expect sufferings. It is strange, that although wee see 30 nothing in the course of this life more frequent then miseries, yet will wee not be perswaded that they may fall into our share: Our griefes come most commonly before we believe they may come. Nothing can make us believe, that we may be miserable, untill misery it selfe assures it to us. The mind therefore should be tryed and prepared for it, with some lusorie or mock-misfortunes. Nor must we give eare to *Democritus,* whose saying is, *That if there be any things for us to suffer, it is good to learn them, but not to suffer them.* It is good indeed to learn them, but if they must be unavoydably suffered, what will our learning of them avail us? 40 A most ridiculous advise, in my Judgement: And if the Author of it had been wise, he had laught at nothing more then at this his

20 *reason*] *reasom 1654*   25 fearing] fearing ? *1654*

owne Conclusion. It is good to learn to *suffer Evills*, but not to *be evill*. It will benefit us much to learn to suffer them, if not as they are Evills, yet lest wee our selves become Evill ; for such we shall be by impatience. Besides the overcomming of reall evills, there remaine other slight hurts, as the discourtesies of nature, chance and furie, of our enemies and our selves also, which we cannot avoyd ; but these last are no *evills*, but the *sheaths* or *quivers* of *evills* ; out of these either our *opinion*, or our *impatience* draw evills upon our selves. *Dion* used to say, *that it was a great evill, not to be able to beare evills.* Without this ability, life cannot 10 be pleasant to any, and in this consists the skill and knowledge of life.

Let the mind then learne to buckle with these rude toyles of life, and by a frequent velitation or light skirmishing with troubles so improve it selfe, that when we come to deale with the serious hand, and close encounters of fortune, we may receive her *at sharpe*, and like active, vigilant *Duellists*, put by her most Artfull and violent thrusts. One *Salustius* that lived in the time of *Simplicius* did put upon his bare thigh a burning cole, and to keepe in the fire did gently blow it, that he might try how long hee could endure 20 it. I beleeve that fire did put out and quite extinguish all the burnings and raging flames of incensed fortune. If crosses foreseen are alwaies held light, those we tast and make experiment of before they come, must needs be lighter, because after tryall we feare them not : feares are the fore-teeth of miseries, which bite us sorest, and most intollerably. It was a most ridiculous judgement which that *Sybarite* (mentioned by *Serinus*) past upon the valour of the *Spartans*. This tender Citizen travelling by chance into *Lacedemon*, was so amazed at the severe discipline of that manly nation, who brought up their children in all rigorous and laborious 30 exercises, that being returned home hee told the *Fidlers* of * *Sybaris*, that the forwardnesse of the *Spartan* Youths to dye in battell was, because they would not be compelled any longer to such a toylsome life. This soft fellow knew not how much *Industry* could prevaile against *misfortune*, and *patience* against *passion*. That valour of the *Spartans* was not despayre, but the virtue of suffering perfected. Their voluntary labours at home had so excellently

* *A towne in the higher Calabria in Italy 20. miles distant from Rome : the Inhabitants were mightily given to pleasure, and taught their horses to dance to the pipes ; which the Crotoniatæ their deadly enemies observing, brought into the field a company of minstrels : the Sybarits horses hearing the pipes 40 began to dance, and disordered their Army, by ordered their Army, by which meanes they were overthrowne to the number of 300000.*

improved them, that they could not onely slight the necessary and common afflictions of life, but overcome also (by a noble *volunteering*,) the very prerogative of fate, violating even the violence of death, while they dyed unconstrayned and undisturbed. *Mithridates* his feare of being poysoned, made him use himselfe to a venomous diet, by which he came at last to disgest all sorts of poysons without any prejudice to his health : so that afterwards when he would have poysoned himselfe in good earnest, he could not possibly doe it.   By this destroyer of mankind did he secure
10 himselfe even from himselfe, and by long acquaintance made this deadly enemie a faithfull friend : he fed life with the provision of death.   By a like sagacity should we forearme our selves against the conspiracies (if I may so say) of nature. Let us labour against labours ; It will much availe us : our very feares will prove comforts ; by using our selves to sufferance, the Antidote of life, which is Patience, becomes effectuall.

Of such great importance is this assiduous exercise in troubles, that it lets in the nature of *Constancie*, and is a sure manuduction to that sincerest vertue.   The *Roman* Fencers, players for prizes,
20 barbarous and dissolute livers, if but indifferently skild, received their wounds without grones, or any alteration of gesture or countenance, because they would not be judged pusillanimous, nor cowardly decliners of danger ; If at any time they fell by the violence of wounds, they sent presently to know their masters pleasures, (because they would satisfie them,) for they themselves were contented to dye ; If their masters (finding them incurable) bad them prepare for death, they would presently hold forth their throats and receive the sword most willingly.   O the serious faith of Playes ! O the faith of Players in serious dangers ! It is all one
30 then, whether thou thinkest fortune a meere pageant and pastime, or not ; Thou shouldest obey with an Immortall faith even to the death.   Let a wise man execute the commands of his creator, let him like a faithfull souldier of JESUS CHRIST certifie his great master, that he is ready and willing to doe him service, that he will lose his life, & choose rather to dye, then not to submit to his pleasure.   The conflicts of a good man with calamities are sacred : he is made a spectacle to the world, to Angels and men, and a hallowed *Present* to the Almighty.   Let him in this state overcome his Enemies ! A more glorious garland then the *Olympick*
40 Olive-branches shall crown an enduring Patience, which by an humble, but overcomming Sufferance wearies the hands of those that beat us.   It is the part of a wise man, to tire and weare out

the malice of his Enemies. I say not by Suffering, but by Patience, which makes him neither their Patient, nor trampled upon, but a trampling overcomer. This was the glory of *Melancoma*, who lived not one day without an Enemy. In the most vehement season of the yeare, hee judged his single-selfe hard enough for his two Adversaries: He could beare with the *Sun*, his most obstinate *Antagonist*, though fighting against him in the heate of the Summer with so many hands as he had Rayes: When he might have gotten the Victory by Opposition, he would not but by Submission. Hee considered, that the best might be 10 overcome by the worst, if force should take place. That Victory was in his Judgement the Noblest, when the Enemy, yet whole and without any hurt, was compell'd to submit. Then is he overthrown, when not by wounds, but by himselfe.

Therefore what vice, and a spurious Patience did in the *Roman* Fencers, let Virtue and true Patience performe in thee: and what custome and exercise wrought in *Melancoma*, let reason and Judgement worke in thee: What reason effected in *Possidonius*, let grace effect in thy heart, and let not grace which workt mightily a in *Eustathius*, and sufficiently in many others, languish and faile in thee alone. The power of God is perfected in weaknesse, giving us some prelibations (as it were) of it self; whither by bearing with our Infirmities, or by our bearing his Operations. I believe this last: for the glory of an almighty power against a weake thing would be very small; how litle then against Infirmity it selfe? That power is truly glorious, and hath matter for glory, which prevailes against the mind, a free unconfined thing, and holds it firme though surrounded with Infirmities: The power of God Glories more in prevailing against us, then against our infirmities.

But if wee seek for more delicate or easie remedies, and dare not arme our selves against misfortunes with this harnesse of proofe, because we think it too heavy; It remaines that we must make use of either *Hope*, or *Expectation*. Evills that are foreseen, lose much of

a *One of the Courtiers of* 20 *the Emperor* Traian, *and afterwards a most glorious Martyr. Being in Chase of a Stagge, he observed betwixt his hornes the signe of the Cross, and heard a voice out of his mouth, speaking to him in the Latin tongue,* Curme persequeris? *Whereupon leaving his game, he retyred presently into his own house, and having called together his wife and children, were all baptized* 30 *and received the Christian Faith. But in the persecution under* Hadrian, *he and his wife* Theophila *for their faithfullnesse to JESUS CHRIST, were burnt together in a brasen bull; And so having overcome and endured unto the end, they received the morning star, and crownes of life, which shall never be taken from them. See* Volater lib. 15. 40

8 Rayes:] Rayes. : *1654*   13 Then *M*: There *1654*

their edge : But because we promise our selves the favours of
Fortune (of whom we have alwaies a good opinion, though wee
seldome speak well of her, and she deservs as ill,) our calamities,
while this credulous remissnesse keepes us from looking to them,
find way to surprize and oppresse us at once. Against violent
misfortunes we may not use violence. Expectation will sometimes
serve us best, if it be accompanied with a strong and irremisse
beliefe, that the *Crosse* is at hand, and will not delay. For what
happens in this life more frequent, than unthought of events ?
10 Wee meete oftentimes even in one day with matter of grief, and
matter of Patience. It is strange, that for those two meales we
eat in the day, wee are all the day, and all our life long providing :
But for trouble, for griefes and sadnesse, which take not up two
houres in the day, but all the houres and daies of our lives, wee
never think to make any preparation. Cast up (if thou canst) how
many things must be had to humor the pride of mans appetite ;
more than for a Sacrifice. It is no small state, nor ceremonie that
the belly is serv'd with : How many men doth this worms-meat
Imploy, Cookes, Bakers, Fishers, Fowlers, Hunters, Sheepfeeders,
20 Herdsmen, Millers, Colliers, and Butchers ? How many Instruments, Spits, Pots, Trivets, Cauldrons, Chafing-dishes, Chargers,
Platters, and a thousand other utensils of gluttonie ? And to what
end is all this preparation ? But to please one palate once in the
day, or twice at most. O foolish men ! Wee are ever providing
for pleasures, but never for troubles, which not twice, but for
a great portion of our time, (if not continually) wee must needs
endure. Who against the certain approach of an Enemy, will be
secure and quiet, and upon the comming of a friend watchfull and
sollicitous ? Why do we provide so much for pleasures and
30 vanitie, and provide nothing against the day of trouble and
miserie ? We are guarded about with Cloaths of state, Cano-
pies, Couches, Silk-Curtains, Feather-Beds and Pillowes ; wee
arme our selves for delights and softnesse, for sleeping and
eating, because they are every daies works ; but hear not
every day telling us, that the Evill day is behind. We labour to
provide for the backe and the belly, why not for the better part,
why not for our fraile condition ? The Sense of the secure
liver is too too delicate : The affliction of the Inconsiderate
or unprepared too bitter. Chance throwes downe the carelesse
40 violently : and Fortune tires the idle even to vexation. The
rude and unexperienced in troubles afflicts and macerates
himselfe with an impatient mind in the very midst of his most

affected blandishments, and in the bosome and calme of all his pleasures.

I hold Impatience to be a kind of *Night-Mare* which comes upon us waking, or the *Day-hag* of life : This troublesome disease (for our time of rest is his time of misrule, and when wee are sleeping, then is he stirring,) sets upon us when wee are most at ease, and with a certain strange heavinesse seemes to oppresse and smother us, when in the meane time that weight which so much oppresseth us, is laid on by our owne Imagination : and this sometimes makes us crye out, as if wee were killed ; others, ac- 10 cording to *Lucretius*,

> *Struggle & grone as if by* Panthers *torne*
> *Or* Lyons *teeth, which makes them lowdly mourn.*
> *Some others seem unto themselves to dy.*
> *Some clime steep solitudes & Mountains high,*
> *From whence they seeme to fall inanely down,*
> *Panting with fear, till wak'd, and scarce their owne,*
> *They feel about them if in bed they lye,*
> *Deceiv'd with dreams, and nights Imagerie.*

But the greatest trouble of all, is, that without any hope of 20 remedy, they vainly strive and endeavour to shake off this shadow of heavinesse ;

> *In vain with earnest struglings they contend*
> *To ease themselves : for when they stir & bend*
> *Their greatest force to do it, even then most*
> *Of all they faint, and in their hopes are crost.*
> *Nor tongue, nor hand, nor foot will serve their turne,*
> *But without speech and strength within they mourne.*

What more expresse Image can there be of Impatience lying heavily especially upon those, who drouse away their time in a 30 vitious rest and Idlenesse? They are opprest, cry out, rage, and vainly resist, without any burthens but what their own fancy layes upon them. They feele the weight the heavier, the more they stirre it, without they shake it quite off. To refuse, or not willingly to undergoe burthens, is the onely burthen of Impatients. But if they would awake to themselves (which of necessity they must, for when can the will be more Rational, than when necessity is unreasonable) all these factitious weights and seeming heavinesse would quickly vanish : Force must not be used against Fortune, but Patience. This excells so much in strength, that it bears all : For it bears 40 what ever it will, and for this very reason because it Wills. *Samson* carryed away the dores, the two posts, and the barre of the Gate of the City of *Gaza* ; but this strength lay in his haire,

like the locks of *Nisus* and *Pterelaus.* A miraculous strength; but weakly secured. The strength of Patience is more safely seated; It lyes not in a lock, which may be cut off by some *Dalilah,* or *Comethe,* or *Scylla,* or any womanish and fearfull hand. To *Will,* is the Sanctuary of its strength; by being willing it is not onely enabled to bear, but also beareth. The backe and shoulder of Patience is the *Will.* This voluntary fortitude of the mind will do all its businesse, without the help of outward Engines; It needs not the assistance of the Armes, nor the weak
10 use of wishes. The strength of Virtue is not external, but in it self.

There remain also other necessary Indurances, though not to those that suffer them allready, yet to others that may, or are about to undergoe them : For the preservation of our Country & liberties we ought patiently to suffer even unto death. It is not too deare a rate to pay that debt wee owe to Nature, for the defense of Nature in our publick Persons : To this we want not the Incouragement of examples. What ever hath been suffered heretofore, may be suffered now by us. But if those presidents
20 rather cool, then provoke our Courage, why dare not wee suffer a little, seeing they suffered so much? To teach us this Virtue of Patience, and strengthen our ruinous brittle condition, the motherly love and fatherly care of the eternal, Divine mind, did provide and disperse through certaine spaces and Intervalls of time (like knots for the strengthning of a weak reed,) persons of such eminent Patience and Piety, as might by their examples sustaine and beare up mankind, untill the *Antient of daies,* and Father of Immortality himself should descend into this mortall life, and be born for Patience, and for death. In the meane time,
30 that the populous World might not want a Glasse to dresse themselves by, he sent these to be the substitutes and forerunners of his mighty and inimitable Patience. The first he consecrated to this dignity was *Abel,* in whom *Patience* (saith holy *Aldhelmus*) *was Original, as Sinne was in Adam.* God joyned Patience to his Innocence by a certain Original Justice or claim in him; but to the rest of the Just it descends together with sufferings, by right of Inheritance : to none more, to none better then to the Innocent. But now even by this, those suffer most, that should suffer least, the good and the Just. But those sufferings are most sacred, that
40 are most unjust. *Adam* found out afflictions, and *Abel* Patience; the medicine presently followed the disease. Evills were the Inventions of Sinne, Patience was the Device of Innocence. So

that Patience as their peculiar Treasure abounds more, and is more beloved by the Just, then by any else. But that Posthume Cry of *Abel* proceeded not from Impatience : For God would not have taken to himself the cause of one dying discontentedly, and with Indignation; but as devout *Alexandrinus* saith, Ἄβελ ὁ δίκαιος, *&c. Abel the Just dying unjustly was the first of men that shewd the foundations of death to be ruinous ; wherefore he being dead yet speaketh.* Death, whose right came by unrighteousnesse, laid ruinous foundations indeed, because ill-layd, upon the Just dying unjustly. It hath cause to grieve, that it erred so fouly in its first 10 stroke, seeing it might have made a better beginning in wicked *Cain.* But there was *Divinitie* in it, that death taking possession of mankind by the Murther of the Just, might be justly exterminated and swallowed up in Victory by the undefiled *Virgin-Prince* of the Just, who for that end was born of a Virgin. *Ephrem* saith, *that death howled or lamented in her very beginning, which shewed what would be her end.* The *Hern* by instinct of Nature Chatters and mourns, before he becomes the prey of the *Falcon.* Death dyed by him, over whom she had no power. Only there is the night of death, where sin, where corruption lives. 20

Another tie of Constancy laid upon the World, after a convenient space, was *Job*, who retained his Patience after prosperity, and after Innocence. Patience is no where merrier, nor better contented with it self, then in the Innocent. Integrity and Fortune seldome lodge together. Adversity is the Whetstone which keepes it from rust, and makes it shine. No Virtues can subsist without troubles, which are their foode. They live not commodiously, where their Provision is farre from them : Wherefore holy and Just men have adversity alwaies (like a *Well*) at their dores. I shall take up then with that saying of *Eliphaz* : 30 *Affliction comes not forth of the dust, nor doth trouble spring out of the ground ;* but rather from Heaven ; and comes oftner to holy and heavenly livers, then to Worldly and unrighteous persons.

After *Job*, and at a convenient distance from his time was *Tobiah* appointed, who instead of *Celandine*, made use of Patience to heal his Eyes : being blinded by the *Swallows*, he found a more pretious medicine then their *Herbe*, and his glory is more by bearing with the living, than burying the dead. This holy man also after Innocence, though not after prosperity, retained his Patience ; untill at last the *Son* of God himselfe, after *Impassi-* 40 *bility* and *Allmightinesse*, became wofully passible, and humbled himself to the death of the *Crosse* : of so great an example was

Patience worthy, and so necessary was this voluntary passion of God himselfe to our fatall necessity of suffering. By this mighty example of himself he hath sanctified Patience to be the *All-heal* or Universal *Antidote* of Evills, and the Soveraign *Lenitive* of sorrowes. Divinely did one sing to the blessed *J E S U S.*

Παυσίπονον νηπενθὲς ἔφυς, ἔναλθες ὄνειαρ.

Thou the Nepenthe *easing griefe*
Art, and the minds healing reliefe.

At this secret Counsel of the Almighty, did the rude Instincts, or
10 hallucinations rather of the old Heathens (proceeding, noe doubt, from their sense of Humane misery) blindly aime. They dreamt of some Son of God to be the great exemplar of Patience, and pattern of Virtue; but finding none, they made and proposed to themselves *Hercules* the Son of *Jupiter*, for a president of continuall Patience, Obedience and Virtue: about whose labours and atchievements, Antiquity hath mightily pleas'd it self with lies and Fables. This (indeed) they rightly apprehended, that labour or troubles are rather repugnant to, then unworthy of Divinity; they held them becomming Virtue, and withall necessary, that they might adorne
20 Patience with these two Jewells, the reward of suffering, and the dignity of the Sufferer. But the *Truth* of God hath now outdone the *Fictions* of men; It hath exceeded all they did licentiously wish, but could not hope for. Our Patience is now sufficiently instructed by the *S O N N E* of God, who is the pleasant remedy and *Panacea* of Evills. The blessed *J E S U S* breathed nothing but Patience, nothing but mildnesse in his life, in his Doctrine.

These are the great examples which true *Christians* should follow; not those of spurious Patience, and a narrow, heathen fortitude, which after it had born some Evills indeed, dyed at the
30 root, and could not bear it self. *Seneca* (otherwise in many things a very true, and sometimes a Christian Philosopher,) proposeth to his readers the example of *Cato*; but I utterly reject it; for he destroyed himselfe, because he could not save his Common-wealth. What Constancy was here, though in a state that concern'd not his private happinesse? or what manner of Constancy was that, which durst not endure and hold out, but was overcome, not by irrecoverable, fallen affaires, but falling: Not collapsed and ruin'd, but tottering and doubtfull? I confesse, it was a spectacle, which the Eye of God Intentive to his great and various
40 works might behold with glory: and I confesse him a brave

22 exceeded all] exceede a ll *1654*   37 collapsed] collasped *1654*

Heathen, Ill-disposed. But I see nothing glorious and excellent in him, nothing of true worth, but what I can find as wel in the most degenerate and womanish *Sardanapalus*. If wee look upon *Cato* amidst the publick ruines, wee shall finde him overthrowne and laid along, where an old wall stands up, no Enemy having touch'd him. A most unworthy man! (if he was a man,) to fall thus basely like a Woman; who at the noyse of any thing suddenly thrown down, casts her self to the ground, and squeaks though untouch'd, and far enough from danger. But thou wilt say, *Though all things became subject to one man, though his legions* 10 *possest the Earth and his Navies the Seas, yea though Cæsars own regiment was in the gates, yet* Cato *made his way out.* An honest voice, if it were not flattery: I tell thee he did not make his way, but sneakt and fled out most shamefully: His legs could not carry him off, and therefore hee ran away upon his hands. But it is all one, flye with which he will, it is a plain flight; his busie and searching fear, which in him (by reason of a sudden, unmanly astonishment) was most Sagacious, shew'd him this postern or backdoor, which he most basely fled out at. *But what could that man be afraid of, that had born so often the Assaults of Fortune?* 20 He feared that very same Fortune: *How can that be,* (say'st thou) *seeing he had coped with her so long before?* For that valour let him thank his errour: He believed Fortune (according to her old vogue) to be still inconstant, he expected that the Tyde should turne; but finding her obstinate, and resolved in earnest to the contrary, he feared her last blow, and providing for himself by a most dastardly tendernesse, did with his owne hands dresse and make a wound to his own liking. To be patient, or to suffer as wee please, is not Patience. He could bear the anger, but not the hatred and feud of Fortune. That is poore valour, that bears 30 onely the flourishes and pickearings of an Enemy, but dares not receive his full charge. A weak man will for some time stand under a great burthen; but he that carries it through, and home, is the strongest. *Cato* then was a most base, pusillanimous combatant; hee quitted his ground, and left Fortune in the field, not only unconquer'd, but untir'd, and flourishing with a whole Arme, which hee had not yet drawn bloud from: What Inconstancy can be greater then his, who was more Inconstant than Vertiginous Fortune? Or who more a Coward then he, that fled and ran away swifter and sooner than her wheeles? To call *Cato* 40 then either constant, wise, or good, is most unjust; nay more, it is an Injurie to mankind, to call him a man, who hath deserved

so ill of Wisedome and men, by thinking that any *Cause,* or *Chance* in this World can be worthy of a wise mans death. I would he had read the Conclusion of *Theodorus,* not the dissertation of *Socrates*! *Theodorus Cythereus* most truly affirmed, that there never can be cause enough for a wise man to cast away his life; And he proves it by invincible reason: *For him* (saith he) *that contemns humane Chances, to cast away his life because of them, how contrary is it to his own Judgment, which esteems nothing good, but what is Virtuous, nothing vitious but what is evill?*
10 I wish, when he did read *Socrates,* that he had also understood him! for then he should have heard him condemning that αὐτοχειρίαν, or mad refuge of selfemurther, and commanding him not to stirre out of his appointed station without full Orders from the great Generall of life. Why then dost thou cry up *Cato* for a great leader, who was a most cowardly common Souldier, that forsook his Charge, and betrayed the Fort intrusted to him by the *Prince* of Life? But here thou wilt reply, *that his last nights contemplation, just before he quitted it, was Immortality.* The end he did study it for, made it then unseasonable: And I know not
20 (seeing he was but an Imperfect speculator in the Doctrine of Immortality,) why hee should be so hasty to try whither Eternity was perishable, or not, by casting away his own. He should have expected it, as he did expect the change of Fortune, which till that night he alwaies esteemed Mortall: He should have prepared for it by makeing triall of his Constancie before Eternity.

What praise then either of Patience, or Fortitude hath he deserved? he did no more then the most effeminate, *Hemon* and *Sardanapalus.* O the glorious Act of *Cato* then, equall to his, that handled the *Spindles*! An Act of Women, *Evadne, Jocasta,*
30 and *Auctolia.* An Act of Whores, *Sappho* and *Phædra.* An Act of Wenches, *Thysbe, Biblis, Phillis* and *Anaxarete.* An Act of Boyes, *Iphis* and *Damocles.* An Act of Doting, decrepit men, *Ægeus, Sesostris* and *Timathes.* An Act of Crazie, diseased Persons, *Aristarchus* and *Eratosthenes.* An Act of Madmen, *Aristotle, Empedocles, Timagoras* and *Lucretius.* A rare commendation indeed for a wise man, to have done that which Whores, Wenches and Boyes, sick men and Madmen did, whome either the Impatience of their lust, or Fortune made Impatient of life. Whither thou wilt say, that *Cato* kill'd himself to fly from Fortune,
40 or to find Immortality, thou canst in neither deny his Impatience either of Joy, or else of feare, and in both of life. I would he had been as patient now of life, as he was sometimes of thirst! That

voice of Honour, upon the Sands of *Libya*, was his! where (the *Roman* Army like to perish with thirst) a Common Souldier that had taken up a litle muddy Water in his Helmet, presenting it to him, had in stead of thanks this bitter rebuke,

> *Base man! & couldst thou think Cato alone*
> *Wants courage to be dry, &, but him, none?*
> *Look'd I so soft? breath'd I such base desires,*
> *Not proofe against this Libyc Sun's weak fires?*
> *That shame and plague on thee more justly lye!*
> *To drinke alone, when all our troops are dry.*   10

Here was a glorious *Voice*, and there followes it a more glorious *hand*:

> *For, with brave rage he flung it on the Sand,*
> *And the spilt draught suffic'd each thirsty band.*

This manly Virtue he degenerated from in his last *Act*, and all his friends wisely bending to the present necessity, hee onely broke. The people being all taken, he only fled. To see *Cato* a sufferer in the publicke miserie, had been a Publick comfort; they would have judged it happinesse to have been unhappy with him. It is Honour to suffer with the Honourable, and the 20 Tyranny of Fortune is much allayed, and almost welcome to us, when shee equally rageth against the good and Noble, as against our private selves. If, as he refused the remedy of thirst, he had also rejected this ill remedy against misfortune, his glory had been perfect.

Wee must then be the Patients of life; and of this Patience (which I thinke the greatest of any,) wee have two eminent examples in *Job* and *Tobiah*, who not onely provoked by Fortune, but by their wives also, defended their Calamities in the defense of life. For the other Patience in death (which is the least,) the 30 example of *Abel* sufficed, designed by the wonderfull Counsell of God (untill the manifestation of his Son, that great *Arch-type* of Patience in life and death,) to suffer, though Innocent, a violent and unexperienced death, that the first onset of fate (which was most furious,) meeting in him with an unconquerable Patience, might be somewhat tamed, and the weapons of death having their edge dulled in the first conflict, might afterwards be of lesse terrour to mankind. Just *Abel* was the first that shew'd us the way of dying, when the name of death, as yet untri'd, was most formidable unto life; that he might teach man Patience in his 40 death, and leave it to posterity as a Medicine found out by him.

16 onely *G*: onley *1654*

But when men (by a sad experience grown wise,) found out a greater Evill then death, which to religious men was this sinfull life, and to the miserable and Impatient their own lives; then were *Job* and *Tobiah* set forth the convincing examples of Patience in life, who endured a life more bitter than death, lest by not enduring, they should, to their misery, adde sinne.   They taught the World that Patience was a better Medicine for Evills than death, and withstood the opinions of the Lunatick people. Falsely did *Euripides* (arrogating a laudable Title to death,)
10 terme it

The greatest medicine of Evills,
Κακῶν μέγιστον φάρμακον.

As if he in another place had not term'd it the greatest of Evills. If death then be not its own Medicine, how can it be the Medicine of Evills?   It is an Evill great enough, that it is not the Medicine of Evills ; but that sufficeth not, it is also the greatest Evill. *Æschylus* is in the like errour, for it is called by him

The Physician of incurable Evils,
τῶν ἀνηκέστων κακῶν ἰατρός.

20   A most ridiculous appellation :   How can that be the Physitian of incurable Evills, which is it selfe such an incurable Evill as their owne *Machaon* could not resist?   Equally false is that of *Sophocles*,

The last Curer of diseases is death.
Ἔσθ᾿ ὁ θάνατος λοῖσθος ἰατρὸς νόσων.

If death it selfe be a disease, which must, and shall be healed, how can it be the last curer of diseases?   But these men (after the Common manner of *Physicians*,) held the cure of great Evills to consist in desperate remedies, as obstinate diseases are expell'd
30 by strong and *Diaphoretick* Medicines :   Health indeed is dear unto us, and death, I confesse, puts an end to all its diseases, and to all Medicaments too.   It takes away the disease sooner and oftner then any other remedy ; but these *Poets* themselves (as sick men say of their *Potions*) deny not but it is bitter.

Κακῶς ζῆν κρεῖττον ἢ καλῶς θανεῖν.
It is better to live ill, then to dye well,

Saith *Euripides* himselfe in another place ; such a good opinion had hee of death.   It had beene but a sorry provision for mankind if God had given us no other Medicine against Temporal Evills
40 but death.   The cure of our miserable condition had been both

imperfect and uncertain, and to our sad necessity there had been added necessarie despair, when the cure of small Evils had been by a greater, and the great Evill it self left incurable.

But (Glory to the blessed *Jesus* !) wee are both fully cured, and faithfully cared for ! That which can cure all Evills, must be something that is not Evill ; Therefore death cannot cure them, because it is an Evill ; for God created it not, but it came into the World through the envy of the Divell : Good men hold it to be Evill, & the bad find it so. Thou wilt ask then, what is the Medicine of Evills ?   I answer, it is that, which is the Medicine that strengthens us to bear the violence, and the pangs of death ; that which the very Enemies of it cannot deny to be good, I mean Patience : that which being made Evill by abuse, yet in that state hath been commended by men that were not Evil, by *Seneca* in his *Cato*, *Dion* in his *Melancoma*, and *Philo* in his *Pancratiastes* : So winning and attractive is the Virtue of Patience, that the very shadow of it procures reverence, and makes the very abuse and corruption of it laudable.   If then the *Counterfeit* of it could beautifie vice, and make it amiable even to wise men, what wonder is it, if the *Substance* be a protection and ornament to Virtuous persons ?   This is the Medicine which *Leonides* gave against death.   Let those Titles therefore which death usurped, be vindicated by the right owner.   Patience then is the best medicine of Evills ; It is the cure of the Incurable, the last Physitian, the Ease in death, the mollifying Oyle, the gentle purge, the pleasant Potion, and that I may recover its right to another Title which death usurped from the pen of *Boetius*, *It is a sanctuary that lies alwaies open to the distressed*.   Lastly, lest I should deny that, which even the envy of Fortune could not deny, *Patience* (as *Zeno* elegantly said,) *is the Queen regent of all things*, yea of that rebellious changling Fortune.   But let us adde to the certainty of the cure, the easinesse of comming by the medicine : We need not send for it into *Forraign Regions*, nor dig it out of *Mines*, nor extract it out of the *Veines* of *Herbs*, or the *vital parts* of *beasts* : Wee need not go for it to the *Apothecary*, nay I shall adde, wee need not wish for it ; It is already in our custody, a manuall *Antidote* that is alwaies about us, and in us, effectuall for all things, and ready for all men.   It is a *Physitian* we need not call upon ; not like death, that forsakes the wretched, and those that earnestly long for it, that hath no pitty upon teares, but keeps off,

—— *And will not hear the Crie*
Of distrest man, not shut his weeping Eye.

Hitherto we have taken view but of one side of Patience, and that halfe of her which she opposeth to *Evills.* Every part of her is lovely and excellent : and if we remove now from this Collateral station to a direct, we shall behold her intire beauty, and how well shee deserves of *good.* The *Sacraments* of this Virtue are two : *To suffer Evill : to do good :* Nobly doth she celebrate both ; with her there is no Evill, without her there is no good. I think her the *Mart,* and *Mother-City* of all that is good. Every Virtue is a *Colonie* of Patience, planted and nourished by her. Virtues owe
10 their Original to her, she is part of it, and in every one of them. She is their *holy fire,* their *Vesta,* and *Lararium,* or private Chappell ; they are her *Nuns* or *Virgins,* what ever they have, either sacred or glorious, is from her : To the perfection of man there is nothing more necessary : For as *Brasse* must be first melted, and afterwards cast ; so the hard and rigid matter of Virtues must be softned and dissolved by Patience, that man may become a glorious and living *Statue* of Divinitie. No marvell, that wee require labour and hardnesse in Virtuous persons, seeing wee expect it from *Smiths* ; A certain Just Law of all the World hath exacted it
20 to be the price of Virtue. Beare what thou wouldst not, and thou shalt enjoy what thou wilt. Labour is the good mans purse : Patience is his Gold : Onely an obstinate, sordid Idlenesse makes men poor, not onely in body, but in mind also : Without Patience they cannot possesse their own Soules. Neither Nature, nor Virtue, nor Fortune (and this last thou wilt perhaps think strange,) trust us with their goods without this. Prosperity, when it is lent to man, dispenseth its treasures to none so plentifully, as to the laborious : Without a blow it stroaks us not. The sweet-meats it brings are not eaten, but in the sweat of the face. It was truly
30 said of Fortune,

> *Give bread to the poor, but give him thy fists for sauce.*
> Δὸς πτωχῷ ἄρτον, καὶ κόνδυλον ὄψον ἐπ᾽ αὐτῷ.

The *Snake* will easily slip through our hands, unlesse we grasp her with *Figleaves,* or some knotty, rough grass ; Fortune is very slippery, and without labour, and a strong hand, she will not be held. Honest gaine breeds most Joy, I shall adde most security, when it is gotten with most pain. Labour is the *earnest* we give for after-Joyes, which are an addition, or consequence rather, attending the other fruits of it. Though it goes before them, yet
40 it is refreshed with their following after ; As hunger, which is a Natural sauce, sweetens the meat, and the Joyes of the eater, even

11 fire] sire *1654*   27 dispenseth] dispensenth *1654*

before he eates: Wee look with most delight upon those things which wee think to be our own, and we think them most, which wee have most labour'd for. Patience is a certain *Title* to possession, but labour gives the *Right.* The Mother loves those children best, and as most hers, which shee brought forth with most pain. *Hony* is gathered of *bitter herbes*; they that love not the bitternesse, must not eate of the Honey. *The drones of Attica* (saith *Tzetzes,*) *will not touch the hony of Hymettus, because it is gather'd of Thyme, which the Attic drone cannot endure to light upon.* The Noble *Xenophon* loved no glory, but that which was purchased 10 by his owne Industry.

The glory of God himselfe is not without labour, which he hath shew'd unto us by his works, and amplified in particular natures according to his wisdome, for our example. Wickedly did *Hermogenes* think of that Supreme, eternally active *Mind,* esteeming him to rest, by reason of idlenesse and inefficacie, though elegantly refuted by *Afer* in these words, *his glory is the more in that he hath laboured.* God doth not onely looke upon, and rule the World, he made it also; And which of these, thinkst thou, is most worthy of glory? is it not to have made it? What is more 20 glorious then to have made glory? In the present *Sabbath* and solemnity of Gods rest, the workes which he hath made, declare his glory unto men, whose task also is, *to work.* Besides, this first curious draught of his Almighty hand contributes something to the perfect beauty of his immortal, last one; for the Divine Eye (reflecting upon this *proofe,*) will adorne that building of holinesse and glory with everlasting strength, and an inviolable, Celestial freshnesse. God made not man by a *Fiat,* as he did the rest of the Creatures, but fell to work himself, and like the *Potter* that first tempers, then fashions the Clay, he made him by makeing, 30 not by speaking. That one royall creature capable of felicity, was consecrated for beatitude, and the Divine likenesse with the ceremony of labour: Here man was instructed, before he was made: he received the exemplar of living before he received life: Idlenesse was forbidden him, before he had the Power given him to be active. But when he gave him life, he gave him also with it another *Specimen,* or *Item* of labour, breathing into him, as if he had used respiration (which refresheth the laborious,) to shew man the use of his breath. All things that were created for the service of mankind, were by the manner of their Creation (which was with 40 a *Fiat,* or command,) taught to be obedient and humble: But man was first ordained for Dominion, afterwards for labour; And

God himself, the Lord of all, labour'd in his Creation, that Hee might make him to be in love with his Ordinance, and that God (plotting as it were against himself,) might by that love of man be induced to love him the more, and to esteeme him more his owne Creature then any other, because he onely (like his Creatour) loved Activity, and the use of life. And this I believe is the meaning of *Xenophon* : *Labour* (saith he) *is a certain over-measure, or extraordinary favour of love.*

So glorious an Ornament is Patience, either in suffering, or else in doing, I believe in both (for Labour, without the good of Patience, is good of it selfe,) that for no other end, but to be thought temperate and wise, the *Pythagoreans* commended abstinence, the *Stoicks* severity, the *Cynicks* exceeded to rigour, the *Gymnosophists* to cruelty, and a face of madnesse and despair. Every one of these adorned his *Heresie* with Patience, and all the rude statues they erected to wisedom, were crowned with this Virtue. *Edesius* being sent by his Father to traffick into *Greece*, quitted the *Merchant*, and turn'd *Philosopher* : His Father upon his return receiving him with stripes, and hee patiently bearing them, asked him, what he had learnt in the Schooles of the Philosophers ? He answered, *To bear your anger dutifully :* With the same testimony did another Scholer of *Zeno* adorne the *Stoa* : but *Possidonius* was hardlier provoked then either ; he was so tortured with bodily pain, as if the disease had maliciously laboured to confute his principles : but how far it prevailed, appeares best by his own words ; *It is to no purpose*, (said he) *vex me as much as thou canst, thou shalt never make me give thee an ill word.* So carefull was he of the reputation of his Master. But *Dionysius Heracleotes*, not able to rule his passions, lost the repute of a Philosopher. So much doth that Majesty and tacite reverence wee admire in Virtue depend upon Patience.

Patience doth that for the private man, which their *life-guards* doe for *Kings* : It keepes him safe, and reverenc'd. It is the minds main-guard, that preserves the Authority of Virtue, and secures the Virtuous person, lest Evills should make him Evill. It is in the oppressed a certain tutelar Angel, and the sacred Guardian of their Spirits from Affliction. Most appositely did *Halitargius* call Patience *the Conservatrix of our Condition.* O how great is the Glory of Virtue, whose Guard and attendant is Patience, the Queene of all things ! She is not onely the Crown and Ornament of Philosophie, but the badge and Garland of the Christian warriour. She is not onely honour'd by the Impatient

13 *Cynicks*] *Cynick 1654* (?)

themselves, but by the furious and Salvage. *Abraames*, almost slaine and martyr'd by the *Indian* Infidels, did with this one weapon not onely resist, but overcome a whole City: And that with more expedition then *Cæsar*, and with better successe then *Alexander*; for to such admiration and reverence of his person did his patience drive them, that in the very midst of the storme his persecutors became suddenly calme, begging forgivenesse with teares, and with the generall consent of the people elected him for their Patron and President, whom a little before (having not seen this pearle of Patience,) they design'd for destruction and death. It 10 was the Majesty of this Immoveable, Serene Virtue, that forced them to this miraculous Election, adjudging it of most royall Excellencie, and most worthy of Soveraignty.

Leander told the Fathers, met at *Toledo*, that *Patience would either win, or overcome her adversaries.* *Solon* knew this : For being checkt by some standers by, because he suffered an uncivill fellow to spit upon him, he answered : *Fisher-men, that they may catch one whiting, suffer themselves to be dashed over with the fome and flowings of the Sea-waves ; and shall not I do the like to catch a man ?* Whither he catched him, or not, I cannot tell : But I 20 am sure, that *John Fernandius*, a Servant of *JESUS CHRIST*, and a Fisher of men, catch'd a whole Kingdome with that very baite. Hee preaching to the *Indians* in the street, one barbarous Infidel, having gathered his mouth full of sordid spittle, came pressing through the crowd to the place where he stood, and delivered it just in his face ; but he nothing moved therewith, and neither rebuking the Barbarian, nor discomposing his former gesture, persisted in his Masters businesse, and preach'd on : His Doctrine though powerfull, after the silent Rhetorick of this publick example, might for that time have beene well spared. 30 Here was the foundation of the Churches of *Japan* and *Amangucia* : This very *Indian* (and none before him) becomming the first fruits of that region unto *CHRIST*. So glorious a document of Patience made him envy our Divine Philosophy, that envy made him Ambitious, and his holy Ambition made him a Christian. So gainfull an Industry is Patience, and such a compendious Art of overcomming. Most wholsome is the advice of *Pimenius* : *Malice* (saith he) *never overcomes malice, you must overcome malice with goodnesse :* But if we could overcome one Evill with another, why will wee not reserve that Glory for Virtue ? By such a blood- 40 lesse Victory did *Motois* overthrow his Adversary ; from whom he fled most valiantly, lest he should offend him ; I do not say with

his hands, but with his sight; for Patience hath no hands, but shoulders.   His Adversary pursues : *Motois* had lockt himself up, & became his own prisoner, esteeming it guilt enough, that another could be angry with him : But hearing that his Enemy was come in (being only Impatient till he had shewed more Patience,) hee breakes open the door, bids him welcome, and like one that had offended, desires to be forgiven, and afterwards feasts him.   This story I have touch'd upon, that thou maist see how powerfull an Instrument of tranquillity, and a quiet, happy life, Patience is, that
10 makes peace to beare fruit in another mans soyl, and civilizeth forraigners.   How fruitfull then is she at home? How prosperous a dresser of Virtues in himselfe is the patient man, that will not suffer the propagation of Vices in another?

But *Leander* said, that Patience doth either overcome, or else win her Enemies; I say, she doth both win and overcome : She wins men, and overcomes Fortune; nay, she makes her (though unwilling) a most officious servant of Goodnesse.   The name of Patience is not an empty, titular Honour; it hath also very large and princely revenues for the maintenance of Virtue.   That Fable
20 of the Divine in holy *Maximus* is truth.   He saith, *that wise men dwell in the shadow of a tree, which the more the people cut it, growes the more.*   It strives, and vies with the *Iron* ; or to borrow the *Poets* expression, θανατῷ ζῇ, καὶ τομῇ φύεται,

> *It lives when kill'd, and brancheth when 'tis lopt.*

His own *Mythology* is most elegant : *By this tree* (saith he) *is signified wisedom, which turnes misfortunes into Ornaments, trouble into Virtue, losse into gain, and scars into beauty:* For the Patient and wise liver, like the Serpent of *Lerna*, when he is most mangled, is most entire ; he drinkes in fresh spirits through
30 his very wounds, his courage is heightned by them, and his spilt blood, like dew, doth cherish and revive him,

> *Like some faire* Oke, *that when her boughes*
> *Are cut by rude hands, thicker growes :*
> *And from those wounds the Iron made,*
> *Resumes a rich and fresher shade.*

The benefit then wee receive from Patience, is twofold : It diminisheth the sorrowes of the body, and increaseth the treasure of the mind : Or to speak more properly, there is one great benefit it doth us, It turnes all that is *Evill* into *Good.*   Most
40 apposite to this, is that of *Nazianzen,*

> *Patience digesteth misery.*

11 home?] home, ? *1654*

Concoction and Digestion of meats are the daily miracles of the stomack : they make dead things contribute unto life, and by a strange *Metamorphosis* turne Herbes, and almost all living Creatures into the Substance of Man, to preserve his particular *Species*: No otherwise doth Virtue by Patience (which is her stomack,) transform and turne all damages into benefits and blessings, and those blessings into it self. *Lupines,* or bitter Pulse, if steep'd in water, will grow sweet and nourishing: Patience doth macerate miseries, to fatten it selfe with them. Certaine Divine Raies breake out of the Soul in adversity, like 10 sparks of fire out of the afflicted *flint.* The lesser the Soule minds the body, the lesser she adheres to sensibility, shee is by so much the more capable of Divinity, and her own Nature. When her Den of flesh is secure and whole, then is she in darkness, & sleepes under it : When it is distressed and broken, then is she awake, and watcheth by some Heavenly *Candle,* which shines upon her through those breaches. The wounds of the Body are the windowes of the Soul, through which she looks towards Heaven ; *light* is her *provision,* shee feedes then upon *Divinity.* Sublime is that rapture of the most wise *Gregory,* 20

Τροφὴ μία πᾶσιν ἀρίστη
Δαίνυσθαι μεγάλοιο Θεοῦ νόον ἠδὲ φαεινῆς
Ἕλκειν ἐκ Τριιάδος σελας ἄπλετον.——

——*one food the best for all*
Is to feed on the great Gods mind, & draw
An Immense light from the bright Trinity.

Death it self, which the *lust* of eating brought into the World *inedible,* or as *Zeno* saith, *indigestible,* is eaten, digested and transubstantiated into life by Patience, begun in *Abel,* and per-fected in *JESUS CHRIST.* So that now, that saying of 30 *Pittho,* who affirm'd, *that there was no difference betwixt death and life,* is no longer a *Paradox* ; nor need we make use of that shrewd exaggeration of *Euripides* : *who knowes* (said he) *but this which we call life, is death, and death life? we see, that men, when they are (as we speak) alive, are then only sick, but the dead neither sicken, nor suffer any sorrowes :* Certainly the death of a good liver is eternal life.

Every Action of a wise man is a certain emulation of Death ; wee may see it exprest in his patience. The Soul by this Virtue disintangles, and frees her selfe from the troubles of Mortality : For 40

the frivolous flesh burning with *fevers*, or drown'd in *dropsies*, or any other diseases, the attendants of corruption, which possesse and fill up the narrow Fabrick of Man; the Soul (as in great inundations, when the lower roomes are overflown) ascends to the battlements, where she enjoyes a secure, healthfull ayre, leaving the *ground-roomes* to the tumult and rage of the distemper'd *humours.* She ascends thither, where griefe cannot ascend. *Carneades,* comming to visit *Agesilaus* grievously tormented with the Gout, and turning his back to be gone, as if impatient of the
10 violence and insolencie of the disease (whose custome it is to shew litle reverence towards the best men, the prerogative of Virtue can give no protection to Nature,) *Agesilaus* pointing from his feet to his brest, calls him back with this Check, *stay* Carneades, *the pain is not come from thence hither.* Hee shew'd by this, that his mind was in health, though his feet were diseased, and that the pain had not ascended thither, where the Soule sate in-throned. At this height she hath two priviledges more then ordinary; she is lesse affected with the body, because at some distance from it; and hovers above griefe, because above sensi-
20 bility; shee is nearer to God, and dresseth her selfe by his beames which she enjoyes more freely, as from a kind of *Balconie,* or refreshing place, having onely a *Knowledge,* but no *Sense* of the bodies affliction. From this place she overlookes the labours and conflicts of the flesh, as *Angels* from the windowes of Heaven behold Warre, and the Slaughter of distracted men. One bene-fit more shee hath by Patience, that though shut up in the body, yet shee can have a tast of her glorious posthume liberty. Death looseth the Soule from the body, it breaks in sunder the secret bonds of the blood, that she may have the full use of her
30 wings, and be united to Divinity. Patience, though it doth not quite loosen the chaine, yet it lengthens it, that she may take the aire, and walk some part of the way towards Home: Though it frees not the Soul from the body, yet it gives her liberty and dominion over it. He that is tyed up by a long Cord, is within the compasse allowed him untyed, and a free man. The Spirit of man incensed by adversities, and collected into it selfe, is by a certain *Antiperistasis* made more ardent and aspiring: *Fire* is never stronger, nor more intense then amongst *Water*; In the bosome of a cloud it breakes forth into thunder: So this Divine
40 Spark, which God hath shut up in Vessels of Clay, when all the passages of pleasures are stopt, his raies (which before were

24 distracted men *G*: distractem en *1654*

diffused and extravagant) returne into it selfe, and missing their usuall vent, break forth with such violence, as carries with it sometimes the very body, and steales the whole man from passion and mortality. The *Levitie* of fire is of greater force, then the *Gravity* and Massinesse of Earth : His *Spirit* is unresistable, and the unknown force of it will blow up the greatest *Mountains*, and the strongest *Castles* this earth affords.

Hitherto have I discoursed of outward *Evills*, I shall now consider the Inward, and how Patience is their Antidote. You have seen her Prerogative over Fortune, and reputed *Evills*, which 10 are called *Evills*, because they seem to be so, not because they are so; as disgrace, grief, and poverty. All these are but fictitious *Evils*, which Custom and Humane error have branded with that injurious denomination : for in these contingencies there is no reall *Evill*, but the *Evill* of opinion; neither is any man miserable but in his own conceit, and by comparison. The glory of Patience would be but poor and trivial, if it could doe no more then take away, or beare with such frivolous and fictitious troubles as these : If it prevailed onely against *Evills*, which we do not suffer, but invent. Its true glory is, that it subdues true 20 *Evills* : Not that it bears them, but that it removes them far from us : Not that it endures them, but that it abstaines from them : For truly to suffer *Evil*, is to do *Evil*, whose *Agent* alwaies the *Patient* is, by reason of a most ill impatience : But Patience is onely excellent, because it suffers not. This worst kind of *Evil* is therefore the greater, because when 'tis in acting, it is not seen ; and were it not afterwards felt, there would be no place left for Virtue. This is the usuall method of Vice, a flattering, *Comical* entrance, and a *Tragical exit.* The force and malice of Evil Actions may be gathered by their Nature : They are so powerfully 30 hurtful, that when they cease to be, they cease not to torment us : and so malignant, that while we act them, they flatter us, that being Acted, they may afflict us : While we are doing them, they conceal and deny themselves ; but being done, they appear to our sorrow. Wherefore he that will lead a blessed, a joyfull, and a peaceful life, must make it his whole work, to do no work, but what Religion and Virtue shall approve of. What peace and security can he enjoy that will revenge himselfe, (what more would cruelty have?) according to his own lust ? What life can he be said to live, that kills himselfe to please his inordinate 40 affections ? What joy can he have, whose troubled conscience is his continual Executioner, racking and tormenting him in the

22 but that] but than *1654*

very embraces of smiling Fortune? No outward *Fomentations* will serve turne against that *Indisposition* to which *fevers* and *fire* are but *coolers.* Wee can provide against the violence of winter and Summer-weather when and how we please: But the inward *heats* and *colds*, the raging *accessions* of the *Spirit* admit no cure. Patience, though Fortune should assist her, will never heal the wounds of conscience.

He that suffers by the guilt of Conscience, endures worse torments then the *wheel*, and the *saw*: As that heat which ascending
10 from the liver, and the region of the heart, doth diffuse it selfe through the body, is greater then the united flames of the *dog-star* and the *Sun.* What torturing invention of *Amestris, Pherotima,* or *Perillus* did ever so afflict distress'd wretches, as the fury of his owne Conscience did torment *Orestes*, though freed from all men but himself? no Tyrant is so cruel as a guilty spirit: Not *Scylla* with his *prison, Sinis* with his *Isthmian pine, Phalaris* with his *bull, Sciron* with his *Rock*, nor *Faunus* in his *Inne.* The *Pelusians* when they punished *Parricides*, conceived no torture so answerable to the heynousnesse of the crime, as this inward
20 *ª Pliny mentions this punishment: the parricide after his apprehension, to augment the horror of his conscience, was first whipt with rods dipt in the blood of his murthered parents: and afterwards together with a dog, an ape, and a cock, (Creatures which shew litle reverence towards their sires) he was thrust alive into a strong sack, and so thrown into the Sea.*
30
Divine revenge; neither the ª *Sack*, nor the *Limekil* pleased them so much as this gnawing worm, the terrible and luctual excogitation of the wise *Father* of Nature. They ordered therefore, and enacted it for a Law, that the murtherer for three daies and three nights should be pent up in some narrow roome together with the naked body of the slaine, and be forced to look upon it, whither he would, or not; which was effected by putting him in such a posture, as permitted him not to look any way, but just upon the dead. The *Sicilian* Tyrant himselfe knew that conscience was a more cruell torment then the *bull* of *brasse.* This made him spare the most unnaturall and bloody offenders, that they might be tormented, not with scalding metalls, and glowing Iron, but by a damning conscience. The first penaltie for murther was conscience: The first Actor of a violent death was punished with life: He that first saw, and introduced death, was thought worthy of no other punishment, but the security of life, which he
40 first shewed to be not secure: for it is a more mercilesse punishment then death, to have long life secured with a killing conscience. So he that brought murther first into the World, was first punished

with the terrours of conscience: Which are then most torturing, when health and strength are the capital punishments. The *Protoplasts* themselves, the parents of death, and of mankind too, who gave us death before they gave us life, thought it a greater plague then death, to be still alive, and yet to be guilty of death? They would have fled to death, to flye from themselves. Apposite to this is that of *Marius Victor*,

> ——*They faine would (if they might)*
> *Descend to hide themselves in Hell. So light*
> *Of foot is vengeance, and so near to sin,* 10
> *That soon as done, the Actors do begin*
> *To fear and suffer by themselves: Death moves*
> *Before their Eyes: Sad dens, and duskie groves*
> *They haunt, and hope (vain hope which fear doth guide!)*
> *That those dark shades their inward guilt can hide.*

You see now that conscience, even amongst ᶜ the *Pelusians*, was held a legal and politick punishment, that in *Phalaris* it was a Tyrannical devise, in *Cain* the Divine vengeance, and in *Adam* and *Eve*, the Justice of Nature. God, Nature, Reason, and fury it selfe (which in this case must not be defined madnesse,) do all beare witnesse, that selfe-condemnation, or the guilt of conscience is of all others the most bitter and avenging torment.

ᶜ *The inhabitants of Pelusium, a town in the borders of* Egypt, *now called* Damiata; *It was built by* Peleus *the fratricide, from whom the Citizens descended.* 20

Adde to this, that the certainty of it is as infallible, and inevitable, as the extremity and fiercenesse of it are implacable: there was never any Tyrant so cruel, but would pardon some offender: There was none so severely inquisitive, but some might either escape from him, or deceive him: But the rigour of conscience permits neither favour, flight, nor fraud. It is utterly 30 inexorable, and neither our feete will serve us to run away, nor our hands to free us: whither shall a man run from himselfe, from the secrets of his own spirit, from his life? No man can be an Impostour or dissembler with his own heart, no man can undo what he hath already done: to have sinned is the remediless plague of the Soul. It was a slow expression of *Victor*, that *Vengeance is near to sinne.* It is swifter then so: It is not *consectaneous*, or in chase of it, but *coetaneous* with it, and its *fostersister*: The punishment hath the same birth with the offence, and proceeds from it; It is both the *Sister*, and the *Daughter* of it: 40 Wickednesse cannot be brought forth without its penalty: The

brest that conceives the one, is big with the other, and when the
one is borne, he is delivered of both. It is a fruitfullnesse like
that of *Mice*, whose young ones are included the one in the other,
and generate in the very wombe. Conscience, while man thinkes
of Evill, even before he acts, doth rebuke that thought : so that
the punishment is præexistent to the crime, though in the reigne
of Virtue it is noiselesse and uselesse ; as penal Lawes are dead
letters, untill they are quickned by offenders. It is then in its
minority, and without a *sting,* or else it is asleep, untill the Cry of
10 Sinne awakes it. In the state of Evill, Conscience is the first and
the last revenger : when smal offences are wiped out, enormous
crimes like capital letters will still remain.

No man can find a Sanctuary to save *him* from *himself.* No
evill doer can so fly for refuge, as to be *secure,* though he may be
safe : Hee will be afraid in that place, where he thought not to fear :
Though he fears not the friends of the murthered, yet he finds
that within him, which makes him sore afraid : He may escape
the Executioner and the sword, but he will be overtaken by
himselfe ; and being safe, hee will be afraid even of his safety :
20 Though he may find fidelity in his fellow-Tyrants, yet shall he
find none in his own bosome, which is ever clamorous, and spues
out blood and guilt. Nature deviseth such a punishment for evill
doers, as that which tyed living Malefactors unto the putrid
Carkasses of dead men, that the horrour and stench of them
might afflict their spirits, and the quick flesh be infected and
devoured by the dead and rotten. The *punishment* sticks fast
unto us after the *offence,* whose carkasse is terrour of Conscience,
Shame, and a gnawing remorse, that feeds still upon the faulty,
but is not satisfied. The guilty person can have noe peace,

30   *But night and day doth his owne life molest,*
         And bears his Judge and witnesse in his brest.

Adde to this, that Reason which in all other pressures and
misfortunes is the great Auxiliary and Guardian of man, is in an
offended Conscience his greatest Enemy, and imploys all her
forces to his vexation and ruine.

Fortune therefore is not the onely cause of our contristation ;
we our selves do arm adversities, and put a sword into the hand
of griefe to wound us with ; we are sticklers against our selves.
Evill Actions afflict more then Evill Fortune ; We are not onely
40 troubled that it was *Chaunce,* but that it was our *Choice.* It is the
worst kind of misery, to be made miserable by our owne approbation. That evill which we procure to our selves, must needs

grieve us more, then that which we casually suffer : Noe damage is so dolefull, as a condemning conscience. Truly, I do believe, that the onely misfortune of Man is *Sinne.* And so very bad and mischievous a Cheat it is, that when it is most punished, wee think it most prospers ; neither can Fortune be justly termed Evil, but when she is the Assistant of Evill men, and the surety for Evill doing. This permitted successe makes the affaires of the most unrighteous to be esteemed Just : This is a felicity like that of beasts, which we put into pleasant and well watered pastures, that they may be fed for slaughter. Against this true misfortune, 10 as well as the false and seeming, Patience must be our Antidote ; not by bearing, but by abstaining from it. Patience in this Case must elevate it selfe, and passe into a virtuous anger and contempt of sinfull prosperity : We must be piously impatient of all their proffers and poisonous allurements ; Impatient, I say, that we may patiently overcome them.

Therefore as I have formerly exhibited the *Art* of *bearing well* to be the onely remedy against Fortune : So now I shall demonstrate to you, that the *Art* of *abstaining well,* is the sole medicine against these true and inward misfortunes : Differing diseases must 20 have different cures. Patience is the poyson that kills Fortune, and the Balm that heales her stripes : but a sacred impatience, or abstinence from Sinne is the Antidote of Conscience ; and the *Basis* or foundation of this holy impatience is transcendent and triumphant Patience. To mitigate or overcome Fortune is a trivial trick : Flattery will do it, if we can but descend to approve of, and commend all that she doth. To preserve the peace of Conscience, wee must be rigid, and censorious : We must speak home, and truly : We must examine before we Act, and admit of no Action that wil be a just cause but for to blush. The approaches of 30 Fortune are abstruse : She moves not within the light of Humane wisedome ; or if she doth, the strength of her Prerogative lies betwixt *Willingnesse* and *Constraint* : It is a kind of *fatal fooling* : Man playes with his *Stars* untill they hurt him : But the cause of an evill Conscience is within our view, and may be prevented by Counsell ; For no man can Sinne against his *Will,* or without his *Knowledge.* One naile must drive out another : He that would avoyd damnation, must avoid also those things which are damnable : He cannot grieve too much, that grieves only to prevent Eternal griefe. The helps we use against Fortune are *after-games.* But the *Salves* 40 of Conscience must precede the wound ; the cure of spirituall diseases is their *prevention.* In the affaires of this World the best

man is the experienced : But in the distresses and affaires of Conscience, he is the wisest that is most ignorant.   A noxious Knowledge is death, and every Sinner is a Fool.   The wisedome of *Doves* is innocence, and that which makes the *light* to shine is its *simplicity*.   Light is a Type of Joy, and Darknesse of Sorrow : Joy is the fruit of innocence, and sorrow of Sinne.   The sorrow we take for Fortune is hurtfull : Those teares, like tempestuous droppings, if not kept out, will rot the house : But the sorow for sinne is healing.   Penitential tears are the *Oile* of the Sanctuary :
10 God gives them, and afterwards accepts them : they both cleanse us and cherish us.   When *Marble* weepes, it washeth off the dust : Worldly teares are the waters of *Marah* ; the tree that sweetens them, must be shewed by the Lord : The waters of the pool
* *the word in the* * *Bethesda* heal'd not, untill the *Angel* stirred
Hebrew   signifies, them ; without true remorse teares profit not :
the house of pow- but if they have that Ingredient, they are
ring out : *which in*
a secret Allegorie showers which the Lord hath blessed, and must
may very well con- not be stopped, although they might.   As
cerne man. courage, and a joyfull heart are the *ripe fruits* of
20 innocence, so shame and sorrow are the hopefull *buds* and *prim-roses* of it.   Contrition is the infancie of Virtue : Therefore that sadnesse must not be expelled which expelleth Vice.   It is an invention of the Deity to destroy Sinnes :   That they might be either unfruitfull, or fruitfull onely to their owne destruction : For this we have two instances from Nature, in the *Mule* and the *Viper* :   Whereof the one is barren, and the other unhappily fruitfull.   Nature is carefull that Evills may not multiply, or if they do, that they may not prosper.   The *Mule* is barren, lest there should be an increase of Monsters.   Apposite to this, is that
30 saying of *Gregory Cerameus*, H᾿ γάρ κακία &c, *Evils* (saith he) *are denyed from God the power of propagating, as mules have not the faculty to preserve their kind by generating one another.*   The *Viper* notwithstanding is a mother, but shee brings forth her owne destruction :   The birth of her young ones is her death.   So sorrow, that is the child of sinne, is the death of it also.   Let therefore this saving destroyer of sins be made much off, let this godly sorrow be still cherished, and never rebuked : he that dryes up his teares, before he is cleansed, takes delight in his filthinesse, and like the lothsome drunkard, would sleep in his vomit :
40 Penitent afflictions should never be resisted but by precaution.

Hee then that would not drink of this *Wormwood*, must be sure to refuse the *sugred venom* of sinne :   No man is Evill for nothing. Every defect in life is occasioned by a defect of Patience: because we cannot endure to be constantly good: because we are impatient of continuall holinesse. Two Evills attend upon Sinners, the *Evill* of *sin*, and the *Evill* of *Punishment*, which is the *Evil* of *sorrow* : To escape the last, we must abstain from the first : wee must be either impatient of the first, or else the patients of the last : Unlesse wee will suffer a litle to avoid offences, wee must suffer much after we have fallen into them. A short displeasure is better then a long torment : This previous Patience of abstaining, frees us from two subsequent Evils : The ro *pain* of *Conscience* untill we repent, and after that the *pain* of *Penitence* : These two are the *Appendants*, or retinue of every sinne ; A seasonable, innocent forbearance is the *sense* against them both : one small griefe averts these two great ones : How wholesome and comfortable is that Patience which prevents sinne and sorrow, the Consequent of it? But Virtue, when it is most healthfull, is in the estimation of some reputed to be poyson : For no other reason do they reject it, of whome *Theodotus* elegantly sings,

> *Virtues faire cares some people measure*   20
> *For poys'nous works, that hinder pleasure.*

This Patient abstinence from Evill is the Mother of holy Joy, it keeps the mind pleasant and serene : What is there, or what can there be more beneficial, or delightfull to man, then a pure, innocent conscience, where all the *Virtues* (like busie *Bees*) are in constant action, as in a fair, *flowry field*, or rather in *Paradise*? where all is Divine, all Peacefull, nothing polluted, no feare, no distraction. In this state, as *Theophanes* saith, *The wise man is adorned with a Godlike Conscience, and a mind becomming the very Deity*. What is there more joyful, then to be master of such 30 a Power, as cannot be violated by Tyrants and Torments? It was a golden and Victorious saying of *Tiburtius* : *Every punishment is poor, when a pure Conscience keepes us company*: For as the guilty can receive no comfort : So the Innocent cannot lose his Joy. The Joy of Conscience is Natures recompence, the coalescent reward, or fruite of integrity, an entailed happinesse, the native blandishment of life, and the minds mighty purchase : What happier gaine can be, then to rejoice alwaies, for what wee have done but once? or what greater damage then an unrighteous gain? It was bravely said by *Chilo, that the heaviest losse was to* 40 *bee chosen before base gain :* That will grieve us but once, the other alwaies. The losse of temporal goods will trouble us but for a time, but a lost Conscience will torment us Eternally. What greater liberty can there be, then not to fear any thing? And what can he be affeard of, that is not frighted by the guilt of his own spirit? when *Periander* was asked, *what liberty was?* he answered, *A good Conscience.* And another saith, that

> *Man should with Virtue arm'd, and hearten'd be,*
> *And innocently watch his Enemy :*
> *For fearlesse freedom, which none can controule,*
> *Is gotten by a pure and upright Soul.*

Sinne makes remisse and cowardly spirits to be the constant slaves of misery : what liberty, yea, what joy can he have, or what dares he do,

> *Whose guilty soul with terrours fraught, doth frame*
> *New torments still, and still doth blow that flame*
> *Which still burns him : nor sees what end can be*
> *Of his dire plagues, and fruitful penalty ?*
> *But fears them living, and fears more to dye.*
> *Which makes his life a constant Tragedy.*

Therefore to preserve the mirth and peace of Conscience, righteous, or honest Actions are mainly conducing, and should be alwaies our imployment ; for this is the appointed *task* of man, and it is his *mysterie* too. The *hand* is the best *Sacrifice.* The Antient *Portugals* used to dedicate to their Gods the right hands of their captives ; but offer thou thine own, and not anothers. To be onely without Vice, is a vitious commendation : Nay, it is not commendable at all, but self-indulgence, or a flattering of our owne corrupt inactivity. To such a passe is man come, that he is not ashamed to do lesse for Virtue, then the vitious will do for Vice. It is a most poore and sordid glory, to be onely not numbred amongst the bad : It is a base degree of praise, to be reputed onely not base. To be without Vice, is not to be good : Not to be vitious, and to be Virtuous, are two things. To refrain from Evill, is scarse not Evill, especially if we proceed no further: For to be able to be good, and not to be throughly so, is, if not Evill, a neighbourhood to Evill. True praise consists not in a bare abstinence from Evill, but in the pursuance & the perform-ance of good. It sufficeth not therefore that we doe nothing which may *afflict* us, but we must withall doe something that may *exhilarate* us. This we must remember, that to do good is one thing, and to become good is another; Although we cannot become good, unlesse wee doe good; But we become good, not because we have done good works, but because we did them well. Discretion, which considers the manner of doing good, orders the Action so excellently, that oftentimes there is more goodnesse in the *manner*, then in the *Action* : What will it availe us to do good, if it be not well done ? It is to write faire, and then to poure the Inke upon it. Actions cease to be good, unlesse well acted, they are like excellent *colours* ill layed on. The more glorious thy intention is, the more carefully thou must manage it. Indiscretion is most evident in matters of importance : One *drop* of *Oyle* upon *Purple*, is sooner seen, then a whole *quart* that is spilt upon *Sack-cloath.*

The *Ermyn* keepes his whitenesse unstained with the hazard of his life : Hee values himselfe at a most sordid rate, that esteems lesse of *Virtue*, then this beast doth of his *skin* ; that prefers a foule life to a fair death, that loves his blood more then his honour, and his body more then his Soule. *Ennius* saith, *that the way to live, is, not to love life.* Life is given us for another cause, then meerly to live : he is unworthy of it, that would live onely for the love of life; the greatest cause of life is Virtue : what more absolute madnesse can there be, then to make life the cause of sin, yea the cause of death,

And for lifes sake to lose the crown of life ?

What greater unhappinesse, then to dye eternally by refusing death ? The Virtuous youth *Pelagius*, rather then he would lose his Innocence, suffered the most exquisite and studyed torments of that impure Tyrant *Habdarrhagmanus* : He suffered many deaths before he was permitted to dye : Hee saw his limbs, his hands, and his sinewes cut in sunder, and lying dead by him, while he yet lived. This preservation of their *honour* some chast *beauties* have paid dearly for. It cost *Nicetas* his tongue, *Amianus* his Eye, Saint *Briget* her face, *Apollonia* her teeth, and *Agatha* her breasts : The lovely *Cyprian Virgin* paid her life for it.

Nature even for her self doth lay a snare,
And handsome faces their own traitours are.

The beauty of Chastity is best preserved by deformity, and the purity of life by a contemptible shape.

The *Shoomaker* is carefull of the neatnesse of a *shooe*, which is made to be worn in durt and mire: And shall man be negligent to adorn his Soul, which is made for Heaven, and the service of the deity ? Every artificer strives to do his worke so, as none may find fault with it ; And shall we do the works of life perfunctorily and deceitfully ? All that makes man to be respected, is his worke, as the fruite doth make the Tree : and a good work can never be too much respected. Keepe thy selfe alwaies in respect by doing good : Thy own dignity is in thy own power : If thy works be good, thou shalt be accounted good too ; If better then any, thou shalt be acknowledged for the best. Man is the *effect* of his own *Act,* he is made by those things which he himself makes : Hee is the work of his own hands. A rare priviledge, that permits men, and impowers them to make themselves : Thou hast leave to be whatsoever thou wouldst be. God would not limit thy happinesse : He left thee power to encrease it, to polish and beautifie thy selfe according to thy own mind. Thy friend, or thy neighbour cannot do it : Thy owne good must be thy owne industry. Virtue, because she would be crosse to Fortune, is not adventitious. It is our great happinesse, that this great good must not be borrowed. *Blessed be that Divine mercy, which hath given us means to be saved without the assistance of our neighbours, who have endeavoured to damn us !* That almighty hand which first Created man in the Image of his Creatour, finished him not, but left some things for him to doe, that he might in all things resemble his maker. It is one thing to be an *Idol,* or *Counterfeit,* and another to be a *lively Figure* and *likenesse* : There are many *Coppies,* which are not assimilant to their *Originals,* like *Pictures* that have not so much as an *ayre* of those *faces* they were drawn by. To the *Politure* and *sweetning* of the Divine *Image,* there are some *lines* expected from thine owne hand. If some expert Statuary, suppose *Phidias* himselfe, should leave unfinished some excellent peece, like that Statue of *Minerva* at *Athens,* and out of an incurious wearinesse, give himself to some obscure and Artlesse imployment, or to meere Idlenesse, wouldst not thou much blame and rebuke him for it ? And canst thou deserve any lesse, if by a loose and vitious life thou wilt either totally deface the Image of God in thy selfe, or else leave it unfinished ? Doest thou think that God is maimed, seeing thou doest leave his Image without hands, I mean, without good works ? Dost thou think that he is blind, seeing thou dost extinguish, or put quite out that discerning light and informing wisdome which hee hath given thee ? Hee that doth not integrally compose himself, and will not carefully strive for perfection, would represent God to be imperfect, and a Monster. *Virtuous manners* (saith holy *Maximus*) *are types of the Divine goodnesse, by which*

God descends to be represented by man, assuming for a body those holy habits, and for a soule the Innocent dictates of wisdome in the spirit, by which he makes those that are worthy, to become Gods, and seals them with the true character of Virtue, bestowing upon them the solid riches of his infallible and immortal Knowledge.

Work then while it is day, while it is life-time; work and cease not : Finish this expectation, this great spectacle, not of men onely, but of God and Angels. Remember that the rewards and applause of this World are but a *Paint* of eternity : The solid and perma-nent glory is given in Heaven, *When every man shall have praise* 10 *of God.* The *Limbner* is carefull to beautifie and shew his utmost skill in that *peece*, which hee knowes to be intended for judicious eyes : Thou art not to paint, but really to make a living Image of the Divine mind, which also must be examined and judged by that searching eye, from which nothing can be hidden : have a care that no *ill mixture*, nothing *disproportionable*, nothing *uneven* or *adul-terate* may be found in it. The presents we offer to the true God, must be true and solid works, not the fictitious oblations of *Jupiter Milichus* : Why wilt thou delight in a maimed Soule, or which is worse, in a Soul whose best part is dead ? Thou hadst rather have 20 a member cut off, then hanging dead by thee : Thou wouldst then onely wish for its company, when it would be no hindrance to thee. And canst thou endure the immortal Soul to be sick of death, to be sick in his best part, in the head ? wilt thou suffer thy mind to drowse, to be paralytical and senselesse, never thinking of God, nor of doing good ? In such a *liver*, the beauty of his immortal part is crusted over with an incurable leprosie ; and reason, which is the Soules *Countenance*, is most ingloriously ecclipsed. The Task of life is to labour, and the Sacrament of the Soule is to work rationally. Idlenesse is a *Parenthesis* in the *line* of life : When 30 we do nothing, wee do not live.

Slothfullnesse is a dead *Existence*, a kind of *sleep* when we are awake : That life is empty, that is not filled with the care of living well. It was truly said by *Possidonius*, that one day of a learned mans life, was more pleasant, then all the years of the unlearned : One houre, one minute well spent, is to be preferred before a sin-full, voluptuous *for-ever*. *Time* is a sacred thing : it flowes from Heaven, it is a thred spun from thence by the motion and circum-volution of the spheres. It is an emanation from that place, where eternity springs. The right use of it, is to reduce it to its Original : 40 If we follow time close, it will bring us to its Fountain. It is a *clue* cast down from Heaven to guide us thither. It is the younger

T

brother of eternity, the one must be sought in the other. It hath some assimilation to Divinity: it is partly knowable, and partly not: Wee move in it, and wee see it not: It is then most invisible; when most present. If we be carefull of it, the benefit is ours: If wee neglect it, we cast away our selves. Hee lives not at all, that lives not well: And hee that lives ill, shall dye worse: Hee suffers a living and sensible death: It is death, because it wants the fruit of life; and it is sensible, because it is with losse and punishment. Many ill livers comfort themselves with 10 a vain conceit, that the state of death is senselesse: But Vice and Idlenesse are more malitious deaths, they carry with them the penalty of sense: They are fertill in evills, and barren of good, like a cursed ground that bringes forth nothing but thornes and thistles.

You expect *grapes* from your *vines*, & *corn* from your *Fields,* but no Fruit at all from your selves: Were you made to be good for nothing? for shame be your own *dressers*, *Manure* your selves, and *prune* your vain and noxious affections. *Man* himself is his own pretious *Soile,* his own fruitfull *field,* and thriving *Plant*: let him 20 that expects fruits from extraneous things, tast first of his own. *Good workes* are the *apples* of this Heavenly *Plant.* The *Vine* and the *Field,* though they bear not for themselves, pay their annual proventions. If they had beene left to their first fruitfullnesse before the *Curse,* they had exceeded in a most uberous, spontaneous fertility; if they should yeild nothing now, they would be good for nothing. Man bears fruit for himselfe, and may bear as much as he pleaseth: Wilt thou then keepe backe thy own provision? Wilt thou pine thy selfe? or by burying thy talent in the dust, be an enemy to thy own soule, and envious towards others?

30 Virtue in my opinion is like to *Musick*: it pleaseth most of all the Virtuous man himself; and it pleaseth also the vitious, whose Conscience doth force him to admire that in others, which he neglects in himselfe. *Musick* delighteth both the *Musician,* and the unskillfull. *Musick* built the Walls of *Thebes*; and *Virtue* must build the new *Hierusalem.* Musick and Virtue are the performances of the *hand,* and the Cordials of the *mind.* Every lover of Virtue is *Musical,* that is to say, he is pleased with the suffrages of his own Conscience, and solaced with the Celestiall flights of his pure Spirit: Hee loves the works of Virtue (not to gain the 40 peoples applause,) but for Virtues sake, whose beauty and power are best seene in her workes. Honesty is one of the liberal *Arts,* it is a trade of Conscience, not of gaine. Craftsmen shew their

10 conceit] conceir *1654*   37 to] so *1654*

skill in their works : The *Sculptor* in his *Cuts,* the *Painter* in his *limnings,* and the *Goldsmith* in his *Plate.* To do something, not the manner of doing it, is their care : Their worke may be well done, though negligently, and without much *Art.* The *Limner* may give a *stroke* in hast or anger, which neither Judgement, nor curiosity can ever match. *Giotto's* circle, though drawn perfunctorily, surpassed the most elaborate peeces of other *Artists.* Virtue alone makes no use either of errour or chance, and this she doth meerly to oppose Fortune. In virtuous actions, if wee erre in doing, though we do good, yet the worke of Virtue is not well done. 10 In other *Arts,* one *Exemplar,* or *Act* may serve to shew the Artificers skill, though he should never work more : But it is not so in Virtue ; As we cannot know a skillfull *Musician,* unlesse he plaies upon some *Instrument ;* so Virtuous men are not manifested untill they *Act :* He that will give any *proofe* of himselfe, must needs be active ; but to be so once, is not activity.

Virtue is a most usefull thing, and the use of it dyeth not after it is used : For allthough all the actions of man are transitory, yet when they proceed from Virtue, they are permanent. I advise thee therefore to be permanent, yea to be immortal. Care not for 20 those things which the World esteems to be enduring, as Gold, and the Wealth of Fortune ; those will make them wings and fly away, when thou doest least look for it. Care thou for those things which the people, and their Hypocritical rulers value not, because they believe them to proceed from a sheepish and rewardlesse *tamenesse,* and not from *grace,* and the secret dispensations of the God of peace. Care, I say, for Righteousnesse and Innocence ; Care that thy Actions be upright : These are the treasures which the World believing to be transient, shall find one day to be truly solid and permanent. Thou hast read somtimes that advice of 30 the Apostle, *Redeem the times :* That is to say, what thou doest well at one time, thou shalt have it at all times : Thy good Actions, withersoever thou goest, will bear thee company : They are Companions of a most rare fidelity, and will leave thee neither in the hour of death, nor after death. When our friends cannot follow us, then do our good works travell with us, they are then our best friends, and overcome our foes. Envy it selfe is appeased with death, it falls off with the body. Malice knowes no posthume persecution, and the glory of Virtue in that *state* is above the reach of her Enemies : though they may disturb our temporal rights, 40 they are too short to oppose our claime to immortality : The onely peaceful possession of the dead, is his good life, and righteous

24 Hypocritical] Hypocritital *1654*

dealings : what wil it avail the rich oppressours of this World, to have their Carkasses buried in the abundance of their treasures, unlesse they mean by it, to restore that unto the Earth which was digged out of her bowells ? Gold and Silver are no ransome for unrighteousnesse. Virtue alone, which survives death, is the refreshment of the dead : He cannot be affeard to dy, who is assured of a better subsistance after death : Their dissolution is onely fearful to those, who lose all by it, and their life to boot. The Posthume Inheritance of man is his righteousnesse and integrity, which death takes not from him, but puts him in possession of them. Thou maist gather, that good or Virtuous works are proper and necessary to the Soul, out of mans natural desire of fame, and that innate appetite of immortality which is planted in his Spirit : Nature desires nothing which is not rational, and her perswasions, even when they degenerate, strain, and point at some primitive delights, and innocent priviledges which she was free to before her corruption. All secular glories dye with the body, goodnesse only is above the power of death : That faire part of life is kin to the Supreme good, and death cannot hurt it ; yea it is secured by death, which kills envy, and frees the virtuous both from the malice of their Enemies, and the possibility of failing in themselves.

Therefore the best imployment for man (if he will consider either his own benefit, or the approbation and liking of nature, which aimes also at immortality) is the work of *virtue*, yea far better then the work of *reason*. Many, while they study the reason of virtuous works, passe by virtue it self. By a fruitless study how to do good, they lose their time, and doe none at all. *Theorie* is nothing so beneficial as *Practice*. It is a true saying that *Jamblichus* cites out of *Pythagoras* ; *Every good thing consists of substance and use, and not of meer knowledge*. To be good, is to doe good. The knowledge of a skilfull *Physitian* profits not the *sick*, unlesse he falls to practise, and gives him something towards his cure. Learned *Aphorisms* heal not the diseased, but bitter *Medicines*. That Soul which can reason subtilly, and discourse elegantly, is not saved but the Soul which doth good works : Knowledge and Faith without actual Charity are both dead.

Neverthelesse there is amongst men a certain covetousnesse of Wisdome and Knowledge, as well as of Money. The acquisition pleaseth them, but they will not set it out to use. As Usurers hoard up their mony, laying it out neither in pious works, nor for their own necessities, but suffer it to lye under rust and darknesse

42 lye] lye : *catchword 1654*

So some Learned men neither practise those excellent rules of Living which they have learnt, nor will they impart them unto others : They study stil more curiosities, being in the mean time incurious of their salvation. I will say of them, as *Anacharsis* said of the *Athenians, They know no use of money but to count it.* There is no man poorer then the rich miser, and none more un-learned then the unpractised. Nature is contented with mediocrity : The World hath many things in it which humane affairs have no need of. Virtue also is perfected in few precepts : Though we fill the world with our Writings, it is not our *Volumes* that can make us 10 good, but a *Will* to be so. Book-men write out of no other design, but to reform and civilize Mankind : They make several Assayes, numerous attempts, and then renew them. The *Dice* run not well alwaies, the last cast may carry more then all the former. There-fore to stir up and incline the *Will* to goodnesse, many things are necessarie ; but to be good there is nothing needfull but *willing-nesse.* We suffer our selves to be cheated by hope ; we trust that when we have gathered so much knowledge as we covet, then we shall do all that we can desire. O foolish and vain procrastination ! *Alchuvius* terms it a *Palsie*, I am sure it is a *madnesse*. We stay 20 like that foolish Beggar for a Mess from the Kings table, and in the mean time starve. We care not to use this present life which is our own, but study the secrets of another, which as yet is not ours. We would learn Mysteries, and some things that are either out of our way, or else beyond it. Christians should neither wander, nor sit down, but goe on ; *What is that to thee ? follow thou me.* Content is a private sphere, but wants nothing, and is ever calme. They that study the world are (of the two) the worst Speculators. Popular, politick persons live alwayes by events : Their ambition and firienesse makes their lives uneven, and 30 uncertaine : innocent, and undisturbed *habits* are the companions of Humility. Giant-spirits, though they may flash sometimes with faire *thoughts*, have alwaies dark and stormy *affections*. Men, or the most part of men, are like *Swans*, whose *feet* though ever in a living *Bath*, are alwaies *black* ; but their *wings* and *doune*, which keep above those streames, are pure *white*. That part of our lives which is ever *padling* with the *current* of Time, is foul and defiled ; but that which soares above it, is fair and holy. Worldly businesse is the Soules Idlenesse.

Man, ordained to be *King* of the Worlds Republick, had been 40 a meer Cypher, if without *Soul-imployment*. He had been created to no *end* without this *Aime*. If he for whom all things

were made, will not endeavour to secure himself being made, he
was made in vain. An ornament to the World he cannot be :
He was not made with any great gaity, & his decaies are both
numerous and hastie. If to be seen only, were the duty of
created things, the *Stars* should have been onely fixt, and not
moving. Stop (if thou canst) the course of the *Sun*, his restlesse
and vast circumvolution : As motion makes him bright and lively
(for hee rejoyceth to run his race) so standing still, and slothful-
nesse would make him sad and sullied ; the beauty of the
10 *Firmament* would be darken'd, the freshnesse of the *earth* would
fade, and the whole *family* of *Nature* missing those cherishing
beames, would pine and decay : *Rivers* would fall asleep, *Minerals*
would prove abortive, and the mourning world would wast away
under darknesse and sterility. But the *Sunne* though he should
not move, would not be uselesse ; his very sight is beneficial.
Hee is the created light of the visible world, a *marvellous vessel,*
and *an ornament in the high places of the Lord.* But man for
whom all these things were made, without he be active and
serviceable to his own Soule, is good for nothing. There is
20 nothing more pleasant, nothing more peacefull, nothing more
needfull then an industrious, *Wise man,* and nothing more im-
pertinent, and uselesse then the sluggard. The *rest* of the mind
is the *motion* of Virtue, and the *idlenesse* of the idle is the *disturbance* of his Spirit. He that doth nothing, is of lesse use, and
by much worse then nothing it selfe. Wouldst thou be reduced
into that unnaturall *Vacuity* of *not being,* which is without form
and void ? Cease to do good, and it is done. The fruitlesse tree
must be cut down : Doest thou ask why ? That it may not be ;
yea, that it may be nothing, and not cumber the ground. *Anni-*
30 *hilation* is more profitable then a fruitlesse *being.* In this *Family*
of Nature, every one hath his *task* : None may be idle. The best
and the Noblest are the most laborious. Consider *Heaven*, the first
Exemplar of agility ; the brightest and the most active *Elements*
are the next to it, and above them move the *Stars. Fire* is the
Suburb of *Heaven* : The *Earth* which is cold and dull, like an
Iland lies most remote, and cut off (as it were) from the *neighbourhood* of *light.* Nothing hath commerce with *Heaven,* but
what is pure : he that would be *pure,* must needs be *active* : Sin
never prevailes against us, but in the absence of Virtue, and
40 Virtue is never absent, but when wee are idle. To preserve the
peace of Conscience, wee must not feare sufferings ; if the hand
of man wound us, God himselfe will cure us : But if wee wound

our selves by resisting him, the hands of all his creatures will be against us, because *ours* was against *his*.

Having now taught you how to master *Adventitious, Personal Evils*, and to prevent the *Evils* of *Conscience*; It orderly followes, that I should teach you how to subdue and triumph over *Publick Evils*, or *National Calamities*. The sufferings of just persons wound the heart of a wise man, when his own cannot grate upon it. Fortune, that could neither hurt him by force, nor by fraud, drawes blood from him through the sides of others. The righteous liver is troubled more with the losses of his neighbours, then 10 with his own. Hee whose patience could not be overcome by *passion,* lies open and naked to the assaults of *compassion.* The life of the wise man is the most pretious and profitable, he lives not only for himself, but for others, and for his Country: The safety of the imprudent is his care, as well as his own: Hee is not onely their compatriot, but their patriot and defender. Excellent is that rapture of *Menander,*

> ———*True life in this is shown,*
> *To live for all mens good, not for our own.*

He onely truly lives, that lives not meerly for his own ends. To 20 live is not a *private*, but a *publick* good: The Treasure of good living is diffusive. The *Civil Guardian* lookes to the goods of his *Wards*: but the wise man is the naturall *Tutor* of the people, and lookes to the publick good, and to the *aged* as well as those that are in their *Minority.* It will therefore be worthy our paines, to consider and enquire how such men should carry themselves in popular and grand mutations; Whither they should change their *Nature,* or their *Maners,* or retain them both, when both fortune, knaves and fooles are most changing. In National alterations, a wise man may change his outward carriage, but 30 not his inward: His mind must be dry and unmoved, when his Eyes flow with teares: Hee must bestow a compassionate, Fatherly look upon the afflicted, and those that are soe weak, as to believe that temporal sufferings can make them miserable. But neither his tears, nor those that he bewailes, must work so far upon him, as to break his inward peace by admitting of *fear,* or *hope,* or the *desire* of *revenge ;* and though hee himself stands in a secure station, from whence he can both distresse & defeat Fortune, yet must he helpe also to redeem others; he must take the field with his Forces, and set upon her with open valour, 40 *doing good* (as *Tzetzes* saith) *to all men, and abolishing every where*

30 wise man] wiseman man *1654*

the power of Fortune. If hee finds that the brests of others are too narrow to entertaine Royall Reason, hee must labour by Stratagems, by Manuductions, and inducing circumstances to incourage and strengthen them; Hee must not leave them, untill he hath secured them. *Antisthenes* said, *that a good man was a troublesome burthen.* Who but insipid wretches, that have no feeling of their misery, will assent to this position? A good liver is troublesome to none, but to the bad, and he is by so much the more pretious and desirable. That wound which makes the patient
10 senselesse; is more dangerous then that which smarts and grieves him. But if their misery when it is made apparent to them by the good man is thereby diminished, and they acknowledge themselves to have been made so by their own vain opinion; it is just that they confesse Virtue to be healing, and that by her meanes they found helpe from a strangers hand, when their own were infirm and helplesse. O Virtue, the great *lenitive* of man-kind! Yea of those who are thine Enemies! Thy hand heals him, that would hurt thee,

> *As* Egypts *drought by* Nilus *is redrest,*
20   *So thy wise tongue doth comfort the opprest.*

Yea, the Evill by whose association thy purity was never defiled, thou dost helpe by the good. In every virtuous man I hold that saying to be true, which *Venantius* spoke of the great Captain *Bonegissus*: *His hand restores, his Counsel secures: whom Fortune rejects or casts out of her armes, he taketh up and guards them in his.* And hence I am induced to differ in my opinion from *Philo*, about that saying of the *Jews* Law-giver, *that a wise man hath heavy hands.* What wonder is it if they be so, seeing the imprudent, the afflicted, and the disconsolate, who are grievous
30 and heavy to themselves, do all depend and hang upon his armes, like Infants upon their mothers?

To help these hangers on, he must needs be bowed, and by speaking faire to their grievances, begin to redress them. This is the property, or rather the prerogative of the constant and wise man; Hee can descend safely from the Sphere of his owne happinesse to mingle with, and to comfort the miserable. Noe man by standing still can rescue one that is carryed away by a violent torrent, and ready to be drowned; nor if he also be overcome by the same stream, can he save the other. It is one thing to be
40 thrown down, and another to be bowed down. He that would not be thrown down, must look to the liberty of his *Will*, and not

submit it to Fortune. But to restore, or raise up others, it is
necessary that he must bow. No man can take up a Child that
is fallen, but by bending himselfe : To cure the ill-affected, we
must in some things incline to their affections. Comfort is
a *potion* of that nature, that heals not the sick, without an appearance of the same *indisposition* in the very *Physitian* : The *patient*
will otherwise suspect that for *poyson*, which is meant for his
health. Hee that is ill-affected, wil be unwilling to believe that
another which is not so, can have any skill to cure him : And he
that labours with the same disease, can neither cure others, nor 10
himself. Therefore he that would minister comfort unto the
distressed, must of necessity have his *will* above the Tyranny of
Fortune, he must have a mind that is invulnerable, and yet seem
to be very tender and sensible of her lightest strokes. It is one
thing to be subject to these affections, and another to rule them :
To be had of them, and to have them. He that would loose
others, must not be bound himselfe. When *Musonianus* observed
a Troop of horse, that was under his command, to *halt*, and
make a stand, expecting some *Omen* from a bird that had
suddenly pitched before them, he bent his bow, and riding up to 20
the front of the Troop, shot at the bird, and killed him : Then
laughing at their folly, he told them, that *there was but litle
advice or help to be expected from such irrational creatures, that
were not onely ignorant of the destiny of others, but could not foresee
their own ill luck.* Wee must look first to our own safety, afterwards to others : The hand of the helper should make the first
assay upon himself : He that experimentally knowes, he can *swim*,
is fit to save another that is in danger to be *drowned*.

But when I speak of tendernesse, and a seeming complyance
with the weaknesse of others ; I mean not dissimulation. I allow 30
a community of tears, but not of the *cause* of tears. Let the
miserable bewail their misery, and let the wise man mourne with
those that mourn, because they mourne amisse, not because they
suffer. Let him not mourne for the power of Fortune, but for
the weaknesse of man. When a friend of *Solon* found him
weeping, hee told him, *That tears were not the potion against
Fortune, and would therefore profit nothing ; I know it well* (said
Solon) *and that is it which I Lament.* He bewailed the tears of
others, not the cause of their tears : That is it which a wise man
(the enemy and the avenger upon Fortune,) may justly bewail, 40

28 fit to] fi to *1654*   drowned] drtowned *1654*.   *The* t *has slipped
out of place in the original from* fit *in line above*

to see men weep, when weeping availes not. He is troubled, not because they suffer, but because they will not be comforted; yea, because they will not be men: He thinkes not that it is Evill to suffer worldly afflictions; Nay, hee knowes it is good, but he knowes withall that worldly sorrowes slay the Soul. This is the consideration that calls forth his tears: Hee wisely distinguisheth, that man is not made miserable by any *outward accidents*, but by his own *opinion*: For no man is made unhappy, because he *exists*, or *is*, but because he thinks himselfe to be so: The wise man 10 bewailes a greater *Evil* then the *Evil* of misfortune, and that is the *inability* of some men to beare *Evil*. Hee mourns not because they are *Patients*, but for their *impatience*. The true or reall *Evil* which he knowes to be in them, is their ignorance of false or reputed *Evills*. That which causeth him to weep, is their causelesse weeping. He that disguiseth his constancie thus, dissembles not. I make not a wise man to be impassible, but enduring and compassionate, yea the *Patient* of compassions: Though I exempt him from the *crowd* and *populacie*; I place him not above *Humanity*: Though he is no *peere* of the *Multi-* 20 *tude*, yet he *descends* to pitty them: But we doe not therefore disturb his peace and serenity, because he is mercifull and condoling; but because it is his expectation, his desire. He is not stormy, nor treacherous, nor base, but courteous, liberal and happy; he is in all estates master of himself; he is kept fresh and pleasant by the secret Joyes and vivifications of an unoffended Conscience. It was well said by the *School-Divine*; *That the tears of the righteous were the smiles of their Soules.*

Gregory *Nazianzen* commended his Brother *Cesarius* for his honest dissimulation with the dissembling Court. He was in- 30 wardly an *Anachorite*, and outwardly a *Courtier*. In publick and splendid affaires (which are more seducing and inconstant then private,) this policie is necessary: Wee should alwaies have a snare ready for them, that we may escape theirs. In the downright blowes of Fortune, that is, in our own domestick losses, We should be sincere and naked; we should put on nothing but our native complexion, and a serene mind. In this Case, wee should be so undaunted, as to looke upon Fortune, and overcome her without any weapons, we should set naked upon her, not onely without defensive armes, but without cloaths. In the 40 dangers of others, we must deal otherwise; wee must use all means to secure them: Wee must deal with Fortune as she deals

37 upon] upon upon *1654*

with us, by disguises and stratagems: All her *wares* are but *gilded clouds*, a *Superficiall wash*; they are not that which they seem to be; to be true to our selves, wee must be false to these, wee must not trust them. Shee cannot require more from us, or better, then what shee gives: Her *Good*, and her *Evill* are both counterfeits, and he that dissembles with them, offends not. The riches of this world are not sound within: Wee may not for their sakes corrupt our Soules, and be made like unto them. Let the peace of Conscience shine within, upon a white and undefiled Throne, though wee look mournfull and ragged without. No 10 Man deals better, or more justly with this World, then he that lends her his *face*, but keeps his *heart*. This is the Nature of the World, to give us a fair *looke*, and an empty hand. Consider thy selfe: How often hast thou been that Creature, which thou didst not seem to be? All the accoutrements of Fortune, all her pomp, and the transitory course thereof, when laid out with the best advantage, seemes to me but a *Stage-play*. Her most glorious favourits passe by like *Whifflers*, which carry Torches in their hands onely to shew the deformity of their vizards: They hasten away, and like 20

To speedy posts, bear hence the Lamp of life.

All the glory of this World, hath darknesse, and treachery in it. It passeth gloomily by us, like high-way-men that traverse the road with veiled faces: hee that will be even with this Counterfeit, must clap on a vizard too, and by an honest dissimulation, preserve himself.

In the funeralls of our friends, our kindred and benefactors, wee may moderately mourne; but we must not lose our Patience, nor that Christian peace, which is the golden fruit of faith and hope. The great mercy of God hath so provided, that *Evill* 30 when it sets upon us, is but an apparition; there comes good presently after it. To live well, we have in our selves more then enough: we need not any extraneous help; our very desiring of it, makes us miserable. So excellently best is our condition, that the blessed life is ours *gratis*, but misery we must hunt after. The happy life needes neither riches nor wishes; Misery cannot be had without *desiring*, and it is never given without Covetous-nesse, which is the price paid for it. Wee suffice of our selves for a happy life; why not for meere life, which is something lesse? shall we think our selves poor, because we abound with 40

the means of happinesse? As long as the batteries of Fortune cannot shake the *mind*, nor make the *wil* to fly into shivers; the *heart* is whole, and our *peace* is secure: Her musters and preparations seem formidable but to children only: Take off the helmet, or vizard of *Evil*, and underneath it, you will find *good*: Hast thou lost a friend that took care for thee like a mother, and furnished the like a Father? that very losse is an occasion of greater gain, though at first it appears not. Parents sometimes to sport with their Children disguise themselves: The Child at the
10 first sight is dejected, but having taken off the Masque, he findes his Mother: He laughs, kisseth and embraceth her, and if shee comes again in that dresse, he fears her not. Who would not be astonished at that furious Army of Evils, which fought against holy *Job*? It was a sad sight to see a Father, after the losse of his Children, and substance, to lye languishing under the Tyranny of a devouring Ulcer. And where? upon a dunghill, the very sink of uncleannesse and corruption. But this frighted him not: Hee was so farre from thinking it an *Evil*, that he played with the worms, and made that, which his friends esteemed for vengeance
20 and misery, to be his meditation and mirth: Hee was sure that he was innocent, and retaining his integrity, he could not misse of joy. He saw through that *Crust* and *Scab*, the sure mercies of God: His beautifull and healing *hand*, shined through that lothsome *Veyle*. He desired not the comforts of his kinred, nor his friends: he said to *corruption, thou art my Father*, and *to the worms, you are my Sisters*. This was onely a *shel*, or seeming *Evil*; but the *kernel*, or substance that lay within it, was solid and reall *good*. As Children deal with *nuts*, so good and wise men deal with *Calamities*; they break the *shell*, and eate the
30 *kernell*: both the *Good* and *Evill* of this World have their *fucus*, and outside: Hee that knowes that, and knowes how to take it off, is a knowing man, and knowes how to use them.

This lesson Saint *Paul* taught the Citizens of *Corinth*. *Let them that weep* (saith he) *be as though they wept not: and they that rejoyce, as though they rejoyced not: And they that buy, as though they possessed not.* He allowes onely an illusive and seeming commerce with the World: Hear his *reason*, and you will acknowledge his *Justice*: *The fashion of this World* (saith he) *passeth away*, or is transient and deceiving: That which men call *fruition* in this
40 World, is but *face-acquaintance*: All temporall possession is but a *looking on*, the things themselves passe away. They are still in a Cryptical, unperceived motion, when we suppose them to be

fast lockt, and fettered in our armes : They creep from us like a *mist* or *smoke*, which in confused and silent *Evolutions* steales out at the top of the chimney, after it hath fouled it within.

> *All worldly things, even while they grow, decay,*
> *As smoke doth, by ascending, wast away.*

Saith *Dionysius Lyrinensis*. The Apostle would have us to put on the same disposition, and to be even with this great deceiver by a like deception. Let us give it but a glimpse, and halfe a face, as it gives us but a transient and flattering salute. Let us weep and not weepe, rejoyce and not rejoyce, use it and not use it. This wee can never *Act* handsomly without personating, or rather mocking this Arch-cheat. When our Eyes flow with tears, we must keep our Consciences smiling and pleasant : Wee must have *Heraclitus* his face, and *Democritus* his heart. The forehead is the *Index* of the mind ; but the Soul of the just must *shine*, when his face is most *clouded*. Wee must not give our strength unto the World, that is to say, we must not seriously affect it : In all our negotiations with it, we must stand at a distance, and keepe our affection for him, who must be loved with all the heart, with all the strength, and with all the Soul. Saint *Paul* (when he made use of this expression,) had respect, I believe, unto the *rites* of the *Roman Theater*, the *Comick* and *Tragick Lawes* of their *Poets*, which together with their Government, were dispersed into all civill climates : He applied to the various representations, suddain changes and successive showes of the *Stage*, where *Truth* moved in *disguise*, and the serious travels of the Sons of Men, were by *Masquers* and personating *Counterfeits* solidly Acted : Where the short flourish of humane affaires did wither by degrees, and ended in a sad *Catastrophe*, while the *Poets plot* upbrayded the vanity of *States-mens* policie. The *World* is a meer *Stage* ; the *Master* of the *Revels* is *God* ; the *Actors* are *Men* ; the *Ornaments* and flourishes of the *Scenes* are honour, power and pomp ; the transitory and painted *Streams* of Mortality, which passe along with the *current* of time, and like *flowers*, do but onely appeare, when they stay longest : Hee that enjoyes them most, doth but *smell* to them, and the shortest fruition permits as much.

What else was the Majesty of the *Assyrian* Empire, but a tractitious, vanishing apparition, a slight *Flash* of transient glory ? It shot by like a falling star, and was presently succeeded by the *Medes* and *Persians* : after them came the *Macedon*, and last of all the *Roman*. The Kingdomes of mortall men are not Immortal : they are no better then their Rulers.   Where is *Ninus* now, where is *Semiramis, Cyrus, Darius, Alexander, Antipater, Ptolomie, Julius Cæsar, Octavian,* and *Tiberius* ?   Where now are these Patriarchs of ambition, these weak roots of the *Assyrian, Median, Persian, Macedonian, Asian, Egyptian,* and *Roman* greatnesse ?   What is become of these *Primats* of pride, these eldest Sons of Fortune, these prosperous disturbers of mankinds peace, before whom the world became dumb, like a *Sparrow* before a *Kite* ? what a deep

10 Silence ! What a thick darkness is now drawn over them ! Nothing remaines of them but their names, and the bare *Skeleton* of glory : Their onely *boast*, is, that they have been : Our onely *Knowledge*, is, that they are vanished.   Nay, it is most certain, that we

ᵃ know not all their names ; those we are acquainted with, are not many : so ruinous a thing is humane glory, though held by mortal men to be immortal.   They are deceived :   It leaves neither *Reliques*, as their *bodies* do ; nor *Inscriptions*, like their *Sepulchers*.   The glory of men

ᵃ *Vixere fortes ante Agamemnona multi; sed omnes Illachrymabiles urgentur, ignotique longâ nocte, carent quia vate sacro.*

20 is more mortal then their Carkasses.   Their bones remain after their Funerals, after the fire, & the Executioner ; And their teeth may be seen, when they can neither snarle, nor bite.   But their fame is edible, it is devoured by time without *Fire*, yea, without *Aire* ; for by not reaching posterity, it becomes dumb, and misseth their tongues, by whose speaking it lives.   All the felicity of men is a dream, it comes on they know not how, and when it vanisheth, they cannot so much as discern its Back-parts. If these recorded *Empires*, these famous *Yoaks* and *Burthens* of the World came so suddenly to nothing ; what will be the lot of

30 these *petty fetters*, these *leaden manacles* that we are bound with ? If those massie and mighty *weights* were so clearly blown off ; what will become of these *loose Packes*, which have nothing to balasse them, but feathers, but chaffe and motes ?   Those universall *Monarchies* founded upon the principall *Cities* of the World, whose *Colony* was the whole Earth : Those *Cities* whose *bulwarks* did threaten the Clouds, whose *Armies* and *Fleets* made the *Earth* to tremble, and the *Seas* to grone : whose *Lawes* (like *Oracles*) were held sacred and unalterable ; found no security against the *Arm* of God, which tears the *Crowne* from the *Head*

40 and the *Scepter* from the *right hand* of the *Lawgiver*.   *He considers in his dwelling place, like a clear heat upon herbs : he appoints the things that are to come : He sifteth the Nations with the Sive*

21 & the] the *catchword only, not text*

of Vanity : He blowes upon them, and they wither, and shall not be planted. And why think you then that these dry and fading leaves shall flourish for ever ? All temporall triumphs have their date : they passe away in a sure and uninterrupted course, and when they begin to decay and unloade themselves, then they are swiftest. All the pomp of this World, is but gilded emptinesse, a nine daies blossome, whose beauty drops into the same Mould from whence it sprung. It is the Consciousnesse of their delusion, that makes these worldly honours fly from us so fast, lest if they should stay long, wee should discover their Cosenage ; the *dis-* 10 *coverer* then would be ashamed of his *dotage,* and the *discovered* would blush at his *deceit.*

Therefore Saint *Paul,* in these versible and transitory fashions of the World, would have us to personate *Stage-players,* who when they weep, grieve not ; when they buy, they possesse not ; when they command, they are without authority. Seeing the World is but a *play,* and a *fable,* hee would not have us to *act* in earnest. Players *Act* the lives of others, not their owne : I wish that we could do so too. Excellent is that advice of the *divine,*

To live a stranger unto life.   20

Why should I be troubled with the affaires of others, more then with their *Agues* or *Feavers* ? he that lives without the *Affections* of this life, is master of himself, and looks upon all things, as *Spectators* do upon *Stage-playes,* who are without *passion,* because without *Interest.* The *Actors* care not how the *Scenes* varie : they know, that when the *Play* is ended, the *Conquerour* must put off his *Crown* in the same *Ward-robe* where the *Fool* puts off his *Cap.* Take this wholsome Counsel of resting quiet in the *degree* appointed thee, not from the mouth of *Musonius, Teletes,* or *Epictetus,* who adviseth thee to be a *Pantomime,* or *shifting* 30 *Masquer* in these worldly *Enterludes,* but from the mouth of Saint *Paul,* that great *Doctour* of the *Universe.*

Let every man wherein he is called, therein abide with God.

That Supreme, Eternall mind is the master and deviser of this worldly *Drama* : Hee brings on the *persons,* and assignes them their *parts.* Art thou called to be a servant ? be not troubled at it : Hath he ordained thy life to be short ? desire not to have it lengthned : If poor, desire not to be made rich. What *part* soever he hath appointed for thee, be contented therewith, and Act it faithfully. It is thy duty to represent the *person* thou wert 40 chosen for, and not to choose ; that is the prerogative of thy

great master.   If it be his will, that thou shouldst *Act* a begger, a sick man, or an afflicted, let it be thy care to *act* it well, and to meddle with no other action.   The *stageplayer* is not commended, because he *acts* the *part* of a *Prince*, but because hee *acts* it well, and like a *Prince*.   It is more commendable to *act* a foole, a begger, or a mourner to the life ; then to *act* a King, or a Philosopher foolishly.   In the beginning, the midle, and the end of thy Course, keep thou to thy *part*.   The best way of *acting* is to make thy *heart* consentaneous to thy *tongue*, thy *deeds* to thy
10 *words*, and thy *conversation* to thy *doctrine*.   In all the tumults and combustions of this World, keepe constant to thy *station* ; comfort the *afflicted*, and envy not the *wicked* ; despise not the *one*, and flatter not the *other* : remember thy *Creator*, and forget not thy end.

Gloria tibi mitissime Jesu !

OF
LIFE and DEATH.

The People think Life to be the greatest *good*, and Death the greatest *evill*. They are mightily deceived : And as in the least blessings, so in this, which is the greatest, they greatly erre. For Life, if thou livest not well, is the greatest evill ; and Death, if thou dyest not ill, is the greatest good ; and dye ill thou canst not, unlesse thou livest ill. A life that is not good encreaseth evils and wickednesse ; and the death of the good sets an end to afflictions and miseries. Those that are sick of the *Jaundis*, judge the sweetest honcy to be the most bitter : So evil men esteem Death to be evill, because of their evill conscience ; but Death is not so to 10 any, but to those onely, whose evill lives end in the evill of endlesse death. This controversie I shall decide with such reasons as must not be numbred, but weighed. If wee look upon *Philosophy*, it takes part with Death ; and is the first that marcheth into the field against this popular error. It teacheth us that this hideous nothing, this imaginary fear of the multitude should be always contemned, and sometimes desired. How many wise men hath this contempt of Death made Immortall ? For those, who by a continual remembrance of death, did compose and regulate their lives, are now by the memory of their virtuous lives vindicated 20 from death. *Socrates* perfected his wisdom by his willingnesse to dye ; *Pythagoras* by his gentlenesse ; *Anaxagoras* dyed merrily ; *Calanus resolutely ; hee would not stay to be tamely besieged by her, but sallyed out, and took her : he surprized death and all of them despised her. No definitions we can give will suffice to make Death odious, every one will make it desirable. Whither you consider what Death is, or what are the effects, or consequents of it ; whether the *evil* or the *good* attending it ; or whether Death it self be a meer *evill*, or meer *good*, all make for it. For though it should be an *evill*, yet the good that comes by it exceeds that *evill* ; and being evill, it cannot be so great an *evill* as all those *evils* it puts an end to.

* One of the Indian Gymnosophists, who feeling himself a little sick made a great Bone-fire, and in the presence of Alexander burnt himselfe therein. Alexander a little before asked him, What he would 30 have ? hee answered, I shall see thee shortly. Which fel out, for he dyed at Babylon few days after.

14 the] this *catchword 1654* : thus the G   25 her : *G* : her. *1654*

What one thing hath Life that is desirable? Contentions, and obstinate, busie miseries, whose frequency and number hath made them lesse feared then Death, which comes but once : Whose assiduity, or daily malice to afflict us, hath by a long custome made us not valiant, but senslesse and blockish. *Orpheus* defined Life to be *the penalty of Soules*; and *Aristotle* added, *That it was a punishment like to that, which tied the living to the dead, mouth to mouth, and breast to breast.* The pure and eternal Soul is tyed to the putrid and wasting carkasse. If God should
10 now suddenly create a man, giving him withall in that very instant the perfect and free use of his mind, and should then bring before him all Mankind (as he did all living creatures before the first man) and shew him in this mixt multitude some weeping and sighing; some without eyes to weep; some without hands; others without legs; some sick and languishing; others eaten up with horrid, impure ulcers; some beging; others quarrelling; some plotting treason, and washing their hands in innocent blood; some old and decrepit, quivering, trembling, and leaning upon staves; some distracted, and bound up in chains; others plun-
20 dered, tortured, murthered, and martyred; their murtherers in the mean time pretending Religion, Piety, and the Glory of God : And after all this outward *Scene*, should so enlighten his eyes, that he might discover another inward one, I meane their secret thoughts, and close devices, their tyranny, covetousnesse, & sacriledge varnished outwardly with godly pretences, dissembled purity, and the stale shift of liberty of Conscience : Is there any doubt to be made, think you, but after such impious, and aston-ishing spectacles, he would quickly repent of his existence or being, and earnestly desire to be dissolved again, that he might
30 rest in peace, and not be cast into this hospital, and valley of villanies which we call the World. It is for this cause, that wise Nature is so slow and niggardly in her dispensations of reason and maturity unto man, lest a sudden perfection should make us loath her, and lest the necessary evils of life understood in grosse, and upon our first entrance into life should discourage us from under-going those miseries which by degrees, and successive conflicts we more willingly struggle with. *Abner* the *Eastern* King, so soon as his son was born, gave order for his confinement to a stately and spatious Castle, where he should be delicately
40 brought up, & carefully kept from having any knowledg of humane calamities; he gave speciall command that no distressed person should be admitted into his presence; nothing sad, nothing

1 desirable] desirarable *1654*

lamentable, nothing unfortunate ; no poor man, no old man, none weeping nor disconsolate was to come near his Palace. Youthfulnesse, pleasures, and joy were alwaies in his presence, nothing else was to be seen, nothing else was discoursed of in his company. A most ridiculous attempt to keep out sorrow with bars and walls, and to shut the gates against sadnesse, when life is an open door by which it enters. His very delights conveigh'd displeasure to him, and grief by a distast of long pleasure found way to invade him. So constant is pleasure in inconstancy, that continual mirth turns it into sadnesse. Certainly though *Abner* by this device might keep 10 all sorrows from the presence of his son, hee could not keep them from his sense : Hee could keep out, and restrain external evils, but could not restraine his inherent affections. His son longed ; this made him sad in the very midst of his joyes. And what thinkst thou did he long for ? Truly, not to be so cumberd with delights. The grief of pleasures made him request his father to loose the bonds of his miserable felicity. This suit of the Son crost the intentions of the Father, who was forced to give over his device to keep him from sadnesse, lest by continuing it, he should make him sad. He gave him his liberty, but charged his 20 attendants, to remove out of his way all objects of sorrow : The blind, the maimed, the deformed, and the old must not come near him. But what diligence is sufficient to conceal the miseries of Mortality? they are so numerous, that they may as soon be taken out of the world, as hidden from those that are in the world. Royal power prevailed lesse here then humane infirmity ; for this last took place in spight of the first. The *Prince* in his Recreations meets with an old man, blind, and leprous ; the sight astonisheth him ; he startles, trembles, and faints, like those that swound at the apparition of a Spirit ; enquires of his 30 followers what that thing might be ? And being inwardly perswaded that it was some fruit of humane life, he became presently wise, disliked pleasures, condemned mirth, and despised life. And that his life might have the least share here, where Fortune hath the greatest, he rejected the hopes and blandishments of life, yea that which is to many the price of two lives, his Kingdom, and royal Dignity : He laboured with all diligence to live so in the world as if he had been dead, that by avoyding sin, the cause of sorrow, he might be, though not safe, at least secure. If this single accident made him so much offended with life, what (think 40 you) would he have done, had his liberty been universal, and unbounded ? What if he had seen the inside of those stately

Tombes wee build for the worms to eat us in, where they feed upon such fat oppressors as have been fed here with the tears and pillage of the oppressed? What if he had narrowly searched every corner of the world, and seen those necessary uncleannesses in which the birth of man is celebrated, in which this miserie is inaugurated, by the paines of the Mother, and the cries of the Infant? What if he had entred into their bedchambers and bosomes, where some sit weeping, others wishing; some surfeited and sick with fruition? where some mourn for their wives, others
10 for their children; some pine and starve with want, others are full and vomit; some are troubled with lack of necessaries, and others are as much vexed with abundance and superfluity? What if after all this search, and wide disquisition he could not have found one house without some misfortune, and none without tears? What if he had been admitted into the breasts of all those, whom either domestick, hidden griefs, lingring diseases, worldly cares, or an insatiable covetousness is ever tormenting? Perhaps the sight of so many evils had driven him to a refusall of life, in which we doe so dye with miseries, and by which miseries doe so live in us; at
20 least he had earnestly wished and groaned for some means of redemption from so miserable a bondage. If any had brought him the joyful news of liberty, and affirmed that some were already made free, he had certainly envyed them very much, and would have been impatient to know the means. But when it had been told him that the device and release was death, I do not onely think, but I verily beleeve that he had both approved of it, and would have sought for it more then for hidden treasure. He had judged it not onely desirable and convenient, but necessary, and the greatest felicity, and favour that the living could expect.
30   If some solitary travellour, shut up in a wilderness, and surrounded with wild beasts, should on the one side see a *Tiger* making towards him, on the other a *Lyon*, and from some third place a scalie, winding *Serpent*, or a *Basilisk*, which kils with his very looks,

> *Whose hissings fright all Natures monstrous Ills,*
> *His eye darts death, more swift then poison kils.*
> *All Monsters by instinct to him give place,*
> *They fly for life, for death lives in his face;*
> *And hee alone by Natures hid commands*
40   *Reigns* Paramont, *and* Prince *of all the sands.*

If these, with a thousand more, as *Bears, Leopards, Wolves,*

17 the] thei *1654*

Dragons, Adders, and *Vipers* were gathered together about him, and ready to seize upon him, what would not he give to be freed from the violence and rage of such destroyers? What greater felicity could he desire, then to be redeemed from such an horrid and fatall distresse? And is it a lesser blessing to be delivered from greater evills? We are surrounded with calamities, torn by inordinate wishes, hated by the world, persecuted, prest, and trodden upon by our enemies, disquieted with threatnings, which also torture and dishearten some; for in pusillanimous dispositions fear makes words to be actions, and threats to be torments. Death is a divine remedy which cures all these evils. Death alone is the cause that temporal miseries are not eternal. And I know not how that came to be feared, which brings with it as many helps, as the world brings damages. Danger it self is a sufficient motive to make us in love wth security. Death only secures us from troubles: Death heals, and glorifies all those wounds which are received in a good cause. When *Socrates* had drank off his *potion* of *hemlock*, he commanded that sacrifices should be offered to *Æsculapius,* as the *Genius* of *Medicine.* He knew that Death would cure him. It was the *Antidote* against that poysonous *Recipe* of the *Athenian Parliament.* Tyranny travels not beyond Death, which is the Sanctuary of the good, and the *Lenitive* of all their sorrows.

Most ridiculous were the tears of *Xerxes,* and worthily checkt by his Captain *Artabazus*; when seated on the top of an hill, and viewing his great Army (wherein were so many hands as would have served to overturn the world, to levell mountains, and drain the seas, yea to violate Nature, and disturb Heaven with their noyse, and the smoak of their Camp) he fell to a childish whining, to consider in what a short portion of time all that haughty multitude, which now trampled upon the face of the earth, would be layd quietly under it. He wept to think, that all those men (whose lives notwithstanding hee hastned to sacrifice to his mad ambition) should dye within the compasse of an hundred yeares The secular death, or common way of mortality, seemed very swift unto him, but the way of war & slaughter he minded not. It had been more rational in him to weep, because death was so slow and lazie, as to suffer so many impious, inhumane souldiers to live an hundred years, and disturb the peace and civill societies of Mankind. If as hee saw his Army from that hill, he had also seen the calamities and mischief they did, with the tears and sorrows of those that suffered by them, he had dried his eyes, and would not have mourned, though he had seen death seising upon all those salvages, and easing the world of so vast an affliction. He would not have feared that, which takes away the cause of fear : That is not evill, which removes such violent and enormous evills.   If I might ask those that have made experiment of life and death, whither they would chuse (if it were granted them) either to live again, or to continue in their state of dissolution, I am sure none would chuse life but the wicked, & those that are unworthy of it ; for no pious liver did ever repent of death, and 10 none ever will.   The Just desire not this life of the unjust, which (were it offered them,) they would fear it more, (now being at rest,,) then ever they feared death, when they lived.   The story runnes that *Stanislaus* the *Polonian*, a man of marvellous holinesse and constancy ; had the opportunity to put this *question*, and the *respondent* told him, that *he had rather suffer the paines of dissolution twice over again, then live once* : He feared one life, but did not fear to dy thrice.

Having this Solution from the experienced, it is needless, and fruitlesse to question the living.   If Soules were *Præexistent*, as 20 one *Origen* dreamt, as *Cebes, Plato, Hermes*, and other *Philosophers*, the great Fathers of *Hereticks*, have affirmed ; Wee might have reason to conclude, that they would obstinately refuse to be imprisoned in the wombs of women, and wallow in Seminal humours.   What if it were told them, that they must dwell nine monthes in a thick darknesse, and more then nine years (perhaps all the years of their sojourning) in hallucinations, and the darknesse of ignorance ? what if the paines, the exigencies, the hunger and thirst they must endure, before they can be acquainted with the miseries of life, were laid before them ?   The Infant while he 30 is yet in the womb, is taught necessity.   Quest for foode makes him violate that living Prison, and force his way into the World. And now comes he forth, (according to the Sentiment of *Hippocrates*,) to seek for Victualls ; the provision which proceeded from his Mother, being grown too little for him.   But he comes from one prison into another, and breaks through the *first* to enlarge his own, which he carries with him : But if the Soules thus incarcerated (like Prisoners through a grate) might behold the various plagues and diseases of those that are at liberty, as *Palsies, Passions* of the heart, *Convulsions, Stranguries*, the *Stone*, the *Gout*, the 40 *Wolfe*, the *Phagedœna*, and an hundred other horrid incurable *Evils*, such as *Pherecides, Antiochus*, and *Herod* were tormented

with, or that fearful sicknesse of *Leuthare*, which was so raging
and furious, that she did eat her own flesh, and drink her blood
in the extremity of the pain : Or if they might see those Evills,
which man himselfe hath sought and found out for himself; as
emulations, warres, bloodshed, confusion, and mutual destruction ;
Is there any doubt to be made, think you, but they would wish
themselves freed from such a miserable estate ; or that their intellectuall light were quite extinguished, that they might not behold
such horrid and manifold calamities. *Plato* imputed the *suspension*
of Reason in Infants, and the *hallucinations* of Childhood to the 10
terrour and astonishment of the *Soules*, which he supposed *them*
to be possessed with, because of their sudden translation from the
Empyreal light, into the darke and grosse prisons of flesh, and
this inferiour World ; as if such a strange and unexpected change
(like a great and violent fall,) had quite doated them, and cast
asleep their intellectuall faculties. *Proclus* assisted this conjecture
of *Plato*, with another argument drawne from the mutability, and
the multitude of Worldly Events, which in the uncertaine state of
this life, the Soules were made subject unto. Adde to this, that
the merriest portion of life, which is youth, is in both sexes be- 20
dewed with tears, and the flowers of it are sullied, and fade away
with much weeping, and frequent sadnesse. Children also want
not their sorrowes : The *Rod* blasteth all their innocent joyes, and
the sight of the School-master turnes their mirth into mourning.
Nay that last *Act* of life, which is the most desirable to the Soul,
I mean old Age, is the most miserable.

> *The plenteous Evills of frail life fill the old :*
> *Their wasted Limbs the loose skin in dry folds*
> *Doth hang about ; their joynts are numm'd and through*
> *Their veines not blood, but rheumes and waters flow.*   30
> *Their trembling bodies with a staffe they stay,*
> *Nor doe they breath, but sadly sigh all day :*
> *Thoughts tire their hearts, to them their very mind*
> *Is a disease ; their Eyes no sleep can find.*

Adde to these usuall infirmities, the confluence of adventious
maladies : For all the former distempers and corruptions of life
gather themselves together, and make head in old age ; when the
inward strength, and expulsive power of Nature is decayed, when
wee are almost dead, then do they revive and rage most of all.
Rivers are no where more full, nor more foule then towards the 40
Channell-end. But this generall decay I acknowledge to be
a great benefit, because it drives away all voluptuous and unseemly

delights from the aged, that their Soules may be lively and in health, when the hour of dissolution comes. And indeed it is necessary, that griefes and unpleasantnesse should lay hold upon age, because men (who are alwaies unwilling to think of dying,) may be thereby weaned from the delights of life, and learn to dye before the day of death. Seeing then, that the temporal life is in all its portions so full of misery, it is not irrational to conclude, that Soules (if they were *præexistent,*) would be very unwilling to submit to this sad Bondage of flesh and blood. Nor do I wonder

10 that *Isis,* in his *sacred Book,* writes, that the Soules, when they were commanded to enter into the bodies, were astonished, and suffered a kind of *Deliquium,* or traunce ; and that they did hisse and murmure, like to the suspirations of wind. *Camephes* sets down their complaints : Τί ταῖς δυστήναις ἡμῖν ἀπρεπὲς ὄντως πέπρακται, *&c. Miserable wretches ! in what have we so foulely trespassed, what offense so heinous and worthy of so horrible a punishment have we committed, as to be shut up and imprisoned for it, in these moist and cold carkasses ? Our Eyes from henceforth shall not behold the Divine spirits, for wee shall onely peepe through two*

20 *small Spheres made of grosse and corrupt humours. When we look towards Heaven, we shall have onely the liberty to grone for the presence of our Creatour, but see him we may not ; for we shall see then by a Secondary light, which is the light of the lower World, and not be permitted to use our own discerning light,* &c. *We shall hear our* Kinred *rejoycing in the air, and mourn that we are not partakers of their liberty,* &c. *But thou great Father and maker of Spirits, who doest dispose of all thy works as it pleaseth thee, appoint we beseech thee some terme to our sad bondage, and let this punishment passe quickly over us, that we may be restored again to our celestiall liberty, to*

30 *behold (without obstruction) the perfect beauty of all thy works,* &c. They comforted themselves with the thought of the bodies dissolution, and petitioned before their captivity, that their inlargement might be hastned : when they were excluded from the heavenly life, there was no greater blessing then the death of the body, which sets an end to the earthly. Hee that loves death, hates a transitory corrupt condition, and he that hates his own life here, shall keep it unto life eternall.

I do verily believe, that to him that throughly considers it, no part of life can be desireable. It is altogether so full of sorrowes ;

40 It is a peece weaved of calamities and troubles, yea, life it selfe is its owne vexation. As those that travell in rough, uneven and mountainous roades are alwaies gasping and weary, which makes

them sit down often, to recover their spent breath, and refresh themselves, that having reach'd the brow and crown of the hill, they may walk onwards with more delight, and be at leasure to feed their Eyes with the beauteous prospect, and freshnesse of those green & flowry plaines which lye extended before them : So this troublesome and tumultuous life hath need of death, for its ease and repast, as a state in which it doth repaire and strengthen it selfe against the fair Journey and progresse of eternity. Frail and weary life cannot last, and hold out untill the *Indiction* of immortality ; So long a journey cannot be performed without 10 subsiding ; A resting place must be had : Death is the *Inne* where we take up, that we may with more chearfullnesse set forwards, and be enabled to overtake, and to keep company with eternity. Nay, so fraile is life, that it cannot expect, or stay for the day of death without some prevening recreations : It travells by Stages, and Periodical Courses, where it breathes, and gathers strength against the next motion. As tyred travellours make frequent Pauses in the very Roade, and cannot stay for the refreshment of lodging ; So life, by reason of the importunity, and the multitude of humane troubles, cannot endure or hold out till it reacheth the *Inne*, which 20 is death ; but is driven to rest in the shade upon the way-side ; for sleep (the shadow of death) is nothing else but a reparation of weary and fainting life. So much more excellent then life is death, that life is driven to be sustained by so many deaths, that is to say, the mortal life is necessarily preserved by sleep, which is the usher & *Masquerade* of death. Reedes, because they are very weak and brittle, are strengthned with distinct knots or joynts, which makes their length firme, and keepes them from cleaving : So life, if it were not refreshed and mantained still by successive, set alleva- tions of certain prolusions of death, would fall asunder and vanish 30 upon its first appearance.

Hitherto we have discoursed of life, let us now consider death, and compare it with life. If death in its shadow and projection be the recreation of life, how delightfull will it be at home, or in it self ! Wearinesse is a preparative which makes rest pleasant : That *Recipe* which succeedes bitternesse, must needs be sweet. *Charidemus* used to say, *That through all temporal things there was a chaine drawne, whereof one link was* pain, *and the other* pleasure : *That these succeeded one another, and so* (said he) *after great sorrowes there come greater joyes.* What greater sorrowes can there be, then 40 the sorrowes of life ? There is therefore no greater pleasure then the pleasure of death, which succeeds those great sorrows. *Phalaris*

42 succeeds] su cceed *1654*

said, *That men held life to be pleasant, because they suspected death to be grievous and irksome.*   He speaks after the sense of the people, and abuseth life, not esteeming it to be good, but because he thinks death to be Evill.   I shall crosse his saying, and inferre that death should be esteemed pleasant, because wee are sure that life is painfull : But there is an appearance of something like errour, because we see many here, that passe through their whole lives without any troubles or discontents.   That felicity is rare and adulterate, and happens most commonly to
10 those that desire it not : look not upon those few which escape in this storme, but upon those which are drowned : these last are innumerable, though it is thought otherwise, because they are sunk into the bottom, and cannot be seen.

Admit not, I beseech thee, for a testimony against Death, those ejulations and tears which darken Funerals, and make foul weather in the fairest faces.   Opinion makes the people compassionate, and they bewail not the party that is dead, but their owne frailty.   Call not for evidence to the teares of strangers, because thou knowest not whence they flow ; but call for it to thine own,
20 for none of us is happy or miserable but in his own sense which makes us any thing.   What reason hast thou to think life better then death, because others mourne when thou dyest, who when thou wert born, didst weep thy selfe?   It is madnesse to judge our selves miserable, because others think so.   The solemnities of death are contrary to the ceremonies of life.   At the birth of man others laugh, but he himself weeps.   At his death others weep, but surely hee rejoyceth, unlesse his ill life hath made his death deadly.   Nor must thou think that his joy is either little or none at al, because it is not manifested unto thee : Thou mayst lye
30 watching by the side of one that dreams of Heaven, & is conversing with Angels, but unlesse hee tells it thee when he is awaked, thou canst discover no such thing while he sleepes.   The Infant that is born weeping, learns to laugh in his sleep, as *Odo* and *Augustine* have both observed : So, he that bewailed his birth with tears, welcomes the shadow of his death with smiles : He presaged miseries to follow his nativity, and beatitude his dissolution. Weeping is natural ; tears know their way without a guide : Mirth is rude, and comes on slowly, and very late, nor comes it then without a supporter and a leader : It must be taught, and acquired.
40 Weeping comes with the Infant into the world ; Laughing is afterwards taught him ; the Nurse must both teach, and invite

12 though] thought *1654*

him to it. When he sleeps, then he sips and tasteth joy; when he dies, then he sucks and drinkes it. Mourning and grief are natural, they are born with us ; Mirth is slow-paced, and negligent of us : The sense of rejoycing (if we beleeve *Avicenna*) comes not to the most forward child till after the fortieth day. Men therefore weep at thy death, because it is an experiment they have not tryed ; and they laugh at thy birth, because the miseries of thy life must not be born by them. Thou onely art the infallible diviner of thy own frail condition, who refusest it with teares, which are the most proper expressions of unwilling, & constrained nature.　　10

But as the ceremonies of Life and Death are contrary, so he that is born, and he that dyes, have different events. Death to some seems to destroy all, but she restores all : By discomposing things she puts them in their order : For he that inverts things that were before inverted, doth but reduce them to their right Positure. The Funeral rite of the *Tebitenses* (who are certain *East-Indians*) is to turn the inside of their garments outward ; they manifest that part which before was hidden, and conceale that part which before was manifest ; by which they seeme, in my opinion, to point at the liberty of the soul in the state of death, 20 and the captivity of the body, whose redemption must bee expected in the end of the world. This inversion by death is reparation, and a preparative for that order wherein *all things shall be made new*. Most true is that saying of the Royal Preacher, Ἀγαθὸν ὄνομα ὑπὲρ ἔλαιον ἀγαθὸν, καὶ ἡμέρα τοῦ θανάτου ὑπὲρ ἡμέραν γενέσεος. *A good name is above precious ointment, and the day of death is better then the day of ones birth.* But thou wilt ask, To whom is the day of death better than the day of his nativity ? It is in the first place to him that dies ; True (thou wilt say) if he be a just and holy man ; Yea (say I) though he be wicked. Who doubts that 30 there can happen in all their lives a better day to the just and honest, then the day of death, which frees them both from seeing, and from feeling the miseries which are in this world ? As for the unjust, it is most certain, that no day can be more beneficiall to them, then that which sets an end to their impieties, tyranny, perjury, and sacriledge. To deny a sword to one that would murther himself, is benevolence; to deny money to a Gamester that would presently cast it away, is courtesie ; and to deny life to those that would use it to their owne damnation, is Mercy, and not Judgement. But to whom besides these is the day of death better then the day of 40 life ? Certainly to God Almighty ; because in that day when the wicked dye, his Justice on them, and his Mercy towards his own are

conspicuous to all, and acknowledged by all.   And to whom else ?
Not to speak of the rich and ambitious, It is good to all men, to
the whole Creation, and to Nature it self: For in that day the
fair order and prerogative of Nature is vindicated from the rage
and rape of lustfull, intemperate persons : It becomes constant,
consonant, and inviolable, by putting off those gross vestiments
wch make her productions subject to the assaults and violence of
man, who is the most perverse and shamelesse defacer of Gods
Image in himself, and the most audacious and abhominable con-
10 temner of his Ordinances in his works, by using them to a contrary
end, and quite different from that which their wise Creator made
them for.

But let us not consider the goodnesse of death by those evils
onely which it freeth us from, but by the blessings also which it
brings along with it.   Their soules are by some men less valued
then Fortune and temporal power ; Some cast away their lives to
winne a Crowne, yea the Crowne, and the Kingdome of another.
They plot to forfeit a Crown of Eternall glory, by usurping a
transitory one : They murther their owne soules by shedding the
20 blood of some innocent persons, permitted to be overcome by
men, that they might have power with God, and prevail.   Shall the
short soveraignty and sway of some small corners and spots of
earth be compared to the everlasting triumphs in the Kingdom of
Heaven ?   The death of the sufferer is in this case the most gainfull ; the more he loseth by it upon earth, his gain is by so much
the greater in heaven.   The shorter our stay is here, our time
above (if reckon'd from the day of our death) is the longer, but
hath no end at all ; and the more our sufferings are, the greater
shall our glory be.   *Hegesias* the *Cyrenian*, when he praised death,
30 promised not these blessings of Immortality, but onely an end of
temporall miseries ; and yet he did so far prevail with his Auditors,
that they preferred death to life ; they contemned the one, and so
lusted after the other, that they would not patiently expect it, but
did impatiently long for it ; they fel upon their own swords, and
forced death to come on, by turning life out of doors before her
lease was out ; and had not *Ptolomie* by a special *Edict* silenced
his Doctrine, he had robbed him of more subjects then ever War
or the Plague could have taken from him.   Before the blessed
Jesus had made his entrance through the veile, and opened the
40 way to heaven, the reward of righteousnesse and sanctity was long
life, the peculiar blessing of the *Patriarchs* : It was a favour then
not to appear before *perfect purity*, a *Judge* of infinite, and all-

seeing *brightnesse*, without an *Advocate* or friend to speak for us, in the strength and heat of irregular youthfulnesse, when not so much as time had subdued or reformed the affections; but now because Christ is gone thither before, and hath provided a place for us, the greatest blessing, and highest reward of holynesse, is short life, and an unseasonable, or a violent death: For those harsh *Epithets* (which are but the inventions of fearfull, and sinful livers) are swallowed up of immortality, & an unspeakable heavenly happinesse which crowns and overflowes all those that dye in *Christ*. Wee consider not those blessings which death leads us to, and therefore it is, that we so frequently approve of our most frivolous, worldly wishes, and sit weeping under the burthens of life, because we have not more laid upon us. A certain groundlesse suspition, that death is evill, will not suffer us to believe it to be good, though the troubles of life make us complement, and wish for it every day. This foolish fear and inconstancy of man, *Locmannus* (one of the most antient *Sages* of *Persia*, and admitted also into the Society of the *Arabian Magi*,) hath pleasantly demonstrated in the *person* of an *Old man*, loaded with a great burthen of *Wood*; which having quite tyred him, he threw down, and called for *death* to come and ease him: Hee had no sooner called, but *death* (which seldome comes so quickly to those that call for it in earnest,) presently appeared, and demands the reason, *why he called? I did call thee* (said he) *to help me to lift this burthen of wood upon my back, which just now fell off.* So much are we in love with miseries, that we fear to exchange them with true happinesse: we do so doate upon them, that we long to resume them again, after wee have once shaked them off; being either faithlesse and wavering, or else forgetfull of those future joyes, which cannot be had without the funerall and the death of our present sorrowes.

What man distrest with hunger, if hee sate upon some Barren and Rockie bank, bounded with a deep River, where nothing could be expected but Famine, or the Fury of wild·beasts; and saw beyond that stream a most secure and pleasant *Paradise*, stored with all kinds of bearing Trees; whose yielding boughes were adorned and plenteously furnished with most fair and delicate fruites; If it were told him that a little below, there was a boate, or a bridge to passe over, would refuse that secure conveyance, or be affeard to commit himself to the calm and perspicuous streames, choosing rather to starve upon the brink, then

13 worldly] wordly *1654*

to passe over, and be relieved ? O foolish men ! For Gold, which is digged out of the *Suburbs* of Hell, we trust our selves to the raging and unstable Seas, guarded with a few planks, and a little pitch ; *where onely a Tree* (as *Aratus* saith) *is the partition betwixt death and us :* And after many rough disputes with violent perills, and the sight of so many more ; wee perish in the unhappy acquisition of false happinesse ; the Sea either resisting, or else punishing our covetousnesse. But to passe into our Heavenly Country, into the bosome and embraces of Divinity, into a Realm where
10 Fortune reigns not, wee dare not so much as think of it. Who after long banishment, and a tedious pilgrimage, being now come near to his native Country, and the house of his Father, where his Parents, his brethren, and friends expect him with longing, would then turn back, and choose to wander again, when he might have joy, when he might have rest ? God the *Father* expects us, the blessed *Jesus* expects us, the mild and mourning *Dove* doth long and grone for us : The holy Virgin-mother, the Angells our friends, and the Saints our kindred, are all ready to receive us. It is through death that wee must passe unto them : Why grieve
20 we then, yea, why rejoyce wee not to have this passage opened ?

But let us grant that death were not inevitable, yea, that it were in the power of man, and that every one had a particular prerogative given him over destinie ; So that this greatest *Necessity* were the greatest freedome, yea, that man could not dye, though he desired death : Yet in this very state, would hee be troubled with *Fortune* and *Hope.* He would be a fool that would not venture to dye, to enjoy true felicity : That would choose rather to live alwaies in the changeable state of most unchangeable and lasting miseries, then to put an end to them all by dying once. It is madnesse to
30 feare death, which (if it reigned not upon the Earth) wee would both desire and pray for. It was wisely adjudged by *Zaleucus,* that death ought to be publickly proclaimed, though men had been immortall. Had death been arbitrary, and at every mans pleasure, I believe we had esteemed it as desireable as any other joy ; now because it is Imperial, and above us, let it not seem too much, if wee grant it to be tollerable. It was absurdly said by one, *that death was a necessary Evill, and ought therefore to be patiently born.* His *Inference* was good, though from a bad *Principle* : Death is rather a necessary good : And if necessity makes Evils to
40 be tolerable, there is more reason, it should make good so. Death because it is good, should be made much of ; and wee should rejoyce that it is necessary, because that makes it certain. How

great a good is that, by which it is necessary that we be not miserable! Which frees the captive without ransome, dismisseth the oppressed without the consent of the oppressour, brings home the banished in spite of the banisher, and heales the sicke without the pain of *Physick*: Which mends all that Fortune marred; which is most just; which repaires and makes even all the disorders and inequalities made by time and chance; which is the blessed necessity that takes away necessary Evills? He had erred lesse, if he had mentioned a necessity of bearing life patiently, whose more proper definition that sorry proverbe is; for it casts us into necessary Evills against our will, and is the cause that wee willfully meddle with Evills that are unnecessary. It is a discreet method of nature, that infuseth the Soules into the body in such a state that is not sensible of their captivity, lest they should murmur at the decrees of the great *Archiplast.* What wise man that were neare the terme of his appointed time, if he were offered to have life renew'd, would consent to be born again, to be shut up in flesh, & fed for nine months with excrementitious obscenities, to bear all the ignominies of Nature, all the abuses of Fortune, to resume the ignorance of Infancie, the feares of Childhood, the dangers of youth, the cares of manhood, and the miseries of old age? I am of beliefe that no man did ever live so happily, as to be pleased with a repetition of past life. These Evills which with our owne consent wee would not have reiterated, wee are driven into without our consent: They are necessarily inferred, that they may be willingly borne, to shew the necessity of Patience. Wee are born on condition, that wee must dye. Death is the price or reward of life: It is the Statute-law of mankind, and that ought to be born as a publick good, which (were it not already enacted) would be the spontaneous petition of all men. Certainly if life were without the *Jubile* of death, it were just to refuse it, as a servitude which hath no year of release.

Let us now clearly prove, that death is not Evill, out of her assimilation and conformity to those things, which are most excellently good. None leade a better life, then those that live so, as if they were dead, *Rom. Chap. 6. ver. 7. For he that is dead, is freed from Sinne.* Therefore that which is the exemplar of goodnesse, cannot be Evill: The onely true praise of the living, is to assimilate death: He is the most commendable liver, whose life is dead to the World, and he is the most honest that lives the least to it; whose Soul listens not to the body, but is at a constant distance from it, as if they were dissolved; or though it sojournes in

it, yet is not defiled by it, but is separated from sensuality, and
united to Divinity. What is the reason (thinkest thou,) that the
Divine *Secrets* are revealed to men most commonly in their sleep ;
because that similitude of death is most pleasing to God. Life is
a wild and various madnesse, disturbed with passions, and distracted with objects ; Sleepe (like death) settles them all ; it is the
minds *Sabbath*, in which the Spirit, freed from the Senses, is well
disposed and fitted for Divine intimations. The Soul is then alive
to it selfe, while the body reigns not, and the affections are
10 ecclipsed in that short *Interlunium* of the temporall life.

Philosophie, or humane Knowledge is nothing else but a Contemplation of death ; not to astonish or discourage men, but first
to informe, and then to reform them : for the fruit of Philosophy
is Virtue, and Virtue is nothing else but an imitation of death, or
the Art of dying well, by beginning to dye while we are alive.
Virtue is a certain *Primrose*, a *prolusion* or *Assay* of dying.
Therefore that by which man becomes immortall and eternall is
the *preface*, and the *Inchoation* of death. This is the main drift of
Philosophy, to make life comfortable by conforming it unto death,
20 and to make death immortality by regulating life. Death is
intollerable to him only that hath not mortified his desires, while
he yet lives ; but expects to swallow up death, and all the powers
of it at once ; that is to say, in the hour of death. We cut our
meate, and feed on it by bits, lest we should be choaked by
swallowing it whole ; so death, if it be assayed and practised by
degrees, will be both pleasant in the tast, and wholsome in the
digestion ; if we mortifie one affection to day, and another to
morrow. Hee that cannot carry a great burthen at once, may
carry it all by portions. *Philosophy* acts the part of death upon
30 the Stage of life : it kills sensuality, and makes death most easie
to be born by teaching us to dye dayly. What can be more
grievous then death unto him, who together with his own, feeles
the paine of a thousand other dying cupidities ? We faile not to
bewaile the losse of one thing, whither honour, pleasure, or a friend :
How much more when we loose all at a blow, and loose eternal
life in one short minute ? The Soule of the wise man frees her
selfe from the body in an acceptable time, she casts off the
delectations of the flesh, and the cares of this World while it is
day-light, that shee may enjoy her self, and be acquainted with God
40 before the night comes. She finds by experience, that her forces
are more vigorous, and her light more discerning, when she is not
sullied with Earthly negotiations, and the grosse affections of the

body ; she finds that covetousnesse, love and feare permit her not to see the truth, and that the affaires of the body are the *Remora's* of the Spirit : and therefore she concludes, that he must neglect the cryes of the flesh, and be attentive onely to the voyce of God ; and upon these considerations, shee shakes off that Bondage ; she deserts the familiarity and consultations of blood, that she may advise with, and discerne the most clear light of truth ; she casts off pleasures, by which even Spirits are made subject to sense and pollution. The truth is most pure, and will not be manifested, but to the pure and the undefiled : Therefore all the scope and the end of Virtue is, to separate the Soul from the body, and to come as near death as possibly may be, while wee are yet alive. This is the cause that wise men do so much love and long for death, at least they fear it not. How can he feare death, who by dying passeth into the life of the blessed ? Who hath already delivered himselfe from more feares and inconveniences then death can free him from ? Yea from those dangers which make death fearfull ? Who before his dying day, hath disarmed and overcome death ? Shall he that all his life-time desired to be separated from the body, repine at the performance and fullfilling of it ? It were most ridiculous, if hasting towards home, thou wouldst refuse the helpe of another to convey thee thither with more speed, and be angry at thy arrivall in that Port, whither thou didst bend thy course since the first day thou didst set forth. There is no man that seeking for a friend, will not rejoyce when he hath found him. No man will be angry if another perfects what he did begin, but was not able to finish. Nature by death perfects that which Virtue had begun in life, and the endeavour dies not, but is continued, and thrives by a necessary transplantation. While he yet lived, he denyed himselfe the use of the body, because it hindred the course of the Soul ; and the body dying, he doth but persist in the same just denyall. It is a greater pleasure to want, then not to use what wee doe not want.

This *Correlation* of *Death* and *Virtue* I shall exhibite, or lay out to your view, by a discussion of those honours which each of them procures. As Virtue by the Consideration of death, ordereth and preserves her Majesty ; so by imitating death, she obtaines the reverence and admiration of all : What more reverend thing can wee labour for, then that, which by our reverence of it, makes the worst livers to be reputed not bad ? As those who are Evill, are loath to believe themselves to be such, because of an innate reverence due from every man to Virtue, which makes them love

the repute of Excellencie, though not inherent, and rejoyce to be accounted good of themselves, or in their own esteem, though they be evill, taking pleasure in that self-deception : So those who have beene vitious in their lives (out of the reverence wee owe to death,) wee dare not speak evill of when they are once dead ; Nay, it is not civil, nor pious, to mention the dead without commendation, either by *praise*, or else by *prayer*, & our *Christian well wishes*, as if they had been most deserving in their lives. So powerfull is the Majesty of death, that it makes the most contemptible, vener-
10 able. Those we most envie while they live, we speak well of when they are dead. Excellent is that observation of *Mimnermus*,

> *Against the Virtuous man we all make head,*
> *And hate him while he lives, but praise him dead.*

Envy pursues us not beyond the grave, and our honour is not free and secure til we are layd in it. That humble and quiet *dust* stops the lying and malicious mouth. *Socrates* foresaw that his *draught* of *hemlock* would (after his death) make his very enemies his worshippers : He saw his *Statues* erected by the same *decree* that did cast him downe : And what was the *motive* (thinkst
20 thou) that made his enemies worship him dead, whom they per-secuted living? There is amongst the people a secret tradition that whispers to them, that *those who are freed from the miseries of this life, live happily in another world.* Now happinesse even in their opinion is worthy of honour; therefore the honour or veneration which death exacts, is a certain tribute, or a debt rather that is due to happinesse; and if for this thou wilt advise with thy *Aristotle*, he will not deny it. The *Lacedemonians* bestowed the *Olympick* palms and honours (which whosoever won in his life time, he was accounted most happy) upon all that dyed,
30 without exception, or extenuation; adorning the *statutes* of some, and the *tombes* of all with the green and flourishing *Laurel*, esteeming every one of the dead as happy as the most fortunate Victor that lived. The antient *Romans* held the greatest honour of the living to consist in the renown of their dead Ancestors : They judged him to be highly honoured, that was enjoyned by any dying persons to perform some extraordinary service for them, as an Embassie, or some other weighty negotiation : And * *Calli-stratus* in his first book of *Questions* affirmes,

* *One of the Coun-* *That Embassadors so employed are the most*
sellors of Alexand.
40 *the great.* *honourable ; because that the suffrages and election of dying men is most venerable, as being then upon the borders of*

immortality, and discerning more then those who are yet in the midst of life, and more in the clouds of thick-sighted humanity. That honour is the greatest which is done us by the honourable. Nor is this glory of death a *Relative* of the Soul only; Looke well upon the body, that provision of the worms, a frail and perishing object, but ful of Majesty. We arc nothing so moved, nor doe we so gravely compose our selves at the presence of a King, as at the sight of a dead body. With how much awfulnesse doth it lye along! with what a secret mysterious command doth it check all about it! It is a silent, abstruse *Philosopher*, and makes others so too: 10 Nor is it onely venerable, but sacred, and the *Depositum,* and *Index* of an almighty Restauratour. The honour of Sepulture is a part of Religion.

Now, if it be argued that goodnesse consists onely in utility, or benefits, it follows that nothing is good, but that which profiteth: Death then is the best, and the greatest subordinate good of all; for the death of others benefits those that see it, and their own death is most profitable to those that mind it. The *Lamæ* (who are the Priests of the *Tebitenses*) are in this point the most excellent Philosophers in the world: When they prepare 20 to celebrate prayers, they summon the people   *The pipes of death* together with the hollow, whispering sounds of *used by the* Lamæ. certain Pipes made of the bones of dead men; they have also Rosaries, or Beads made of them, which they carry alwayes about them, and they drink constantly out of a Skull: Being asked the reason of this Ceremony by *Antonie Andrada*, who first found them out; one that was the chiefest amongst them, told him, that they did it,

Ad Fatorum memoriam.

They did therefore pipe with the bones of dead men, that those 30 sad whispers might warn the people of the swift and invisible approach of death, whose *Musick* they termed it, and affirmed it to be the most effectuall of any; That the Beads they wore did put them in minde of the fraile estate of their bodies, and did in prayer-time regulate and humble their thoughts; That a constant commemoration of death was as beneficial to the Soul as devotion, & therefore they carryed them alwaies about them as the powerfull *Memento's* of their approaching departure out of the Land of the living. To this he added, that their drinking in a skull did mortifie their affections, represse pleasures, and imbitter their tast, 40 lest they should relish too much the delights of life; Lastly, he added that this constant representation of death, was an Antidote

37 powerfull] powefull *1654*

against all the sinfull Excesses and deviations of man. With the
same Medicine they secured themselves from other iniquities :
When they were to swear concerning any thing, they laid their
hands upon certain *Images* set with the bones of dead men, by
which ceremony they were put in mind of the last Judgement,
and the Account which the *dead* and the *Quick* must give in that
great, that impartiall and censorious day.   Certainly this was no
barbarous, but a very humane and elegant *Philosophy*, which
taught men to season, and redeeme all the daies of their lives,
10 with the memory of the one day of their death.   Admirable was
the memory of *Mithridates*, who was master of two and twenty
Languages, and could readily discourse in every one of them ;
and no lesse happy was that of *Cyrus*, *Themistocles* and *Seneca* ;
but a constant memory of mans miseries, and his death exceeds
them all.   As the rootes of the tree in the Ile of *Malega*, upon
that side which lookes towards the *East*, are an Antidote or
preservative, but those which spread *Westward* are poysonous and
deadly : So the *Cogitations* of a Christian, which are the *Roots* by
which hee stickes to Heaven (for every Christian is a *Tree*
20 reversed,) when they look towards the *West*, or setting point of
life, are healing and salutiferous ; but those which reflect still upon
temporall things, and his abode in this World are destructive and
deadly.   Nature doth every minute commend unto us this memoriall of death.   *Hermes* in his *sacred book* contends, that respiration was given to man, as a sign of that last efflation, in which
the Soul parts from the body.   Wee should therefore as often as
wee breath, remember death, when we shall breath our last, when
the Spirit shall returne unto him that gave it.   Our whole life is
nothing else but a repeated resemblance of our last expiration ; by
30 the emission of our breath we doe retaine it, and (as I may say)
spin it out.   God gave it not *continual* and *even*, like fluent *streames*,
or the calme and unwearied *Emanations* of light, but refracted and
shifting, to shew us that we are not permanent but transitory, and
that the Spirit of life is but a *Celestial Gale* lent us for a time, that
by using it well, we may secure it Eternally.   Another *Hermetist*
adviseth us, *Adorare relliquias ventorum*, to make much of, and to
honour our Soules, which are the *breathings*, and last *dispensations* of
the still fruitful, and liberal creator : This we can never do but by a
frequent study of our dissolution, and the frailty of the body.   Of
40 such an effectuall goodness is death, that it makes men good before
it comes, and makes sure of Eternity by a virtuous disposing of
time.   Thinke not that evill, which sends from so far the beams

of its goodnesse. There is no good liver but is a debtor to death, by whose lendings, and premunitions we are furnished and fitted for another world.

The certainty of it, and the incertainty of the time and manner, (which is the oncly circumstance that seemes to offend us,) if it were seriously considered, deserves to be the most pleasing & acceptable ; for amongst all the wondrous Ordinances of Divine providence, there is none more Excellent for the Government of man then death, being so wisely disposed of, that in the height of incertainty it comprehends and manifests an infallible certainty. 10 God would have us to be alwaies good, to keepe in his likenesse and Image : Therfore it is his will, that we should be alwaies uncertaine of our most certain death. Such is his care of us, lest the knowledge of a long life, and a late death should encourage us to multiply our transgressions, as the notice of a swift dissolution might dishearten and astonish us. But being left now in a possibility of either, we are taught to live soberly, and to expect the time of our change in all holynesse and watchfullnesse. The possibility of dying shortly, doth lessen the cares of life, and makes the difficulties of Virtue easie. Bondage and Slavery (if it 20 be but short,) is to those that suffer it the lighter by so much : And a large allowance of time makes us slow to Virtue, but a short portion quickens us, and the incertainty of that very shortnesse makes us certaine to be good. For who would weep, and vexe himself for worldly provisions, if he certainly knew that he should live but one month ? and how dares he laugh, or be negligent of his Salvation, that knowes not whither hee shall live to see one day more, yea, one hour ? The incertainty of death makes us suspect life, and that suspition keepes us from sinning. The world was never fouler, nor more filled with abominations, then 30 when life was longest, when abused Nature required an Expiation by waters, and the generall submersion of her detestable defilers. *Theophrastus* did unjustly to raile at Nature, and condemne her of partiality, when he envyed the long life of some *plants* and inferiour *creatures*, as the *Oake*, the *Hart*, the *Ravens* ; some of which live to *feed* and *flye* up and down in the World above *five hundred* years. He quarrelled with the wise dispensations of Divinity, because a slight *suite* of feathers, and a renew'd *dresse* of greene leaves could weare out a building that lodged a rationall Soul, and the breath of the Almighty. Both his *wish* and his 40 *reason* were erroneous : He erred in desiring long life, and in judging happinesse to consist in the multitude of yeares, and not

the number of good workes. The shortnesse of life is lengthned by living well: When life was reckond by centuries, the innumerable sins of the living so offended God, that it repented him to have made impenitent man: Those that sinned out of confidence of life he punished with sudden destruction. That long-liv'd generation had made the world unclean, and being polluted by their lives, it was purged by their deaths. He shorten'd afterwards the lease of life, reducing it to an hundred and twenty years, that by the diligence of frequent death, he might reform the past
10 disorders of long life, and prevent them for the future, teaching both sexes to amend their lives by giving them death for their next neighbours. So beneficiall is death, so much profits the certainty of it, and as much the incertainty: The ignorance of the day of death is in effect the same with the knowledge of it; the first makes us watch, lest it come upon us unawares; and the last (though it might name the day to us) yet could it not arme us better against it, perhaps not so well. This incertainty of dying, certainly secures us from many errors; it makes us prudent, provident, and not evill. Death therefore is a device of the
20 Almighty, and a wise instrument of divine policy. *Zaleucus* so highly approved of it, that he was about to enact and proclaime a Law for dying, had he not found it already published by the edict of Nature: And in his Preface to those Laws made for the *Locrenses*, he warns them, Τίθεσθαι πρὸ ὀμμάτων τὸν καιρὸν τοῦτον, &c. To have alwayes before their eyes that time, which is to every one the end of life, because a hearty repentance for all former injuries seiseth upon all men that thinke of death, and an earnest desire or wishing, that all their actions in life had been just. Wherefore it is expedient that in all our dealings and
30 thoughts death should act a part, and be our familiar counsellor, ever present with us; so shall we be carefull to doe all things virtuously and justly. Death then is most necessary to govern mankinde, because the memory of it keeps us in awe, and conformable to virtue. All Commonwealths that follow the method of Nature, must approve of this Law of *Zaleucus*, and death in all their consultations should guide their lives.

Certainly in the Government of the rebellious Generation of Man, Death hath been the most awfull Engine of the Deity; without this stern he guided them not: When man was immortall,
40 God saw it necessary to preserve his immortality by death; he injoyned the Law of Abstinence to *Adam*, under the penalty of dying, which is continued still by the same artifice of death, lest

iniquities should be immortal, & wickedness should escape punishment : by the patience and submission of his only Son to death he restored dead men to life, he conferred upon him all his lost honours, renewd and confirmed his old prerogative, and together with the salvation of his Soule gave him a sure promise, that his body allso should be made Immortal ; but in all these favours, and after full reconciliation, he would not remove death, but continued it still, and the incertainty as well as the certainty of it. This divine devise of death so pleased God, and was so necessary for the good of man, that though by the merits of his dying Son 10 he changed all the former things, blotting out ordinances, abolishing Ceremonies, & opening the gates of Heaven to all believers, yet would not he Exterminate death. It was out of his mercy that he refused to abrogate it, that while corruption reigned, death also might reign over it, lest this poyson should want its Antidote. We have therefore no just cause to complain of death, which is an Invention conducing to our great good, and the incertainty of the time (though it most vexeth us) is notwithstanding the most beneficial Circumstance that attends it. The time of life is certainly known, & there is but one entrance into the light of this 20 World : The Ceremony of dying is not formal ; It keeps not to one time, nor one manner, but admits of all times, and many manners. Life comes into the World but one way, but hath many waies to go out. It was the benevolence of God to open so many doors to those that flye for refuge. One way is more then enough to find out dangers, but to escape them, many are but necessary. Death is not a burthen of seaven or nine monthes, but life must have time before it sets forth. And what are the first encounters of it ? Tears and Bonds. It cannot avoyd Evills, and it is afeared to bear them ; therefore it delaies time, and 30 when it cannot lurk any longer, it comes forth Crying. Death leads us forth to joy and liberty : Therefore it stayes not, it seeks no corners nor protractions. Nor doth death free us onely from suffering Evills, but keeps us also from doing any : To be good every day, thou must dye dayly. The incertainty also of the time of death, and the manner of it, like a busie Monitour, warnes thee to do good, and to be good at all times, and in every place, private or publick : And the inevitablenesse of it takes away all Excuse or pretensions for thy impreparation.

The Glory of death, is also much augmented by its facility, in 40

---

1 immortal,] tall, *catchword 1654*　　　20 into] to *1654* : in- *catchword*
40 *space for fresh paragraph end of original page* 170. *Catchword* mented
follows space.

redressing the difficulties of life. It is not without the Divine counsel, and a speciall priviledge that the Soule of man is so easily parted from the body; the life of beasts is more tenacious, and will suffer much indignitie and fury before it leaves them. There is no living creature more fraile, none more weak then man; the lightest stroake fells him; the Soul is very nice, and will quickly cast off the body if it persists but in the least Indisposition. A single hair killed *Fabius*, and a Grape *Anacreon*; these contemptible instruments destroy'd them as effectually as
10 the thunderbolt did *Esculapius*. *Coma* dyed as easily as he could wish, and *Baptista Mirandulus* as he could think: His Soule quitted his body without any grudging, without a disease, without poyson, without violence, or any fatall mischance. No door can keep death out, it defeats life with its own weapons, and kills us with the very Cordials and comforts of it. Perhaps no kind of death is more violent then that which sets upon us with the forces of life, because it kills when life is most vigorous and pleasant. Their owne wishes have destroyed many: And life hath oftentimes perished by her own contrivements.
20 *Clidemus* was killed with honour, *Diagoras* with joy, *Plato* with rest, and *Philemon* with laughter. This last is both a merry, and a frequent destroyer, and freed *Sicily* from one Tyrant. Death also makes use sometimes of our very virtues to exanimate us: Shame killed *Diodorus*, and the Mother of *Secundus* the Philosopher dyed with blushing, and an excessive modestie. Life is a fraile possession, it is a flower that requires not rude and high winds, but will fall in the very whispers and blandishments of fair weather. It is folly to labour to retain that which wil away; to fly from that which will meet us every where, yea, in the way we
30 fly, is a vain and foolish industry. Whither we seek death or avoyd it, it will find us out: Our way to fly, and our very flight end both in death; by hasting from it, we make hast to it. Life is a journey, whose end cannot be mist; it is a steady ayming at dissolution: Though we fetch wide Compasses, and traverse our way never so often, we can neither lengthen it, nor be out of it: What path soever we take, it is the Port-roade to death. Though youth and age are two distant *Tropicks* of life, yet death is as near to the one, as to the other: And though some live more, and some lesse, yet death is their equal neighbour, and will visit
40 the young as soon as the old. Death is a Crosse, to which many waies leade, some direct, and others winding, but all meet in one Center: It matters not which thou takest, nor whither thou art

young or aged: But if thou beest young, thou maist come sooner
thither, then the old, who is both doting and weary. It was
necessary that a Sanctuary being provided for the distressed, the
way to it should be easie, pervious, and at an indifferent distance
from all parts. Good should be diffusive, and the gate that leads
to it, must be without doors and bolts. The entrance into this
life, is narrow and difficult, it is difficultly attained, difficultly
retained, and lyes alwaies in the power of another. Every man
may take life from us, none can take death. Life is subject to
the Tyranny of men, but death is not; life makes Tyrants, and 10
death unmakes them. Death is the slaves prerogative royall, and
the Sabbath of the afflicted. *Leo Iconomachus* the Emperor, made
the birth of both sexes tributary: but death never paid taxation.
It was not lawfull in his reigne to get Children without paying for
them; every Infant so soon as borne, was to give him contribution,
they paid then the Excise of life. Death onely frees us from
these Impositions of Tyrants.

And wilt thou then condemn liberty, and that maturity of death
by which it ripens every age? wilt thou the divine liberality
blame, because thy life is short, or may be so? thou hast no 20
reason to find fault with the years already given thee, because thou
shalt not have more: thou mayst as well quarrel with Nature,
because she made not thy dimensions larger, and thy body heavier
by eighty or a hundred pounds: he that measured thy proportion,
measured thy time too: and too much of this last would have been
as troublesome and unweildy as too much of the first: for

> *Long life, opprest with many woes,*
> *Meets more, the further still it goes.*

Death in every age is seasonable, beneficial, and desirable: It
frees the old man from misery, the youthfull from sin, and the 30
infant from both. It takes the aged in the fullnesse of their time;
It turnes the flowers of youth into fruit; and by a compendious
secret improvement, matures infancy, leading it into the Gate of
Heaven, when it cannot go one step upon Earth, and giving it the
wings of a Dove to flye, and be at rest, before it can use its feet.

To these past arguments of the goodnesse of death, I shall adde
another. Death in the old world, (before the manifestation of God
in the flesh,) was the publick index, or open signe of hidden
divinity. It is the gift of God, who gives nothing but what is good.
The Divell playing the Ape, and labouring to imitate the Inimi- 40
table *Jehovah*, did by asserting death to be the greatest good,

19 the (*space*) *1654*: then (?)

mainly fortifie those abominable rites and honours conferred upon
him by his blind worshipers : When they petitioned him for the
greatest blessing that the Gods could give to man, he (by the permission of the true God whom they had deserted) would within
three daies strangle them in their beds, or use some other invisible
meanes to set an end to their daies.   Thus he served *Triphonius,*
Agamedes, and *Argia* for her three Sons : This miserable mother
requested of him, that hee would give the best thing to her children, that could be given to men : her petition was granted, and
10 within a very short time they received that which she thought to be
the worst, namely death.   So great is the ods betwixt seeming to
be, and being really : betwixt opinion and truth : yea that death
which we judge to be the worst, I meane the immature, is oftentimes the best.

> *What greater good had deckt great* Pompey's *Crown*
> *Then death, if in his honours fully blown,*
> *And mature glories he had dyed?* *those piles*
> *Of huge successe, lowd fame & lofty stiles*
> *Built in his active youth, long, lazie life*
> 20 *Saw quite demolished by ambitious strife:*
> *He lived to weare the weake and melting snow*
> *Of lucklesse Age, where garlands seldom grow.*
> *But by repining fate torne from the head*
> *Which wore them once, are on another shed.*

Neither could I ever grant that the death of Infants and Children, though commonly bewail'd as unseasonable, were the parents
misfortunes, but the courtesies rather, and mercies of the almighty.
To omit *Amphiaraus,* and other Ethnick instances ; I shall make
use of a true and Christian History, which in these later years,
30 was the great admiration of King *Philips* Court.   *Didacus Vergara,*
a most noble hopefull youth, adorned with all those vertues which
beautifie a blooming life, was famous in the mouths of all good
men, and as deare in their hearts.   But what was the reward
(thinkest thou) of his virtuous life?   An immature and almost a
sudden death ; So that it is not to be doubted, but it was a divine
favour.   Being to go into bed, he spoke to his sister, O what
manner of night will this be unto me ! I beseech you, deare
sister, furnish me with some candles, and leave one to burn by me.
Abought midnight he suddenly called, so that all the familie was
40 awaked, and got up ; to whom he told that he should dye that
night ; and desired them to send presently for his Confessour.
They all imagined that he had been troubled with some dream,
especially his Father, a most renowned Physitian, when he

felt his pulse to beate well and orderly. But notwithstanding all this, they omitted not to send for his Confessour, who was *Gasper Pedroza*: He (as if touched with some Divine presension) was at that dead time of the night awake, and being come to the sorrowfull Father, he told him, that *Didacus* was expected in another World before day, that the Virgin-Queene of Heaven had revealed so much to him, and that hee would be gone as soon as the Sacraments could be administred unto him. It fell out just so : For those sacred solemnities were no sooner ended, but he was dissolved, as if he had stayed onely for that 10 spirituall refection to strengthen him in his Journey. He left this dark and low World towards the first breakings of the day, and ascending to eternity upon the wings of the morning. He might have past from thence with lesser noise, and in a shorter time ; but he expired more solemnly then so ; and yet without weary accessions, and the Tyranny of sicknesse : He stayed for the saving institutions of his redeemer, the businesse that detain'd him so long, was Heaven, and not the tumults of a tyring and obstinate dissolution ; all this proves it to have been the hand of God, and not an unfortunate, sudden death ; the precise Actions of the 20 deity must be attended with unusuall circumstances.

> *Whome God doth take care for and love,*
> *He dies young here, to live above.*

There is room enough for life within the compasse of few years, if they be not cast away : Think not that to last long, and to live long is the same thing : every one that hath stayd long upon earth, hath not lived long.

Some men find fault with death, because no experiment can be made of it, without an absolute dissolution : they would dye twice, to trye what kind of state it is, that they may be fitly 30 furnished against the second time, when they must dye in earnest. But this is madness, and were it granted them, the good they pretend would not be performed. For he that will cast away one life without preparing for death, wil not fear to hazard another ; desperate malefactors will take no warning by reprieves. Besides, what benefit would there be by dying twice, seeing that of necessity they must live twice too, and so be twice miserable, if not twice impious ? It is strange, that these men who fear death, and adjudge it to be evill, should desire to have it doubled, and that which, by their good will, they would not tast once, they will beg 40 to chew and swallow downe twice ; whereas if death were an Evill, it would be so much the lesser by comming but once. The

miseries of life are nothing so civill ; they are instant, importunate, and outragious ; they will reinforce themselves, and set upon us twice or thrice, yea, a thousand times. Death is more modest, she wearies us not as long as wee are well : When our disorders have turned the harmony of life into discord and noise, then shee comes to cast those murmurers asleep, and to give the Soul peace : He is no troublesome guest that comes but once. But it were a great happinesse, thou wilt say, if men did experimentally know what it is to dye : Truely this Felicity is not wanting : Death is
10 a most admirable, ingenious Excogitation : Though we dye but once, yet do not we dye at once : We may make, yea we do make many assaies or tryals of dying : Death insinuates it selfe, and seizeth upon us by peecemeals ; it gives us a tast of it self : It is the Cronie, or Consort of life : So soon as we begin to be, wee begin to wast and vanish ; we cannot ascend to life, without descending towards death : Nay we begin to dye before we appeare to live ; the perfect shape of the Infant is the death of the *Embryo*, childhood is the death of Infancie, youth of Childhood, Manhood of youth, and old age of Manhood. When we are arrived at this
20 last stage, if we stay any long time in it, and pay not the debt we owe, death requires interest ; she takes his hearing from one, his sight from another, and from some she takes both : The extent and end of all things touch their beginning, neither doth the last minute of life do any thing else, but finish what the first began. We may know also what death is, by the apparition or Image of it. We see it, and make tryal of it assiduously : we cannot act life one day, but wee must act death at night : Life is a Terrace-walke with an Arbour at one end, where we repose, and dream over our past perambulations. This lesser rest, shewes us the
30 greater ; the Soule watcheth when wee sleepe, and Conscience in the Just as well as the unjust will be ruminating on the works of life, when the body is turned into dust. Sleepe is nothing else but death painted in a night-peece ; it is a prelibation of that deepe slumber, out of which we shall not be awaked untill the Heavens be no more : We go to bed under a Scene of Stars and darknesse, but when we awake, we find Heaven changed, and one great luminary giving light to all : We dye in the state of corruption, errours, and mistinesse : But wee shall be raised in glory, and perfection, when these clouds of blacknesse that are carried
40 about with diverse winds, and every Enemy of truth shall vanish for ever, and God alone shall be all in all. We affect sleepe naturally, it is the reparation of man, & a laying by of cares. The

Coppy cannot match the pattern : if we love sleep then, why should wee hate the Idæa of it ; why should we feare death, whose shadow refresheth us, which nature never made, nor meant to fright us with ? It was her intention to strengthen our hope of dying, by giving us the fruition of this resemblance of death ; lest we should grow impatient with delay, she favour'd us with this shadow and Image of it, as Ladies comfort themselves with the pictures of their absent lovers. There is no part of life without some portion of death, as dreames cannot happen without sleepe, so life cannot be without death. As sleepe is said to be the shadow of death ; So I think dreams to be the shadowes of life, for nothing deceives us more frequent then it : When we shal be raised from death, we shal not grieve so much because the joys of life were not real, as because there were none at all. It was said by one, that he had rather dream of being tormented in Hell, then glorified in *Paradise* : for being awaked, he should rejoyce to find himselfe in a soft featherbed, and not in a lake of unquenchable fire : But having dreamt of Heaven, it would grieve him that it was not reall. *Paracelsus* writes, that the watching of the body is the sleep of the Soul, and that the day was made for Corporeall Actions, but the night is the working-time of Spirits. Contrary natures run contrary courses : Bodies having no inherent light of their own, make use of this outward light, but Spirits need it not. Sunbeams cannot stumble, nor go out of their way. Death frees them from this dark Lantern of flesh. *Heraclitus* used to say, that men were both dead and alive, both when they dyed, and when they lived : when they lived their Soules were dead, and when they dyed, their Soules revived. Life then is the death of the Soule, and the life of the body : But death is the life of the Soule, and the death of the body.

I shall return now to prosecute the Commendations of death, because it comes but once. Death (like the Phœnix) is onely one, lest any should be ill. That which comes but once, is with most longing looked for, and with most welcome entertained. That poor man, the owner of one Ewe, nourished her in his bosome, she did eate of his meat, and drank out of his Cup, as *Nathan* exemplified. The Father that hath but one Son, hath more cares, then he that hath many ; so should we be more carefull to provide for death which comes but once, then for the numerous and daily calamities of life : By providing for that one, wee turne the rest all into so many joyes. Whatsoever is rare, whatsoever is pretious, it is single, and but one. There is nothing

so rare, nothing that is comparable to a good death. But it is
not the universality or diffusivenesse of it that makes it so, but
the contempt and the subduing of it; his death is most pretious,
by whom death is contemned. Dissolution is not a meere merit,
but a debt we owe to nature, which the most unwilling must pay.
That wisedome which can make destiny to be her servant, which
can turne necessity into virtue, Mortality into Immortality, and the
debt we owe to nature into a just right and Title to eternall glory, is
very great. What greater advantage can there be, then to make
10 Heaven due to us, by being indebted to nature, and to oblige
Divinity by paying a temporal debt ? *Clemens* called them *Golden
men*, who dyed thus ; that is to say, when it was necessary to dye.
They made necessity their free will, when either the publick liberty,
the prerogative of reason, or the word of God called for their sufferings : For though death be a debt due to Nature, yet in these
causes, Nature doth willingly resigne her right, and God becomes
the Creditor. If we pay it unto him before the time of pure
resolution, Nature is better pleased with that anticipation, then if
we kept our set day : He is the best debtour, that paies before
20 the time of payment. The day of payment by the Covenant of
Nature is old age, but the good man paies before the day. If the
noblenesse of thy mind will not incite thee to such a forward
satisfaction; let the desire of gaine move thee, for the sooner
thou payest, the more thou dost oblige. Hee that suffers an
immature death for the good of his Country, for the sacred lawes,
or the vindication of the truth of God, and not for his owne vain
glory, doth free himselfe from the Natural debt, and doth at the
same time make God his debtour, and all mankind ? To a man
that dyes thus, all men are indebted : God owes him for the Cause,
30 and men for the effect : The last doth at least set us an example,
and the first improves the faith, and gives life to Charity.

Adde to this, that this great good of a passive death, is
a voluntary imitation of the Son of God, who laid down his life for
the life of the World : And it is also done without our industry ;
this great virtue, this glorious perfection requires not our care and
activity to bring it about. This death is most pretious and the
best, because it is executed by others, and not by our selves : To
suffer death, not to dye, is glorious. If prisoners break their
40 chaines, it is neither their glory, nor their security, but augments
their Guilt, and hastens their condemnation : So he that violates
his own body, and makes way for the Soul to flye out with his own

13 when] *not inserted as catchword ad loc., 1654*

hands, is damned by the very Act : but if another doth it to him, it is both his Salvation and his Crown. The heathens esteemed it no honour for Captives to have their bonds loosed : It was their freedome, but not their glory. When the judge himself did break off their Chaines, that they accounted honorable. By this Ceremony did *Vespasian* and *Titus* acknowledge the worth of *Joseph* the *Jew* : This vindicated his integrity : By cutting his bonds with their Imperial hand, they freed him both from captivity and disgrace. *Titus* said, that if they would break off 10 his fetters, and not stay to take them off, his honour would be so perfectly repaired by it, as if he had been never bound, nor overcome. The same difference (in point of honour) is betwixt the naturall death and the violent : betwixt dying when wee are full of daies, and the death which Tyrants impose upon us, when we are mangled and grinded by their fury. This honour is then greatest, when the body is not dissolved, but distorted and broken into peeces. Certainly the best men have ever perished by the violence of Tyrants ; nature (to preserve her innocence) being very backward and unwilling (as it were) to take away such great and needfull examples of goodnesse. Treachery and violence were 20 ordained for the just in the death of *Abel* ; who dyed by the wicked. This better sort of death was (in him) consecrated to the best men ; those persons whom Nature respects, and is loath to medle with, envy laies hands upon : Whom the one labours to preferre, the other plotteth to destroy. Nor deals she thus with the good only, but with the eminent and mighty too : thus she served *Hector*, *Alexander* and *Cæsar* : the goodliest object is alwaies her aim. When *Thrasybulus* the Astrologer told *Alexander* the *Roman*, that he should end his daies by a violent death, he answered, that he was very glad of it, for then (said he) I shall dye like an Emperour, 30 like the best and the greatest of men, and not sneak out of the World like a worthlesse, obscure fellow. But the death of these *Glorioli* was not truly glorious : I have onely mentioned them, because that a passive death (though wanting religion) hath made their honour permanent. That death is the truly glorious, which is seald with the joy of the sufferers spirit, whose Conscience is ravished with the kisses of the Dove : Who can look upon his tormentour with delight, and grow up to Heaven without diminution, though made shorter on Earth by the head.

This is the death which growes pretious by contempt, and 40 glorious by disgrace : Whose sufferer runs the race set before him

4 judge] jugde *1654*

with patience, and finisheth it with joy.   We are carefull that those
things which are our own, may be improved to the utmost ; and
why care wee not for death ? what is more ours then mortality ?
Death should not be feared, because it is simply, or of it self,
a great good, and is evill to none but to those that by living ill
make their death bad : What ever evil is in death, it is attracted
from life.   If thou preservest a good Conscience while thou livest,
thou wilt have no feare when thou dyest, thou wilt rejoyce and
walke homeward singing.   It is life therefore that makes thee fear
10 death : If thou didst not fear life, if life had not blasted the joyes
of death, thou wouldst never be afraid of the end of sorrowes.
Death therefore is of it self innocent, sincere, healthfull, and
desirable.   It frees us from the malignancie and malice of life,
from the sad necessities and dangerous errours we are subject to
in the body.   That death, whose leaders are Integrity and virtue,
whose cause is Religion, is the *Elixir* which gives this life its true
tincture, and makes it immortal.   To dye is a common and trivial
thing, for the good and the bad dye, and the bad most of all : but
to dye willingly, to dye gloriously is the peculiar priviledge of good
20 men.   It is better to leave life voluntarily, then to be driven out of
it forcibly : let us willingly give place unto posterity.   Esteem not
life for its own sake, but for the use of it : Love it not, because
thou wouldst live, but because thou mayst do good works while
thou livest.   Now the greatest work of life is a good death.   If
life then ought to be lesse esteemed then good works, who
would not purchase a good death with the losse of life ? why
should we be afeared of politick, irreligious Tyrants, and an arm
of flesh though guarded with steele ?   Nature it selfe threatens us
with death, and frailty attends us every hour : Why will we refuse
30 to dye in a good cause when 'tis offered us, who may dye ill the
very next day after ? let us not promise our selves a short life,
when our death assures us of eternal glory.

   But if it were granted that death were neither good nor honourable, but evill and fearfull, why will not we take care for that
which we fear ? Why do we neglect that which we suspect ? Why,
if it be evill, do not wee arme and defend our selves against it ?
we provide against dangerous contingencies, we labour against
casuall losses, and we neglect this great and enevitable perill.   To
neglect death, and to contemn death are two things : none are
40 more carefull of it, then those that contemne it ; none feare it
more then those that neglect it ; and which is strange, they fear it
not because they have neglected it, but they neglect it, when they

fear it: they dare not prepare for it, for fear of thinking of it.
O the madnesse and Idlenesse of mankind! to that, which they
adjudge to be most Evill, they come not onely unprepared, but
unadvisedly, and without so much as forethought. What mean
we, what do we look for? Death is still working, and wee are
still idle, it is still travelling towards us, and we are still
slumbering and folding our hands. Let us awake out of this
darke and sleepy state of mind, let us shake off these dreams and
vain propositions of diverse lusts: let us approve of truth and
realities, let us follow after those things which are good; let us 10
have true joy made sure unto us, and a firm security in life, in
death.

> *Sickness and death, you are but sluggish things,*
> *And cannot reach, a heart that hath got wings.*

FINIS.

THE WORLD
CONTEMNED,
IN A
Parenetical Epiſtle written by
the Reverend Father

EUCHERIUS,

Biſhop of *Lyons*, to his Kinſman
UALERIANUS.

---

*Love not the VVorld, neither the things that are
in the world. If any man love the world, the love
of the Father is not in him.* 1 Ioh. 2. 15.

*They are of the world, therefore ſpeake they of the
world, and the world heareth them.* Chap. 4. verſ. 5.

*If the world hate you, ye know that it hated me
before it hated you.* Ioh. 15. verſe 18.

*If ye were of the world, the world would love his
own, but becauſe ye are not of the world, but I have
choſen you out of the world, therfore the world hateth
you.* ver. 19.

*Remember the word that I ſaid unto you, the Ser-
vant is not greater than the Lord: if they have perſe-
cuted me, they will alſo perſecute you : If they have
kept my ſaying, they will keepe yours alſo.* v. 20.

London, Printed for *Humphrey Moſeley,*
at the *Princes Armes* in St *Pauls*
Church-yard. 1654.

Advertisement.

Heribert Ros-weyd *published this peece at* Antwerp 1621. *It is mentioned by* Gennadius cap. 63. De Scriptoribus Ecclesiasticis; *and* Erasmus (*long before* Ros-weyd's *Edition*) *writ some Notes upon it.* The Author Eucherius *was a* Roman *Senatour, but being converted to the Faith, he left the* Senate, *and lived in a poor* Cell *by the river* Druentium, *where his Wife* Galla *died. His two daughters,* Consortia, *and* Tullia, *having learnt* Christ, *continued both in the Virgin-life,* & signorum gloriâ claruerunt. *He sate Bishop in the chair of* Lyons (*as I find him placed by* Helvicus) *in the year of our*
10 Lord 443. *Some will have him a Century lower, but that difference weakens not the certainty of it. The peece it self* (*in the Original*) *is most elaborate and judicious, and breaths that* togatam elegantiam *which in most of the* Roman *Senatours was not more acquired, then natural. What this* Valerian *was* (*more then our Authors Kinsman, by whose pen his name lives*) *is not certainly known. Some will have him to be* Priscus Valerianus, *the Præfect, or Deputy of* France, *mentioned by* Sidonius Apollinaris : *Others are willing to let him passe for that* Valerian, *whose* Homilies *now extant were published by* Sirmondus. *But as it is not determinable, so is it not material :*
20 *This we may safely conclude, that he was a very eminent, noble* Personage, *and one that followed too much after temporal* pomp, *and the* powers *of this* world ; *though neither of them could lend him so much* light, *as would keep him from* obscuritie. *To bring down these top-branches,* Eucherius *layes the* Axe to the root of the tree, *by shewing him the* vanity, *and the* iniquity *of* riches *and* honours, *the two grand inticements of* popular spirits. *And this he doth with such powerfull and clear reasons, that to virtuous and peaceful minds he hath renderd them not only* contemptible, *but* odious. *Much more might have been spoken against them, but* (*seeing the* Age *we*
30 *live in hath made all his* Arguments, Demonstrations) *he hath in my judgement spoken enough.*

H. V. S.

E U C H E R I U S

to his Kinsman

VALERIANUS, &c.

They are happily linked in the bond of blood, who are held together by the bond of love. And for this gift (which is descended upon us from the Father of lights,) both you and my selfe may greatly rejoyce: Whom love as well as kindred hath united, and those two faire obligations have betrothed in one entire affection. One of them wee tooke from the Fathers of our flesh, and the other from our private dispositions. This double tye by which (love binding us on the one side, and blood on the other,) we are mutually knit together; hath inforced me to inlarge my selfe in this Epistle with some excesse more then usuall; that 10 I might commend unto your Consideration the Cause of your owne Soul, and assert the work of our profession to be, that Supreme beatitude which is onely true, and capable of those things which are Eternal.

And indeed your own pious propension is not repugnant to the profession of holy living, who already by a forward felicity of manners have in some points prevented, and met with many things which are taught unto us by sacred learning: So that by the meanes of provident and discreet Nature, you seem unto me to have seized upon many duties of Religion ; as the Concessions and 20 Indulgences of our good God towards you, whose gift it is, that the Divine wisedome should partly find in you, and partly conferre upon you the riches of his Kingdome.

But although (by the hands of your Father, and Father in law,) you have been allready advanced and seated upon the highest pinnacles of temporall honours, and are still adorned and surrounded with illustrious titles descending from them both ; Yet I desire, and long to find in you a thirst of greater and far higher honours, and shall now call you not to Earthly, but Heavenly honours, not to the dignities and splendour of one short age, but to 30 the solid and enduring glories of eternity : For the onely true and indelible glory is, to be glorified in Eternity.

I shall therefore speak unto you, not the wisedome of this

World, but that secret and hidden wisdome which God ordained befor the World unto our glory. I shall speake with much care and affection towards you, and with very little respect or anim-adversion of my selfe; for I have in this attempt considered more, what I wish to see perfected in you, than what I am able to do in my self.

The first duty of Man ordained and brought forth into this World for that end, (my most dear *Valerian*!) is to know his Creatour, and being known, to confesse him, and to resigne or
10 give up his life (which is the wonderfull and peculiar gift of God,) to the service and worship of the giver ; that what he received by Gods free donation, may be imployed in true devotion, and what was conferred upon him in the state of wrath and unworthinesse, may by an obedient resignation make him pretious and beloved. For of this saving opinion are we ; That as it is most certain, that we came forth first from God, so should we believe it, and presse on still towards him : Whereupon we shall conclude, that he onely, rightly and divinely apprehends the purpose of God in making man, who understands it thus, *That God himself made us for*
20 *himself.*

It is then our best course, to bestow our greatest care upon the Soul; So shall that which is the first and highest in dignity, be not the lowest, and last in consideration.   Amongst us *Christians*, let that which is the first in order, be the first cared for ; let Salvation which is the chiefest profit be our chiefest imployment. Let the safeguard and the defense of this, take up all our forces ; let it be not only our chiefest, but our sole delight. As it sur-passeth all other things in excellencie, so let it in our care and consideration.

30   Our Supreme duty is that which wee owe to God, and the next to it appertaines to the Soul.   And yet these two are such loving correlates, that though every one of them is a duty of Supreme con-sequence, and such as by no means we may presume to neglect or omit, yet cannot wee possibly performe any one of them without the other.   So that whosoever will serve God, doth at the same time provide for his own Soul ; and he that is carefull for his own Soul, doth at the same time serve God.   So that the state of these two soveraign duties in man, is by a certain compendious depen-dencie and co-intention rendred very easie, while the faithfull
40 performance of the one, is a perfect consummation of both : For by the unspeakable tendernesse and mercy of God, the good wee

19 understands] understand *1654*

do to our own Soules, is the most acceptable service and sacrifice that we can offer unto him.

Much Physicall curiosity, much care and many strict observations are bestowed upon the body ; much pain it undergoes in hope of health ; and deserves the Soule no Medicine? If it be but fit and necessary, that diverse helps and means of healing are sought for the body, for the recovering onely of a temporall and transitory health, is it not unjust that the Soul should be excluded, and be suffered to languish and putrifie with deadly and spirituall diseases? Shall the Soul onely be a stranger to those proper and pretious remedies ordained for it by the great Physitian? Yea rather, if so many things are provided for the body, let the provision for the Soul be far more abundant: for if it was truly said by some, that this *fleshly frame is the servant, and the Soul the Mistris*, then will it be very undecent and injurious, if we shall preferre and place the servant before the Mistris. It is but a just claim, that the better part should require the better attendance ; for with constant and intentive diligence should wee look on that side, where the greater dignity and our most pretious treasure is laid up. It is not agreeable to reason, and it takes from the honour of our imployment, that we should subject it to the unworthier party. The flesh being allwaies inclined to vitiousnesse, drawes us back to the Earth, as to its proper center and Originall : But the Soul being descended from the Father of lights, is like the sparks of fire still flying upwards. The Soule is the Image of God in us, and the pretious pledge of his future munificence. Let us imploy all our innate forces, and all outward Auxiliaries for the preservation of this : if we manage and defend it faithfully, wee take care for, and protect the intrusted pledge and purchased possession of God. What conveniencie can wee have to build, unless we do first of all lay the foundation? but to him that hath design'd a superstructure of true blessings, the fundamentall must be Salvation. And if hee hath not laid that foundation, upon what can the Consequences he hopes for be builded? how shall he be filled with the Increase of those remunerations and after-blessings, that wants the first fruits, and denies the rewarder? what portion can he have in the joyes of Eternity, that will be wanting to his own Salvation? How can he live the life of the blessed, that wil not rise from death? or what will it benefit him to heape up temporal provision, and the materials of this World ; when he hath stored up nothing for the comfort of his Soule? Or as our Lord *JESUS CHRIST* hath said, *What is a man*

profited, if hee gain the whole World, and lose his own Soul? There
can therefore be no cause for sparing and laying up, where it is
manifest, that the Soul is already lost ; where Salvation is forfeited,
what gaine or profit can be hoped for ?   Or wherein shall the true
treasure be laid up, or wherewith shall he receive it, when the
Soules pretious vessell, and the storehouse of Eternal joyes is
utterly ruined and broken ? let us therefore while we have time,
labour for true riches, and make earnest hast to that holy and
Heavenly commerce, which is worth our looking and longing
10 after.

Eternall life may be obtained in a very few daies : Which daies
though they should be blest with an inoffensive and untainted
holinesse of life, yet because they are but few, are to be lightly
esteem'd of : for nothing can be rich in value, which is but short
in duration : Nor can that procure any long or durable joyes,
whose time of existence or abode is narrow and transient.   The
short Accommodations of this life have but short effects.   It seems
therefore but just unto me, that to the joyes of this present life (if
it hath any) we should preferre the true and indubitable joyes of
20 that which is everlasting.   For the felicity we enjoy here, is at
best but temporal, but the other is eternal ; and the fruition of
a transitorie, uncertaine happinesse is but a frailty and accident ;
but the possession of inviolable and never ending joyes, is triumph
and security.

It is clear then, that the Eternal life is most blessed ; for what
other thing can be named, or thought upon, that is more happy
then everlasting life ?   As for this present short life, it is so very
short, that it is withall most miserable.   It is prest and assaulted
on every side with surrounding, inevitable sorrowes, it is distrest
30 with many evill defects, and tost to and fro by secret and penal
accidents.   For what is there in all the whole World that is so
uncertain, so various, and so replenished with troubles, as the
course of this life ?   Which is full of labour, full of anguish,
fraught with cares, and made ominous with dangers : which is
distracted with violent and suddaine mutations, made unpleasant
with bodily distempers, afflicted with thoughtfullnesse, and mentall
agonies, and lies naked and open to all the Whirlwinds of time
and Chance ?   What benefit then, yea, what reason have you to
turne aside, and run away from Eternal joyes, that you may pursue
40 and follow after temporall miseries.

Do not you see, my dear *Valerian,* how every one that is
provident (even in this life,) doth with plenty of all necessaries

furnish that cottage or field, where hee knowes he shall reside?
and where he abides but for a short time, his provision is accordingly, where he intends a longer stay, he provides likewise
a greater supply? unto us also, who in this present World (being
straightned on every side) have but a very short time, are Eternall
ages reserv'd in the World which is to come; if so be that wee
competently provide for an Eternall state, and seeke onely
what is sufficient for the present, not perversely bestowing the
greatest care upon the shortest and smallest portion of time,
and the smallest care upon the time of greatest and endlesse 10
extent.

And indeed I know not, which should soonest, or most
effectually incite us to a pious care of life Eternal, either the
blessings which are promised us in that state of glory, or the
miseries which we feel in this present life. Those from above
most lovingly invite and call upon us; these below most rudely
and importunately would expell us hence. Seeing therefore that
the continuall Evills of this life, would drive us hence unto a better,
if we will not be induced by the good, let us be compelled by the
Evill: Both the good and the bad agree to incite us to the best, 20
and though at difference amongst themselves; yet both consent to
make us happy. For while the one invites us, and the other
compells us, both are sollicitous for our good.

If some eminent and powerfull Prince having adopted you for
his Son, and co-partner, should forthwith send for you by his
Embassador; you would (I believe) break through all difficulties,
and the wearisome extent of Sea and Land, that you might appear
before him, and have your adoption ratified. God Almighty, the
Maker and the Lord of Heaven and Earth, and all that is in them,
calls you to this adoption, and offers unto you (if you will receive 30
it,) that dear stile of a Sonne, by which he calls his onely begotten, and your glorious Redeemer. And will you not be
inflamed and ravished with his Divine love? will you not make
hast, and begin your Journey towards Heaven, lest swift destruction
come upon you, and the honors offered you be frustrated by a sad
and sudden death?

And to obtain this adoption, you shall not need to passe through
the unfrequented and dangerous Solitudes of the Earth, or to
commit your selfe to the wide and perillous Sea: When you will,
this adoption is within your reach, and lodgeth with you. And 40
shall this blessing, because it is as easie in the getting, as it is great
in the consequence, find you therefore backward or unwilling to

attain it? How hard a matter to the lukewarme and the dissembler will the making sure of this adoption prove? for as to the faithfull and obedient it is most easie, so to the hypocrite and the rebellious, it is most difficult.

Certainly, it is the love of life that hath inslaved us so much to a delectation, and dotage upon temporal things. Therefore do I now advise you, who are a lover of life, to love it more. It is the right way of perswading, when we do it for no other end but to obtain that from you, which of your owne accord you desire to
10 grant us. Now for this life which you love, am I an Embassadour; and intreat that this life which you love in its transient and momentary state, you would also love in the Eternal. But how, or in what manner you may be said to love this present life, unlesse you desire to have it made most excellent, perfect, and eternally permanent, I cannot see; for that which hath the power to please you when it is but short and uncertain, wil please you much more, when it is made eternal and immutable: And that which you dearly love and value, though you have it but for a time, will be much more deare and pretious to you, when you shall enjoy it
20 without end. It is therefore but fit, that the temporall life should look still towards the Eternal, that through the one, you may passe into the other. You must not rob your selfe of the benefits of the life to come, by a crooked and perverse use of the present. This life must not oppose it selfe to the damage and hurt of the future: For it were very absurd and unnatural, that the love of life should cause the destruction and the death of life.

Therefore whither you judg this temporall life worthy of your love, or your Contempt; my present argument will be every way very reasonable.   * For if you contemne it,
An excellent Dilemma.
30   your reason to do so, is, that you may obtain a better: and if you love it, you must so much the more love that life which is eternall.

But I rather desire, that you would esteem of it, as you have found it; and judge it to be (as it is indeed) full of bitternesse and trouble, a race of tedious and various vexations; and that you would utterly forsake and renounce both it, and its occupations. Cut off at last that wearisome and endlesse chain of secular imployments, that one and the same slavery, though in severa negotiations. Break in sunder those cords of vain cares, in whose
40 successive knots you are alwayes intangled, and bound up, and in every one of which your travell is renewed and begun again. Let this rope of sands, this coherencie of vaine causes be taken away:

In which (as long as men live) the tumult of affairs (being still lengthen'd by an intervening succession of fresh cares) is never ended, but runnes on with a fretting and consuming sollicitousness, which makes this present life, that is already of it selfe short and miserable enough, far more short and more miserable. Which also (according to the successe or crosnesse of affairs) lets in divers times vain and sinfull rejoycings, bitter sorrows, anxious wishes, and suspitious fears. Let us last of all cast off all those things which make this life in respect of their imployment but very short, but in respect of cares and sorrows very long. Let us reject, and resolutely contemn this uncertain world, and the more uncertain manners of it, wherein the Peasant as well as the Prince is seldom safe, where things that lye low are trodden upon, and the high and lofty totter and decline. Chuse for your self what worldly estate you please: There is no rest either in the *mean*, or the *mighty*. Both conditions have their miseries, and their misfortunes: The private and obscure is subject to disdain, the publick and splendid unto envy.

Two prime things I suppose there are, which strongly enchain, and keep men bound in secular negotiations; and having bewitch'd their understanding, retaine them still in that dotage; the *pleasure* of *riches*, & the *dignity* of *honours*. The former of which ought not to be called pleasure, but poverty; and the latter is not dignity, but vanity. These two (being joyn'd in one subtile league) set upon man, and with alternate, insnaring knots disturb and intangle his goings. These (besides the vain desires which are peculiar to themselves) infuse into the mind of man other deadly and pestiferous lustings, which are their consequents; and with a certaine pleasing inticement sollicite and overcome the hearts of Mankind.

As for Riches (that I may speake first of them) what is there, I pray, or what can there be more pernicious? They are seldom gotten without Injustice; by such an Administrator are they gathered, and by such a Steward they must be kept; for Covetousnesse is the root of all evils. And there is indeed a very great familiarity betwixt these two, Riches * and Vices in their names, as well as in their nature. And * *Divitiæ & Vitia.* are they not also very frequently matter of disgrace, and an evill report? Upon which consideration it was said [a] *Every rich man* by one, that [a] *Riches were tokens of Injuries.* In *is either a tyrant* *himself, or the son* the possession of corrupt persons they publish *of a tyrant.* to the world their bribery and unrighteousnesse, and elswhere, they allure the eyes, and incite the spirits of seditious men to rebellion, and in the custody of such they bear witnesse of the sufferings, and the murther of innocent persons, & the plundering of their goods.

But grant that these disasters should not happen, can we have any certainty, whither these things that make themselves wings, will fly away after our decease? *He layeth up treasure* (saith the *Psalmist*) *and knoweth not for whom he gathers it.*

But suppose that you should have an heir after your own heart,
10 doth hee not oftentimes destroy and scatter what the Father hath gathered? doth not an ill-bred son, or our ill choice of a Son-in-law prove the frequent ruin of all our labours and substance in this life? What pleasure then can there be in such riches, whose collection is sin and sorrow, and our transmission, or bequeathing of them anxious and uncertaine?

Whither then at last will this wild and devious affection of men carry them? You know how to love accidental and external goods, but cannot love your own self. That which you so much long for is abroad, and without you; you place your affection
20 upon a forraigner, upon an enemy. Returne, or retire rather into your self, and be you dearer, and nearer to your own heart then those things which you call yours. Certainly if some wise man, and skilfull in the affaires of this world, should converse, and come to be intimate with you, it would better please you, that he should affect your person, then affect your goods; and you would choose, that he should rather love you for your self, then for your riches; you would have him to be faithful unto man, not to his money. What you would have another to performe towards you, that doe you for your self, who ought to be the most faithfull to
30 your self. Our selves, our selves wee should love, not those things which wee phantastically call ours.

And let this suffice to have been spoken against Riches.

As for the Honours of this world (to speak generally, and without exception, for I shall not descend to particulars) what dignity can you justly attribute to those things which the base man, and the bad, as well as the noble and good, promiscuously obtain, and all of them by corruption and ambition? The same honour is not conferred upon men of the same merits, and dignity makes not a difference betwixt the worthy and the unworthy, but
40 confounds them. So that which should be a character of deserts, by advancing the good above the bad, doth most unjustly make

22 wise man] wiseman *1654*

them equal; and after a most strange manner there is in no state of life lesse difference made betwixt the worst men, and the best, then in that state which you term honourable. Is it not then a greater honour to be without that honour, and to be esteemed of according to our genuine worth, and sincere carriage, then according to the false gloss of promiscuous, deceiving honours?

And these very things (how big soever they look) what fleeting and frail appearances are they? We have seen of late men eminently honourable, seated upon the very spires, and top of dignity, whose incredible treasures purchased them a great 10 part of the world; their successe exceeded their own desires, and their prodigious fortunes amazed their very wishes: But these I speak of were private prosperities. Kings themselves with all their height and imperiousnesse, with all their triumphs and glory shined but for a time. Their cloathings were of wrought gold, their diadems sparkled with the various flames, and differing relucencies of precious stones; their Palaces were thronged with Princely attendants, their roofs adorned with gilded beams, their Will was a Law, and their words were the rules and coercive bounds of Mankind. But who is he, that by a temporal felicity 20 can lift his head above the stage of humane chances? Behold now, how the vast sway and circumference of these *mighty* is no where to be found! their riches and precious things too are all gone, and they themselves the possessors and masters of those royal treasures! most late, and most famous Kingdoms (even amongst us) are now become a certaine fable. All those things which sometimes were reputed here to be very great, are now become none at all.

Nothing I think, nay I am sure, of all these riches, honours, powers went along with them from hence: All they took with 30 them was the pretious substance of their faith and piety. These onely (when they were deprived of all other attendants) waited on them, and like faithfull, inseparable companions, travelled with them out of this world. With this provision are they now fed; with these riches, and with these honours are they adorned. In these they rest, and this goodnesse is now their greatnesse.

Wherefore, if we be taken at all with honours and riches, let us be taken with the true and durable ones: Every good man exchangeth these earthly dignities for those which are celestiall, and earthen treasures for the heavenly. He layes up treasure 40 there, where a most exact and inconfused difference is made

15 of wrought] of wrought of *1654*

betwixt the good and the bad ; where that which is once gotten shall be for ever enjoyed ; where all things may be obtained, and where nothing can be lost.

But seeing we are fallen into a discourse of the frailty of temporal things, let us not forget the frail condition of this short life. What is it, I beseech you, what is it ? Men see nothing more frequently then death, and minde nothing more seldome. Mankinde is by a swift mortality quickly driven into the *West*, or setting point of life, and all posterity by the unalterable Law of
10 succeeding ages and generations follow after. Our fathers went from hence before us ; we shall goe next, and our children must come after. As streames of water falling from high, the one still following the other, doe in successive circles break and terminate at the banks ; so the appointed times and successions of men are cut off at the boundary of death. This consideration should take up our thoughts night and day ; this memoriall of our fraile condition should keep us still awake. Let us alwayes thinke the time of our departure to be at hand ; for the day of death, the farther we put it off, comes on the faster, and is by so much the nearer to us. Let
20 us suspect it to be near, because we know not how far. Let us, as the *Scripture* saith, *make plain our wayes before us.*

If we make this the businesse of our thoughts, and meditate still upon it, wee shall not be frighted with the fear of death. Blessed and happy are all you who have already reconciled your selves unto *Christ*! no great fear of death can disturb them, who desire to be dissolved that they may be with *Christ*; who in the silence of their own bosomes, quietly, and long since prepared for it, expect the last day of their pilgrimage here. They care not much how soon they end this temporal life, that passe from it
30 into life eternal.

Let not the populacy and throng of loose livers, or hypocriticall time-pleasers perswade us to a neglect of life, neither be you induced by the errours of the *many* to cast away your particular salvation. What wil the multitude in that day of Gods judgement avail us, when every private person shall be sentenced, where the examinations of works, and every mans particular actions, not the example of the common people shall absolve him ? Stop your ears, and shut your eyes against such damnable Precedents that invite you to destruction. It is better to sow in tears, and to plant
40 eternal life with the few, then to lose it with the multitude. Let not therefore the number of sinfull men weaken your diligence of not sinning ; for the madnesse of those that sin against their

own soules, can be no authority unto us; I beseech you look alwayes upon the vices of others as their shame, not your example.

If it be your pleasure to look for examples, seek them rather from that party, which though the least, yet if considered as it is a distinct body, is numerous enough : Seek them (I say) from that party, wherein you shall find those ranged, who wisely understood, wherefore they were born, and accordingly while they lived, did the businesse of life ; who eminent for good works, and excelling in virtue, pruned and drest the present life, and planted the future. Nor are our examples (though of this rare kind) only copious, but 10 great withall, and most illustrious.

For what worldly nobility, what honours, what dignity, what wisdom, what eloquence, or learning have not betaken themselves to this heavenly warfare? what soveraignty now hath not with all humility submitted to this easie yoke of *Christ?* And certainly it is a madnesse beyond error and ignorance for any to dissemble in the cause of their salvation. I could (but that I will not be tedious to you) out of an innumerable company produce many by name, and shew you what eminent and famous men in their times have forsaken this World, and embraced the most strict rules of 20 *Christian* Religion. And some of these (because I may not omit all,) I shall cursorily introduce.

Clement the *Roman,* of the stock of the *Cæsars,* and the Antient Linage of the Senatours, a person fraught with Science, and most skillfull in the liberall *Arts,* betook himself to this path of the just ; and so uprightly did he walk therein, that he was elected to the Episcopal dignity of *Rome.*

Gregorie of *Pontus,* a Minister of holy things, famous at first for his humane learning and eloquence, became afterwards more eminent by those Divine 30 Graces conferr'd upon him. For (as the Faith of Ecclesiastical History testifies,) amongst other miraculous signes of his effectual devotion, he removed a Mountain by prayer, and dried up a deep lake. *Gregorius Thaumaturgus.*

Gregory Nazianzen, another holy Father, given also at first to Philosophie and humane literature, declined at last those Worldly rudiments, and embraced the true and Heavenly Philosophy : To whose industry also wee owe no meaner a person then *Basil* the Great; for being his intimate acquaintance, and fellow-student in secular Sciences, he entred one day into his *Auditory,* where 40 *Basilius* was then a Reader of *Rhetorick,* and leading him by the hand out of the School, disswaded him from that imployment with this gentle reproofe, *Leave this Vanity, and study thy Salvation.* And shortly after both of them came to be famous and faithfull Stewards in the house of God, and have left us in the Church, most usefull and pregnant Monuments of their Christian learning.

Thou hast his life annexed to this Epistle: as a precedent after these precepts.

Paulinus Bishop of *Nola,* the great Ornament and light of *France,* a person of Princely revenues, powerfull eloquence, and most accomplish'd learning, so highly approved of this our profession, that *choosing for himself the better* 10 *part,* he divided all his Princely Inheritance amongst the poor, and afterward filled most part of the World with his elegant and pious writings.

Hilarius of late, and *Petronius* now in *Italie,* both of them out of the fulnesse of Secular honours and power, betook themselves

[a] Hilarius *about this time (which was* 435. *years after* Christ) *did lead a monastical life: but upon the death of* Honoratus, *he was elected his successour in the Bishoprick of* Orleans, 20 *in which dignity he continued not long, for being addicted to solitarinesse, he resigned it, and turned into the Wildernesse.*

St. Augustine.

to this Course ; the one entring [a] into the religion, the other into the Priesthood.

And when shall I have done with this great cloud of witnesses, If I should bring into the field all those eloquent Contenders for the Faith, *Firmianus, Minutius, Cyprian, Hilary, Chrysostome* and *Ambrose?* These I believe spoke to themselves in the same words which [a] another of our profession used as a spurre to drive himselfe out of the Secular life into this blessed and Heavenly vocation ; They said, I believe : *What is this? The unlearned get up, and lay hold upon the Kingdome of Heaven, and we with our learning, behold where we wallow in flesh and blood.* This (sure) they said, and upon this consideration they also rose up, and tooke 30 the Kingdome of Heaven by force.

Having now in part produced these reverend witnesses, whose zeal for the Christian faith hath exceeded most of their successours, though they also were bred up in secular rudiments, perswasive eloquence, and the Pomp and fulnesse of honours ; I shall descend unto Kings themselves, and to that head of the World, the *Roman* Empire. And here I think it not necessary that those Royal, religious Antients of the old World should be mentioned at all. Some of their posterity, and the most renowned in our *Sacred* Chronicles I shall make use of ; as *David* for Piety, *Josiah* 40 for Faith, and *Ezechias* for Humility. The later times also have been fruitfull in this kinde, nor is this our age altogether barren of pious Princes, who draw near to the Knowledge of the onely true and Immortal King, and with most contrite and submissive hearts acknowledge and adore the Lord of Lords. The *Court,* as well as the *Cloyster,* hath yeelded Saints, of both Sexes. And these in my opinion are more worthy your Imitation, then the mad and giddy Commonalty ; for the examples of these, carry with them in the World to come Salvation, and in the present World, Authority.

You see also how the dayes and the years, and all the bright Ornaments and Luminaries of Heaven, do with an unwearied duty execute the commands and decrees of their Creatour ; and in a constant, irremissive tenour continue obedient to his ordinances. 10 And shall wee (for whose use these lights were created, and set in the firmament,) seeing we know our Masters will, and are not ignorant of his Commandements, stop our ears against them ? And to these Vast members of the Universe it was but once told, what they should observe unto the end of the World ; but unto us line upon line, precept upon precept, and whole volumes of Gods Commandements are every day repeated. Adde to this, that man (for this also is in his power) should learn to submit himself to the will of his Creator, and to be obedient to his Ordinances ; for by paying his whole duty unto God, he gives withall a good 20 example unto men.

But if there be any that will not returne unto their maker and be healed, can they therefore escape the Arme of their Lord, in whose hand are the Spirits of all flesh ? Whither will they fly, that would avoyd the presence of God ? What Covert can hide them from that *Eye* which is every where, and sees all things ? Let them heare thee, holy *David,* let them heare thee.

Psalm 139.

Whither shall I go from thy presence, or whither shall I flee from thy Spirit? 30

If I ascend up into Heaven, thou art there : if I make my bed in Hell, behold thou art there.

If I take the wings of the morning, and dwell in the uttermost parts of the Sea ;

Even there shall thy hand lead me, and thy right hand shall hold me.

If I say, surely the darknesse shall cover me : even the night shall be light about thee.

Yea the darknesse hideth not from thee, but the night shineth as the day : the darkness and the light are both alike to thee. 40

6 Authority.] Authority, *1654*   35 *hand shall*] *hand stall 1654*

Therefore (willing or unwilling) though they should absent themselves from the Lord of all the world by their Wills, yet shall they never be able to get their persons out of his Jurisdiction and Supreme right. They are absent from him indeed in their love and affections: But he is present with them in his prerogative and anger. So then being runagates, they are shut up, and (which is a most impious madnesse) they live without any consideration or regard of God, but within his power. And if these being earthly Masters, when their servants run away from them ; with a furious 10 and hasty search pursue after them ; or if they renounce their service, prosecute them for it, and become the assertours of their owne right over them ; why will not they themselves render unto their Master which is in Heaven his most just right ? Why will they not stay in his Family, and freely offer themselves unto his service, and be as impartial Judges in the cause of God as in their own ?

Why with so much dotage do we fixe our Eyes upon the deceitfull lookes of temporal things? Why do we rest our selves upon those thornes onely, which wee see beneath us ? Is it the 20 Eye alone that wee live by? Is there nothing usefull about us but that wanderer? We live also by the eare, and at that Inlet wee receive the glad tydings of Salvation, which fill us with earnest grones for our glorious liberty and the consummation of the promises ; Whatsoever is promised, whatsoever is preached unto us, let us wait for it with intentive wishes, and most eager desires. That faithfull one, the blessed Author of those promises assures us frequently of his fidelity and performance, let us covet earnestly his best promises.

But notwithstanding this which hath been spoken, if a sober 30 and virtuous use were made of the Eye, we might by that very faculty be drawn to a certaine sacred longing after Immortality, and the powers of the World to come ; if that admiration, which by contemplating the rare frame of the World wee are usually filled with, were returned upon the glorious Creatour of it, by our praises and benediction of him ; Or if we would meditate what a copious, active and boundlesse light shall fill our eyes in the state of Immortality, seeing so fair a luminary is allowed us in the state of corruption : Or what transcendent beauty shall be given to all things in that eternall World, seeing this transitory one is so full 40 of Majesty and freshnesse ; There can be no excuse for us, if we sollicite the faculties of these members to abuse and perversenesse : Let them rather be commodiously applied to both lifes, and so

minister to the use of the temporall, as not to cast off their duty
to the Eternal.

But if pleasure and love delight us, and provoke our Senses,
there is in Christian Religion, a love of infinite comfort, and such
delights as are not nauseous and offensive after fruition. There
is in it, that which not onely admits of a most vehement and overflowing love, but ought allso to be so beloved; namely, God, blessed
for evermore, the onely beautifull, delightfull, immortal and
Supreme good, whom you may boldly and intimately love as well
as piously; if in the room of your former earthly affections, you 10
entertain Heavenly and holy desires. If you were ever taken with
the magnificence and dignity of another person, there is nothing
more magnificent then God. If with any thing that might conduce to your honour and glory; there is nothing more glorious
then him: If with the splendour and excellencie of pompous
showes, there is nothing more bright, nothing more excellent. If
with fairnesse and pleasing objects, there is nothing more beautifull.
If with verity and righteousnesse, there is nothing more just,
nothing more true. If with liberality, there is nothing more
bountifull. If with incorruption and simplicity, there is nothing 20
more sincere, nothing more pure then that Supreme goodnesse.
Are you troubled that your treasure and store is not proportionable
to your mind? The Earth and the fullnesse thereof are under his
lock: Do you love any thing that is trusty and firm? There is
nothing more friendly, nothing more faithfull then him: Do you
love any thing that is beneficial? There is no greater benefactor.
Are you delighted with the gravity or gentleness of any object?
there is nothing more terrible then his Almightinesse, nothing
more mild then his goodnesse. Do you love refreshments in
a low estate, and a merry heart in a plentifull? Joy in prosperity, 30
and comforts in adversity are both the dispensations of his hand.
Wherefore it stands with all reason, that you should love the giver
more then his gifts, and him from whom you have all these things,
more then the things themselves. Riches, Honours, and all
things else, whose present lustre attracts and possesseth your heart,
are not onely with him, but are now also had from him.

Recollect your dispersed, and hitherto ill-placed affections,
imploy them wholly in the Divine service. Let this dissolute love
and compliance with worldly desires become chast piety, and wait
upon sacred affaires. Call home your devious and runnagate 40
thoughts, which opinion and custome have sadly distracted; and
having supprest old errors, direct your love to his proper object,

bestow it wholy upon your Maker. For all that you can love now is his, his alone, and none else. For of such infinitenesse is he, that those who do not love him, deale most injuriously : because they cannot love any thing, but what is his.

But I would have an impartial judgement to consider, whether it be just for him to love the work, and hate the Workman ; and having cast by, and deserted the Creator of all things, to run and seize upon his creatures every where, and without any difference, according to his perverse and insatiable lust. Whereas it behoved
10 him rather to invite God to be gratious and loving to him, by this very affection to his works, if piously layd out. And now man gives himself over to the lusts and service of his own detestable figments, and most unnaturally becomes a lover of the Art, and neglects the Artificer, adores the Creature, and despiseth the Creator.

And what have we spoken all this while of those innumerable delights which are with him ? or of the infinite and ravishing sweetnesse of his ineffable Goodnesse ? the sacred and inexhaustible treasure of his Love ? or when will it be that any shall be able
20 to expresse or conceive the dignity and fulnesse of any one Attribute that is in him ? To love him then is not onely delightfull, but needfull : For not to love him, whom even then when we love, we cannot possibly requite, is impious ; and not to returne him such acknowledgements as we are able, whom if we would, we can never recompence, is most unjust : For what shall we render unto the Lord for all his benefits towards us ? What shall we render unto him for this one benefit, that he hath given salvation to man by faith, and ordained that to be most easie in the *fact*, by which he restored hope to the subjected world, and
30 eternal life unto lost man ?

And that I may now descend unto those things which were sometimes out of his Covenant, I mean the Nations and Kingdomes of the Gentiles, doe you think that these were made subject to the *Roman* power, and that the dispersed multitude of Mankind were incorporated (as it were) into one body under one head for any other end, but that (as Medicines taken in at the mouth are diffused into all parts of the body) so the Faith by this means might with more ease be planted and penetrated into the most remote parts of the world. Otherwise by reason of different
40 powers, customs, and languages, it had met with fresh and numerous oppositions, and the passage of the Gospel had been much more difficult. Blessed *Paul* himself describing his course

in planting the Faith amongst this very people, writes in his Epistle to the *Romans, That from Hierusalem and round about to Illyricum he had fully preached the Gospel of Christ.* And how long (without this preparation in the fulnesse of time) might this have been in doing, amongst Nations, either innumerable for multitude, or barbarous for immanitie? Hence it is that the whole earth now from the rising of the Sun unto the going down thereof, from the farthest North and the frozen sea breaks forth into singing, and rings with the glorious name of *Jesus Christ.* Hence it is, that all parts of the world flock and run together to the Word of Life: The *Thracian* is for the Faith, the *African* for the Faith, the *Syrian* for the Faith, and the *Spaniard* hath received the Faith. A great argument of the divine clemency may be gathered out of this, that under *Augustus Cæsar,* when the *Roman* power was in the height, and *Acmie,* then the Almighty God came down upon the earth and assumed flesh. Therfore that I may now make use of those things, which you also are versed in, it may be clearly proved (if any skilled in your Histories would assert the truth) that from the first foundation of the *Roman* Empire (which is now one thousand one *This letter was* hundred and eighty five years ago) what ever *written in the year* additions and growth it gathered either in the *of our Lord* 435. reign of their first *Kings,* or afterwards under the administration of *Consuls,* all was permitted by the onely wise, and almighty God to prepare the world against the coming of *Christ,* and to make way for the propagation of the Faith.

But I return thither, from whence I have digrest. *Love not the world* (saith *St. John*) *neither the things that are in the world;* for all those things with delusive, insnaring shews, captivate our sight, and will not suffer us to look upwards. Let not that faculty of the eye which was ordained for light, be applyed to darknesse, being created for the use of life, let it not admit the causes of death. Fleshly lusts (as it is divinely spoken by the Apostle) war against the soul, and all their accoutrements are for the ruin and destruction of it. A vigilant guard doe they keep, when they are once permitted to make head, and after the manner of forraign and expert enemies, with those forces they take from us, they politickly strengthen and increase their own.

Thus hitherto have I discoursed of those splendid allurements, which are the chiefest and most taking baits of this subtile world, I mean Riches and Honours. And with such earnestnesse have I argued against them, as if those blandishments had still some

force. But what beauty soever they had, when cast over heretofore with some pleasing adumbrations, it is now quite worn away, and all that paint and cousenage is fallen off. The world now hath scarce the art to deceive. Those powerfull and bewitching lookes of things, beautiful sometimes even to deception, are now withered, and almost loathsome. In former times it laboured to seduce us with its most solid and magnificent glories, and it could not. Now it turnes cheat, and would entice us with toyes, and slight wares, but it cannot. Reall riches it never had, and now it
10 is so poor, that it wants counterfeits. It neither hath delectable things for the present, nor durable for the future; unlesse wee agree to deceive our selves, the world in a manner cannot deceive us.

But why delay I my stronger arguments? I affirm then that the forces of this world are dispersed and overthrown, seeing the world it self is now drawing towards its dissolution, and pants with its last gasps, and dying anhelations. How much more grievous and bitter will you think this assertion, that for certain it cannot last very long? What should I trouble my self to tell you that all
20 the utensils and moveables of it are decayed and wasted? And no marvell that it is driven into these defects, and a consumption of its ancient strength, when now grown old and weary it stoopes with weaknesse, and is ready to fall under the burthen of so many ages.

These latter years and decrepitness of time are fraught with evils and calamities, as old age is with diseases. Our forefathers saw, and we still see in these last dayes the plagues of famine, pestilence, war, destruction, and terrours. All these are so many acute fits and convulsions of the dying world. Hence it is that such frequent signs are seen in the firmament, excessive Ecclipses,
30 and faintings of the brightest Luminaries, which is a shaking of the powers of heaven; sudden and astonishing Earthquakes under our feet, alterations of times and governments, with the monstrous fruitfulnesse of living creatures; all which are the prodigies, or fatall *symptomes* of time going indeed still on, but fainting, and ready to expire. Nor is this confirmed by my weak assertions onely, but by sacred authority and the Apostolical Oracles: For there it is written, that *upon us the ends of the world are come,* 1 *Cor.* 10. 11. Which divine truth seeing it hath been spoken so long agoe, what is it that we linger for, or what can we expect? That day,
40 not onely ours, but the last that ever the present world shall see, calls earnestly for our preparation. Every hour tels us of the

coming on of that inevitable hour of our death, seeing a double danger of two finall dissolutions threatens every one in particular, and all the world in generall. Wretched man that I am! the mortality of this whole frame lyes heavily upon my thoughts, as if my own were not burthensome enough. Wherefore is it that we flatter our selves against these sure fears. There is no place left for deviation: A most certain decree is past against us, on the one side is written every mans private dissolution, and on the other the publick and universal.

How much more miserable then is the condition of those men (I will not say, in these out-goings, or last walks of time, but in these decayes of the worlds goodly things) who neither can enjoy ought that is pleasant at the present, nor lay up for themselves any hope of true joyes hereafter. They misse the fruition of this short life, and can have no hope of the everlasting: They abuse these temporal blessings, and shall never be admitted to use the eternall. Their substance here is very little, but their hope there is none at all. A most wretched and deplorable condition! unless they make a virtue of this desperate necessity, and lay hold on the onely soveraign remedy of bettering their estate, by submitting in time to the wholsome rules of heavenly and saving reason. Especially because the goodliest things of this present time, are such rags and fragments, that he that loseth the whole fraught, and true treasure of that one precious life which is to come, may be justly said to lose both.

It remaines then, that we direct and fixe all the powers of our minds upon the hope of the life to come. Which hope (that you may more fully and clearly apprehend it) I shall manifest unto you, under a type or example taken from temporal things. If some man should offer unto another five peeces of silver this day, but promise him five hundred peeces of gold, if he would stay till the next morning, and put him to his choice, whither he would have the silver at present, or the gold upon the day following, is there any doubt to be made, but he would chuse the greater sum, though with a little delay? Goe you and doe the like: Compare the Crummes and perishing pittance in this short life, with the glorious, and enduring rewards of the eternall: And when you have done, chuse not the least and the worst, when you may have the greatest and the best. The short fruition of a little is not so beneficial, as the expectation of plenty. But seeing that all the fraile goods of this world are not onely seen of us, but also possessed by us: It is most manifest that hope cannot belong unto this world, in which we both see and enjoy those things we delight in: For *Hope that is seen is not hope; for what a man seeth, why doth he yet hope for?* Rom. 8. *ver.* 24. Therefore however hope may be abused, and misapplyed to temporal things, it is most certaine that it was given to man and ordained for the things that are eternal; otherwise it cannot be called hope, unlesse something bee hoped for, which as yet (or for the present life) is not had. Therefore the substance of our hope in the world to come is more evident and manifest, then our hope of substance in the present.

Consider those objects which are the clearest and most visible; when we would best discern them, we put them not into our eyes, because they are better seen and judged of at a distance. It is just so in the case of present things and the future: For the present (as if put into our eyes) are not rightly and undeceivably seen of us; but the future, because conveniently distant, are most clearly discerned.

Nor is this trust and Confidence wee have of our future happinesse built upon weak or uncertain Authors, but upon our Lord and Master *JESUS CHRIST,* that allmighty and faithfull witnesse, who hath promised unto the just, a Kingdome without end, and the ample rewards of a most blessed eternity. Who also by the ineffable Sacrament of his humanity, being both God and Man, reconciled Man unto God, and by the mighty and hidden mystery of his passion, absolved the World from sinne. For which cause he was manifested in the flesh, justified in the Spirit, seen of Angels, preached unto the Gentiles, believed upon in the World, and received into glory. Wherefore God also hath highly *Philip. Chap.* 2. exalted him, and given him a name which is *ver.* 9, 10. above every name: that at the name of *JESUS* every knee should bow, of things in Heaven, and things in Earth, and things under the Earth. And that every tongue should confesse that the Lord *JESUS* is in glory, both God and King before all ages.

Casting off then the vaine and absurd precepts of Philosophy, wherein you busie your selfe to no purpose, embrace at last the true and saving Knowledge of Christ. You shall find even in that, imployment enough for your eloquence and wit, and will quickly discern how far these precepts of piety and truth surpasse the conceits and delirations of Philosophers. For in those rules which they give, what is there but adulterate virtue, and false wisedom? and what in ours, but perfect righteousnesse and sincere truth? Whereupon I shall Justly conclude, that they indeed usurpe the name of Philosophy, but the substance and life of it is with us.   For what manner of rules to live by could they give, who were ignorant of the first Cause, and the Fountain of life?   For not knowing God, and deviating in their first principles from the Author, and the Wel-spring of Justice; they necessarily erred in the rest: Hence it happened, that the end of all their studies was vanity and dissention.   And if any amongst them chanced to hit upon some more sober and honest Tenets, these presently ministred matter of pride and Superstitiousnesse, so that their very Virtue was not free from vice.   It is evident then, that these are they, whose *Knowledge is Earthy, the disputers of this world, the blind guides,* who never saw true justice, nor true wisedome.   Can any one of that School of *Aristippus* be a teacher of the truth, who in their Doctrine and Conversation differ not from swine and unclean beasts, seeing they place true happinesse in fleshly lusts? whose God is their belly, and whose glory is in their shame.   Can he be a Master of Sobriety and Virtue, in whose School the riotous, the obscene, and the adulterer are Philosophers?   But leaving these blind leaders, I shall come againe to speak of those things which were the first motives of my writing to you.

I advise you then, and I beseech you, to cast off all their *Axioms,* or general *Maxims* collected out of their wild and irregular disputations, wherein I have knowne you much delighted; & to imploy those excellent abilities bestowed upon you in the study of holy Scripture, & the wholsom instructions of Christian Philosophers.   There shall you be fed with various and delightfull learning, with true and infallible wisedome.   There (to incite you to the Faith) you shall hear the Church speaking to you, though not in these very words, yet to this purpose, *He that believes not the word of God, understands it not.*   There you shall hear this frequent admonition; *Feare God, because he is your Master, honour him because he is your Father.*   There it shall be told you, *that the most acceptable Sacrifice to God are justice and mercy.*   There you shall be taught, that, *If you love your self, you must necessarily love your neighbour; for you can never do your selfe a greater Courtesie, then by doing good to another.*   There you shall be taught, that, *there can be no worldly cause so great, as to make the death of a man legal or needfull.*   There you shall hear this precept against unlawfull desires.   *Resist lust as a most bitter enemy, that useth to glory in the disgrace of those bodies he overcommeth.*   There it will

be told you of Covetousnesse, *That it is better not to wish for those things you want, than to have all that you wish.* There you shall hear, that *he that is angry, when he is provoked, is never not angry, but when not provoked.* There it will be told you of your Enemies, *Love them that hate you, for all men love those that love them.* There you shall hear, *that he laies up his treasure safeliest, who gives it to the poor, for that cannot be lost which is lent to the Lord.* There it will be told you, *that the fruite of holy marriage is chastity.* There you shall hear, *that the troubles of this World*
10 *happen as well to the just, as the unjust.* There it will be told you, *that it is a more dangerous sicknesse to have the mind infected with vices, then the body with diseases.* There to shew you the way of peace and gentlenesse you shall hear, *that amongst impatient men, their likenesse of manners is the cause of their discord.* There to keepe you from following the bad examples of others, it will be told you, *That the wise man gains by the fool, as well as by the prudent: the one shewes him what to imitate, the other what to eschew.* There also you shall hear all these following precepts. *That the ignorance of many things is better then their Knowledge;*
20 *and that therefore the goodnesse or mercy of God is as great in his hidden will, as in his revealed. That you should give God thanks as well for adversity, as for prosperity; and confesse in prosperity, that you have not deserved it. That there is no such thing as Fate, and for this let the Heathens examine their owne Lawes, which punish none but willfull and premeditating offenders.* There to keep you stable in faith, it will be told you, *That he that will be faithfull, must not be suspitious; for we never suspect, but what wee slowly believe.* There also you shall hear, *that Christians when they give any attention to the noyse and inticements of their passions,*
30 *fall headlong from Heaven unto Earth.* It will be also told you there, *that seeing the wicked do sometimes receive good things in this world, and the just are afflicted by the unrighteous, those that believe not the final Judgement of God after this life, do (as far as it lies in them) make God unjust,* and far be this from your thoughts. There it will be told you about your private affaires, *that what you would have hidden from men, you should never do, what from God, ye should never think.* There you shall here this rebuke of deceivers; It is lesser damage to be deceived, then to deceive. Lastly you shall hear this reproofe of self-conceit, or a fond
40 opinion of our owne worth; flye vanity, and so much the more, the better thou art: all other vices increase by vitiousnesse, but vanity is oftentimes a bubble that swims upon the face of Virtue.

These few rules, as a tast and invitation, I have (out of many more) inserted here for your use.

But if you will now turn your Eyes towards the sacred Oracles, and come your self to be a searcher of those Heavenly treasures, I know not which will most ravish you, the *Casket*, or the *Jewell*, the *Language* or the *Matter*. For the Booke of God, while it shines and glitters with glorious irradiations within, doth after the manner of most pretious gems, drive the beholders Eyes into a strong and restlesse admiration of its most rich and inscrutable brightnesse. But let not the weaknesse of your Eyes make you shun this Divine light, but warme your Soul at the beames of it, and learne to feede your inward man with this mystical and health-full foode.

I doubt not but (by the powerful working of our mercifull God upon your heart,) I shall shortly find you an unfeyned lover of this true Philosophie, and a resolute opposer of the false; renouncing also all worldly oblectations, and earnestly coveting the true and eternall. For it is a point of great impiety and impru-dence, seeing God wrought so many marvellous things for the Salvation of man, that he should do nothing for himself: and see-ing that in all his wonderfull works he had a most speciall reguard of our good, we our selves should especially neglect it. Now the right way to care for our Soules, is to yeild our selves to the love and the service of God : For true happinesse is obtained by con-temning the false felicities of this World, and by a wise abdication of all earthly delights, that we may become the Chast and faithfull lovers of the Heavenly. Wherefore henceforth let all your words and actions be done either to the glory of God, or for Gods sake. Get Innocence for your Companion, and she is so faithfull, that she will be also your defendresse. It is a worthy enterprise to follow after Virtue, and to perform something while we live, for the example and the good of others : nor is it to be doubted, but the mind, by a virtuous course of life, will quickly free it selfe from those intanglements and deviations it hath been formerly accustomed to. That great Physition to whose cure and care we offer our selves, will daily strengthen and perfect our recovery.

And what estimation or value (when in this state) can you lay upon those glorious remunerations that will be laid up for you against the day of recompence? You see that God, even in this life, hath mercifully distributed unto all (without any difference) his most pleasant and usefull light. The pious and the impious

26 delights] d lights *1654*

are both allowed the same Sunne, all the creatures obediently submit themselves to their service : And the whole Earth with the fullnesse thereof is the indifferent possession of the just and unjust. Seeing then that he hath given such excellent things unto the impious, how much more glorious are those things which he reserves for the pious ? he that is so great in his free gifts, how excellent will he be in his rewards ? He that is so Royal in his daily bounty, and ordinary magnificence ; how transcendent will hee be in his remunerations and requitalls ? Ineffable and beyond
10 all conception are those things which God hath prepared for those that love him ; And that they are so is most certain : For it is altogether incomprehensible, and passeth the understanding of his most chosen vessels to tell, how great his reward shall be unto the just, who hath given so much to the unthankfull and the unbelieving.

Take up your Eyes from the Earth, and look about you, my most dear *Valerian* ; spread forth your sailes, and hasten from this stormy Sea of Secular negotiations, into the calme and secure harbour of Christian Religion. This is the onely Haven into
20 which we all drive from the raging Surges of this malitious World. This is our shelter from the lowd and persecuting whirlwinds of time : Here is our sure station and certain rest : Here a large and silent recesse, secluded from the World, opens and offers it selfe unto us. Here a pleasant, serene tranquillity shines upon us. Hither when you are come, your weather-beaten Vessell (after all your fruitlesse toiles) shall at last find rest, and securely ride at the Anchor of the *Cross*.

But it is time now that I should make an end. Let then (I beseech you,) the truth and the force of Heavenly Doctrine
30 Epitomized here by me, be approved of and used by you to the glory of God and your own good. These are all my precepts at present : pardon the length, and acknowledge my love.

Gloria tibi mitissime Jesu !

Primitive Holiness,

Set forth in the

L I F E

of blessed

PAULINUS,

The most Reverend, and
Learned B I S H O P of
NOLA:

Collected out of his own Works,
and other Primitive Authors by

Henry Vaughan, Silurist.

---

2 Kings *cap.* 2. *ver.* 12.
*My Father, my Father, the Chariot of
Israel, and the Horsmen thereof.*

L O N D O N,
Printed for *Humphrey Moseley* at
the *Prince's Armes* in St. *Paul's* ·
Church-yard. 1 6 5 4.

TO THE
READER.

If thou lovest Heaven, *and the beauty of Immortality, here is*
a guide *will lead thee into that* house of light. *The* earth *at*
present is not worth the enjoying, it is corrupt, and poysoned with
the curse. *I exhort thee therefore to look after a* better country, an
inheritance that is undefiled and fadeth not away. *If thou doest*
this, thou shalt have a portion given thee here, when all things shall
be made new. *In the mean time I commend unto thee the memorie*
of that restorer, *and the* reward *he shall bring with him in the* end
of this world, *which truely draws near, if it be not* at the door.
10 *Doat not any more upon a withered, rotten* Gourd, *upon the*
seducements and falshood of a most odious, decayed Prostitute; *but*
look up to Heaven, where wealth *without* want, delight *without*
distast, and joy *without* sorrow (*like undefiled and incorruptible*
Virgins) *sit cloathed with* light, *and crowned with* glory. *Let me*
incite thee to this speculation *in the language of* Ferarius: Desine
tandem aliquando prono in terram vultu, vel præter naturam
brutum animal, vel ante diem silicernium videri. Cœlum suspice,
ad quod natus, ad quod erectâ staturâ tuendum tenendumque
factus es. Immortalia sydera caducis flosculis præfer, aut eadem
20 esse Cœli flores existimato nostratibus Amaranthis diuturniores.
Farewel, and neglect not thy own happiness.

H. V.

THE LIFE OF
HOLY
PAULINUS,
THE
BISHOP of *NOLA*.

Ben Sirach finishing his Catalogue of holy men (to seal up the summe, and to make his list compleat) brings in *Simon* the Sonne of *Onias* : And (after a short narration of his pious care in repairing and fortifying the Temple) hee descends to the particular excellencies, and sacred perfections of his person. Which to render the more fresh and sweet unto posterity, he adornes with these bright and flowrie *Encomiums.*

1. *He was as the Morning-star in the midst of a cloud, and as the Moon at the full.*

2. *As the Sunne shining upon the temple of the most high, and* 10 *as the Rain-bow giving light in the bright clouds.*

3. *As the flower of Roses in the spring of the year, as Lilies by the rivers of waters, and as the branches of the Frankincense-tree in the time of summer.*

4. *As fire and Incense in the Censer, and as a vessel of beaten gold set with all manner of precious stones.*

5. *As a fair Olive-tree budding forth fruit, and as a Cypresse tree which groweth up to the clouds.*

6. *When he put on the robe of honour, and was cloathed with the perfection of glory, when he went up to the holy Altar, he made the* 20 *garment of holinesse honourable.*

Most great (indeed) and most glorious Assimilations, full of life, and full of freshnesse ! but in all this beauty of holinesse, in all these spices and flowers of the Spouse, there is nothing too much, nothing too great for our most great and holy *Paulinus.* The Saints of God (*though wandring in sheep-skins, and goat-skins, in caves, and in mountains*) become eminently famous, and leave behind them a more glorious and enduring memory, then the most prosperous tyrants of this world ; which like noysome exhalations, moving for a time in the Eye of the Sun, fall after- 30 wards to the earth, where they rot and perish under the *chaines of darkness.* The fame of holy men (like the *Kingdome of God*) is a *seed that grows secretly*; the dew that feeds these plants comes from him, that *sees in secret, but rewards openly.* They are those *trees* in the Poet,

> *Which silently, and by none seen,*
> *Grow great and green.*

While they labour to conceal, and obscure themselves, they shine the more. And this (saith *Athanasius* in the life of *Antonie* the great) *is the goodnesse of God, who useth to glorifie his servants, though unwilling, that by their examples he may condemn the world,* 10 *and teach men, that holinesse is not above the reach of humane nature.* Apposite to my present purpose is all this prolusion, both because this blessed Bishop (whose life I here adventure to publish) was a person of miraculous perfections and holynesse, and because withall he did most diligently endeavour to vilifie his own excellent abilities, and to make himselfe of no account. But Pearls, though set in *lead*, will not lose their brightnesse; and a virtuous life shines most in an obscure livelyhood.

In the explication of his life I shall follow first the method of *Nature*, afterwards of *Grace*: I shall begin with his *Birth,* 20 *Education*, and *Maturitie*; and end with his *Conversion, Improvements*, and *Perfection.* To make my entrance then into the work, I finde that he was born in the City of *Burdeaux* in *Gascoyne*, in the year of our Lord three hundred and fifty three, *Constantius* the *Arian* reigning in the East, and *Constans* in the West, and * *Liberius* being Bishop of *Rome* : In a Golden Age, when Religion and Learning kissed each other, and equally flourished. So that he had the happines to shine in an age that loved light, and to multiply his own by the 30 light of others. It was the fashion then of the *Roman* Senatours to build them sumptuous houses in their Country-livings, that they might have the pleasure and conveniency of retiring thither from the tumult and noyse of that great City, which sometimes was, and would be yet the head of the World. Upon such an occasion (without doubt) was *Burdeaux* honoured with the birth of *Paulinus*, his Fathers estate lying not far off, about the town of *Embrau,* upon the River *Garumna*, which rising out of the *Pyrene* hils washeth that part of *Guienne* with a pleasant stream, and then runs into the *Aquitane* sea. By this happy accident came *France* 40 to lay claime to *Paulinus*, which she makes no small boast of at this day. But his Country indeed (if we follow his descent, which is the right way to find it) is *Italie*, and *Rome* it self; his Ancestors

* *He subscribed to the damnable heresie of* Arius, *as both* Hierome *and* A-thanasius *testifie against him.*

were all *Patricians*, and honour'd (by a long succession) with the
Consular *purple*. His Patrimonies were large, and more becomming
a Prince then a private man; for besides those possessions in the
City of *Burdeaux*, and by the River *Garumna*, he had other most
ample Inheritances in *Italy* about *Narbone* and *Nola*, and in *Rome* it
self. And for this we have a pregnant testimony out of *Ausonius*,
who labouring to disswade him from *Evangelical poverty*, and
that obscure course of life (as he is pleased to term it) layes before
him (as the most moving arguments) the desolation of his ancient
house, with the ruin and *sequestration* (as it were) of his large 10
possessions; his words are these.

> *Ne raptam sparsamḍ domum,* &c.

> *Let me not weep to see thy ravish'd house*
> *All sad & silent, without Lord or Spouse,*
> *And all those vast dominions once thine owne,*
> *Torn 'twixt a hundred slaves to me unknown.*

But what account he made of these earthly possessions, will
appear best by his own words in his fifth Epistle to *Severus* :
Ergo nihil in hunc mundum inferentibus substantiam rerum tem-
poralium quasi tonsile vellus apponit, &c. " God (saith he) layes 20
" these temporal accommodations upon us that come naked into
" this world, as a fleece of wooll which is to be sheared off. He
" puts it not as a load to hinder us, whom it behoves to be born
" light and active, but as a certain matter which rightly used may
" be beneficial. And when he bestoweth any thing upon us, that
" is either dear or pleasant to us, he gives it for this end, that by
" parting with it, it may be a testimonial, or token of our love and
" devotion towards God, seeing we neglect the fruition of our best
" present things for his sake, who will amply reward us in the
" future. 30

He had conferred upon him all the ornaments of humane life
which man could be blest with. He was nobly born, rich, and
beautifull, of constitution slender and delicate, but every way fitted
for virtuous imployment; of an excellent wit, a happy memory,
and, which sweeten'd all these gracious concessions, of a most
mild and modest disposition. To bring these seeds to perfection,
his Father (having a care of him equall to his degree) caused him
to be brought up under the regiment of *Decius magnus Ausonius*,
a famous *Poet* and *Oratour*, who at that time kept a School of
Grammar and *Rhetorick* in the City of *Burdeaux*. The Ingenuity 40
and sweetnesse of *Paulinus* so overcame and ravished *Ausonius*,
that he used all possible skill and diligence, to adorne and perfect

those natural abilities which he so much loved and admired in this hopefull plant. The effect was, that he exceeded his Master. *Ausonius* upon this being called to the Court by the old Emperor *Valentinian*; *Paulinus* gave himselfe to the study of the *Civill Law*, and the acute and learned pleadings of that age, wherein he was so excellent, that the Emperor taking notice of his Abilities, took order for his Election into the *Senate*, and this a very long time before his *Tutor* attained to that honour. This præcedence of eloquence and honour * *Ausonius* himself confesseth; but having a greater witnesse, I shall leave his testimony to the *Margin*, to make room for the other. Take then (if it please you) the Judgement of that glorious and Eloquent Doctour Saint *Hierome*, for thus he writes in his thirteenth Epist. to *Paulinus, O si mihi liceret istiusmodi ingenium non per Aonios montes & Heliconis vertices, ut poetæ canunt, sed per Sion,* &c. "O that I were able (saith he) to "extoll and publish your ingenuity and holy learning, not upon "the *Aonian* hills, or the tops of *Helicon* (as the Poets sing) but "upon the Mountaines of *Sion* and *Sinai*; that I might preach "there what I have learnt from you, and deliver the sacred "mysteries of Scripture through your hands; I might then have "something to speak, which learned *Greece* could never boast of. "And in another place, A most pregnant wit you have, and an "infinite treasure of words, which easily and aptly flow from you, "and both the easinesse and the aptness are judiciously mixt.

To these Divine favours already conferred upon him, God added another great blessing, the Crown of his youth, and the Comfort of his age; I meane *Therasia*, a Noble *Roman* Virgin, whom he tooke to wife in the midst of his honours, and who afterwards (of her owne free will) most joyfully parted with them all, and with her own pleasant possessions to follow *Christ* in the regeneration.

At this height of honours, & growing repute, he was employ'd (upon some concernments of the *Empire*) into *Italy, France,* and *Spain*; Where he was detained (together with his dear consort) for the space of almost fifteen years; during which time, he secretly laboured to make himself acquainted with the glorious *Fathers* of that age, and (the Spirit of God now beginning to breath upon him) hee was strongly moved to embrace the *Christian* Faith. In these travells of his, it was his fortune to

* *Cedimus ingenio quantum prœcedimus ævo, Assurgit Musæ nostra Camœna tuæ. Sic & fastorum titulo prior, & tua Romæ Præcessit nostrum sella curulis ebur.*

3 *(note) ævo] ayo 1654*

arrive at *Millaine*, where Saint *Augustine*, and *Alypius*, the Bishop of *Tagasta* in *Africk*, did then Sojourne ; here by accident he was known of *Alypius*, though unknown to him ; as we see it often fall out, that great persons are known of many, which to them are unknown.

Much about this time (which was the eight and thirtieth year of his age,) he retired privately with his wife into the City of *Burdeaux*. And the hour being now come, that *the singing of birds should be heard, and the lips which were asleep should speak* : Hee was there by the hands of holy *Delphinus* (who then sate Bishop in the *Sea* of *Burdeaux*,) publickly baptized, from which time forward he renounced all his Secular acquaintance, associating himself to the most strict and pious livers in that age, especially to Saint *Ambrose* the Bishop of *Millan*, and Saint *Martin* the Bishop of *Tours*. That he was baptized about the eight and thirtieth yeare of his age, is clear by his owne words in his first Epistle to Saint *Augustine*, *Nolo in me corporalis ortus, magis quam spiritalis exortus ætatem consideres*, &c. " I would not (saith he) that you consider my " temporall age, so much as my spiritual ; my age in the flesh is " the same with that Cripple, who was healed in the beautifull gate " by the power of Christ working by his Apostles ; but my age in " the regeneration is the same with the blessed Infants, who by " the wounds intended for Christ himself, became the first fruits " unto Christ, and by the losse of their innocent blood, did fore- " shew the slaughter of the Lamb, and the passion of our Lord. Now for the first, Saint *Luke* tells us, *That the Cripple upon whom this miracle of healing was shown, was above forty years of age* (Acts Chap. 4. ver. 22.) and for the Infants, the *Evangelists* words are, that *Herod sent forth his messengers, and slew all the Male Children that were in* Bethlem, *and the Coasts thereof, from two years old and under.* So that considering all the Circumstances which offer themselves for the clearing of this point, it will evidently appear, that he was baptized (as I have said before) in the eight and thirtieth year of his age.   The onely Instrument which God was pleas'd to ordain, and imploy upon the Earth for his Conversion, was his dear and Virtuous Wife *Therasia* ; Which makes me conjecture, that she was borne of Christian parents, and had received the faith from her infancie.   This *Ausonius* his old *Tutor*, (who was scarce a good Christian,) forgat not to upraid him with in most injurious termes, calling her *Tanaquil*, and the *Imperatrix* of her Husband : To which passionate passages (though sadly resented) *Paulinus* replyed with all the humanity and sweetnesse which language could expresse. Thus *Ausonius* barks at him.

Undè istam meruit non fœlix Charta repulsam?
Hostis ab hoste tamen, &c.

——— how could that paper sent,
That luckless paper, merit thy contempt?
Ev'n foe to fo (though furiously) replies;
And the defied, his Enemy defies:
Amidst the swords and wounds ther's a Salute.
Rocks answer man, and though hard, are not mute.
Nature made nothing dumb, nothing unkind:
The trees and leaves speak trembling to the wind.
If thou doest feare discoveries, and the blot
Of my love, *Tanaquil* shal know it not.

To this Poetical fury, *Paulinus* reposeth with that Native mildnesse, which he was wholly composed of.

Continuata meæ durare silentia linguæ,
Te nunquam tacito memoras; placitamq; latebris
Desidiam exprobras; neglectæq; insuper addis
Crimen amicitiæ; formidatamq; Jugalem
Objicis, & durum iacis in mea viscera versum, &c.

Obdurate still, and tongue-tyed you accuse
(Though yours is ever vocall) my dull muse;
You blame my Lazie, lurking life, and adde
I scorne your love, a Calumny most sad;
Then tell me, that I fear my wife, and dart
Harsh, cutting words against my dearest heart.
Leave, learned Father, leave this bitter Course,
My studies are not turn'd unto the worse;
I am not mad, nor idle; nor deny
Your great deserts, and my debt, nor have I
A wife like *Tanaquil*, as wildly you
Object, but a *Lucretia*, chast and true.

To avoid these clamours of *Ausonius*, and the dangerous sollicitations of his great kindred and friends, he left *Burdeaux* and *Nola*, and retyred into the Mountanous and solitary parts of *Spaine*, about *Barcinoe* and *Bilbilis* upon the River *Salo*. Two journeyes he made into *Spain*, this last, and his first (before his baptism) upon the Emperours affairs; he Sojourned then in new *Castile*, in the City of *Complutum* now called *Alcala de henares*, where his wife *Therasia* was delivered of her onely Son *Celsus*, who died upon the eighth day after his birth. Holy *Paulinus* in his *Panegyrick* upon the death of *Celsus* the Son of *Pneumatius*,

3 *Undè*] *Unde catchword 1654* 15 reposeth] reponeth *Gu*

by his Wife *Fidelis*, takes occasion to mention the early death of
this blessed infant,

Hoc pignus commune superno in lumine Celsum
    Credite vivorum lacte favisq́ frui.
Aut cum Bethlæis infantibus in Paradiso
    (Quos malus Herodes perculit invidiâ,)
Inter odoratum ludit nemus, &c.

This pledge of your joint love, to Heaven now fled,
With honey-combs and milk of life is fed.
Or with the *Bethlem*-Babes (whom *Herods* rage   10
Kill'd in their tender, happy, holy age)
Doth walk the groves of Paradise, and make
Garlands, which those young Martyrs from him take.
With these his Eyes on the mild lamb are fixt,
A Virgin-Child with Virgin-infants mixt.
Such is my *Celsus* too, who soon as given,
Was taken back (on the eighth day) to Heaven,
To whom at *Alcala* I sadly gave
Amongst the Martyrs Tombes a little grave.
Hee now with yours (gone both the blessed way,)   20
Amongst the trees of life doth smile and play ;
And this one drop of our mixt blood may be
A light for my *Therasia*, and for me.

These distant and obscure retirements he made choice of,
because he would not be known of any, nor hindred in his course ;
Which at *Nola*, and the adjacent parts of *Rome* (where his Secular
honours and antient descent made all the people obsequious to
him) could not possibly be effected.   Besides very few in those
Western parts (especially of the Nobility) had at that time received
the *Christian* Faith ; for they look'd upon it as a most degenerate, 30
unmanly profession: such a good opinion had those rough times
of peace and humility.   This made him lesse looked after by the
Inhabitants of those parts ; and his own friends not knowing what
became of him, began to give him over, and not onely to withdraw
from him in their care, but in their affections also, giving out that
he was mad, and besides himself.   But all this moved him not :
he was *not ashamed of the Gospel of Christ, he counted all things
dung that he might gaine* his Saviour, and hee fainted not, but
endured, as seeing him that is invisible.   The first step to Christianity (saith Saint *Hierome*) is to contemne the *St. Hierome Ep.* 26. 40
censures of men.   This foundation he laid, and
upon this he built ; he had given himselfe wholly to *Christ*, and
rejected the world ; he tooke part with that *man of sorrowes*, and
suffered the scoffs and reproaches of these men of mirth.   The

people are the many waters, he turn'd their froth and fome into pearls, and wearied all weathers with an unimpaired *Superstitie.* Hee was founded upon that Rock, which is not worne with time, but wears all that oppose it. Some dispositions love to stand in raine, and affect wind and showers beyond Musick. *Paulinus* sure was of this temper ; he preferred the indignation and hatred of the multitude to their love, he would not buy their friendship with the losse of Heaven, nor call those Saints and propagators, who were Devills and destroyers. What courage he had in such
10 tempests, may be seen in every line almost of his workes; I shal insert one or two out of his 6th Epistle to *Severus* : *Utinam, frater mi, digni habeamur qui maledicamur, & notemur, & conteramur, atque etiam interficiamur in nomine Jesu Christi, dum non ipse occidatur Christus in nobis.* &c. " I would (saith he) my dear " brother, that we might be counted worthy to suffer reproach, to " be branded and troden upon ; Yea, and to be killed for the " name of Christ, so that Christ be not killed in us. Then at last " should we tread upon the Adder, and the Dragon, and bruise "the head of the old Serpent. But (alas !) wee as yet relish this
20 " World, and do but pretend to love Christ ; we love indeed to be " commended and cherished for professing his name, but wee love "not to be troubled and afflicted for his sake. And in his first " Epistle to *Aper*; O blessed displeasures (saith he) to displease " men by pleasing Christ ! Let us take heed of the love of such, "who will be pleased without Christ. It is an observation of the Readers of Saint *Cyprian, quod in ejus scriptis singula propè verba Martyrium spirant,* that through all his writings, almost every word doth breath Martyrdome. His expressions are all Spirit and Passion, as if he had writ them with his blood, and conveyed the
30 anguish of his sufferings into his writings. I dare not say so much of *Paulinus,* nor of any other Father of the Church ; but I fear not to say that *Paulinus* both durst, and (had he beene called to it) would have laid downe his life for the love of Christ.

Four yeares hee spent in these remote parts of *Spain,* during which time, he did lead a most solitary and austere life, labouring by all meanes to conceale and vilifie himself. *But a City that is built upon a hill cannot be hidden ;* his holinesse and humility had so awaked the Common people dwelling about the place of his abode, that they would not rest again till they had him for their
40 Minister. This most honourable and sacred charge he would by no meanes adventure to undergo, judging himselfe a most unworthy vile sinner, not fit to deale in holy Scripture, much lesse to handle

and administer the mystical Elements of life. But God, who had ordained him for it, would not suffer this. For the people (not without violence and some rudeness,) carried him away to *Barcinoe*, where holy *Lampius*, then Bishop of that Sea, did upon *Christmasse* day by the laying on of his hands, consecrate him a faithfull steward and learned dispenser of the Mysteries of God. This passage we have fully related in his sixth Epistle to *Severus*, *Nos modo in Barcinonensi (ut ante Scripseram) civitate consistimus*, &c. "I live now (saith he) as I formerly writ to you in the City of "*Barcinoe*, where (since the last letters received from you) I was by 10 "the violence of the people (God, I believe, having foreordained "it) compell'd to enter into holy Orders upon that day in which "our Lord was born. I confesse it was done against my will, not "for any dislike that I have to the place (for Christ is my witnesse, "that my highest desire was to begin my imployment in his house "with the office and honour of a door-keeper) but having designed "my selfe (as you know) * elsewhere, I was   * *For Nola.* "much terrified with this sudden and unexpected "pleasure of the Divine will: However I refused it not, but "submitted with all humility, and have put my necke into the 20 "Yoke of Christ, though altogether unworthy and unable. I see "now that I have medled with things that are too wonderful for "me; I am made a Steward of the Secrets of the Almighty, and "honourd with the dispensation of Heavenly things, and being "called nearer to my Master, I am exercised about the Body, "about the Spirit, and the glory of Jesus Christ. The narrownesse "of my understanding cannot comprehend the signification of "this high and sacred dignity, and I tremble every minute (when "I consider my own infirmities) to thinke of the great burthen "that is laid upon me. But he that gives wisedome to his little 30 "ones, and hath perfected praise out of the mouths of babes and "sucklings, is able to finish what he begun in me, that by his "mighty working, I may be made worthy, who was most unworthy "to be called. The Priesthood is an Office belonging to the Kingdome of Heaven. It is an honour that is ranged upon holy ground, and by it selfe. Worldly dignities, which are but humane inventions, are, and may be acquired (with lesse offence) by humane meanes, as bribery, ambition, and policie. But to take hold of this white robe with such dirty hands, is nothing lesse then to spit in the face of *Christ*, and to dishonour his Ordinance. 40 He that doth it, and he that permits it to be done, agree like *Herod* and *Pilate*, to dispise and crucifie him. They that

Countenance and ratifie such disorders, take care to provide so many *Judasses* to betray Christ, and then vote the treason to be lawfull. Every man can speak, but every man cannot preach: Tongues and the gift of tongues are not the same things: The wisdome of God hath *depth* and *riches*, and *things hard to be spoken*, as well as *milk*, and *the first principles of his Oracles*. Wee have amongst us many builders with *hay and stubble*, but let them, and those that hired them, take heed how they build; The tryal will be by fire, and by a consuming fire. The *hidden things of* 10 *dishonesty, the walking in Craftinesse*, and *the handling deceitfully of the word of God* they are well versed in; but true sanctitie, and the Spirit of God (which Saint *Paul* thought he had) I am very sure they have not.

A modest reader would now thinke that *Paulinus* had removed himselfe farre enough from the elaborate temptations, and clamorous pursuits of *Ausonius*; But even in this will he be deceived. For at the fourth years end, did the Incantations of this busie and obstinate Charmer find him out. God (no doubt) providing for the security of his servant all that while, by delaying them in severall 20 regions, or else by concealing the abode of his beloved votary, from this pursuer of Soules. For with all the artifice and strength of wit, did he set upon him in this last letter, which the divine providence suffered not to come into his hand, till he had set both his *hands to the plough*, and seald his conformation with that indelible Character. And now having set a hedge about his beloved, he suffered this *Fowle* of the Evening to fly over, which chattered to him in these melodious numbers.

> *Vertisti*, Pauline, *tuos dulcissime mores ?* &c.
> *Sweet* Paulinus, *is thy nature turn'd ?*
> 30 *Have I so long in vaine thy absence mourn'd ?*
> *Wilt thou, my glory, and great* Romes *delight,*
> *The Senates prop, their oracle, and light,*
> *In* Bilbilis *and* Calagurris *dwel,*
> *Changing thy Ivorie-chair for a dark Cell ?*
> *Wilt bury there thy Purple, and contemn*
> *All the great honours of thy noble stem ?*

To this *Roman Magick*, and most pernicious Elegancy, *Paulinus* replyed with a certain sacred and serene simplicity, which proved so piercing, and powerful, that he was never after troubled with 40 the Poetry of *Ausonius*.

> ———*Revocandum me tibi credam,*
> *Cum steriles fundas non ad divina precatus ?*
> *Castalidis supplex averso numine musis*, &c.

42 *precatus*] *percatus 1654*

Shall I beleeve you can make me return,
Who pour your fruitless prayers when you mourn,
Not to your Maker ?   Who can hear you cry :
But to the fabled Nymphs of *Castalie*?
You never shall by such false Gods bring me
Either to *Rome*, or to your company.
As for those former things you once did know,
And which you still call mine, I freely now
Confesse, I am not he, whom you knew then ;
I have dyed since, and have been borne agen.   10
Nor dare I think my sage instructor can
Believe it errour, for redeemed man
To serve his great redeemer.   I grieve not,
But glory so to erre.   Let the wise knot
Of worldlings call me fool ; I slight their noise,
And heare my God approving of my choice.
Man is but glass, a building of no trust,
A moving shade, and, without *Christ*, meer dust :
His choice in life concerns the Chooser much :
For when he dyes, his good or ill (just such   20
As here it was) goes with him hence, and staies
Still by him, his strict Judge in the last dayes.
These serious thoughts take up my soul, and I
While yet 'tis day-light, fix my busie eye
Upon his sacred Rules, lifes precious sum,
Who in the twilight of the world shall come
To judge the lofty looks, and shew mankind
The diff'rence 'twixt the ill and well inclin'd.
This second coming of the worlds great King
Makes my heart tremble, and doth timely bring   30
A saving care into my watchfull soul,
Lest in that day all vitiated and foul
I should be found : That day, times utmost line,
When all shall perish, but what is divine.
When the great Trumpets mighty blast shall shake
The earths foundations, till the hard Rocks quake,
And melt like piles of snow, when lightnings move
Like hail, and the white thrones are set above.
That day, when sent in glory by the Father,
The Prince of life his blest Elect shall gather ;   40
Millions of Angels round about him flying,
While all the kindreds of the earth are crying,
And he enthron'd upon the clouds shall give
His last just sentence, who must die, who live.
   This is the fear this is the saving care,
That makes me leave false honours, and that share
Which fell to mee of this fraile world ; lest by
A frequent use of present pleasures I
Should quite forget the future, and let in
Foul Atheism, or some presumptuous sin.

Now by their loss I have secur'd my life,
And bought my peace ev'n with the cause of strife.
I live to him, who gave me life & breath,
And without feare expect the houre of death.
If you like this, bid joy to my rich state,
If not, leave me to *Christ* at any rate.

Being now ordained a Minister of holy things, and a feeder of
the flock of *Christ*, that he might be enabled to render a joyfull account at the appearance of the great Shepheard, he resolved
10 with all convenient expedition to sell and give away all his large and
Princely Possessions in *Italy* and *France*, which hitherto he had not
disposed of; for he looked upon his great Patrimonies as matters of
distraction and backsliding, the thoughts and solicitousnesse about
such vast revenues disturbing his pious affections, and necessarily
intruding into his most holy exercitations. Upon this rare resolution
he returnes with his faithfull Consort into *France*, leaving *Barcinoe*
and holy *Lampius* in much sorrow for his departure. For though
hee had entred there into the Ministery, yet was he no member of
that Diocesse. And here (saith *Uranius*, who was his Presbyter,
20 and wrote a brief narration of his life) did he open his Treasuries
to the poor and the stranger. He did not only refresh his neighbours, but sent messengers into other remote parts to summon the
naked, and the hungry to this great Feast, where they were both
fed and cloathed with his own hands. He eased the oppressed,
freed the captives, payd the debts of whole families, and redeemed
divers persons that were become bondslaves to their creditors.
Briefly, he sold all that he had, and distributed the money amongst
the poor, not reserving one penny either for himself, or his dear
Therasia. Saint *Ambrose* in his thirtieth Epistle to *Sabinus* con-
30 firmeth this relation : *Paulinum splendore generis in partibus
Aquitaniæ nulli secundum, venditis facultatibus tam suis quam etiam
conjugalibus, &c.* " *Paulinus* (saith he) the most eminent for
" his Nobility in all the parts of *Aquitane*, having sold away all his
" patrimonies, together with the goods of his wife, did out of pure
" love to Jesus Christ divide all that vast Summe of Money amongst
" the poor ; and he himself from a rich Senator is become a most
" poor man, having cast off that heavy secular burthen, and forsaken
" his own house, his country, and his kindred, that he might with
" more earnestnesse follow Christ. His Wife also, as nobly de-
40 " scended, and as zealous for the Faith as himself, consented to all
" his desires, and having given away all her own large possessions,
" lives with her husband in a little thatch'd cottage, rich in

32 (saith *text 1654* : saith *catchword 1654*

"nothing but the hidden treasures of Religion and holinesse. Saint *Augustine* also in his first book *de Civitate Dei*, and the tenth Chapter, celebrates him with the like testimony : " Our *Paulinus* " (saith hee) from a man most splendidly rich, became most poor " most willingly, and most richly holy. He laboured not to adde field unto field, nor to inclose himself in Cedar and Ivory, and the drossie darke gold of this world, but to enter through the gates into the precious light of that City, which is of *pure gold like unto cleare glasse.* He left some few things in this world, to enjoy all in the world to come. A great performance certainly, and a most fair approach towards the Kingdom of heaven. He that fights with dust, comes off well, if it blinds him not. To slight words, and the names of temptations, is easie, but to deale so with the matter, and substance of them, is a task. Conscience hath Musick, and light, as well as discord and darknesse : And the triumphs of it are as familiar after good works, as the Checks of it after bad. It is no heresie in devotion to be sensible of our small-est Victories over the World. But how far he was from thinking this a Victory, may be easily gathered out of his owne words in his second Epistle to *Severus* ; *Facilè nobis bona*, &c. " The "goods (saith he) I carried about me, by the slipping of my skirt "out of my hand, fell easily from me : And those things which "I brought not into this World, and could not carry out of it, being "only lent me for a time, I restored again. I pulled them not "as the skin off my back, but laid them by, as a garment I had "sometimes worne. But now comes the difficulty upon me, "when those things which are truly mine, as my heart, my Soul, "and my works must be presented and given a living Sacrifice "unto God. The abdication of this World, and the giving of our "temporall goods amongst the poore, is not the running of the race, "but a preparing to run ; it is not the end, but the beginning, and "first step of our Journey. Hee that striveth for masteries, shall "not be crowned, except he first strive lawfully ; And he that is "to swimme over a River, cannot do it by ·putting off his "cloathes onely, he must put his body also into the stream, and "with the motion of his armes, his hands and feete, passe through "the violence of the Brook, and then rest upon the further side "of it. And in his 12th Epistle, he cries out, " O miserable and "vaine men ! Wee believe that wee bestow something upon the "poor : wee trade and lend, and would be counted liberall, when "we are most covetous. The most unconscionable userers upon

10

20

30

40

" Earth are not so greedy as we are, nor their interest and exactions
" so unreasonable as ours. We purchase Heaven with Earth,
" happinesse with misery, and immortality with rust and rotten-
" nesse. Such another Divine rapture is that in his Poems.

>—— *Et res magna videtur,*
> *Mercari propriam de re pereunte salutem ?*
> *Perpetuis mutare caduca ?* &c.

>—— And is the bargain thought too dear,
> To give for Heaven our fraile subsistence here ?
> To change our mortall with immortall homes,
> And purchase the bright Stars with darksome stones ?
> Behold ! my God (a rate great as his breath !)
> On the sad crosse bought me with bitter death,
> Did put on flesh, and suffer'd for our good,
> For ours, (vile slaves !) the losse of his dear blood.

Wee see by these *Manifesto's* what account he made of this
great deed ; so great, that none now adaies thinke of doing it. *Go
thy way, sell whatsoever thou hast, and give to the poor,* is a commandement, as well as, *take up the Crosse and follow me.* This last
cannot be done, but by doing the first. Wee sell oftentimes, but
seldome give : and happily that is the reason we sell so often. He
that keeps all to himselfe, takes not the right way to thrive. The
Corn that lies in the Granarie will bring no harvest. It is most
commonly the foode of vermine, and some creatures of the night
and darknesse. Charity is a relique of Paradise, and pitty is
a strong argument that we are all descended from one man : He
that carries this rare Jewell about him, will every where meete with
some kindred. He is quickly acquainted with distressed persons,
and their first sight warmes his blood. I could believe, that the
word *stranger* is a notion received from the posterity of *Cain,* who
killed *Abel.* The *Hebrewes* in their own tribes, called those of the
farthest degree, *brothers ;* and sure they erred lesse from the law
of pure Nature, then the rest of the Nations, which were left to
their owne lusts. The afflictions of man are more moving then of
any other Creature ; for he onely is a stranger here, where all things
else are at home. But the losing of his innocency, and his device
of Tyranny have made him unpittied, and forfeited a prerogative,
that would have prevailed more by submission, then all his posterity shall do by opposition. Not to give to one that lacks, is
a kind of murther : Want and famine are destroyers as well as the
sword, and rage very frequently in private, when they are not

14 suffer'd] suffe'rd *1654*   18 *whatsoever]* *whatsover 1654*   20
Wee *M* : Well *1654* : We'll *G Gu*

thought of in the Publick. The blessed *JESUS* who came into the World to rectifie Nature, and to take away the inveterate corruptions of man, was not more in any of his precepts, then in that which bids us *Love one another.* This is the cement not onely of this World, but of that other which is to come. *Blessed are the mercifull;* and, *give to him that asketh thee*, proceeded from the same lips of truth. And in his description of the last judgement, he grounds the sentence of condemnation pronounced against the wicked upon no other fact, but because they did not *cloath the naked, feed the hungry, and take in the stranger. Love covers a* 10 *multitude of sins, and God loves the chearfull giver.* But this is not our whole duty : though we give our bodies to be burnt, and give all our goods unto the poor, yet *without holinesse we shall never see the face of God.* Darknesse cannot stand in the presence of light, and *flesh and blood cannot inherit the Kingdome of God.* The great difficulty then (as our holy Bishop here saith) is to become a living sacrifice ; and truly the next way to it, is by an Evangelical disposing of these outward incumbrances ; this will open and pre-pare the way before us, though it takes nothing from the length of it. The Hawke *proines* and *rouseth* before she flyes, but that brings 20 her not to the *mark* : Preparations, and the distant flourishes of *Array* will not get the field, but action, and the pursuance of it.

His Estate in *France* being thus disposed of, he retyred into *Italy* ; where having done the like to his Patrimonies there, hee came to *Millaine*, and was honourably received by holy *Ambrose*, then Bishop of that *Sea*. But these gay feathers of the World, being thus blown off him, by the breath of that Spirit which makes *the dry tree to become green*, and *the spices of the Garden to flow out*, all his kindred and former acquaintance became his deadly Enemies. Flyes of estate follow Fortune, and the Sun-shine ; 30 friendship is a thing much talked off, but seldome found ; I never knew above two that loved without selfe-ends. That which passeth for love in this age, is the meere counter to it ; It is policie in the cloathes of love, or the hands of *Esau* with the tongue of *Jacob*. These smooth Cheats the World abounds with : There is *Clay enough for the potter, but little dust whereof commeth Gold.* The best direction is Religion ; find a true Christian, and thou hast found a true friend. He that fears not God, will not feare to do thee a mischiefe.

From *Millaine* he came to *Rome*, where he was honourably 40 entertained by all, but his own kindred, and *Siricius* the great Bishop. It was the ill Fortune of this zealous Pope, to be offended

not onely with *Paulinus,* but with that glorious Father Saint *Hierome.* It was a perillous dissolutenesse of some Bishops in that Century, to admit of Lay-men, and unseason'd persons into the Ministry. This rash and impious practice *Siricius* had, by severall strict Sanctions or decrees, condemned and forbidden ; and it is probable that the reason of his strange carriage towards *Paulinus* and *Hierome* was, because he would not seem to connive at any persons that were suddenly ordained, though never so deserving, lest he should seeme to offend against his own edicts.   It is a sad truth that
10 this pernicious rashnesse of Bishops (fighting *ex diametro* with the Apostolical cautions) hath oftentimes brought boars into the Vineyard, and Wolves into the sheep-fold ; which complying afterwards with all manner of Interests, have torne out the bowels of their Mother.   Wee need no examples : Wee have lived to see all this our selves.   Ignorance and obstinacie make *Hereticks* : And ambition makes *Schismaticks* ; when they are once at this passe, they are on the way toward *Atheisme.*   I do not say that *Ecclesiastical polity* is an inviolable or sure fense against Church-rents ; because there is a necessity that *offences must come*, though *wo to*
20 *them by whom* ; but rules of prevention are given, and therefore they should not be slighted.   The Bridegroom adviseth his spouse to *take these foxes while they are litle.*

In a pleasant field halfe a mile distant from *Nola* lies the Sepulcher of the blessed Martyr *Felix.*   To this place (which from his youth hee was ever devoted to,) did *Paulinus* now retire.   It was the custom of holy men in that age, not onely to live near the Tombs of the Martyrs, but to provide also for their buriall in those places ; because they were sure, that in the Resurrection, and the terrours of the day of Judgement God would descend upon
30 those places in *the soft voyce*, that is to say in his love and mercies. *Eusebius* in his fourth Book, and the sixth Chapter of the life of *Constantine* tells us, how that great Emperour gave strict order for his buriall amongst the Tombes of the Apostles, and then adds, Ὠφέλειαν ψυχῆς ὀνησιφόρον τὴν τῶνδε μνήμην ποιεῖσθαι αυτῶ πιστεύων.   Saint *Chrysostome* in that homilie which hee writ to prove that *Christ is God,* gives the same relation, Καὶ ἐν τῇ Κωνσταντίνου πόλει δε, &c.   The Emperors of *Constantinople* (saith he) esteeme it for a great honour, if they be buried not within the shrines of the Apostles, but at the Gates of their
40 Temple, that they may be the door-keepers of those poor fishers. So *Marcellina*, descended from the consular Nobility of *Rome*,

15 *Hereticks*] *Heretick catchword 1654*   31 in] is *1654*

refused to be buried amongst her Ancestors, that she might sleepe at *Millaine* with her great Brother Saint *Ambrose*, where shee lies under this *Epitaph.*

> *Marcellina, tuos cum vita resolveret artus :*
> *Sprevisti patriis,* &c.

> Life, *Marcellina*, leaving thy faire frame,
> Thou didst contemne those Tombes of costly fame,
> Built by thy Roman Ancestours, and lyest
> At *Millaine*, where great *Ambrose* sleeps in Christ.
> Hope, the deads life, and faith, which never faints,   10
> Made thee rest here, that thou may'st rise with Saints.

To this place therefore near *Nola* in *Campania* (a Country lying within the Realm of *Naples*, and called now by the Inhabitants *Terra di Lavoro*,) as to a certain Harbour and recesse from the clamours of their friends, and the temptations of the World, did *Paulinus* and *Therasia* convey themselves. His affection to this holy [a] Martyr was very great : for frequenting *Nola*, when he was yet a youth, he would oftentimes steale privately to visit his Sepulcher : and he loved the possessions which his 20 Father had left him in those parts above any other, because that under pretence of looking to his estate there, he had the convenience of resorting to the Tombe of *Felix* ; where he took in his *first love*, and in the seaven and twentieth year of his age, made a private vow to become a Servant of *Jesus Christ*. This *Felix* was by descent a *Syrian*, though born in *Nola*, where his Father (trafficking from the *East* into *Italie*,) had purchased a very fair estate, which he divided afterward betwixt him and his Brother *Hermias* ; but *Felix* following *Christ*, gave all to his brother. The frequent miracles manifested at his Tombe, made 30 the place famous, and resorted to from most parts of the world. Saint *Augustine*, upon a Controversie betwixt his Presbyter *Boniface*, and another fellow that accused him, when the truth of either side could not be certainly known, sent them both from *Hippo* to *Nola*, to have the matter decided upon Oath, before the Tombe of *Felix* ; and in his 137th Epistle, hee sets down the reason, why he sent them so farre. His words are these : *Multis notissima est sanctitas loci, ubi Felicis Nolensis corpus conditum est, quò volui ut peragrent, quia inde nobis facilius fideliusque scribi potest, quicquid in eorum aliquo divinitus fuerit propalatum.* "The 40 "holinesse (saith he) of that place where the body of *Felix* of

Paulinus calls him [a] Martyr, quia multa pro Christo passus, etsi non occisus.

"*Nola* lies interred, is famously knowne to many ; I have there-
"fore sent them thither, because that from thence, I shall be
"more easily and truly informed about any thing that shall be
"miraculously discovered concerning either of them.

Paulinus had not lived very long in this place, but it pleas'd
God to visit him with a very sharpe and tedious sicknesse. Hee
had now (upon Earth) no Comforter but *Therasia* ; His Estate
was gone, and his contempt of that made the World contemne
him. In this solitude and poverty, he that tries the reines and
10 the heart, begins to take notice of this his new servant, and the first
favour he conferred upon him was a disease. Good Angels doe
not appeare without the Ecstasie and passion of the Seere :
without afflictions and trialls God will not be familiar with us.
Fruit-trees, if they be not pruned, will first leave to beare, and
afterwards they will dye. Nature, without she be drest by the
hand that made her, will finally perish. He that is not favour'd
with visitations, is (in Saint *Pauls phrase*) a bastard, and no Son
of the Superiour *Jerusalem*. *Paulinus* had put from him all
occasions of worldly sorrowes, but he wanted matter for Heavenly
20 Joyes. Without this disease, hee had not known so soone, how
acceptable his first Services were unto his Master. This sicknesse
was a pure stratagem of love, God visited him with it for this very
purpose, that he himselfe might be his Cordial.

Man and the *Eagle* see best in the day-time, they see by the
light of this World : but the ᵃ *night-Raven*
is a bird of Mysterie, and sees in the darke
by a light of her own. *Paulinus* thought
now (like the servant of *Elisha*) that hee
had not a friend in all the World to be of
his side ; but God removes the mist from
his Eyes, and shewed him a glorious Army
of *Saints* and *Confessours*, who during the
time of his sicknesse, did so throng and
fill up his Cottage, and the fields about it,
that neither his Palace in *Rome*, nor his

ᵃ *Paulinus will have the
word which is commonly
used in the Latin, to be
Nicticora, from νυξ and
χορη, which signifies the
apple or candle of the eye,
and not from χορα. And
30 this he saith was told him
by a holy man, that had
lived a long time in the
deserts of* Egypt, *where he
observed the nature of this
bird of night, and the
Pelican.*

house in *Burdeaux* could ever boast of such a number. These
Comforters he hath recorded with his own pen in his first Epistle
to *Severus* ; *viderunt pueri tui*, &c. "Your men (saith he) that
"were here with me, have seen, and can tell you with what
40 "constant diligence all the Bishops, and my brethren the Clergy,
"with the common people my neighbours, did minister unto me

14 if] if, *1654*   27 thought] hought *1654*   38 *viderunt Vita : viderant 1654*

"all the time of my sicknesse. Unto you, who are unto me as
"my own soul, I take leave to boast and glory in this mercy of
"the Lord, whose goodnesse it is, that I am so plentifully
"comforted. There is not one Bishop in all *Campania* that did
"not come personally to visit me, and those whom either a farther
"distance, or their own infirmities would not permit to travel,
" fail'd not to visit me by their Presbyters & letters. The Bishops
"of *Africk* allso with the beginning of the spring, sent their
" particular letters and messengers to comfort me. Thus *he that* 10
forsakes houses and brethren, and lands to follow Christ, shall
receive an hundred fold even in this World, and in the world to
come life everlasting.

As touching the letters, or Embassage rather of the *African*
Bishops to *Paulinus*, it happened on this manner. *Alypius*, the
Bishop of *Tagasta* in *Africk*, had at *Millain* (as I intimated
before) taken speciall notice of *Paulinus* : And the rumour of his
Conversion (as the actions of eminent and noble personages passe
quickly into the most distant regions,) had filled with joy not
onely the Churches of *Africk*, but the most remote corners of 20
Christianity, even the very wildernesse and the scattered Isles,
which in those daies were more frequented by Christians, then
populous Continents and splendid Cities. *Alypius* upon this
(because he would not loose so fair an opportunity to ground his
acquaintance,) dispatcheth a letter from *Tagasta* to *Paulinus*, to
gratulate his conversion to the Faith; encouraging him withall
to hold fast his Crown ; and for a token, sent him five of Saint
Augustines bookes against the *Manichæans*, which in that age
(when the Invention of the *Presse* was not so much as thought
of,) was a rich present. *Paulinus* was so taken with the reading
of these Volumes, that he conceived himself not only engaged to 30
Alypius, but to *Augustine* also. Whereupon he sent his servant
from *Nola* with letters full of modestie and sweetnesse to them
both, and with particular commendations to other eminent lights
of the Church then shining in *Africk*. These letters received by
Augustine and *Alypius*, and communicated by them to the other
Bishops, and the *African* Clergy, were presently Coppied out by
all, and nothing now was more desired by them, then a sight of
this great Senatour, who was turned a *poor Priest, and a fool* (as
Saint *Paul* saith) *for Christ his sake*, and *the off-scouring of the*
World. But above all, the Soules of holy *Augustine* and *Paulinus* 40
(like *Jonathan* and *David*, or *Jacob* and *Joseph*) were *knit together*,

7 fail'd] fai'd *1654*

and *the life of the one was bound up in the life of the other.* The perfect love and union of these two, can by none be more faithfully, or more elegantly described, then it is already by Saint *Augustine* himself. I shall therefore insert his own words, the

August. Epistol. 22. words of that tongue of truth and Charity ; O
ad Paulin. *bone vir, O bone frater ! latebas animam meam ; & ei dico ut toleret, quia adhuc lates oculos meos, & vix obtemperat, immo non obtemperat. Quomodo 'ergo non doleam quod nondum faciem tuam novi, hoc est, domum animæ tuæ, quam sicut meam*
10 *novi? legi enim literas tuas fluentes lac & mel, præferentes simpli citatem cordis, in quâ quæris dominum, sentiens de illo in bonitate & afferens ei claritatem & honorem. Legerunt fratres & gaudent infatigabiliter & ineffabiliter tam uberibus & tam excellentibus donis dei, bonis tuis. Quotquot eas legerunt, rapiunt ; quia rapiun tur, cum legunt. Quàm suavis odor Christi, & quàm fragrat ex eis dici non potest, illæ literæ cum te offerunt ut videaris, quantum no. excitent ut quæraris: nam et perspicabilem faciunt, & desidera bilem. Quantò enim præsentiam tuam nobis quodammodò exhibent tantò absentiam nos ferre non sinunt. Amant te omnes in eis, &*
20 *amari abs te cupiunt. Laudatur & benedicitur deus, cujus gratic tu talis es. Ibi excitatur Christus, ut ventos & Maria tibi placar tendenti ad stabilitatem suam dignetur. Ibi conjux excitatur, nor dux ad mollitiem viro suo, sed ad fortitudinem redux in ossa viri sui quam in tuam unitatem redactam, in spiritualibus tibi tantò firmiori bus quantò castioribus nexibus copulatam, officijs vestræ sanctitat debitis in te, uno ore salutamus. Ibi cedri Libani ad terram deposita & in arcæ fabricam compagine charitatis erectæ, mundi hujus fluctu imputribilitèr secant. Ibi gloria ut acquiratur, contemnitur ; & mun dus, ut obtineatur, relinquitur. Ibi parvuli, sive etiam grandiuscul*
30 *filij Babylonis eliduntur ad petram, vitia scilicet confusionis, super biæque secularis. Hæc atque hujusmodi suavissima & sacratissim spectacula literæ tuæ præbent legentibus ; literæ illæ, literæ fide non fictæ, literæ spei bonæ, literæ puræ charitatis. Quomod nobis anhelant sitim tuam, & desiderium defectumque animæ tua in atria domini? Quid amoris sanctissimi spirant? Quantam opulentiam sinceri cordis exæstuant? Quas agunt gratias deo Quas impetrant à deo? blandiores sunt, an ardentiores? luminosiores an fæcundiores? Quid enim est, quòd ita nos mulcent, ita accendun*

5 *So Vita. Misprinted in 1654 as follows : O bone vir, O bone frater lei dico ut toleret, quia adhuc lates oculos meos, latebas animâ meâ, & & vi obtemperat immo,*
32 *legentibus ; literæ illæ, Vita : legentibus ; 1654*

ita compluunt; & ita serenæ sunt? Quid est, quæso te, aut quid tibi pro eis rependam, nisi quia totus sum tuus in eo, cujus totus es tu ? si parùm est, plus certê non habeo. "O good man, O good "brother! you lay hidden from my Soul, and I spoke to my "Spirit, that it should patiently bear it, because you are also "hidden from my Eyes ; but it scarse obeyes, yea it refuseth to "obey. How then shall I not grieve, because I have not as yet "knowne your face, the habitation of your Soul, which I am as "well acquainted with as my owne? For I have read your letters "flowing with milk and honey, manifesting the simplicity of your "heart, in which you seek the Lord, thinking rightly of him, and "bringing him glory and honor. Your brethren here have read "them, and rejoyce with an unwearied and unspeakable Joy, for "the bountifull and excellent gifts of God in you, which are your "riches. As many as have read them, snatch them from me ; "because when they read them, they are ravished with them. "How sweet an Odour of Christ, and how fragrant proceeds from "them ? It cannot be exprest how much those letters, while they "offer you to be seen of us, excite us to seek for you : They "make you both discerned and desired : For the more they "represent you unto us, wee are the more impatient of your absence. "All men love you in them, & desire to be beloved of you. God "is blessed and praised by all, through whose grace you are such. "There do we find that Christ is awaked by you, and vouchsafeth "to rebuke the winds and the Seas, that you may find them calme "in your Course towards him. There is your dear wife stirred "up, not to be your leader to softnesse and pleasures, but to "Christian fortitude ; becomming Masculine again, and restored "into the bones of her Husband : whom we all with one voice "salute and admire, being now united unto you, serving you in "spiritual things, wherein you are coupled with mutuall embraces, "which the more chast they be, are by so much the more firm. "There do we see two Cedars of *Libanus* fell'd to the Earth, "which joyned together by love, make up one Arke, that cuts "through the Waves of this World without detriment or putre- "faction. There glory, that it may be acquired, is contemned ; "and the World, that it may be obtained, is forsaken. There the "Children of *Babylon,* whither litle ones, or of Maturer age ; "I mean the Evils of Confusion and secular pride, are dashed "against the stones. Such sacred and delightfull spectacles do "your letters present unto us : O those letters of yours ! Those

2 *cuius] cu us 1654*

" letters of an unfained faith, those letters of holy hope, those letters
"of pure Charity! How do they sigh and gaspe with your pious
" thirst, your holy longings, and the Ecstatical faintings of your Soul
"for the Courts of the Lord? What a most sacred love do they
" breath? with what treasures of a sincere heart do they abound?
" How thankfull to God? How earnest for more grace? How
"mild? How zealous? How full of light? How full of fruite?
" Whence is it that they do so please us, and so provoke us, so
" showre and raine upon us, and yet are so calm and so serene?
10 "What is this I beseech you? or what shall I returne unto you
"for these letters, unlesse I tell you, that I am wholly yours in
" him, whose you are altogether? If this be too little, in truth
" I have no more.

These were the first effects of *Paulinus* his letters; but shortly
after, St. *Augustine* sent him others, nothing inferiour to this first,
either in affection, or Piety. And the year following, being
elected by *Valerius* to sit his Coadjutor in the Sea of *Hippo*, where
he afterwards succeeded him; It was resolved by them all, namely
by *Valerius, Augustine, Alypius, Severus,* and *Profuturus,* the
20 *African* Bishops, that a messenger should be dispatched into
Campania to present *Paulinus* with their several letters, and the
sincere gratulations of their respective Clergy; which accordingly
was performed.

In the beginning of this year, which was the three hundred
ninety and fifth after *Christ, Theodosius Augustus* the first,
a most pious Emperour, and a *Nursing Father* of the Church
departed this life. The *Ethnick* writers hating his memory as
virulently as his person, laboured with all manner of lyes and
Libels to render him odious and detestable to posterity. Holy
30 *Endelechius* awaked with these scandalous clamours, and the
insolent aspersions cast upon so religious an Emperour, writes
earnestly to *Paulinus,* and prevailes with him, to imploy those
excellent abilities bestowed on him, in the defense of this faithfull
Souldier of *Jesus Christ,* and Champion of his Spouse. This task
Paulinus performed, as appears by his owne words in his 9th
Epistle to *Severus,* to whom hee sent a Coppy of his learned
Panegyrick; however posterity have suffered in the losse of it. But
we want not another witnesse: That learned Father, and happy
translator of the booke of God in his thirteenth Epistle to *Paulinus,*
40 gives us a very fair and full account of it. *Librum tuum quem
pro Theodosio principe prudenter ornateque,* &c. "Your booke

7 light?] light?? *1654*   8 so showre *Gu*: to showre *1654*   37 *Panegyrick*]
Panegyrick 1654   41 booke] Book *catchword 1654*

" (saith he) which elegantly and judiciously you composed in the
" defense of the Emperor *Theodosius,* and sent to me by [a] *Vigi-*
" *lantius,* I have with much delight read over. [a] *He proved after-*
" What I admire in it, is your Method : For *wards a most detes-*
" having excelled all other writers in the first parts, *table Heretick.*
" you excell your selfe in the last. Your stile is compact and
" neat, and with the perspicuity and purenesse of *Cicero,* and yet
" weighty and sententious ; for that writing which hath nothing
" commendable in it, but words, is (as one saith) meer prating.
" The consequence besides is very great, and the coherence exact. 10
" What ever you infer, is either the confirmation of the antece-
" dent, or the inchoation of the subsequent. Most happy *Theo-*
" *dosius,* to be vindicated by such a learned Oratour of *Christ* !
" You have added to the glory of his Imperial robe, and made the
" utility of his just lawes sacred to posterity. But this rare peece,
with many more mentioned by *Gennadius,* either through the
envie of the Heathen, or the negligence of our own, are unfortunately lost ; especially a *Volume of Epistles* written to his *Sister,*
with some *controversial peeces* against the *Ethnick* Philosophers,
mentioned also by Saint *Augustine* in his four and thirtieth 20
Epistle ; and a most learned *Treatise of true Repentance,* and *the
glory of Martyrs.*

Much about this time, the name of *Paulinus* began to be
famous in the *East* ; and not onely there, but in all parts of the
Christian World. It is almost incredible (especially in this age
of Impieties and Abominations) how much the example of this
one man prevailed over all. The Course he ran, drew another
wealthy and noble *Roman* (I mean *Pammachius*) from the Senate
to the Cell ; and all the Fathers of that age, when they prest any
to holy living, and a desertion of the World, brought in *Paulinus* 30
for their great exemplar, and a star to lead them unto *Christ.*
St. *Augustine* propounds him to *Romanianus* & *Licentius,* Saint
Hierome to *Julian,* and the Daughters of *Geruntius* ; and Saint
Chrysostome in his thirteenth homily upon *Genesis,* sets him
downe for a pattern to the husbands, and *Therasia* to the wives. The
reverend Bishop of *Hippo* did very earnestly sollicite him to come
over into *Africk,* & he gives his reason for it in these words : *Non
imprudenter ego vos rogo, & flagito, & postulo,* &c. " Not un-
" advisedly doe I intreat and earnestly desire, and require you to
" come into *Africk,* where the Inhabitants labour more now with 40
" the thirst of seeing you, then with the famous thirstinesse of the

1 which] whihc *1654*

"Climate. God knowes, I ask it not for my private satisfaction, nor
"for those onely, who either by my mouth, or by the publick fame
"have heard of you ; but for the rest, who either have not heard,
"or else having heard will not believe so great a change ; but when
"they themselves shall see the truth, they will not onely believe,
"but love and imitate. It is for their sakes therefore, that I desire
"you to honour these parts with your bodily presence: Let the Eyes
"of our flocks also behold the glory of Christ in so eminent
"a Couple, the great exemplars to both Sexes, to tread pride under
10 "their feet, and not to despaire of attaining to perfection. And in
his fifty ninth Epistle to *Paulinus*, when (according to the custome
of those holy times) hee had sent his Presbyter to him to be
instructed, *he cannot* (saith he) *profit more by my Doctrine, then he
can by your life.* Saint *Hierome* useth the same Engine to bring
down the high thoughts of *Julian* : "Art thou (saith he) nobly
"descended? So were *Paulinus* and *Therasia*, and far nobler in
"Christ. Art thou rich and honourable? So were they : and from
"the height of honours and worldly riches became poor and
"inglorious, that they might gain Christ. Dearly did *Anastasius*,
20 who succeeded *Siricius* in the Sea of *Rome*, affect this holy
Bishop, as appears by his owne words in his sixteenth Epistle to
Delphinus the Bishop of *Burdeaux*.

But amidst all these triumphs of the Church of God, for the
conversion of so eminent a person, and the frequent gratulations
of learned men, exprest by their letters or personall visits, there
were none that raged with so much hatred and malice against him
as his own kindred, and former acquaintance. *A Prophet hath
no honour in his own Country, and those of his owne house will be
his Enemies.* There are no such persecutors of the Church, as
30 those that do it for selfe-ends, and their private advantage.
Sweetly doth he complain of these bitter, unnatural dealings in
his fifth Epistle to *Severus*. *Potiore mihi parente germanus es,
quam illi quos caro tantùm & sanguis mihi sociat,* &. "You
"are my Brother now by a greater Father, then those who are
"tyed to me by flesh and blood onely. For where is now my
"great affinity by blood? Where are my old friends? where is my
"former acquaintance? I am become as a dream before them all,
"and as a stranger to my owne brothers, the Sons of my Mother.
"My kinsmen and my friends stand looking upon me afar off, and
40 "they passe by me like hasty floods, or the streames of a brook
"that will not be stay'd. They convey themselves away, and are
10 perfection] prefection *1654*

"ashamed of me, who displeased them by pleasing God. And in "his first Epistle, I beseech you (saith he) If I shall have need "(for now my servants, and those I made free-men, are become "my despisers,) that you would take care to send the old Wine, "which I beleive I have still at *Narbon*, hither unto me, and to "pay for the carriage: Do not fear, dear brother, to make the "poor your debtor, &c. The Noble Spirit is the bravest bearer of indignities: and certainly extraction and a virtuous descent (let popular flatterers preach what they will to the contrary,) is attended with more Divinity, and a sweeter temper, then the indiscrete Issue of the multitude. There is an eminent difference betwixt flowers and weedes, though they spring from the same mould. The Ape contending with the Lyonesse, told her, that she was a very fair creature, but very barren: For you (said the Ape) bring forth but one at a birth, and I bring six, or more; 'Tis true (replyed the Lionesse,) but thy six are six Apes, and my one is a Lyon. The greatest part of men, which we commonly terme the populacy, are a stiffe, uncivill generation, without any seed of honour or goodnesse, and sensible of nothing but private interest, & the base waies of acquiring it. What Virtue, or what humanity can be expected from a *Raymond Cabanes*, a *Massinello*, or some Son of a Butcher? They have one barbarous shift, which Tigers and Beares would blush to commit: They will cut the throats of their most generous and Virtuous Benefactours, to comply with times, and advantage themselves; Yea, they will rejoyce to see them ruined, and like inhumane Salvages, insult over their innocent and helplesse posterity. I could compare those fawning Hypocrits, that waite not upon men, but upon their Fortunes, to that smiths bitch in the *Apologues* of *Locmannus* the *Persian*, which sleeping in the forge, could not be awaked with all the noise of the hammers, the Anvile, and the Bellowes: but if the smith would offer to stirre his teeth to eat, shee would start up presently, and attend upon him with all officiousnesse. She would share with him in the fruits of his labours; but would not watch and look to the shop one minute while he laboured.

Paulinus had now first lost these false friends, but was loaded for it with the love and commendations of true ones; And I know not which offended him most, to be despised by the first, or commended by the last. He had (like Saint *Paul*,) great heavinesse, and continuall sorrow of heart, to see that his brethren and kinsmen according to the flesh, hated him because he loved

25 times] [the] times *Gu*

Christ : And on the other side, his humility would not suffer him to beare the *labour of love,* I meane the generall applause and sincere commendations conferred upon him by his Christian friends. *Severus* in one of his Epistles written to him (after hee had spent some lines in the commendation of his zeale and constancie,) contrary to the custome of that plaine age, subscribed

Te multa dilectio ad himself, his Servant. To the first he replyed, *mendacii peccatum* that *his excessive love had drawn him to the sin traxit.* *of untruth* : And the last he desired him to
10 desist from, for this reason ; *Cave ergo ne posthac,* &c. " Have " a care hereafter (saith he) that you who are a Servant of Christ, " called unto liberty, terme not your self the servant of a sinner, " and of one that is not worthy to be called your fellow-servant. " The virtue of humility will not excuse the vice of flattery. Thus *Gregorie* the great, when Pope *Anastasius* had exceeded towards him in his laudatory elocutions, blasted them all with this humble reply ; *Quod verò me os domini, quod lucernam,* &c. " Your " calling me the mouth of the Lord, a shining light, and a strong " helper, is nothing else but an augmentation of my iniquity ; for
20 " when I deserve to be punished for my sins, then do I instead of " punishment receive praise. *Severus,* in another of his Epistles to *Paulinus,* earnestly intreated him to suffer his picture to be taken by a limner, which he had sent to him for that purpose, that he might have it to set up, together with the picture of Saint *Martin,* before the sacred font in a fair Church which *Severus* was then in building. This friendly motion *Paulinus* was very much offended with, and would by no means consent unto, teling *Severus, that too much love had made him mad* ; And in his eighth Epistle, reasoning with him about this request, *What kind of picture* (saith he) *would*
30 *you have from me, the picture of the earthly, or the Heavenly man ? I know you love onely that incorruptible image, which the King of Heaven doth love in you. I am ashamed to picture what I am, and I dare not picture what I am not.* But *Severus* resolving to force it from him, would not be satisfied with any other returne ; wherupon he sent it to him, with these following verses, the elegant expresse of his unfeined humility. The first coppy relates to the *pictures,* and the latter to the *Font.*

> *Abluitis quicunq̃ animas & membra lavacris,*
> *Cernite propositas ad bona facta vias,* &c.

40 You that to wash your flesh and Soules draw near, Ponder these two examples set you here.

Great *Martin* shewes the holy life, and white ;
Paulinus to repentance doth invite.
Martins pure, harmlesse life tooke Heaven by force,
Paulinus tooke it by teares and remorse.
Martin leads through victorious palms and flowers,
Paulinus leades you through the pooles and showres.
You that are sinners, on *Paulinus* look,
You that are Saints, great *Martin* is your book.
The first example bright and holy is,
The last, though sad and weeping, leads to blisse.   10

The verses relating to the *Font*, were these.

Hic reparandarum generator fons animarum
   Vivum viventi lumine flumen agit, &c.

Here the great well-spring of wash'd Soules, with beams
Of living light quickens the lively streams ;
The Dove descends, and stirs them with her wings,
So weds these waters to the upper springs,
They strait conceive : A new birth doth proceede
From the bright streams by an immortall seed.
O the rare love of God ! sinners wash'd here,   20
Come forth pure Saints, all justified and clear.
So blest in death and life, man dyes to sins,
And lives to God ; Sin dies, and life begins
To be reviv'd : Old *Adam* falls away,
And the new lives, born for eternal sway.

Nor did the manners of holy *Paulinus* differ from his mind : all
his Garments, all the Utensils of his poor Cot, were so many
emblems and memento's of humility.   Grace is an Elixir of a
contrary Nature to the Philosophers stone, it turn'd all the gold
and Silver vessells of this great Senatour into earthen dishes and 30
wooden spoons.   Righteousnesse and honesty are alwaies poor.
In his first Epist. to *Severus*, he presents him with some of this
innocent furniture ; *Misimus testimonialem divitiarum scutellam*
buxeam, &c. " I have sent you (saith he) a platter made of a box-
" tree, for a testimoniall of my riches ; receive it as a pledge or
" earnest of Evangelicall poverty, and let it be an example to you,
" if as yet you will make use of any Silver platters.   To this he
addes, that he was very desirous to be supplyed with some more
earthen dishes, which (saith he) *I do very much love* ; and then
subscribes his reason, *quòd secundum Adam cognata nobis sint, &* 40
domini thesaurum in talibus vasis commissum habeamus; because they
are near kin to us by *Adam*, and because the treasure of the Lord
is committed to our care in such vessells.   Certainly poverty (as

man is now to be considered) is his best, and his true estate. Riches, though they make themselves wings, yet do they not fly to Heaven. The home or house of gold, is the heart of the Earth, and mineralls are a fuel of hell-fire. Poverty was the Inauguration of the first man, who was made naked, and all his posterity are born so. *This onely have I found* (saith *Solomon*) *that God made man upright, but he hath sought out many inventions.* By Covetousnesse we loose our uprightnesse : Wee come here light and easie, but we load our selves afterwards with unnecessary
10 burthens. *Perditio tua ex te*, these weights that we take up, sink us down : Our temporall misery as well as the Eternal is from our

* Paulinus calls Christ (mistically) a sparrow: Hic est ille passer, qui requirentibus se in viis hilaritèr ostendit; nunc in portis fit obvius, nunc in platis occurrit, nunc in muris vel turribus sublimis convocat ad se amatores suos, & invitat eos in alti-
20 tudines habitationum sua- rum, ut impleat verbum suum, & exaltatus omnia ad se trahat. Quis dabit nobis pennas columbæ deargentatas, ut pennati pervolemus ad bravîum supernæ vocationis, se- quentes istum passerem solitarium, qui est unicus dei filius, supervolitantem, qui in altis habitat, & hu- milia respicit ?

selves. The merriest creature that I can see, is the * *Sparrow*. This makes me think, that hee is not troubled with fore-thoughts, which are the hands of covetousnesse. What man and beasts scatter and leave behind them, is his provision : his table is laid every where, and the first bush he meets with, is his bed. Our Saviour, who knew the nature and thoughts of all created things, was pleased to send us to school to the birds. They are alwaies full of Musical livelinesse, and a certain bright freedome, which descends not so low as men and beasts. Spirits, when they have businesse upon Earth, must assume bodies. Clarity and purifi-cation is a kind of poverty : it is a state that hath cast off dregs & burthens. Divine is that saying of
30 *Gr. Pisides.*

Τὸ πτωχὸν ἦθος οὐρανόδρομον φύσει.
Poor habits are naturally heaven-seekers.

But *Paulinus*, though he was poor, yet was he charitable, and withall liberall. The widowes mite is more then the rich mens abundance. In the four hundred and tenth year after *Christ*, when the *Gothes* raged in *Italy*, and had sackt *Nola*, *Paulinus*
Lib. I. de Civitate (amongst many others,) was taken prisoner by
dei. them ; *And thus* (saith Saint *Augustine*) *as I afterwards learnt from him, did he then pray in his heart.*
40 Domine, ne excrucier propter aurum & argentum ; ubi enim

omnia mea sunt, tu scis. *O Lord suffer me not to be troubled with the losse of Gold & Silver, for thou knowest where all my riches are laid up.* His treasure was laid up in Heaven, where he commanded us to lay it, who foretold, that these calamities should come upon the World. And God (without doubt) had reguard unto his prayer, for the barbarous enemie leading all the rest into captivity, he onely was left behind. But amongst all these plunderings and outward afflictions, hee never failed in his daily almes to the poor, nor was the hand of his faithfull *Therasia* any way shortned. At last his store failing, and no more provision being left, then onely one loafe of bread ; A poor man comming to the door for reliefe, *Paulinus* commands it should be given him. But *Therasia* (arguing with her selfe, that no begger could be poorer then *Paulinus* now was, and that it was as much charity to keepe it for him, as to give it to another,) conceal'd the loafe, and suffered the poor man to go without it. A day or two after, some men that were sent with relief to *Paulinus*, from his friends, arrive at *Nola*, and tell him that they had been there much sooner, had not one of the ships, which was loaden with corn, been cast away almost in the Harbour ; the rest that were fraught with Wine and other Victualls, being come safe to shore. Whereupon *Paulinus* turning towards *Therasia*, put her in mind of her overmuch carefullnesse, with these words, *Understand now* Therasia, *that this great ship full laden with Corne, was cast away for that one loafe of bread which thou didst steale from the poore man.*

But passe we now to his *Episcopall* dignity. In his own Workes we have not one line that mentions this Ecclesiasticall honour, nor any other passage of his life, that might but seem to conduce to his own glory. They breath nothing but humility, nothing but self-deniall and dedignation. Wee must be guided then through this part of his life by other Authors, and such faithfull records as are come unto us, from the hands of learned and publick persons ; who either upon the generall interest and concernments of the Church, or their own private merits, and not by reflection were acquainted with him. The first that offers himself to us, is *Uranius*, his own Presbyter, who in that short narration which he wrote of his life, sets him forth to posterity in this following Character ; *Cum autem ad summum sacerdotij gradum*, &c. " When he was honoured (saith he) with the highest degree in " the Priesthood, he did not shew himself such a Bishop that " desired to be feared, but one that endeavoured to be beloved. " He was never so farre angry, as not in his anger to shew mercy.

"Nor could that man indeed be angry, for he regarded not
"calumnies, and he avoyded hatred. He never sate in Judge-
"ment, but mercy sate close by him. He was truly such a Bishop
"as laboured to get the love of all. For hee lived a Consolation
"to all, and their great example to make sure their Salvation.
"Nor is this my voyce onely : even the barbarous Nations who
"knew my Lord *Paulinus* by report onely, will testifie as much.
"And worthily was hee beloved of all, who was a friend to all.
"For who was there cast down, and he did not lift him up ? who
10 "ever called to him for help, and was not piously and comfortably
"answered ? For he was pious, tender hearted, humble and
"courteous, hating none, despising none. He gave to all, he
"cherished all : he encouraged the fearfull, pacified the violent,
"those with his words, these with his example ; Some he com-
"forted with his letters, and those that wanted, with his mony.
"He loved not any riches, nor any treasures, but those which
"Christ promised to his followers. Gold and Silver, and the
"other accommodations of life he approved of, if they were liberally
"given to the poor, not covetously hoorded up. Briefly, he had
20 "in him all goodnesse, for he loved Christ. Hee had Faith,
"Meeknesse, love towards his neighbours, a constant care of the
"poor, compassion upon the weak, and laboured for nothing in
"his life, but peace and charity. All his endeavours were to make
"men good, and to save their Soules. What place is there in the
"World, what solitude, what Seas which acknowledge not the
"good wòrks of holy *Paulinus* ? All men desired his acquaintance,
"and did extreamly long to have a sight of him. Who ever came
"to him without joy, or who went from him, but he desired to
"stay longer ? those that could not see him in the body, desired
30 "to see him in his writings ; for he was sweet and gentle in his
"Epistles, elegant and ravishing in his Poems. What more shall
"I say ? The relations that may be given of him, would be scarse
"credible, but that his knowne integrity is above falshood.

Nola was at this time a very famous and splendid City, nothing
inferiour to the best *Emporiums* of *Italie*, and had withall a very
rich *Sea*; which questionlesse was a great occasion, that the piety
of this blessed Bishop was so renowned, and so familiarly spoken
of in the most remote parts of the World. So the just and
faithfull God exalteth those that humble themselves, and honours
40 those that honour him. He had beene faithfull in those things
that were his own, and was therefore intrusted with the treasures
of the Church. *Prosper* in his second book, *de vitâ Contemplativâ,*

and the ninth Chapter, tells us, how hee disposed of them ; *Sanctus Paulinus (ut ipsi meliùs nostis) ingentia prædia quæ fuerunt sua, vendita pauperibus erogavit : sed cum posteà factus esset Episcopus, non contempsit Ecclesiæ facultates, sed fidelissime dispensavit.* " Holy *Paulinus* (saith he) as you best know, sold all those " princely Possessions which were his own, and gave of them to " the poor : but when he was afterwards consecrated Bishop, he " neglected not the revenues of the Church, but was a most faith- " full Steward and dispenser of them. So faithfull, that when he lay upon his death bed, hee had not one piece left to relieve him- 10 self, but was driven to lay out for some Cloathes which he had given to the poor, a small summe of mony, which God ordained to be sent to him for that very purpose a litle before the hour of his dissolution. So that living and dying, he kept to the Apostles rule, and *owed no man any thing but love* : Hee was a great lover of learned and holy men, and confesseth in one of his Epistles to *Alypius*, that his affection to Saint *Ambrose*, was the first induce- ment which he felt to incline him to Christianity. His dearest and most intimate friends were Saint *Augustine*, Saint *Ambrose*, Saint *Hierome*, Saint *Martin* the Bishop of *Tours*, *Delphinus* the 20 Bishop of *Burdeaux*, and *Amandus* his Successour ; *Alypius* the Bishop of *Tagasta*, *Januarius* the Bishop of *Naples*, afterwards a Martyr, *Victricius* the *Rhotomagensis*, *Aper*, *Severus*, and *Nicetas* of *Dacia*. I may say of him as the Scripture saith of *Moses*, he was the meekest man upon the face of the Earth. He was not onely obedient and serviceable to these Fathers, and pillars of the Church, but to his own *Presbyters* and *Domesticks* : he judged himself the most unworthy, and the most unable of all his brethren. *Victor* the Monk, sent from *Severus* to see him (according to the custome of those times) washed his feete. This 30 was a ceremony, which in that age of holinesse could not be refused. But *Victor* by this did not onely wash his feet, but his face also ; for he drew tears from him, because hee might not deny him the performance of that Evangelical service. *Servivit ergo mihi peccatori, & væ misero mihi quod passus·sum ; he served me a sinner* (saith the holy Bishop) *and woe is to me because I suffered him.* But he staid not at tears, for as soone as *Victor* had done washing his feet, to requite his service, he fetched him clean water, and held the bason while he wash'd his hands. He was not like that insolent *Abbot* that did cast off his humility with his 40 *Cowle*, and being asked by his brethren, *why he was then so proud, that was formerly such an humble Monk*, made answer ; *that in his*

Monachisme, when he went so low, and stooping, he was searching for the keyes of the Abbey; but now having found them, he did hold up his head to ease himself.

This true carriage of an Evangelist, made him both honourd and beloved; the *Church* rejoyced, and glorified God for him, and the *Court* admired him. Holynesse is a light that cannot be hidden: It is a candle set upon a hill: stars never shine more glorious, then when they are neare black Clouds. In the year of our Lord, four hundred and nineteen (a grievous *Schism* then
10 happening in the Church,) there was a convention of certain Bishops and Fathers at *Rome*, to quiet those groundlesse perturbations, and stop the breach. But *Honorius* the Emperour, judging by his skil in the temper of those Church-men, that no good would be done without the presence of *Paulinus*, who then lay sick at *Nola*, dispatched his Imperial letter to this holy Bishop, wherein he earnestly intreated him (if possible) to shake off his present indisposition, and to repaire in person to the Synod, lest that great blessing of peace, which he and the Church did earnestly hope and long for, might by his absence unfortunately miscarry.
20 This royall record (because it is a monument of no lesse sincerity then concernment, and discovers unto us much of the face of those times) I shall *verbatim* insert.

Sancto & venerabili Patri, *Paulino*,
Episcopo *Nolensi*.

Tantùm fuit apud nos certa sententia, nihil ab his sacerdotibus, qui ad Synodum convenerant, posse definiri, cum beatitudo tua de corporis inæqualitate causata, itineris non potuit injuriam sustinere, ut propter absentiam sancti viri, non quidem obtentura: Interim tamen vitia gratulantur, cùm prava & vetus ambitio, & cum
30 *benedicto viro sanctæ̧ vitæ diù velit habere certamen, ut contra hæc Apostolicæ institutionis bona, de præsumptis per vim parietibus existimet confidendum. O verè digna causa quam non nisi coronæ tuæ beata vita designat! Dilatum itaq̧ Judicium nuntiamus, ut divina præcepta ex venerationis tuæ ore promantur, qui ea secutus implesti; nec potest alius eorum præceptorum lator existere, quam qui dignus Apostolicis disciplinis est approbatus. Specialiter itaq̧ domine sancte, meritò venerabilis pater, Justus dei famulus, divinum opus, contempto labore, tributum hoc nobis visitationis tuæ (si ita dicendum est) munus indulge, ut postpositis omnibus, quantùm tem-*

perantia his & tranquillitas suffragantur, Synodo profuturus, sine intermissione etiam desideriis nostris, & benedictioni quam cupimus, te præstare digneris.

To the holy and reverend Father P A U L I N U S, *Bishop of* Nola.

"Such a firm opinion have we that nothing can be agreed and
" concluded upon by the Bishops met in this Synod, (your Holi-
" nesse by reason of your bodily indisposition being not able to
" travel hither) that for your onely absence it is not like to con-
" tinue : In the mean time offences triumph and rejoyce at it, and 10
" the old and wicked sinne of ambition, which of a long time
" desires to contend even with your holynesse and upright life,
" presumes now, and is confident that having forcibly taken the
" wall from us, it will carry you also against the wholsomnesse of
" Apostolicall institution. O! a cause truly worthy not to be
" determined, but by your holy life, which is your Crown! we
" therfore declare unto you, that we have suspended our judge-
" ment for the present, that we may have the truth of these Divine
" precepts pronounced by your reverend mouth, who have both
" followed them, and fullfilled them : For none can be a fit arbiter 20
" of those rules, but he that hath approved himself worthy and
" conformable to Apostolicall discipline. Wherefore, holy Sir,
" worthily reverend Father, the faithfull Servant of God, and his
" Divine work, we intreat you particularly, that slighting the
" troubles of this Journey, you would favour us with this gift and
" tribute (if I may so speak) of your presence : and laying aside
" all other concernments (so far as your health and ease will per-
" mit,) be in your owne person at this Synod, and vouchsafe to
" lend your assistance to our desires, and that blessing which wee
" earnestly long for. 30

Wee see by this letter in what account hee was with the
Emperour, and that his integrity and holyness were not dissimula-
tions and popular Fables, but experimentall truths so known and
so believed ; hee was a true Christian, and no Impostour. It
was not the Custome, but the nature (if I may so say) of those
Primitive times to love holy and peacefull men. But some *great
ones* in this later age, did nothing else but countenance *Schismaticks*
and *seditious raylers, the despisers of dignities,* that covered their
abominable villanies with a pretence of *transcendent holinesse,* and
a certain *Sanctimonious excellencie* above the Sons of men. This 40
Vaile (which then *cousend* weak eyes) is now fallen off their *faces,*

and most of their patrons have by an unthought of Method received their rewards : The rest without doubt (though they shift themselves into a thousand shapes) shall not escape him, *whose anger is not yet turned away, but his hand is stretched out still.* But returne we to *Paulinus* : Whose Charity and tendernesse towards the poor, was both inimitable and incredible ; This iron age wants faith as well as mercy : When he had given them all he had, to the last that begged he gave himself. *Gregorie* the great, in the third Book of his *Dialogues*, and the first Chapter, hath
10 recorded this memorable passage. I shall cut it short, and in as few words, as conveniently may be, give you all that is material. When the *Vandals* had miserably wasted *Campania*, and carried many of the inhabitants into *Africk*, blessed *Paulinus* gave all that he had both towards his own sustenance, and the reliefe of the poor, amongst the prisoners and Captives. The Enemy being departed, and his prey with him ; a poor Widow (whose onely Son was (amongst the rest of the Natives) by a Son in law of the King of the *Vandals* carried into Bondage,) comes to petition *Paulinus* for so much Money as might serve to redeem him.
20 *Paulinus* told her that he had nothing then left, either in money or other goods, but promised, if shee would accept of him, to go with her into *Africk*, and to be exchanged for her Son. The poore Widow taking this for a meere scoffe, turnes her back to be gone. *Paulinus* followes after, and with much adoe made her believe, that he meant it (as he did indeed) in earnest. Upon this, they travell'd both into *Africk*, and having opportunity to speake with the Kings Son in Law, the poor widow begged of him first, to have her son restor'd unto her *Gratis* : but the youthfull and haughty *Vandal* averse to all such requests, would hear her
30 no farther ; whereupon she presents him with *Paulinus*, and petitioned to have her Son set at liberty, and the other to serve in his stead. The Prince taken with the comely and reverend countenance of *Paulinus*, asked him, what his occupation or trade was ? *Paulinus* answered, that he never followed any trade, but that he had good skill in dressing of Herbes and Flowers. Upon this, the Prince delivered her Son to the Widow, who took him home with her, and sent *Paulinus* to work into his Gardens.

The Prince delighting much in Flowers and Sallets, would very frequently visit *Paulinus*, and took such delight in him, that he
40 forsook all his Court-associates to enjoy the company of his new Gardiner. In one of these visits, *Paulinus* taking occasion to

confer seriously with him, advised him to be very carefull of himselfe, and to consider speedily of some means to secure and settle
the Kingdome of the *Vandals* [n] in *Mauri-*
tania ; for (said he) the King your Father
in law will shortly dye.   The Prince something troubled with the suddain newes,
without further delay acquaints the King
with it; and tells him withall, that his
Gardiner (whose prediction this was)
excelled all other men both in wisedome
and learning.   Whereupon the King
requested, that he might see him ; you
shall, replyed the Prince, for to morrow
when you are at dinner, I will give order that hee shall come in
person with the dishes of Sallate to the Table.   This being agreed
upon, and accordingly performed, the old Tyrant upon the first sight
of *Paulinus* exceedingly trembled, and speaking to his Daughter,
who sate next to him, to call to her husband, he told him, that the
prediction of his Gardiner was very true ; for *yesternight* (said he)
I saw in a dream a great tribunal with judges sitting thereon, and
amongst them this Gardiner, by whose judgement a scourge which had
been formerly put into my hands, was taken from me.   But learn of
him what his profession is, and what dignity he had conferred upon
him in his own Country, for I cannot believe him to be (as he
pretends) an inferiour or ordinary person.

This was about the year
of our L. 428. *about which*
time the Vandals after their
excursions through Polonia,
Italy, Franconia, *and* An-
dalusia *had setled in* Africk,
where they continued quiet-
ly until the reigne of Justinian, *but rebelling against*
him, they were together
with their King Gillimer
totally overthrown by the
great Captaine Belisarius
An. Christi 533.

As soon as dinner was ended, the Prince stole from the *presence*
into the Garden, and earnestly intreated *Paulinus* to tell him, who
he was ; I am (said he) your Gardiner, which you received in
exchange for the Widowes Son.   I know that, replyed the Prince,
but I desire to know your profession in your own Country, and
not the servitude you have put your self in with me for the present ;
To this *Paulinus* answered, that he was by profession a *Bishop,*
and a servant of Jesus Christ the Son of the living God.   At these
words the Prince was mightily troubled, and requested him to
depart againe into his own Country, assuring him, that before he
departed, he would give him any thing that he should please
demand.   *Paulinus* replyed, that he would desire nothing, but to
have those Captives which were carried out of *Campania*, set at
liberty, and transported to their Native Country.   To this the
Prince consented, and for *Paulinus* his sake, furnished them with
shipping and all other necessaries for their voyage, and sent them
home joyfull in the Company of their blessed and beloved Bishop.

2 (*note*) *which*] *which 1654*

Some few daies after, the old Tyrant (as God had foretold by his holy Servant) departed out of this World *into his owne place*; And so that scourge which God had put into his hand for the punishment of a great part of the Christian World, was taken away, and the instrument cast into the fire. Wherefore whoever thou beest, that readest this book, and art a sufferer thy selfe, or doest see and grieve for the calamities of the Church, *the oppression of the poor, & the violent perverting of judgement & justice in a province, do not thou marvel at the matter,* nor vex thy self; *for he that is*
10 *higher then the highest, regardeth it, and there be higher then they. Envy not the glory of Sinners, for thou knowest not what will be their end :* but *submit thy self under the mighty hand of God,* expecting with patience the time of refreshing, and I do assure thee upon my Soul, thou shalt not be deceived.

Paulinus, with all his joyfull Captives, was now landed in *Campania,* where all the Inhabitants, as upon a solemne feast-day flocked together to welcome him, and to poure their joyes into his bosome ; some received their Sonnes, some their brothers, and some their husbands : both the receivers and the received were
20 beholding to *Paulinus.* They commended, honoured and admired him : He exhorted, incouraged and confirmed them. Mutuall Consolations are a double banquet, they are the Churches *Eulogiæ,* which we both give and take. What the *Campanians* most admired in *Paulinus,* was that which the Scripture commends in *Moses : youthfullnesse in old age.* He was now as earnest, as hearty, and as active for the glory of God, as in his most vigorous years. *His spiritual force was not abated, nor the Eye of his Soul any way dimmed.* Hee did not coole towards his *setting,* but grew more large, more bright, and more fervent. Bearing trees, when their
30 fruit is ripe, bend their boughes, and offer themselves to the gatherers hands. He knew that his time of departure was at hand, and therefore *Moses*-like he made his *Doctrine to drop as the raine, and his speech distilled as the dew. Hee poured out his milk and his Wine, and made them drink abundantly.* To labour in the heat of the day, and to give over in the cool, is great indiscretion, the contention should be alwaies hottest towards the end of the race.

I am now come to my last *Paragraph,* which all this while I did reserve for his *Works of Piety.* And these indeede (if wee consider his unworldlinesse, and religious poverty) were very great and very
40 sumptuous. He repaired and beautified the four old *Basilica's,* or Churches, dedicated to the Martyr *Felix,* and built the *fifth,* which

exceeded them all, both for beauty and largenesse. This he
dedicated to our Lord and Saviour *Jesus Christ.* It was adorned
with two stately Porches, the one opend towards the way of
Publick resort, the other was a private *Postern*; and the path
leading to it, was through a pleasant *green field* set with *fruit-trees*
and other *shady wood*, fenced about with a very high and sumptuous
wall; The entrance into this Court was through a fair Marble-
Gate, in whose Front were cut these following verses.

> *Cælestes intrate vias per amœna vireta*, &c.
>
> Through pleasant green fields enter you the way   10
> To blisse; and wel through shades and blossoms may
> The walkes leade here, from whence directly lyes
> The good mans path to sacred *Paradise.*

This Church was joyned to the other four, and an entrance made
from the one into the other, by high and spatious *Arches*, supported with pillars of Marble. Through these pillars (whose height
did almost reach to the roof,) as through a *traverse* was to be
seene, by those that came from the old Church into the new, the
picture of the Crosse, limned in most lively and glorious Colours,
and hung with Garlands of palms and flowers; above it shined 20
a cleare and luminous skie, and on the Crosse, which was all
Purple, sate perching a flock of white Doves; at the bottome of
this *Paisage* were written these verses.

> *Ardua floriferæ Crux,* &c.
>
> The painfull Crosse with flowers and Palms is crown'd,
> Which prove, it springs; though all in blood 'tis drown'd:
> The Doves above it shew with one consent,
> Heaven opens onely to the innocent.

In the Courts belonging to this Church, were very faire and
spatious walks, paved with stone, and covered over head against 30
the violence of weather. The outside was supported with Pillars,
and the Inner was divided into neat and cleanly Cells, opening
towards the Walks, where the people that came thither to celebrate
the *Vigils* of *Felix*, reposed themselves. Round about these Courts
were great *Cisterns*, and *Lavers* of severall kinds of Marble most
curiously polished, whose diverse formes and colours were very
delightfull, and much recreated the beholders. The Porches,
which were very large, and contained within them many private
Oratories, or places of prayer, were all richly pictured with sacred
Histories out of the *Pentateuch*, the book of *Joshuah*, *Judges* and 40
Ruth; This Church is fully described in his twelfth Epistle to

Severus, and his ninth *Natalis*, when *Nicetas* came out of *Dacia*
to see him.

Ecce vidès quantus splendor velut æde renatâ
Rideat, insculptum camerâ crispante lacunar
In ligno mentitur ebur ; tectoque supernè
Pendentes lychni spiris retinentur ahenis,
Et medio in vacuo laxis vaga lumina nutant
Funibus, undantes flammas levis aura fatigat, &c.

You see what splendour through the spatious Isle,
10 As if the Church were glorified, doth smile.
The Ivory-wrought beams seem to the sight
Ingraven, while the carv'd roofe looks curl'd and bright.
On brasse hoopes to the upmost vaults we tie
The hovering Lamps, which nod and tremble by
The yeelding Cords ; fresh Oyle doth still repair
The waving flames, vex'd with the fleeting aire.

Having finished this Church, hee built another, not far from
Nola, in a litle Town called *Fundi*, where his possessions (which
he afterwards sold and gave to the poor,) were situate ; this also
20 he dedicated to our Lord *Jesus*, whom he used to call the *Saint of*
Saints, and the Martyr of Martyrs. In this Church in the great
Isle leading to the Altar, he caused to be put up another peece of
Limning, or sacred *Paisage*, which for beauty and excellencie
exceeded all the former. We have it most lively described and
explained in these following verses.

Sanctorum labor & merces sibi rite cohærent,
Ardua Crux, pretiumque crucis sublime, corona, &c.

The paines of Saints, and Saints rewards are twins,
The sad Crosse, and the Crowne which the Crosse wins.
30 Here *Christ* the Prince both of the Cross and Crown
Amongst fresh Groves and Lillies fully blown,
Stands, a white Lamb bearing the purple Crosse,
White shewes his purenesse, *Red* his bloods dear losse :
To ease his sorrowes the Chast *Turtle* sings,
And fans him swetting blood with her bright wings ;
While from a shining Cloud the *Father* Eyes
His Sons sad conflict with his Enemies,
And on his blessed head lets gently down
Eternal glory made into a Crown.
40 About him stand two flocks of differing notes,
One of white sheepe, and one of speckled goates,
The first possesse his right hand, and the last
Stand on his left : The spotted Goates are cast
All into thick, deep shades, while from his right
The white sheepe passe into a whiter light.

20 he dedicated] de dedicated *1654*   21 *Martyr*] *Marty 1654*

But in all these sacred buildings, our most pious and humble Bishop did not so much as dream of *Merit.* He thought (as blessed Mr. *Herbert* did) that they were good works, if sprinkled with the blood of *Christ*; otherwise hee thought them nothing. It will not be amisse, nor perhaps needlesse, to produce his own words in his own defense : *Nisi dominus ædificaverit domum, vano ædificantes labore sudabimus. Oremus ergo dominum, ut dum nos illi ædificamus domicilia quæ videntur, ille nobis intus ædificet illa quæ non videntur, domum videlicet illam non manufactam.* "Unlesse "the Lord build the house, wee labour in vaine to build it. Let us "therefore (saith he) pray to the Lord, that while wee outwardly "build unto him these visible buildings, hee would build inwardly "in us those which are invisible, that is to say, the house not "made with hands. How can a servant merit by making use of his masters goods? All we do, and all we give are but his concessions and favours first given unto us. *Cum suis & hic & ibi rebus locupletamur,* in this World, and in the World to come all our magnificence is but his munificence. But *Paulinus* was not onely outwardly pious, but inwardly also. He did so abound with private devotions, that all the time from his Baptism to his buriall, may be truly called his *Prayer-time.* All that he did think, all that he did speak, and all that he did write, was pure devotion. Either publick or private prayers took up all his time. Our Saviour tells us, that *Gods Elects cry day and night unto him,* and Saint *Paul* adviseth us *to pray without ceasing, and in every thing to give thanks, for this* (saith he) *is the will of God in Christ Iesus concerning you.* Holy *Paulinus* called Saint *Paul* his Master, having made himselfe his Disciple, hee would not neglect his commands : *If you continue in my word* (saith our Saviour) *then are you my Disciples indeed.*

Luk. 18.

To this I shall adde his Conformity and obedience to the Church, a blessing of no small consequence in all ages, especially in this age of *Schismes* and *Heresies.* Hee highly honoured the memory of the Saints of God, and was a most chearfull and devout observer of Sacred Festivals, or holy daies. His pious affection to these blessed seasons, together with the necessity and convenience of them, he hath most elegantly and learnedly demonstrated in his Poems.

——— *hos per longa morantes*
Tempora, dum tardi splendens rota vertitur anni
Sustineo intentis affecto pectore votis :
Quos cupio totis mihi prælucere diebus,

Vel quando veniunt ita compensare moras, ut
Æstivis possent spatiis producere lucem,
Aut illum pensare diem, qui sistere Jussis
Syderibus, longo lassavit lumine mundum,
Humanos duplicans dilatâ nocte labores.
 Ergo velut cælum stellis, & floribus arva
Temporibusque annos dominus, sic ipse diebus
Tempora distinxit festis, ut pigra diurnis
Ingenia obsequiis, saltem discrimine facto,
Post intervallum reduci sollemnia voto   10
Sancta libenter agant, residesque per annua mentes
Festa parent domino, quia jugiter intemeratos
Justitiæ servare piget: delinquere suetis,
Parcere peccato labor est: decurritur omni
Valle, per ascensum non est evadere cursu.
 Inde bonus dominus cunctos pietatis ut alis
Contegat, invalidis niti virtutis ad arcem
Congrua sanctorum dedit intervalla dierum,
Ut saltem officiis mediocribus ultima Christi
Vestimenta legant, & eos sacra fimbria sanet.   20
 Primus enim gradus est cælo pertexere cunctos
Continuâ bonitate dies, & tempore toto
Pascha sacrum Christi Cultu celebrare pudico.
Quod si mista seges tribulis mihi germinat, & cor
Incultum stimulat terreni spina laboris,
Vel festis domino studeam me offere diebus,
Ut vel parte mei tangam confinia Vitæ,
Corpore ne toto trahar in Consortia mortis.

Englished thus.

Those sacred daies by tedious time delai'd   30
While the slow years bright line about is laid,
I patiently expect, though much distrest
By busie longing, and a love-sicke brest:
I wish, they may outshine all other daies,
Or when they come, so recompence delaies
As to outlast the Summer-hours bright length,
Or that fam'd day, when stopt by Divine strength,
The Sun did tyre the World with his long light,
Doubling mens labours, and adjourning night.
 As the bright Skye with stars, the fields with flowers, 40
The years with diff'ring seasons, months and houres
God hath distinguished and mark'd; so he
With sacred feasts did ease and beautifie
The working dayes: because that mixture may
Make men (loath to be holy ev'ry day,)

12 *jugiter Paulinus: Jupiter 1654*   19 *ultima*] *ultimæ 1654*

27 *tangam Paulinus : tanquam 1654*

After long labours with a freer will
Adore their maker, and keepe mindfull still
Of holynesse, by keeping holy daies :
For otherwise they would dislike the wayes
Of piety as too severe.   To cast
Old customes quite off, and from sinne to fast
Is a great work.   To runne which way we will,
On plaines is easie, not so up a hill.
   Hence 'tis our good God (who would all men bring
Under the Covert of his saving wing,)   10
Appointed at set times his solemne feasts,
That by mean services, men might at least
Take hold of Christ as by the hemme, and steal
Help from his lowest skirts their Soules to heal.
   For the first step to Heaven, is to live well
All our life long, and each day to excel
In holynesse ; but since that tares are found
In the best Corn, and thistles will Confound
And prick my heart with vaine cares, I will strive
To weed them out on feast-daies, and so thrive   20
By handfuls, 'till I may full life obtaine,
And not be swallow'd of Eternall paine.

Two places upon Earth were most renowned with the memory
of our Saviour, *Bethlem* for his *birth*, and mount *Calvarie* for his
passion.   To extirpate all remembrance of his *Humanity* out of
these places, *Hadrian* the persecutor caused the Idol of *Jupiter* to
be set up, and worshiped in *Mount Calvarie* ; and in *Bethlem* he
built a *Mosquie* for that *Egyptian* block *Adonis*, which the Idolatrous *Jewes* called *Thamuz*.   Some men amongst us have done the
like : Two *Seasons* in the year were consecrated by the *Church* to 30
the memory of our *Saviour*: The *Feast* of his *Nativity* and
Circumcision, and the *Feast* of his *Passion* and *Resurrection*.   These
two they have utterly taken away : endeavouring (in my opinion)
to extinguish the *memory* of his *Incarnation* and *Passion*, and to
race his blessed name out of those *bright columnes of light*, which
the *Scripture* calls *daies*.   They will not allow him two daies in the
year, who made the dayes and the nights.   But it is much to be
feared, that he who hath appointed their daies here, will allow them
for it long nights.

Holy *Paulinus* had now attained a good old age, the fore- 40
runners (as Master *Herbert* saith) were come, and the *Almond tree
did flourish*: hee was all white with years, and worshiped (like
Jacob) *leaning upon the top of his staffe*.   His virtuous and deare
Therasia had died (I believe) long before this time ; God having

ordained him to be hindmost, who was the stronger Vessell, and best able to bear her absence, and the unavoydable disconsolations of flesh and blood. And now (having for some time stood gazing after her,) he begins to follow, God visiting him with a strong paine in the side, which in a few daies did set him at liberty to overtake her, by breaking the prison.

Three daies before his dissolution, *Symmachus* and *Hyacinthinus*, two Bishops of his acquaintance came to visit him ; whereupon hee spoke to *Uranius* his Presbyter, that hee should prepare to attend
10 him in the administration of the Sacrament ; for (said he) I desire to receive it in the company of my brethren, which are now come to see mee. This sacred Solemnity was no sooner ended, but suddenly hee began to ask, *where his brothers were?* One that stood by, supposing that he had asked for the two Bishops, answered, *Here they be* : I know that, replyed *Paulinus*, but I aske

Januarius was Bishop of Naples, and a Martyr ; and Martinus was the Bishop of Tours in France. for my brothers * *Januarius* and *Martinus, who were here with me just now, and promised to come to me again.* And having thus spoken, he looked up towards Heaven, and with a voyce as
20 chearfull as his countenance, which seemed to shine and revive with joy, he sung out the one hundred and twentieth Psalme, *I lift up mine Eyes unto the hills from whence cometh my help. My help commeth from the Lord, who made Heaven and Earth.*

This being done *Posthumianus*, another Presbyter that was then present, told *Paulinus, that there were forty shillings unpaid for the Cloathes which he had given to the poor, before he fell sick.* To this *Paulinus* replyed with a smile, that he remembred it very well : *and Son* (said he) *take no thought for it, for beleive me, there
30 is one that will not be wanting to pay the debt of the poor.* The words were no sooner out of his mouth, but presently there comes in from the parts of *Lucania* (now called *Basilicata*) a Presbyter sent from the holy Bishop *Exuperantius* to visit *Paulinus* ; who brought him fifty shillings for a token from the Bishop. *Paulinus* receiving the money, blessed God, saying, *I thank thee O Lord, that hast not forsaken them that seek thee.* Of these fifty shillings he gave two with his owne hand to the Presbyter that brought them, and the rest he delivered to *Posthumianus* to pay for the Cloathes which were given to the poor.
40 The Evening now drawing on, hee remained quiet and well at

20 (*note*) France.] France *1654*   27 *he fell*] *he fell 1654*   33 *Paulinus*] *Paul nus 1654*

ease untill midnight : but the paine then increasing in his side, he was troubled with a great difficulty, and shortnesse of breathing, which held him till five in the morning. The day begining to break, he felt the usuall motions of holynesse awaking his Spirit, to which (though weak) he chearfully obeyed, and sitting up in his bed, celebrated *Mattins* himselfe. By this time all the *Deacons* and *Presbyters* of his diocesse were gathered together at the door, and came (like the *Sons* of the *Prophets*) to see the translation of their aged Father. After some short exhortations to holynesse and Christian courage, he lifted up his hands and blessed them, 10 mindfull (it seems) of our Saviours carriage at his ascension, whose peace he prayed might rest upon them.

Shortly after (the pain still encreasing and prevailing against him) hee became speechlesse, and so continued untill the Evening ; when suddenly sitting up (as if hee had been awaked out of his sleep) he perceived it to be the time of the *Lucernarium*, or Evening-Office, and lifting up his hands towards Heaven, he repeated with a low voyce, this verse out of the Psalmes, *Thy word is a Lantern unto my feet, and a light unto my paths.* About the fourth hour of the night, when all that were present sate diligently 20 watching about him ; his poor Cottage did suddenly shake with such a strong Earth-quake, that those who kneeled about his bed were something disordered with it, and fell all trembling to their prayers. The Guests of Eternal Glory were now entred under that narrow roof, where (after the abdication of his great worldly honours) he had lived so long in all holynesse and humility. For in that instant of time (saith *Uranius*) he was dissolved, the blessed Angels testifying that they were present to conduct his happy and glorious Soul into the joy of his Master. By the like signe did *Christ* signifie to his Church in *Hierusalem*, that he 30 heard their prayers when they were persecuted by the mercilesse *Jews*. *Gregory* the great, in the place before cited, makes expresse mention of this Earthquake. And thus we see after what manner the righteous are taken away, though no man will lay it to his heart.

Three daies (saith *Uranius*) before *John* the Bishop of *Naples* departed out of this life, he affirmed that he saw *Paulinus* all clothed with Angelicall brightnesse, which shined like the stars, holding in his hand a kind of Heavenly foode in form like a honey-combe, but white as the light, and speaking to him, *brother Iohn, what do you here? pray, that you may be dissolv'd, & come unto* 40 *us, where we have enough of this provision which you see in my hand.*

5 sitting] sittting *1654*

This pious Bishop did not long survive this vision, for the Sunday following, after he had ended his Sermon, and blessed the people (having the day before celebrated the Communion, and distributed to the poor,) he fell sicke and dyed in the Church. So that I may say of him, *Episcopos Concionantes, & Concionatores stantes mori docuit*: Hee taught Bishops to dye preaching, and preachers to die standing.

Blessed *Paulinus* departed out of this life in the year of our Lord four hundred and thirty one, in the seaven and seaventieth year of his age, upon the tenth of the kalends of *Iuly*, which according to our account is the two and twentieth day of *Iune*. His body was carried from *Nola* to *Rome*, and decently interred in the Church of St. *Bartholomew*, neare the Apostles own Tombe: where they both lye expecting the second comming of our Lord and Saviour *JESUS CHRIST*; which of his great mercy I earnestly beseech him to hasten, and to appeare himselfe the onely faithfull Judge, and most just Determiner of *Right* and *Wrong*, of *Truth* and *Falshood*.

Gloria tibi mitissime Jesu !

St. *Paulinus* to his Wife
Therasia.

Come my true Consort in my Joyes and Care !
Let this uncertaine and still wasting share
Of our fraile life be giv'n to God. You see
How the swift dayes drive hence incessantlie,
And the fraile, drooping World (though still thought gay,)
In secret, slow consumption weares away.
All that we have, passe from us : and once past
Returne no more ; like clouds, they seeme to last,
And so delude loose, greedy mindes. But where
Are now those trim deceits ? to what darke sphere   10
Are all those false fires sunck, which once so shin'd
They captivated Soules, and rul'd mankind ?
He that with fifty ploughes his lands did sow,
Will scarse be trusted for two Oxen now,
His rich, lowd Coach known to each crowded street
Is sold, and he quite tir'd walkes on his feet.
Merchants that (like the Sun) their voyage made
From East to West, and by whole-sale did trade,

Are now turn'd Sculler-men, or sadly swett
In a poore fishers boat with line and nett.   20
Kingdomes and Cities to a period tend,
Earth nothing hath, but what must have an end :
Mankind by plagues, distempers, dearth and warre,
Tortures and prisons dye both neare and farre ;
Furie and hate rage in each living brest,
Princes with Princes, States with States contest ;
An Vniversall discord mads each land,
Peace is quite lost, the last times are at hand ;
But were these dayes from the last day secure,
So that the world might for more yeares endure,   30
Yet we (like hirelings) should our terme expect,
And on our day of death each day reflect.
*For what (*Therasia!*) doth it us availe*
That spatious streames shall flow and never faile,
That aged forrests live to tyre the Winds,
And flowers each spring returne and keepe their kinds ?
Those still remaine : but all our Fathers dyed,
And we our selves but for few dayes abide.
    This short time then was not giv'n us in vaine,
To whom tyme dyes, in which we dying gaine,   40
But that in time eternall life should be
Our care, and endlesse rest our industrie.
And yet, this Taske which the rebellious deeme
Too harsh, who god's mild lawes for chaines esteem
Suites with the meeke and harmelesse heart so right
That 'tis all ease, all comfort and delight.
" To love our God with all our strength and will ;
" To covet nothing ; to devise no ill
"Against our neighbours ; to procure or doe
" Nothing to others, which we would not to   50
" Our very selves ; not to revenge our wrong ;
" To be content with little ; not to long
" For wealth and greatnesse ; to despise or jeare
" No man, and if we be despised, to bear ;
" To feede the hungry ; to hold fast our Crown ;
" To take from others naught ; to give our owne ;
These are his precepts : and (alas !) in these
What is so hard, but faith can doe with ease ?
He that the holy Prophets doth beleeve,

      35 *live LGu: hie 1654*

And on Gods words relies, words that still live   60
And cannot dye ; that in his heart hath writ
His Saviour's death and tryumph, and doth yet
With constant care, admitting no neglect,
His second, dreadfull comming still expect :
To such a liver earthy things are dead,
With Heav'n alone, and hopes of heav'n hee's fed ;
He is no Vassall unto worldly trash,
Nor that black knowledge, which pretends to wash,
But doth defile : A knowledge, by which Men
With studied care loose Paradise agen.   70
Commands and titles, the vaine worlds device,
With gold, the forward seed of sin and vice,
He never minds : his Ayme is farre more high,
And stoopes to nothing lower than the skie ;
Nor griefe, nor pleasures breede him any pain,
He nothing feares to loose, would nothing gaine ;
What ever hath not God, he doth detest :
He lives to Christ, is dead to all the rest.
This Holy one sent hither from above
A Virgin brought forth, shadow'd by the Dove ;   80
His skin with stripes, with wicked hands his face,
And with foule spittle soyl'd and beaten was ;
A Crown of thornes his blessed head did wound,
Nayles pierc'd his hands and feet, and he fast bound
Stuck to the painefull Crosse, where hang'd till dead
With a cold speare his hearts dear blood was shed.
All this for man, for bad, ungratefull Man
The true God suffer'd ! not that sufferings can
Adde to his glory ought, who can receive
Accesse from nothing, whom none can bereave   90
Of his all-fullnesse : but the blest designe
Of his sad death was to save me from mine ;
He dying bore my sins, and the third day
His early rising rais'd me from the clay.
To such great mercies what shall I preferre,
Or who from loving God shall me deterre ?
Burne me alive, with curious, skilfull paine
Cut up and search each warme and breathing vaine :
When all is done, death brings a quick release,
And the poore mangled body sleepes in peace.   100
Hale me to prisons, shut me up in brasse :

My still free Soule from thence to God shall passe ;
Banish or bind me, I can be no where
A stranger, nor alone ; My God is there.
I feare not famine ; how can he be sed
To sterve, who feedes upon the living bread ?
And yet this courage springs not from my store,
Christ gave it me, who can give much, much more ;
I of my selfe can nothing dare or doe,
He bids me fight, and makes me conquer too :   110
If (like great Abr'ham,*) I should have command*
To leave my fathers house and native Land,
I would with joy to unknown regions run,
Bearing the Banner of his blessed Son.
On worldly goods I will have no designe,
But use my owne, as if mine were not mine ;
Wealth I'le not wonder at, nor greatnesse seeke,
But chuse (though laugh'd at,) to be poore & meeke.
In woe and wealth I'le keepe the same stay'd mind,
Griefe shall not breake me, nor joyes make me blind :   120
My dearest Jesus I'le still praise, and he
Shall with *Songs of Deliverance compasse me.*

    Then come my faithfull Consort ! joyne with me
In this good fight, and my true helper be ;
Cheare me when sad ; advise me when I stray ;
Let us be each the others guide and stay ;
Be your Lords Guardian *: give joynt ayde and due ;*
Helpe him when falne ; rise, when he helpeth you ;
That so we may not onely one flesh be,
But in one Spirit, and one Will agree.   130

FINIS.

Authoris (de se) Emblema.

Tentâsti, fateor, sine vulnere sæpius, & me
  Consultum voluit Vox, sine voce, frequens ;
Ambivit placido divinior aura meatu,
  Et frustrà sancto murmure præmonuit.
Surdus eram, mutusq; Silex : Tu, (quanta tuorum
  Cura tibi est !) aliâ das renovare viâ,
Permutas Curam ; Jamq; irritatus Amorem
  Posse negas, & vim, Vi, superare paras,
Accedis propior, molemq, & Saxea rumpis
  Pectora, fitq; Caro, quod fuit ante Lapis.   10
En lacerum ! Cælosq; tuos ardentia tandem
  Fragmenta, & liquidas ex Adamante genas.
Sic olim undantes Petras, Scopulosq; vomentes
  Curâsti, O populi providus usq; tui !
Quam miranda tibi manus est ! Moriendo, revixi ;
  Et fractas jam sum ditior inter opes.

Emblem and Poem only in 1650.   4 præmonuit.] præmonuit 1650.   10 Lapis.]
Lapis 1650.

Silex Scintillans:
or
SACRED POEMS
and
Private Eiaculations
By
Henry Vaughan Silurist

LONDON Printed by T. W. for H. Blunden
at ye Castle in Cornehill . 1650

Engraved title-page of *Silex Scintillans* (1650)

Silex Scintillans:

SACRED

POEMS

And private

EJACULATIONS.

The fecond Edition, In two Books;
By *Henry Vaughan*, Silurift.

Job chap. 35. ver. 10, 11.

*Where is God my Maker, who giveth Songs in
the night ?
Who teacheth us more then the beafts of the
earth, and maketh us wifer then the fowls
of heaven ?*

London, Printed for *Henry Crips*, and *Lodo-
wick Lloyd*, next to the Caftle in *Cornhil*,
and in *Popes-head Alley*. 1655.

The Authors

P R E F A C E

To the following

H Y M N S.

That this Kingdom hath abounded with those ingenious persons, which in the late notion are termed *Wits*, is too well known. Many of them having cast away all their fair portion of time, in no better imployments, then a deliberate search, or excogitation of *idle words*, and a most vain, insatiable desire to be reputed *Poets*; leaving behinde them no other Monuments of those excellent abilities conferred upon them, but such as they may (with a *Predecessor* of theirs) term *Parricides*, and a soul-killing Issue; for that is the Βραβεῖον, and Laureate *Crown*, which idle
10 *Poems* will certainly bring to their unrelenting Authors.

And well it were for them, if those willingly-studied and wilfully-published vanities could defile no *spirits*, but their own; but the *case* is far worse. These *Vipers* survive their *Parents*, and for many ages after (like *Epidemic* diseases) infect whole Generations, corrupting always and unhallowing the best-gifted *Souls*, and the most capable *Vessels*: for whose sanctification and well-fare, the glorious *Son* of God laid down his *life*, and suffered the pretious *blood* of his blessed and innocent *heart* to be poured out. In the mean time it cannot be denyed, but these men are

20 had in remembrance, though we cannot say with any comfort, *Their memorial is blessed*; for, that I may speak no more then the truth (let their passionate *worshippers* say what they please) all the commendations that can be justly given them, will amount to no more, then what *Prudentius* the Christian-sacred *Poet* bestowed upon *Symmachus*;

> *Os dignum æterno tinctum quod fulgeat auro*
> *Si mallet laudare deum : cui sordida monstra*
> *Prætulit, & liquidam temeravit crimine vocem ;*
> *Haud aliter, quàm cum rastris qui tentat eburnis*
> 30 *Cænosum versare solum, &c. ——*

Preface and texts (page 393) only in 1655.

In English thus,

A wit most worthy in tryed Gold to shine,
Immortal Gold ! had he sung the divine
Praise of his Maker : to whom he preferr'd
Obscene, vile fancies, and prophanely marr'd
A rich, rare stile with sinful, lewd contents ;
No otherwise, then if with Instruments
Of polish'd Ivory, some drudge should stir
A dirty sink, *&c.* ———

This *comparison* is nothing odious, and it is as *true*, as it is 10
apposite; for a *good* wit in a *bad* subject, is (as *Solomon* said of the
fair and *foolish woman*) *Like a jewel of gold in a swines snowt*,
Prov. 11. 22. Nay, the more acute the *Author is*, there is so
much the more danger and death in the *work*. Where the *Sun*
is busie upon a *dung-hill*, the *issue* is always some unclean
vermine. Divers persons of eminent piety and learning (I meddle
not with the seditious and *Schismatical*) have, long before my
time, taken notice of this *malady*; for the complaint against
vitious verse, even by peaceful and obedient *spirits*, is of some
antiquity in this Kingdom. And yet, as if the evil consequence 20
attending this inveterate *error*, were but a small thing, there is
sprung very lately another prosperous *device* to assist it in the
subversion of *souls*. Those that want the *Genius* of *verse*, fall to
translating; and the people are (every *term*) plentifully furnished
with various *Foraign vanities*; so that the most lascivious compositions of *France* and *Italy* are here *naturalized* and made
English: And this (as it is sadly observed) with so much favor
and success, that nothing *takes* (as they rightly phrase it) like
a *Romance*. And very frequently (if that *Character* be not an
Ivy-bush) the *buyer* receives this lewd ware from *persons of honor*: 30
who want not reason to forbear, much private misfortune having
sprung from no other *seed* at first, then some infectious and dissolving *Legend*.

To continue (after years of discretion) in this *vanity*, is an
inexcusable desertion of *pious sobriety* : and to persist so to the
end, is a wilful despising of Gods *sacred exhortations*, by a constant,
sensual volutation or wallowing in *impure thoughts* and *scurrilous
conceits*, which both defile their Authors, and as many more, as
they are communicated to. If *every idle word shall be accounted
for*, and if *no corrupt communication should proceed out of our* 40
mouths, how desperate (I beseech you) is their condition, who all
their life time, and out of meer design, study *lascivious fictions* :

then carefully record and publish them, that instead of *grace* and
life, they *may minister sin and death* unto their readers? It was
wisely considered, and piously said by one, *That he would read
no idle books ; both in regard of love to his own soul, and pity unto
his that made them, for* (said he) *if I be corrupted by them, their
Composer is immediatly a cause of my ill : and at the day of
reckoning (though now dead) must give an account for it, because
I am corrupted by his bad example, which he left behinde him .
I will write none, lest I hurt them that come after me ; I will read*
10 *none, lest I augment his punishment that is gone before me. I will
neither write, nor read, lest I prove a foe to my own soul : while
I live, I sin too much ; let me not continue longer in wickedness,
then I do in life.* It is a sentence of sacred authority, that *he that
is dead, is freed from sin* ; because he cannot in that *state,* which
is without the *body,* sin any more ; but he that writes *idle books,*
makes for himself another *body,* in which he always *lives,* and
sins (after *death*) as *fast* and as *foul,* as ever he did in his *life ;*
which very consideration, deserves to be a sufficient *Antidote*
against this evil disease.

20 And here, because I would prevent a just *censure* by my free
confession, I must remember, that I my self have for many years
together, languished of this very *sickness* ; and it is no long time
since I have recovered. But (blessed be God for it !) I have
by his saving assistance supprest my *greatest follies,* and those
which escaped from me, are (I think) as innoxious, as most of
that *vein* use to be ; besides, they are interlined with many
virtuous, and some pious mixtures. What I speak of them, is
truth ; but let no man mistake it for an *extenuation* of faults, as
if I intended an *Apology* for *them,* or my *self,* who am conscious
30 of so much *guilt* in *both,* as can never be expiated without *special
sorrows,* and that cleansing and pretious *effusion* of my Almighty
Redeemer : and if the world will be so charitable, as to grant my
request, I do here most humbly and earnestly beg that none
would read them.

 But an idle or sensual *subject* is not all the *poyson* in these
Pamphlets. Certain Authors have been so irreverendly bold, as to
dash *Scriptures,* and the *sacred Relatives* of *God* with their impious
conceits ; And (which I cannot speak without grief of heart) some
of those desperate *adventurers* may (I think) be reckoned amongst
40 the principal or most learned Writers of *English verse.*

 Others of a later *date,* being corrupted (it may be) by that evil
Genius, which came in with the publique distractions, have stuffed

their books with *Oathes, horrid Execrations,* and a most gross
and studied *filthiness.* But the *hurt* that ensues by the publi-
cation of *pieces* so notoriously ill, lies heavily upon the *Stationers*
account, who ought in conscience to refuse them, when they are
put into his hands. No *loss* is so doleful as that *gain,* that will
endamage the soul; he that *prints* lewdness and impieties, is that
mad man in the *Proverbs,* who *casteth firebrands, arrows and
death.*

The suppression of this pleasing and prevailing *evil,* lies not
altogether in the power of the *Magistrate;* for it will flie abroad 10
in *Manuscripts,* when it fails of entertainment at the *press.* The
true remedy lies wholly in their bosoms, who are the gifted
persons, by a wise exchange of *vain* and *vitious subjects,* for *divine
Themes* and *Celestial praise.* The *performance* is easie, and were
it the most difficult in the world, the *reward* is so glorious, that
it infinitely transcends it: for *they that turn many to righteousness,
shall shine like the stars for ever and ever:* whence follows this
undenyable *inference,* That the *corrupting of many,* being a contrary *work,* the *recompense* must be so too; and then I know
nothing reserved for them, but *the blackness of darkness for ever;* 20
from which (O God!) deliver all penitent and reformed *Spirits*!

The first, that with any effectual success attempted a *diversion*
of this foul and overflowing *stream,* was the blessed man, Mr.
George Herbert, whose holy *life* and *verse* gained many pious
Converts, (of whom I am the least) and gave the first check to
a most flourishing and admired *wit* of his time. After him
followed diverse,—*Sed non passibus æquis;* they had more of
fashion, then *force:* And the *reason* of their so vast *distance* from
him, besides differing *spirits* and *qualifications* (for his *measure*
was eminent) I suspect to be, because they aimed more at *verse,* 30
then *perfection;* as may be easily gathered by their frequent *impressions,* and numerous *pages:* Hence sprang those wide, those
weak, and lean *conceptions,* which in the most inclinable *Reader*
will scarce give any nourishment or help to *devotion;* for not
flowing from a true, practick piety, it was impossible they should
effect those things abroad, which they never had acquaintance
with at home; being onely the productions of a common spirit,
and the obvious ebullitions of that light humor, which takes the
pen in hand, out of no other consideration, then to be seen in
print. It is true indeed, that to give up our thoughts to pious 40
Themes and *Contemplations* (if it be done for pieties sake) is
a great *step* towards *perfection;* because it will *refine,* and *dispose*

17 *like*] *l ke 1655* (?)

to devotion and sanctity. And further, it will *procure* for us (so easily communicable is that *loving spirit*) some small *prelibation* of those heavenly *refreshments*, which descend but seldom, and then very sparingly, upon *men* of an ordinary or indifferent *holyness*; but he that desires to excel in this kinde of *Hagiography*, or holy writing, must strive (by all means) for *perfection* and true *holyness*, that a *door may be opened to him in heaven*, Rev. 4. 1. and then he will be able to write (with *Hierotheus* and holy *Herbert*) A *true Hymn.*

10   To effect this in some measure, I have begged leave to communicate this my poor *Talent* to the *Church*, under the *protection* and *conduct* of her *glorious Head* : who (if he will vouchsafe to *own* it, and *go along* with it) can make it as useful now in the *publick*, as it hath been to me in *private*. In the *perusal* of it, you will (peradventure) observe some *passages*, whose *history* or *reason* may seem something *remote* ; but were they brought *nearer*, and plainly exposed to your view, (though that (perhaps) might quiet your *curiosity*) yet would it not conduce much to your greater *advantage*. And therefore I must desire you to 20 accept of them in that *latitude*, which is already alowed them. By the last *Poems* in the book (were not that *mistake* here prevented) you would judge all to be *fatherless*, and the *Edition* posthume ; for (indeed) *I was nigh unto death*, and am still at no great distance from it ; which was the necessary reason for that solemn and accomplished *dress*, you will now finde this *impression* in.

    But *the God of the spirits of all flesh*, hath granted me a further use of *mine*, then I did look for in the *body* ; and when I expected, and had (by his assistance) prepared for a *message* of *death*, then 30 did he *answer* me with *life*; I hope to his *glory*, and my great *advantage* : that I may flourish not with *leafe* onely, but with some *fruit* also ; which *hope* and earnest *desire* of his poor *Creature*, I humbly beseech him to perfect and fulfil for his dear *Sons* sake, unto *whom*, with *him* and the most holy and loving *Spirit*, be ascribed by *Angels*, by *Men*, and by all his *Works*, All Glory, and Wisdom, and Dominion, in this the *temporal* and in the *Eternal* Being. *Amen.*

    Newton by *Usk*, near
    Sketh-rock, Septem. 30.
40   1 6 5 4.

O Lord, the hope of Israel, all they that forsake thee shall be ashamed ; and they that depart from thee, shall be written in the earth, because they have forsaken the Lord, the fountain of living waters.

Heal me, O Lord, and I shall be healed ; save me, and I shall be saved, for thou art my health, and my great deliverer.

I said in the cutting off of my days, I shall go to the gates of the grave ; I have deprived my self of the residue of my years.

I said, I shall not see the Lord, even the Lord in the Land of the living : I shall behold man no more with the Inhabitants of the 10 *world.*

O Lord! by thee doth man live, and from thee is the life of my spirit : therefore wilt thou recover me, and make me to live.

Thou hast in love to my soul delivered it from the pit of corruption ; for thou hast cast all my sins behinde thy back.

For thy names sake hast thou put off thine anger ; for thy praise hast thou refrained from me, that I should not be cut off.

For the grave cannot praise thee, death cannot celebrate thee : they that go down into the pit, cannot hope for thy truth.

The living, the living, he shall praise thee, as I do this day : the 20 *Father to the children shall make known thy truth.*

O Lord! thou hast been merciful, thou hast brought back my life from corruption : thou hast redeemed me from my sin.

They that follow after lying vanities, forsake their own mercy.

Therefore shall thy songs be with me, and my prayer unto the God of my life.

I will go unto the altar of my God, unto God, the joy of my youth ; and in thy fear will I worship towards thy holy temple.

I will sacrifice unto thee with the voice of thanksgiving ; I will pay that which I have vowed : salvation is of the Lord. 30

To my most merciful, my most
loving, and dearly loved Redeemer, the ever blessed,
the onely Holy and

JUST ONE,

JESVS CHRIST,

The Son of the living

G O D,

And the sacred

Virgin Mary.

I.

My God! thou that didst dye for me,
These thy deaths fruits I offer thee;
Death that to me was life and light,
But dark and deep pangs to thy sight.
Some drops of <u>thy all-quickning blood</u>
Fell on my heart; those made it bud
And put forth thus, though Lord, before
The ground was curst, and void of store.
Indeed I had some here to hire
Which long resisted thy desire,   10
That ston'd thy servants, and did move
To have the murthred for thy love;
But Lord, I have expell'd them, and so bent,
Beg, thou wouldst take thy Tenants Rent.

II.

Dear Lord, 'tis finished! and now he
That copyed it, presents it thee.
<u>'Twas thine first, and to thee returns,</u>
From thee it shin'd, though here it burns;

The first verse alone appears in 1650 and is headed simply The Dedication.
1 God!] God, *1650*   2 thee;] thee. *1650*   3 life] life, *1650*   6 heart;]
heart, *1650*   those] these *1650*   9 Indeed] Indeed, (*set in*) *1650*   12 love;]
Love, *1650*   13 But] But, *1650*   bent,] bent *1650*   14 Beg,] Begge *1650*

If the Sun rise on rocks, is't right,
To call it their inherent light? 20
No, nor can I say, this is mine,
For, dearest Jesus, 'tis all thine.
As thy cloaths, (when thou with cloaths wert clad)
Both light from thee, and virtue had,
And now (as then within this place)
Thou to poor rags dost still give grace.
This is the earnest thy love sheds,
The *Candle* shining on some heads,
Till at thy charges they shall be,
Cloath'd all with immortality. 30

My dear Redeemer, the worlds light,
And life too, and my hearts delight!
For all thy mercies and thy truth
Shew'd to me in my sinful youth,
For my sad failings and my wilde
Murmurings at thee, when most milde:
For all my secret faults, and each
Frequent relapse and wilful breach,
For all designs meant against thee,
And ev'ry publish'd vanity 40
Which thou divinely hast forgiven,
While thy blood wash'd me white as heaven:
I nothing have to give to thee,
But this thy own gift, given to me;
Refuse it not! for now thy *Token*
Can tell thee where a heart is broken.

Revel. cap. 1. *ver.* 5, 6, 7.
Unto him that loved us, and washed us from our sins in his own
blood.
And hath made us Kings and Priests unto God and his Father;
to him be glory and dominion, for ever and ever. Amen.
Behold, he cometh with clouds, and every eye shall see him, and
they also which pierced him; and all kinreds of the earth shall wail
because of him: even so. Amen.

6 (*prose*) *of*] *af 1655*

¶

Vain Wits and eyes
Leave, and be wise :
Abuse not, shun not holy fire,
But with true tears wash off your mire.
Tears and these flames will soon grow kinde,
And mix an eye-salve for the blinde.
Tears cleanse and supple without fail,
And fire will purge your callous veyl.
Then comes the light! which when you spy,
And see your nakedness thereby,
Praise him, who dealt his gifts so free
In tears to you, in fire to me.

These verses in 1655 only

10

Silex Scintillans, &c.

Regeneration.

A Ward, and still in bonds, one day
        I stole abroad,
It was high-spring, and all the way
      Primros'd, and hung with shade ;
        Yet, was it frost within,
           And surly winds
Blasted my infant buds, and sinne
      Like Clouds ecclips'd my mind.

2.

Storm'd thus ; I straight perceiv'd my spring
      Meere stage, and show,   10
My walke a monstrous, mountain'd thing
      Rough-cast with Rocks, and snow ;
        And as a Pilgrims Eye
           Far from reliefe,
Measures the melancholy skye
      Then drops, and rains for griefe,

3.

So sigh'd I upwards still, at last
      'Twixt steps, and falls
I reach'd the pinacle, where plac'd
      I found a paire of scales,   20
      I tooke them up and layd
        In th'one late paines,
The other smoake, and pleasures weigh'd
      But prov'd the heavier graines ;

4.

With that, some cryed, *Away* ; straight I
      Obey'd, and led
Full East, a faire, fresh field could spy
      Some call'd it, *Jacobs Bed* ;
      A Virgin-soile, which no
        Rude feet ere trod,   30
Where (since he stept there,) only go
      Prophets, and friends of God.

6 And surly winds] The surly wind *L 1847* : And surly wind *L 1858–1883*
17 still] till *conj. GM*   31 stept] slept *anonymous conjecture in G*

5.

Here, I repos'd; but scarse well set,
A grove descryed
Of stately height, whose branches met
And mixt on every side;
I entred, and once in
(Amaz'd to see't,)
Found all was chang'd, and a new spring
Did all my senses greet;   40

6.

The unthrift Sunne shot vitall gold
A thousand peeces,
And heaven its azure did unfold
Checqur'd with snowie fleeces,
The aire was all in spice
And every bush
A garland wore; Thus fed my Eyes
But all the Eare lay hush.

7.

Only a little Fountain lent
Some use for Eares,   50
And on the dumbe shades language spent
The Musick of her teares;
I drew her neere, and found
The Cisterne full
Of divers stones, some bright, and round
Others ill-shap'd, and dull.

8.

The first (pray marke,) as quick as light
Danc'd through the floud,
But, th'last more heavy then the night
Nail'd to the Center stood;   60
I wonder'd much, but tyr'd
At last with thought,
My restless Eye that still desir'd
As strange an object brought;

48 Eare] Earth *G* : ear[th] *C*   63 desir'd] desir'd, *LGCB*

9.

It was a banke of flowers, where I descried
(Though 'twas mid-day,)
Some fast asleepe, others broad-eyed
And taking in the Ray,
Here musing long, I heard
A rushing wind   70
Which still increas'd, but whence it stirr'd
No where I could not find ;

10.

I turn'd me round, and to each shade
Dispatch'd an Eye,
To see, if any leafe had made
Least motion, or Reply,
But while I listning sought
My mind to ease
By knowing, where 'twas, or where not,
It whisper'd ; *Where I please.*   80

Lord, then said I, *On me one breath,*
And let me dye before my death !

Cant. Cap. 5. ver. 17.
Arise O North, and come thou South-wind, and blow upon my
garden, that the spices thereof may flow out.

Death.

A Dialogue.

Soule. 'Tis a sad Land, that in one day
Hath dull'd thee thus, when death shall freeze
Thy bloud to Ice, and thou must stay
Tenant for Yeares, and Centuries,
How wilt thou brook't ?

Body. I cannot tell,——
But if all sence wings not with thee,
And something still be left the dead,
I'le wish my Curtaines off to free
Me from so darke, and sad a bed ;   10

A neast of nights, a gloomie sphere,
Where shadowes thicken, and the Cloud
Sits on the Suns brow all the yeare,
And nothing moves without a shrowd ;

Soule. 'Tis so : But as thou sawest that night
    Wee travell'd in, our first attempts
    Were dull, and blind, but Custome straight
    Our feares, and falls brought to contempt,

    Then, when the gastly *twelve* was past
    We breath'd still for a blushing *East,*   20
    And bad the lazie Sunne make hast,
    And on sure hopes, though long, did feast ;

    But when we saw the Clouds to crack
    And in those Cranies light appear'd,
    We thought the day then was not slack,
    And pleas'd our selves with what wee feard ;

    Just so it is in death.   But thou
    Shalt in thy mothers bosome sleepe
    Whilst I each minute grone to know
    How neere Redemption creepes.   30

Then shall wee meet to mix again, and met,
'Tis last good-night, our Sunne shall never set.

Job. Cap: 10. *ver.* 21. 22.
Before I goe whence I shall not returne, even to the land of dark-
nesse, and the shadow of death ;
*   A Land of darknesse, as darkenesse it selfe, and of the shadow of*
death, without any order, and where the light is as darknesse.

Resurrection and Immortality :

Heb. cap. 10. *ve:* 20.
By that new, and living way, which he hath prepared for us,
through the veile, which is his flesh.

Body.

1.

Oft have I seen, when that renewing breath
        That binds, and loosens death
Inspir'd a quickning power through the dead
        Creatures a bed,
   Some drowsie silk-worme creepe
     From that long sleepe

And in weake, infant hummings chime, and knell
    About her silent Cell
Untill at last full with the vitall Ray
    She wing'd away,
    And proud with life, and scnce,
      Heav'ns rich Expence,
Esteem'd (vaine things!) of two whole Elements
    As meane, and span-extents. —
Shall I then thinke such providence will be
    Lesse friend to me?
Or that he can endure to be unjust
Who keeps his Covenant even with our dust.

    Soule.

    2.

Poore, querulous handfull! was't for this
    I taught thee all that is?   20
Unbowel'd nature, shew'd thee her recruits,
    And Change of suits
    And how of death we make
      A meere mistake,
For no thing can to *Nothing* fall, but still
    Incorporates by skill,
And then returns, and from the wombe of things
    Such treasure brings
As *Phenix*-like renew'th
    Both life, and youth;   30
For a preserving spirit doth still passe
    Untainted through this Masse,
Which doth resolve, produce, and ripen all
    That to it fall;
    Nor are those births which we
    Thus suffering see
Destroy'd at all; But when times restles wave
    Their substance doth deprave
And the more noble *Essence* finds his house
    Sickly, and loose,
He, ever young, doth wing   40
    Unto that spring,
And *source* of spirits, where he takes his lot
    Till time no more shall rot

His passive Cottage; which (though laid aside,)
    Like some spruce Bride,
Shall one day rise, and cloath'd with shining light
    All pure, and bright
   Re-marry to the soule, for 'tis most plaine
   Thou only fal'st to be refin'd againe.   50

      3.
Then I that here saw darkly in a glasse
     But mists, and shadows passe,
And, by their owne weake *Shine*, did search the springs
     And Course of things
    Shall with Inlightned Rayes
     Peirce all their wayes;
And as thou saw'st, I in a thought could goe
    To heav'n, or Earth below
To reade some *Starre*, or *Min'rall*, and in State
     There often sate,   60
   So shalt thou then with me
    (Both wing'd, and free,)
Rove in that mighty, and eternall light
   Where no rude shade, or night
Shall dare approach us; we shall there no more
    Watch stars, or pore
  Through melancholly clouds, and say
    Would it were Day!
One everlasting *Saboth* there shall runne
Without *Succession*, and without a *Sunne*.   70

Dan: Cap: 12. ver: 13.
*But goe thou thy way untill the end be, for thou shalt rest, and
stand up in thy lot, at the end of the dayes.*

Day of Judgement.

When through the North a fire shall rush
   And rowle into the East,
And like a firie torrent brush
   And sweepe up *South*, and *West*,

When all shall streame, and lighten round
   And with surprizing flames
Both stars, and Elements confound
   And quite blot out their names,

When thou shalt spend thy sacred store
      Of thunders in that heate   10
And low as ere they lay before
      Thy six-dayes-buildings beate,
When like a scrowle the heavens shal passe
      And vanish cleane away,
And nought must stand of that vast space
      Which held up night, and day,
When one lowd blast shall rend the deepe,
      And from the wombe of earth
Summon up all that are asleepe
      Unto a second birth,   20
When thou shalt make the Clouds thy seate,
      And in the open aire
The Quick, and dead, both small and great
      Must to thy barre repaire ;
O then it wilbe all too late
      To say, *What shall I doe?*
Repentance there is out of date
      And so is *mercy* too ;
Prepare, prepare me then, O God !
      And let me now begin   30
To feele my loving fathers *Rod*
      Killing the man of sinne !
Give me, O give me Crosses here,
      Still more afflictions lend,
That pill, though bitter, is most deare
      That brings health in the end ;
Lord, God ! I beg nor friends, nor wealth
      But pray against them both ;
Three things I'de have, my soules chief health !
      And one of these seme loath,   40
A living *F A I T H,* a *H E A R T* of flesh,
      The *W O R L D* an Enemie,
This last will keepe the first two fresh,
      And bring me, where I'de be.

        1 Pet. 4. 7.
Now the end of all things is at hand, be you therefore sober, and
watching in prayer.

37 Lord, God] Lord God *C*   40 seme] semes *L* : same *G*

Religion.

My God, when I walke in those groves,
And leaves thy spirit doth still fan,
I see in each shade that there growes
An Angell talking with a man.

Under a *Juniper*, some house,
Or the coole *Mirtles* canopie,
Others beneath an *Oakes* greene boughs,
Or at some *fountaines* bubling Eye ;

Here *Jacob* dreames, and wrestles ; there
Elias by a Raven is fed,   10
Another time by th' Angell, where
He brings him water with his bread ;

In *Abr'hams* Tent the winged guests
(O how familiar then was heaven !)
Eate, drinke, discourse, sit downe, and rest
Untill the Coole, and shady *Even* ;

Nay thou thy selfe, my God, in *fire*,
Whirle-winds, and *Clouds*, and the *soft voice*
Speak'st there so much, that I admire
We have no Conf'rence in these daies ;   20

Is the truce broke ? or 'cause we have
A mediatour now with thee,
Doest thou therefore old Treaties wave
And by appeales from him decree ?

Or is't so, as some green heads say
That now all miracles must cease ?
Though thou hast promis'd they should stay
The tokens of the Church, and peace ;

No, no ; Religion is a Spring
That from some secret, golden Mine   30
Derives her birth, and thence doth bring
Cordials in every drop, and Wine ;

But in her long, and hidden Course
Passing through the Earths darke veines,
Growes still from better unto worse,
And both her taste, and colour staines,

Then drilling on, learnes to encrease
False *Ecchoes*, and Confused sounds,
And unawares doth often seize
On veines of *Sulphur* under ground ;   40

So poison'd, breaks forth in some Clime,
And at first sight doth many please,
But drunk, is puddle, or meere slime
And 'stead of Phisick, a disease ;

Just such a tainted sink we have
Like that *Samaritans* dead *Well*,
Nor must we for the Kernell crave
Because most voices like the *shell.*

Heale then these waters, Lord ; or bring thy flock,
Since these are troubled, to the springing rock,   50
Looke downe great Master of the feast ; O shine,
And turn once more our *Water* into *Wine* !

Cant. cap. 4. ver. 12.
My sister, my spouse is as a garden Inclosed, as a Spring shut
up, and a fountain sealed up.

The Search.

'Tis now cleare day : I see a Rose
Bud in the bright East, and disclose
The Pilgrim-Sunne ; all night have I
Spent in a roving Extasie
To find my Saviour ; I have been
As far as *Bethlem*, and have seen
His Inne, and Cradle ; Being there
I met the *Wise-men*, askt them where
He might be found, or what starre can
Now point him out, grown up a Man ?   10
To *Egypt* hence I fled, ran o're
All her parcht bosome to *Nile's* shore
Her yearly nurse ; came back, enquir'd
Amongst the *Doctors*, and desir'd
To see the *Temple*, but was shown
A little dust, and for the Town
A heap of ashes, where some sed
A small bright sparkle was a bed,
Which would one day (beneath the pole,)
Awake, and then refine the whole.   20

E e

Tyr'd here, I come to *Sychar*; thence
To *Jacobs wel*, bequeathed since
Unto his sonnes, (where often they
In those calme, golden Evenings lay
Watring their flocks, and having spent
Those white dayes, drove home to the Tent
Their *well-fleec'd* traine ;) And here (O fate !)
I sit, where once my Saviour sate ;
The angry Spring in bubbles swell'd
Which broke in sighes still, as they fill'd,
And whisper'd, *Jesus had been there*
But *Jacobs children would not heare.*
Loath hence to part, at last I rise
But with the fountain in my Eyes,
And here a fresh search is decreed
He must be found, where he did bleed ;
I walke the garden, and there see
Idæa's of his Agonie,
And moving anguishments that set
His blest face in a bloudy sweat ;
I climb'd the Hill, perus'd the Crosse
Hung with my gaine, and his great losse,
Never did tree beare fruit like this,
Balsam of Soules, the bodyes blisse ;
But, O his grave ! where I saw lent
(For he had none,) a Monument,
An undefil'd, and new-heaw'd one,
But there was not the *Corner-stone* ;
Sure (then said I,) my Quest is vaine,
Hee'le not be found, where he was slaine,
So mild a Lamb can never be
'Midst so much bloud, and Crueltie ;
I'le to the Wilderness, and can
Find beasts more mercifull then man,
He liv'd there safe, 'twas his retreat
From the fierce *Jew*, and *Herods* heat,
And forty dayes withstood the fell,
And high temptations of hell ;
With Seraphins there talked he
His fathers flaming ministrie,
He heav'nd their *walks*, and with his eyes
Made those wild shades a Paradise,

Thus was the desert sanctified
To be the refuge of his bride ;
I'le thither then ; see, It is day,
The Sun's broke through to guide my way.
But as I urg'd thus, and writ down
What pleasures should my Journey crown,
What silent paths, what shades, and Cells,
Faire, virgin-flowers, and hallow'd *Wells*
I should rove in, and rest my head   70
Where my deare Lord did often tread,
Sugring all dangers with successe,
Me thought I heard one singing thus ;

1.

Leave, leave, thy gadding thoughts ;
Who Pores
and spies
Still out of Doores
descries
Within them nought.   80

2.

The skinne, and shell of things
Though faire,
are not
Thy wish, nor pray'r
but got
By meer Despair
of wings.

3.

To rack old Elements,
or Dust
and say
Sure here he must   90
needs stay
Is not the way,
nor just.

Search well another world ; who studies this,
Travels in Clouds, seeks *Manna*, where none is.

Acts Cap. 17. ver. 27, 28.
That they should seek the Lord, if happily they might feel after him,
and finde him, though he be not far off from every one of us, for in
him we live, and move, and have our being.

84 pray'r] Pray'r, *1650*   89 Dust] Dust ; *1650*

Isaacs Marriage.

Gen. cap. 24. ver. 63.

And Isaac *went out to pray in the field at the Even-tide, and he lift up his eyes, and saw, and behold, the Camels were coming.*

Praying ! and to be married ? It was rare,
But now 'tis monstrous ; and that pious care
Though of our selves, is so much out of date,
That to renew't were to degenerate.
But thou a Chosen sacrifice wert given,
And offer'd up so early unto heaven
Thy flames could not be out ; Religion was
Ray'd into thee, like beams into a glasse,
Where, as thou grewst, it multipli'd and shin'd
The sacred Constellation of thy mind.   10
But being for a bride, prayer was such
A decryed course, sure it prevail'd not much.
Had'st ne'r an oath, nor Complement ? thou wert
An odde dull sutor ; Hadst thou but the art
Of these our dayes, thou couldst have coyn'd thee twenty
New sev'ral oathes, and Complements (too) plenty ;
O sad, and wilde excesse ! and happy those
White dayes, that durst no impious mirth expose !
When Conscience by lew'd use had not lost sense,
Nor bold-fac'd custome banish'd Innocence ;   20
Thou hadst no pompous train, nor *Antick* crowd
Of young, gay swearers, with their needlesse, lowd
Retinue ; All was here smooth as thy bride
And calm like her, or that mild Evening-tide ;
Yet, hadst thou nobler guests : Angels did wind
And rove about thee, guardians of thy minde,
These fetch'd thee home thy bride, and all the way
Advis'd thy servant what to do, and say ;
These taught him at the *well*, and thither brought
The Chast, and lovely object of thy thought ;   30

But here was ne'r a Complement, not one
Spruce, supple cringe, or study'd look put on,
All was plain, modest truth : Nor did she come
In *rowles* and *Curles*, mincing and stately dumb,
But in a Virgins native blush and fears
Fresh as those roses, which the day-spring wears.
O sweet, divine simplicity ! O grace
Beyond a Curled lock, or painted face !
A *Pitcher* too she had, nor thought it much
To carry that, which some would scorn to touch ;   40
With which in mild, chast language she did wooe
To draw him drink, and for his Camels too.

   And now thou knewest her coming, It was time
To get thee wings on, and devoutly climbe
Unto thy God, for Marriage of all states
Makes most unhappy, or most fortunates ;
This brought thee forth, where now thou didst undress
Thy soul, and with new pinions refresh
Her wearied wings, which so restor'd did flye
Above the stars, a track unknown, and high,   50
And in her piercing flight perfum'd the ayer
Scatt'ring the *Myrrhe*, and incense of thy pray'r.
So from * *Lahai-roi's* Well some spicie cloud
Woo'd by the Sun swels up to be his shrowd,
And from his moist wombe weeps a fragrant showre,
Which, scatter'd in a thousand pearls, each flowre
And herb partakes, where having stood awhile
And something coold the parch'd, and thirstie Isle,
The thankful Earth unlocks her self, and blends,
A thousand odours, which (all mixt,) she sends
Up in one cloud, and so returns the skies
That dew they lent, a breathing sacrifice.   62
   Thus soar'd thy soul, who (though young,) didst inherit
Together with his bloud, thy fathers spirit,
Whose active zeal, and tried faith were to thee
Familiar ever since thy Infancie.

* A wel in the South Country where Ja-cob dwelt, between Cadesh, & Bered ; Heb. the well of him that liveth, and seeth me.

35-6   But in a frighted, virgin-blush approach'd
         Fresh as the morning, when 'tis newly Coach'd ; *1650*
38 lock, *1650*: lock. *1655*   43 knewest] knewst *1650*   48 refresh
1650: refrsh *1655*   49 restor'd *1650*: resto'd *1655*   flye *1650*: flee *1655*
51 ayer] ayre *1650*: ayer. *1655*   52 pray'r. *1650*: pray'r *1655*   53 Well]
Well, *1650*   55 his] her *LGCB*   58 thirstie *1650*: thirst *1655*
62 sacrifice. *1650*: sacrifice *1655*   66 Infancie.] Infancie, *1650*

Others were tym'd, and train'd up to't but thou
Diddst thy swift yeers in piety out-grow,
Age made them rev'rend, and a snowie head,
But thou wert so, e're time his snow could shed ;   70
Then, who would truly limne thee out, must paint
First, a *young Patriarch*, then a *marri'd Saint.*

The Brittish Church.

Ah ! he is fled !
And while these here their *mists*, and *shadows* hatch,
My glorious head
Doth on those hills of Mirrhe, and Incense watch.
Haste, hast my dear,
The Souldiers here
Cast in their lots again,
That seamlesse coat
The Jews touch'd not,
These dare divide, and stain.   10

2.

O get thee wings !
Or if as yet (until these clouds depart,
And the day springs,)
Thou think'st it good to tarry where thou art,
Write in thy bookes
My ravish'd looks
Slain flock, and pillag'd fleeces,
And hast thee so
As a young Roe
Upon the mounts of spices.   20

*O Rosa Campi! O lilium Convallium! quomodò nunc
facta es pabulum Aprorum!*

The Lampe.

'Tis dead night round about : Horrour doth creepe
And move on with the shades ; stars nod, and sleepe,
And through the dark aire spin a firie thread
Such as doth gild the lazie glow-worms bed.

67 to't] to't, *1650*   3 head *1650* : head. *1655*

Yet, burn'st thou here, a full day ; while I spend
My rest in Cares, and to the dark world lend
These flames, as thou dost thine to me ; I watch
That houre, which must thy life, and mine dispatch ;
But still thou doest out-goe me, I can see
Met in thy flames, all acts of piety ;   10
Thy light, is *Charity* ; Thy heat, is *Zeale* ;
And thy aspiring, active fires reveale
Devotion still on wing ; Then, thou dost weepe
Still as thou burn'st, and the warme droppings creepe
To measure out thy length, as if thou'dst know
What stock, and how much time were left thee now ;
Nor dost thou spend one teare in vain, for still
As thou dissolv'st to them, and they distill,
They're stor'd up in the socket, where they lye,
When all is spent, thy last, and sure supply,   20
And such is true repentance, ev'ry breath
Wee spend in sighes, is treasure after death ;
Only, one point escapes thee ; That thy Oile
Is still out with thy flame, and so both faile ;
But whensoe're I'm out, both shalbe in,
And where thou mad'st an end, there I'le begin.

Mark Cap. 13. ver. 35.

*Watch you therefore, for you know not when the master of the
house commeth, at Even, or at mid-night, or at the Cock-crowing, or
in the morning.*

Mans fall, and Recovery.

Farewell you Everlasting hills ! I'm Cast
Here under Clouds, where stormes, and tempests blast
        This sully'd flowre
Rob'd of your Calme, nor can I ever make
Transplanted thus, one leafe of his t'awake,
        But ev'ry houre
He sleepes, and droops, and in this drowsie state
Leaves me a slave to passions, and my fate ;
        Besides I've lost
A traine of lights, which in those Sun-shine dayes   10
Were my sure guides, and only with me stayes
        (Unto my cost,)

One sullen beame, whose charge is to dispense
More punishment, than knowledge to my sense;
   Two thousand yeares
I sojourn'd thus; at last *Jeshuruns* king
Those famous tables did from *Sinai* bring;
   These swell'd my feares,
Guilts, trespasses, and all this Inward Awe,
For sinne tooke strength, and vigour from the Law. 20
   Yet have I found
A plenteous way, (thanks to that holy one!)
To cancell all that e're was writ in stone,
   His saving wound
Wept bloud, that broke this Adamant, and gave
To sinners Confidence, life to the grave;
   This makes me span
My fathers journeys, and in one faire step
O're all their pilgrimage, and labours leap,
   For God (made man,) 30
Reduc'd th'Extent of works of faith; so made
Of their *Red Sea*, a *Spring*; I wash, they wade.

(handwritten note in margin: X both Redeemer and Creator)

Rom. Cap. 18. ver. 19.
As by the offence of one, the fault came on all men to condem-
nation; So by the Righteousness of one, the benefit abounded
towards all men to the Justification of life.

The Showre.

'Twas so, I saw thy birth: That drowsie Lake
From her faint bosome breath'd thee, the disease
Of her sick waters, and Infectious Ease.
   But, now at Even
   Too grosse for heaven,
Thou fall'st in teares, and weep'st for thy mistake.

     2.

Ah! it is so with me; oft have I prest
Heaven with a lazie breath, but fruitles this
Peirc'd not; Love only can with quick accesse
   Unlock the way, 10
   When all else stray
The smoke, and Exhalations of the brest.

3.

Yet, if as thou doest melt, and with thy traine
Of drops make soft the Earth, my eyes could weep
O're my hard heart, that's bound up, and asleep,
<u>   Perhaps at last</u>
<u>   (Some such showres past,)</u>
<u>My God would give a Sun-shine after raine.</u>

Distraction.

O knit me, that am crumbled dust! the heape
            Is all dispers'd, and cheape;
         Give for a handfull, but a thought
               And it is bought;
                  Hadst thou
Made me a starre, a pearle, or a rain-bow,
            The beames I then had shot
               My light had lessend not,
                  But now
I find my selfe the lesse, the more I grow;   10
               The world
Is full of voices; Man is call'd, and hurl'd
            By each, he answers all,
               Knows ev'ry note, and call,
                  Hence, still
Fresh dotage tempts, or old usurps his will.
Yet, hadst thou clipt my wings, when Coffin'd in
            This quicken'd masse of sinne,
         And saved that light, which freely thou
               Didst then bestow,   20
                  I feare
I should have spurn'd, and said thou didst forbeare;
            Or that thy store was lesse,
               But now since thou didst blesse
                  So much,
I grieve, my God! that thou hast made me such.
               I grieve?
O, yes! thou know'st I doe; Come, and releive
            And tame, and keepe downe with thy light
         Dust that would rise, and dimme my sight,   30
               Lest left alone too long
            Amidst the noise, and throng,
               Oppressed I
Striving to save the whole, by parcells dye.

The Pursuite.

Lord! what a busie, restles thing
   Hast thou made man?
Each day, and houre he is on wing,
   Rests not a span;
Then having lost the Sunne, and light
   By clouds surpriz'd
He keepes a Commerce in the night
   With aire disguis'd;
Hadst thou given to this active dust
   A state untir'd,   10
The lost Sonne had not left the huske
   Nor home desir'd;
That was thy secret, and it is
   Thy mercy too,
For when all failes to bring to blisse,
   Then, this must doe.
Ah! Lord! and what a Purchase will that be
To take us sick, that sound would not take thee?

Mount of Olives.

Sweete, sacred hill! on whose fair brow
My Saviour sate, shall I allow
   Language to love
And Idolize some shade, or grove,
Neglecting thee? such ill-plac'd wit,
Conceit, or call it what you please
   Is the braines fit,
   And meere disease;

2.

Cotswold, and *Coopers* both have met
With learned swaines, and Eccho yet   10
   Their pipes, and wit;
But thou sleep'st in a deepe neglect
Untouch'd by any; And what need
The sheep bleat thee a silly Lay
   That heard'st both reed
   And sheepward play?

9 *Cotswold,*] *Cottswold, catchword 1655*

3.

Yet, if Poets mind thee well
They shall find thou art their hill,
    And fountaine too,
Their Lord with thee had most to doe ;   20
He wept once, walkt whole nights on thee,
And from thence (his suff'rings ended,)
      Unto glorie
      Was attended ;

4.

Being there, this spacious ball
Is but his narrow footstoole all,
    And what we thinke
Unsearchable, now with one winke
He doth comprise ; But in this aire
When he did stay to beare our Ill   30
      And sinne, this Hill
      Was then his Chaire.

The Incarnation, and Passion.

Lord ! when thou didst thy selfe undresse
Laying by thy robes of glory,
To make us more, thou wouldst be lesse,
And becam'st a wofull story.

To put on Clouds instead of light,
And cloath the morning-starre with dust,
Was a translation of such height
As, but in thee, was ne'r exprest ;

Brave wormes, and Earth ! that thus could have
A God Enclos'd within your Cell,   10
Your maker pent up in a grave,
Life lockt in death, heav'n in a shell ;

Ah, my deare Lord ! what couldst thou spye
In this impure, rebellious clay,
That made thee thus resolve to dye
For those that kill thee every day ?

O what strange wonders could thee move
To slight thy precious bloud, and breath !
Sure it was *Love*, my Lord ; for *Love*
Is only stronger far than death.   20

The Call.

Come my heart ! come my head
    In sighes, and teares !
'Tis now, since you have laine thus dead
    Some twenty years ;
    Awake, awake,
    Some pitty take
    Upon your selves——
Who never wake to grone, nor weepe,
Shall be sentenc'd for their sleepe.

2.

Doe but see your sad estate,   10
    How many sands
Have left us, while we careles sate
    With folded hands ;
    What stock of nights,
    Of dayes, and yeares
    In silent flights
    Stole by our eares,
How ill have we our selves bestow'd
Whose suns are all set in a Cloud ?

3.

Yet, come, and let's peruse them all ;   20
    And as we passe,
What sins on every minute fall
    Score on the glasse ;
    Then weigh, and rate
    Their heavy State
    Untill
The glasse with teares you fill ;
That done, we shalbe safe, and good,
Those beasts were cleane, that chew'd the Cud.

¶

Thou that know'st for whom I mourne,
    And why these teares appeare,
That keep'st account, till he returne
    Of all his dust left here ;

As easily thou mightst prevent
    As now produce these teares,
And adde unto that day he went
    A faire supply of yeares.
But 'twas my sinne that forc'd thy hand
    To cull this *Prim-rose* out,   10
That by thy early choice forewarn'd
    My soule might looke about.
U what a vanity is man !
    How like the Eyes quick winke
His Cottage failes; whose narrow span
    Begins even at the brink !
Nine months thy hands are fashioning us,
    And many yeares (alas !)
E're we can lisp, or ought discusse
    Concerning thee, must passe ;   20
Yet have I knowne thy slightest things
    A *feather,* or a *shell,*
A *stick,* or *Rod* which some Chance brings
    The best of us excell,
Yea, I have knowne these shreds out last
    A faire-compacted frame
And for one *Twenty* we have past
    Almost outlive our name.
Thus hast thou plac'd in mans outside
    Death to the Common Eye,   30
That heaven within him might abide,
    And close eternitie ;
Hence, youth, and folly (mans first shame,)
    Are put unto the slaughter,
And serious thoughts begin to tame
    The wise-mans-madnes *Laughter* ;
Dull, wretched wormes ! that would not keepe
    Within our first faire bed,
But out of *Paradise* must creepe
    For ev'ry foote to tread ;   40
Yet, had our Pilgrimage bin free,
    And smooth without a thorne,
Pleasures had foil'd Eternitie,
    And *tares* had choakt the *Corne.*
Thus by the Crosse Salvation runnes,
    Affliction is a mother,

Whose painfull throws yield many sons,
　　Each fairer than the other;
A silent teare can peirce thy throne,
　　When lowd Joyes want a wing,　　　　　　　　50
And sweeter aires streame from a grone,
　　Than any arted string;
Thus, Lord, I see my gaine is great,
　　My losse but little to it,
Yet something more I must intreate
　　And only thou canst doe it.
O let me (like him,) know my End!
　　And be as glad to find it,
And whatsoe'r thou shalt Commend,
　　Still let thy Servant mind it!　　　　　　　　60
Then make my soule white as his owne,
　　My faith as pure, and steddy,
And deck me, Lord, with the same Crowne
　　Thou hast crownd him already!

Vanity of Spirit.

Quite spent with thoughts I left my Cell, and lay
Where a shrill spring tun'd to the early day.
　　I beg'd here long, and gron'd to know
　　Who gave the Clouds so brave a bow,
　　Who bent the spheres, and circled in
　　Corruption with this glorious Ring,
　　What is his name, and how I might
　　Descry some part of his great light.
I summon'd nature: peirc'd through all her store,
Broke up some seales, which none had touch'd before,　　10
　　Her wombe, her bosome, and her head
　　Where all her secrets lay a bed
　　I rifled quite, and having past
　　Through all the Creatures, came at last
　　To search my selfe, where I did find
　　Traces, and sounds of a strange kind.
Here of this mighty spring, I found some drills,
With Ecchoes beaten from th' eternall hills;
　　Weake beames, and fires flash'd to my sight,
　　Like a young East, or Moone-shine night,　　　　20
　　Which shew'd me in a nook cast by

21 Which] Wich *1655* (*from* With *l.* 23?)

A peece of much antiquity,
With Hyerogliphicks quite dismembred,
And broken letters scarce remembred.
I tooke them up, and (much Joy'd,) went about
T" unite those peeces, hoping to find out
The mystery ; but this neer done,
That little light I had was gone :
It griev'd me much.   At last, said I,
Since in these veyls my Ecclips'd Eye
May not approach thee, (for at night
Who can have commerce with the light ?)
I'le disapparell, and to buy
But one half glaunce, most gladly dye.

30

The Retreate.

Happy those early dayes ! when I
Shin'd in my Angell-infancy.
Before I understood this place
Appointed for my second race,
Or taught my soul to fancy ought
But a white, Celestiall thought,
When yet I had not walkt above
A mile, or two, from my first love,
And looking back (at that short space,)
Could see a glimpse of his bright-face ;   10
When on some *gilded Cloud,* or *flowre*
My gazing soul would dwell an houre,
And in those weaker glories spy
Some shadows of eternity ;
Before I taught my tongue to wound
My Conscience with a sinfull sound,
Or had the black art to dispence
A sev'rall sinne to ev'ry sence,
But felt through all this fleshly dresse
Bright *shootes* of everlastingnesse.   20
    O how I long to travell back
And tread again that ancient track !
That I might once more reach that plaine,
Where first I left my glorious traine,
From whence th' Inlightned spirit sees
That shady City of Palme trees ;

    10 see *1650*: fee *B. M. copy of 1655* (?)

"Exequy"
(metrical)

But (ah !) my soul with too much <u>stay</u>
Is drunk, and staggers in the way.
Some men a forward motion love,
But I by backward steps would move,   30
And when this dust falls to the urn
In that state I came return.

¶

Come, come, what doe I here?
    Since he is gone
Each day is grown a dozen year,
    And each houre, one ;
      Come, come !
     Cut off the sum,
     By these soil'd teares !
     (Which only thou
     Know'st to be true,)
    Dayes are my feares.   10

2.

Ther's not a wind can stir,
    Or beam passe by,
But strait I think (though far,)
    Thy hand is nigh ;
      Come, come !
     Strike these lips dumb :
     This restles breath
     That soiles thy name,
     Will ne'r be tame
    Untill in death.   20

3.

Perhaps some think a tombe
    No house of store,
But a dark, and seal'd up wombe,
    Which ne'r breeds more.
      Come, come !
     Such thoughts benum ;
     But I would be
     With him I weep
     A bed, and sleep
    To wake in thee.   30

¶ Midnight.

When to my Eyes
(Whilst deep sleep others catches,)
Thine hoast of spyes
The starres shine in their watches,
I doe survey
Each busie Ray,
And how they work, and wind,
And wish each beame
My soul doth streame,
With the like ardour shin'd ;　　　　　　10
What Emanations,
Quick vibrations
And bright stirs are there ?
What thin Ejections,
Cold Affections,
And slow motions here ?

2.

Thy heav'ns (some say,)
Are a firie-liquid light,
Which mingling aye
Streames, and flames thus to the sight.　　　20
Come then, my god !
Shine on this bloud,
And water in one beame,
And thou shalt see
Kindled by thee
Both liquors burne, and streame.
O what bright quicknes,
Active brightnes,
And celestiall flowes
Will follow after　　　　　　30
On that water,
Which thy spirit blowes !

Math. Cap. 3. ver. xi.
I indeed baptize you with water unto repentance, but he that com-
meth after me, is mightier than I, whose shooes I am not worthy to
beare, he shall baptize you with the holy Ghost, and with fire.

Title Midnight] Mid-night *catchword 1655*

F f

¶ Content.

Peace, peace ! I know 'twas brave,
　　But this corse fleece
I shelter in, is slave
　　To no such peece.
　　When I am gone,
I shall no ward-robes leave
　　To friend, or sonne
But what their own homes weave,

2.

Such, though not proud, nor full,
　　May make them weep,　　　　　　10
And mourn to see the wooll
　　Outlast the sheep ;
　　Poore, Pious weare !
Hadst thou bin rich, or fine
　　Perhaps that teare
Had mourn'd thy losse, not mine.

3.

Why then these curl'd, puff'd points,
　　Or a laced story ?
Death sets all out of Joint
　　And scornes their glory ;　　　　20
　　Some Love a *Rose*
In hand, some in the skin ;
　　But crosse to those,
I would have mine *within*.

¶

Joy of my life ! while left me here,
　　And still my Love !
How in thy absence thou dost steere
　　Me from above !
　　A life well lead
　　This truth commends,
　　With quick, or dead
　　It never ends.

2.

Stars are of mighty use : The night
    Is dark, and long ;   10
The Rode foul, and where one goes right,
    Six may go wrong.
    One twinkling ray
    Shot o'r some cloud,
    May clear much way
    And guide a croud.

3.

Gods Saints are shining lights : who stays
    Here long must passe
O're dark hills, swift streames, and steep ways
    As smooth as glasse ;   20
    But these all night
    Like Candles, shed
    Their beams, and light
    Us into Bed.

4.

They are (indeed,) our Pillar-fires
    Seen as we go,
They are that Cities shining spires
    We travell too ;
    A swordlike gleame
    Kept man for sin   30
    First *Out* ; This beame
    Will guide him *In.*

The Storm.

I see the use : and know my bloud
    Is not a Sea,
But a shallow, bounded floud
    Though red as he ;
Yet have I flows, as strong as his,
    And boyling stremes that rave
With the same curling force, and hisse,
    As doth the mountain'd wave.

2.

But when his waters billow thus,
  Dark storms, and wind
Incite them to that fierce discusse,
  Else not Inclin'd,
Thus the Enlarg'd, inraged air
  Uncalmes these to a floud,
But still the weather that's most fair
  Breeds tempests in my bloud ;   10

3.

Lord, then round me with weeping Clouds,
  And let my mind
In quick blasts sigh beneath those shrouds
  A spirit-wind,
So shall that storme purge this *Recluse*
  Which sinfull ease made foul,   20
And *wind*, and *water* to thy use
  Both *wash*, and *wing* my soul.

The Morning-watch.

O Joyes ! Infinite sweetnes ! with what flowres,
And shoots of glory, my soul breakes, and buds !
  All the long houres
  Of night, and Rest
  Through the still shrouds
  Of sleep, and Clouds,
 This Dew fell on my Breast ;
  O how it *Blouds*,
And *Spirits* all my Earth ! heark ! In what Rings,
And *Hymning Circulations* the quick world   10
  Awakes, and sings ;
  The rising winds,
  And falling springs,
  Birds, beasts, all things
 Adore him in their kinds.
  Thus all is hurl'd
In sacred *Hymnes*, and *Order*, The great *Chime*
And *Symphony* of nature. Prayer is
  The world in tune,
  A spirit-voyce,
  And vocall joyes   20

Whose *Eccho is* heav'ns blisse.   *through spheres*
        O let me climbe
When I lye down !   The Pious soul by night
Is like a clouded starre, whose beames though sed
                To shed their light
                Under some Cloud
                Yet are above,
                And shine, and move   30
            Beyond that mistie shrowd.
                So in my Bed
That Curtain'd grave, though sleep, like ashes, hide   *death is return*
My lamp, and life, both shall in thee abide.—

Christ?

The Evening-watch.

A Dialogue.

Farewell ! I goe to sleep ; but when   *Body.*
The day-star springs, I'le wake agen.
    Goe, sleep in peace ; and when thou lyest   *Soul.*
Unnumber'd in thy dust, when all this frame
Is but one dramme, and what thou now descriest
    In sev'rall parts shall want a name,
Then may his peace be with thee, and each dust
Writ in his book, who ne'r betray'd mans trust !
    Amen ! but hark, e'r we two stray,   *Body.*
    How many hours do'st think 'till day ?   10
    Ah ! go ; th'art weak, and sleepie.   Heav'n   *Soul.*
Is a plain watch, and without figures winds
All ages up ; who drew this Circle even
    He fils it ; Dayes, and hours are *Blinds.*
Yet, this take with thee ; The last gasp of time
Is thy first breath, and mans *eternall Prime.*

¶

Silence, and stealth of dayes ! 'tis now
            Since thou art gone,
Twelve hundred houres, and not a brow
            But Clouds hang on.
As he that in some Caves thick damp
        , Lockt from the light,
Fixeth a solitary lamp,
            To brave the night

And walking from his Sun, when past
    That glim'ring Ray   10
Cuts through the heavy mists in haste
    Back to his day,
So o'r fled minutes I retreat
    Unto that hour
Which shew'd thee last, but did defeat
    Thy light, and pow'r,
I search, and rack my soul to see
    Those beams again,
But nothing but the snuff to me
    Appeareth plain ;   20
That dark, and dead sleeps in its known,
    And common urn,
But those fled to their Makers throne,
    There shine, and burn ;
O could I track them ! but souls must
    Track one the other,
And now the spirit, not the dust
    Must be thy brother.
Yet I have one *Pearle* by whose light
    All things I see,   30
And in the heart of Earth, and night
    Find Heaven, and thee.

Church-Service.

Blest be the God of Harmony, and Love !
    The God above !
    And holy dove !
(Whose Interceding, spirituall grones
    Make restless mones
    For dust, and stones,
    For dust in every part,—
    But a hard, stonie heart.

        2.

O how in this thy Quire of Souls I stand
    (Propt by thy hand)
    A heap of sand !   10
Which busie thoughts (like winds) would scatter quite

And put to flight,
But for thy might;
Thy hand alone doth tame
Those blasts, and knit my frame,

Divine Organist

from the organ

Sub.

3.

So that both stones, and dust, and all of me
Joyntly agree
To cry to thee,
And in this Musick by thy Martyrs bloud
Seal'd, and made good
Present, O God!
The Eccho of these stones
—— My sighes, and grones.

20

of the Church bldg.
Church Triumphant
can be created
out of sinful men's
stony hearts.

Buriall.

O thou! the first fruits of the dead
And their dark bed,
When I am cast into that deep
And senseless sleep
The wages of my sinne,
O then,
Thou great Preserver of all men!
Watch o're that loose
And empty house,
Which I sometimes liv'd in.

10

2.

It is (in truth!) a ruin'd peece
Not worth thy Eyes,
And scarce a room but wind, and rain
Beat through, and stain
The seats, and Cells within;
Yet thou
Led by thy Love wouldst stoop thus low,
And in this Cott
All filth, and spott,
Didst with thy servant Inne.

20

3.

And nothing can, I hourely see,
   Drive thee from me,
Thou art the same, faithfull, and just
    In life, or Dust;
   Though then (thus crumm'd) I stray
     In blasts,
Or Exhalations, and wasts
     Beyond all Eyes
     Yet thy love spies
 That Change, and knows thy Clay.   30

4.

The world's thy boxe: how then (there tost,)
    Can I be lost?
But the delay is all; Tyme now
    Is old, and slow,
   His wings are dull, and sickly;
     Yet he
Thy servant is, and waits on thee,
    Cutt then the summe,
    Lord haste, Lord come,
 O come Lord *Jesus* quickly!   40

Rom. Cap. 8. ver. 23.
And not only they, but our selves also, which have the first fruits
of the spirit, even wee our selves grone within our selves, waiting for
the adoption, to wit, the redemption of our body.

Chearfulness.

Lord, with what courage, and delight
   I doe each thing
When thy least breath sustaines my wing!
    I shine, and move
    Like those above,
   And (with much gladnesse
   Quitting sadnesse,)
Make me faire dayes of every night.

2.

Affliction thus, meere pleasure is,
   And hap what will,   10
If thou be in't, 'tis welcome still;

But since thy rayes
In Sunnie dayes
Thou dost thus lend
And freely spend,
Ah! what shall I return for this?

3.

O that I were all Soul! that thou
Wouldst make each part
Of this poor, sinfull frame pure heart!
Then would I drown
My single one,
And to thy praise
A Consort raise
Of *Hallelujahs* here below.

¶

Sure, there's a tye of Bodyes! and as they
Dissolve (with it,) to Clay,
Love languisheth, and memory doth rust
O'r-cast with that cold dust;
For things thus *Center'd*, without *Beames*, or *Action*
Nor give, nor take *Contaction*,
And man is such a Marygold, these fled,
That shuts, and hangs the head.

2.

Absents within the Line Conspire, and *Sense*
Things distant doth unite,
Herbs sleep unto the *East*, and some fowles thence
Watch the Returns of light;
But hearts are not so kind: false, short delights
Tell us the world is brave,
And wrap us in Imaginary flights
Wide of a faithfull grave;
Thus *Lazarus* was carried out of town;
For 'tis our foes chief art
By distance all good objects first to drown,
And then besiege the heart.
But I will be my own *Deaths-head*; and though
The flatt'rer say, *I live*,
Because Incertainties we cannot know
Be sure, not to believe.

Peace.

My Soul, there is a Countrie
    Far beyond the stars,
Where stands a winged Centrie
    All skilfull in the wars,
There above noise, and danger
    Sweet peace sits crown'd with smiles,
And one born in a Manger
    Commands the Beauteous files,
He is thy gracious friend,
    And (O my Soul awake !)   10
Did in pure love descend
    To die here for thy sake,
If thou canst get but thither,
    There growes the flowre of peace,
The Rose that cannot wither,
    Thy fortresse, and thy ease ;
Leave then thy foolish ranges ;
    For none can thee secure,
But one, who never changes,
    Thy God, thy life, thy Cure.   20

The Passion.

O my chief good !
My dear, dear God !
When thy blest bloud
Did Issue forth forc'd by the Rod,
    What pain didst thou
    Feel in each blow !
    How didst thou weep,
    And thy self steep
In thy own precious, saving teares !
    What cruell smart   10
    Did teare thy heart !
    How didst thou grone it
    In the spirit,
O thou, whom my soul Loves, and feares !

Peace 2 Far] Afar *LB*

2.

Most blessed Vine !
Whose juice so good
I feel as Wine,
But thy faire branches felt as bloud,
How wert thou prest
To be my feast !   20
In what deep anguish
Didst thou languish,
What springs of Sweat, and bloud did drown thee !
How in one path
Did the full wrath
Of thy great Father
Crowd, and gather,
Doubling thy griefs, when none would own thee !

3.

How did the weight
Of all our sinnes,   30
And death unite
To wrench, and Rack thy blessed limbes !
How pale, and bloudie
Lookt thy Body !
How bruis'd, and broke
With every stroke !
How meek, and patient was thy spirit !
How didst thou cry,
And grone on high
Father forgive,   40
And let them live,
I dye to make my foes inherit !

4.

O blessed Lamb !
That took'st my sinne,
That took'st my shame
How shall thy dust thy praises sing !
I would I were
One hearty tear !
One constant spring !
Then would I bring   50
Thee two small mites, and be at strife

Silex Scintillans,

Which should most vie,
My heart, or eye,
Teaching my years
In smiles, and tears
To weep, to sing, thy *Death*, my *Life.*

Rom. Cap. 8. ver. 19.
Etenim res Creatæ exerto Capite observantes expectant revela-
tionem Filiorum Dei.

And do they so? have they a Sense
  Of ought but Influence? — *of the stars [astral]* *Yeates'*
Can they their heads lift, and expect,
  And grone too? why th'Elect
Can do no more: my volumes sed
  They were all dull, and dead,
They judg'd them senslesse, and their state
  Wholly Inanimate.
    Go, go; Seal up thy looks,   *anti - Aristotelian*
    And burn thy books.   10

2.

I would I were a stone, or tree,
  Or flowre by pedigree,
Or some poor high-way herb, or Spring
  To flow, or bird to sing!
Then should I (tyed to one sure state,)
  All day expect my date;
But I am sadly loose, and stray
  A giddy blast each way;
  O let me not thus range!
    Thou canst not change. — *why should I?*   20

3.

Sometimes I sit with thee, and tarry
  An hour, or so, then vary.
Thy other Creatures in this Scene
  Thee only aym, and mean;
Some rise to seek thee, and with heads
  Erect peep from their beds;
Others, whose birth is in the tomb,
  And cannot quit the womb,
    Sigh there, and grone for thee,
      Their liberty.   30

suggestion that redemption of men + nature are identified

4.

O let not me do lesse ! shall they
    Watch, while I sleep, or play ?
Shall I thy mercies still abuse
    With fancies, friends, or newes ?
O brook it not ! thy bloud is mine,
    And my soul should be thine ;
O brook it not ! why wilt thou stop
    After whole showres one drop ?
      Sure, thou wilt joy to see
      Thy sheep with thee.   40

The Relapse.

My God, how gracious art thou ! I had slipt
    Almost to hell,
And on the verge of that dark, dreadful pit
    Did hear them yell,
But O thy love ! thy rich, almighty love
    That sav'd my soul,
And checkt their furie, when I saw them move,
    And heard them howl ;
O my sole Comfort, take no more these wayes,
    This hideous path,   10
And I wil mend my own without delayes,
    Cease thou thy wrath !
I have deserv'd a thick, Egyptian damp,
    Dark as my deeds,
Should *mist* within me, and put out that lamp
    Thy spirit feeds ;
A darting Conscience full of stabs, and fears ;
    No shade but *Yewgh,*
Sullen, and sad Ecclipses, Cloudie spheres,
    These are my due.   20
But he that with his bloud, (a price too deere,)
    My scores did pay,
Bid me, by vertue from him, chalenge here
    The brightest day;
Sweet, downie thoughts ; soft *Lilly*-shades ; Calm streams ;
    Joyes full, and true ;
Fresh, spicie mornings ; and eternal beams
    These are his due.

The Resolve.

I have consider'd it ; and find
　　　　A longer stay
Is but excus'd neglect.　To mind
　　　　One path, and stray
Into another, or to none,
　　　　Cannot be love ;
When shal that traveller come home,
　　　　That will not move ?
If thou wouldst thither, linger not,
　　　　Catch at the place,　　　　　　　10
Tell youth, and beauty they must rot,
　　　　They'r but a *Case* ;
Loose, parcell'd hearts wil freeze : The Sun
　　　　With scatter'd locks
Scarce warms, but by contraction
　　　　Can heat rocks ;
Call in thy *Powers* ; run, and reach
　　　　Home with the light,
Be there, before the shadows stretch,
　　　　And *Span* up night ;　　　　　　20
Follow the *Cry* no more : there is
　　　　An ancient way
All strewed with flowres, and happiness
　　　　And fresh as *May* ;
There turn, and turn no more ; Let wits,
　　　　Smile at fair eies,
Or lips ; But who there weeping sits,
　　　　Hath got the *Prize*.

The Match.

Dear friend ! whose holy, ever-living lines
　　　　Have done much good
　　　To many, and have checkt my blood,
My fierce, wild blood that still heaves, and inclines,
　　　　But is still tam'd
　　　By those bright fires which thee inflam'd ;

11 beauty] beautie, *WR* (*1650*)　　　　16 heat rocks] heat the rocks *LG*
17 run] run on, *L*　　　18 light,] light; *WR* (*all editions*)　　　20 night;]
night : *WR* (*1667*)　　　25 wits,] wits *WR* (*1663, 1667*)　　　27 lips;] lips
WR (*1667*)

Here I joyn hands, and thrust my stubborn heart
      Into thy *Deed*,
   There from no *Duties* to be freed,
And if hereafter *youth*, or *folly* thwart   10
      And claim their share,
   Here I renounce the pois'nous ware.

ii

Accept, dread Lord, the poor Oblation,
      It is but poore,
   Yet through thy Mercies may be more.
O thou ! that canst not wish my souls damnation,
      Afford me life,
   And save me from all inward strife !
Two *Lifes* I hold from thee, my gracious Lord,
      Both cost thee deer,
   For one, I am thy Tenant here ;
The other, the true life, in the next world   10
      And endless is,
   O let me still mind *that* in *this* !
To thee therefore my *Thoughts*, *Words*, *Actions*
      I do resign,
   Thy will in all be done, not mine.
Settle my *house*, and shut out all distractions
      That may unknit
   My heart, and thee planted in it ;
Lord *Jesu* ! thou didst bow thy blessed head
      Upon a tree,   20
   O do as much, now unto me !
O hear, and heal thy servant ! Lord, strike dead
      All lusts in me,
   Who onely wish life to serve thee ?
Suffer no more this dust to overflow
      And drown my eies,
   But seal, or pin them to thy skies.
And let this *grain* which here in tears I sow
      Though *dead*, and *sick*,
   Through thy *Increase* grow *new*, and *quick*.   30

Rules *and* Lessons.

When first thy Eies unveil, give thy Soul leave
To do the like; our Bodies but forerun
The spirits duty; True hearts spread, and heave
Unto their God, as flow'rs do to the Sun.
    Give him thy first thoughts then; so shalt thou keep
    Him company all day, and in him sleep.

Yet, never sleep the Sun up; Prayer shou'd
Dawn with the day; There are set, awful hours
'Twixt heaven, and us; The *Manna* was not good
After Sun-rising, far-day sullies flowres.
    Rise to prevent the Sun; sleep doth sins glut,
    And heav'ns gate opens, when this world's is shut.

Walk with thy fellow-creatures: note the *hush*
And *whispers* amongst them. There's not a *Spring*,
Or *Leafe* but hath his *Morning-hymn*; Each *Bush*
And *Oak* doth know *I AM*; canst thou not sing?
    O leave thy Cares, and follies! go this way
    And thou art sure to prosper all the day.

Serve God before the world; let him not go
Until thou hast a blessing, then resigne
The whole unto him; and remember who
Prevail'd by *wrestling* ere the *Sun* did *shine*.
    Poure *Oyle* upon the *stones*, weep for thy sin,
    Then journey on, and have an eie to heav'n.

Mornings are *Mysteries*; the first worlds *Youth*,
Mans *Resurrection*, and the futures *Bud*
Shrowd in their births: The Crown of life, light, truth
Is stil'd their *starre*, the *stone*, and *hidden food*.
    Three *blessings* wait upon them, two of which
    Should move; They make us *holy*, *happy*, rich.

When the world's up, and ev'ry swarm abroad,
Keep thou thy temper, mix not with each Clay;
Dispatch necessities, life hath a load
Which must be carri'd on, and safely may.
    Yet keep those cares without thee, let the heart
    Be Gods alone, and choose the better part.

Through all thy *Actions, Counsels,* and *Discourse,*
Let *Mildness,* and *Religion* guide thee out,
If truth be thine, what needs a brutish force?
But what's not *good,* and *just* ne'r go about.   40
    Wrong not thy Conscience for a rotten stick,
    That gain is dreadful, which makes spirits sick.

To God, thy Countrie, and thy friend be true,
If *Priest,* and *People* change, keep thou thy ground.
Who sels Religion, is a *Judas Jew,*
And, oathes once broke, the soul cannot be sound.
    The perjurer's a devil let loose : what can
    Tie up his hands, that dares mock God, and man?

Seek not the same steps with the *Crowd* ; stick thou
To thy sure trot ; a Constant, humble mind   50
Is both his own Joy, and his Makers too ;
Let folly dust it on, or lag behind.
    A sweet *self-privacy* in a right soul
    Out-runs the Earth, and lines the utmost pole.

To all that seek thee, bear an open heart ;
Make not thy breast a *Labyrinth,* or *Trap* ;
If tryals come, this wil make good thy part,
For honesty is safe, come what can hap ;
    It is the good mans *feast* ; The prince of flowres
    Which thrives in *storms,* and smels best after *showres.*   60

Seal not thy Eyes up from the poor, but give
Proportion to their *Merits,* and thy *Purse* ;
Thou mai'st in Rags a mighty Prince relieve
Who, when thy sins call for't, can fence a Curse.
    Thou shalt not lose one *mite.* Though waters stray,
    The Bread we cast returns in fraughts one day.

Spend not an hour so, as to weep another,
For tears are not thine own ; If thou giv'st words
Dash not thy *friend,* nor *Heav'n* ; O smother
A vip'rous thought ; some *Syllables* are *Swords.*   70
    Unbitted tongues are in their penance double,
    They shame their *owners,* and the *hearers* trouble.

63 Prince] Prlnce *1655*   69 not thy *friend*] not with them thy
friend L : not thyself, thy friend *G*

Injure not modest bloud, whose *spirits* rise
In judgement against *Lewdness* ; that's base wit
That voyds but *filth,* and *stench.*   Hast thou no prize
But *sickness,* or *Infection* ? stifle it.
    Who makes his jests of sins, must be at least
    If not a very *devill,* worse than a *Beast.*

Yet, fly no friend, if he be such indeed,
But meet to quench his *Longings,* and thy *Thirst* ;   80
Allow your Joyes *Religion* ; That done, speed
And bring the same man back, thou wert at first.
    Who so returns not, cannot pray aright,
    But shuts his door, and leaves God out all night.

To highten thy *Devotions,* and keep low
All mutinous thoughts, what busines e'r thou hast
Observe God in his works ; here *fountains* flow,
Birds sing, *Beasts* feed, *Fish* leap, and th'*Earth* stands fast ;
    Above are restles *motions,* running *Lights,*
    Vast Circling *Azure,* giddy *Clouds,* days, nights.   90

When *Seasons* change, then lay before thine Eys
His wondrous *Method* ; mark the various *Scenes*
In heav'n ; *Hail, Thunder, Rain-bows, Snow,* and *Ice,*
Calmes, Tempests, Light, and *darknes* by his means ;
    Thou canst not misse his Praise ; Each *tree, herb, flowre*
    Are shadows of his *wisedome,* and his Pow'r.

To *meales* when thou doest come, give him the praise
Whose *Arm* supply'd thee ; Take what may suffice,
And then be thankful ; O admire his ways
Who fils the worlds unempty'd granaries !   100
    A thankles feeder is a *Theif,* his feast
    A very *Robbery,* and himself no *guest.*

High-noon thus past, thy time decays ; provide
Thee other thoughts ; Away with friends, and mirth ;
The Sun now stoops, and hasts his beams to hide
Under the dark, and melancholy Earth.
    All but preludes thy End.   Thou art the man
    Whose *Rise, hight,* and *Descent* is but a span.

[handwritten marginalia: Sense of nature in motion - characteristic of V's poetry]

Yet, set as he doth, and 'tis well. Have all
Thy Beams home with thee : trim thy *Lamp*, buy *Oyl*,   110
And then set forth ; who is thus drest, The *Fall*
Furthers his glory, and gives death the foyl.
  Man is a *Summers day* ; whose *youth*, and *fire*
  Cool to a glorious *Evening*, and Expire.

When night comes, list thy deeds ; make plain the way
'Twixt Heaven, and thee ; block it not with delays,
But perfect all before thou sleep'st ; Then say
Ther's one Sun more strung on my Bead of days.
  What's good score up for Joy ; The bad wel scann'd
  Wash off with tears, and get thy *Masters* hand.   120

Thy Accounts thus made, spend in the grave one houre
Before thy time ; Be not a stranger there
Where thou may'st sleep whole ages ; Lifes poor flowr
Lasts not a night sometimes.   Bad spirits fear
  This Conversation ; But the good man lyes
  Intombed many days before he dyes.

Being laid, and drest for sleep, Close not thy Eys
Up with thy Curtains ; Give thy soul the wing
In some good thoughts ; So when the day shall rise
And thou *unrak'st* thy *fire*, those *sparks* will bring   130
  New *flames* ; Besides where these lodge vain *heats* mourn
  And die ; That *Bush* where God is, shall not burn.

When thy *Nap's* over, stir thy fire, unrake
In that *dead age* ; one beam i'th' dark outvies
Two in the day ; Then from the *Damps*, and *Ake*
Of night shut up thy *leaves*, be Chast ; God prys
  Through thickest nights ; Though then the Sun be far
  Do thou the works of *Day*, and rise a *Star*.

Briefly, *Doe as thou would'st be done unto,*
Love God, and Love thy Neighbour ; Watch, and Pray.   140
These are the *Words*, and *Works* of life ; This do,
And live ; who doth not thus, hath lost *Heav'ns way.*
  O lose it not ! look up, wilt Change those *Lights*
  For *Chains* of *Darknes*, and *Eternal Nights* ?

   125 Conversation] Coversation *1655*

Corruption.

Prelapsarian

Sure, It was so. Man in those early days
    Was not all stone, and Earth,
He shin'd a little, and by those weak Rays
    Had some glimpse of his birth.
He saw Heaven o'r his head, and knew from whence
    He came (condemned,) hither,
And, as first Love draws strongest, so from hence
    His mind sure progress'd thither.
Things here were strange unto him : Swet, and till
    All was a thorn, or weed,   10
Nor did those last, but (like himself,) dyed still
    As soon as they did *Seed*,
They seem'd to quarrel with him ; for that Act
    That fel him, foyl'd them all,
He drew the Curse upon the world, and Crackt
    The whole frame with his fall.
This made him long for *home*, as loath to stay
    With murmurers, and foes ;
He sigh'd for *Eden*, and would often say
    Ah! what bright days were those?   20
Nor was Heav'n cold unto him ; for each day
    The vally, or the Mountain
Afforded visits, and still *Paradise* lay
    In some green shade, or fountain.
Angels lay *Leiger* here ; Each Bush, and Cel,
    Each Oke, and high-way knew them,
Walk but the fields, or sit down at some *wel*,
    And he was sure to view them.
Almighty *Love*! where art thou now? mad man
    Sits down, and freezeth on,   30
He raves, and swears to stir nor fire, nor fan,
    But bids the thread be spun.
I see, thy Curtains are Close-drawn ; Thy bow
    Looks dim too in the Cloud,
Sin triumphs still, and man is sunk below
    The Center, and his shrowd ;
All's in deep sleep, and night ; Thick darknes lyes
    And hatcheth o'r thy people ;
But hark ! what trumpets that? what Angel cries
    Arise! Thrust in thy sickle.   40

H. Scriptures.

Welcome dear book, souls Joy, and food !   The feast
  Of Spirits, Heav'n extracted lyes in thee ;
  Thou art lifes Charter, The Doves spotless neast
Where souls are hatch'd unto Eternitie.

In thee the hidden stone, the *Manna* lies,
  Thou art the great *Elixir*, rare, and Choice ;
  The Key that opens to all Mysteries,
The *Word* in Characters, God in the *Voice*.

O that I had deep Cut in my hard heart
  Each line in thee ! Then would I plead in groans 10
  Of my Lords penning, and by sweetest Art
Return upon himself the *Law*, and *Stones*.
  Read here, my faults are thine.   This Book, and I
  Will tell thee so ; *Sweet Saviour thou didst dye !*

Unprofitablenes.

How rich, O Lord ! how fresh thy visits are !
'Twas but Just now my bleak leaves hopeles hung
  Sullyed with dust and mud ;
Each snarling blast shot through me, and did share
Their Youth, and beauty, Cold showres nipt, and wrung
  Their spiciness, and bloud ;
But since thou didst in one sweet glance survey
Their sad decays, I flourish, and once more
  Breath all perfumes, and spice ;
I smell a dew like *Myrrh*, and all the day 10
Wear in my bosome a full Sun ; such store
  Hath one beame from thy Eys.
But, ah, my God ! what fruit hast thou of this ?
What one poor leaf did ever I yet fall
  To wait upon thy wreath ?
Thus thou all day a thankless weed doest dress,
And when th' hast done, a stench, or fog is all
  The odour I bequeath.

C H R I S T s Nativity.

Awake, glad heart! get up, and Sing,
It is the Birth-day of thy King,
  Awake! awake!
  The Sun doth shake
Light from his locks, and all the way
Breathing Perfumes, doth spice the day.

2.

Awak, awak! heark, how th' *wood* rings,
Winds whisper, and the busie *springs*
  A Consort make;
  Awake, awake!   10
Man is their high-priest, and should rise
To offer up the sacrifice.

3.

I would I were some *Bird*, or Star,
Flutt'ring in woods, or lifted far
  Above this *Inne*
  And Rode of sin!
Then either Star, or *Bird*, should be
Shining, or singing still to thee.

4.

I would I had in my best part
Fit Roomes for thee! or that my heart   20
  Were so clean as
  Thy manger was!
But I am all filth, and obscene,
Yet, if thou wilt, thou canst make clean.

5.

Sweet *Jesu*! will then; Let no more
This Leper haunt, and soyl thy door,
  Cure him, Ease him
  O release him!
And let once more by mystick birth
The Lord of life be borne in Earth.   30

   7 Awak] Awake *catchword 1655*

I I.

How kind is heav'n to man !   If here
    One sinner doth amend
Strait there is Joy, and ev'ry sphere
    In musick doth Contend ;
And shall we then no voices lift ?
    Are mercy, and salvation
Not worth our thanks ? Is life a gift
    Of no more acceptation ?
Shal he that did come down from thence,
    And here for us was slain,   10
Shal he be now cast off ? no sense
    Of all his woes remain ?
Can neither Love, nor suff'rings bind ?
    Are we all stone, and Earth ?
Neither his bloudy passions mind,
    Nor one day blesse his birth ?
Alas, my God ! Thy birth now here
    Must not be numbred in the year.

The Check.

Peace, peace ! I blush to hear thee ; when thou art
    A dusty story
A speechlesse heap, and in the midst my heart
    In the same livery drest
    Lyes tame as all the rest ;
When six years thence digg'd up, some youthfull Eie
    Seeks there for Symmetry
But finding none, shal leave thee to the wind,
    Or the next foot to Crush,
        Scatt'ring thy kind   10
And humble dust, tell then dear flesh
    Where is thy glory ?

2.

As he that in the midst of day Expects
    The hideous night,
Sleeps not, but shaking off sloth, and neglects,
    Works with the Sun, and sets
    Paying the day its debts ;

That (for Repose, and darknes bound,) he might
    Rest from the fears i'th' night ;
So should we too.   All things teach us to die   20
    And point us out the way
      While we passe by
    And mind it not ; play not away
      Thy glimpse of light.

3.

View thy fore-runners : Creatures giv'n to be
    Thy youths Companions,
Take their leave, and die ; Birds, beasts, each tree
    All that have growth, or breath
    Have one large language, *Death.*
O then play not ! but strive to him, who Can   30
    Make these sad shades pure Sun,
Turning their mists to beams, their damps to day,
    Whose pow'r doth so excell
      As to make Clay
    A spirit, and true glory dwell
      In dust, and stones.

4.

Heark, how he doth Invite thee ! with what voice
    Of Love, and sorrow
He begs, and Calls ; *O that in these thy days*
    Thou knew'st but thy own good !   40
    Shall not the Crys of bloud,
Of Gods own bloud awake thee ?   He bids beware
    Of drunknes, surfeits, Care,
But thou sleep'st on ; wher's now thy protestation,
    Thy Lines, thy Love ?   Away,
      Redeem the day,
The day that gives no observation,
      Perhaps to morrow.

Disorder *and* frailty.

When first thou didst even from the grave
And womb of darknes becken out
My brutish soul, and to thy slave
Becam'st thy self, both guide, and Scout ;

42 thee] thet *1655*

Even from that hour
Thou gotst my heart; And though here tost
 By winds, and bit with frost
  I pine, and shrink
  Breaking the link
'Twixt thee, and me; And oftimes creep   10
Into th' old silence, and dead sleep,
  Quitting thy way
  All the long day,
Yet, sure, my God! I love thee most.
 Alas, thy love!

2.

I threaten heaven, and from my Cell
Of Clay, and frailty break, and bud
Touch'd by thy fire, and breath; Thy bloud
Too, is my Dew, and springing wel.
  But while I grow
And stretch to thee, ayming at all   20
  Thy stars, and spangled hall,
  Each fly doth tast,
  Poyson, and blast
My yielding leaves; sometimes a showr
Beats them quite off, and in an hour
  Not one poor shoot
  But the bare root
Hid under ground survives the fall.
 Alas, frail weed!   30

3.

Thus like some sleeping Exhalation
(Which wak'd by heat, and beams, makes up
Unto that Comforter, the Sun,
And soars, and shines; But e'r we sup
  And walk two steps
Cool'd by the damps of night, descends,
  And, whence it sprung, there ends,)
  Doth my weak fire
  Pine, and retire,
And (after all my hight of flames,)   40
In sickly Expirations tames

23 tast,] tast *1655*

Leaving me dead
On my first bed
Untill thy Sun again ascends.
Poor, falling Star !

4.

O, is ! but give wings to my fire,
And hatch my soul, untill it fly
Up where thou art, amongst thy tire
Of Stars, above Infirmity ;
  Let not perverse,   50
And foolish thoughts adde to my Bil
  Of forward sins, and Kil
   That seed, which thou
   In me didst sow,
But dresse, and water with thy grace
Together with the seed, the place ;
   And for his sake
   Who died to stake
His life for mine, tune to thy will
  My heart, my verse.   60

Hosea Cap. 6. ver. 4.

*O Ephraim what shall I do unto thee ? O Judah how shall I
intreat thee ? for thy goodness is as a morning Cloud, and as the
early Dew it goeth away.*

Idle Verse.

Go, go, queint folies, sugred sin,
  Shadow no more my door ;
I will no longer Cobwebs spin,
  I'm too much on the score.

For since amidst my youth, and night,
  My great preserver smiles,
Wee'l make a Match, my only light,
  And Joyn against their wiles ;

Blind, desp'rate *fits*, that study how
  To dresse, and trim our shame,   10
That gild rank poyson, and allow
  Vice in a fairer name ;

46 is] yes *LGCB*

The *Purles* of youthfull bloud, and bowles,
    Lust in the Robes of Love,
The idle talk of feav'rish souls
    Sick with a scarf, or glove ;

Let it suffice my warmer days
    Simper'd, and shin'd on you,
Twist not my Cypresse with your Bays,
    Or Roses with my Yewgh ;   20

Go, go, seek out some greener thing,
    It snows, and freezeth here ;
Let Nightingales attend the spring,
    Winter is all my year.

Son-dayes.

Bright shadows of true Rest ! some shoots of blisse,
        Heaven once a week ;
The next worlds gladnes prepossest in this ;
        A day to seek

Eternity in time ; the steps by which
We Climb above all ages ; Lamps that light
Man through his heap of dark days ; and the rich,
And full redemption of the whole weeks flight.

2.

The Pulleys unto headlong man ; times bower ;
        The narrow way ;   10
Transplanted Paradise ; Gods walking houre ;
        The Cool o'th' day ;

The Creatures *Jubile*; Gods parle with dust ;
Heaven here , Man on those hills of Myrrh, and flowres ;
Angels descending ; the Returns of Trust ;
A Gleam of glory, after six-days-showres.

3.

The Churches love-feasts ; Times Prerogative,
        And Interest
Deducted from the whole ; The Combs, and hive,
        And home of rest.   20

The milky way Chalkt out with Suns ; a Clue
That guides through erring hours ; and in full story
A taste of Heav'n on earth ; the pledge, and Cue
Of a full feast ; And the Out Courts of glory.

Repentance.

Lord, since thou didst in this vile Clay
  That sacred Ray
Thy spirit plant, quickning the whole
With that one grains Infused wealth,
My forward flesh creept on, and subtly stole
Both growth, and power ; Checking the health
And heat of thine : That little gate
And narrow way, by which to thee
The Passage is, He term'd a grate
And Entrance to Captivitie ;   10
Thy laws but nets, where some small birds
(And those but seldome too) were caught,
Thy Promises but empty words
Which none but Children heard, or taught.
This I believed : And though a friend
Came oft from far, and whisper'd, *No* ;
Yet that not sorting to my end
I wholy listen'd to my foe.
Wherefore, pierc'd through with grief, my sad
Seduced soul sighs up to thee,   20
To thee who with true light art Clad
And seest all things just as they be.
Look from thy throne upon this Rowl
Of heavy sins, my high transgressions,
Which I Confesse withall my soul,
My God, Accept of my Confession.
   It was last day
(Touch'd with the guilt of my own way)
I sate alone, and taking up
   The bitter Cup,   30
Through all thy fair, and various store
Sought out what might outvie my score.
  The blades of grasse, thy Creatures feeding,
  The trees, their leafs ; the flowres, their seeding ;

4 Infused *1650* : Infufed *B. M. copy of 1655* (?)   5 flesh] flest *1655*

The Dust, of which I am a part,
The Stones much softer than my heart,
The drops of rain, the sighs of wind,
The Stars to which I am stark blind,
The Dew thy herbs drink up by night,
The beams they warm them at i'th' light,　　　　40
All that have signature or life,
I summon'd to decide this strife,
And lest I should lack for Arrears,
A spring ran by, I told her tears,
But when these came unto the scale,
My sins alone outweigh'd them all.
O my dear God ! my life, my love !
Most blessed lamb ! and mildest dove !
Forgive your penitent Offender,
And no more his sins remember,　　　　50
Scatter these shades of death, and give
Light to my soul, that it may live ;
Cut me not off for my transgressions,
Wilful rebellions, and suppressions,
But give them in those streams a part
Whose spring is in my Saviours heart.
Lord, I confesse the heynous score,
And pray, I may do so no more,
Though then all sinners I exceed
O think on this ; *Thy Son did bleed ;*　　　　60
O call to mind his wounds, his woes,
His Agony, and bloudy throws ;
Then look on all that thou hast made,
And mark how they do fail, and fade,
The heavens themselves, though fair and bright
Are dark, and unclean in thy sight,
How then, with thee, Can man be holy
Who doest thine Angels charge with folly ?
O what am I, that I should breed
Figs on a thorne, flowres on a weed !　　　　70
I am the gourd of sin, and sorrow
Growing o'r night, and gone to morrow,
In all this *Round* of life and death
Nothing's more vile than is my breath,
Profanenes on my tongue doth rest,
Defects, and darknes in my brest,

Pollutions all my body wed,
And even my soul to thee is dead,
Only in him, on whom I feast,
Both soul, and body are well drest,   80
    His pure perfection quits all score,
    And fills the Boxes of his poor ;
He is the Center of long life, and light,
I am but finite, He is Infinite.
O let thy *Justice* then in him Confine,
And through his merits, make thy mercy mine !

The BURIAL
Of an Infant.

Blest Infant Bud, whose Blossome-life
Did only look about, and fal,
Wearyed out in a harmles strife
Of tears, and milk, the food of all ;

Sweetly didst thou expire : Thy soul
Flew home unstain'd by his new kin,
For ere thou knew'st how to be foul,
Death *wean'd* thee from the world, and sin.

Softly rest all thy Virgin-Crums !
Lapt in the sweets of thy young breath,   10
Expecting till thy Saviour Comes
To *dresse* them, and *unswadle* death.

Faith.

Bright, and blest beame ! whose strong projection
    Equall to all,
Reacheth as well things of dejection
    As th' high, and tall ;
How hath my God by raying thee
    Inlarg'd his spouse, — *Church*
And of a private familie
    Made open house ?
All may be now Co-heirs ; no noise
    Of *Bond*, or *Free*   10
Can Interdict us from those Joys
    That wait on thee,

The Law, and Ceremonies made
    A glorious night,
Where Stars, and Clouds, both light, and shade
    Had equal right;
But, as in nature, when the day
    Breaks, night adjourns,
Stars shut up shop, mists pack away,
    And the Moon mourns;   20
So when the Sun of righteousness
    Did once appear,
That Scene was chang'd, and a new dresse
    Left for us here;
Veiles became useles, Altars fel,
    Fires smoking die;
And all that sacred pomp, and shel
    Of things did flie;
Then did he shine forth, whose sad fall,
    And bitter fights   30
Were figur'd in those mystical,
    And Cloudie Rites;
And as i'th' natural Sun, these three,
    Light, motion, heat,
So are now *Faith, Hope, Charity*
    Through him Compleat;
Faith spans up blisse; what sin, and death
    Put us quite from,
Lest we should run for't out of breath,
    Faith brings us home;   40
So that I need no more, but say
    I do believe,
And my most loving Lord straitway
    Doth answer, *Live.*

The Dawning.

Ah! what time wilt thou come? when shall that crie
    The *Bridegroome's Comming*! fil the sky?
    Shall it in the Evening run
    When our words and works are done?
    Or wil thy all-surprizing light
        Break at midnight?

When either sleep, or some dark pleasure
Possesseth mad man without measure ;
Or shal these early, fragrant hours
    Unlock thy bowres ?   10
And with their blush of light descry
Thy locks crown'd with eternitie ;
Indeed, it is the only time
That with thy glory doth best chime,
All now are stirring, ev'ry field
    Ful hymns doth yield,
The whole Creation shakes off night,
And for thy shadow looks the light,
Stars now vanish without number,
Sleepie Planets set, and slumber,   20
The pursie Clouds disband, and scatter,
All expect some sudden matter,
Not one beam triumphs, but from far
    That morning-star ;

O at what time soever thou
(Unknown to us,) the heavens wilt bow,
And, with thy Angels in the *Van,*
Descend to Judge poor careless man,
Grant, I may not like puddle lie
In a Corrupt securitie,   30
Where, if a traveller water crave,
He finds it dead, and in a grave ;
But as this restless, vocall *Spring*
All day, and night doth run, and sing,
And though here born, yet is acquainted
Elsewhere, and flowing keeps untainted ;
So let me all my busie age
In thy free services ingage,
And though (while here) of force I must
Have Commerce somtimes with poor dust,   40
And in my flesh, though vile, and low,
As this doth in her Channel, flow,
Yet let my Course, my aym, my Love,
And chief acquaintance be above ;
So when that day, and hour shal come
In which thy self wil be the Sun,
Thou'lt find me drest and on my way,
Watching the Break of thy great day.

Admission.

How shril are silent tears ? when sin got head
    And all my Bowels turn'd
To brasse, and iron ; when my stock lay dead,
    And all my powers mourn'd ;
  Then did these drops (for Marble sweats,
    And Rocks have tears,)
  As rain here at our windows beats,
    Chide in thine Ears ;

2.

No quiet couldst thou have : nor didst thou wink,
    And let thy Begger lie,   10
But e'r my eies could overflow their brink
    Didst to each drop reply ;
  Bowels of Love ! at what low rate,
    And slight a price
  Dost thou relieve us at thy gate,
    And stil our Cries ?

3.

Wee are thy Infants, and suck thee ; If thou
    But hide, or turn thy face,
Because where thou art, yet, we cannot go,
    We send tears to the place,   20
  These find thee out, and though our sins
    Drove thee away,
  Yet with thy love that absence wins
    Us double pay.

4.

O give me then a thankful heart ! a heart
    After thy own, not mine ;
So after thine, that all, and ev'ry part
    Of mine, may wait on thine ;
  O hear ! yet not my tears alone,
    Hear now a floud,   30
  A floud that drowns both tears, and grones,
    My Saviours bloud.

H h

Praise.

King of Comforts ! King of life !
    Thou hast cheer'd me,
And when fears, and doubts were rife,
    Thou hast cleer'd me !

Not a nook in all my Breast
    But thou fill'st it,
Not a thought, that breaks my rest,
    But thou kill'st it ;

Wherefore with my utmost strength
    I wil praise thee,   10
And as thou giv'st line, and length,
    I wil raise thee ;

Day, and night, not once a day
    I will blesse thee,
And my soul in new array
    I will dresse thee ;

Not one minute in the year
    But I'l mind thee,
As my seal, and bracelet here
    I wil bind thee ;   20

In thy word, as if in heaven
    I wil rest me,
And thy promise 'til made even
    There shall feast me.

Then, thy sayings all my life
    They shal please me,
And thy bloudy wounds, and strife
    They wil ease me ;

With thy grones my daily breath
    I will measure,   30
And my life hid in thy death
    I will treasure.

    Though then thou art
    Past thought of heart
All perfect fulness,
    And canst no whit
    Accesse admit
From dust and dulness ;

    Yet to thy name
      (As not the same   40
With thy bright Essence,)
      Our foul, Clay hands
      At thy Commands
Bring praise, and Incense;

    If then, dread Lord,
      When to thy board
Thy wretch comes begging,
      He hath a flowre
      Or (to his pow'r,)
Some such poor Off'ring;   50

    When thou hast made
      Thy begger glad,
And fill'd his bosome,
      Let him (though poor,)
      Strow at thy door
That one poor Blossome.

Dressing.

O thou that lovest a pure, and whitend soul!
That feedst among the Lillies, 'till the day
Break, and the shadows flee; touch with one Coal
My frozen heart; and with thy secret key

Open my desolate rooms; my gloomie Brest
With thy cleer fire refine, burning to dust
These dark Confusions, that within me nest,
And soyl thy Temple with a sinful rust.

Thou holy, harmless, undefil'd high-priest!
The perfect, ful oblation for all sin,   10
Whose glorious conquest nothing can resist,
But even in babes doest triumph still and win;

    Give to thy wretched one
  Thy mysticall *Communion,*
    That, absent, he may see,
    Live, die, and rise with thee;
Let him so follow here, that in the end
He may take thee, as thou doest him intend.

      3 flee] ssee *1655*

Give him thy private seal,
Earnest, and sign ; Thy gifts so deal   20
That these forerunners here
May make the future cleer ;
Whatever thou dost bid, let faith make good,
Bread for thy body, and Wine for thy blood.
Give him (with pitty) love,
Two flowres that grew with thee above ;
Love that shal not admit
Anger for one short fit,
And pitty of such a divine extent
That may thy members, more than mine, resent.   30

Give me, my God ! thy grace,
The beams, and brightnes of thy face,
That never like a beast
I take thy sacred feast,
Or the dread mysteries of thy blest bloud
Use, with like Custome, as my Kitchin food.
Some sit to thee, and eat
Thy body as their Common meat,
O let not me do so !
Poor dust should ly still low,   40
Then kneel my soul, and body ; kneel, and bow ;
If *Saints*, and *Angels* fal down, much more thou.

Easter-day.

Thou, whose sad heart, and weeping head lyes low,
Whose Cloudy brest cold damps invade,
Who never feel'st the Sun, nor smooth'st thy brow,
But sitt'st oppressed in the shade,
Awake, awake,
And in his Resurrection partake,
Who on this day (that thou might'st rise as he,)
Rose up, and cancell'd two deaths due to thee.

Awake, awake ; and, like the Sun, disperse
All mists that would usurp this day ;   10
Where are thy Palmes, thy branches, and thy verse ?
Hosanna ! heark ; why doest thou stay ?
Arise, arise,
And with his healing bloud anoint thine Eys,
Thy inward Eys ; his bloud will cure thy mind,
Whose spittle only could restore the blind.

Easter Hymn.

Death, and darkness get you packing,
Nothing now to man is lacking,
All your triumphs now arc cnded,
And what *Adam* marr'd, is mended ;
Graves are beds now for the weary,
Death a nap, to wake more merry ;
Youth now, full of pious duty,
Seeks in thee for perfect beauty,
The weak, and aged tir'd, with length
Of daies, from thee look for new strength,   10
And Infants with thy pangs Contest
As pleasant, as if with the brest ;
   Then, unto him, who thus hath thrown
Even to Contempt thy kingdome down,
And by his blood did us advance
Unto his own Inheritance,
To him be glory, power, praise,
From this, unto the last of daies.

The Holy Communion.

Welcome sweet, and sacred feast ; welcome life !
  Dead I was, and deep in trouble ;
But grace, and blessings came with thee so rife,
That they have quicken'd even drie stubble ;
  Thus soules their bodies animate,
  And thus, at first, when things were rude,
    Dark, void, and Crude
They, by thy Word, their beauty had, and date ;
    All were by thee,
    And stil must be,   10
   Nothing that is, or lives,
But hath his Quicknings, and reprieves
   As thy hand opes, or shuts ;
    Healings, and Cuts,
Darkness, and day-light, life, and death
Are but meer leaves turn'd by thy breath.
   Spirits without thee die,
    And blackness sits
    On the divinest wits,
As on the Sun Ecclipses lie.   20

    Title (1) Easter] Easter- *catchword 1655*

But that great darkness at thy death
When the veyl broke with thy last breath,
    Did make us see
    The way to thee;
And now by these sure, sacred ties,
    After thy blood
    (Our sov'rain good,)
    Had clear'd our eies,
    And given us sight;
Thou dost unto thy self betroth   30
    Our souls, and bodies both
    In everlasting light.

Was't not enough that thou hadst payd the price
    And given us eies
When we had none, but thou must also take
    Us by the hand
    And keep us still awake,
    When we would sleep,
    Or from thee creep,
Who without thee cannot stand?   40

Was't not enough to lose thy breath
And blood by an accursed death,
    But thou must also leave
    To us that did bereave
Thee of them both, these seals the means
    That should both cleanse
    And keep us so,
    Who wrought thy wo?
O rose of *Sharon*! O the Lilly
    Of the valley!   50
How art thou now, thy flock to keep,
Become both *food*, and *Shepheard* to thy sheep

Psalm 121.

Up to those bright, and gladsome hils
    Whence flowes my weal, and mirth,
I look, and sigh for him, who fils
    (Unseen,) both heaven, and earth.

He is alone my help, and hope,
    That I shall not be moved,
His watchful Eye is ever ope,
    And guardeth his beloved ;

The glorious God is my sole stay,
    He is my Sun, and shade,   10
The cold by night, the heat by day,
    Neither shall me invade.

He keeps me from the spite of foes,
    Doth all their plots controul,
And is a shield (not reckoning those,)
    Unto my very soul.

Whether abroad, amidst the Crowd,
    Or els within my door,
He is my Pillar, and my Cloud,
    Now, and for evermore.   20

Affliction.

Peace, peace ; It is not so.   Thou doest miscall
    Thy Physick ; Pils that change
Thy sick Accessions into setled health,
This is the great *Elixir* that turns gall
To wine, and sweetness ; Poverty to wealth,
  And brings man home, when he doth range.
    Did not he, who ordain'd the day,
        Ordain night too ?
    And in the greater world display
    What in the lesser he would do ?   10
All flesh is Clay, thou know'st ; and but that God
    Doth use his rod,
And by a fruitfull Change of frosts, and showres
    Cherish, and bind thy *pow'rs*,
Thou wouldst to weeds, and thistles quite disperse,
    And be more wild than is thy verse ;
Sickness is wholsome, and Crosses are but curbs
    To check the mule, unruly man,
They are heavens husbandry, the famous fan
    Purging the floor which Chaff disturbs.   20

Were all the year one constant Sun-shine, wee
    Should have no flowres,
All would be drought, and leanness ; not a tree
    Would make us bowres ;
Beauty consists in colours ; and that's best
    Which is not fixt, but flies, and flowes ;
The settled *Red* is dull, and *whites* that rest
    Something of sickness would disclose.
    Vicissitude plaies all the game,
        Nothing that stirrs,   30
        Or hath a name,
    But waits upon this wheel,
Kingdomes too have their Physick, and for steel,
    Exchange their peace, and furrs.
Thus doth God *Key* disorder'd man
        (Which none else can,)
Tuning his brest to rise, or fall ;
And by a sacred, needfull art
Like strings, stretch ev'ry part
Making the whole most Musicall.   40

The Tempest.

How is man parcell'd out ? how ev'ry hour
    Shews him himself, or somthing he should see ?
    This late, long heat may his Instruction be,
And tempests have more in them than a showr.

    When nature on her bosome saw
        Her Infants die,
    And all her flowres wither'd to straw,
        Her brests grown dry ;
    She made the Earth their nurse, & tomb,
        Sigh to the sky,   10
    'Til to those sighes fetch'd from her womb
        Rain did reply,
    So in the midst of all her fears
        And faint requests
    Her Earnest sighes procur'd her tears
        And fill'd her brests.

O that man could do so ! that he would hear
    The world read to him ! all the vast expence
    In the Creation shed, and slav'd to sence
Makes up but lectures for his eie, and ear.   20

Sure, mighty love foreseeing the discent
    Of this poor Creature, by a gracious art
    Hid in these low things snares to gain his heart,
And layd surprizes in each Element.

All things here shew him heaven ; *Waters* that fall
    Chide, and fly up ; *Mists* of corruptest fome
    Quit their first beds & mount ; trees, herbs, flowres, all
Strive upwards stil, and point him the way home.

How do they cast off grossness ? only *Earth*,
    And *Man* (like *Issachar*) in lodes delight,   30
    Water's refin'd to *Motion*, Aire to *Light*,   * *Light,*
Fire to all * three, but man hath no such mirth.   *Motion,*
                                      heat.

Plants in the *root* with Earth do most Comply,
    Their *Leafs* with water, and humiditie,
    The *Flowres* to air draw neer, and subtiltie,
And *seeds* a kinred fire have with the sky.

All have their *keyes*, and set *ascents* ; but man
    Though he knows these, and hath more of his own,
    Sleeps at the ladders foot ; alas ! what can
These new discoveries do, except they drown ?   40

Thus groveling in the shade, and darkness, he
    Sinks to a dead oblivion ; and though all
    He sees, (like *Pyramids*,) shoot from this ball
And less'ning still grow up invisibly,

Yet hugs he stil his durt ; The *stuffe* he wears
    And painted trimming takes down both his eies,
    Heaven hath less beauty than the dust he spies,
And money better musick than the *Spheres*.

Life's but a blast, he knows it ; what ? shal straw,
    And bul-rush-fetters temper his short hour ?   50
    ·Must he nor sip, nor sing ? grows ne'r a flowr
To crown his temples ? shal dreams be his law ?

O foolish man ! how hast thou lost thy sight ?
   How is it that the Sun to thee alone
   Is grown thick darkness, and thy bread, a stone ?
Hath flesh no softness now ? mid-day no light ?

Lord ! thou didst put a soul here ; If I must
   Be broke again, for flints will give no fire
   Without a steel, O let thy power cleer
Thy gift once more, and grind this flint to dust !   60

Retirement.

Who on yon throne of Azure sits,
   Keeping close house
   Above the morning-starre,
   Whose meaner showes,
And outward utensils these glories are
   That shine and share
   Part of his mansion ; He one day
   When I went quite astray
   Out of meer love
   By his mild Dove   10
Did shew me home, and put me in the way.

2.

Let it suffice at length thy fits
   And lusts (said he,)
   Have had their wish, and way ;
   Presse not to be
Still thy own foe, and mine ; for to this day
   I did delay,
   And would not see, but chose to wink,
   Nay, at the very brink
   And edge of all
   When thou wouldst fall   20
My *love-twist* held thee up, my *unseen link.*

3.

I know thee well ; for I have fram'd
   And hate thee not,
   Thy spirit too is mine ;
   I know thy lot,

Extent, and end, for my hands drew the line
     Assigned thine ;
  If then thou would'st unto my seat,
    'Tis not th'applause, and feat   30
     Of dust, and clay
     Leads to that way,
But from those follies a resolv'd Retreat.

4.

  Now here below where yet untam'd
     Thou doest thus rove
    I have a house as well
     As there above,
In it my *Name*, and *honour* both do dwell
     And shall untill
  I make all new ; there nothing gay   40
    In perfumes, or Array,
     Dust lies with dust
     And hath but just
The same Respect, and room, with ev'ry clay.

5.

  A faithful school where thou maist see
     In Heraldrie
  Of stones, and speechless Earth
     Thy true descent ;
Where dead men preach, who can turn feasts, and mirth
     To funerals, and *Lent.*   50
  There dust that out of doors might fill
    Thy eies, and blind thee still,
     Is fast asleep ;
     Up then, and keep
Within those doors, (my doors) dost hear ? *I will.*

Love, and Discipline.

Since in a land not barren stil
(Because thou dost thy grace distil,)
My lott is faln, Blest be thy will !

And since these biting frosts but kil
Some tares in me which choke, or spil
That seed thou sow'st, Blest be thy skil !

Blest be thy Dew, and blest thy frost,
And happy I to be so crost,
And cur'd by Crosses at thy cost.

The Dew doth Cheer what is distrest,   10
The frosts ill weeds nip, and molest,
In both thou work'st unto the best.

Thus while thy sev'ral mercies plot,
And work on me now cold, now hot,
The work goes on, and slacketh not,

For as thy hand the weather steers,
So thrive I best, 'twixt joyes, and tears,
And all the year have some grean Ears.

The Pilgrimage.

As travellours when the twilight's come,
And in the sky the stars appear,
The past daies accidents do summe
With, *Thus wee saw there, and thus here.*

Then *Jacob*-like lodge in a place
(A place, and no more, is set down,)
Where till the day restore the race
They rest and dream homes of their own.

So for this night I linger here,
And full of tossings too and fro,   10
Expect stil when thou wilt appear
That I may get me up, and go.

I long, and grone, and grieve for thee,
For thee my words, my tears do gush,
O that I were but where I see !
Is all the note within my Bush.

As Birds rob'd of their native wood,
Although their Diet may be fine,
Yet neither sing, nor like their food,
But with the thought of home do pine ;   20

So do I mourn, and hang my head,
And though thou dost me fullnes give,
Yet look I for far better bread
Because by this man cannot live.

O feed me then ! and since I may
Have yet more days, more nights to Count,
So strengthen me, Lord, all the way,
That I may travel to thy Mount.

Heb. Cap. xi. ver. 13.

And they Confessed, that they were strangers, and Pilgrims on the earth.

The Law, and the Gospel.

Lord, when thou didst on *Sinai* pitch
And shine from *Paran*, when a firie Law
Pronounc'd with thunder, and thy threats did thaw
Thy Peoples hearts, when all thy weeds were rich
    And Inaccessible for light,
      Terrour, and might,
How did poor flesh (which after thou didst weare,)
      Then faint, and fear !
Thy Chosen flock, like leafs in a high wind,
Whisper'd obedience, and their heads Inclin'd.   10

2.

But now since we to *Sion* came,
And through thy bloud thy glory see,
With filial Confidence we touch ev'n thee ;
And where the other mount all clad in flame,
    And threatning Clouds would not so much
      As 'bide the touch,
We Climb up this, and have too all the way
      Thy hand our stay,
Nay, thou tak'st ours, and (which ful Comfort brings)
Thy Dove too bears us on her sacred wings.   20

3.

Yet since man is a very brute
And after all thy Acts of grace doth kick,
Slighting that health thou gav'st, when he was sick,
Be not displeas'd, If I, who have a sute
    To thee each houre, beg at thy door
      For this one more ;
O plant in me thy *Gospel*, and thy *Law*,
      Both *Faith*, and *Awe* ;
So twist them in my heart, that ever there
I may as wel as *Love*, find too thy *fear* !   30

4.

Let me not spil, but drink thy bloud,
Not break thy fence, and by a black Excess
Force down a Just Curse, when thy hands would bless;
Let me not scatter, and despise my food,
   Or nail those blessed limbs again
      Which bore my pain;
So Shall thy mercies flow : for while I fear,
      I know, thou'lt bear,
But should thy mild Injunction nothing move me,
I would both think, and Judge I did not love thee.   40

John Cap. 14. ver. 15.
If ye love me, keep my Commandements.

The World.

I saw Eternity the other night
Like a great *Ring* of pure and endless light,
      All calm, as it was bright,
And round beneath it, Time in hours, days, years
      Driv'n by the spheres
Like a vast shadow mov'd, In which the world
      And all her train were hurl'd;
The doting Lover in his queintest strain ⟩ Petrarchan
      Did their Complain,
Neer him, his Lute, his fancy, and his flights,   10
      Wits sour delights,
With gloves, and knots the silly snares of pleasure
      Yet his dear Treasure
All scatter'd lay, while he his eys did pour
      Upon a flowr.

2.

The darksome States-man hung with weights and woe
Like a thick midnight-fog mov'd there so slow
      He did nor stay, nor go;
Condemning thoughts (like sad Ecclipses) scowl
      Upon his soul,   20
And Clouds of crying witnesses without
      Pursued him with one shout.
Yet dig'd the Mole, and lest his ways be found
      Workt under ground,

11 sour] so our *1655*

Where he did Clutch his prey, but one did see
  That policie,
Churches and altars fed him, Perjuries
  Were gnats and flies,
It rain'd about him bloud and tears, but he
  Drank them as free.   30

3.

The fearfull miser on a heap of rust
Sate pining all his life there, did scarce trust
  His own hands with the dust,
Yet would not place one peece above, but lives
  In feare of theeves.
Thousands there were as frantick as himself
  And hug'd each one his pelf,
The down-right Epicure plac'd heav'n in sense
  And scornd pretence
While others slipt into a wide Excesse   40
  Said little lesse ;
The weaker sort slight, triviall wares Inslave
  Who think them brave,
And poor, despised truth sate Counting by
  Their victory.

4.

Yet some, who all this while did weep and sing,
And sing, and weep, soar'd up into the *Ring*,
  But most would use no wing.
O fools (said I,) thus to prefer dark night
  Before true light,
To live in grots, and caves, and hate the day 50
  Because it shews the way,
The way which from this dead and dark abode
  Leads up to God,
A way where you might tread the Sun, and be
  More bright than he.
But as I did their madnes so discusse
  One whisper'd thus,
This Ring the Bride-groome did for none provide
  But for his bride.   60

John Cap. 2. ver. 16, 17.

 All that is in the world, the lust of the flesh, the lust of the Eys,
and the pride of life, is not of the father, but is of the world.
 And the world passeth away, and the lusts thereof, but he that
doth the will of God abideth for ever.

The Mutinie.

Weary of this same Clay, and straw, I laid
Me down to breath, and casting in my heart
The after-burthens, and griefs yet to come,
  The heavy sum
So shook my brest, that (sick and sore dismai'd)
My thoughts, like water which some stone doth start
Did quit their troubled Channel, and retire
Unto the banks, where, storming at those bounds,
They murmur'd sore ; But I, who felt them boyl
  And knew their Coyl,
Turning to him, who made poor sand to tire
And tame proud waves, If yet these barren grounds
  And thirstie brick must be (said I)
  My taske, and Destinie,

2.

Let me so strive and struggle with thy foes
(Not thine alone, but mine too,) that when all
Their Arts and force are built unto the height
  That Babel-weight
May prove thy glory, and their shame ; so Close
And knit me to thee, That though in this vale
Of sin, and death I sojourn, yet one Eie
May look to thee, To thee the finisher
And Author of my faith ; so shew me home
  That all this fome
And frothie noise which up and down doth flie
May find no lodging in mine Eie, or Eare,
  O seal them up ! that these may flie
  Like other tempests by.

3.

Not but I know thou hast a shorter Cut
To bring me home, than through a wildernes,
A Sea, or Sands and Serpents ; Yet since thou
  (As thy words show)
Though in this desart I were wholy shut,
Canst light and lead me there with such redress
That no decay shal touch me ; O be pleas'd
To fix my steps, and whatsoever path
Thy sacred and eternal wil decreed
  For thy bruis'd reed

Ɔ give it ful obedience, that so seiz'd
Ɔf all I have, I may nor move thy wrath   40
   Nor grieve thy *Dove*, but soft and mild
     Both live and die thy Child.

Revel. Cap. 2. *ver.* 17.
To him that overcometh wil I give to eate of the hidden Manna,
*and I wil give him a white stone, and in the stone a new name
written, which no man knoweth, saving he that receiveth it.*

The Constellation.

Fair, order'd lights (whose motion without noise
   Resembles those true Joys
Whose spring is on that hil where you do grow
   And we here tast sometimes below,)

With what exact obedience do you move
   Now beneath, and now above,
And in your vast progressions overlook
   The darkest night, and closest nook !

Some nights I see you in the gladsome East,
   Some others neer the West,   10
And when I cannot see, yet do you shine
   And beat about your endles line.

Silence, and light, and watchfulnes with you
   Attend and wind the Clue,
No sleep, nor sloth assailes you, but poor man
   Still either sleeps, or slips his span.

He grops beneath here, and with restless Care
   First makes, then hugs a snare,
Adores dead dust, sets heart on Corne and grass
   But seldom doth make heav'n his glass.   20

Musick and mirth (if there be musick here)
   Take up, and tune his year,
These things are Kin to him, and must be had,
   Who kneels, or sighs a life is mad.

Perhaps some nights hee'l watch with you, and peep
   When it were best to sleep,
Dares know Effects, and Judge them long before,
   When th' herb he treads knows much, much more.

I i

But seeks he your *Obedience, Order, Light,*
    Your calm and wel-train'd flight,
Where, though the glory differ in each star,
    Yet is there peace still, and no war?   3

Since plac'd by him who calls you by your names
    And fixt there all your flames,
Without Command you never acted ought
    And then you in your Courses fought.

But here Commission'd by a black self-wil
    The sons the father kil,
The Children Chase the mother, and would heal
    The wounds they give, by crying, zeale.   4

Then Cast her bloud, and tears upon thy book
    Where they for fashion look,
And like that Lamb which had the Dragons voice
    Seem mild, but are known by their noise.

Thus by our lusts disorder'd into wars
    Our guides prove wandring stars,
Which for these mists, and black days were reserv'd,
    What time we from our first love swerv'd.

Yet O for his sake who sits now by thee
    All crown'd with victory,   5
So guide us through this Darknes, that we may
    Be more and more in love with day;

Settle, and fix our hearts, that we may move
    In order, peace, and love,
And taught obedience by thy whole Creation,
    Become an humble, holy nation.

Give to thy spouse her perfect, and pure dress,
    Beauty and *holiness,*
And so repair these Rents, that men may see
    And say, *Where God is, all agree.*   6

The Shepheards.

Sweet, harmles livers! (on whose holy leisure
    Waits Innocence and pleasure,)
Whose leaders to those pastures, and cleer springs,
    Were *Patriarchs*, Saints, and Kings,

          1 livers *L 1858 C*: lives *1655*

How happend it that in the dead of night
    You only saw true light,
While *Palestine* was fast a sleep, and lay
    Without one thought of Day?
Was it because those first and blessed swains
    Were pilgrims on those plains   10
When they receiv'd the promise, for which now
    'Twas there first shown to you?
'Tis true, he loves that Dust whereon they go
    That serve him here below,
And therefore might for memory of those
    His love there first disclose;
But wretched *Salem* once his love, must now
    No voice, nor vision know,
Her stately Piles with all their height and pride
    Now languished and died,   20
And *Bethlems* humble Cotts above them stept
    While all her Seers slept;
Her Cedar, firr, hew'd stones and gold were all
    Polluted through their fall,
And those once sacred mansions were now
    Meer emptiness and show,
This made the Angel call at reeds and thatch,
    Yet where the shepheards watch,
And Gods own lodging (though he could not lack,)
    To be a common *Rack*;   30
No costly pride, no soft-cloath'd luxurie
    In those thin Cels could lie,
Each stirring wind and storm blew through their Cots
    Which never harbour'd plots,
Only Content, and love, and humble joys
    Lived there without all noise,
Perhaps some harmless Cares for the next day
    Did in their bosomes play,
As where to lead their sheep, what silent nook,
    What springs or shades to look,   40
But that was all; And now with gladsome care
    They for the town prepare,
They leave their flock, and in a busie talk
    All towards *Bethlem* walk
To see their souls great shepheard, who was come
    To bring all straglers home,
        12 'Twas] 'Iwas *1655*

Where now they find him out, and taught before
   That Lamb of God adore,
That Lamb whose daies great Kings and Prophets wish'd
   And long'd to see, but miss'd.   50
The first light they beheld was bright and gay
   And turn'd their night to day,
But to this later light they saw in him,
   Their day was dark, and dim.

Misery.

   Lord, bind me up, and let me lye
   A Pris'ner to my libertie,
   If such a state at all can be
   As an Impris'ment serving thee ;
   The wind, though gather'd in thy fist,
   Yet doth it blow stil where it list,
   And yet shouldst thou let go thy hold
   Those gusts might quarrel and grow bold.
     As waters here, headlong and loose
   The lower grounds stil chase, and choose,   10
   Where spreading all the way they seek
   And search out ev'ry hole, and Creek ;
   So my spilt thoughts winding from thee
   Take the down-rode to vanitie,
   Where they all stray and strive, which shal
   Find out the first and steepest fal ;
   I cheer their flow, giving supply
   To what's already grown too high,
   And having thus perform'd that part
   Feed on those vomits of my heart.   20
   I break the fence my own hands made
   Then lay that trespasse in the shade,
   Some fig-leafs stil I do devise
   As if thou hadst nor ears, nor Eyes.
   Excesse of friends, of words, and wine
   Take up my day, while thou dost shine
   All unregarded, and thy book
   Hath not so much as one poor look.
   If thou steal in amidst the mirth
   And kindly tel me, *I am Earth*,   30
   I shut thee out, and let that slip,
   Such Musick spoils good fellowship.

Thus wretched I, and most unkind,
Exclude my dear God from my mind,
Exclude him thence, who of that Cel
Would make a Court, should he there dwel.
He goes, he yields ; And troubled sore
His holy spirit grieves therefore,
The mighty God, th' eternal King
Doth grieve for Dust, and Dust doth sing.   40
But I go on, haste to Devest
My self of reason, till opprest
And buried in my surfeits I
Prove my own shame and miserie.
Next day I call and cry for thee
Who shouldst not then come neer to me,
But now it is thy servants pleasure
Thou must (and dost) give him his measure.
Thou dost, thou com'st, and in a showr
Of healing sweets thy self dost powr   50
Into my wounds, and now thy grace
(I know it wel,) fils all the place ;
I sit with thee by this new light,
And for that hour th'art my delight,
No man can more the world despise
Or thy great mercies better prize.
I School my Eys, and strictly dwel
Within the Circle of my Cel,
That Calm and silence are my Joys
Which to thy peace are but meer noise.   60
At length I feel my head to ake,
My fingers Itch, and burn to take
Some new Imployment, I begin
To swel and fome and fret within.
   " *The Age, the present times are not*
   " *To snudge in, and embrace a Cot,*
   " *Action and bloud now get the game,*
   " *Disdein treads on the peaceful name,*
   " *Who sits at home too bears a loade*
   " *Greater than those that gad abroad.*   70
Thus do I make thy gifts giv'n me
The only quarrellers with thee,

58 Cel, *M* : Cel *1655* : Cel ; *LGCB*

I'd loose those knots thy hands did tie,
Then would go travel, fight or die.
Thousands of wild and waste Infusions
Like waves beat on my resolutions,
As flames about their fuel run
And work, and wind til all be done,
So my fierce soul bustles about
And never rests til all be out.   80
Thus wilded by a peevish heart
Which in thy musick bears no part
I storm at thee, calling my peace
A Lethargy, and meer disease,
Nay, those bright beams shot from thy eys
To calm me in these mutinies
I stile meer tempers, which take place
At some set times, but are thy grace.

    Such is mans life, and such is mine
The worst of men, and yet stil thine,   90
Stil thine thou know'st, and if not so
Then give me over to my foe.
Yet since as easie 'tis for thee
To make man good, as bid him be,
And with one glaunce (could he that gain,)
To look him out of all his pain,
O send me from thy holy hil
So much of strength, as may fulfil
All thy delight (what e'r they be)
And sacred Institutes in me ;   100
Open my rockie heart, and fil
It with obedience to thy wil,
Then seal it up, that as none see,
So none may enter there but thee.

    O hear my God ! hear him, whose bloud
Speaks more and better for my good !
O let my Crie come to thy throne !
My crie not pour'd with tears alone,
(For tears alone are often foul)
But with the bloud of all my soul,   110
With spirit-sighs, and earnest grones,
Faithful and most repenting mones,
With these I crie, and crying pine
Till thou both mend and make me thine.

        99 delight] delights (?)

The Sap.

Come sapless Blossom, creep not stil on Earth
　　Forgetting thy first birth ;
'Tis not from dust, or if so, why dost thou
　　Thus cal and thirst for dew ?
It tends not thither, if it doth, why then
　　This growth and stretch for heav'n ?
Thy root sucks but diseases, worms there seat
　　And claim it for their meat.
Who plac'd thee here, did something then Infuse
　　Which now can tel thee news.　　　　　　　10
There is beyond the Stars an hil of myrrh
　　From which some drops fal here,
On it the Prince of *Salem* sits, who deals
　　To thee thy secret meals,
There is thy Country, and he is the way
　　And hath withal the key.
Yet liv'd he here sometimes, and bore for thee
　　A world of miserie,
For thee, who in the first mans loyns didst fal
　　From that hil to this vaie,　　　　　　　20
And had not he so done, it is most true
　　Two deaths had bin thy due ;
But going hence, and knowing wel what woes
　　Might his friends discompose,
To shew what strange love he had to our good
　　He gave his sacred bloud
By wil our sap, and Cordial ; now in this
　　Lies such a heav'n of bliss,
That, who but truly tasts it, no decay
　　Can touch him any way,　　　　　　　　30
Such secret life, and vertue in it lies
　　It wil exalt and rise
And actuate such spirits as are shed
　　Or ready to be dead,
And bring new too.　Get then this sap, and get
　　Good store of it, but let
The vessel where you put it be for sure
　　To all your pow'r most pure ;
There is at all times (though shut up) in you
　　A powerful, rare dew,　　　　　　　　40

Which only grief and love extract; with this
 Be sure, and never miss,
To wash your vessel wel : Then humbly take
 This balm for souls that ake,
And one who drank it thus, assures that you
 Shal find a Joy so true,
Such perfect Ease, and such a lively sense
 Of grace against all sins,
That you'l Confess the Comfort such, as even
 Brings to, and comes from Heaven.   50

Mount of Olives.

When first I saw true beauty, and thy Joys
Active as light, and calm without all noise
Shin'd on my soul, I felt through all my powr's
Such a rich air of sweets, as Evening showrs
Fand by a gentle gale Convey and breath
On some parch'd bank, crown'd with a flowrie wreath ;
Odors, and Myrrh, and balm in one rich floud
O'r-ran my heart, and spirited my bloud,
My thoughts did swim in Comforts, and mine eie
Confest, *The world did only paint and lie.*   10
And where before I did no safe Course steer
But wander'd under tempests all the year,
Went bleak and bare in body as in mind,
And was blow'n through by ev'ry storm and wind,
I am so warm'd now by this glance on me,
That, midst all storms I feel a Ray of thee ;
So have I known some beauteous *Paisage* rise
In suddain flowres and arbours to my Eies,
And in the depth and dead of winter bring
To my Cold thoughts a lively sense of spring.   20
 Thus fed by thee, who dost all beings nourish,
My wither'd leafs again look green and flourish,
I shine and shelter underneath thy wing
Where sick with love I strive thy name to sing,
Thy glorious name ! which grant I may so do
That these may be thy *Praise*, and my *Joy* too.

Man.

Weighing the stedfastness and state
Of some mean things which here below reside,
Where birds like watchful Clocks the noiseless date
 And Intercourse of times divide,
Where Bees at night get home and hive, and flowrs
  Early, aswel as late,
Rise with the Sun, and set in the same bowrs;

2.

I would (said I) my God would give
The staidness of these things to man! for these
To his divine appointments ever cleave,   10
 And no new business breaks their peace;
The birds nor sow, nor reap, yet sup and dine,
  The flowres without clothes live,
Yet *Solomon* was never drest so fine.

3.

Man hath stil either toyes, or Care,
He hath no root, nor to one place is ty'd,
But ever restless and Irregular
 About this Earth doth run and ride,
He knows he hath a home, but scarce knows where,
  He sayes it is so far   20
That he hath quite forgot how to go there.

4.

He knocks at all doors, strays and roams,
Nay hath not so much wit as some stones have
Which in the darkest nights point to their homes,
 By some hid sense their Maker gave;
Man is the shuttle, to whose winding quest
  And passage through these looms
God order'd motion, but ordain'd no rest.

7 bowrs] howrs *G*

¶

I walkt the other day (to spend my hour)
     Into a field
Where I sometimes had seen the soil to yield
     A gallant flowre,
But Winter now had ruffled all the bowre
     And curious store
I knew there heretofore.

2.

Yet I whose search lov'd not to peep and peer
     I'th' face of things
Thought with my self, there might be other springs   10
     Besides this here
Which, like cold friends, sees us but once a year,
     And so the flowre
Might have some other bowre.

3.

Then taking up what I could neerest spie
     I digg'd about
That place where I had seen him to grow out,
     And by and by
I saw the warm Recluse alone to lie
     Where fresh and green   20
He lived of us unseen.

4.

Many a question Intricate and rare
     Did I there strow,
But all I could extort was, that he now
     Did there repair
Such losses as befel him in this air
     And would e'r long
Come forth most fair and young.

5.

This past, I threw the Clothes quite o'r his head,
     And stung with fear   30
Of my own frailty dropt down many a tear
     Upon his bed,
Then sighing whisper'd, *Happy are the dead !*
     What peace doth now
     Rock him asleep below ?

6.

And yet, how few believe such doctrine springs
  From a poor root
Which all the Winter sleeps here under foot
  And hath no wings
To raise it to the truth and light of things,   40
  But is stil trod
  By ev'ry wandring clod.

7.

O thou! whose spirit did at first inflame
  And warm the dead,
And by a sacred Incubation fed
  With life this frame
Which once had neither being, forme, nor name,
  Grant I may so
  Thy steps track here below,

8.

That in these Masques and shadows I may see   50
  Thy sacred way,
And by those hid ascents climb to that day
  Which breaks from thee
Who art in all things, though invisibly;
  Shew me thy peace,
  Thy mercy, love, and ease,

9.

And from this Care, where dreams and sorrows raign
  Lead me above
Where Light, Joy, Leisure, and true Comforts move
  Without all pain,   60
There, hid in thee, shew me his life again
  At whose dumbe urn
  Thus all the year I mourn.

57 Care] Cave *conj.* G

Self comp-to flo-; X will guide growth of 6th

Begging.

King of Mercy, King of Love,
In whom I live, in whom I move,
Perfect what thou hast begun,
Let no night put out this Sun ;
Grant I may, my chief desire !
Long for thee, to thee aspire,
Let my youth, my bloom of dayes
Be my Comfort, and thy praise,
That hereafter, when I look
O'r the sullyed, sinful book,   10
I may find thy hand therein
Wiping out my shame, and sin.
O it is thy only Art
To reduce a stubborn heart,
And since thine is victorie,
Strong holds should belong to thee ;
Lord then take it, leave it not
Unto my dispose or lot,
But since I would not have it mine,
O my God, let it be thine !   20

Jude ver. 24, 25.

*Now unto him that is able to keep us from falling, and to present us
faultless before the presence of his glory with exceeding joy,
To the only wise God, our Saviour, be glory, and majesty, Dominion
and power, now and ever, Amen.*

FINIS.

Silex Scintillans, &c.

Ascension-day.

Lord Jesus ! with what sweetness and delights,
Sure, holy hopes, high joys and quickning flights
Dost thou feed thine ! O thou ! the hand that lifts
To him, who gives all good and perfect gifts.
Thy glorious, bright Ascension (though remov'd
So many Ages from me) is so prov'd
And by thy Spirit seal'd to me, that I
Feel me a sharer in thy victory.
   I soar and rise
   Up to the skies,   10
    Leaving the world their day,
   And in my flight,
   For the true light
    Go seeking all the way ;
I greet thy Sepulchre, salute thy Grave,
That blest inclosure, where the Angels gave
The first glad tidings of thy early light,
And resurrection from the earth and night.
I see that morning in thy *Converts tears,
Fresh as the dew, which but this dawning wears ? 20
I smell her spices, and her ointment yields,
As rich a scent as the now Primros'd-fields :
The Day-star smiles, and light with the deceast,
Now shines in all the Chambers of the East.
What stirs, what posting intercourse and mirth
Of Saints and Angels glorifie the earth ?
What sighs, what whispers, busie stops and stays ;
Private and holy talk fill all the ways ?
They pass as at the last great day, and run
In their white robes to seek the risen Sun ; 30
I see them, hear them, mark their haste, and move
Amongst them, with them, wing'd with faith and love.

   * St. Mary Magdalene.

23 light with the deceast] light, with Thee deceas'd, C : light with Thee
deceased B   30 risen] tisen 1655

Thy forty days more secret commerce here,
After thy death and Funeral, so clear
And indisputable, shews to my sight
As the Sun doth, which to those days gave light.
I walk the fields of *Bethani* which shine
All now as fresh as *Eden,* and as fine.
Such was the bright world, on the first seventh day,
Before man brought forth sin, and sin decay ;   40
When like a Virgin clad in *Flowers* and *green*
The pure earth sat, and the fair woods had seen
No frost, but flourish'd in that youthful vest,
With which their great Creator had them drest :
When Heav'n above them shin'd like molten glass,
While all the Planets did unclouded pass ;
And Springs, like dissolv'd Pearls their Streams did pour
Ne'r marr'd with floods, nor anger'd with a showre.
With these fair thoughts I move in this fair place,
And the last steps of my milde Master trace ;   50
I see him leading out his chosen Train,
All sad with tears, which like warm Summer-rain
In silent drops steal from their holy eyes,
Fix'd lately on the Cross, now on the skies.
And now (eternal Jesus !) thou dost heave
Thy blessed hands to bless, these thou dost leave ;
The cloud doth now receive thee, and their sight
Having lost thee, behold two men in white !
Two and no more : *what two attest, is true,*
Was thine own answer to the stubborn Jew.   60
Come then thou faithful witness ! come dear Lord
Upon the Clouds again to judge this world !

Ascension-Hymn.

Dust and clay
Mans antient wear !
Here you must stay,
But I elsewhere ;
Souls sojourn here, but may not rest ;
Who will ascend, must be undrest.

And yet some
That know to die

Before death come,
Walk to the skie
Even in this life ; but all such can
Leave behinde them the old Man.

     If a star
Should leave the Sphære,
She must first mar
Her flaming wear,
And after fall, for in her dress
Of glory, she cannot transgress.

     Man of old
Within the line
Of *Eden* could
Like the Sun shine
All naked, innocent and bright,
And intimate with Heav'n, as light ;

     But since he
That brightness soil'd,
His garments be
All dark and spoil'd,
And here are left as nothing worth,
Till the Refiners fire breaks forth.

     Then comes he !
Whose mighty light
Made his cloathes be
Like Heav'n, all bright ;
The Fuller, whose pure blood did flow
To make stain'd man more white then snow.

     Hee alone
And none else can
Bring bone to bone
And rebuild man,
And by his all subduing might
Make clay ascend more quick then light.

¶

They are all gone into the world of light !
   And I alone sit lingring here ;
Their very memory is fair and bright,
   And my sad thoughts doth clear.

It glows and glitters in my cloudy brest
    Like stars upon some gloomy grove,
Or those faint beams in which this hill is drest,
    After the Sun's remove.

I see them walking in an Air of glory,
    Whose light doth trample on my days :   10
My days, which are at best but dull and hoary,
    Meer glimering and decays.

O holy hope ! and high humility,
    High as the Heavens above !
These are your walks, and you have shew'd them me
    To kindle my cold love,

Dear, beauteous death ! the Jewel of the Just,
    Shining nowhere, but in the dark ;
What mysteries do lie beyond thy dust ;
    Could man outlook that mark !   20

He that hath found some fledg'd birds nest, may know
    At first sight, if the bird be flown ;
But what fair Well, or Grove he sings in now,
    That is to him unknown.

And yet, as Angels in some brighter dreams
    Call to the soul, when man doth sleep :
So some strange thoughts transcend our wonted theams,
    And into glory peep.

If a star were confin'd into a Tomb
    Her captive flames must needs burn there ;   30
But when the hand that lockt her up, gives room,
    She'l shine through all the sphære.

O Father of eternal life, and all
    Created glories under thee !
Resume thy spirit from this world of thrall
    Into true liberty.

Either disperse these mists, which blot and fill
    My perspective (still) as they pass,
Or else remove me hence unto that hill,
    Where I shall need no glass.   40

White Sunday.

Wellcome white day! a thousand Suns,
Though seen at once, were black to thee;
For after their light, darkness comes,
But thine shines to eternity.

Those flames which on the Apostles rush'd
At this great feast, and in a tyre
Of cloven Tongues their heads all brush'd,
And crown'd them with Prophetic fire:

Can these new lights be like to those,
These lights of Serpents like the Dove?   10
Thou hadst no *gall*, ev'n for thy foes,
And thy two wings were *Grief* and *Love*.

Though then some boast that fire each day,
And on Christs coat pin all their shreds;
Not sparing openly to say,
His candle shines upon their heads:

<u>Yet while some rays of that great light
Shine here below within thy Book,
They never shall so blinde my sight
But I will know which way to look.</u> 20

For though thou doest that great light lock,
And by this lesser commerce keep:
Yet by these glances of the flock
I can discern Wolves from the Sheep.

Not, but that I have wishes too,
And pray, *These last may be as first,
Or better;* but thou long ago
Hast said, *These last should be the worst.*

Besides, thy method with thy own,
Thy own dear people pens our times, 30
Our stories are in theirs set down
And penalties spread to our Crimes.

Again, if worst and worst implies
A State, that no redress admits,
Then from thy Cross unto these days
The *rule* without *Exception* fits.

And yet, as in nights gloomy page
One silent star may interline :
So in this last and lewdest age,
Thy antient love on some may shine.   40

For, though we hourly breath decays,
And our best *note* and highest *ease*
Is but meer changing of the *keys*,
And a *Consumption* that doth please ;

Yet thou the great eternal Rock
Whose height above all ages shines,
Art still the same, and canst unlock
Thy waters to a soul that pines.

Since then thou art the same this day
And ever, as thou wert of old,   50
And nothing doth thy love allay
But our hearts dead and sinful cold :

As thou long since wert pleas'd to buy
Our drown'd estate, taking the Curse
Upon thy self, so to destroy
The knots we tyed upon thy purse,

So let thy grace now make the way
Even for thy love ; for by that means
We, who are nothing but foul clay,
Shal be fine gold, which thou didst cleanse.   60

Q come ! refine us with thy fire !
Refine us ! we are at a loss.
Let not thy stars for *Balaams* hire
Dissolve into the common dross !

The Proffer.

Be still black Parasites,
          Flutter no more ;
Were it still winter, as it was before,
          You'd make no flights ;
But now the dew and Sun have warm'd my bowres,
     You flie and flock to suck the flowers.

But you would honey make :
　　These buds will wither,
And what you now extract, in harder weather
　　　Will serve to take ;　　　　　　　　　10
Wise husbands will (you say) there wants prevent,
　　Who do not so, too late repent.

　　O poys'nous, subtile fowls !
　　　The flyes of hell
That buz in every ear, and blow on souls
　　　Until they smell
And rot, descend not here, nor think to stay,
　　I've read, who 'twas, drove you away.

　　Think you these longing eyes,
　　　Though sick and spent,　　　　　　20
And almost famish'd, ever will consent
　　　To leave those skies,
That glass of souls and spirits, where well drest
　　They shine in white (like stars) and rest.

　　Shall my short hour, my inch,
　　　My one poor sand,
And crum of life, now ready to disband
　　　Revolt and flinch,
And having born the burthen all the day,
　　Now cast at night my Crown away ?　　　30

　　No, No ; I am not he,
　　　Go seek elsewhere.
I skill not your fine tinsel, and false hair,
　　　Your Sorcery
And smooth seducements : I'le not stuff my story
　　With your Commonwealth and glory.

　　There are, that will sow tares
　　　And scatter death
Amongst the quick, selling their souls and breath
　　　For any wares ;　　　　　　　　　40
But when thy Master comes, they'l finde and see
　　There's a reward for them and thee.

11 husbands *LGCB* : husband *1655*

Then keep the antient way!
Spit out their phlegm
And fill thy brest with home; think on thy dream:
A calm, bright day!
A Land of flowers and spices! the word given,
If these be fair, O what is Heaven!

Cock-crowing.

Father of lights! what Sunnie seed,
What glance of day hast thou confin'd
Into this bird? To all the breed
This busie Ray thou hast assign'd;
      Their magnetisme works all night,
      And dreams of Paradise and light.

Their eyes watch for the morning hue,
Their little grain expelling night
So shines and sings, as if it knew
The path unto the house of light.
      It seems their candle, howe'r done,
      Was tinn'd and lighted at the sunne.

If such a tincture, such a touch,
So firm a longing can impowre
Shall thy own image think it much
To watch for thy appearing hour?
      If a meer blast so fill the sail,
      Shall not the breath of God prevail?

O thou immortall light and heat!
Whose hand so shines through all this frame,
That by the beauty of the seat,
We plainly see, who made the same.
      Seeing thy seed abides in me,
      Dwell thou in it, and I in thee.

To sleep without thee, is to die;
Yea, 'tis a death partakes of hell:
For where thou dost not close the eye
It never opens, I can tell.
      In such a dark, Ægyptian border,
      The shades of death dwell and disorder.

Title Cock-crowing] Cock crowing *catchword 1655*

If joyes, and hopes, and earnest throws,
And hearts, whose Pulse beats still for light
Are given to birds ; who, but thee, knows
A love-sick souls exalted flight?
    Can souls be track'd by any eye
    But his, who gave them wings to flie?

Onely this Veyle which thou hast broke,
And must be broken yet in me,
This veyle, I say, is all the cloke
And cloud which shadows thee from me.
    This veyle thy full-ey'd love denies,
    And onely gleams and fractions spies.

O take it off! make no delay,
But brush me with thy light, that I
May shine unto a perfect day,
And warme me at thy glorious Eye!
    O take it off! or till it flee,
    Though with no Lilie, stay with me!

The Starre.

What ever 'tis, whose beauty here below
Attracts thee thus & makes thee stream & flow,
    And wind and curle, and wink and smile,
      Shifting thy gate and guile:

Though thy close commerce nought at all imbarrs
My present search, for Eagles eye not starrs,
    And still the lesser by the best
      And highest good is blest:

Yet, seeing all things that subsist and be,
Have their Commissions from Divinitie,
    And teach us duty, I will see
      What man may learn from thee.

First, I am sure, the Subject so respected
Is well disposed, for bodies once infected,
    Deprav'd or dead, can have with thee
      No hold, nor sympathie.—

Next, there's in it a restless, pure desire
And longing for thy bright and vitall fire,
    Desire that never will be quench'd,
      Nor can be writh'd, nor wrench'd.

These are the Magnets which so strongly move
And work all night upon thy light and love,
  — As beauteous shapes, we know not why,
    Command and guide the eye.

For where desire, celestiall, pure desire
Hath taken root, and grows, and doth not tire,
  There God a Commerce states, and sheds
    His Secret on their heads.

This is the Heart he craves; and who so will
But give it him, and grudge not; he shall feel
  That God is true, as herbs unseen
    Put on their youth and green.   30

The Palm-tree.

Deare friend sit down, and bear awhile this shade
As I have yours long since; This Plant, you see
So prest and bow'd, before sin did degrade
Both you and it, had equall liberty

With other trees: but now shut from the breath
And air of *Eden,* like a male-content
It thrives no where.   This makes these weights (like death
And sin) hang at him; for the more he's bent

The more he grows.   Celestial natures still
Aspire for home; This *Solomon* of old   10
By flowers and carvings and mysterious skill
Of Wings, and Cherubims, and Palms foretold.

This is the life which hid above with Christ
In God, doth always (hidden) multiply,
And spring, and grow, a tree ne'r to be pric'd,
A Tree, whose fruit is immortality.

Here Spirits that have run their race and fought
And won the fight, and have not fear'd the frowns
Nor lov'd the smiles of greatness, but have wrought
Their masters will, meet to receive their Crowns.   20

15 pric'd] prick'd *1655*

Here is the patience of the Saints : this Tree
Is water'd by their tears, as flowers are fed
With dew by night ; but One you cannot see
Sits here and numbers all the tears they shed.

Here is their faith too, which if you will keep
When we two part, I will a journey make
To pluck a Garland hence, while you do sleep
And weave it for your head against you wake.

Joy.

Be dumb course measures, jar no more ; to me
There is no discord, but your harmony.
False, jugling sounds ; a grone well drest, where care
Moves in disguise, and sighs afflict the air :
Sorrows in white ; griefs tun'd ; a sugerd Dosis
Of Wormwood, and a Deaths-head crown'd with Roses.
He weighs not your forc'd accents, who can have
A lesson plaid him by a winde or wave.
Such numbers tell their days, whose spirits be
Lull'd by those Charmers to a Lethargy.   10
    But as for thee, whose faults long since require
More eyes then stars ; whose breath could it aspire
To equal winds : would prove too short : Thou hast
Another mirth, a mirth though overcast
With clouds and rain, yet full as calm and fine
As those *clear heights* which above tempests shine.
        Therefore while the various showers
        Kill and cure the tender flowers,
        While the winds refresh the year
        Now with clouds, now making clear,   20
        Be sure under pains of death
        To ply both thine eyes and breath.
            As leafs in Bowers
            Whisper their hours,
            And Hermit-wells
            Drop in their Cells :
        So in sighs and unseen tears
        Pass thy solitary years,
And going hence, leave written on some Tree,
Sighs make joy sure, and shaking fastens thee.   30

The Favour.

O thy bright looks ! thy glance of love
Shown, & but shown me from above !
Rare looks ! that can dispense such joy
As without wooing wins the coy.
And makes him mourn, and pine and dye
Like a starv'd Eaglet, for thine eye.
Some kinde herbs here, though low & far,
Watch for, and know their loving star.
O let no star compare with thee !
Nor any herb out-duty me !   10
So shall my nights and mornings be
Thy time to shine, and mine to see.

The Garland.

Thou, who dost flow and flourish here below,
To whom a falling star and nine dayes glory,
Or some frail beauty makes the bravest shew,
Hark, and make use of this ensuing story.

When first my youthfull, sinfull age
Grew master of my wayes,
Appointing errour for my Page,
And darknesse for my dayes ;
I flung away, and with full crie
Of wild affections, rid   10
In post for pleasures, bent to trie
All gamesters that would bid.
I played with fire, did counsell spurn,
Made life my common stake ;
But never thought that fire would burn,
Or that a soul could ake.
Glorious deceptions, gilded mists,
False joyes, phantastick flights,
Peeces of sackcloth with silk-lists,
These were my prime delights.   20
I sought choice bowres, haunted the spring,
Cull'd flowres and made me posies :
Gave my fond humours their full wing,
And crown'd my head with Roses.

The Garland 1 below,] below. *1655*   21 bowres,] bowres *1655*
23 their] the r *1655* (?)

But at the height of this Careire
   I met with a dead man,
Who noting well my vain Abear,
   Thus unto me began :
Desist fond fool, be not undone,
   What thou hast cut to day   30
Will fade at night, and with this Sun
   Quite vanish and decay.

Flowres gather'd in this world, die here ; if thou
Wouldst have a wreath that fades not, let them grow,
And grow for thee ; who spares them here, shall find
A Garland, where comes neither rain, nor wind.

Love-sick.

Iesus, my life ! how shall I truly love thee ?
O that thy Spirit would so strongly move me,
That thou wert pleas'd to shed thy grace so farr
As to make man all pure love, flesh a star !
A star that would ne'r set, but ever rise,
So rise and run, as to out-run these skies,
These narrow skies (narrow to me) that barre,
So barre me in, that I am still at warre,
At constant warre with them. O come and rend,
Or bow the heavens ! Lord bow them and descend,   10
And at thy presence make these mountains flow,
These mountains of cold Ice in me ! Thou art
Refining fire, O then refine my heart,
My foul, foul heart ! Thou art immortall heat,
Heat motion gives ; Then warm it, till it beat,
So beat for thee, till thou in mercy hear,
So hear that thou must open : open to
A sinfull wretch, A wretch that caus'd thy woe,
Thy woe, who caus'd his weal ; so far his weal
That thou forgott'st thine own, for thou didst seal   20
Mine with thy blood, thy blood which makes thee mine,
Mine ever, ever ; And me ever thine.

Trinity-Sunday.

O holy, blessed, glorious three,
Eternall witnesses that be
In heaven, One God in trinitie !

    31 Will *catchword* : Whll *text 1655*

As here on earth (when men with-stood,)
The Spirit, Water, and the Blood,
Made my Lords Incarnation good :

So let the *Anty-types* in me
Elected, bought and seal'd for free,
Be own'd, sav'd, *Sainted* by you three !

Psalme 104.

Up, O my soul, and blesse the Lord.   O God,
      My God, how great, how very great art thou !
Honour and majesty have their abode
            With thee, and crown thy brow.

Thou cloath'st thy self with light, as with a robe,
      And the high, glorious heav'ns thy mighty hand
Doth spread like curtains round about this globe
            Of Air, and Sea, and Land.

The beams of thy bright Chambers thou dost lay
      In the deep waters, which no eye can find ;   10
The clouds thy chariots are, and thy path-way
            The wings of the swift wind.

In thy celestiall, gladsome messages
      Dispatch'd to holy souls, sick with desire
And love of thee, each willing Angel is
            Thy minister in fire.

Thy arm unmoveable for ever laid
      And founded the firm earth ; then with the deep
As with a vail thou hidst it, thy floods plaid
            Above the mountains steep.   20

At thy rebuke they fled, at the known voice
      Of their Lords thunder they retir'd apace :
Some up the mountains past by secret ways,
            Some downwards to their place.

For thou to them a bound hast set, a bound
      Which (though but sand) keeps in and curbs whole seas :
There all their fury, fome and hideous sound
            Must languish and decrease.

And as thy care bounds these, so thy rich love
      Doth broach the earth, and lesser brooks lets forth,   30
Which run from hills to valleys, and improve
            Their pleasure and their worth.

These to the beasts of every field give drink ;
    There the wilde asses swallow the cool spring :
And birds amongst the branches on their brink
      Their dwellings have and sing.

Thou from thy upper Springs above, from those
    Chambers of rain, where Heav'ns large bottles lie,
Doest water the parch'd hills, whose breaches close
      Heal'd by the showers from high.   40

Grass for the cattel, and herbs for mans use
    Thou mak'st to grow ; these (blest by thee) the earth
Brings forth, with wine, oyl, bread : All which infuse
      To mans heart strength and mirth.

Thou giv'st the trees their greenness, ev'n to those
    Cedars in *Lebanon*, in whose thick boughs
The birds their nests build ; though the Stork doth choose
      The fir-trees for her house.

To the wilde goats the high hills serve for folds,
    The rocks give Conies a retyring place :   50
Above them the cool Moon her known course holds,
      And the Sun runs his race.

Thou makest darkness, and then comes the night ;
    In whose thick shades and silence each wilde beast
Creeps forth, and pinch'd for food, with scent and sight
      Hunts in an eager quest.

The Lyons whelps impatient of delay
    Roar in the covert of the woods, and seek
Their meat from thee, who doest appoint the prey
      And feed'st them all the week.   60

This past, the Sun shines on the earth, and they
    Retire into their dens ; Man goes abroad
Unto his work, and at the close of day
      Returns home with his load.

O Lord my God, how many and how rare
    Are thy great works !   In wisdom hast thou made
Them all, and this the earth, and every blade
      Of grass, we tread, declare.

So doth the deep and wide sea, wherein are
    Innumerable, creeping things both small   70
And great : there ships go, and the shipmens fear
      The comely spacious Whale.

These all upon thee wait, that thou maist feed
    Them in due season : what thou giv'st, they take ;
Thy bounteous open hand helps them at need,
    And plenteous meals they make.

When thou doest hide thy face (thy face which keeps
    All things in being) they consume and mourn :
When thou with-draw'st their breath, their vigour sleeps,
    And they to dust return.   80

Thou send'st thy spirit forth, and they revive,
    The frozen earths dead face thou dost renew.
Thus thou thy glory through the world dost drive,
    And to thy works art true.

Thine eyes behold the earth, and the whole stage
    Is mov'd and trembles, the hills melt & smoke
With thy least touch : lightnings and winds that rage
    At thy rebuke are broke.

Therefore as long as thou wilt give me breath
    I will in songs to thy great name imploy   90
That gift of thine, and to my day of death
    Thou shalt be all my joy.

Ile *spice* my thoughts with thee, and from thy word
    Gather true comforts ; but the wicked liver
Shall be consum'd.   O my soul, bless thy Lord !
    Yea, blesse thou him for ever !

The Bird.

Hither thou com'st : the busie wind all night
Blew through thy lodging, where thy own warm wing
Thy pillow was.   Many a sullen storm
(For which course man seems much the fitter born,)
    Rain'd on thy bed
    And harmless head.

And now as fresh and chearful as the light
Thy little heart in early hymns doth sing
Unto that *Providence*, whose unseen arm
Curb'd them, and cloath'd thee well and warm.   10
    All things that be, praise him ; and had
    Their lesson taught them, when first made.

        75 Thy] They *catchword 1655*

So hills and valleys into singing break,
And though poor stones have neither speech nor tongue,
While active winds and streams both run and speak,
Yet stones are deep in admiration.
Thus Praise and Prayer here beneath the Sun
Make lesser mornings, when the great are done.

For each inclosed Spirit is a star
    Inlightning his own little sphere,
Whose light, though fetcht and borrowed from far,
    Both mornings makes, and evenings there.

But as these Birds of light make a land glad,
Chirping their solemn Matins on each tree:
So in the shades of night some dark fowls be,
Whose heavy notes make all that hear them, sad.

    The Turtle then in Palm-trees mourns,
      While Owls and Satyrs howl;
    The pleasant Land to brimstone turns
      And all her streams grow foul.

Brightness and mirth, and love and faith, all flye,
Till the Day-spring breaks forth again from high.

The Timber.

Sure thou didst flourish once! and many Springs,
Many bright mornings, much dew, many showers
Past ore thy head: many light *Hearts* and *Wings*
Which now are dead, lodg'd in thy living bowers.

And still a new succession sings and flies;
Fresh Groves grow up, and their green branches shoot
Towards the old and still enduring skies,
While the low *Violet* thrives at their root.

But thou beneath the sad and heavy *Line*
Of death, dost waste all senseless, cold and dark;
Where not so much as dreams of light may shine,
Nor any thought of greenness, leaf or bark.

And yet (as if some deep hate and dissent,
Bred in thy growth betwixt high winds and thee,
Were still alive) thou dost great storms resent
Before they come, and know'st how near they be.

14 tongue] tongu *1655*   13 if] is *1655*

Else all at rest thou lyest, and the fierce breath
Of tempests can no more disturb thy ease ;
But this thy strange resentment after death
Means onely those, who broke (in life) thy peace.

So murthered man, when lovely life is done,
And his blood freez'd, keeps in the Center still
Some secret sense, which makes the dead blood run
At his approach, that did the body kill.

And is there any murth'rer worse then sin ?
Or any storms more foul then a lewd life ?
Or what *Resentient* can work more within,
Then true remorse, when with past sins at strife ?

He that hath left lifes vain joys and vain care,
And truly hates to be detain'd on earth,
Hath got an house where many mansions are,
And keeps his soul unto eternal mirth.

But though thus dead unto the world, and ceas'd
From sin, he walks a narrow, private way ;
Yet grief and old wounds make him sore displeas'd,
And all his life a rainy, weeping day.

For though he should forsake the world, and live
As meer a stranger, as men long since dead ;
Yet joy it self will make a right soul grieve
To think, he should be so long vainly lead.

But as shades set off light, so tears and grief
(Though of themselves but a sad blubber'd story)
By shewing the sin great, shew the relief
Far greater, and so speak my Saviors glory.

If my way lies through deserts and wilde woods ;
Where all the Land with scorching heat is curst ;
Better, the pools should flow with rain and floods
To fill my bottle, then I die with thirst.

Blest showers they are, and streams sent from above
Begetting *Virgins* where they use to flow ;
And trees of life no other waters love,
These upper springs and none else make them grow.

---

42 story)] story *1655*   50 *Virgins*] verdure *conj. Firth in* C

But these chaste fountains flow not till we dye;
Some drops may fall before, but a clear spring
And ever running, till we leave to fling ——
Dirt in her way, will keep above the skie.

(handwritten note: Welsh idiom ("stop flinging"))

Rom. Cap. 6. ver. 7.
He that is dead, is freed from sin.

The Jews.

When the fair year
 Of your deliverer comes,
And that long frost which now benums
Your hearts shall thaw; when Angels here
 Shall yet to man appear,
And familiarly confer
Beneath the Oke and Juniper:
 When the bright *Dove*
Which now these many, many Springs
 Hath kept above,
 Shall with spread wings
Descend, and living waters flow
To make drie dust, and dead trees grow;

(handwritten note: Dove, traditionally 3rd Person, has life-giving function) 10

 O then that I
Might live, and see the Olive bear
Her proper branches! which now lie
 Scattered each where,
And without root and sap decay
Cast by the husband-man away.
 And sure it is not far! 20
For as your fast and foul decays
Forerunning the bright morning star,
Did sadly note his healing rayes
Would shine elsewhere, since you were blind,
And would be cross, when God was kinde:
 So by all signs
Our fulness too is now come in,
And the same Sun which here declines
And sets, will few hours hence begin
To rise on you again, and look 30
Towards old *Mamre* and *Eshcols* brook.

For surely he
Who lov'd the world so, as to give
His onely Son to make it free,
Whose spirit too doth mourn and grieve
To see man lost, will for old love
From your dark hearts this veil remove.

Faith sojourn'd first on earth in you,
You were the dear and chosen stock :
The Arm of God, glorious and true,   40
Was first reveal'd to be your rock.

You were the *eldest* childe, and when
Your stony hearts despised love,
The *youngest*, ev'n the Gentiles then
Were chear'd, your jealousie to move.

Thus, Righteous Father ! doest thou deal
With Brutish men ; Thy gifts go round
By turns, and timely, and so heal
The lost Son by the newly found.

Begging.

I, do not go ! thou know'st, I'le dye !
My *Spring* and *Fall* are in thy book !
Or, if thou goest, do not deny
To lend me, though from far, one look !

My sins long since have made thee strange,
A very stranger unto me ;
No morning-meetings since this change,
Nor evening-walks have I with thee.

Why is my God thus slow and cold,
When I am most, most sick and sad ?   10
Well fare those blessed days of old
When thou didst hear the *weeping Lad* !

O do not thou do as I did,
Do not despise a Love-sick heart !
What though some clouds defiance bid
Thy Sun must shine in every part.

1 I,] I *1655* : O *1654*   go !] goe, *1654*   know'st,] know'st *1654*   dye !]
dye, *1654*   3 Or,] Or *1654*   7 since this change,] (since this change) *1654*
9 slow] hard *1654*   11 old] old, *1654*   15 bid] bid, *1654*

Though I have spoil'd, O spoil not thou !
Hate not thine own dear gift and token !
Poor birds sing best, and prettiest show,
When their nest is faln and broken.

Dear Lord ! restore thy ancient peace,
Thy quikning friendship, mans bright wealth !
And if thou wilt not give me ease
From sicknesse, give my spirit health !

[handwritten marginal note: pre-historical-X life-giver *]*

Palm-Sunday.

Come, drop your branches, strow the way
                Plants of the day !
Whom sufferings make most green and gay.

The King of grief, the man of sorrow
Weeping still, like the wet morrow,
Your shades and freshness comes to borrow.

Put on, put on your best array ;
Let the joy'd rode make holy-day,
And flowers that into fields do stray,
Or secret groves, keep the high-way.   10

Trees, flowers & herbs ; birds, beasts & stones,
That since man fell, expect with groans
To see the lamb, which all at once,
Lift up your heads and leave your moans !
                For here comes he
                Whose death will be
Mans life, and your full liberty.

Hark ! how the children shril and high
                Hosanna cry,
Their joys provoke the distant skie,   20
Where thrones and Seraphins reply,
And their own Angels shine and sing
                In a bright ring :
                Such yong, sweet mirth
                Makes heaven and earth
Joyn in a joyful Symphony,

17 thou !] thou, *1654*   22 wealth !] wealth ; *1654*
13 which] come *LG* : whist *conj. M*

The harmless, yong and happy Ass,
Seen long before * this came to pass,
Is in these joys an high partaker
Ordain'd, and made to bear his Maker.   30

X is Creator

Dear feast of Palms, of Flowers and Dew !
Whose fruitful dawn sheds hopes and lights ;
Thy bright solemnities did shew,
The third glad day through two sad nights.

I'le get me up before the Sun,
I'le cut me boughs off many a tree,
And all alone full early run
To gather flowers to wellcome thee.

Then like the *Palm*, though wrong, I'le bear,
I will be still a childe, still meek   40
As the poor Ass, which the proud jear,
And onely my dear *Jesus* seek.

If I lose all, and must endure
The proverb'd griefs of holy *Job*,
I care not, so I may secure
But one *green Branch* and a *white robe*.

        * *Zechariah, chap.* 9. *ver.* 9.

Jesus weeping.

S. Luke 19. *ver.* 41.

Blessed, unhappy City ? dearly lov'd
But still unkinde ! art this day nothing mov'd !
    Art senseless still ?   O can'st thou sleep
    When God himself for thee doth weep !
    Stiff-necked *Jews* ! your fathers breed
    That serv'd the calf, not *Abr'ams* seed,
    Had not the Babes *Hosanna* cryed,
    The stones had spoke, what you denyed.

Dear *Jesus* weep on ! pour this latter
Soul-quickning rain, this living water   10
    On their dead hearts ; but (O my fears !)
    They will drink blood, that despise tears.

39 though wrong] though wronged *L 1847 1858 C* : through wrong *G*
8 denyed.] denyed *1655*

My dear, bright Lord! my Morning-star!
Shed this live-dew on fields which far
From hence long for it! shed it there,
Where the starv'd earth groans for one tear!

This land, though with thy hearts blest extract fed,
Will nothing yield but thorns to wound thy head.

The Daughter of *Herodias.*

St. Matth. chap. 14. *ver.* 6. *&c.*

Vain, sinful Art! who first did fit
Thy lewd loath'd *Motions* unto *sounds,*
And made grave *Musique* like wilde *wit*
Erre in loose airs beyond her bounds?

What fires hath he heap'd on his head?
Since to his sins (as needs it must,)
His *Art* adds still (though he be dead,)
New fresh accounts of blood and lust.

Leave then * yong Sorceress; the *Ice*
Will those coy spirits cast asleep,   10
Which teach thee now to please * his eyes
Who doth thy lothsome mother keep.

But thou hast pleas'd so well, he swears,
And gratifies thy sin with vows:
His shameless lust in publick wears,
And to thy soft arts strongly bows.

Skilful Inchantress and true bred!
Who out of evil can bring forth good?
Thy mothers nets in thee were spred,
She tempts to *Incest,* thou to *blood.*   20

* *Her name was* Salome; *in passing over a frozen river, the ice broke under
her, and chopt off her head.*
* Herod Antipas.

Jesus weeping.

St. John chap. 11. *ver.* 35.

My dear, Almighty Lord! why dost thou weep?
  Why dost thou groan and groan again,
      And with such deep,
  Repeated sighs thy kinde heart pain,

Since the same sacred breath which thus
Doth Mourn for us,
Can make mans dead and scatter'd bones
Unite, and raise up all that dyed, at once?

O holy groans! Groans of the Dove!
O healing tears! the tears of love!   10
Dew of the dead! which makes dust move
And spring, how is't that you so sadly grieve,
Who can relieve?

Should not thy sighs refrain thy store
Of tears, and not provoke to more?
Since two afflictions may not raign
In one at one time, as some feign.
Those blasts, which o'r our heads here stray,
If showers then fall, will showers allay,
As those poor Pilgrims oft have tryed,   20
Who in this windy world abide.

Dear Lord! thou art all grief and love,
But which thou art most, none can prove.
Thou griev'st, man should himself undo,
And lov'st him, though he works thy wo.

'Twas not that vast, almighty measure
Which is requir'd to make up life,
(Though purchas'd with thy hearts dear treasure,)
Did breed this strife
Of grief and pity in thy brest,   30
The throne where peace and power rest:
But 'twas thy love that (without leave,)
Made thine eyes melt, and thy heart heave;
For though death cannot so undo
What thou hast done, (but though man too
Should help to spoil) thou canst restore
All better far then 'twas before;
Yet, thou so full of pity art
(Pity which overflows thy heart!)
That, though the Cure of all mans harm   40
Is nothing to thy glorious arm,
Yet canst not thou that free Cure do,
But thou must sorrow for him too.

Then farewel joys ! for while I live,
My business here shall be to grieve :
A grief that shall outshine all joys
For mirth and life, yet without noise.
A grief, whose silent dew shall breed
Lilies and Myrrhe, where the curs'd seed
Did sometimes rule.   A grief so bright   50
'Twill make the Land of darkness light ;
And while too many sadly roam,
Shall send me (*Swan-like*) singing home.

Psal. 73. ver. 25.

Whom have I in heaven but thee ? and there is none upon earth,
that I desire besides thee.

Providence.

Sacred and secret hand !
By whose assisting, swift command
The Angel shewd that holy Well,
Which freed poor *Hagar* from her fears,
And turn'd to smiles the begging tears
Of yong, distressed *Ishmael.*

How in a mystick Cloud
(Which doth thy strange sure mercies shroud)
Doest thou convey man food and money
Unseen by him, till they arrive   10
Just at his mouth, that thankless hive
Which kills thy Bees, and eats thy honey !

If I thy servant be
(Whose service makes ev'n captives free,)
A fish shall all my tribute pay,
The swift-wing'd Raven shall bring me meat,
And I, like Flowers shall still go neat,
As if I knew no moneth but *May.*

I will not fear what man,
With all his plots and power can ;   20
Bags that wax old may plundered be,
But none can sequester or let
A state that with the Sun doth set
And comes next morning fresh as he.

Poor birds this doctrine sing,
And herbs which on dry hills do spring
Or in the howling wilderness
Do know thy dewy morning-hours,
And watch all night for mists or showers,
Then drink and praise thy bounteousness   30

May he for ever dye
Who trusts not thee ! but wretchedly
Hunts gold and wealth, and will not lend
Thy service, nor his soul one day :
May his Crown, like his hopes, be clay,
And what he saves, may his foes spend !

If all my portion here,
The measure given by thee each year
Were by my causless enemies
Usurp'd ; it never should me grieve   40
Who know, how well thou canst relieve,
Whose hands are open as thine eyes.

Great King of love and truth !
Who would'st not hate my froward youth,
And wilt not leave me, when grown old ;
Gladly will I, like *Pontick* sheep,
Unto their wormwood-diet keep
Since thou hast made thy Arm my fold.

The Knot.

Bright Queen of Heaven ! Gods Virgin Spouse
        The glad worlds blessed maid !
Whose beauty tyed life to thy house,
        And brought us saving ayd.

Thou art the true Loves-knot; by thee
        God is made our Allie,
And mans inferior Essence he
        With his did dignifie.

For Coalescent by that Band
        We are his body grown,   10
Nourished with favors from his hand
        Whom for our head we own.

And such a Knot, what arm dares loose,
  What life, what death can sever?
Which us in him, and him in us
  United keeps for ever.

The Ornament.

The lucky world shewd me one day
Her gorgeous Mart and glittering store,
Where with proud haste the rich made way
To buy, the poor came to adore.

Serious they seem'd and bought up all
The latest Modes of pride and lust,
Although the first must surely fall,
And the last is most loathsome dust.

But while each gay, alluring wear
With idle hearts and busie looks   10
They viewd, (for idleness hath there
Laid up all her Archives and books.)

Quite through their proud and pompous file
Blushing, and in meek weeds array'd
With native looks, which knew no guile,
Came the sheep-keeping *Syrian* Maid.

Whom strait the shining Row all fac'd
Forc'd by her artless looks and dress,
While one cryed out, We are disgrac'd
For she is bravest, you confess.   20

St. Mary Magdalen.

Dear, beauteous Saint! more white then day,
When in his naked, pure array;
Fresher then morning-flowers which shew
As thou in tears dost, best in dew.
How art thou chang'd! how lively-fair,
Pleasing and innocent an air,
Not tutor'd by thy glass, but free,
Native and pure shines now in thee!
But since thy beauty doth still keep
Bloomy and fresh, why dost thou weep?   10

  19 one] once *1655*   6 an] and *1655*

This dusky state of sighs and tears
Durst not look on those smiling years,
When *Magdal·*castle was thy seat,
Where all was sumptuous, rare and neat.
Why lies this *Hair* despised now
Which once thy care and art did show?
Who then did dress the much lov'd toy,
In *Spires, Globes,* angry *Curls* and coy,
Which with skill'd negligence seem'd shed
About thy curious, wilde, yong head?   20
Why is this rich, this *Pistic* Nard
Spilt, and the box quite broke and marr'd?
What pretty sullenness did hast
Thy easie hands to do this waste?
Why art thou humbled thus, and low
As earth, thy lovely head dost bow?
Dear *Soul*! thou knew'st, flowers here on earth
At their Lords foot-stool have their birth;
Therefore thy wither'd self in haste
Beneath his blest feet thou didst cast,   30
That at the root of this green tree
Thy great decays restor'd might be.
Thy curious vanities and rare
Odorous ointments kept with care,
And dearly bought, (when thou didst see
They could not cure, nor comfort thee,)
Like a wise, early Penitent
Thou sadly didst to him present,
Whose interceding, meek and calm
Blood, is the worlds all-healing *Balm.*   40
This, this Divine Restorative
Call'd forth thy tears, which ran in live
And hasty drops, as if they had
(Their Lord so near) sense to be glad.
Learn, *Ladies,* here the faithful cure
Makes beauty lasting, fresh and pure;
Learn *Marys* art of tears, and then
Say, *You have got the day from men.*
Cheap, mighty Art! her Art of love,
Who lov'd much and much more could move;   50

33 rare *LGCB*: rare, *L*: rare; *1655*

Her Art! whose memory must last
Till truth through all the world be past,
Till his abus'd, despised flame
Return to Heaven, from whence it came,
And send a fire down, that shall bring
Destruction on his ruddy wing.

Her Art! whose pensive, weeping eyes,
Were once sins loose and tempting spies,
But now are fixed stars, whose light
Helps such dark straglers to their sight.   60

Self-boasting *Pharisee*! how blinde
A Judge wert thou, and how unkinde?
It was impossible, that thou
Who wert all false, should'st true grief know;
Is't just to judge her faithful tears
By that foul rheum thy false eye wears?

This Woman (say'st thou) *is a sinner:*
And sate there none such at thy dinner?
Go Leper, go; wash till thy flesh
Comes like a childes, spotless and fresh;   70
He is still leprous, that still paints:
Who Saint themselves, they are no *Saints*.

The Rain-bow.

Still yong and fine! but what is still in view
We slight as old and soil'd, though fresh and new.
How bright wert thou, when *Shems* admiring eye
Thy burnisht, flaming *Arch* did first descry!
When *Terah, Nahor, Haran, Abram, Lot*,
The youthful worlds gray fathers in one knot,
Did with intentive looks watch every hour
For thy new light, and trembled at each shower!
When thou dost shine darkness looks white and fair,   10
Storms turn to Musick, clouds to smiles and air:
Rain gently spends his honey-drops, and pours
Balm on the cleft earth, milk on grass and flowers.
Bright pledge of peace and Sun-shine! the sure tye
Of thy Lords hand, the * object of his eye.

* *Gen. chap.* 9. *ver.* 16.

10 Storms *conj. H. H. Vaughan in G*: Forms *1655 LCB*

When I behold thee, though my light be dim,
Distant and low, I can in thine see him,
Who looks upon thee from his glorious throne
And mindes the Covenant 'twixt *All* and *One.*
O foul, deceitful men ! my God doth keep
His promise still, but we break ours and sleep.
After the *Fall*, the first sin was in *Blood*,
And *Drunkenness* quickly did succeed the flood ;
But since *Christ* dyed, (as if we did devise
To lose him too, as well as *Paradise*,)
These two grand sins we joyn and act together,
Though blood & drunkeness make but foul, foul weather.
Water (though both Heavens windows and the deep,
Full forty days o'r the drown'd world did weep,)
Could not reform us, and blood (in despight)
Yea Gods own blood we tread upon and slight.
So those bad daughters, which God sav'd from fire,
While *Sodom* yet did smoke, lay with their sire.

Then peaceful, signal bow, but in a cloud
Still lodged, where all thy unseen arrows shrowd,
I will on thee, as on a Comet look,
A Comet, the sad worlds ill-boding book ;
Thy light as luctual and stain'd with woes
I'le judge, where penal flames sit mixt and close.
For though some think, thou shin'st but to restrain
Bold storms, and simply dost attend on rain,
Yet I know well, and so our sins require,
Thou dost but Court cold rain, till *Rain* turns *Fire.*

The Seed growing secretly.
S. Mark 4. 26.

If this worlds friends might see but once
What some poor man may often feel,
Glory, and gold, and Crowns and Thrones
They would soon quit and learn to kneel.

My dew, my dew ! my early love,
My souls bright food, thy absence kills !
Hover not long, eternal Dove !
Life without thee is loose and spills.

26 weather.] weather *1655.*

Somthing I had, which long ago
Did learn to suck, and sip, and taste,   10
But now grown sickly, sad and slow,
Doth fret and wrangle, pine and waste.

O spred thy sacred wings and shake
One living drop! one drop life keeps!
If pious griefs Heavens joys awake,
O fill his bottle! thy childe weeps!

Slowly and sadly doth he grow,
And soon as left, shrinks back to ill;
O feed that life, which makes him blow
And spred and open to thy will!   20

For thy eternal, living wells
None stain'd or wither'd shall come near:
A fresh, immortal *green* there dwells,
And spotless *white* is all the wear.

Dear, secret *Greenness*! nurst below
Tempests and windes, and winter-nights,
Vex not, that but one sees thee grow,
That *One* made all these lesser lights.

If those bright joys he singly sheds
On thee, were all met in one Crown,   30
Both Sun and Stars would hide their heads;
And Moons, though full, would get them down.

Let glory be their bait, whose mindes
Are all too high for a low Cell:
Though Hawks can prey through storms and winds,
The poor Bee in her hive must dwel.

Glory, the Crouds cheap tinsel still
To what most takes them, is a drudge;
And they too oft take good for ill,
And thriving vice for vertue judge.   40

What needs a Conscience calm and bright
Within it self an outward test?
Who breaks his glass to take more light,
Makes way for storms into his rest.

Then bless thy secret growth, nor catch
At noise, but thrive unseen and dumb;
Keep clean, bear fruit, earn life and watch
Till the white winged Reapers come!

¶

As time one day by me did pass
 Through a large dusky glasse
 He held, I chanc'd to look
 And spyed his curious book
Of past days, where sad Heav'n did shed
A mourning light upon the dead.

Many disordered lives I saw
 And foul records which thaw
 My kinde eyes still, but in
 A fair, white page of thin   10
And ev'n, smooth lines, like the Suns rays,
Thy name was writ, and all thy days.

O bright and happy Kalendar!
 Where youth shines like a star
 All pearl'd with tears, and may
 Teach age, *The Holy way*;
Where through thick pangs, high agonies
Faith into life breaks, and death dies.

As some meek *night-piece* which day quails,
 To candle-light unveils: 20
 So by one beamy line
 From thy bright lamp did shine,
In the same page thy humble grave
Set with green herbs, glad hopes and brave.

Here slept my thoughts dear mark! which dust
 Seem'd to devour, like rust;
 But dust (I did observe)
 By hiding doth preserve,
As we for long and sure recruits,
Candy with sugar our choice fruits.   30

O calm and sacred bed where lies
 In deaths dark mysteries
 A beauty far more bright
 Then the noons cloudless light
For whose dry dust green branches bud
And robes are bleach'd in the *Lambs* blood.

22 shine, *M*: shine ; *1655* : shine *LGCB*   36 blood.] blood *1655*

Sleep happy ashes! (blessed sleep!)
   While haplesse I still weep;
   Weep that I have out-liv'd
   My life, and unreliev'd   40
Must (soul-lesse shadow!) so live on,
Though life be dead, and my joys gone.

¶

Fair and yong light! my guide to holy
Grief and soul-curing melancholy;
Whom living here I did still shun
As sullen night-ravens do the Sun,
And lead by my own foolish fire
Wandred through darkness, dens and mire.
How am I now in love with all
That I term'd then meer bonds and thrall,
And to thy name, which still I keep,
Like the surviving turtle, weep!   10
O bitter curs'd delights of men!
Our souls diseases first, and then
Our bodies; poysons that intreat
With fatal sweetness, till we eat;
How artfully do you destroy,
That kill with smiles and seeming joy?
If all the subtilties of vice
Stood bare before unpractic'd eyes,
And every act she doth commence
Had writ down its sad consequence,   20
Yet would not men grant, their ill fate
Lodged in those false looks, till too late.
O holy, happy, healthy heaven,
Where all is pure, where all is even,
Plain, harmless, faithful, fair and bright,
But what Earth breaths against thy light!
How blest had men been, had their *Sire*
Liv'd still in league with thy chaste fire,

5-8, *the last four lines on the original page* 43, *are repeated on page* 44
as follows:
        And led by my own foolish fire,
        Wandred through darkness dens and mire.
        How am I now in love withal
        That I term'd then mere bonds and thrall,

Nor made life through her long descents,
A slave to lustful Elements! 30
I did once read in an old book
Soil'd with many a weeping look,
That the seeds of foul sorrows be
The finest things that are, to see.
So that fam'd fruit which made all dye
Seem'd fair unto the womans eye.
If these supplanters in the shade
Of Paradise, could make man fade,
How in this world should they deter
This world, their fellow-murtherer! 40
And why then grieve we to be sent
Home by our first fair punishment,
Without addition to our woes
And lingring wounds from weaker foes?
Since that doth quickly freedom win,
For he that's dead, is freed from sin.

O that I were winged and free
And quite undrest just now with thee,
Where freed souls dwel by living fountains
On everlasting, spicy mountains! 50
    Alas! my God! take home thy sheep;
    This world but laughs at those that weep.

The Stone.

Josh. chap. 24. ver. 27.

    I have it now:
But where to act, that none shall know,
Where I shall have no cause to fear
    An eye or ear,
      What man will show?
If nights, and shades, and secret rooms,
    Silent as tombs,
Will nor conceal nor assent to
My dark designs, what shall I do?
Man I can bribe, and woman will 10
Consent to any gainful ill,
But these dumb creatures are so true,
No gold nor gifts can them subdue.

Hedges have ears, said the old *sooth*,
And ev'ry bush is somethings booth ;
This cautious fools mistake, and fear
Nothing but man, when ambush'd there.

     But I (Alas !)
Was shown one day in a strange glass
That busie commerce kept between   20
God and his Creatures, though unseen.

     They hear, see, speak,
And into loud discoveries break,
As loud as blood.   Not that God needs
Intelligence, whose spirit feeds
All things with life, before whose eyes,
Hell and all hearts stark naked lyes.
But * he that judgeth as he hears,
He that accuseth none, so steers
His righteous course, that though he knows   30
All that man doth, conceals or shows,
Yet will not he by his own light
(Though both all-seeing and all right,)
Condemn men ; but will try them by
A process, which ev'n mans own eye
Must needs acknowledge to be just.
     Hence sand and dust
Are shak'd for witnesses, and stones
Which some think dead, shall all at once
With one attesting voice detect   40
Those secret sins we least suspect.
For know, wilde men, that when you erre
Each thing turns Scribe and Register,
And in obedience to his Lord,
Doth your most private sins record.

     The *Law* delivered to the *Jews*,
Who promis'd much, but did refuse
Performance, will for that same deed
Against them by a *stone* proceed ;
Whose substance, though 'tis hard enough,   50
Will prove their hearts more stiff and tuff.

     * *John chap.* 5. *ver.* 30. 45.

But now, since God on himsclf took
What all mankinde could never brook,
If any (for he all invites)
His easie yoke rejects or slights,
The *Gospel* then (for 'tis his word
And not himself * shall judge the world)
Will by loose *Dust* that man arraign,
As one then dust more vile and vain.

> * *St. John, chap.* 12. *ver.* 47, 48.

The dwelling-place.

S. John, chap. 1. *ver.* 38, 39.

What happy, secret fountain,
  Fair shade, or mountain,
Whose undiscover'd virgin glory
Boasts it this day, though not in story,
Was then thy dwelling? did some cloud
Fix'd to a Tent, descend and shrowd
My distrest Lord? or did a star
Becken'd by thee, though high and far,
In sparkling smiles haste gladly down
To lodge light, and increase her own? 10
My dear, dear God! I do not know
What lodgd thee then, nor where, nor how;
But I am sure, thou dost now come
Oft to a narrow, homely room,
Where thou too hast but the least part,
My God, I mean *my sinful heart.*

The Men of War.

S. Luke, chap. 23. *ver.* 11.

If any have an ear
*Saith holy * John, then let him hear.*
He that into Captivity
Leads others, shall a Captive be.
Who with the sword doth others kill,
A sword shall his blood likewise spill.
Here is the patience of the Saints,
And the true faith, which never faints.

> * *Revel. cap.* 13. *ver.* 10.

Were not thy word (dear Lord !) my light,
How would I run to endless night,   10
And persecuting thee and thine,
Enact for *Saints* my self and mine.
But now enlighten'd thus by thee,
I dare not think such villany ;
Nor for a temporal self-end
Successful wickedness commend.
For in this bright, instructing verse
Thy Saints are not the Conquerers ;
But patient, meek, and overcome
Like thee, when set at naught and dumb.   20
Armies thou hast in Heaven, which fight,
And follow thee all cloath'd in white,
But here on earth (though thou hast need)
Thou wouldst no legions, but wouldst bleed.
The sword wherewith thou dost command
Is in thy mouth, not in thy hand,
And all thy Saints do overcome
By thy blood, and their Martyrdom.
But seeing Soldiers long ago
Did spit on thee, and smote thee too ;   30
Crown'd thee with thorns, and bow'd the knee,
But in contempt, as still we see,
I'le marvel not at ought they do,
Because they us'd my Savior so ;
Since of my *Lord* they had their will,
The servant must not take it ill.

　　Dear *Jesus* give me patience here,
And faith to see my Crown as near
And almost reach'd, because 'tis sure
If I hold fast and slight the *Lure.*   40
Give me humility and peace,
Contented thoughts, innoxious ease,
A sweet, revengeless, quiet minde,
And to my greatest haters kinde.
Give me, my God ! a heart as milde
And plain, as when I was a childe ;
That when *thy Throne is set*, and all
These *Conquerors* before it fall,

23　hast] hadst *LGB*

M m

I may be found (preserv'd by thee)
Amongst that chosen company,   50
Who by no blood (here) overcame
But the blood of the *blessed Lamb.*

The Ass.

St. Matt. 21.

Thou! who didst place me in this busie street
Of flesh and blood, where two ways meet:
The *One* of goodness, peace and life,
The *other* of death, sin and strife;
Where frail visibles rule the minde,
And present things finde men most kinde:
Where obscure cares the *mean* defeat,
And splendid vice destroys the *great*;
As thou didst set no law for me,
But that of perfect liberty,   10
Which neither tyres, nor doth corrode,
But is a *Pillow*, not a *Load*:
So give me grace ever to rest,
And build on it, because the best;
Teach both mine eyes and feet to move
Within those bounds set by thy love;
Grant I may soft and lowly be,
And minde those things I cannot see;
Tye me to faith, though above reason,
Who question power, they speak treason: 20
Let me thy Ass be onely wise
To carry, not search mysteries;
Who carries thee, is by thee lead,
Who argues, follows his own head.
To check bad motions, keep me still
Amongst the dead, where thriving ill
Without his brags and conquests lies,
And truth (opprest here) gets the prize.
At all times, whatsoe'r I do,
Let me not fail to question, who   30
Shares in the *act*, and puts me to't?
And if not thou, let not me do't.
Above all, make me love the poor,
Those burthens to the rich mans door,

Let me admire those, and be kinde
To low estates, and a low minde.
If the world offers to me ought,
That by thy book must not be sought,
Or though it should be lawful, may
Prove not expedient for thy way ;⠀⠀⠀⠀⠀⠀⠀40
To shun that peril, let thy grace
Prevail with me to shun the place.
Let me be wise to please thee still,
And let men call me what they will.

⠀⠀When thus thy milde, instructing hand
Findes thy poor *foal* at thy command,
When he from wilde is become wise,
And slights that most, which men most prize ;
When all things here to thistles turn
Pricking his lips, till he doth mourn⠀⠀⠀⠀⠀50
And hang the head, sighing for those
Pastures of life, where the Lamb goes :
O then, just then ! break or untye
These bonds, this sad captivity,
This leaden state, which men miscal
Being and life, but is dead thrall.
And when (O God !) the Ass is free,
In a state known to none but thee ;
O let him by his *Lord* be led,
To living springs, and there be fed⠀⠀⠀⠀⠀60
Where light, joy, health and perfect peace
Shut out all pain and each disease ;
Where death and frailty are forgotten,
And bones rejoyce, which once were broken !

The hidden Treasure.

S. Matt. 13. 44.

What can the man do that succeeds the * *King?*
Even what was done before, and no new thing.
Who shews me but one grain of sincere light ?
False stars and fire-drakes, the deceits of night

⠀⠀* *Ecclesiastes, chap.* 2. 12.

Set forth to fool and foil thee, do not boast;
Such Coal-flames shew but Kitchin-rooms at most.
And those I saw search'd through; yea those and all
That these three thousand years time did let fall
To blinde the eyes of lookers-back, and I
Now all is done, finde all is vanity.   10
Those secret searches, which afflict the wise,
Paths that are hidden from the *Vulturs* eyes
I saw at distance, and where grows that fruit
Which others onely grope for and dispute.
    The worlds lov'd wisdom (for the worlds friends think
There is none else) did not the dreadful brink
And precipice it leads to, bid me flie
None could with more advantage use, then I.
    Mans favorite sins, those tainting appetites
Which nature breeds, and some fine clay invites,   20
With all their soft, kinde arts and easie strains
Which strongly operate, though without pains,
Did not a greater beauty rule mine eyes,
None would more dote on, nor so soon entice.
But since these sweets are sowre, and poyson'd here
Where the impure seeds flourish all the year,
And private Tapers will but help to stray
Ev'n those, who *by them* would finde out the day,
I'le seal my eyes up, and to thy commands
Submit my wilde heart, and restrain my hands;   30
I will do nothing, nothing know, nor see
But what thou bidst, and shew'st, and teachest me.
Look what thou gav'st; all that I do restore
But for one thing, though purchas'd once before.

Childe-hood.

I cannot reach it; and my striving eye
Dazles at it, as at eternity.
    Were now that Chronicle alive,
Those white designs which children drive,
And the thoughts of each harmless hour,
With their content too in my pow'r,
Quickly would I make my path even,
And by meer playing go to Heaven.

Why should men love
A Wolf, more then a Lamb or Dove?   10
Or choose hell-fire and brimstone streams
Before bright stars, and Gods own beams?
Who kisseth thorns, will hurt his face,
But flowers do both refresh and grace,
And sweetly living (*fie on men!*)
Are when dead, medicinal then.
If seeing much should make staid eyes,
And long experience should make wise;
Since all that age doth teach, is ill,
Why should I not love childe-hood still?   20
Why if I see a rock or shelf,
Shall I from thence cast down my self,
Or by complying with the world,
From the same precipice be hurl'd?
Those observations are but foul
Which make me wise to lose my soul.

And yet the *Practice* worldlings call
Business and weighty action all,
Checking the poor childe for his play,
But gravely cast themselves away.   30

    Dear, harmless age! the short, swift span,
Where weeping virtue parts with man;
Where love without lust dwells, and bends
What way we please, without self-ends.

An age of mysteries! which he
Must live twice, that would Gods face see;
Which *Angels* guard, and with it play,
Angels! which foul men drive away.

How do I study now, and scan
Thee, more then ere I studyed man,   40
And onely see through a long night
Thy edges, and thy bordering light!
O for thy Center and mid-day!
For sure that is the *narrow way.*

        15 *men!*)] *men!* *1655*

The Night.

John 2. 3.

Through that pure *Virgin-shrine*,
That sacred vail drawn o'r thy glorious noon
That men might look and live as Glo-worms shine,
  And face the Moon:
  Wise *Nicodemus* saw such light
  As made him know his God by night.

Most blest believer he!
Who in that land of darkness and blinde eyes
Thy long expected healing wings could see,
  When thou didst rise,   10
  And what can never more be done,
  Did at mid-night speak with the Sun!

O who will tell me, where
He found thee at that dead and silent hour!
What hallow'd solitary ground did bear
  So rare a flower,
  Within whose sacred leafs did lie
  The fulness of the Deity.

No mercy-seat of gold,
No dead and dusty *Cherub*, nor carv'd stone,   20
But his own living works did my Lord hold
  And lodge alone;
  Where *trees* and *herbs* did watch and peep
  And wonder, while the *Jews* did sleep.

Dear night! this worlds defeat;
The stop to busie fools; cares check and curb;
The day of Spirits; my souls calm retreat
  Which none disturb!
  Christs * progress, and his prayer time;
  The hours to which high Heaven doth chime.   30

Gods silent, searching flight:
When my Lords head is fill'd with dew, and all
His locks are wet with the clear drops of night;
  His still, soft call;

* *Mark, chap.* 1. 35. *S. Luke, chap.* 21. 37.

27 retreat] retaeat *1655*

His knocking time; The souls dumb watch,
When Spirits their fair kinred catch.

Were all my loud, evil days
Calm and unhaunted as is thy dark Tent,
Whose peace but by some *Angels* wing or voice
    Is seldom rent;   40
  Then I in Heaven all the long year
  Would keep, and never wander here.

    But living where the Sun
Doth all things wake, and where all mix and tyre
Themselves and others, I consent and run
    To ev'ry myre,
  And by this worlds ill-guiding light,
  Erre more then I can do by night.

    There is in God (some say)
A deep, but dazling darkness; As men here   50
Say it is late and dusky, because they
    See not all clear;
  O for that night! where I in him
  Might live invisible and dim.

Abels blood.

Sad, purple well! whose bubling eye
Did first against a Murth'rer cry;
Whose streams still vocal, still complain
    Of bloody *Cain*,
And now at evening are as red
As in the morning when first shed.
    If single thou
(Though single voices are but low,)
Could'st such a shrill and long cry rear
As speaks still in thy makers ear,   10
What thunders shall those men arraign
Who cannot count those they have slain,
Who bath not in a shallow flood,
But in a deep, wide sea of blood?
A sea, whose lowd waves cannot sleep,
But *Deep* still calleth upon *deep*:
Whose urgent *sound* like unto that
Of many waters, beateth at

The everlasting doors above,
Where souls behinde the altar move,   20
And with one strong, incessant cry
Inquire *How long?* of the most high.
   Almighty Judge!
At whose just laws no just men grudge ;
Whose blessed, sweet commands do pour
Comforts and joys, and hopes each hour
On those that keep them ; O accept
Of his vow'd heart, whom thou hast kept
From bloody men ! and grant, I may
That sworn memorial duly pay   30
To thy bright arm, which was my light
And leader through thick death and night!
   I, may that flood,
That proudly spilt and despis'd blood,
Speechless and calm, as Infants sleep !
Or if it watch, forgive and weep
For those that spilt it ! May no cries
From the low earth to high Heaven rise,
But what (like his, whose blood peace brings)
Shall (when they rise) *speak better things*,   40
Then *Abels* doth ! may *Abel* be
Still single heard, while these agree
With his milde blood in voice and will,
Who pray'd for those that did him kill !

Righteousness.

Fair, solitary path ! Whose blessed shades
The old, white Prophets planted first and drest :
Leaving for us (whose goodness quickly fades,)
A shelter all the way, and bowers to rest.

Who is the man that walks in thee ? who loves
Heav'ns secret solitude, those fair abodes
Where turtles build, and carelesse sparrows move
Without to morrows evils and future loads ?

Who hath the upright heart, the single eye,
The clean, pure hand, which never medled pitch ?   10
Who sees *Invisibles*, and doth comply
With hidden treasures that make truly rich ?

33 I,] I *1655* 40 *things, M*: *things. 1655*: *things LGCB* 6 Heav'ns]
Heav ns *1655* 7 carelesse] carelese *1655*

He that doth seek and love
The things above,
Whose spirit ever poor, is meek and low;
Who simple still and wise,
Still homewards flies,
Quick to advance, and to retreat most slow.

Whose acts, words and pretence
Have all one sense,   20
One aim and end; who walks not by his sight:
Whose eyes are both put out,
And goes about
Guided by faith, not by exterior light.

Who spills no blood, nor spreds
Thorns in the beds
Of the distrest, hasting their overthrow;
Making the time they had
Bitter and sad
Like *Chronic* pains, which surely kill, though slow.   30

Who knows earth nothing hath
Worth love or wrath,
But in his *hope* and *Rock* is ever glad.
Who seeks and follows peace,
When with the ease
And health of conscience it is to be had.

Who bears his cross with joy
And doth imploy
His heart and tongue in prayers for his foes;
Who lends, not to be paid,   40
And gives full aid
Without that bribe which Usurers impose.

Who never looks on man
Fearful and wan,
But firmly trusts in God; the great mans measure
Though high and haughty must
Be ta'en in dust,
But the good man is Gods peculiar treasure.

30 pains *LGCB*: prayers *1655* (*from* 39 ?)

Who doth thus, and doth not
These good deeds blot   50
With bad, or with neglect; and heaps not wrath
By secret filth, nor feeds
Some snake, or weeds,
Cheating himself; That man walks in this path.

Anguish.

My God and King! to thee
I bow my knee,
I bow my troubled soul, and greet
With my foul heart thy holy feet.
Cast it, or tread it! It shall do
Even what thou wilt, and praise thee too.

My God, could I weep blood,
Gladly I would;
Or if thou wilt give me that Art,
Which through the eyes pours out the hart,   10
I will exhaust it all, and make
My self all tears, a weeping lake.

O! 'tis an easie thing
To write and sing;
But to write true, unfeigned verse
Is very hard! O God, disperse
These weights, and give my spirit leave
To act as well as to conceive!

O my God, hear my cry;
Or let me dye! ——   20

Tears.

O when my God, my glory brings
His white and holy train,
Unto those clear and living *Springs*,
Where comes no *stain*!

Where all is *light*, and *flowers*, and *fruit*,
And *joy*, and *rest*,
Make me amongst them ('tis my suit!)
The last one, and the least.

And when they all are fed, and have
    Drunk of thy living stream,   10
Bid thy poor Ass (with tears I crave !)
    Drink after them.

Thy love claims highest thanks, my sin
    The lowest pitch :
But if he pays, who *loves much,* then
    Thou hast made beggers rich.

Jacobs Pillow, and Pillar.

I see the Temple in thy Pillar rear'd,
And that dread glory, which thy children fear'd,
In milde, clear visions, without a frown,
Unto thy solitary self is shown.
'Tis number makes a Schism : throngs are rude,
And God himself dyed by the multitude.
This made him put on clouds, and fire and smoke,
Hence he in thunder to thy Off-spring spoke ;
The small, still voice, at some low Cottage knocks,
But a strong wind must break thy lofty rocks.   10

    The first true worship of the worlds great King
From private and selected hearts did spring,
But he most willing to save all mankinde,
Inlarg'd that light, and to the bad was kinde.
Hence Catholick or Universal came
A most fair notion, but a very name.
For this rich Pearl, like some more common stone,
When once made publique, is esteem'd by none.
Man slights his Maker, when familiar grown,
And sets up laws, to pull his honor down.   20
This God foresaw : And when slain by the crowd
(Under that stately and mysterious cloud
Which his death scatter'd) he foretold the place,
And form to serve him in, should be true grace
And the meek heart, not in a Mount, nor at
Jerusalem, with blood of beasts, and fat.
A heart is that dread place, that awful Cell,
That secret Ark, where the milde Dove doth dwell
When the proud waters rage : when Heathens rule
By Gods permission, and man turns a Mule.   30

This litle *Goshen*, in the midst of night,
And Satans seat, in all her Coasts hath light,
Yea *Bethel* shall have Tithes (saith *Israels* stone)
And vows and visions, though her foes crye, None.
Thus is the solemn temple sunk agen
Into a Pillar, and conceal'd from men.
And glory be to his eternal Name !
Who is contented, that this holy flame
Shall lodge in such a narrow pit, till he
With his strong arm turns our captivity.   40

But blessed *Jacob*, though thy sad distress
Was just the same with ours, and nothing less ;
For thou a brother, and blood-thirsty too
Didst flye, * whose children wrought thy childrens wo :
Yet thou in all thy solitude and grief,
On stones didst sleep and found'st but cold relief ;
Thou from the Day-star a long way didst stand
And all that distance was Law and command.
But we a healing Sun by day and night,
Have our sure Guardian, and our leading light ;   50
What thou didst hope for and believe, we finde
And feel a friend most ready, sure and kinde.
Thy pillow was but type and shade at best,
But we the substance have, and on him rest.

* *Obadiah chap.* I. II.   *Amos chap.* I. II.

The Agreement.

I wrote it down.   But one that saw
And envyed that Record, did since
Such a mist over my minde draw,
It quite forgot that purpos'd glimpse.
    I read it sadly oft, but still
    Simply believ'd, 'twas not my Quill ;

At length, my lifes kinde Angel came,
And with his bright and busie wing
Scatt'ring that cloud, shewd me the flame
Which strait, like Morning-stars did sing,   10
    And shine, and point me to a place,
    Which all the year sees the Suns face.

52 feel] feel, *LGCB*

O beamy book ! O my mid-day
Exterminating fears and night !
The mount, whose white Ascendents may
Be in conjunction with true light !
  My thoughts, when towards thee they move,
  Glitter and kindle with thy love.

Thou art the oyl and the wine-house :
Thine are the present healing leaves,   20
Blown from the tree of life to us
By his breath whom my dead heart heaves.
  Each page of thine hath true life in't,
  And Gods bright minde exprest in print.

Most modern books are blots on thee,
Their doctrine chaff and windy fits :
Darken'd along, as their scribes be,
With those foul storms, when they were writ ;
  While the mans zeal lays out and blends
  Onely self-worship and self-ends.   30

Thou art the faithful, pearly rock,
The Hive of beamy, living lights,
Ever the same, whose diffus'd stock
Entire still, wears out blackest nights.
  Thy lines are rays, the true Sun sheds ;
  Thy leaves are healing wings he spreads.

For until thou didst comfort me,
I had not one poor word to say :
Thick busie clouds did multiply,
And said, I was no childe of day ;   40
  They said, my own hands did remove
  That candle given me from above.

O God ! I know and do confess
My sins are great and still prevail,
Most heynous sins and numberless !
But thy *Compassions* cannot fail.
  If thy sure mercies can be broken,
  Then all is true, my foes have spoken.

But while time runs, and after it
Eternity, which never ends,   50

Quite through them both, still infinite
Thy Covenant by *Christ* extends ;
 No sins of frailty, nor of youth
 Can foil his merits, and thy truth.

And this I hourly finde, for thou
Dost still renew, and purge and heal :
Thy care and love, which joyntly flow
New Cordials, new *Cathartics* deal.
 But were I once cast off by thee
 I know (my God !) this would not be.   60

Wherefore with tears (tears by thee sent)
I beg, my faith may never fail !
And when in death my speech is spent,
O let that silence then prevail !
 O chase in that *cold calm* my foes,
 And hear my hearts last private throws !

So thou, who didst the work begin
(For *I till* * *drawn came not to thee*)
Wilt finish it, and by no sin
Will thy free mercies hindred be.   70
 For which, O God, I onely can
 Bless thee, and blame unthankful man.

   * *St. John, chap.* 6. *ver.* 44. 65.

The day of Judgement.

O day of life, of light, of love !
The onely day dealt from above !
A day so fresh, so bright, so brave
Twill shew us each forgotten grave,
And make the dead, like flowers, arise
Youthful and fair to see new skies.
All other days, compar'd to thee,
Are but lights weak minority,
They are but veils, and Cypers drawn
Like Clouds, before thy glorious dawn. 10
O come, arise, shine, do not stay
  Dearly lov'd day !
The fields are long since white, and I
With earnest groans for freedom cry,

   58 *Cathartics*] *Catharties 1655*

My fellow-creatures too say, *Come!*
And stones, though speechless, are not dumb.
When shall we hear that glorious voice
    Of life and joys?
That voice, which to each secret bed
    Of my Lords dead,   20
Shall bring true day, and make dust see,
The way to immortality.
When shall those first white Pilgrims rise,
Whose holy, happy Histories
(Because they sleep so long) some men
Count but the blots of a vain pen?
    Dear Lord! make haste,
Sin every day commits more waste,
And thy old enemy, which knows
His time is short, more raging grows.   30
Nor moan I onely (though profuse)
Thy Creatures bondage and abuse;
But what is highest sin and shame,
The vile despight done to thy name;
The forgeries, which impious wit
And power force on Holy Writ,
With all detestable designs
That may dishonor those pure lines.
O God! though mercy be in thee
The greatest attribute we see,   40
And the most needful for our sins;
Yet, when thy mercy nothing wins
But meer disdain, let not man say
Thy arm doth sleep; but write this day
Thy judging one: Descend, descend!
Make all things new! and without end!

Psalm 65.

Sions true, glorious God! on thee
Praise waits in all humility.
All flesh shall unto thee repair,
To thee, O thou that hearest prayer!
But sinful words and works still spread
And over-run my heart and head;
Transgressions make me foul each day,
O purge them, purge them all away!

Happy is he ! whom thou wilt choose
To serve thee in thy blessed house !　　　　　10
Who in thy holy Temple dwells,
And fill'd with joy, thy goodness tells !
King of Salvation ! by strange things
And terrible, Thy Justice brings
Man to his duty.　Thou alone
Art the worlds hope, and but thee, none.
Sailers that flote on flowing seas
Stand firm by thee, and have sure peace.
Thou still'st the loud waves, when most wild
And mak'st the raging people mild.　　　　20
Thy arm did first the mountains lay
And girds their rocky heads this day.
The most remote, who know not thee,
At thy great works astonish'd be.

The *outgoings* of the *Even* and *Dawn*,
In *Antiphones* sing to thy Name.
Thou visit'st the low earth, and then
Water'st it for the sons of men,
Thy upper river, which abounds
With fertil streams, makes rich all grounds,　　30
And by thy mercies still supplied
The sower doth his bread provide.
Thou water'st every ridge of land
And settlest with thy secret hand
The furrows of it ; then thy warm
And opening showers (restrain'd from harm)
Soften the mould, while all unseen
The blade grows up alive and green.
The year is with thy goodness crown'd,
And all thy paths drop fatness round,　　　　40
They drop upon the wilderness,
For thou dost even the desarts bless,
And hills full of springing pride,
Wear fresh adornments on each side.
The fruitful flocks fill every Dale,
And purling Corn doth cloath the Vale ;
They shout for joy, and joyntly sing,
Glory to the eternal King!

43 hills] hills all *L* : the hills *G*

The Throne.

Revel. chap. 20. *ver.* 11.

When with these eyes clos'd now by thee,
        But then restor'd,
The great and white throne I shall see
        Of my dread Lord :
And lowly kneeling (for the most
        Stiff then must kneel)
Shall look on him, at whose high cost
        (Unseen) such joys I feel.

What ever arguments, or skill
        Wise heads shall use,   10
Tears onely and my blushes still
        I will produce.
And should those speechless beggers fail,
        Which oft have won ;
Then taught by thee, I will prevail,
        And say, *Thy will be done !*

Death.

Though since thy first sad entrance by
        Just *Abels* blood,
'Tis now six thousand years well nigh,
And still thy sov'rainty holds good :
Yet by none art thou understood.

We talk and name thee with much ease
        As a tryed thing,
And every one can slight his lease
As if it ended in a Spring,
Which shades & bowers doth rent-free bring.   10

To thy dark land these heedless go :
        But there was *One*,
Who search'd it quite through to and fro,
And then returning, like the Sun,
Discover'd all, that there is done.

And since his death, we throughly see
        All thy dark way ;
Thy shades but thin and narrow be,
Which his first looks will quickly fray :
Mists make but triumphs for the day.   20

As harmless violets, which give
        Their virtues here
For salves and syrups, while they live,
Do after calmly disappear,
And neither grieve, repine, nor fear :

So dye his servants ; and as sure
        Shall they revive.
Then let not dust your eyes obscure,
But lift them up, where still alive,
Though fled from you, their spirits hive.   30

The Feast.

O come away,
Make no delay,
    Come while my heart is clean & steddy !
While Faith and Grace
Adorn the place,
    Making dust and ashes ready.

No bliss here lent
Is permanent,
    Such triumphs poor flesh cannot merit ;
Short sips and sights   10
Endear delights,
    Who seeks for more, he would inherit.

Come then true bread,
Quickning the dead,
    Whose eater shall not, cannot dye,
Come, antedate
On me that state
    Which brings poor dust the victory.

I victory
Which from thine eye   20
    Breaks as the day doth from the east,

When the spilt dew,
Like tears doth shew
    The sad world wept to be releast.

Spring up, O wine,
And springing shine
    With some glad message from his heart,
Who did, when slain,
These means ordain
    For me to have in him a part.   30

Such a sure part
In his blest heart,
    The well, where living waters spring,
That with it fed
Poor dust though dead
    Shall rise again, and live and sing.

O drink and bread
Which strikes death dead,
    The food of mans immortal being!
Under veyls here   40
Thou art my chear,
    Present and sure without my seeing.

How dost thou flye
And search and pry
    Through all my parts, and like a quick
And knowing lamp
Hunt out each damp,
    Whose shadow makes me sad or sick?

O what high joys
The Turtles voice   50
    And songs I hear! O quickning showers
Of my Lords blood
You make rocks bud
    And crown dry hils with wells & flowers!

For this true ease
This healing peace,
    For this taste of living glory,
My soul and all,
Kneel down and fall
    And sing his sad victorious story.   60

57 taste] brief taste *L* : fore-taste *G*

O thorny crown
More soft then down !
   O painful Cross, my bed of rest !
O spear, the key
Opening the way !
   O thy worst state, my onely best !

Oh ! all thy griefs
Are my reliefs,
   And all my sins, thy sorrows were !
And what can I,   70
To this reply ;
   What (O God !) but a silent tear ?

Some toil and sow,
That wealth may flow,
   And dress this earth for next years meat :
But let me heed,
Why thou didst bleed,
   And what in the next world to eat.

            Revel. chap. 19. ver. 9.
Blessed are they, which are called unto the marriage Supper of the
Lamb !

The Obsequies.

Since dying for me, thou didst crave no more
        Then common pay,
   Some few true tears, and those shed for
        My own ill way ;
   With a cheap, plain remembrance still
        Of thy sad death,
Because forgetfulness would kill
        Even lifes own breath :
I were most foolish and unkinde
        In my own sense,   10
Should I not ever bear in minde
If not thy mighty love, my own defense.
Therefore, those loose delights and lusts, which here
        Men call good chear,
   I will close girt and tyed
For mourning sack-cloth wear, all mortified.

Not but that mourners too, can have
        Rich weeds and shrouds ;
For some wore *White* ev'n in thy grave,
And Joy, like light, shincs oft in clouds :   20
But thou, who didst mans whole life earn,
Doest so invite, and woo me still,
That to be merry I want skill,
        And time to learn.
Besides, those Kerchiefs sometimes shed
        To make me brave,
I cannot finde, but where thy head
Was once laid for me in thy grave.
Thy grave ! To which my thoughts shal move
Like Bees in storms unto their Hive,   30
That from the murd'ring worlds false love
Thy death may keep my soul alive.

The Water-fall.

With what deep murmurs through times silent stealth
Doth thy transparent, cool and watry wealth
        Here flowing fall,
        And chide, and call,
As if his liquid, loose Retinue staid
Lingring, and were of this steep place afraid,
        The common pass
        Where, clear as glass,
        All must descend
        Not to an end :   10
But quickned by this deep and rocky grave,
Rise to a longer course more bright and brave.

    Dear stream ! dear bank, where often I
    Have sate, and pleas'd my pensive eye,
    Why, since each drop of thy quick store
    Runs thither, whence it flow'd before,
    Should poor souls fear a shade or night,
    Who came (sure) from a sea of light ?
    Or since those drops are all sent back
    So sure to thee, that none doth lack,   20
    Why should frail flesh doubt any more
    That what God takes, hee'l not restore ?
        16 before] before. *1655*

O useful Element and clear !
My sacred wash and cleanser here,
My first consigner unto those
Fountains of life, where the Lamb goes?
What sublime truths, and wholesome themes,
Lodge in thy mystical, deep streams !
Such as dull man can never finde
Unless that Spirit lead his minde,   30
Which first upon thy face did move,
And hatch'd all with his quickning love.
As this loud brooks incessant fall
In streaming rings restagnates all,
Which reach by course the bank, and then
Are no more seen, just so pass men.
O my invisible estate,
My glorious liberty, still late !
Thou art the Channel my soul seeks,
Not this with Cataracts and Creeks.   40

Quickness.

False life ! a foil and no more, when
                    Wilt thou be gone?
Thou foul deception of all men
That would not have the true come on.

Thou art a Moon-like toil; a blinde
                    Self-posing state ;
A dark contest of waves and winde ;
A meer tempestuous debate.

Life is a fix'd, discerning light,
                    A knowing Joy ;   10
No chance, or fit : but ever bright,
And calm and full, yet doth not cloy.

'Tis such a blissful thing, that still
                    Doth vivifie,
And shine and smile, and hath the skill
To please without Eternity.

Thou art a toylsom Mole, or less
                    A moving mist
But life is, what none can express,
A quickness, which my God hath kist.   20

The Wreath.

Since I in storms us'd most to be
    And seldom yielded flowers,
How shall I get a wreath for thee
    From those rude, barren hours?

The softer dressings of the Spring,
    Or Summers later store
I will not for thy temples bring,
    Which *Thorns*, not *Roses* wore.

But a twin'd wreath of *grief* and *praise*,
Praise soil'd with tears, and tears again 10
Shining with joy, like dewy days,
This day I bring for all thy pain,
Thy causless pain! and sad as death;
Which sadness breeds in the most vain,
(O not in vain!) now beg thy breath;
Thy quickning breath, which gladly bears
Through saddest clouds to that glad place,
Where cloudless Quires sing without tears,
Sing thy just praise, and see thy face.

The Queer.

O tell me whence that joy doth spring
Whose diet is divine and fair,
Which wears heaven, like a bridal ring,
And tramples on doubts and despair?

Whose Eastern traffique deals in bright
And boundless Empyrean themes,
Mountains of spice, Day-stars and light,
Green trees of life, and living streams?

Tell me, O tell who did thee bring
And here, without my knowledge, plac'd,
Till thou didst grow and get a wing,
A wing with eyes, and eyes that taste?

Sure, *holyness* the *Magnet* is,
And *Love* the *Lure*, that woos thee down;
Which makes the high transcendent bliss
Of knowing thee, so rarely known.

The Book.

Eternal God ! maker of all
That have liv'd here, since the mans fall ;
The Rock of ages ! in whose shade
They live unseen, when here they fade.

Thou knew'st this *papyr*, when it was
Meer *seed*, and after that but *grass* ;
Before 'twas *drest* or *spun*, and when
Made *linen*, who did *wear* it then :
What were their lifes, their thoughts & deeds
Whither good *corn*, or fruitless *weeds*.   10

    Thou knew'st this *Tree*, when a green *shade*
Cover'd it, since a *Cover* made,
And where it flourish'd, grew and spread,
As if it never should be dead.

    Thou knew'st this harmless *beast*, when he
Did live and feed by thy decree
On each green thing ; then slept (well fed)
Cloath'd with this *skin*, which now lies spred
A *Covering* o're this aged book,
Which makes me wisely weep and look   20
On my own dust ; meer dust it is,
But not so dry and clean as this.
Thou knew'st and saw'st them all and though
Now scatter'd thus, dost know them so.

    O knowing, glorious spirit ! when
Thou shalt restore trees, beasts and men,
When thou shalt make all new again,
Destroying onely death and pain,
Give him amongst thy works a place,
Who in them lov'd and sought thy face !   30

To the Holy Bible.

O book ! lifes guide ! how shall we part,
And thou so long seiz'd of my heart !
Take this last kiss, and let me weep
True thanks to thee, before I sleep.

16 live] liee *1655*   18 *skin*] *skln 1655*

Thou wert the first put in my hand,
When yet I could not understand,
And daily didst my yong eyes lead
To letters, till I learnt to read.
But as rash youths, when once grown strong
Flye from their Nurses to the throng,   10
Where they new Consorts choose, & stick
To those, till either hurt or sick :
So with that first light gain'd from thee
Ran I in chase of vanity,
Cryed dross for gold, and never thought
My first cheap Book had all I sought.
Long reign'd this vogue ; and thou cast by
With meek, dumb looks didst woo mine eye,
And oft left open would'st convey
A sudden and most searching ray   20
Into my soul, with whose quick touch
Refining still, I strugled much.
By this milde art of love at length
Thou overcam'st my sinful strength,
And having brought me home, didst there
Shew me that pearl I sought elsewhere.
Gladness, and peace, and hope, and love,
The secret favors of the Dove,
Her quickning kindness, smiles and kisses,
Exalted pleasures, crowning blisses,   30
Fruition, union, glory, life
Thou didst lead to, and still all strife.
Living, thou wert my souls sure ease,
And dying mak'st me go in peace :
Thy next *Effects* no tongue can tell ;
Farewel O book of God ! farewel !

S Luke chap. 2. *ver.* 14.

Glory be to God in the highest, and on
Earth peace, good will towards men.

The one send
L'Envoy.

O the new worlds new, quickning Sun !
Ever the same, and never <u>done</u> !
The <u>seers</u> of whose sacred light — *T. V.* :
Shall all be drest in shining white,

And made conformable to his
Immortal shape, who wrought their bliss,
    Arise, arise!
And like old cloaths fold up these skies,
This long worn veyl: then shine and spread
Thy own bright self over each head,   10
And through thy creatures pierce and pass
Till all becomes thy cloudless glass,
Transparent as the purest day
And without blemish or decay,
Fixt by thy spirit to a state
For evermore immaculate.
A state fit for the sight of thy
Immediate, pure and unveil'd eye,
A state agreeing with thy minde,
A state thy birth, and death design'd: 20
A state for which thy creatures all
Travel and groan, and look and call.
O seeing thou hast paid our score,
Why should the curse reign any more?
But since thy number is as yet
Unfinish'd, we shall gladly sit
Till all be ready, that the train
May fully fit thy glorious reign.
Onely, let not our haters brag,
Thy seamless coat is grown a rag,   30
Or that thy truth was not here known,
Because we forc'd thy judgements down.
Dry up their arms, who vex thy spouse,
And take the glory of thy house
To deck their own; then give thy saints
That faithful zeal, which neither faints
Nor wildly burns, but meekly still
Dares own the truth, and shew the ill.
Frustrate those cancerous, close arts
Which cause solution in all parts,   40
And strike them dumb, who for meer words
Wound thy beloved, more then swords.
Dear Lord, do this! and then let grace
Descend, and hallow all the place.
Incline each hard heart to do good,
And cement us with thy sons blood,

That like true sheep, all in one fold *agree*
We may be fed, and one minde hold.
Give watchful spirits to our guides ! *Guardian angels*
For sin (like water) hourly glides 50
By each mans door, and quickly will
Turn in, if not obstructed still.
Therefore write in their hearts thy law, *Bib ref ?*
And let these long, sharp judgements aw
Their very thoughts, that by their clear
And holy lives, mercy may here
Sit regent yet, and blessings flow
As fast, as persecutions now.
So shall we know in war and peace
Thy service to be our sole ease, 60
With prostrate souls adoring thee, *benevolent*
Who turn'd our sad captivity !

S. Clemens apud Basil :

Ζῆ ὁ Θεὸς, καὶ ὁ κύριος Ἰησοῦς Χριστὸς,
καὶ τὸ πνεῦμα τὸ ἅγιον.

58 fast, *M* : fast. *1655* : fast *LGCB*

*The God, And The Lord Jesus Christ
and The breath (inspiration)*

affirmation of Trinity (?)

FINIS.

The God, and The

An Alphabetical

T A B L E,

Containing the several Titles of all
the Hymns or Sacred Poems in
these two Books.

FINIS.

Romans *etc.*] *no page-number 1655*   Trinity] *Yrinity 1655*

HERMETICAL
PHYSICK:
O R,

The right way to pre-
ferve, and to reftore

HEALTH.

BY

That famous and faith-
full Chymift,

HENRY NOLLIVS.

Englifhed by
HENRY VAUGHAN, Gent.

LONDON.

Printed for *Humphrey Mofeley*, and
are to be fold at his fhop, at the
Princes Armes in St. *Pauls Church-
Yard*, 1 6 5 5.

THE
T R A N S L A T O R
To the ingenious
R E A D E R.

If any will be offended with this *Hermeticall* Theorie, I shall
but smile at his frettings, and pitty his ignorance.   Those are bad
Spirits, that have the light; and such are all malicious despisers
of true knowledge, who out of meere envie, scribble and rail at all
endeavours; but such as submit to, and Deifie their rigid superstition, and twice sodden Colworts.   For my owne part, I honour
the truth where ever I find it, whether in an old, or a new Booke,
in *Galen*, or in *Paracelsus*; and Antiquity, (where I find it gray
with errors) shall have as little reverence from me, as *Novelisme.*
10 *Veritatem tempus manu-ducit.*   There is no reason (if they bind
not their owne hands) but the discoveries of Survivers and
Posterity, may and should be more perfect, then the superficiall
searches, and first attempts, or aims rather of their predecessors.
I wish we were all unbiassed and impartiall learners, not the
implicite, groundlesse Proselyts of Authors and opinions, but the
loyall friends and followers of truth.   It would not then be impossible, but that we might in a short time attain to that perfection,
which while it is envied in some, will never bee found in all.   As
men are killed by fighting, so truth is lost by disputing; for while
20 we study the figments and subtilties of Sophisters, wee cannot
search into the operations and virtues of nature.   As many as wil
consider this, it is not improbable, but they may do well.   But
despisers, and such as hate to be quietly instructed, must be
punished with silence, lest by seeking their peace, we lose our
owne.

Plautus.

*Qui mali sunt, habeant mala; qui boni, bona; bonos quòd
oderint mali, sunt mali; malos, quod oderint boni, bonos esse
oportet.*

HERMETICALL
PHYSICK &c.

Chap. I.

Medicine *or* Physick *is an Art, laying down in certain Rules or Precepts, the right way of preserving and restoring the health of Man-kind.*

The word *Medicine,* hath a manifold sense. First, It is taken for some receipt or medicament. So the *Philosophicall Stone* is termed a Medicine. The Lord hath created Medicines out of the Earth, and the wise man will not abhor them. Secondly, It is taken for the habit, or profession of the Physitian, and then it signifies the faculty of curing existent in some learned and expert 10 Professor. This habit or faculty is delineated, or methodically described and laid down in the Dogmaticall Books of Physicians, that others may learne and practise thereby. Thirdly, It is taken for, and signifies a Physicall System or Treatise, and in this latter sence it is to be understood in this place.

The Object of Medicine or Physick in this latter sence is, Man, not in general, but that man onely who desires to learn the Art of Physick, and is to be informed or instructed by this present Treatise : but the Object of Physick, as it is an habit in the mind of the Physician, is man in general, either for the preserving, or 20 the restoring of his health. The operation, use, and end of Physick, is health ; as the work and end of Physical books, is a rightly principled and instructed Physitian ; so far as instruction goes : It is termed *Hermetical Physicke,* because it is grounded upon *Principles* of true *Philosophy,* as the Physick of *Hermes* was. And for this very reason the true Philosophers applyed themselves wholly to the *Hermetic* science, that they might thereby lay a true foundation of Physick, for the *Hermetic* Phylosophy layes open the most private and abstruse closets of nature, it doth most exquisitely search and find out the natures of health and sickness, it provides 30 most elaborate and effectuall Medicines, teacheth the just Dose of them, and surpasseth by many degrees the vulgar Philosophy, and that faculty which is grounded upon the principles of the common, supposititious knowledge, that is to say, it doth much exceed and

outdo the *Galenical Physick.* This appears most evidently, because
the *Hermetical Physicians* both can and frequently doe cure those
diseases, which the *Galenists* adjudge to be incurable, as the
Leprosie, the falling sickness, the Gout, &c. That the Principles
of the *Hermetists,* are more certain then those of *Galen,* is sufficiently
verified by their performances ; besides, it is a truth which cannot
be denyed, that the Certainty and proof of the principles of all
Arts, can by no other meanes, be known and tryed but by practise,
as *Paracelsus* doth rightly urge *In Præfat. Defensionum, page* 252.
10 Now all the knowledge of the *Hermetists,* proceeds from
a laborious manual disquisition and search into nature, but the
Galenists insist wholly upon a bare received *Theorie* and prescribed
Receits, giving all at adventure, and will not be perswaded to
inquire further then the mouth of their leader. I call not those
Hermetists, who know onely to distil a little water from this or
that Herb ; nor those, who seeke to extract from other things by
their sophistical operations a great treasure of Gold, which onely
nature can supply us with : for the most ignorant amongst the
people, may make a very useful Distiller, and the other attempt is
20 most commonly the task of Sophisters and Impostors : but I call
them *Hermetists,* who observe nature in her workes, who imitate
her, and use the same method that she doth, that out of nature, by
the mediation of nature, and the assistance of their owne judgements,
they may produce and bring to light such rare effectual medicines, as
will safely, speedily, and pleasantly cure, and utterly expell the most
deplorable diseases. These are the true *Hermetists* : As therefore
I doe not approve of all those that would be called *Hermetists,* So
neither doe I condemn all those, who diligently and conscientiously
practise the *Galenicall Physick* : for some of them are precize and
30 petulant, others are sober & modest : and these latter sort
acknowledge the imperfection of their medicines, and therefore
they endeavour and take delight to adorne, inlarge, and accomplish
their profession with the secrets of *Hermetical Physick* : but the
other sort ascribe supreme perfection to that Ethnic, Antichristian
writer, and his medicines, and will not for meer envy, or out of a
childish depraved ignorance, looke upon the eminency of *Hermetic
Philosophy,* nor inquire into the secrets of it, but seek rather by
reprehending and carping those things they doe not understand,
to magnifie their own way, and with peevish and virulent language,
40 raile at the *Hermetic* professors. Now as I preferre the *Hermetical*
science to the medicines of these men : so (their Errours being

9 *Defensionum*] *Defensionum 1655*   21 workes,] workes *1655*

first laid aside,) I unite it with the Physick of the more sober *Galenists*, that theirs by consocation with ours, may become perfect and irreprehensible :

This *Joseph Quercetan*, a most expert Physician, and a learned Philosopher, whom as my master in this science I worthily honour, (for I must confess, that by his instructions (God assisting me,) I benefited very much,) did most happily performe. And many learned men even in this Age design the same thing, especially the professors of Physick in *Marburg*, who by an express and memorable decree of the most illustrious and mighty Prince 10 *William Lantgrave* of *Hassia*, proceed in that very course. And who then can justly blame me, for walking in the same path with such eminent men? I shall conclude, and give my judgement with learned *Crollius* (a man who for the advancement of the true Physick, was most worthy of a longer life) that whosoever desires to be eminent in the Art of Physick, (and none can be so, that will study onely the *Placets* of one man) must (above all things) be unbiassed and addicted to no Sect, nor any one Author whatsoever, but passe through them all in pursuit of the sincere truth, and subscribe only unto that, being mindful ever to preserve the 20 same freedome for himself, which *Horace* did.

> *Quo me cunq; rapit tempestas, deferor hospes,*
> *Nullius addictus jurare in verba Magistri.*
> Where-e'r my fancy calls, there I goe still,
> Not sworne a slave to any Masters will.

II.

Health is an incorrupt integrity, and soundnesse of the body preserved by, and depending upon the strength and virtue of the radical Balsame.

Whence followes this Consequence, that the more strong and 30 virtual the Balsame is, so much the more vegetous and healthful is the body.

III.

The strength and virtue of the Balsame, depends upon the equal and mutual conspiration of the Hypostatical Principles, that by their even and peaceful consistency, the Balsame also may legitimately perform his functions, by which he may advantage and strengthen himself with the received aliment or food which is taken in, and may also (when separation is performed by the stomack,) cast out

18 any] a-|any *1655*

*through his proper Emunctories what is not nutritive, and may
further provide that the seeds of diseases (if any lurk in the
flesh, or in the blood, in the disguise of that tincture,) break not
out, and bring suddain destruction to the body, or else may cause
that those ill seeds may by the balsames strength and vigour, be cast
out of the body as superfluous impurities, which cannot consist with
the health of man.*

It is truth therefore which the most noble and learned *Crollius*
speaks in his preface to his *Basilica Chymica*: In what body
10 soever (saith he) the *Hypostatical* principles consist by union, that
body may be judged to be truly sound.

IV.

Medicine *or* Physick, *treats either of the preservation, or of the
restoration of health.*

C H A P. 2.

Of the preservation of Health.

That part of Physick which treates of the preserving of health, is
an Art, which by certaine cautionary Rules, or Precepts, teacheth and prescribeth a certain way and meanes to defend and
20 save people from diseases.
It is by the *Græcians* termed προφυλακτικὴ : To effect what this
Art promiseth, I give these following Precepts.

I.

Lead a pious and an holy life.

For Piety (as the Apostle teacheth) is profitable for all things,
having the promise of this present life, and of that which is to
come. Now all piety consists in this, that we love God with all
our souls, and our Neighbours as our selves. Wonder not therefore, that so many in this age perish so suddainly and so soon.
30 Impiety now bears the sway : true and unfeigned charity hath no
place to abide in; Perjury, Treachery, Tyranny, Usury and
Avarice, or (where these are not,) a vicious, lascivious, and loose
life, are every where in request. The soul, which God made and
ordained to be the nobler essence, and the mistress, is now the
bond-woman, and the servile drudge to the vile body. We daily
see, that one Groom will serve to dresse and look to many Horses,
one sheepheard will keep a thousand sheep, one Herdsman as

many Kine or Oxen: but to dresse and feed one voluptuous
body

> *There's need (betwixt his clothes, his bed and bord,)*
> *Of all that Earth and Sea, and Air afford.*

And I would to God that all these would suffice! A most
unhappy truth was that of the *Stoic*, He is a servant to many,
that serves but one body: for doe but imagine thy selfe placed in
the Clouds, or neare the Starres, and from thence to looke down
and observe our actions upon earth, thou shalt not see one man
quiet, they runne all as busie as Ants over Sea and Land, through
Citty and Country, by right and wrong, to become Lordly and
rich.

> *With restless cares they wast the night and day,*
> *To compasse great Estates, and get the sway.*

What wouldst thou say at such a sight as this ? wouldst not thou
cry out with *Seneca*, *Oh the faith of Gods and men !* how many
persons doth one ambitious stomach imploy ? If brutes and wild
beasts devour or eat one another (unless they be compelled unto
it by extream famine) we presently cry out, it is a prodigie : but
what thing (I beseech thee) amongst mankind, is more frequent
then such prodigies ? The Satyrist askes the question,

> ———*When ever did (I pray,)*
> *One Lyon take anothers life away ?*
> *Or in what Forrest did a wild Bore by*
> *The tusks of his owne fellow wounded, die ?*
> *Tygers with Tygers never have debate,*
> *And Beares amongst themselves abstain from hate.*

> ———*Quando Leoni,*
> *Fortior eripuit vitam leo ? quo nemore unquam,*
> *Expiravit Aper, &c.*

But men, whom God adorned with rationall soules, kill one
another, and those to whom nature, reason, and the faculty of
speech, did (above any other creatures) commend love and unity,
do by troopes (as it were for spectacle and ostentation,) murther
and butcher themselves. Add to this, that (as *Seneca* saith) a Dogge
will bark before he bites ; stormes will threaten us before they
dissolve upon our heads ; buildings will crack before they fall,
and smoke will give us warning that fire is at hand : but the
destruction of man by man is suddain, and without the least
notice : nay, the nearer it is, it is by so much the more diligently

16 *Gods*] God *1655*   36 bark before he bites *G*: bite before he barks *1655*

concealed. And what then is one man to another? who smiles, when he hates, salutes and embraceth, when he intends destruction, who under a serene smooth countenance hides poyson, violence and blood-shed. Certainly thou wilt erre, and erre grievously, if thou wilt trust to those faces, that meet thee civilly, and salute thee fairly : they have (indeed) the complexions of men, but the conditions of Devils. Nay, thou wilt meet with some, who (as the same Satyrist hath observed,)

> *Esteem it no point of revenge to kill,*
> 10   *Unless they may drinke up the blood they spill ;*
> *Who do believe that hands, & hearts, and heads,*
> *Are but a kind of meat, &c.*

> ———*Quorum non sufficit iræ,*
> *Occidisse aliquem, sed pectora, brachia, vultus*
> *Crediderint genus esse cibi, &c.*

But thou wilt reply, that Salvages, Barbarians, and Canibals, may (perhaps) commit such villanies. Art thou no better acquainted with our Saints of *Europe*? that humane society and commerce, that godlinesse and sanctity, which we so much cele-
20 brate and commend our selves for, is nothing else but meere monopolizing, meere deceit, and a mutuall imposture. And amongst us Saints, who (in our owne opinion) are mighty righteous, tender-hearted and brotherly, there is nothing more usuall, then to have store of *Anthropophagi*, or Men-eaters : for the rich, and the great amongst us, not onely feed upon and live by the sweat, the slaughter, and the blood of the poor and opprest, but esteem them (of all others) their choicest dainties, for they are swallowed without much chewing, and there is none to deliver them : Insomuch that those sheepheards, who were said to flay
30 their sheep, robbing them of their Wool, their skins, and their flesh, and leaving them onely their bare bones, may be truly said to be more merciful then those men. So that man to man, is no more a God, but a Woolf and a Devil. Wonder not then (as I said before,) that so many amongst us dye so suddainly, and so soon for they had rather die sooner, yea and die for ever, then become sober, charitable, and truly pious.

II.

Follow after Sobriety.

For as drunkenness and immoderate feeding oppress and weaken
40 the virtue of the radical balsame : so sobriety preserves from sick-

nesse, and diseases. Sober above most Kings was *Massinissa* the *Numidian*, who standing alwaies, and at his Tent-doore, would in the open field eat his meat without sauce, being contented with dry bread, and military Commons. For which very reason he was so vegetous in old age, that at the years of fourscore and six, he begat a Sonne, and after ninety two, did in a pitched field overthrow the *Carthaginians*, who had broken their league made with him ; in which battel he did not onely supply the place of an active, and expert Leader, but performed all the duties of a common Souldier. By the benefit of this virtue of temperance, did M. *Valerius Corvinus* live to be an hundred years old, and retain'd at that age a sound mind in a sound body. And *Socrates* continued all his life long in a perfect undisturbed health : yea, sobriety (if we should fall sick,) will restore us to health. There are some who think, that *Cæsar* used no other remedy to cure his falling sicknesse, which tooke him first at *Corduba* in *Spaine*, so that by a meere spare dyet, hard labours, and tedious watchings, he escaped, and overcame that dangerous and most commonly fatall indisposition.

III.

Eat not greedily, and drink not immoderately.

Nature in Vegetables, doth not swallow down her nutriment, nor take it in ravenously, and all at a time. She doth all things leasurely, and by degrees, that her *motion* may be convenient and useful, or assisting to her *Preservation*. It is thy concernment to imitate Nature, and to do as she doth, when thou dost eat, and when thou dost drink. It is a most foul blemish upon the memory of *Alexander*, that after most of his Victories, he used to riot it with his Officers, inviting them to delicious and sumptuous feasts, in which he used alwaies to drink *Prizes*, and he that could tun in more then all the rest, was rewarded with a Talent : But this intemperate eating and drinking, did cast him into such a violent, suddaine disease, that within three dayes he dyed of it.

IV.

Let thy meat be simple and unarted.

For such victuals (saith the most industrious *Pliny*,) are the most wholesome and agreeable : Nature is but one, therefore she doth most delight in one kinde of meate and drink. Whence followes this consequence,

Thou shouldest never at one meal feed upon divers sorts of meats & drinks.

For they are of an Heterogeneous nature, and the fire of Nature, which is but one and the same, cannot work equally upon them all, and prepare (legitimately) a nutriment for his own body, out of divers and differing cibations. Every thing the nearer it is to unitie, is by so much the more perfect and durable. There are
10 infinite sorts of Trees which live very long, but they use all of them (without change) onely one kind of nutriment : But if it be so, that thou canst not abstaine from variety of meats, yet be sure (if possibly thou canst) that they have some agreement and correlation amongst themselves : For Contraries, (as *Hippocrates* affirmes) will move sedition and differences, while some of them are sooner, some latter digested and communicated to the body. *Octavius Augustus,* would never have above three dishes of meat to his supper : Imitate him, and use not too much indulgence towards thy selfe, so shalt thou live the longer and the better.

20   V.

Accustome not thy selfe suddainly to meats and drinks, which formerly thou hast not been used to feed upon, unlesse they be prescribed thee by some expert and learned Physician for thy healths sake.

For every Change is dangerous. Nature is simple and alwayes the same : and her manner of operation is simple too, and without change, and she delights altogether in constancy, and simple nutriments : but if thou dost change, she also will suffer the like change. We see daily, that those birds which are taken, and put
30 into Cages, by changing their naturall dyet, fall into divers diseases, and dye frequently. A Lamb that is nourished with the milk of a Cow, seldome comes to any improvement, but most commonly dyes.

VI.

Use Antidotes frequently, to preserve thee from poysons, and private or accidental mischiefes.

Lest thou perish by venemous meats or drinks, or by the aire thou livest in, which may be poysoned as well as thy food.

26 and her *G* : Other *1655*

Mithridates by the frequent use of an Antidote, which from him
is still called Mithridate, did so strengthen nature, that no poyson
could hurt him : And when he tooke a venemous, deadly confection of purpose to kill himselfe, it could not so much as make
him sick : So that being overthrown in battel by his Enemies, and
not being able to poyson himselfe, he was forced to command his
Armour-bearer to thrust him through, and so dyed. There be
divers kinds of Antidotes. I shall onely mention the most
effectuall. The first is *Quercetanus,* his confection of *Juniper* and
Vipers, described by him in his private dispensatory, *page* 349. 10
The second is his blessed *Theriac* : the third, his celestiall
Theriac, called so by way of Eminency, and described both in
the same Book. The fourth is *Crollius* his *Theriac* of *Mummie,*
with another very soveraigne, one described by him in his *Basilica
Chymica.* Use these Antidotes according to the Philosophers
prescriptions, and (God assisting) no poyson shall be able to hurt
thee.

VII.

Fly contagious airs, and if the aire thou livest in, be infected, change
thy habitation. 20

VIII.

Take Physick in the spring-time, and in the Autumne.

Let us consider the nature of Serpents and Vipers : these in our
stated seasons of Spring & Fall, cast off their old skins, and are
clothed with new. That Medicine or course of Physick, which in
all its circumstances answers to the great world, will work the
more easily, the more prosperously, and will have the greatest
effect. Seeing therefore that Trees, and all Roots, which in the
Winter time seem dead, doe about the entrance of the Spring
break forth and bud, putting on greenness, and a renew'd youth- 30
fulnesse and fresh vivacity as it were, therefore the wise *Ancients*
did at the very same time (by observing them) take their purging
and restorative Physick, and by that meanes (God cooperating
with them) did mightily strengthen nature, and multiply their
dayes upon earth. Such Physick as this, is the starre of man
impregnated with the Physicall tincture. Others use onely the
Philosophicall stone. These glorious medicines (whomsoever God
shall reveale them to,) may in their just Dose be taken once in
every week to the singular comfort, and incredible improvement

37 stone.] stone *1655*

of nature: So the Philosophers tell me.   The dose of the universall medicine, is the weight of one graine.

IX.

Vse not too frequently, the permissions of Marriage.

Man for procreations sake, should not abhorre the Concessions and Priviledges of lawfull love, but let him eschew all wantonnesse, and confine his desires to naturall and legitimate, and that too within the bounds of Wedlock: But in this also there must be moderation. *Solons* Law was thrice in the moneth.   Emission
10 of seed weakens all bodies: This experience tells us, for men that are addicted to this intemperance, have the most nice and tender constitutions, easily offended, and seldome fruitfull: like Trees, which bearing too much in one year, yeeld nothing but leaves in the next.   You are to understand from this *Paragraph*, that seed is two-fold, *Radical*, and *Prolific*.   The Radical seed, is the innate balsame of the body, which if it be advantaged with perfect digestion, will yeeld effusion, and a balsame of the same nature as it selfe.   In this balsame the body lives as in his proper seed.   Hence *Anonymus Leschus*, Tract. 7. instructs us, that so
20 long as there is seed in the body, it lives; but the seed being consumed, the body dies.   It is no wonder then, that so many have perished by this intemperance, who *
going to bed in a vegetous, perfect health, were found dead next morning.   If you excite a Tree to bear fruit by violent and unnaturall means, or by artificiall, as by kindling fire under his branches in an unseasonable time, you will but kill the Tree, and manifest your own indiscretion.

> * *It was not long before the publishing of this peece, that I was told by a very noble Gentleman, that in his late travailes in* France, *he was acquainted with a young* French *Physician, who for a long time had beene suiter to a very hand-some Lady, and having at length gained her consent,*
30 *was married to her, but his Nuptial bed proved his Grave, for on the next morning he was found dead.   It was the Gentlemans opinion, that this sad accident might be caused by an excessive joy, and for my part I subscribe to it; for a violent joy hath oftentimes done the worke of death: this comes to passe by an extreame attenuation, and diffusion of the animal spirits, which passing all into the exterior parts, leave the heart destitute, whence followes suffocation and death.   Scaliger Exercit.* 310. *gives the reason of this violent effusion and dissipation of the Spirits: Quia similia maxime cupiunt inter se uniri, ideo spiritus veluti exire conantur ad objectum illud externum gratum ac jucundum, ut videlicet cum eo vniantur, Illudq; sibi maxime simile reddant.   If any will*
40 *suspect, that together with this excessive joy, there was a concurrency of the other excess mentioned by my Author, I permit him his liberty, but certainly I thinke he will be deceived.*

3 *frequently*] *frequnently 1655*   12 fruitfull: *G*: fruitfull. *1655*   22 this *G*: the *1655*.   38 *gratum*] *g atum 1655*   41 *liberty*] *lib rty 1655*

Chap. 3.

Of Diseases in Generall.

Hitherto we have spoken onely of that part of Physick, which teacheth us to preserve health ; It remaines now, that we consider the other part, which treats of the restitution of health.

I.

That part of Physick which teacheth us the restoration of health, is an Art laying down in certaine precepts or rules, a sure & safe way to redeem or free sick persons from diseases. It is termed by the Grecians θεραπευτικὴ.

II.

In this we are to consider, first, the disease, and all its circumstances : secondly, the cure of it.

For the true method consists in knowing, first the disease, and afterwards the cure. The Doctrine of diseases, is termed by the *Grecians,* νοσολογία.

III.

Disease or sicknesse, is a privation, or the loss of health.

IV.

Therefore ; because health depends upon the strength and vigour of the radical balsame, sicknesse must needs proceed from the weaknesse and indisposition of it.

V.

But when the strength of the Balsame followes the conspiration of the Hypostatical principles, as his proper πάθος *or inclination, then or in that cause the infirmity of the balsame proceeds from the indisposition of the principles.*
Whence followes this consequence.

That those bodies, whose principles agree not amongst themselves, may be truly judged to be sickly and ill disposed.

VI.

Touching the disease, there are two things to be considered. First, The conjoyn'd and apparent cause of the disease, which we shall terme Extrarious. *Secondly, the cause of that Extrarious or con-joyn'd cause.*

27 *indisposition*] *ind sposition_1655* (?)

Chap. 4.

Of the Extrarious or conjoyned and apparent Cause of the Disease.

I.

The conjoyned apparent cause of the disease, I terme * by reason it is a Cause most remote from, and altogether a stranger to, our nature.

* *Extrarious* signifies such a substance, that is quite another thing, and of another disposition than ours is.

II.

10 *This Extrarious Cause is twofold, Substantial and Accidental.*

The substantial is so termed, because it is the substantiall Essence, or matter of the disease. The other is termed accidental, by reason that the conjoyned cause signified by it, is an accident, not a substance.

III.

The substantial extrarious Cause, is either an impure tincture, or a Meteor.

IV.

An impure tincture, is an impure spiritual nature, so exactly mixt 20 *with the most inward parts of our substance, that at the time of its commixtion, it doth not presently and manifestly hinder nor prejudice the functions of the Balsame, but remaining quiet and inoffensive at first, and for a time, doth afterwards by degrees, discover its enmity and force, and so infects the body.*

To this place must be referred; first, those impure seminal tinctures, by which the prolific seed is tainted, and the child that is borne of it, comes to be Hereditarily infected with the Diseases of his parents.

Secondly, the impurity of the body, that proceeds from the 30 bloud, with which the child is fed and nourished in the wombe: from which last impurity, if the substance of the Childe were not vindicated, and free'd by frequent breakings out, by the Measels, and divers other extrusions, and petty indispositions, besides the dayly discharge of it through the proper Emunctories of the body, it were not absurd to conclude, that his whole nature must needs be depraved and overcome by it. Purgations of this kind happen sometimes sooner, sometimes later, according to the strength of the Radicall balsame, which in some is slower, in others quicker and more vigorous ; as we see it exemplified in our very fields, of which some are more barren, some more fruitfull, according to their scituation, and the aspect of the Sun-beames, shining directly and favourably upon some, upon others glancingly, and for a short time, which makes some places more forward, some more back-ward, and their productions, whether flowers, or Hey, or 10 Corne, to differ accordingly, some being very good, some very bad.

V.

A Meteor is either volatile or coagulated, both kindes are Extrarious.

I call it a Meteor, because I would have the Reader to inquire, how the * Meteors of the greater world are generated, and by their Generation, to learn and find out the true Doctrine of the Microcosmical Meteors.

* I promise my English Reader, that (if God will blesse me with health, and his performing assistance) I will shortly communicate to him, (according to the Hermetic principles) a most accurate Treatise of 20 Meteors, their Generation, Causes, qualities, peculiar Regions and Forms: what spirits governe them, and what they signifie or fore-shew.

VI.

The volatile Meteor, is commonly called an Exhalation, and that is either dry or moist.

The dry Exhalation is termed a *Fume*, and the humid a *Vapour* : the fumid Exhalation, because it is a fume arising from a dry body or Principle, is hot, dry, light and subtile, always tending upwards, and is near to a sulphureous fiery nature, which will easily inflame and kindle, and so is set on fire and burns. Contrarily, a vapour 30 is an humid flux, which if it be deprived by any exterior heat of its owne cold quality and so carried up into the Region of the Air, and there condensed by cold, is presently (because of its thin, Mercurial and aqueous nature,) forced to resume its former state, and is turned againe into the nature of water. For as we see in the greater world, that those Vapors and Exhalations, which by the heat of the Sun, the influence of the Stars, and by their owne proper internall calidity, are excited and stirred up, doe afterwards afford matter for various, miraculous Meteors, and bodies im- perfectly mixt both in the Region of the Air, and in the bowels of 40 the Earth ; and that those which are of a Mercurial, cold, moist, and watry nature, doe alwayes produce Clouds, Raine, Hail-stones, Snow, Frost and winds; but those which are sulphureous, hot and dry generate Coruscations, Lightnings, Fire-drakes, Thunder-bolts, and other burning Meteors: so in the lesser world, that is in the body of man, the like, and the very same vapours and Exhalations, afford matter for the generation of many and different kinds of Meteors.   Hence it is, that so many and such various sorts of Diseases afflict man-kind.   Some of them being Mercurial, cold and moist; others sulphureous, hot and dry: Nor are they so in meer forme and accident, but in substance, that is to say, they are such in their essentiall virtue, and are generated as wel in the inferiour Region, the breast, the stomack, and the belly; as in the superiour, the head and the braine, which parts do exactly quadrate and correspond with the airy Region, and the subterraneous Concavities of the earth.   See *Quercetanus, Tetr. page* 45. 46.

VII.

The Coagulated Meteor, is termed Tartar, *of which we shall treat in the following Chapter.*

Chap. 5.
Of Tartar.
I.

Tartar *is an acrimonious, pricking and corroding, or an aluminous, acid and styptic mucilage, which is bred in the body, and being separated from its proper juyce, is by the supervenient spirit of Salt, according to the various inclination of nature, at a set time, and in those places which are most apt to receive it, collected together, and coagulated; or if that juyce be not separated from it, it putrifies: from whence come worms and other innumerable symptoms.*

Quercetanus in his advice against the Joynt-gout, and the Stone, describes it thus.   *Salsuginous* substances, because they have alwayes mixt in them some portion of earth (though the predominant part in them be Liquefactive,) are in the body of man termed *Tartar*; a most apt (in truth) and most significant terme, which was first given them from the Analogy, or similitude that was found betwixt the humours in mans body, yea betwixt his very blood and the substance of wine: which of all the fruits of vegetables, doth most abound with *Tartar*.   I doe not meane by

Tartar in this place that substance which is dissolved, and flowes in new Wines, while they are thick and turbid, which being afterwards separated, or (as the common phrase is) settled, doth as the grosser, earthy, and more impure part subside into a feculent substance, found alwayes in the bottome, and called Dregs. Neither doe I mean that *Tartar* onely, whose separation is performed by a long Tract of time, and sticks to the Dregs or Lees of old Wine-pipes. But I meane that *Tartar* also, which is in perpetual liquefaction and commixture with the most refined wines, and which gives them their tincture either red, or any other. 10 This true *Tartar*, either by Evaporation, or simple distillation, or a *Balneum Maris,* is easily discerned to be moderately hot, for the more liquid part of the humour (which was the *Vehiculum,* in which the *Tartar* in its dissolution was contained) being separated from it, the *Tartar* alone remaines in the bottom. This liquid humour, though of red wine, distills all bright and limpid, but the heavier red substance, which I call *Tartar,* stayes all behind: a solid substance, and the more you fetch out of the substantifical humour, it becomes by so much the more hard and the dryer. Nor is this *Tartar* onely in red, or white Wines, but in any other 20 though decocted, and also in the humours of mans body. Nor is it there onely in the Chylus, or nutriment, which answers in proportion to wine newly made (for from the Chylus, as from new wine, divers impure and tartareous dregs are separated,) but also in the very blood, yea in the most pure, and after the very same manner, as we described it to be in wine. And as the Art of distilling (even that which is performed by the most gentle fire) discovers and manifests unto us this kind of *Tartar*: so nature also by her naturall fury both canne and daily doth performe such separations of *Tartar,* by a consumption of the humourall parts 30 of our bodies, out of which the Dogmatical Writers of Physick, suppose the stone to be generated. And it is wonderfull to consider, how many sorts of Diseases by the intervening of obstructions or oppilations, arise out of this meere separation, particularly the joynt-gout, and the stone: which diseases according to the sentiment of these Dogmatists themselves, happen most frequently to those, who have the hottest Livers, and consequently the coldest stomacks: Who ingenerate much crudities and mucous matters, which for want of a through-digestion, may be compared to raw fruits, that failing of their due and perfect maturity, (which 40 is performed by a contemperate heat, that is all concocting and

29 canne *G*: ranne *1655*

digesting,) remaine acid, bitter, sowre and green. These being mixt with, and in the whole Masse of blood, are there by the natural heate againe concocted, and a separation is made of the more crude and tartareous portion, which sticks afterwards to the inward parts, and causing divers obstructions, is at length forcibly carried into the joynts, where it stayes and lodgeth. For every part of the body of man doth naturally delight in, and attract to it, that which is most like to it selfe : the fleshie parts are nourished by that portion of the blood, which is most thinly moist, and
10 mercuriall : the fat and marrowish parts, by that which is most oily, or sulphureous, but the joynts which are parts that be naturally glutinous and mucilaginous, love that portion which hath most likenesse and affinity with their nature ; whence it comes to passe, that this Salsuginous and Tartareous matter is taken in by them. Now, when it happens that these parts in some bodyes, either for their weakness, or an innate hereditary disposition, or some such cause cannot by a proper and particular digestion, inoffensively digest, nor expell this crude and indigested Tarta-reous matter, then is this matter, being of a saltish, viscous nature
20 coagulated in them, and the ligaments of the joynts come to be stuffed up and stiffened with it, whence proceed those acute in-tolerable paines which attend this Disease. And this is the true and genuine conjoyn'd cause of the paines and knottines of the Joynt-gout. The same cause is sometimes lesse acute, sometimes more, according to the nature and condition of the *Tartar*. For as we see that there is in the greater world, a great diversity of Salts, for the Earth yeelds first Salt-gemme, which answers in proportion to Sea-salt, that is onely saltish in tast ; then Salt-nitre which is bitter in tast, and Salt-alum which is austere and Astrin-
30 gent : afterwards Salt of Vitriol, and Salt Armoniac which are acid and hot : and lastly, those corrosive sharp Salts which are termed *Alkali*, with others that are sweet and pleasant as Sugar : so in the lesser world, that is in the body of man, there is generated a Tartar or Salt, which being dissolved, causeth onely a saltish humour, which the Dogmatical Physicians term saltish phlegme, in plaine termes, a salt water or humour. There is also generated, a nitrous or bitter Salt, which mixeth with the Urine, and causeth bitter Choler ; and a vitriolated acid salt which predominates in acid phlegme and melancholy. In like manner there be also alumi-
40 nous and austere kinds of *Tartar*, and other sorts which resemble the acrimonie of Salt, as it is manifestly seen by the various affec-

35 phlegme] phegme *1655*

tions of contractures and astrictions of the sinews, and the many perilous troubles of acrimonious humours in Dysenteries, and divers Ulcers as well inward as outward, all which are caused by the many and different kindes of Salts, which are generated in the body. For why should not this be done by those things which are most like to doe it, and most significant, and which do most properly and fully expresse the natures and diversities of Causes, having their derivation and appositenes from the very fountains of nature, who is the best Interpretress of her own concernments. These Salts (believe me) doe better expresse and discover unto us the essences and distinctions of Tartareous or saltish diseases, then those four humours which are commonly termed the Sanguine, the Phlegmatic, the Bilious, and the Melancholy, both because that these latter termes, signifie nothing unto us of the essence or matter of the Disease, and also because that those Dogmatists themselves, Hallucinate and stagger very much both in the formation or aptnesse, and in the application of their said termes.

II.

Tartar *is two-fold, Adventitious and Innate.*

III.

Adventitious Tartar, *proceeds from meat and drinke, and the Impressions of the Firmament.*

Every thing that we eat and drinke, hath in it a Mucilaginous, reddish and sandy Tartar, very noxious to the health of man. Nature receives nothing for her own use, but what is pure. The stomack, which is an instrument of the *Archæus* of man, or an internall, innate Chymist, and implanted there by God, presently upon the reception of that which is chew'd and swallowed down, separates the impure, Tartareous part from the pure nutriment : If the stomack be vigorous, especially in its faculty of separation, the pure portion passeth presently into all the members to nourish and preserve the body, and the impure goes forth into the Draught : if the stomack be weake, the impure portion is through the *Misaraic* veines conveyd to the Liver, where a second digestion or separation is made. Here the Liver separates againe the pure from the impure, the *Rubie* from the *Chrystall*, that is to say, the *Red* from the *White* : The Red is the nutriment of all the members the heart, the brain, &c. The white, or that which is no nutriment, is driven by the Liver to the Reyns and it is Urine,

which is nothing else but Salt, which being exprest from the Mercuriall portions, by the violence of the separation, is forced to a dissolution : It is dissolved into water by the Liver & so cast forth. If the Liver, by reason of its debility, makes no perfect separation, it casts that Mucilaginous and Calculous impurity upon the Reyns, where for want of a right and through separation, it is (according to the concurrency and Method of nature) by the mediation of the spirit of Salt coagulated into Sand, or *Tartar*, either Massie and Solid, or Mucilaginous. This *Tartar* therefore
10 is the Excretion of meat and drinke, which is coagulated in all mens bodies by the spirit of Salt, unless the expulsive faculty by its owne peculiar vigour or virtue, can command it into the Excrements, and so cast it out by dejection.

IV.

There are four kinds of this Adventitious Tartar, *which proceed originally from the four distinct fruits or Cibations which we receive from the four Elements.*

The first kind proceeds from the use of those things that grow out of the Earth, as from all sorts of Pulse, Grains, Fruits, Herbs
20 and Roots, upon which we feed.

The second proceeds from those nutriments which we take out of the Element of Water, as from fish, shel-fish, &c.

The third is from the flesh of Birds and beasts, &c.

The fourth comes from the Firmament, which the spirit of Wine, in respect of its subtilty, doth most resemble. This kind of *Tartar* is of a most forcible impression, while the Air being primarily infected with the vapours of the Earth, the water and the firmament doth afterwards annoy us : as wee frequently see in those acute and pernitious Astral Diseases, the Pleurisie, the
30 Plague, the Prunella, &c.

V.

Tartar *innate, is that which is cogenerated with man in his mothers wombe.*

VI.

Besides these impure Tinctures and Meteors, there is another substantial Extrarious cause, which cannot be reduced to a certaine kind.

To this must be referred, those *Insecta's* or quick Creatures which sometimes (though rarely) are generated in the body, as
40 Snakes, divers worms, &c.

Secondly, those things must be referred hither, which by inchantment and the mediation of evill spirits, are invisibly and insensibly conveyed into the bodies of men and Women.

Thirdly, We are to reduce to this Aphorisme or Canon all Splinters, Bullets, or other weapons, which being violently thrust or shot into the body, lie deeply in the flesh, or under the skin.

VII.

We have now done with the Substantial Extrarious Cause. To the Accidental, I shall referre all disproportions of Limbs, Gibbosities, Luxations, Wounds, and fractures of bones. 10

Chap. 6.

Of God, the first and supreme Cause of the Extrarious Cause.

Having now done with the Extrarious or conjoyned and apparent cause of the disease, I shall consider the cause of that Extrarious Cause.

I.

This Cause I shall divide into six heads or branches. The first of which is God. 2. Excesse and defect of Necessaries. 3. Fire. 4. Hereditary impurity. 5. Imagination. 6. Violent Illation. Of these I shall treat in their order; and first of GOD. 20

Man, because he is made in the Image of God, is bound also to live according to his *Will.* I mean his will revealed and laid down in the Ten Commandements, and the holy Scriptures, namely in those Bookes onely which were left unto us, and which (without scruple) we have received from the holy Prophets, and the Apostles of the Lord and Saviour: but when we transgresse and violate this Law and will of our maker, then doth God send upon us condigne punishments, amongst which *Diseases* are numbred in the very Booke of the Law. For thus saith the Lord: If ye shall despise my statutes, or if your soules abhor my judgements, 30 so that ye will not do my Commandements, but that ye break my Covenants: I also will do this unto you, I will even appoint over you terrour, consumption and the burning ague, that shall consume the eyes, and cause sorrow of heart. I will also smite thee in the knees and the legges with a sore botch, that cannot be healed, from the sole of thy foot unto the top of the Head. I will make the Pestilence cleave unto thee, untill it hath consumed

36 the Head] thy head *G*

thee from off the Land which thou possessest. And in another place, The Lord shall smite thee with a Consumption, with a Feavour, and with an inflammation and extream burning, and with the Sword, and with Blasting, and with Mildew: and they shall pursue thee untill thou perish. And the Heaven that is over thy head, shall be brass, and the Earth that is under thee shal be Iron. The Lord shall make the Raine of thy Land powder and dust, from heaven shall it come down upon thee, untill thou be destroyed. *Levitic.* Cap. 29. 16. *Deuteron.* 28.
10 And in the new Testament, that everlasting and blessed Physitian, the Holy *JESUS,* who came not to destroy, but to save the world; after he had healed the impotent man, who had beene sick of his infirmity eight and thirty years, he dismissed him not without this loving and gracious caution: Behold, thou art made whole, sinne no more, lest a worse thing come unto thee. S. *John* Chap. 5. 14. and S. *Paul* also in his first Epistle to the *Corinthians,* rebuking that new and sinfull custome (which had crept then into that Church) of prophaning the Lords holy Supper, with their own intemperate feasts, objects to them, that sharp visitation by
20 Diseases, which (for that very abuse) God had punished them with: For this cause (saith he) many are weak and sickly among you, and many sleep: for some of them had beene punished with death. Thus is the just and all-seeing God, the first and supreme cause of the Extrarious cause.

CHAP. 7.

Of the excesse and the defect of necessaries, which is the second cause of the Extrarious cause.

Excess of Necessaries, is to be considered, first in Victuals, where the offence is threefold. 1. In superfluousness. 2. In
30 variety. 3. In our manner of receiving them. We offend in superfluousness, when that which is to nourish us is taken in too great a quantity: whence follow frequent and unwholsome evaporations and belchings, which so fill and oppresse the vessels and Organs of the spirits, that they are hindered in their functions; or the meat with its weight and quantity so indisposeth us, that the inordinate operation and digestion is retarded. Innumerable are the Diseases and molestations which proceed from this particular intemperance.

1 thou] thon *1655*   15 whole,] whole *1655*   28 Excess] Fxcess *1655*
30 variety] vairety *1655*

We offend in variety, when at one dinner or supper, we eate many and divers kinds of Meats and Drinkes, for these having a great dissimilitude and enmity amongst themselves, cause divers inconveniences by their various dissents and unequall digestion.

We offend in the manner of receiving, when we eate hastily, or swallow our meat before it be well chew'd and devour our Drinke like Whales, as those are accustomed who drink healths (as they term them) at Meales, taking off whole Bowles and Tankards ἀπνευστί, without so much as breathing time, and thinke the excess very fashionable & praiseworthy.   10

Another Excess in Necessaries, happens about taking of rest and watching: When the Animal spirits by too much sleep, are by degrees habituated into a certaine dulness, so that they perform their functions sluggishly, remitting still something of their due vigour, until at length they lose all their activity, and are naturalized (as it were) into an incurable stupidity. Contrarywise by too much watching they are easily inflamed, so that oftentimes they cause Maniacal fits and phrensies, with divers others most desperate consequences.

A third excess of Necessaries, happens from cold and heat. 20 Excess of heat happens, either when the body is over exercised, or when any other Extraneous heat hath too free an access to it, and the innate fire of nature is beyond measure excited thereby, so that inordinate exhalations are caused in the body, which produce an excessive and dangerous resolution and weakness of parts. Excess of cold happens either by a suddaine Refrigeration, or cooling after Exercise, or when we expose our selves too much to cold weather, which hinders the evaporation of Excrementitious Exhalations by stopping the Pores, and beating them back into the body, where they lodge and remaine: Whence it comes to 30 pass, that being of an Extrarious malignant disposition, they afford matter and foment for many and severall kinds of diseases.

A like excess to this, proceeds frequently from the hardness and thick Callousness of some peoples skins, by which fault (because little or no perspiration is performed) the *secret*, and the *Ambient* Aire of their bodies is intercepted, so that there is no liberty for inspiration or exspiration.

8 ἀπνευστί *M*: ἀπναστῇ *1655*

Defect of Necessaries is first, the want of meat and drink in their due time and proportion. This is either famine or thirst. Secondly, The want of naturall rest, according to the Verse,

Quod caret alterna requie, durabile non est.

The strongest body, and the best
Cannot subsist, without due rest.

Thirdly, The want of Refrigeration or coolness of aire, which by its needfull community and permeation, allayes and tempers the inward heat of the heart.

Fourthly, and lastly, the want of due and requisite heat, by which the Excrementitious Exhalations of the body are vented forth, and the animall spirits incited to their peculiar functions.

C h a p. 8.

Of Fire, the third Cause of the Extrarious Cause.

By Fire in this place, I understand not onely Kitchin-fire, or any other fire that burns, but also the celestiall fire of the Sun, and the native implanted fire of all the parts of mans body.

I.

Externall fire is the producent of Extrarious Causes by its separative power or faculty, by which it separates & extracts them from other bodies, & communicates them afterwards to our nature.

II.

The Internal, innate fire, produceth Extrarious causes, when by digestion it separates the impure part, from that food or matter in which it first resided, whence our natural substance comes to be infected.

So the naturall heat digests our meat, and by the assistance of the innate Salt dissolves it, that man may retain or keep in his body, that which is agreeable to his nature, and joyne it to his essence: but that which is contrariant, he segregates from the other, and casts forth at his proper Emunctories. This Segregated matter, or Excrement, doth oftentimes mightily afflict the body, and that it doth two manner of waies. The first by being retained in the body, or for want of evacuation. The second, by a noysome fetid Exhalation, and sent ascending from it to the nobler parts, when it is so retained. It offends by retention first, when it is carried (indeed) to the naturall Emunctories, or dejicient parts ; but the weakness of the expulsive faculty is so great, that it cannot drive it out. Secondly, When it is left in the very stomack without farther Exclusion. Thirdly, when some subtil poyson, in and together with the nutritive portion or Chylus, doth convey and insinuate it self into the most inward parts of the body : which poyson was first taken in with meat and drink. It happens often (saith the most learned and expert *Quercetanus*) that when the naturall Balsame is tainted by some impurity proceeding from food or nutriment, it doth afterwards give way and occasion for many dangerous symptomes and diseases. This *Paracelsus,* the great Father and leader of the *German* Philosophers, in his Treatise of the *Being, and nature of poyson,* doth most learnedly expound. The Stars also doe frequently powre down into the Aire, and upon the Earth, certaine Astral Emunctions, and Arsenical vapours, with other noxious Excretions and Exudations. See his Treatise of the *Being,* and the power of the Stars over inferiour Bodies. Hence proceed Distraction, Phrensies, Plurisies, the Plague, and frequent, suddaine Dysenteries. Putrified things grow to be noysome and hurtfull, by the meanes of those corrosive Salts and fuliginous Exhalations, which partly by an externall, partly by their own internall heat, are excited out of them and dispersed. Moreover the Excrements of man, when they happen to be retained in the body, are subject to a Re-putrifaction, and frequently doe so, and Wormes are generated out of them : In this Case, the fuliginous, malignant spirits of that foul Masse, ascend to the braine, whence proceed suddaine madnesse, the Vertigo, the Falling-sickness, and divers other lamentable diseases. There are also certaine living Creatures, which (if they be applyed to man) will by their naturall heat, suddainly indispose him, by *emission* of that which is most remote from, and inconsistent with his nature. *Cantharides* are so full of this virulency, that being onely externally applyed, they prove oftentimes pernicious. *Bartholomew Montagnana* reports, that a certain Citizen of *Padua,* applying them onely to one of his knees, did bleed at the Urinary passage, five quarts of blood. He affirms also, that the like inconvenience happened to another, who applyed them to his great Toe, to take off the Leprous scurfe of his Nayls. The

Basilisk hath such a subtil and violent poyson in his eyes, that his very looks infect and kill. How hurtfull Minerals are, when elevated into Mercuriall vapours, may be read at large in *Paracelsus* his books, *Von den Bergkranckheiten.*

III.

That Extrarious Causes, and divers indispositions, are introduced by common fire, none is ignorant.

Alchymists, Goldsmiths, and *Colliers,* can sufficiently prove this point, who are oftentimes so offended with vehement searching, 10 Sulphureous, Arsenical and Mercurial smoaks, that they fall into desperate and most painfull Diseases. The smoake of *Galbanum,* and *Hartshorne,* will induce the Lethargy.

C H A P. 9.

Of Hereditary impurity, which is the fourth Cause of the Extrarious Cause.

I.

Hereditary *infection, is a transplantation of extrarious Causes, performed by impressing a fixt tincture, springing from another fixt salt into the prolific seed, which Parents contribute to the Genera-*
20 *tion of Children.*

Salt alone and onely, is of all the three Principles fixt and firme. Therefore those Diseases which proceed from the indisposition of the Salt, are radically fixt, and for the most part Hereditary, as the *Leprosie,* the *Stone,* the *Joynt-gout,* and the like. But those Diseases which spring from any infirmity of the fluxible and volatile principles, that is to say, from *Mercury* and *Sulphur* (as all manner of Cathars and Feavers do,) cannot so easily infect posterity: for these Diseases neither fix their seeds firmly, nor deeply, because they have not their tinctures so tenaciously imprest. The nature of this 30 kind of fixed Salt or Sulphur, may be perfectly discern'd in the seeds and the roots of Plants: for if you take but some particles of them, and transplant them, those very peeces will take root and grow, and bear fruit: But neither the leaves, nor the flowers in which the volatile Mercury & Sulphur have their seat, will do so. Now the fixed Salt is alwaies conserved in the root, and in some pithy stalks & Siens, or Graffes: but the fixed Sulphur is in the

4 *Bergkranckheiten M*: *Bergfrancfheiten 1655*   18 *another*] *another 1655*

seed. And this is the reason that the transplantation of all *Vegetals*, is performed by these onely : but by the Mercuriall parts, which easily fade and wither, it cannot be done ; nor by those parts, which have onely in them a volatile Sulphur, as the flowers, and the leaves of some Vegetables. See *Quercetan*, in his advice against the joynt-gout, and the stone.

Therefore (saith the same *Quercetanus*) whatever lodgeth in the body of the parents, that with a firm, spirituall, impure, and malignant tincture can affect or infect the radical Balsame, the vital seed, and the very root or fundamentall of humane nature : 10 that same impurity (whatever it be) doth by an Hereditary transplantation pass into, and infect the Children. But if these impure seeds of Diseases, have not taken such a deep root, nor so far corrupted the radicall Balsame : or if by the helpe of nature, and her internall Balsame, there is a separation made of them ; or if by the ministry of Art, and externall, specifical Balsames of Physick, they are effectually allayed and weakned, or are come to their proper terme and utmost duration, so that their virulency and force is quite spent and broken : in any of these Causes, Gouty and Leprous persons, doe not alwaies beget Gouty and 20 Leprous Children. For by these means, the roots of Diseases, even the most fixt and malignant are eradicated, impure seeds are purified, and the morbid tincture by long traduction becomes quite extinct. This Eradication of hereditary Diseases, and Purification of diseased seed comes to passe by the benefit and assistance of good *Seed-plots*, that is, by the excellent, wholesome temperament of the *Matrix*, in vegetous and healthy women : whence it happens, that the Fathers seed, though tainted with some morbific indisposition, is by the laudable vigour of the mothers radical *Balsame* amended, so that Arthritical and Calcu- 30 lous Fathers beget Children, which all their life-time continue healthy and unattempted by such Diseases. Yea, they beget such Children, as are not obnoxious or liable to such indispositions. In like manner also it happens, that a vegetous, healthy Father, contributing good seed, may have a sickly, impure issue, troubled with hereditary infirmities, the Fathers seed attracting to it the malignant propriety of those Diseases which possessed the Mother. Thus good Corne, if it be cast into a bad soile, will degenerate into Tares, or yeeld a very bad and a thin Crop : but sow it againe in good ground, and it will recover its former goodnesse 40 and perfection.

33 indispositions. *G* : indispositions *1655*

Chap. 10.
Of Imagination, the fifth Cause of the Extrarious Cause.

I.
Imagination *is a Star, excited in the firmament of man, by some externall Object.*

II.
When the Imagination is inflamed, or at the height, then strange passions and defections follow.

10
III.
It is inflamed first, when it feigns some object to it selfe, and longs for it, but cannot enjoy it.

Hence it comes to passe, that pregnant or breeding women (whose imagination is most vehement, because of the Starre of the Child, which upon some singular longing, doth most powerfully move them,) doe by the force of an inflamed or exalted imagination (when they faile to come by that Object they long for) impresse into the very child, the perfect forme or figure of it ; yea, it oftentimes causeth miscarriage, and the death of the Child, as
20 may be seen in this following History. A certaine woman great with child, seeing a Baker carrying Bread into the Oven with his Doublet off, longed for a peece of the Bakers shoulder, and when any other meat was offered unto her, or brought in to her sight, she would presently fall to vomit. Her Husband distrest betwixt love and pitty, offered such a large summe of money to the Baker, that he consented, & suffered her to bite off two morsels of his flesh, but being not able to endure the pain the third time, the woman presently fell in Labour, and was delivered of three boyes, whereof two were alive, and the third dead. *Mizaldus* in his first
30 Century, relates it out of *Langius.* To this first Division, must be referred those unfortunate Aspirers, who affecting some great knowledge or science, and missing to attain to it, by reason of a blockish stupidity, or imbecillity of apprehension, come to be distracted and stark mad.

IV.
Secondly, The Imagination comes to be inflamed, when by some unexpected Object or Accident, a man or woman is suddainly frighted.

Such Accidents prove oftentimes very pernicious. A causeless,
40 imaginary fear in times of infection, hath cast many into the

36 *comes to*] *comes tomes to 1655*

Plague, and the Plague hath beene their death. There lives at *Gueilburg,* a certaine Bakers wife, who being young with Child, went into the adjoyning Woods or Forrest, to gather sticks, and being very intent in gathering with her face towards the ground, a Citizen of that place comming suddainly at her, did so fright her, that (not knowing well what to doe,) she struck one hand into the other, and continued rubbing them together with a very strong compression for a good while. This woman was shortly after delivered of a Son with one hand onely, which Childe I my selfe saw, and taught there in the publick free-Schoole. In the like manner, some men that have been frighted by Phantasms, and spiritual Apparitions in the night time, have instantly fallen into grievous diseases, and some have dyed. Others by the excesse and violence of the horrour, had the hairs of their heads changed from the native colour, into a quite contrary, especially that part which they chanced to touch at the time they were so frighted. I my self have known two, who affirmed, that such a change did happen to them upon the like occasion : the one had halfe his Beard turned gray, the other had part of the haires of his head turned perfect white, the rest retaining still their first colour.   20

V.

Thirdly, The imagination is inflamed, when the stomack is offended
by some object of sence.

Such perturbations happen often, and men are frequently inclined to vomit, when they looke earnestly upon those Ejectments which another hath cast up.

VI.

Fourthly, The imagination is inflamed, when any person imagines or
fancies, that paine or trouble he is in, to be intolerable for him, and
incurable.   30

Hence it comes to passe, that men despairing of their health or redemption, contrive their owne death, and make themselves away.

Chap. II.

Of violent Illation, which is the sixth and last
cause of the extrarious Cause.

Violent Illation is performed two wayes, Corporally, and Spiritually.

12 Apparitions *G*: Apparition *1655*   34 Chap.] Cahp. *1655*

I.

Corporally, when a man or woman is wounded, thrust, or shot, or fallen, or their bones broken.

II.

Spiritually, when by the meanes and ministry of evill spirits, a man or woman is either blinded, or maimed, or any extraneous visible matter, is invisibly and without manifest violence, conveyed into, and lodged in their bodies, or when they are by any other preter-natural wayes and meanes set upon and afflicted.

10 That such things may and have been done, we shall prove by the truth of this following relation.   In the year of our Lord, 1539. there lived in the village of *Fugesta*, within the Bishoprick of *Eisteter*, a certaine Husbandman, named *Ulrich Neusesser*, who was grievously pained in the Hypochondriacal Region, with most violent and sharp stitches; whose fury and persistance made him send for a Chirurgion, and (incision being made) there was found, and taken out of his side, an Iron Naile, which lay under the skin, without the least external symptome, or discoloration of the part.   This notwithstanding, the pain ceased not, but was dayly
20 exasperated, and did more and more increase: whereupon this miserable man resolving with himselfe, that there could be no cure for him but death, snatched a knife out of the hand of his attendant, and did therewith cut his own throat.   Upon the third day after, when his body was to be drest for buriall, there were present, *Eucherius, Rosenbader* of *Weisenburg,* and *John* of *Ettenstet,* (a Town in the Dukedome of *Bavaria*,) both Chirurgions, who in the presence of as many persons as came to the Funeral, did cut up the Body, and in the fore-part of his belly, betwixt the Cartilages and the Navill, towards the side-region there were
30 found, and taken out, and seen by them all (a prodigious and wonderfull sight!) a round and long peece of wood, foure knives of steel made partly with edges, and partly with teeth like a saw, and two peeces of sharp and rough Iron, each of them being more then a span in length, and underneath all these, a great lock of haire wrapt close together and made up in the forme of a Ball.   *Mizaldus* in his sixth Century, relates this sad History out of *Langius.*

---

7 afflicted] aff i ted *1655*   19 This notwithstanding, *G* : This, notwithstanding *1655*   23 own] own own *1655*

Chap. 12.

Of the cure of Diseases.

Hitherto we have known the Disease by his Causes: It remains now that we teach the Cure of it; and this we shall doe onely by certain generall Rules or Precepts. But lest we should proceed without method, we shall divide this Chapter concerning the Cure, into seven Sections.

We shall teach, 1. What, and how manifold the Cure is. 2. How a Physician ought to be qualified. 3. Of what sort, kind or quality, the medicines or meanes of the Cure ought to be. 4. Out of what things those Remedies must be sought and taken. 5. Why Medicines sometimes cannot restore and introduce health. 6. How the Remedies or Medicaments ought to be administred. 7. How the sick man must carry or dispose of himselfe, while he is in a course of Physick.

Section 1.

What, and how manifold the Cure is.

I.

The cure of Diseases, is an operation by which a sick person is restored to his former health, and his sicknesse (what ever it be) quite expelled, and radically extirpated.

II.

The cure or healing of all Diseases, (that I may in this place make use of the most apposite, significant termes of Severinus, *out of* Crollius) *is twofold.*

1. Universal, *which is an absolute Extirpation of every radical morbid impurity, whether hereditary, or from the sinister use of food, or by the force of externall impression.*

This universall Cure is performed by a naturall medicinall Balsame, consentaneous to the nature of man, which resolves, discusseth and consumes the Seminary tinctures of all impurities and diseases: but corroborates, confirms, and conserves the innate humane Balsame; for (as *Paracelsus* teacheth) so long as the radicall humour keepes in its due quantity and proportion, no Disease or indisposition can be perceived. And in this way of

3 Disease] Diseases *1655*   5 generall] genenrall *1655*

Cure, the pluralities, particularities, and orderly Rules of Symptoms and Prognosticks, have no place, for all Diseases (what ever they be) are universally & perfectly cured by this one universall medicine. It is not without reason then, that *Raymund Lullie* affirms, that this onely one, supreme, universall medicine (to which, and in which the virtues of all other particular and specificall medicines are reduced and included) may be safely administred unto all sick persons, without inquiring what Disease they are sick of. For wise nature, by an instinct from her selfe,
10 hath given unto this her favourite-medicine, the prerogative and power to cure, and absolutely to exterminate all naturall infirmities whatsoever; yea, and to rectifie and restore her own selfe, when disordered and weakned. There be four chief kinds of Diseases, which if once confirmed, or inveterate, can be expelled by no medicine, but the universall, namely the Falling-sicknesse, the Gout, the Dropsie, and the Leprosie. To these *Paramount* Diseases, all other inferiour sicknesses, as to their proper fountaines and originalls, have relation and affinity. This universall medicine, is a Jewel much to be wished for and worthy the looking after;
20 but few are they whom God blesseth with his favourite-secret. *Lullius* adviseth all Physicians, that diligently and faithfully labour for to search and looke after it : because it is the infallible remedy against all infirmities, and the greatest and most proper restorative and comforter of the spirits in their functions : For in this medicine (as in their onely and proper subject) there is a reall and universall collection and conjunction of all the operative, effectuall virtues of generall Physick, coacted and united together by a natural method, consent and design : which virtues are otherwise, (according to the ordinary course and dispensation of
30 nature) confusedly dispersed and distributed amongst and through
* *Animalls, Vege-* her * three great Families ; and he that hath
tals, and Minerals. such an Antidote against all bodily Diseases, hath the gift of God, which is an incorrupt, incomparable, and invaluable treasure in this life : What ever infirmity cannot be healed by this competent, natural medicine, we may boldly and safely conclude, that the finger of the great God of nature is in the Cause. But the paine (when we find it to proceed from his righteous hand,) is by much the more tolerable, and we ought to beare it patiently, and thankfully, until the Almighty Physician
40 himselfe will be pleased to heal us, by those wayes and means which his divine and unerring wisdome shall judge the best.

3 perfectly] perfecty *1655*   8 Disease] Dis ase *1655* (?)   26 universall] universal *catchword 1655*

III.

2. Next to the universall, is the particular cure, by which the roots of diseases, and the Seminal tinctures themselves, are not alwayes taken away ; but the bitter fruits of them, the Symptoms, Paroxismes, and paines, are oftentimes prevented, mitigated, and so supprest, that they cannot come to their exaltation, or the worst passe, as the common phrase is. By this Cure, the Physicall evacuation of Excrements is instituted, and some considerable succours are communicated to opprest nature by the friendly, consentaneous spirits of those medicines that are administred ; which spirits can onely rightly know, and penetrate into the secret lodges and topicall residencies of the radicall morbific impurity.

Now, though this particular Cure performs no more, than we have told you in the definition of it, yet is it not therefore to be slighted, nor rejected ; for it doth oftentimes in the most desperate diseases, doe the work of the universal, because the most mercifull God hath discovered unto us certain secret-natural universals, of which some containe in them the nature of the whole Heaven, others of the whole Air, and some againe of the whole earth, by whose help most Diseases are easily known and cured. Morcover specifical, appropriate medicines, when they are rightly refined and spiritualized, will emulate the virtue of the universal, by consuming radical impurities & strengthning the virtue of the innate humane Balsame. Seeing then that we want the universal, it will be happy for us, if we may attaine to the true knowledge of (at least) the particular, subordinate, specifical and individual kinds and means of cures.

Section 2.

How a Physician ought to be qualified.

I.

Every Physician that desires to cure sick persons well and happily, must be a sound Christian, and truly religious and holy.

For true and perfect medicines, and the knowledge of them, can no where be had, but from God, whom we can serve by no other means in this life, but onely by piety, and piety hath included in it fervent and incessant supplications unto God, hearty and frequent thanksgivings for his gracious and free benefits, with sincere and actuall love towards our Neighbours. God is so infinitely good and kind, that he doth dayly give, and offer both

to the *good* and to the *bad,* all those things which are necessary both for their *sustenance* and their *health* : but that we use those gifts to the glory of God, and the good of our Neighbours, piety alone is the onely cause.   Therefore, if thou desirest to select, and extract convenient and effectuall Medicines out of those Myriads of Creatures, which by the secret power of their Creator, dayly flow upon thee, & appear about thee, *Fear God, and love thy Neighbour as thy selfe.*   This being done, I affirm it to thee, thou shalt find those things which will fill thee with joy.   Thou
10 maist easily apprehend by what I say, that he is unworthily permitted to be a Physician, whose practise hath no other aim then Covetousness and Usury, and abuseth the gifts of God (I mean his medicinal favours and discoveries,) to hoord up for himselfe the riches of this world.   They are all impostors, and faithlesse Mountebanks, who professe Physick, and its great ornament Chymistry, out of such a sordid, uncharitable, and unjust design.

II.

He must be the servant, not the Master of nature, and according to
20 *the sentiment of* Hippocrates *and* Galen, *he must be a profound Philosopher, and expert, or well vers'd in the Art of healing.*

He must be throughly seen in *Philosophy,* because there be two sorts of Philosophers.   The one (who are in truth but Philosophers by name,) after the common Doctrine of the Schooles, inquire onely into the Elementary qualities of sublunary bodies : but the other sort (who are the true Philosophers indeed) search into the most secret operations, proprieties, and performances of nature : her most private Closets, and Sanctuaries, are ever open unto these ; whence it comes to passe, that they have a perfect
30 experimentall knowledge by the light of Nature, and are indeed true Physicians : For the innate naturall faculty of all productions of the earth, is, by the Chymical dexterity of these latter sort of Philosophers, vindicated from the drossie adherencies of the matter, and united with the firmamentall virtue, or occult quality, which is caused and communicated to them, by the influence of the Stars.   This Art of refining, and uniting inferiours to their superiours, makes a compleat and a successeful Physician.

III.

He must be an Alchymist skilfull in all spagirical operations, to
40 *separate the pure from the impure, the drossie and venemous parts*

of his medicinall Ingredients, from the usefull and sanative, and one that knowes exactly how to prepare, and when to administer Chymical medicines for the restoration of his Patients.

For as Gold is seven times purified, so a Physician ought to try and refine all his Physicall Materials by the ministry of fire, which separates the good from the bad. Also he ought to have in some things, a certain and confirmed knowledge acquired by long experience, and a diligent daily inspection into the works of nature; for true Philosophy is nothing else, but a Physicall practise or triall, communicating daily to industrious and learned 10 operators, most usefull and various conclusions and medicines. And after all the coyl of Academical licenciated Doctors, he onely is the true Physician, created so by the light of Nature, to whom Nature her selfe hath taught and manifested her proper and genuine operations by Experience.

Section 3.

Of Medicines, what their qualities should be,
and how prepared.

I.

Physicall Remedies or Medicines, should both expell the disease, and 20 *strengthen nature.*

Hence came that infallible Rule of Physicians, *Contraries* are cured by their *Contraries.* For *Contraries,* by the consent of all Philosophers, expell and drive out one another, therefore it is necessary, that those Medicines which take away the Disease, be repugnant and contrary to the Disease : and for the same reason, they must be auxiliaries and consentaneous to our nature. Upon which very consideration, that famous principle of the *Hermetists* is grounded : *Every like is cured by its like.* Therefore *Medicines,* as they respect, or look to the Hypostatical principles, ought also 30 to have some correspondence with the nature of the disease, but in their Energie and effect, they must be adversant and quite opposite. Thus the stone which proceeds from *Tartar,* or coagulated Salt, is cured by Salt, but it must be Analytical or resolvent salt. The Joynt-gout also which proceeds from Tartareous, sharp and corrosive Salts, is cured by lenitive and consolidating Salts. In like manner, sulphureous Diseases must be cured by their proper and specificall sulphurs : but to inflammatory sulphur, that causeth Feavers, we must oppose acid, Vitriolated sulphur, which is a most effectuall cooler, and will coagulate and allay those incensed sulphureous spirits. Whence followes this Consequence.

That some Medicines may be corrosive, without any danger or prejudice.

But with this Caution, that they be so qualified, as not to work upon the innate, radical Balsame, but only upon that Extrarious malignant matter, which is the conjoyn'd and apparent cause of the Disease.

II.

It is requisite, that of Medicines, some be Spagyrically prepared, and some otherwise.

For Chymical remedies must not be used at all times, nor in all Causes, but onely then, when our internal natural Alchymist is insufficient of himselfe to separate the pure from the impure, and perfectly to extract out of compound Medicines, that noble Essence in which the force and virtue, or spirit of the medicament, is chiefly resident : or when there is a necessity in fixed and rooted Diseases, to use minerall remedies, that confirmed and obstinate Maladies may be set upon, and brought under by such powerfull and active Medicines that will not be baffled. It is otherwise a foolish and needlesse imployment, to separate that by Chymistry, which nature her selfe will performe with more ease and dexterity. And Nature knowes better what is most convenient for her, then any Physician : for she makes use of her own proper fire, and Magnet, which attracts both from Physick and food, that which is congeneous, and most like to her selfe : whereas an Artist on the contrary, doth not at all times use the like fire, nor exactly in the same degree to perform his operations. For which cause, the true Hermetical Physicians, do not at all times administer Minerals ; but most commonly when they exhibit Minerals, they make use also of Medicines extracted out of Vegetables, or to quicken the operation of these latter, they give a competent and safe quantity of the former.

III.

All Medicines must be specificall and appropriated to the Disease.

That is to say, they must have in them by the gift of God, such a virtue, that is peculiarly proper, and designed (as it were) to remove those diseases against which they are administred. Whether they be universally so gifted, or particularly for some one sort of disease. That body, or subject in nature, which will be easily corrupted, cannot be medicinall for all diseases : and this is the reason, that out of such bodies, the true Philosophers extract onely specifical Antidotes, whose power or virtue is effectual onely against some particular kind of disease. That thou maist have some knowledge of those materials or ingredients which are requisite and proper to make such specifical Medica- ments, thou must diligently read the Bookes of the *Hermetists,* 10 *De signaturis rerum,* That is to say, Of those impressions and Characters, which God hath communicated to, and marked (as I may say) all his Creatures with. These Bookes thou must carefully peruse, and all others which teach us the true and solid practise of Physick. But if it would please God to blesse thee with the universal Medicine, these studies, and all other cures whatsoever, might be safely pretermitted. This glorious uni- versal Medicine (without all doubt) is to be extracted out of such a subject, whose innate Balsame preserves both it *Selfe,* and the *Body* in which it exists from all corruption. This body is so 20 adequate, and temperated with such a just and even proportion of all the foure Elements, that the qualities of no one of them, can ever possibly corrupt it. If thou conceivest it may be had in another kind of subject, thou dost but play the fool and deceive thy selfe. What ever Nature hath, that she can give us; what she hath not, she neither will, nor can afford. To the wise man one word is enough. I speake out of the true light of nature : My Studies also hitherto cannot find any other *Fundamental* of an universal Medicine.

Section 4. 30

Out of what things Medicines must be sought.

I.

They must be sought. 1. *Out of the Word of God.* 2. *Out of Nature : and in nature, out of Vegetals, Animals, and Minerals.*

In this search, we must first pray for Gods assistance ; and in the next place, we must attend to the instructions of the wise Ancients. If thou couldst finde out such a thing as would purge and rectifie nature in the great world so effectually that ever after she would remaine sound and unimpaired, so that nothing of her Homogeneous essence and perfection, could be saved from her by any Extraneous fire, then (without doubt) both the way to, and the miraculous Energie of this onely true and undeceiving medicine were in thy hands.

Section 5.

Why Medicines cannot alwayes restore sick Persons to their former health.

Oswaldus Crollius, a truly learned and expert Physician, in his
10 Preface to his *Basilica Chymica,* doth most fully and judiciously handle this point. His words are these. It is observed sometimes, that sick persons by the most convenient and effectuall Medicines, cannot be healed for some one or more of these eight subsequent reasons.

The first is, because their appointed time or terme of life is come, which by no humane wit or Medicine can be prolonged. For there is no remedy upon earth, by which our corruptible bodies can be freed from death, the decreed penalty, and the wages of our sinnes : But there is one thing, which (if we add
20 holinesse to it,) will keep back and restrain corruption, renew youth, and lengthen our short life, as heretofore in the *Patriarchs.*

* *The terme of life is moveable, not fixed: conditionall, not positive, as appears by that commandement. which* S. Paul *observed to be the* first *with a promise ; and by many other reasons, which cannot be inserted in this place.*

Now though our life may be shortned and * prolonged ; yet because of the punishment for sinne, we must by the immutable decree of the eternal Law, unavoydably die : for a conjunction of different Natures, and things (suppose a Spirit and a Body) must necessarily induce a dissolution, else we should state a Pythagorical Metempsuchosis, or a revertency in
30 ages as Plato did. And in this Case the use of our universall and supreme Medicine, will prove as vaine and ineffectuall, as an old womans *Recipe,* because the Marriage of souls and bodyes, ordained by an inevitable necessity for divorcement and separation, can by no industry of Artists, nor Ayds of nature be rendred perpetuall ; for the statute Lawes of the present things, and their great Law-giver, are inviolable. It is impious therefore to seeke, and impossible to find out such a Medicine, that will carry us alive beyond those bounds, which the very Father of life will not have us to transpasse.

The second reason is, Because that sick persons are tootoo often brought to such a lamentable passe by the ignorance of unlearned Physicians, and their pernicious *Recipe's*, that the best and most virtual medicines can doe them no good, their bodies being utterly poysoned, and made immedicable by those fatal Tormentors and Executioners of mankind. In this desperate Case (most commonly) is the Chymicall Physician called upon ; but then would I have him to call to mind, that saying of *Trophilus* in *Plutarch*, which affirms that man onely to be the compleat Physician, τὰ δυνατὰ, ἔφη καὶ τὰ μὴ δυνατὰ, δυνάμενος ἀναγινω- 10 σκειν : and not to cast away (out of vaine-glory,) their soveraigne and undeserved medicines, to salve the credit of such detestable villaines, whose infamy is past cure : οὐ γὰρ μετανοεῖν, ἀλλὰ προνοεῖν χρὴ τὸν ἄνδρα τὸν σοφὸν : Let them beware also, that they suffer not their Medicaments to be mingled with the sluttish and venemous compositions of others, lest the ill consequence of such doings be laid to their charge, and the success or good event (if any comes to passe,) be arrogated by, and ascribed unto those impudent and clamorous impostors ; for such a perverse and execrable envy possesseth these Medicasters, that to disgrace those that are more 20 learned and expert than themselves, and to keep up their owne decaying repute, they will (if they can have that opportunity) cast those Patients which are curable and towards recovery, into an incurable and hopelesse condition. Hence it comes to pass, that amongst the common sort of people, (who suffer most by them) they are publiquely saluted by the most apposite Title of *Profest Poysoners*.

The third reason is, Because the Physician is called upon too late, when nature is quite mastred or orecome, and the disease hath got his full sway ; otherwise if convenient or proper medicines 30 were seasonably, (that is to say, in a time of prevention, by resisting the beginnings and first attempts of diseases) administred, no doubt but (with Gods blessing and assent) the consequence and effect would be happinesse and health.

The fourth reason is, because the sick person will not punctually observe the Physicians prescriptions : for it happens too often, that Diseased people charge the Physician or his Medicines, with those ill events which by some omission or irregularity (contrary to that golden Law of the *Locrenses* in *Ælianus*,) they have drawne upon themselves. 40

10 ἀναγινωσκειν] ἀνάγινασκειν *1655*   30 medicines] medines *1655*

The fifth reason is, because the nature or peculiar propriety of some persons, are not inclinable or adapted to health, as we see some timber to be so tough and knotty, and out of a certaine natural defect, to degenerate into such an untowardnesse, that by no force or Art it can be cleft or wrought: And it happens very frequently, that the time chosen for healing, together with the indisposition of the Stars, oppose the Cure: for what ever Disease is unseasonably, that is to say, immaturely heal'd, the party will be ever after subject to a relapse, because it is the seasonablenesse
10 or fulnesse of time, that (like harvest) gives a firme and a fixed health.   A ripe Pear will fall off the Tree spontaneously, but if we seeke to have it off, while it is green, we must either bruise the tree by shaking it, or with more violence break off the bough. Therefore, if these considerations be neglected, especially in the Cure of *Astral* diseases, we shall but lose our labour, and come off with prejudice.   Physicians also must religiously provide, that the remedies they give, prove not worse then the Disease, therefore let them never advise their Patients to any impious course, nor consent to doe those things, which by salving the sore, destroy the
20 soule and the body too: let it be their chiefe care not to hurt, if they cannot help.   By doing so, they will keep a good conscience, which is a continuall feast, but for a bad one there is no medicine.

The sixth reason is, because the disease is come to that pitch or confirmation, from whence there can be no regress by the Laws of nature, as in perfect, absolute, and confirmed bituminous, massie, sandy, and stony coagulations: for in such consummated Diseases, no medicines can availe: nor in a native deafnesse or blindness: for what nature her selfe hath once deprived us off, that cannot be restored by any Artists, no more then corporall dispro-
30 portions and birth-maimes, or transpositions can be amended.

The seventh Cause or Reason is, the sordid, tenacious parci-monie of some rich Patients, which makes the Physician (for no Money is better disbursed, nor more honestly gotten) discontented and carelesse: sometimes also the diffidence, incredulity, and suspition of Patients, (though the Physician be never so faithful and diligent,) hinders the operation of the Medicine, and is a great impediment to the Physician himself.

The eighth and last reason is, the wisdome and the goodnesse of God, who (without further toleration) takes away the Patient,
40 lest being recovered, he should commit more, and more heynous offences against his Maker, his Neighbour, and himself, to the

30 transpositions] transpositions *1655* (?)

utter misery and perdition of his soul. For every disease is an expiatory penance, and by this divine affliction, correction and rod of judgement is the patient called upon, and required to amend his life : or else by this fatherly visitation and imposition of the Crosse, which every child of God (in imitation of his blessed Sonne) must patiently bear, he is purposely exercised to be an example of piety, submission, and perfection unto others ; for God doth oftentimes permit some particular persons to be afflicted with many and grievous Diseases, whom the cheerefulness and health of the flesh, with their dayly continuation in sins (if left without 10 rebuke,) had cast at length into some desperate spirituall malady, to the manifest hazard of their eternal welfare : for health, without holinesse, and a penitent resentment of our frequent infirmities, is no token of Gods mercy, but rather of damnation, and the portion of this life. Moreover, sinnes by weakning the forces and activities of the soule, make her impotent and unfit to govern the body ; so that the principall part being sick and unapt to rule, the bodily faculties are profusely wasted and abused, and so death is hastned on, and with it a total and a finall destruction. At least by this yoke and bridle of sicknesse, as by a wholsome kind of 20 purgatory, men will be retained in the ordinary offices of piety, and (though they be but few, who are effectually reclaimed or converted by it,) yet this detainment of their health, (which if still left to them, they had still abused,) will in some measure restrain and cut off from them, both the liberty and the power of sinning. Hitherto the most learned *Crollius.*

Thou wilt now (perhaps) object, that seeing all Diseases are not curable, it is consequently absurd, to terme any Medicine universal. I answer, That it is termed universall, not becaus it takes away all diseases at all times & in all Causes, for that it cannot do ; but 30 because it being but one, can expell and cure all those diseases, which by all other particular or specifical Medicines whatsoever can, or have been healed and eradicated ; yea, and some diseases which by no appropriated particular medicine can be healed, as the Gout, the Falling-sicknesse, the Dropsie, the Leprosie, &c. Therefore it is termed universal, because it hath in it really and effectually, all the manifest and occult virtues of all other specifical medicines, & that eminently, or by way of transcendency, so that all other medicines are subordinate and accomptable unto this.

13 of] of of *1655*   29 That it *M*: That *1655*   36 really *M*: real *1655*

Section 6.

How Medicines ought to be administred to the sick, and after what
manner the Physician must be-
have himself in their administration, and generally
in his practise.

I.

Every professor of Physick, when he is furnished with convenient,
10　　*effectuall, and rightly prepared medicines, before he enters into*
practise, must be conversant with, and acquire the friendship
of some learned and well experienced Physician, whose advise and
assistance in his first attempts, he must make use of, not omitting
his own observations.

For in the multitude of Counsellours there is safety, and a more
exact judgement is given of the Patients present condition, and
the wayes and meanes to restore him are better and surer laid.
By this Course, that opprobrious *German* Proverb, which sticks
too fast to some young Adventurers, (*Ein newer Arzt, Ein newer*
20　*Kirch-hoff:* A new Physician must have a new Church-yard,)
would be easily refuted and quite abolished. This very Course
(after serious and needful considerations) I did heretofore propose
to my selfe, and to effect it throughly, I procured and entred
into mutuall and friendly Covenants with a certaine Doctor of
Physick, who was not unlearned : and that I might by this meanes
proceed farther in my Chymical discoveries, I conversed with him
by frequent Letters, and other more familiar wayes : And this I
did, because I supposed him (at that time) to be a true Philosopher, but I could never receive one line from him, that was not
30　wholly dictated by the spirit of pride and arrogancy. At length,
when it fortuned, that (after a most loving invitation, I could not
for very moving, and extraordinary reasons, attend upon him) he
rail'd at me (though altogether innocent,) with most horrid impre-
cations, and virulent language, terming me an unsanctified villaine,
and laboured by all meanes to vilifie my studies and person, that
by such clamorous and publique discouragements, he might force
me to desist, and give over my profession. But none of these
things shall move me : for God will yet give me such friends, with
whom I may freely deliberate, and advise about Physical opera-
40　tions, and the healing of the sick : too much knowledge is oftentimes foolishness. True Philosophers walk wholly in the plaine

19 *Arzt*] *Arkt 1655*　　28 Philosopher] Philososopher *1655*

path of nature. What profits learning, where pride beares the sway, and blinds the owner? I have ever judged, the modest knowledge to be the most divine. It is true indeed, we are not all equalls: but let him that hath more of the light, walke in that shining path with modesty. I confesse indeed, and it is true, that he was my superiour by many degrees, but had he beene moved to this harsh-dealing, by a meer conceit of his superiority in learning, perhaps he would not have cast me off so as he hath done. God resisteth the proud, and gives grace even to the humble. Yea, the most wise, and the blessed *JESUS*, did humble himselfe in the very forme of a servant, that he might familiarly live and converse with the most obscure and inferiour sort of people: and he was not ashamed, nor disdained to teach those poore spirits, not a sublunary, transient knowledge, but the glorious and permanent mysteries of the Kingdome of heaven. I love still the learning of so eminent a person because others whom I love, commend it unto me: But that great knowledge, which he abuseth to an injurious scorn and undervaluing of me, I heartily hate. God Almighty (it may be) for some secret respects, which his all-discerning spirit onely knowes, would not suffer me to impart any longer, (as we were mutually bound,) my private affaires unto him. Therefore from henceforth let him live to himselfe, onely I would have him understand by this which is published, that his vehement and bitter Letters made me very sad. But to returne to what we have proposed in the Contents of this Section; A Physician that would practise successfully, must

First and before all things find out the disease, and what the cause of it is.

For in vain wilt thou either seek or apply remedies, if the cause of the disease be not perfectly knowne unto thee: the beginning of the Cure, is a right knowledge of the Disease: but the disease cannot be known, without knowing the cause: For then are we confident, that we know the matter and effect, when we have discovered the cause or efficient of it.

II.

He must appiy and appropriate his remedies to the root and originall apparent cause of the disease, and not otherwise.

III.

He must administer no Medicines, whose forces or operative virtues in taking away the disease, he is not throughly acquainted with,

40 *acquainted*] acquaintd 1655

*unlesse he be well assured that they cannot indanger nor prejudice
a person that is in health : by such trials he may safely and
profitably discern what his Medicines can, and what they cannot
effect.*

IV.

*He must administer nothing that hath in it a manifest poyson,
unlesse the venome be first wholly and actually separated or
taken out.*

V.

10 *He must before the administration of his Medicines, remove all
impediments that are likely to oppose or weaken their virtues ;
and this must be done either by himself, or by another, viz. by a
Surgeon.*

He must let blood, take away all luxations, set broken bones, &c.
And afterwards apply his Medicines inwardly or outwardly, or
both wayes, as need requires.

VI.

*He must prescribe such a Dyet both of Meat and Drinke, as will be
agreeable to his Patients present exigencie, and for the furtherance
20 or assistance of nature, and the restoration of health.*

VII.

*He must carefully observe a just Dose in all his Medicines, with
respect had to their operations, and to the strength of the Patient.*

VIII.

*He must never administer any of his Medicines, without sanctifying
them in, and with the blessed name of JESUS CHRIST.
Whatsoever ye doe (saith the Apostle of the Gentiles) in word or
deed, doe all in the name of the Lord JESUS, giving thankes to
God and the Father by him.*   Colos. 3. 17.

30 ### Section. 7.
How the sick man should behave himself, while
he is in a course of Physick.

I.

*Let the sick person acknowledge, that he hath deserved, and drawn
upon himseife, the just anger of God, by his frequent sinnes : and
that it is by his righteous permission, that he is visited with sicknesse.*

II.

*Let him by an unfeigned penitence, and a godly sorrow reconcile him-
40 selfe unto God through the merits of his Saviour, putting on an*

39 *himselfe*] *him-*|*himselfe 1655*

holy resolution to become a new man ; and afterwards let him draw near to the throne of Grace, and intreat God for mercy, and his healing assistance.

III.

After reconciliation and invocation of the divine Aide, let him send for the Physician, and Physick being taken, let him not doubt of Gods mercy, and his own recovery.

That is to say, let him certainly believe that there is communicated and infused (by the gift of God) into the medicine which he hath taken, such an innate vertue, as is effectual and proper to expell 10 his Disease. If he doth this, the event will be answerable to his faith, and the Medicine will in all circumstances work successfully. A firm credulity, chearfull hope and true love and confidence towards the Physician, and the Medicine, (saith that great Philosopher *Oswaldus Crollius,*) conduce as much to the health of the Patient, yea sometimes more, then either the remedy, or the Physician. Naturall faith (I meane not the faith of Grace which is from Christ, but the *imaginative faith,* which in the day that the first man was created, was then infused and planted in him by God the Father, and is still communicated to his posterity,) is 20 so powerfull, that it can both expell and introduce Diseases : as it manifestly appeares in times of infection, when man by his owne private imagination, out of meere feare and horrour, generates a *Basiliscum Cæli,* which infects the Microcosmical Firmament by means of the Imaginants superstition, according as the Patients faith assists, or resists. To the faithfull all things are possible, for faith ascertaines all those things which are uncertaine : God can by no meanes be reach'd and injoy'd of us, but onely by faith : whosoever therefore believes in God, he operates by the power of God, and to God all things are possible. But how this 30 is performed, no humane wit can find out : This onely we can say, that faith is an operation or work not of the Believer but of him in whom he believes. Cogitations or thoughts, surpasse the operations of all Elements and Stars : for while we imagine and believe, such a thing shall come to passe, that faith brings the worke about, and without it is nothing done. Our faith that it will be so, makes us imagine so : imagination excites a Star, that Star (by conjunction with Imagination) gives the effect or perfect operation. To believe that there is a medicine which can cure us, gives the spirit of Medicine : that spirit gives the knowledge 40 of it and the Medicine being known, gives health. Hence it appeares, that a true Physician, whose operations are natural, is born of this faith, and the spirit (I meane this spirit of nature, or star of medicine,) furthers and assists him, according to his faith. It happens oftentimes, that an illiterate man performes those cures by this imaginative faith, which the best Physicians cannot doe with the most soveraigne medicines. Sometimes also, this bare perswasion or imaginative faith heales more, and more effectually, then any virtue in the exhibited Medicine, as it was manifestly found of late years, in that famous *Panacea*, or *All-heal* of *Amwaldus*, and since his time, in that new medicinall spring, which broke out this present yeare in the Confines of *Misnia* and *Bohemia*, to which an incredible number of sick persons doe daily resort. No other cause can be rendred of these *Magnalia*, or rare Physical operations, then the firme and excessive affection of the Patient; for the power, which worketh thus, is in the Spirit of the receiver, when taking the medicine without any fear or hesitation, he is wholly possessed and inspired (as it were) with an actual desire and beliefe of health : for the rationall soule, when stirred up, and enkindled by a vehement imagination, overcomes nature, and by her own effectuall affections, renewes many things in her own body or mansion, causing either health or sicknesse, and that not onely in her own body, but Extraneously, or in other bodies. The efficacy of this naturall faith, manifested it selfe in that woman with the bloody Issue, and in the Centurion. Hitherto are the words of *Crollius.*

IV.

When the Patient is delivered from his disease, and restored to his former health, let him heartily and solemnly give all the glory to the Supreme, All-mighty Physician : let him offer the sacrifice of Thankes-giving, and acknowledge the goodness and the tender mercies of the Lord. And let not the Physitian forget to performe his duty, by a thankeful and solemn acknowledgement of Gods gracious concessions, by choosing and enabling him to be his unworthy instrument to restore the sick. And this he must do, not onely because it is his duty, and a most deserved and obliged gratitude, but also out of a wise Christian caution, to avoid those judgements which are poured upon the negligent and ungratefull, by the most just jealousie of the irresistible and everlasting GOD ; unto whom alone be rendred by Angels and Men, and by all his creatures, All Praise and Glory, and perpetual thanks in this the Temporall, and in the eternall Being. *Amen.*

FINIS.

THE
CHYMISTS
KEY

To ſhut, and to open:

OR

The true doctrin of *Corruption* and
Generation, in ten brief *Aphoris-*
mes, illuſtrated with moſt plain
and faithful commentaries out
of the pure light of
NATURE:

By that *Judicious* & *Induſtreous* Artiſt
HENRY NOLLIVS.

Rob. Flud Tract: 1.º lib. 6.
de Creaturis Cæli elementaris

Non aliter appevit materia terræ forman
cæli, quam fœmina virum.

Publiſhed by *Eugenius Philalethes.*

LONDON,
Printed by *E. B.* for *L. Lloyd* at the
Caſtle in *Cornhill.* 1657.

To the READER.

This *little Book* having *Worth* enough in it *self,* needes not my *Commendation:* the *Author* in his life time, being an eminent *Physician,* and a most able *Philosopher,* as the *discourse* it selfe can best *testifie.*

The *Translator* also wanted not *Judgement* to choose what was *Best* in this *kind:* nor *Abilities* to performe, the *Choyse* being made. It is I alone, that appear here, as *Menelaus* did at that Feast in the *Iliads: who came though not invited.* I shall not indeavour to excuse my selfe, for I come not *Emptie,* but will con-
10 tribute somewhat to the *Collation.*

The *Author* builds on *good Principles,* so that his *Theorie* is as *True,* as it is *Plausible;* and I presume he aymed at *nothing more,* leaving all *Particulars,* and their *Application* to the Industry of the R E A D E R. He is sometimes pleased to descend to *Examples,* but to such onely as are *Naturall:* and they indeed are *good* to *Teach,* but *hard* to *Imitate;* we *see not all,* that *Nature doth.*

When he speakes of *Rain,* and *Dew,* I am contented to think he means *something else* then what is *vulgarly* so called: and I doubt not but his *Salt-peter* is much *different* from that which is
20 *combustible,* and *Common.* The Philosophers *Dew,* if I know it at all, is a *drie water,* and their *Salt-peter* is a most *White incombustible Body,* of a *Gummie Aereall nature:* and indeed (if my Eyes have not deceived me) it is so *Aereall,* and *Unctuous,* that it will no more *mingle* with *water,* then *common Oyle* will. I have, for Tryall, taken it in it's *gross Body,* and putting it in a *Quart* of *Raine distilled,* I digested these *two* without any other *third Thing,* for a full Fortnights time; but they would never mix, the *nitre* (notwithstanding many *long* and *violent Agitations* of the *glasse*) keeping still *a part,* in the forme of *Butter* or *Oyle,* more
30 *white* then *Snow.*

The Truth is, there is no *Affinitie* betweene this *Saltpeter,* and *water* for it is not *made* of *Water:* but of *Ayre hid,* and *Condensed* in *Water.* We see also, that the *Ayre* is a *Drie Spirit,* and *Wets nothing:* but the *mist,* or *vapour* of the *water incorporating* with

24 for] fot *1657*

the *Aire, wets all things.* Even so those *Bodies* or *Substances,* which are *generated of Ayr,* retaine the First *Complexion* of their *Parent,* this drie *Aereall Humiditie* being *Prædominant* in them, as it is evident in *Common Quick-silver,* and in all *resinous Substances,* as vegetable and minerall *Gums* which will not *mix with water.* But this will be more *apparent* to *those,* who know that *Universall Gumme* or *sperme* whereof *nitre* is *made,* which is neither Dew, nor Raine, but a *Water and no Water;* that is, it is a *drie Water,* whereof see *D. Espagnet* in the nine & fortieth *Canon* of his first *Aphoristicall part.* Here is the *reason* then, why 10 *Nitre Philosophicall* will not *disolve in,* nor *mix* with *common water;* for it is a *fat, Oleous, Ayrie substance,* made by naturall *congelation* of a *Mercuriall drie Humiditie,* which *separats* from *Phlegme,* as it is *evident* in that *Succus vitalis* and *great Lunarie* of *Lullie.*

Aire then or *Mercurie philosophicall* is to be found in *severall places* and of *severall Complexions.*

In the Great *Hali-Caly* of *Nature,* it is *congeled* and in a manner crucifi'd between *two extreames,* & *both* of them *venemous,* and *Caustic.* If thou knowest how to *extract* it thence, in the forme of *Butter,* or a most *White sweet Oyle* then the Ἁλὸς χυμὸς, whence 20 the *Art* hath it's *Name,* is in thy power, and *D. Espagnet* in his two hundred and twenty fift *Canon,* will tell thee what thou hast attained to.

Thus thou seest where the *Ayre,* or *radicall Humiditie* is *congealed*: and now I must instruct thee where it is *volatil* and not *congealed.* It is *so* in the *sperme* whereof *Nature* immediatly *makes* the *Hali-cali*: to which purpose the former Auther hath left us a considerable Maxim, in his two hundred and fourtenth Canon: *Rerum Seminibus plurimum Humidi Radicalis inest*; for this *volatil Ayre,* which is *in* the *seed* or *sperme reincrudates* the *fixed* 30 *Ayre,* which is in the *Hali-Cali.* I say this *volatil spermatic Ayre* or *Oyle* doth it, and not *Oyle* of *soape* or *Sallad,* as some fooles have dreamed: for nothing *reincrudates,* and *naturally dissolves* a *Body,* but that *Crude sperme,* whereof the *Body* was *made.* Most excellent in this respect, is that passage of *Raymond Lullie,* in the 48[th.] Chapter of his *great Testament*;

Quando volumus quod siccum convertatur in Humidum, capimus

Instrumentum, quod est in AQUA, quæ quidem participat de Humido
radicali viz. in vapore Humiditatis Aireæ discordante a suo phlegmate
aquatico in quo vapore spiritus Quintus delatus est, &c.

Thus hee : and now I think I have sufficiently introduced thee
but if this be not enough I am afraid the whole discourses will not
satisfie.   I should have said much more but that I intend shortly
to publish a *Discourse* of my *owne*, wherein I have indeavoured to
give out some *Reasons* for a most *excellent,* and a *mysterious ex-*
perience which I have *lately seen.*

10   Farewell.

Eugenius Philalethes.

11 *Philalethes*] *Philalathes 1657*

The *Authour's* Epistle dedicatory to his noble Friend and Kinsman, the Lord *Wigand Heymel,* President of *Dresden, &c.*

It is no long time (my honoured Lord and Patron) since there came to *Gueilburg* (in quest of me) a most learned man, a professour of Logic, and a Tutour of Undergraduates in a certaine famous Universitie, who did earnestly intreat me to discover unto him those principles by which he might be introduced into the true knowledge of our more secret *Philosophie;* finding him therefore to be a Person of singular humanity, of most excellent abilities, and (as I perceived by frequent discourse) of a most acute and discerning apprehension, I resolved to grant his request; and for that end I did purposely lead him into a dissertation or 10 reasoning about the generation of natural bodies, and having brought him thither, I advised him to search curiously after what manner, and by what meanes this great and secret (though daily) work was performed : signifying farther unto him, that the foundation of our Art did (next to the divine assistance) consist chiefly in the perfect knowledge of Corruption and Generation.   Now, though this answer and advice of mine did nothing like this learned man, seeming in his Book-Judgement to be very simple and wide : neverthelesse, that which I told him is the very truth ; for he that perfectly knowes the wayes of Generation, will easily 20 come to be acquainted with the true Menstruum of every body, which in our Philosophy is the most usefull and difficult matter to come by ; yea, he will finde out a way or processe, which if he by a right imitation of nature, will wisely practise, he shall out of a convenient body (dissolved first, and digested in its own most naturall or proper vinegar) perfectly extract and attaine to a most noble and matchlesse medicine : A medicine I say, and not gold ; for the Sophisters or Pseudo-chymists pining with an insatiable hunger after gold, doe by most covetous, chargeable and fruitlesse processes infuse into their silly readers a strong desire of gold 30 making, and promise them golden mountains ; but Art cannot make gold, nature only produceth substances ; but how to perfect and purifie imperfect mettals by nature only and a natural way (not by adding to them, or mixing with them any extraneous

R r

Substance or Ingredient) and to separate and purge from them
those obstructing, discordant impurities, which are the cause of
their imperfection, the Philosophers doe know very well.   Art
(I say) cannot produce or make any substance ; but how to propagate and multiply natures in their owne Species by transplantation
and insition she doth know, but not without nature.   This I am
sure of by the light of nature, whose only contemplation with
Gods blessing & gracious assistance hath enabled me to write
this short discourse of generation, and wholly perswades me to
10 beleeve, that the soveraigne true medicine must be sought out
and prepared, *ad modum Generationis*, after the same method
that natural generations are performed.   Every thing that nature
affords for the subsistence and health of man is crude, and needs
a further digestion, before it can be converted either into the
substance of man, or into a wholesome medicine : let us consider
our daily foode, this growes in our gardens, is fed in our houses,
and sowne in our fields ; but it is not turned into a bloud and
nutriment, before it is (after the manner of generation) altered,
putrified, and dissolved in our stomacks : that from this masse so
20 dissolved within us, the natural spirit may be extracted and communicated to the heart, and the other members for their conservation and strength, and so after other various digestions, the bloud
may become seed, and turne into that radicall balsame, by whose
virtue mankind is both preserved and propagated : what hinders
then, seeing our internall vessell of putrefaction is insufficient, but
we may after the same manner by natural means and a Philosophic skill so imitate and assist nature, that all Crude bodies
whatsoever, may externally (without the *Officina Ciborum*) be set
to putrifie, to be digested and dissolved, untill their spirituall
30 nature may (after that Solution) be easily extracted, or taken out
of them ; by which spirit so extracted our internal, vital spirit
(for the singular harmony that is betwixt them) would be so
marvellously comforted and strengthend, that by this excellent
kind of assistance, it would be brought to exercise all its faculties
with such effectuall activity and virtue, as would quickly expell
and exterminate all the enemies and disturbers of life ; I mean all
diseases, though never so desperate.   If we certainly knew what
that is which putrifies all seeds, and how it is done, without doubt
we might and would by a constant, judicious industry (God
40 assisting us) find out and prepare medicines truly Philosophical,

to the great advantage and comfort of mankind. To this purpose
Chymistry serves ; for by the help of this Art we know how to
digest, to dissolve, to putrifie, to separate the impure from the
pure, and so to come by most perfect medicines : And verily, so
great and precious a blessing it is, that God never imparts it to
any fraudulent *Mountebanks*, nor to *Tyrants*, nor to any impure,
lascivious persons, nor to the effeminate and idle, nor to gluttons,
nor usurers, nor to any worshippers of *Mammon :* but in all ages,
the pious, the charitable, the liberal, the meek, the patient, and
indefatigable spirit, who was a diligent observer and admirer 10
of his marvellous works, found it out. This truth is elegantly
sung and expresly taught by that famous Philosopher and Poet,
the excellent *Augurellus !*

> *The greedy cheat with impure hands may not*
> *Attempt this Art, nor is it ever got*
> *By the unlearn'd and rude : the vitious mind*
> *To lust and softnesse given, it strikes stark blind,*
> *So the slye, wandring factour, &c.* _____

And shortly after.

> *But the sage, pious man, who stil adores*   20
> *And loves his Maker, and his love implores,*
> *Who ever joyes to search the secret cause*
> *And series of his works, their love and lawes,*
> *Let him draw near, and joyning will with strength*
> *Study this Art in all her depth and length ;*
> *Then grave experience shall his consort be*
> *Skill'd in large nature's inmost mysterie.*
> *The knots and doubts his busie course and cares*
> *Will oft disturb, till time the truth declares,*
> *And stable patience (through all trials past)*   30
> *Brings the glad end and long hop'd for, at last.*

Give ear all you Medicasters, who hate and persecute this
Divine Science : give ear I say, and tell me with what conscience
or honest confidence can you professe your selves to be Physicians,
seeing that all Physick or medicines are, without Chymistery,
imperfect ? without that Chymistry I say, which out of the manifested light of nature hath its invincible grounds and canons laid
down in this little Book. This is the only Art, which (by supply-
ing us, out of the light of nature, with convenient means and

particular natures to separate the impure from the pure) will teach us first how to heal all diseases of the Macrocosmicall substances, and afterwards by examples & experiments deduced from those exteriour cures, will shew us the right and infallible cure of all diseases in our own bodies.   He that knows not how to heal and purge metals, how can he restore the decayed or weakend radical balsam in Man, and excite it by comfortable and concordant medicines to perform perfectly all his appointed functions, which must necessarily be put into action, before any
10 disease can be expelled?   He that knows not what that is in *Antimony* which purgeth gold, how can he come by an effectuall and wholesome medicine, that will purge and cast out those extrarious peccant causes and humours that afflict and destroy the body of man?   He that knows not how to fix *Arsenic,* to take away the corrosive nature of *sublimate,* to coagulate *Sulphureous* spirits, and by a convenient specifical Medium to break and analyze stones in the greater world, will never in the body of man allay and tame the Arsenical spirits of the Microcosmic salt, nor take quite away the venemous indisposition of the Sulphur, nor
20 dissolve the stone in the bladder, and drive it out being dissolved. It is a noble, safe and pious course to examine and trye the force and virtue of medicines upon the Macrocosmical substances, before we apply them to our fellow creatures, and the rare fabrick of man.

   This was the very consideration, that moved the Antients, who were true Philosophers, to a carefull and effectuall study of true Chymistry, the only genuine Philosophic Science, that by imitating *Hermes,* the Father and the Prince of all true and loyall Philosophers, they might find out most effectual and proper medicines
30 against all griefes & diseases, especially that glorious & supream natural remedy, which is termed the universal one, and is really without deception or exception (unlesse the finger of God oppose it) the most sure Antidote of all Diseases : for the obtaining of which soveraign medicine, because this my treatise of generation is no meane help, I would have it no longer conceald from the ingenious lovers of this Art, but resolved to expose it to the publike view, that the enemies of the truth may see and know, that this our Science is grounded upon, and proceeds from the clear light of nature, and that all the Sons of Art may be more

27 Philosophic] Philophic *1657*

and more encouraged to a studious inquiry and a laborious search after the truth. If they benefit any thing by this my Book, let them give God the glory, and lend me what further assistance they shall think fit to communicate.

What ever it is, unto you (most noble and prudent Sir, my intimate friend, and my kinsman,) I humbly dedicate it: that you may see, how willing I am to requite (in some measure) those numerous favours, which from the first day I enterd upon this study, you have chearfully conferred upon me, to this very houre. Therefore I must entreat you to accept of this small remuneration 10 with your usual good will and benignity, to be still favourable to my endeavours, and to defend me from the calumnies and envy of the malitious, who from all parts set upon me and defame my studies. This undeserved malignity I suffer under, will require your permanent favours and affection: And I do here solemnly promise, that I will never (God willing,) do any thing that shall tend to the violation of so sacred a friendship, but shall daily endeavour that we may be more and more endeard, and closelier united, which the only wise and good God mercifully grant, Amen! farewell most noble Sir, and as you really do, so continue 20 still to further the studies of

Your

Henry Nollius.

The Authour's Preface to his Treatise of Generation.

Being to write of the generation of naturall things, I must ingenuously confesse, that I learnt it not in the Books of the *Athenian Sophisters*, (he meanes the Schoolemen, and the followers of *Aristotle*; this term he borrowed from *Paracelsus*, for he first called them so, and writing his *Mysterium magnum*, intituled it *Philosophy for the Athenians*, for Aristotles Schoole was at Athens,) but by the true light of nature : neither will I borrow any thing from them, or their Books, and convert it in this discourse (like a Plagiary) to my own use or glory; for the truth
10 is not to be found in their Bookes, but most grosse ignorance and errour, grounded upon and supported by the vaine opinions and contentions of most vaine men, which opinions the credulous people esteem and crye up as the utmost bounds and *non ultra* of all wisedome and perfection. As men are killed by fighting, so truth is lost by disputing; for while they onely dispute and wrangle about nature, every one of them in particular, and all of them in generall are so fild and swolne up with such a testie, intolerable pride and selfe worship, that each of them arrogating a kind of infallibility to his owne Chymera's or monstrous con-
20 ceits, doth with all might and maine labour to refute and demolish the airy Castles and fond imaginations of the other. And by this ridiculous continued feud they wander from the Bath and fundamentals of true knowledge, intangling both themselves and too credulous posterity in an inextricable labyrinth of quarrels and errours, fortified with fictitious and groundless principles never reduced to practice or tryal, but meerely supposed and implicitely beleeved; so that he that would get out of this spacious and wearisome wildernesse, cannot do it without much difficulty and laboriousnesse, and shall not doe it without their general
30 envy and opposition. Leaving therefore these lewd contenders and their verbosity, let us (the divine mercy assisting us,) goe directly to the house of wisedome by the light of nature, that by the simple and peaceable contemplation of the creatures, and her operations in them, we may truly discover and describe unto

others the perfect manner of generation, and so come not only to
the certain knowledge of our selves, but learne also how to produce
and prepare out of perfect bodies and substances such a medicine
or medicines as will innoxiously and faithfully cure all diseases
that are incident to our owne fraile bodies : for as men, corn and
herbs are (every one of them) generated and born out of their
own specific seed : so or in the same manner is the true medicine
of the Antients (then which there cannot be a better,) generated
and prepared out of the most perfect bodies and essences.   Look
not therefore with carelesse and transient eyes upon what is offer'd 10
thee in this Book : but know and be assured that this doctrine is
the most profitable and advantagious for thee, by whose light &
guidance thou wilt be most prosperously lead to the true knowledge of the secret generation of all Vegetals, Animals and
Minerals, and to the finding out of that rich and rare medicine
which perfectly cures all imperfect metals.

Of the Generation of naturall things.

To begin then, thou art to know in the first place that
Generation is twofold.

$$1 \left.\begin{array}{l} \text{Ordinarie} \\ \& \\ \text{Extraordinarie.} \end{array}\right\} 2 \qquad 20$$

1 Extraordinary generation is that, by which an unlike thing is
generated out of an unlike ; as mice are generated out of dung
and putrefaction by the sun.   This generation is termed in the
Schooles, Equivocal.

2 The Ordinarie is that, by which a like thing begets his like,
as when a man begets a manchild, and a lyon a lyon.   This in the
Schooles is termed Univocal.   This generation with the method
and the means of it, I shall include in these ten following 30
Aphorismes, or Propositions.

I.

Every thing generated or begotten, is generated and born of his
owne specific (1) seed, and in his proper (2) matrix.

The Commentarie or Illustration.

(1) Seed is a spiritual or subtile body, out of which the included spirit (by attraction of nutriment to it,) forms and produceth

in his proper matrix a living body indued with the like prolific
and multiplicable seed. This very spirit is by some Philosophers
(κατ᾽ ἐξοχὴν) termed seed, and the body in which it resides, they
call sperm ; but while we agree about the matter, I shall not
quarrel about words. This seminal spirit is the most subtile
essence of the seed, exalted by nature out of some perfect body,
and containing in it (after the most eminent or perfect manner)
all the virtues and faculties of the said body, and a seminific
power besides, which enables it (in its own species) to propagate
10 and multiply its own body.

(2) No kind of seed is of any virtue or effect, unless it be
placed by nature, or by Art in its proper Matrix. *Lesch.* tract. 8.
That Matrix is only proper and fostering, which is naturally agreeable and ordained for the seed, according to its particular species
and regiment. Therefore mineral seeds require a mineral Matrix :
vegetable seeds a vegetable, and animal seeds an animal Matrix.
The Matrix of mineral seeds are subterraneous mines, the earth is
the matrix of vegetables, and the females wombe is the Matrix of
animal seeds.

20   II.

Before any perfect thing can be generated, the seed must necessarily putrifie, and then be nourished.

The Commentary.

Believe our Saviour, *John* 12. 24. *Verily, verily I say unto you,*
except a corn of wheat fall into the ground and dye, it abideth alone ;
but if it dye, it bringeth forth much fruit. Nothing can be animated and borne, unless it first suffer corruption, putrefaction
and mortification, saith *Raymond Lullie* in his testament. See
Rosar. Phil. page 254. Therefore saith *Parmenides*, unless the
30 body be dissolved & broken and putrified and suffer a change in
its substantial substance, that secret, centrall virtue cannot be
extracted, nor be at liberty to mix with another body.

III.

The seed then putrifies, when a (1) salt of the same nature with
it, dissolved in a convenient (2) liquor, doth by the assistance
of a gentle heat (3) penetrate, analize and rarifie the substance

13 That] that *1657*   29 Therefore] therefore *1657*

of the seed, that the included spirit may out of its subject matter forme a convenient (4) habitation or body for it selfe : in which it may performe the offices of naturall propagation and seminall multiplication.

The Commentary.

(1) Therefore every mineral seed requires to its putrefaction a mineral salt & liquor ; vegetable seeds a vegetable salt and liquor (which is common water impregnated with Salt-peter ; and animal seeds require an animal salt and liquor, which is the females *menstruum* impregnated with the salt of the animal matrix. By 10 this doctrine, that passage of the most acute *Philosopher, Basil Valentine,* in his treatise of *The worlds great mystery, and its Medicine,* is easily understood. The words are these, *metals and minerals must be dissolved and reduced againe to their first matter by minerals* ; but in doing this, you must in every sort of mineral consider the species or kind ; for every kind mixeth only with his own kind, and so yeilds his seed, unlesse you will have a monster; *the virtue and propension of every seed* (saith the most subtile *Leschus* tract. 7.) *is to joyne and mix it selfe with every thing that is of or within its owne order and latitude* ; for no seed naturally applyes 20 to any thing that is *extra regnum suum* ; therefore in ordinary and lawfull generations, that one like may beget another, man applyes to woman, the lyon to the lyonesse, &c.

(2) *Without the humour of water* (saith *Basil Valentine* in his eighth *Key,*) *true putrefaction can never be performed* ; for humours or liquors are the true Mediums by which the salt doth by his dissolving and searching nature enter into and open the most intricate and inmost recesses of the seed ; for when this humour or liquor is by a due degree of heat rarified and provoked, then also is the salt in it attenuated and renderd fit to passe into, and 30 open the most compacted body of the seed ; and there stirs up and incites to vegetation a spirit of salt, that is the like, and the same with it selfe, which before lay hid and inactive.

(3) A spirit that is at liberty will easily and quickly free another spirit of the same nature, that is bound up and restrained ; This is done, *first* by reason of that activity & permeability, wch the free spirit is endued with. *Secondly* by reason of the harmonie, likenesse and love betwixt them ; this correlation is the cause

18 *Leschus*] *Leshus* 1657

that the exteriour free spirit makes way unto, and joynes with that spirit of salt included in the seed, and so doth with more ease work upon him, and excite him: for (as the Proverb hath it) *like will easily go to like,* and their unity is most intimate; Now, you must know, that every spirit, when loose & floating in liquid bodies or liquors, is at liberty in this state; by the mediation of heate, it doth (like a Loadstone) attract to it the spirit that is under restraint: opening and dissolving the body, which holds it in; and the restrained spirit it selfe (like a sensible prisoner,)

10 labours for liberty, conspiring and striving to be in action, and a full communion with the other; the free spirit by his sudden and subtile accession still exciting and strengthening him, and by this means so provokes him to action, as fire doth inkindle fire; so that the body holding it, must necessarily suffer a change and labefaction, and come to be putrified by its own included spirit, whose operation before was obstructed and kept under; for the included spirit having acquired liberty, and a power to be in action from the other, strives to get out and inlarge it selfe, and to that end breaks and destroyes its first body, and produceth

20 another new one. So the spirit of the salt of the earth, when it is dissolved in the immixt humour of that element (now every salt melts and is dissolved in its proper liquor,) is then at liberty; for every salt, when it is once dissolved in its own liquor, becomes active. Hence it is, that a corne of wheat (in whose body, as if under lock and key, the spirit of vegetable salt is bound up and fetterd,) as soon as it is cast into the ground, is by the free spirit of the salt of the earth penetrated and opend, that the salt which lies dissolved or loose in that liquor or immixt humour, may excite the vegetable spirit in the corne of wheat to action and

30 vegetation, which spirit being thus set at liberty, doth presently by putrefaction of the corne or graine, produce in the wheats proper matrix the substance of the roote (which is a new body) by whose mediation and deferency the earth must afterwards (the spirit attracting it) communicate nutriment to the blade, and the rest of this vegetable, as it growes up and increaseth. You must observe here, that this salt which conduceth to the solution and opening of bodies, is somtimes weak, sometimes strong. If it be weak, you must strengthen it with a salt that is of the same nature and property with the seed; and the liquor which hath the weak

40 salt in it, must be impregnated with it; that the solution may be

more effectuall and more convenient for nature in her operations.
Let us consider the generation of wheat. There is in raine-water
a volatile salt, by solution made in the earth ; but when that salt,
by reason of the earths over drinesse, is not sufficient to cause
a perfect and fruitfull solution of the seed-corne : then do the
husbandmen strengthen and manure their ground with muck and
dung, in which there is a salt of the same nature with the seed
(for muck is made of straw, and the straw growes out of the seed :)
so that when the raine descends and mixeth it selfe with the compost or mold, there proceeds from the muck and the ground a   10
nitro-sulphureous salt, which the immixt humour of the earth
imbibes or takes in, and being strengthend by it, opens the most
compacted and firmest seeds, whence comes a fruitfull and a
joyfull harvest. If thou desirest to see the secrets of nature, now
open thine eyes.

(4) Seeing that the seminal virtue lurkes in the most intimate
recesses of the seed, and consists in the most subtile portion of
the Sulphureous salt, it is most clear, that it cannot be exalted
and multiplyed but in an humour that is most eminently subtile
and pure. But because the seed sowne doth not at the first, or   20
presently take in that subtile humour out of those places, which
supply it with nutriment, therefore nature doth before all things,
take care first to produce and forme those vessels, in which that
humour taken afterwards out of the elements is digested, rarified
and most accurately purged ; that out of the whole body when
formed and perfected, she may contribute and produce a most
pure seminal essence, for the conservation and the multiplication
of that Species, which yeilds it ; for which very reason, provident
nature doth (by the intervening of putrefaction) out of the seeds
of herbs form first the roote, and out of the roote she doth after-   30
wards shoote forth the blade, dividing it in the growth into several
sections or joynts, that the humour taken out of the soyle, in
which the seed is sowne, may at first in the roote, and afterwards
in the body of the herb (when grown up and flourishing,) be more
and more digested, and drive the seminal virtue (through all the
vessels and joynts) from the very roote, to the upmost top-branches,
wherein a matrix purposely formed for the reception of this seminal
matter, a most perfect seed, and fit for the propagation of the same
Species, is (by the assistance of the suns heat maturing it,) found

1–2 operations. Let] operations, let *1657*

and gathered. But it happens oftentimes (and this you are concernd to know,) that, though nature formes alwayes these *vessels*
and *vehicula* of the seminal progression : yet those bodies, which
are thus furnished, do not alwayes yeild seed ; And this comes to
passe, because in those bodies the pores through which the Sper-
matical virtue should be promoted and driven into their super-
ficies and upper parts, are (before the seed is stirred, or can be
produced,) stopt up by external colds, or else by the predominant
virtue of their innate fixed salt are so bound up and obstructed,
10 that the seed either cannot come to any effectual maturity and
perfection, or else is wholly supprest and shut up. An example of
this we may manifestly see in the Orange trees, which grow
(indeed) in this Climate as well as other Plants, but in this cold
region they will yeild no fruite : whereas in *Italy* and other places,
which are their native soyle, they both yeild and bring forth fruite
to perfection. In the like manner gold and the other metals,
which come to our hands can make no emission of their included
seed, because their pores are by the vigour and excellency of their
innate fixed salt so bound and shut up, that they are wholly
20 restrained from effusion of seed ; so that the seminal virtue in them
is not at liberty to act and come forth ; for which very reason the
Philosophers, who knew this and were willing to assist nature, did
with most happy successe reduce gold and the other mettals into
their first matter : that by this course they might open their pores,
which by the supereminent vigour & power of the innate fixed
salt were shut up and lockt : and so bring the metals to that passe
and condition, in which they might with a marvellous increase
and to their great benefit, yeild seed and propagate : No otherwise
than the Orange-trees in the Maurice-garden at Casels are all
30 winter long cherished with an external, artificial heate, which
makes them put forth, and brings their fruits to maturity. *He
that hath eares to heare, let him heare.*

IV.

The humour or liquor which, serves for putrefaction, must be
proportionable to that body which is to be putrified.

The Commentary.

The humour must be thus proportioned both for quantity and
for receptivity. The humour is then proportioned for quantity,

when so much of the humour is taken in by the body, as is
sufficient for its subtiliation. It is proportioned for receptivity, or
the manner of reception, when the humour is not suddenly and
at once, but gently and by degrees or by little and little taken in
and drunk up by the body or seed: for a sudden imbibition of
the humour cannot so conveniently vivifie the seed, but causeth
by its sudden and unequal penetration, that some parts of the
body or seed are insufficiently opend or dissolved, hence it happens
that Darnel doth sometimes come up instead of Corne; therefore
the Philosophers advise the Sons of this Science to irrigate or 10
moysten our earth by long delay, and a frequent and wearisome
attrition.

V.

The heate which promotes this putrefaction, must be so mild
and temperate, that the liquor in which the resolving salt lyeth,
may remaine still in and about the matter, and not be laved or
evapourated from it.

The Commentary.

This must be done for two reasons. 1 Because the body putrefying must receive life in this liquor. 2 Because such a gentle 20
heat dissolves the salt in the liquor without violence and disperseth it into the matter after a natural tenour and manner, that
the body may more commodiously putrifie: but if the liquor were
agitated by an excessive burning heat, the matter in it would be
destroyed or spoyled, so that it could neither be animated, nor
receive such a putrefaction as is convenient for it, and therefore
nothing (in this case) could be generated out of the matter.
Listen to this Pamphilus! Thou that aimest at the universal
medicine.

VI. 30

The body putrefying must not be removed out of that Matrix,
in which the putrefaction was begun, untill that which is intended
be fully perfected.

The Commentary.

Therefore when we would out of one graine of Corne get a
whole eare, we leave it in the earth, untill the appointed time of
harvest, and then we find the eare ripe, and carry it home. Seeds
(saith *Avicen*) should not be gatherd, untill the harvest come.

VII.

The more pure the Matrix is, the thing generated is by so much the more perfect and sound.

For a pure Matrix (saith *Leschus*) will yeild pure fruit. Now the more pure any thing is, it is so much the more perfect and durable in its kind : on the contrary the more impure it is, it is so much the more imperfect and fraile ; and therefore an impure Matrix, because it yeilds impure fruit, must necessarily also produce it weak, impermanent and uselesse.

10 Which inconvenience being found in every thing, wise men willing to assist nature, attempted to purifie and heale the impure Matrix, wherever they found it ; from these attempts sprang a most wise and a sure experience which taught them, that all impurities and extrarious natures which hinderd the generation or fostering of the birth in the Matrix, were either by a natural or else by an artificial assistance to be removed and taken away. Now, when for the separation of subtile delitescent impurities or the removeal of any weaknesse nature requires help, this must be done by a judicious and discerning knowledg : but after separa-
20 tion, when these impurities are once excluded from the Matrix, and are only an hinderance to generation by their incumbrance and abode in the place then there is only required a manual operation, as evulsion or ejection : we find a plain demonstration of this in the Art of tillage or husbandrie : where the infirme salt of the earth is by the sulphureous, fat salt of the dung assisted and strengthend : but the stones and thistles which lye separated from the Matrix, and hinder its fertilitie only by their weight and incumbrance are by meere handie-work cast out and rooted up ; that the Matrix of the Corn thus drest may become and be called
30 a fruitfull field. The same method do the Philosophers use in their magisterie or secret practice, for they do first purge their field or matrix, then they inrich and strengthen it with the sulphur of nature : and lastly cast in their seed, that it may be vivified and multiply, and be turned into a most noble and effectuall medicine.

VIII.

That Matrix is only convenient and adapted to generation, which permits an easy entrance to the seed.

The Commentary.

This is to say, which receives it with ease, and is no hinderance

by its hardnesse or closenesse to the entrance of the seed : here
you must know that when the Matrix by reason of hardnesse, is
growne callous and impenetrable, it is then opend and renderd
porous againe by frequent agitation that it may be fitted for the
concoption of seed : so the husbandmen do plough up first, then
mattock and afterward harrow their green sword or untiled lands
and bend every clot asunder that by this Rarefaction and discussion
the earth may receive and take easily in the seed, and put it forth
againe with increase. If thou desirest to come by the secrets of
God, and to use them rightly to his glory, and the good of thy 10
neighbour ; then do thou in this Philosophic Task set before thine
eyes the laborious and patient husbandman, and be sure to imitate
him ; then will God without doubt favour thy righteous attempts,
and give that into thy possession, which will perfectly satisfie all
the longings of thy heart.

IX.

Out of that body, which is either corrupted or destroyed by
strange or extrarious natures : or whose spermatic vessels are by
some violence maymed or cut off, no seed can be had.

The Commentary. 20

It will be a very vain and unprofitable attempt for any to hope
for issue or healthfull seed by a man, whose body and radical
balsam is depraved or dryed up by an excesse of aromatic wines
or hot waters, or by some contagious incurable disease. Evenucks
because their genitals are cut off, cannot propagate their owne
Species. Let the Sons of this Science know (saith the most ingenious *Leschus*.) that it is a very fruitlesse search to look for
that in dry trees and lopt branches, which can never be found but
in the green and living. Give ear to this my Son, and follow the
Philosophers. 30

X.

That body which is preserved or sustained by one simple kind
of nutriment, is far more perfect and durable, & yeilds more sound
and prolific seed, than that which is nourished with many & different
kinds of nutriment.

The Commentary.

For the nearer any thing is to unity, it is so much the more

6 mattock] mattoik *1657*   7 bend] bent *1657*   8 and take] atd take *1657*

durable: for in unity there is no division or discord which is the cause of corruption: and where no corruption is, there is a permanent integrity and conservation, therefore that which is nearest to unity, must needs keep better and endure longer than that which is remoter from it; because there is in the one lesse discord and more in the other. Now the more durable any thing is, the seed it yeilds is by so much the more perfect and permanent.

THE END.

The Authours Postscript to his Readers.

10 This is the short and solid doctrine of generation: which if the *Athenians* understood, they would neither deride nor despise the most perfect and eminent science of *Hermes*, a science, that whosoever is *Adeptus* : and Master in it, he is truely rich and wise.

But least I should be mistaken in the latitude of this Nation and the ingenious reader might think that so often as I speak against the *Athenians,* I doe thereby meane all manner of persons that professe Physic and Philosophie in the Universities, I shall heere (before I goe off) acquaint him that by that notion or name of *Athenians,* I mean only those envious ignorants, who being 20 bewitched by authority and custome of other blinde guides are clearly of opinion that there is no Philosophie nor truth to be found, or left for us, but in one *Aristotle* and *Galen,* perversly maintaining and persisting in the great and manifest errours of *Aristotles* Physicks, and the evident imperfections of the *Galenical* medicines: and further do out of a lewd disposition or malignity of mind, and as much ridiculous willfull dotage disswade other growing and hopefull wits from applying to the Hermetic Science, and with pittifull wretched arguments (reasons they call them,) impede and keep them back from a study so excellent and 30 eminently salutiferous. These are the Men whome I aime at, and whose odious wayes and persons my writings strike at, and these I do openly assert, and shall prove to be Sophisters or deceivers, farewell Courteous Reader, and favour his attempts, whose greatest aime is thy good.

12 *Hermes,*] *Hermes 1657*

Thalia Rediviva:

THE

Pass-Times and *Diversions*
OF A
COUNTREY-MUSE,

In Choice

POEMS

On several Occasions.

WITH

Some Learned *Remains* of the Eminent
Eugenius Philalethes.

Never made Publick till now.

———Nec erubuit fylvas habitare Thalia. *Virgil.*

Licenfed, *Roger L'Eftrange.*

London, Printed for *Robert Pawlet* at the Bible in
Chancery-lane, near *Fleetftreet,* 1 6 7 8.

TO THE

Most Honourable and truly Noble

H E N R Y

Lord Marquis and Earl of

WORCESTER, &c.

My Lord,

Though *Dedications* are now become a kind of Tyranny over
the Peace and Repose of great Men ; yet I have confidence I shall
so manage the present Address as to entertain your Lordship
without much disturbance ; and because my purposes are govern'd
by deep Respect and Veneration, I hope to find your Lordship
more facile and accessible.   And I am already absolv'd from
a great part of that fulsome and designing guilt, being sufficiently
remov'd from the causes of it : for I consider, my Lord ! that you
10 are already so well known to the World in your several Characters,
and advantages of Honour ; it was yours by traduction, and the
adjunct of your Nativity, you were swaddl'd and rock'd in't, bred
up and grew in't to your now wonderful height and eminence :
that for me under pretence of the inscription to give you the
heraldry of your family, or to carry your person through the fam'd
Topicks of Mind Body, or Estate, were all one as to perswade the
World that Fire and Light were very bright Bodies, or that the
Luminaries themselves had Glory.   In point of Protection I beg to
fall in with the common wont, and to be satisfied by the reason-
20 ableness of the thing, and abundant worthy precedents ; and
although I should have secret prophecy and assurance that the
ensuing Verse would live eternally, yet would I, as I now do,
humbly crave it might be fortifi'd with your Patronage ; for so the
Sextile Aspects and Influences are watch'd for, and applied to the
actions of Life, thereby to make the Scheme and good Auguries
of the Birth pass into Fate, and a success infallible.

My Lord ! By a happy obliging Intercession, and your own
consequent Indulgence, I have now recourse to your Lordship ;
hopeing, I shall not much displease by putting these Twin
30 Poets into your Hands.   The Minion and Vertical Planet of the
Roman Lustre and Bravery was never better pleased, than

when he had a whole Constellation about him : not his finishing Five several Wars to the promoting of his own Interest, nor par-ticularly the prodigious success at *Actium*, where he held in chase the Wealth, Beauty and Prowess of the East ; not the Triumphs and absolute Dominions which followed, all this gave him not half that serene Pride and Satisfaction of Spirit as when he retir'd himself to umpire the different Excellencies of his insipid Friends, and to distribute Lawrels among his Poetick Heroes : If now upon the Authority of this, and several such Examples I had the Ability and Opportunity of drawing the Value and strange Worth 10 of a Poet, and withall of applying some of the Lineaments to the following pieces ; I should then do my self a real Service, and attone in a great measure for the present insolence. But best of all will it serve my Defence and Interest to appeal to your Lord-ships own conceptions and image of *Genuine* Verse ; with which so just, so regular Original, if these Copies shall hold proportion and resemblance, then am I advanced very far in your Lordships pardon : the rest will entirely be supplied me by your Lordships Goodness, and my own awful Zeal of being,

My Lord !   20

Your Lordships most
obedient, most humbly
devoted Servant

J. W.

7 insipid] inward *MS. alteration in Bodleian copy*

To the Reader.

The Nation of Poets *above all Writers has ever challeng'd perpetuity of Name, or as they please by their Charter of Liberty to call it,* Immortality. *Nor has the World much disputed their claim, either easily resigning a Patrimony in it self not very substantial; or, it may be, out of despair to controule the authority of Inspiration and Oracle. Howsoever the price as now quarrell'd for among the* Poets *themselves is no such rich bargain: 'tis only a vanishing interest in the Lees and Dreggs of Time, in the Rear of those Fathers and Worthies in the Art, who if they know anything of the heats* 10 *and fury of their Successors must extreamly pity them.*

I am to assure, that the Author has no portion of that aiery happiness to lose by any injury or unkindness which may be done to his Verse: his Reputation is better built in the sentiment of several judicious Persons, who know him very well able to give himself a lasting Monument, by undertaking any Argument of note in the whole Circle of Learning.

But even these his Diversions have been valuable with the matchless Orinda, *and since they deserv'd her esteem and commendations; who so thinks them not worth the publishing, will put himself in the* 20 *opposite Scale, where his own arrogance will blow him up.*

I. W.

To Mr. Henry Vaughan *the Silurist : upon these and his former* Poems.

Had I ador'd the Multitude, and thence
Got an Antipathy to wit and sence,
And hugg'd that Fate, in hope the World would grant
'Twas *good Affection* to be Ignorant :
Yet the least Ray of thy bright fancy seen
I had converted, or excuseless been.
For each Birth of thy Muse to after-times
Shall expiate for all this Ages Crimes.
First shines thy *Amoret*, twice crown'd by thee :
Once by thy Love, next by thy Poetrie,   10
Where thou the best of Unions dost dispense
Truth cloath'd in Wit, and Love in Innocence.
So that the muddie Lover may learn here,
No Fountains can be sweet, that are not clear.
There *Juvenal*, by thee reviv'd declares
How flat man's Joys are, and how mean his Cares ;
And wisely doth upbraid the World, that they
Should such a value for their ruine pay.
   But when thy sacred Muse diverts her Quill
The Landskip to design of *Sions* Hill,   20
As nothing else was worthy her, or thee :
So we admire almost t' Idolatrie.
What savage Breast would not be rap'd to find
Such Jewels in such Cabinets enshrin'd ?
Thou fill'd with joys (too great to see or count :)
Descend'st from thence, like *Moses* from the Mount,

---

4 be *KP*: the *1678*   13 muddie Lover] muddiest Lovers *KP*
15 by thee reviv'd] reviv'd by thee *KP*   17 wisely doth upbraid] generally
upbraids *KP 1664*: generously (gen'rously *1710*) upbraids *KP 1667–1710*
20 *Sions*] *Leon's KP*

And with a candid, yet unquestion'd awe
Restor'st the Golden Age, when Verse was Law.
Instructing us, thou so secur'st thy Fame,
That nothing can disturb it, but my name.   30
Nay I have hopes, that standing so near thine
'Twill loose its dross, and by degrees refine.
Live ! till the disabused World consent
All Truths of Use, of Strength or Ornament
Are with such Harmony by thee display'd
As the whole World was first by number made ;
And from the charming rigour thy Muse brings
Learn, there's no pleasure but in serious things !

Orinda

Upon the Ingenious Poems *of his Learned Friend,* Mr. Henry Vaughan *the Silurist.*

Fairly design'd ! to charm our *Civil* Rage
With *Verse*, and plant *Bayes* in an *Iron* Age.
But hath steel'd *Mars* so ductible a Soul,
That *Love* and *Poesie* may it controule ?
Yes : brave *Tyrtæus*, as we read of old,
The *Grecian* Armies, as he pleas'd cou'd *mold ;*
They march'd to his high *Numbers*, and did fight
With that *instinct* and *rage*, which he did write.
When he fell *lower*, they would strait *retreat*,
Grow soft and calm : and temper their bold heat.   10
Such *Magick* is in *Vertue* !   See hear a young
Tyrtæus too, whose sweet persuasive Song
Can lead our *Spirits* any way, and move
To all *Adventures* : either *War* or *Love*.

Then veil the bright *Etesia*, that choice *She*,
Lest *Mars*, (*Timander's* Friend) his Rival be.
So fair a *Nymph*, drest by a *Muse* so neat,
Might warm the *North*, and thaw the frozen *Gete*.

Tho. Powel, D.D.

To the ingenious Author of Thalia
Rediviva.
Ode I.

Where Reverend Bards of old have sate
And sung the pleasant enterludes of Fate,
    Thou takest the hereditary shade
    Which Natures homely Art had made,
And thence thou giv'st thy Muse her swing, and she
       Advances to the Galaxie ;
There with the sparkling *Cowley* she above
Does hand in hand in graceful Measures move.
   We groveling Mortals gaze below,
     And long in vain to know   10
  Her wondrous paths, her wondrous flight
    In vaine ; alas ! we grope,
  In vain we use our earthly Telescope,
   We'r blinded by an intermedial night :
    Thine *Eagle-Muse* can only face
    The fiery Coursers in their race,
  While with unequal paces we do try
To bear her train aloft, and keep her company.

II.

  The loud harmonious *Mantuan*
Once charm'd the world, and here's the *Uscan* Swan   20
    In his declining years does chime,
And challenges the last remains of Time.
    Ages run on, and soon give o're,
    They have their Graves as well as we,
    Time swallows all that's past and more,
Yet time is swallow'd in eternity :
This is the only profits Poets see.
There thy triumphant Muse shall ride in state
    And lead in Chains devouring Fate ;
    Claudian's bright Phœnix she shall bring   30
    Thee an immortal offering ;
  Nor shall my humble tributary Muse
  Her homage and attendance too refuse,
    She thrusts her self among the Crowd
And joyning in th' applause she strives to clap aloud.

12 vaine *GC* : raine *1678*

III.

Tell me no more that Nature is severe
    Thou great Philosopher!
Lo she has laid her vast Exchequer here.
    Tell me no more that she has sent
    So much already she is spent;   40
Here is a vast *America* behind
Which none but the great Silurist could find.
    Nature her last edition was the best,
    As big, as rich as all the rest
    So will we here admit
    Another world of Wit.
No rude or savage fancy here shall stay
    The travailing Reader in his way,
But every coast is clear: go where he will
Vertu's the road *Thalia* leads him still: 50
Long may she live, and wreath thy sacred head
For this her happy resurrection from the dead.
                   N. W. Jes. Coll. *Oxon.*

To my worthy Friend, Mr. Henry Vaughan the Silurist.

See what thou wert! by what Platonick round
Art thou in thy first youth and Glories found!
Or from thy Muse does this Retrieve accrue,
Do's she which once inspir'd thee, now renew!
Bringing thee back those Golden years which time
Smooth'd to thy Lays, and polisht with thy Rhyme.
Nor is't to thee alone she do's convey
Such happy change, but bountiful as day
On whatsoever Reader she do's shine
She makes him like thee, and for ever thine.   10

And first thy manual op'ning gives to see
Ecclipse and suff'rings burnish Majesty,
Where thou so artfully the draught hast made
That we best read the lustre in the shade,
And find our Sov'raign greater in that shroud:
So Lightning dazzles from its night and cloud;
So the *first Light himself* has for his Throne
Blackness, and Darkness his Pavilion.

    7 is't] i'st *1678*   11 manual] manu'al *1678*

Who can refuse thee company, or stay,
By thy next charming summons forc'd away,   20
If that be force which we can so resent
That only in its joys 'tis violent :
Upward thy *Eagle* bears us e're aware
Till above Storms and all tempestuous Air
We radiant Worlds with their bright people meet,
Leaving this little *All* beneath our feet.
But now the pleasure is too great to tell,
Nor have we other bus'ness than to dwell
As on the hallow'd Mount th' Apostles meant
To build and fix their glorious banishment.   30
Yet we must know and find thy skilful Vein
Shall gently bear us to our homes again ;
By which descent thy former flight's impli'd
To be thy extasie and not thy pride.
And here how well do's the wise *Muse* demeane
Her self, and fit her song to ev'ry Scene !
Riot of Courts, the bloody wreaths of War,
Cheats of the Mart, and clamours of the Bar,
Nay, life it self thou dost so well express
Its hollow Joyes, and real Emptiness,   40
That *Dorian* Minstrel never did excite,
Or raise for dying so much appetite.

Nor does thy other softer Magick move
Us less thy fam'd *Etesia* to love ;
Where such a *Character* thou giv'st that shame
Nor envy dare approach the Vestal Dame :
So at bright Prime *Idea's* none repine,
They safely in th' *Eternal Poet* shine.

Gladly th' *Assyrian Phœnix* now resumes
From thee this last reprizal of his Plumes ;   50
He seems another more miraculous thing
Brighter of Crest, and stronger of his Wing ;
Proof against Fate in spicy Urns to come,
Immortal past all risque of Martyrdome.

Nor be concern'd, nor fancy thou art rude
T' adventure from thy Cambrian solitude,
Best from those lofty Cliffs thy *Muse* does spring
Upwards, and boldly spreads her Cherub-wing.

51 another] anothet *1678*

So when the *Sage* of *Memphis* would converse
With boding Skies, and th' Azure Universe,   60
He climbs his starry Pyramid, and thence
Freely sucks clean prophetique influence,
And all Serene, and rap't and gay he pries
Through the Æthereal volum's Mysteries,
Loth to come down, or ever to know more
The *Nile's* luxurious, but dull foggy shore.

                              I. W. A.M. Oxon.

Choice P O E M S on several occasions.

To his Learned Friend and Loyal Fellow-Prisoner, Thomas Powel *of* Cant. *Doctor of Divinity.*

If sever'd Friends by *Sympathy* can joyn,
And absent *Kings* be honour'd in their *coin*;
May they do both, who are so curb'd ! but we
Whom no such *Abstracts* torture, that can see
And pay each other a full self-return,
May laugh, though all such *Metaphysics* burn.
  'Tis a kind Soul in *Magnets*, that attones
Such two hard things as *Iron* are and *Stones*,
And in their dumb *compliance* we learn more
Of Love, than ever Books could speak before.   10
For though *attraction* hath got all the name,
As if that *power* but from one side came,
Which both unites; yet, where there is no *sence*,
There is no *Passion*, nor *Intelligence* :
And so by consequence we cannot state
A Commerce, unless both we animate.
For senseless things, though ne'r so call'd upon,
Are deaf, and feel no Invitation ;
But such as at the last day shall be shed
By the great Lord of Life into the Dead.   20
  'Tis then no *Heresie* to end the strife
With such rare Doctrine as gives *Iron* life.
  For were it otherwise (which cannot be,
And do thou judge my bold Philosophie :)
Then it would follow that if I were dead,
Thy love, as now in life, would in that Bed
Of Earth and darkness warm me, and dispense,
Effectual informing Influence.
Since then 'tis clear, that Friendship is nought else
But a Joint, kind propension : and excess   30

The pagination of 1678 begins with the next poem

In none, but such whose equal easie hearts
Comply and meet both in their *whole* and *parts* :
And when they cannot meet, do not forget
To mingle Souls, but secretly reflect
And some third place their Center make, where they
Silently mix, and make an unseen stay :
Let me not say (though *Poets* may be bold,)
Thou art more hard than *Steel,* than *Stones* more cold,
But as the *Mary-gold* in Feasts of Dew
And early Sun-beams, though but thin and few   40
Unfolds its self, then from the Earths cold breast
Heaves gently, and salutes the hopeful *East* :
So from thy quiet *Cell,* the retir'd Throne
Of thy fair thoughts, which silently bemoan
Our sad distractions, come : and richly drest
With reverend mirth and manners, check the rest
Of loose, loath'd men ! why should I longer be
Rack't 'twixt two Ev'ls ? *I see and cannot see.*

Thalia Rediviva.

The King Disguis'd.

Written about the same time that Mr. John
Cleveland *wrote his.*

A King and no King ! Is he gone from us,
And stoln alive into his Coffin thus ?
This was to ravish Death, and so prevent
The Rebells treason and their punishment.
He would not have them damn'd, and therefore he
Himself deposed his own Majesty.
Wolves did pursue him, and to fly the Ill
He wanders (Royal Saint !) in sheep-skin still.
Poor, obscure shelter ! if that shelter be
Obscure, which harbours so much Majesty.   10
Hence prophane Eyes ! the mysterie's so deep,
Like *Esdras* books, the vulgar must not see't.
    Thou flying Roll, written with tears and woe,
Not for thy Royal self, but for thy Foe :
Thy grief is prophecy, and doth portend,
Like sad *Ezekiel's* sighs, the Rebells end.
Thy robes forc'd off, like *Samuel's* when rent,
Do figure out anothers Punishment.
Nor grieve thou hast put off thy self a while,
To serve as Prophet to this sinful Isle ;   20
These are our days of *Purim*, which oppress
The Church, and force thee to the Wilderness.
But all these Clouds cannot thy light confine,
The Sun in storms and after them, will shine.
Thy day of life cannot be yet compleat,
'Tis early sure ; thy shadow is so great.
    But I am vex'd, that we at all can guess
This change, and trust great *Charles* to such a dress.
When he was first obscur'd with this coarse thing,
He grac'd *Plebeians*, but prophan'd the King.   30
Like some fair Church, which Zeal to Charcoals burn'd,
Or his own Court now to an Ale-house turn'd.

15 portend, *G C* : portend. *1678*

But full as well may we blame Night, and chide
His wisdom, who doth light with darkness hide :
Or deny Curtains to thy Royal Bed,
As take. this sacred cov'ring from thy Head.
Secrets of State are points we must not know ;
This vizard is thy privy Councel now,
   Thou Royal Riddle, and in every thing
The true white Prince, our Hieroglyphic King !   40
Ride safely in his shade, who gives thee Light :
And can with blindness thy pursuers smite.
O may they wander all from thee as farr
As they from peace are, and thy self from Warr !
And wheresoe're thou do'st design to be
With thy (now spotted) spottles Majestie,
Be sure to look no Sanctuary there,
Nor hope for safety in a temple, where
Buyers and Sellers trade : O strengthen not
With too much trust the Treason of a Scot !   50

The Eagle.

'Tis madness sure ; And I am in the *Fitt*,
To dare an *Eagle* with my *unfledg'd* witt.
For what did ever *Rome* or *Athens* sing
In all their *Lines*, as loftie as his wing ?
He that an Eagles *Powers* would rehearse
Should with his plumes first feather all his Verse.
   I know not, when into thee I would prie,
Which to admire, thy *Wing* first : or thine *Eye* ;
Or whether Nature at thy birth design'd
More of her *Fire* for thee, or of her *Wind.*   10
When thou in the clear *Heights* and upmost *Air*
Do'st face the Sun, and his dispersed Hair,
Ev'n from that distance thou the *Sea* do'st spie
And sporting in its deep, wide Lap the *Frie.*
Not the least *Minoe* there, but thou can'st see ;
Whole Seas are narrow spectacles to thee.
   Nor is this Element of water here
Below, of all thy miracles the sphere.

43 wander *GC* : wonder *1678*

If Poets ought may add unto thy store,
Thou hast in Heav'n of wonders many more.   20
For when just *Jove* to Earth his thunder bends
And from that bright, eternal Fortress sends
His louder vollies : strait this Bird doth fly
To *Ætna*, where his Magazine doth lye :
And in his active Talons brings him more
Of ammunition, and recruits his store.
Nor is't a low, or easie *Lift.* He soares
'Bove *Wind* and *Fire* ; gets to the *Moon*, and pores
With scorn upon her duller face ; for she
Gives him but shadows and obscurity.   30
Here much displeas'd, that any thing like night
Should meet him in his proud and loftie flight,
That such dull *Tinctures* should advance so farr,
And rival in the glories of a star :
Resolv'd he is a nobler Course to try
And measures out his voyage with his Eye.
Then with such furie he begins his flight,
As if his *Wings* contended with his sight.
Leaving the Moon, whose humble light doth trade
With *Spotts*, and deals most in the *dark* and *shade* :   40
To the day's Royal *Planet* he doth pass
With daring Eyes, and makes the Sun his glass.
Here doth he plume and dress himself, the Beams
Rushing upon him, like so many Streams ;
While with direct looks he doth entertain
The thronging flames, and shoots them back again.
And thus from star to star he doth repaire
And wantons in that pure and peaceful air.
Sometimes he frights the starrie *Swan*, and now
Orion's fearful *Hare* and then the Crow.   50
Then with the *Orbe* it self he moves, to see
Which is more swift th' *Intelligence* or *He.*
Thus with his wings his body he hath brought
Where man can travell only in a thought.
   I will not seek, rare bird, what *Spirit* 'tis
That mounts thee thus ; I'le be content with this ;
To think, that Nature made thee to express
Our souls bold *Heights* in a material dress.

To Mr. M. L. *upon his reduction of the*
Psalms *into Method.*

SIR,

You have oblig'd the *Patriarch.*   And tis known
He is your Debtor now, though for his own.
What he wrote, is a *Medley.*   We can see
Confusion trespass on his Piety.
Misfortunes did not only Strike at him ;
They charged further, and oppress'd his pen.
For he wrote as his *Crosses* came, and went
By no safe *Rule,* but by his *Punishment.*
His *quill* mov'd by the *Rod* ; his witts and he   10
Did know no *Method,* but their *Misery.*

You brought his *Psalms* now into *Tune.*   Nay, all
His measures thus are more than musical.
Your *Method* and his *Aires* are justly sweet,
And (what's *Church-musick* right) like *Anthems* meet.
You did so much in this, that I believe
He gave the *Matter,* you the *form* did give.
And yet I wish you were not understood,
For now *'tis a misfortune to be good* !

Why then, you'l say, all I would have, is this ;   20
None must be good, because the time's amiss.
For since wise Nature did ordain the *Night,*
I would not have the *Sun* to give us Light.
Whereas this doth not take the *Use* away :
But urgeth the *Necessity* of day.
Proceed to make your pious work as free,
Stop not your seasonable charity.
Good works despis'd, or censur'd by bad times,
Should be sent out to aggravate their Crimes.
They should first *Share* and then *Reject* our store :   30
Abuse our *Good,* to make their *Guilt* the more.
'Tis *Warr* strikes at our *Sins,* but it must be
A *Persecution* wounds our *Pietie.*

To the pious memorie of C. W. Esquire *who finished his Course here, and made his Entrance into Immortality upon the* 13 *of* September, *in the year of* Redemption 1653.

Now, that the publick Sorrow doth subside,
And those slight tears which *Custom* Springs, are dried;
While all the rich & *out-side-Mourners* pass
Home from thy *Dust* to empty their own *Glass*:
I (who the throng affect not, nor their state:)
Steal to thy grave undress'd, to meditate
On our sad loss, accompanied by none,
An obscure mourner that would weep alone.
   So when the world's great Luminary setts,
Some scarce known Star into the *Zenith* gets,   10
Twinkles and curls a weak but willing spark:
As Gloworms here do glitter in the dark.
Yet, since the dimmest flame that kindles there,
An humble love unto the light doth bear,
And true devotion from an Hermits Cell
Will Heav'ns kind King as soon reach and as well
As that which from rich Shrines and Altars flyes
Lead by ascending Incense to the Skies:
'Tis no malicious rudeness, if the might
Of love makes dark things wait upon the bright,   20
And from my sad retirements calls me forth
The Just Recorder of thy death and worth.
   Long did'st thou live (if length be measured by
The tedious Reign of our Calamity:)
And Counter to all storms and changes still
Kept'st the same temper, and the self same will.
Though trials came as duly as the day,
And in such mists, that none could see his way:
Yet thee I found still virtuous, and saw
The Sun give Clouds: and *Charles* give both the Law.   30
When private Interest did all hearts bend
And wild dissents the public peace did rend:
Thou neither won, nor worn wer't still thy self;
Not aw'd by force, nor basely brib'd with pelf.
   What the insuperable stream of times
Did dash thee with, those *Suff'rings* were, not *Crimes*.

T t

So the bright *Sun* Ecclipses bears ; and we
Because then passive, blame him not, should he
For inforc'd shades, and the *Moon's* ruder veile
Much nearer us, than him ; be Judg'd to fail ?   40
Who traduce thee, so erre.   As poisons by
Correction are made Antidotes, so thy
Just Soul did turn ev'n hurtful things to Good ;
Us'd bad Laws so, they drew not Tears, nor Blood.
Heav'n was thy Aime, and thy great rare Design
Was not to Lord it here, but there to shine.
Earth nothing had, could tempt theé.   All that e're
Thou pray'dst for here, was *Peace*; and *Glory* there.
For though thy Course in times long progress fell
On a sad age, when Warr and open'd Hell   50
Licens'd all Artes and Sects, and made it free
To thrive by fraud and blood and blasphemy :
Yet thou thy just Inheritance did'st by
No sacrilege, nor pillage multiply ;
No rapine swell'd thy state : no bribes, nor fees
Our new oppressors best Annuities.
Such clean, pure hands had'st thou !   And for thy heart
Man's secret region and his noblest part ;
Since I was privy to't, and had the Key
Of that faire Room, where thy bright Spirit lay :   60
I must affirm, it did as much surpass
Most I have known, as the clear Sky doth glass.
Constant and kind, and plain and meek and Mild
It was, and with no new Conceits defil'd.
Busie, but sacred thoughts (like *Bees*) did still
Within it stirr, and strive unto that Hill,
Where redeem'd Spirits evermore alive
After their Work is done, ascend and *Hive*.
No outward tumults reach'd this inward place,
'Twas holy ground : where peace, and love and grace   70
Kept house : where the immortal restles life
In a most dutiful and pious strife
Like a fix'd *watch*, mov'd all in order, still ;
The *Will* serv'd God, and ev'ry *Sense* the Will !
    In this safe state death mett thee.   Death which is
But a kind Usher of the good to bliss.

41 thee, so] thee so, *GC*   53 did'st] di'dst *1678*

Therefore to Weep because thy Course is run,
Or droop like Flow'rs, which lately lost the *Sun* :
I cannot yield, since faith will not permitt,
A *Tenure* got by *Conquest* to the *Pitt*.   80
For the great Victour fought for us, and Hee
Counts ev'ry dust, that is lay'd up of thee.
Besides, Death now grows decrepit and hath
Spent the most part both of its time and wrath.
That thick, black night which mankind fear'd, is torn
By *Troops* of Stars, and the bright day's *Forlorn*.
The next glad news (most glad unto the Just !)
Will be the Trumpet's summons from the dust.
Then Ile not grieve ; nay more, I'le not allow
My Soul should think thee absent from me now.   90
Some bid their Dead *good night !* but I will say
Good morrow to dear Charles ! for it is day.

In Zodiacum Marcelli Palingenii.

It is perform'd ! and thy great *Name* doth run
Through ev'ry *Sign* an everlasting *Sun*.
Not Planet-like, but *fix'd* ; and we can see
Thy *Genius* stand still in his *Apogie*.
For how canst thou an *Aux* eternal miss,
Where ev'ry *House* thine *Exaltation* is ?
Here's no *Ecclyptic* threatens thee with night,
Although the wiser few take in thy light.
They are not at that glorious *pitch*, to be
In a *Conjunction* with *Divinitie*.   10
Could we partake some oblique *Ray* of thine,
Salute thee in a *Sextile*, or a *Trine*,
It were enough ; but thou art flown so high,
The *Telescope* is turn'd a Common Eye.
Had the grave *Chaldee* liv'd thy Book to see,
He had known no *Astrologie*, but thee ;
Nay more, (for I believ't,) thou shouldst have been
Tutor to all his Planets, and to him.
Thus whosoever reads thee, his charm'd sense
Proves captive to thy *Zodiac's* influence.   20
Were it not foul to erre so, I should look
Here for the *Rabbins* universal Book :

8 wiser few *GC* : wiser, few *1678*

And say, their fancies did but dream of thee,
When first they doted on that mystery.
Each line's a *via lactea*, where we may
See thy fair steps, and tread that happy way
Thy *Genius* lead thee in.   Still I will be
Lodg'd in some *Sign*, some *Face* and some *Degree*
Of thy bright *Zodiac*,   Thus I'le teach my *Sense*
To move by that, and thee th' *Intelligence*.   30

To Lysimachus, *the Author being with him in* London.

Saw not, *Lysimachus*, last day, when wee
Took the pure Air in its simplicity,
And our own too : how the trim'd *Gallants* went
Cringing, & past each step some Complement?
What strange, phantastic *Diagrams* they drew
With Legs and Arms ; the like we never knew
In *Euclid*, *Archimed* : nor all of those
Whose learned lines are neither Verse nor Prose?
What store of *Lace* was there ? how did the *Gold*
Run in rich *Traces*, but withall made bold   10
To measure the proud *things*, and so deride
The *Fops* with that, which was part of their pride?
How did they point at us, and boldly call,
As if we had been Vassals to them all,
Their poor *Men-mules* sent thither by hard fate
To yoke our selves for their *Sedans* and State?
Of all ambitions, this was not the least,
Whose drift translated man into a beast.
What blind discourse the *Heroes* did afford?
This *Lady* was their Friend, and such a *Lord*.   20
How much of *Blood* was in it? one could tell
He came from *Bevis* and his *Arundel*;
Morglay was yet with him, and he could do
More feats with it, than his old Grandsire too.
    Wonders my Friend at this ? what is't to thee,
Who canst produce a nobler Pedigree,
And in meer truth affirm thy Soul of kin
To some bright *Star*, or to a *Cherubin*?
When these in their profuse *moods* spend the night
With the same sins, they drive away the light,   30

Thy learned *thrift* puts her to use ; while she
Reveals her firy Volume unto thee ;
And looking on the separated skies
And their clear Lamps with careful thoughts & eyes
Thou break'st through Natures upmost rooms & bars
To Heav'n, and there conversest with the Stars.
   Well fare such harmless, happy *nights* that be
Obscur'd with nothing but their *privacie* :
And missing but the false world's *glories*, do
Miss all those *vices*, which attend them too !   40
Fret not to hear their ill-got, ill-giv'n praise ;
Thy darkest nights outshine their brightest dayes.

On Sir Thomas Bodley's *Library ; the Author being then in* Oxford.

Boast not proud *Golgotha* : that thou can'st show
The ruines of mankind, and let us know
How fraile a thing is flesh ! though we see there
But empty Skulls, the *Rabbins* still live here.
They are not dead, but full of *Blood* again,
I mean the *Sense*, and ev'ry *Line* a *Vein*.
Triumph not o're their Dust ; whoever looks
In here, shall find their *Brains* all in their Books.
   Nor is't old *Palestine* alone survives,
Athens lives here, more than in *Plutarch's* lives.   10
The stones which sometimes danc'd unto the strain
Of *Orpheus*, here do lodge his muse again.
And you the *Roman* Spirits, learning has
Made your lives longer, than your Empire was.
Cæsar had perish'd from the World of men,
Had not his *Sword* been rescu'd by his *pen*.
Rare *Seneca* ! how lasting is thy breath ?
Though *Nero* did, thou could'st not bleed to Death.
How dull the expert Tyrant was, to look
For that in thee, which lived in thy Book ?   20
Afflictions turn our *Blood* to *Ink*, and we
Commence when *Writing*, our *Eternity*.
Lucilius here I can behold, and see
His *Counsels* and his *Life* proceed from thee.
But what care I to whom thy *Letters* be ?
I change the *Name*, and thou do'st write to me ;

And in this Age, as sad almost as thine,
Thy stately *Consolations* are mine.
Poor Earth! whát though thy viler dust enrouls
The frail Inclosures of these mighty Souls? 30
Their graves are all upon Record; not one
But is as bright, and open as the Sun.
And though some part of them obscurely fell
And perish'd in an unknown, private Cell:
Yet in their books they found a glorious way
To live unto the Resurrection-day.
   Most noble *Bodley*! we are bound to thee
For no small part of our *Eternity*.
Thy treasure was not spent on *Horse* and *Hound*,
Nor that new Mode, which doth old *States* confound. 40
Thy legacies another way did go:
Nor were they left to those would spend them so.
Thy safe, discreet Expence on us did flow;
Walsam is in the mid'st of *Oxford* now.
Th' hast made us all thine *Heirs*: whatever we
Hereafter write, 'tis thy *Posterity*.
This is thy *Monument*! here thou shalt stand
Till the times fail in their last grain of Sand.
And wheresoe're thy silent *Reliques* keep,
This *Tomb* will never let thine honour sleep. 50
Still we shall think upon thee; all our fame
Meets here to speak one *Letter* of thy name.
Thou can'st not dye! here thou art more than safe
Where every *Book* is thy large *Epitaph*.

The importunate Fortune, written to Doctor Powel *of* Cantre.

For shame desist, why should'st thou seek my fall?
It cannot make thee more Monarchical.
Leave off; thy Empire is already built;
To ruine me were to inlarge thy guilt,
Not thy Prerogative. I am not he
Must be the measure to thy victory.
The Fates hatch more for thee; 'twere a disgrace
If in thy Annals I should make a Clause.

28 Consolations are] *Bodleian copy inserts (MS) all between these two words*

The future Ages will disclose such men,
Shall be the glory, and the end of them. 10
Nor do I flatter.   So long as there be
Descents in Nature, or Posterity,
There must be Fortunes ; whether they be good,
As swimming in thy Tide and plenteous Flood,
Or stuck fast in the shallow Ebb, when we
Miss to deserve thy gorgeous charity.
Thus, Fortune, the great World thy period is ;
Nature and you are *Parallels* in this.
   But thou wilt urge me still.   Away, be gone ;
I am resolv'd, I will not be undone. 20
I scorn thy trash and thee : nay more, I do
Despise my self, because thy Subject too.
Name me Heir to thy malice, and I'le be ;
Thy hate's the best Inheritance for me.
I care not for your wondrous *Hat* and *Purse* :
Make me a *Fortunatus* with thy Curse.
How careful of my self then should I be,
Were I neglected by the world and thee?
Why do'st thou tempt me with thy dirty Ore,
And with thy Riches make my Soul so poor ? 30
My Fancy's pris'ner to thy Gold and thee,
Thy favours rob me of my liberty.
I'le to my Speculations.   Is't best
To be confin'd to some dark narrow chest
And Idolize thy Stamps, when I may be
Lord of all Nature, and not slave to thee?
The world's my Palace.   I'le contemplate there,
And make my progress into ev'ry Sphere.
The Chambers of the *Air* are mine ; those three
Well furnish'd *Stories* my possession be. 40
I hold them all *in Capite*, and stand
Propt by my Fancy there.   I scorn your Land,
It lies so far below me.   Here I see
How all the Sacred Stars do circle me.
Thou to the *Great* giv'st rich Food, and I do
Want no Content ; I feed on *Manna* too.
They have their *Tapers* ; I gaze without fear
On flying *Lamps*, and flaming *Comets* here.
Their wanton flesh in *Silks* and *Purple* Shrouds,
And Fancy wraps me in a *Robe* of *Clouds*. 50

There some delicious beauty they may woo,
And I have *Nature* for my Mistris too.
　But these are mean ; the *Archtype* I can see,
And humbly touch the *hem* of Majestie.
The power of my Soul is such, I can
Expire, and so *analyse* all that's man.
First my dull Clay I give unto the *Earth*,
Our common Mother, which gives all their birth.
My growing Faculties I send as soon
Whence first I took them, to the humid *Moon*.　60
All Subtilties and every cunning Art
To witty *Mercury* I do impart.
Those fond Affections which made me a slave
To handsome Faces, *Venus* thou shalt have.
And saucy Pride (if there was ought in me,)
Sol, I return it to thy Royalty.
My daring Rashness and Presumptions be
To *Mars* himself an equal Legacy.
My ill-plac'd Avarice (sure 'tis but small ;)
Jove, to thy Flames I do bequeath it all.　70
And my false *Magic*, which I did believe,
And mystic Lyes to *Saturn* I do give.
My dark Imaginations rest you there,
This is your grave and Superstitious Sphære.
　Get up my disintangled Soul, thy fire
Is now refin'd & nothing left to tire,
Or clog thy wings.　Now my auspicious flight
Hath brought me to the *Empyrean* light.
I am a sep'rate *Essence*, and can see
The *Emanations* of the Deitie,　80
And how they pass the *Seraphims*, and run
Through ev'ry *Throne* and *Domination*.
So rushing through the Guard, the Sacred streams
Flow to the neighbour Stars, and in their beams
(A glorious Cataract !) descend to Earth
And give Impressions unto ev'ry birth.
With Angels now and Spirits I do dwell.
And here it is my Nature to do well,
Thus, though my Body you confined see,
My boundless thoughts have their *Ubiquitie*.　90

87, 88 dwell. . . . well,] dwell, . . . well. *GC*

And shall I then forsake the *Stars* and *Signs*
To dote upon thy dark and cursed *Mines*?
Unhappy, sad exchange! what, must I buy
Guiana with the loss of all the skie?
Intelligences shall I leave, and be
Familiar only with mortalitie?
Must I know nought, but thy Exchequer? shall
My purse and fancy be Symmetrical?
Are there no Objects left but one? must we
In gaining that, lose our Varietie?　　　　　　　100
 Fortune, this is the reason I refuse
Thy Wealth; it puts my Books all out of use.
'Tis poverty that makes me wise; my mind
Is big with speculation, when I find
My purse as *Randolph's* was, and I confess
There is no Blessing to an Emptiness!
The *Species* of all things to me resort
And dwell then in my breast, as in their port.
Then leave to Court me with thy hated store,
Thou giv'st me that, to rob my Soul of more.　　　110

To I. Morgan *of* White-Hall Esq; *upon his sudden Journey and succeeding Marriage.*

So from our cold, rude World, which all things tires
To his warm *Indies* the bright sun retires.
Where in those provinces of Gold and spice
Perfumes his progress: *pleasures* fill his Eyes.
Which so refresh'd in their return convey
Fire into *Rubies*, into *Chrystalls* day;
And prove, that *Light* in kinder Climates can
Work more on senseless *Stones*, than here on *man*.
 But you, like one ordain'd to shine, take in
Both *Light* and *Heat*: can *Love* and *Wisdom* spin　　　10
Into one thred, and with that firmly tye
The same bright Blessings on posterity;
Which so intail'd, like *Jewels* of the Crown,
Shall with your *Name* descend still to your own.
 When I am dead, and malice or neglect
The worst they can upon my dust reflect,
(For *Poets* yet have left no names, but such
As men have *envied*, or *despis'd* too much;)

You above both (and what *state* more excells
Since a just Fame like *Health*, nor *wants*, nor *swells* ?) 20
To after ages shall remain Entire,
And shine still spottles, like your planets Fire.
No single lustre neither ; the access
Of your fair *Love* will yours adorn and bless ;
Till from that bright *Conjunction*, men may view
A *Constellation* circling her and you :
  So two sweet *Rose-buds* from their *Virgin-beds*
First peep and blush, then kiss and couple heads ;
Till yearly blessings so increase their store
Those two can number two and twenty more, 30
And the fair *Bank* (by heav'ns free bounty Crown'd)
With choice of *Sweets* and *Beauties* doth abound ;
Till time, which *Familys* like *Flowers* far spreads ;
Gives them for *Garlands* to the best of heads.
Then late posterity (if chance, or some
Weak *Eccho*, almost quite expir'd and dumb
Shall tell them, who the *Poet* was, and how
He liv'd and lov'd thee too ; which thou do'st know)
Strait to my grave will *Flowers* and *spices* bring
With *Lights* and *Hymns*, and for an *Offering* 40
There vow this truth ; That *Love* (which in old times
Was censur'd *blind*, and will contract worse Crimes
If hearts mend not ;) did for thy sake in me
Find both his *Eyes*, and all foretell and see.

F I D A : *Or The Country-beauty* : *to* Lysimachus.

Now I have seen her ; And by *Cupid*
The young *Medusa* made me stupid !
A face, that hath no Lovers slain,
Wants forces, and is near disdain.
For every *Fop* will freely peep
At Majesty that is asleep.
But she (fair Tyrant !) hates to be
Gaz'd on with such impunity.
Whose prudent Rigor bravely bears
And scorns the trick of whining tears : 10

43 not ;)] not ; *1678*   3 slain *GC* : stain *1678*

Or sighs, those false All-arms of grief,
Which kill not, but afford relief.
Nor is it thy hard fate to be
Alone in this Calamity,
Since I who came but to be gone,
Am plagu'd for meerly looking on.
    Mark from her forhead to her foot
What charming *Sweets* are there to do't.
A *Head* adorn'd with all those glories
That *Witt* hath shadow'd in quaint stories :   20
Or *pencill* with rich colours drew
In imitation of the true.
    Her *Hair* lay'd out in curious *Setts*
And *Twists*, doth shew like silken *Nets*,
Where (since he play'd at *Hitt* or *Miss* :)
The God of *Love* her pris'ner is,
And fluttering with his skittish Wings
Puts all her locks in Curls and Rings.
    Like twinkling Stars her *Eyes* invite
All gazers to so sweet a light,   30
But then two *arched Clouds* of brown
Stand o're, and guard them with a frown.
    Beneath these rayes of her bright Eyes
Beautie's rich *Bed* of *blushes* lyes.
Blushes, which lightning-like come on,
Yet stay not to be gaz'd upon ;
But leave the *Lilies* of her Skin
As fair as ever, and run in :
Like swift *Salutes* (which dull *paint* scorn,)
Twixt a *white* noon, and *Crimson* Morne.   40
    What *Corall* can her *Lips* resemble ?
For hers are warm, swell, melt and tremble :
And if you dare contend for *Red*,
This is *alive*, the other *dead*.
    Her equal *Teeth* (above, below :)
All of a *Cise*, and *Smoothness* grow.
Where under close restraint and awe
(Which is the Maiden, Tyrant law :)
Like a cag'd, sullen *Linnet*, dwells
Her *Tongue*, the *Key* to potent spells.   50

49 dwells] dwells. *1678*

Her *Skin*, like heav'n when calm and bright,
Shews a rich *azure* under *white*,
With *touch* more soft than heart supposes,
And *Breath* as sweet as new blown *Roses*.
   Betwixt this *Head-land* and the *Main*,
Which is a rich and flowry *Plain* :
Lyes her fair *Neck*, so fine and slender
That (gently) how you please, 'twill bend her.
   This leads you to her *Heart*, which ta'ne
Pants under *Sheets* of whitest *Lawn*,   60
And at the first seems much distrest,
But nobly treated, lyes at rest.
   Here like two *Balls* of new fall'n snow,
Her *Breasts*, Loves native *pillows* grow ;
And out of each a *Rose-bud* Peeps
Which *Infant* beauty sucking, sleeps.

   Say now my *Stoic*, that mak'st soure faces
At all the *Beauties* and the *Graces*,
That criest *unclean !* though known thy self
To ev'ry coorse, and dirty shelfe :   70
Could'st thou but see a *piece* like this,
A piece so full of *Sweets* and *bliss* :
In *shape* so rare, in *Soul* so rich,
Would'st thou not swear she is a witch ?

Fida forsaken.

Fool that I was ! to believe blood
While swoll'n with greatness, then most good ;
And the false thing, forgetful man :
To trust more than our true God, *Pan*,
Such swellings to a dropsie tend,
And meanest things such great ones bend.

Then live deceived ! and *Fida* by
That life destroy fidelity.
For living wrongs will make some wise,
While death chokes lowdest Injuries :   10
And skreens the *faulty*, making Blinds
To hide the most unworthy minds.

And yet do what thou can'st to hide
A bad trees fruit will be descri'd
For that foul guilt which first took place
In his dark heart, now damns his face :
And makes those Eyes, where life should dwell,
Look like the pits of Death and Hell.

Bloud, whose rich *purple* shews and seals
Their faith in *Moors*, in him reveals   20
A blackness at the heart, and is
Turn'd *Inke*, to write his faithlesness.
Only his lips with bloud look *red*,
As if asham'd of what they sed.

Then, since he wears in a dark skin
The shadows of his hell within,
Expose him no more to the light,
But thine own *Epitaph* thus write.
Here burst, and dead and unregarded
Lyes Fida's *heart ! O well rewarded !*   30

To the Editor of the matchless Orinda.

Long since great witts have left the Stage
Unto the *Drollers* of the age,
And noble numbers with good sense
Are like good works, grown an offence.
While much of verse (worse than old story,)
Speaks but *Jack-Pudding*, or *John-Dory*.
Such trash-admirers made us poor,
And *Pyes* turn'd *Poets* out of door.
For the nice Spirit of rich verse
Which scorns absurd and low commerce,   10
Although a flame from heav'n, if shed
On *Rooks* or *Daws* : warms no such head.
Or else the Poet, like bad priest,
Is seldom good, but when opprest :
And wit, as well as piety
Doth thrive best in adversity ;
For since the thunder left our air
Their *Laurels* look not half so fair.
However 'tis 'twere worse than rude
Not to profess our gratitude   20

And debts to thee, who at so low
An Ebbe do'st make us thus to flow :
And when we did a Famine fear,
Hast blest us with a fruitful year.
So while the world his absence mourns
The glorious Sun at last returns,
And with his kind and vital looks
Warms the cold Earth and frozen brooks :
Puts drowsie nature into play
And rids impediments away, 30
Till Flow'rs and Fruits and spices through
Her pregnant lap get up and grow.
But if among those sweet things, we
A miracle like that could see
Which nature brought but once to pass :
A *Muse*, such as *Orinda* was,
Phœbus himself won by these charms
Would give her up into thy arms ;
And recondemn'd to kiss his *Tree*,
Yield the young *Goddess* unto thee. 40

Upon sudden news of the much lamented death of *Judge* Trevers.

Learning and *Law* your *Day* is done,
And your *work* too ; you may be gone !
Trever, that lov'd you, hence is fled :
And *Right*, which long lay *Sick*, is *dead*.
Trever! whose rare and envied *part*
Was both a wise and winning heart,
Whose sweet civilitys could move
Tartars and *Goths* to noblest love.
Bold *Vice* and *blindness* now dare act,
And (like the *gray groat*,) pass, though crack't ; 10
While those sage lips lye dumb and cold,
Whose words are well-weigh'd and tried gold.
O how much to descreet desires
Differs pure *Light* from foolish *fires* !
But nasty *Dregs* out last the *Wine*,
And after Sun-set *Gloworms* shine.

4 *Sick,*] *Sick 1678* (?)

To Etesia *(for* Timander,*) the first Sight.*

What smiling *Star* in that fair *Night*,
Which gave you *Birth* gave me this *Sight*,
And with a kind *Aspect* tho keen
Made me the *Subject*: you the *Queen*?
That sparkling *Planet* is got now
Into your Eyes, and shines below;
Where nearer force, and more acute
It doth dispence, without dispute,
For I who yesterday did know
Loves fire no more, than doth cool Snow   10
With one bright look am since undone;
Yet must adore and seek my Sun.
 Before I walk'd free as the wind,
And if but stay'd (like it,) unkind.
I could like daring Eagles gaze
And not be blinded by a face;
For what I saw, till I saw thee,
Was only not deformity.
Such shapes appear (compar'd with thine,)
In *Arras*, or a tavern-sign,   20
And do but mind me to explore
A fairer piece, that is in store.
So some hang *Ivy* to their Wine,
To signify, there is a *Vine.*
 Those princely Flow'rs (by no storms vex'd,)
Which smile one day, and droop the next:
The gallant *Tulip* and the *Rose*,
Emblems which some use to disclose
Bodyed *Idea's*: their weak grace
Is meer imposture to thy face.   30
For nature in all things, but thee,
Did practise only *Sophistry*;
Or else she made them to express
How she could vary in her dress:
But thou wert form'd, that we might see
Perfection, not Variety.
 . Have you observ'd how the Day-star
Sparkles and smiles and shines from far:
Then to the gazer doth convey
A silent, but a piercing Ray?   40

So wounds my love, but that her Eys
Are in *Effects*, the better Skys.
A brisk bright *Agent* from them Streams
Arm'd with no arrows, but their beams,
And with such stillness smites our hearts,
No noise betrays him, nor his darts.
He working on my easie Soul
Did soon persuade, and then controul ;
And now he flyes (and I conspire)
Through all my blood with wings of fire,   50
And when I would (which will be never)
With cold despair allay the fever :
The spiteful thing *Etesia* names,
And that new-fuells all my flames.

The Character, *to* Etesia.

Go catch the *Phœnix*, and then bring
A *quill* drawn for me from his wing.
Give me a Maiden-beautie's *Bloud*,
A pure, rich *Crimson,* without mudd :
In whose sweet *Blushes* that may live,
Which a dull verse can never give.
Now for an untouch'd, spottles *white*,
For blackest things on paper write ;
Etesia at thine own Expence
Give me the *Robes* of innocence.   10

Could we but see a *Spring* to run
Pure *Milk*, as sometimes Springs have done,
And in the *Snow-white* streams it sheds
Carnations wash their *bloudy* heads.
While ev'ry *Eddy* that came down
Did (as thou do'st,) both *smile* and *frown*.
Such objects and so fresh would be
But dull Resemblances of thee.

Thou art the dark worlds Morning-star,
Seen only, and seen but from far ;   20
Where like Astronomers we gaze
Upon the glories of thy face,
But no acquaintance more can have,
Though all our lives we watch and Crave.
Thou art a world thy self alone,
Yea three great worlds refin'd to one.

The Character (heading)   *to* Etesia.] *to* Etesia *1678*

Which shews all those, and in thine Eyes
The shining *East*, and *Paradise*.
　Thy Soul (a *Spark* of the first *Fire*,)
Is like the *Sun*, the worlds desire ;　　　　　30
And with a nobler influence
Works upon all, that claim to sense ;
But in *Summers* hath no *fever*,
And in frosts is chearful ever.
　As *Flowr's*, besides their curious *dress*
Rich *odours* have, and *Sweetnesses*.
Which tacitely infuse desire
And ev'n oblige us to admire :
Such and so full of innocence
Are all the *Charms*, thou do'st dispence ;　　40
And like fair *Nature*, without *Arts*
At once they seize, and please our hearts.
O thou art such, that I could be
A lover to Idolatry !
I could, and should from heav'n stray,
But that thy life shews mine the way,
And leave a while the *Diety*,
To serve his *Image* here in thee.

To Etesia *looking from her Casement at the full* Moon.

See you that beauteous *Queen*, which no age tames?
Her Train is *Azure*, set with *golden* flames.
My brighter *fair*, fix on the *East* your Eyes,
And view that bed of Clouds, whence she doth rise.
Above all others in that one short hour
Which most concern'd me, she had greatest pow'r.
This made my *Fortunes* humorous as wind,
But fix'd *Affections* to my constant mind.
She fed me with the *tears* of *Starrs*, and thence
I suck'd in *Sorrows* with their *Influence*.　　　10
To some in *smiles*, and store of *light* she broke :
To me in sad *Eclipses* still she spoke.
She bent me with the motion of her *Sphere*,
And made me feel, what first I did but fear.
　But when I came to Age, and had o'regrown
Her Rules, and saw my freedom was my own,
　　　6 me *C* : in *1678*

I did reply unto the Laws of Fate,
And made my Reason, my great Advocate:
I labour'd to inherit my just right;
But then (O hear *Etesia* !) lest I might   20
Redeem my self, my unkind Starry Mother
Took my poor Heart, and gave it to another.

To Etesia *parted from him, and looking back.*

O Subtile Love ! thy Peace is War ;
It wounds and kills without a scar :
It works unknown to any sense,
Like the Decrees of Providence,
And with strange silence shoots me through ;
The *Fire* of Love doth fall like *Snow.*
   Hath she no *Quiver*, but my Heart ?
Must all her Arrows hit that part ?
Beauties like Heav'n, their Gifts should deal
Not to destroy us, but to heal.   10
   Strange *Art* of Love ! that can make sound,
And yet exasperates the wound ;
That *look* she lent to ease my heart,
Hath pierc't it, and improv'd the smart.

In Etesiam lachrymantem.

O dulcis luctus, risuque potentior omni!
   Quem decorant lachrymis Sydera tanta suis.
Quam tacitæ spirant auræ ! vultusque nitentes
   Contristant veneres, collachrymantque suæ !
Ornat gutta genas, oculisque simillima gemma :
   Et tepido vivas irrigat imbre rosas.
Dicite Chaldæi *! quæ me fortuna fatigat,*
   Cum formosa dies & sine nube perit?

To Etesia *going beyond Sea.*

Go, if you must ! but stay—and know
And mind before you go, my vow.
   To ev'ry thing, but *Heav'n* and *you,*
With all my Heart, I bid Adieu !
Now to those happy *Shades* I'le go
Where first I saw my beauteous Foe.

In Etesiam 8 *perit GC* : *peruit 1678* : *pluit conj. Moore Smith*

I'le seek each silent *path*, where we
Did walk, and where you sate with me
I'le sit again, and never rest
Till I can find some *flow'r* you prest.　　　　　10
That near my dying Heart I'le keep,
And when it wants *Dew*, I will weep :
Sadly I will repeat past Joyes,
And Words, which you did sometimes voice :
I'le listen to the *Woods*, and hear
The *Eccho* answer for you there.
But famish'd with long absence I
Like *Infants* left, at last shall cry,
And Tears (as they do *Milk*) will sup
Until you come, and take me up.　　　　　20

Etesia *absent.*

Love, the Worlds Life ! what a sad death
Thy absence is ? to lose our breath
At once and dye, is but to live
Inlarg'd, without the scant reprieve
Of *Pulse* and *Air* : whose dull *returns*
And narrow *Circles* the Soul mourns.
　But to be dead alive, and still
To wish, but never have our will :
To be possess'd, and yet to miss ;
To wed a true but absent bliss :　　　　　10
Are lingring tortures, and their smart
Dissects and racks and grinds the Heart !
As Soul and Body in that state
Which unto us seems separate,
Cannot be said to live, until
Reunion, which dayes fulfill
And slow-pac'd seasons : So in vain
Through hours and minutes (Times long *train*,)
I look for thee, and from thy sight,
As from my Soul, for life and light.　　　　　20
For till thine Eyes shine so on me,
Mine are fast-clos'd and will not see.

Translations.

Some *Odes* of the Excellent and Knowing *Severinus*, Englished.

Metrum 12. *Lib.* 3.

Happy is he, that with fix'd Eyes
The Fountain of all goodness spies !
Happy is he, that can break through
Those Bonds, which tie him here below !
   The *Thracian* Poet long ago
Kind *Orpheus*, full of tears and wo
Did for his lov'd *Euridice*
In such sad Numbers mourn, that he
Made the *Trees* run in to his mone,
And *Streams* stand still to hear him grone.   10
The *Does* came fearless in one throng
With *Lyons* to his mournful Song,
And charm'd by the harmonious sound
The *Hare* stay'd by the quiet *Hound*.
   But when *Love* heightned by *despair*
And deep *reflections* on his *Fair*
Had swell'd his Heart, and made it rise
And run in Tears out at his Eyes :
And those sweet *Aires*, which did appease
Wild Beasts, could give their Lord no ease ;   20
Then vex'd, that so much grief and Love
Mov'd not at all the gods above,
With desperate thoughts and bold intent,
Towards the *Shades* below he went ;
For thither his fair Love was fled,
And he must have her from the dead.
There in such *Lines*, as did well suit
With sad *Aires* and a Lovers *Lute*,
And in the richest Language drest
That could be thought on, or exprest,   30
Did he complain, whatever *Grief*,
Or *Art*, or *Love* (which is the chief,

30 exprest, *GC* : exprest. *1678*

And all innobles,) could lay out ;
In well-tun'd woes he dealt about.
And humbly bowing to the *Prince*
Of Ghosts, begg'd some Intelligence
Of his *Euridice,* and where
His beauteous *Saint* resided there.
Then to his *Lutes* instructed grones
He sigh'd out new melodious mones ;　　　　40
And in a melting charming *strain*
Begg'd his dear *Love* to life again.
　　The *Music* flowing through the shade
And darkness, did with ease invade
The silent and attentive Ghosts ;
And *Cerberus,* which guards those coasts
With his lowd barkings, overcome
By the sweet *Notes,* was now struck dumb.
The *Furies,* us'd to rave and howl
And prosecute each guilty Soul,　　　　50
Had lost their rage, and in a deep
Transport did most profusely weep.
Ixion's wheel stopt, and the curst
Tantalus almost kill'd with thirst,
Though the *Streams* now did make no haste,
But waited for him, none would taste.
That *Vultur,* which fed still upon
Tityus his liver, now was gone
To feed on *Air,* and would not stay
Though almost famish'd, with her prey.　　　　60
　　Won with these wonders, their fierce Prince
At last cry'd out, *We yield !* and since
Thy merits claim no less, take hence
Thy Consort for thy Recompence.
But, Orpheus, *to this law we bind*
Our grant, you must not look behind,
Nor of your fair Love have one Sight,
Till out of our Dominions quite.
　　Alas ! what laws can Lovers awe ?
Love is it self the greatest Law !　　　　70
Or who can such hard bondage brook
To be in Love, and not to Look ?
Poor *Orpheus* almost in the light
Lost his dear Love for one short sight ;

And by those Eyes, which Love did guide,
What he most lov'd unkindly dyed!
   This tale of *Orpheus* and his *Love*
Was meant for you, who ever move
Upwards, and tend into that light,
Which is not seen by mortal sight.   80
For if, while you strive to ascend,
You droop, and towards Earth once bend
Your seduc'd Eyes, down you will fall
Ev'n while you look, and forfeit all.

Metrum 2. Lib. 3.

What fix'd *Affections*, and lov'd *Laws*
(Which are the hid, magnetic *Cause* ;)
Wise *Nature* governs with, and by
What fast, inviolable *tye*
The whole Creation to her ends
For ever provident she bends :
All this I purpose to rehearse
In the sweet *Airs* of solemn Verse.
   Although the *Lybian Lyons* should
Be bound with chains of purest Gold,   10
And duely fed, were taught to know
Their keepers voice, and fear his blow :
Yet, if they chance to taste of bloud,
Their rage which slept, stirr'd by that food
In furious roarings will awake,
And fiercely for their freedom make.
No chains, nor bars their fury brooks,
But with inrag'd and bloody looks
They will break through, and dull'd with fear
Their keeper all to pieces tear.   20
   The *Bird*, which on the *Woods* tall boughs
Sings sweetly, if you Cage or house,
And out of kindest care should think
To give her honey with her drink,
And get her store of pleasant meat,
Ev'n such as she delights to Eat :
Yet, if from her close prison she
The *shady-groves* doth chance to see,

2 (Which . . . Cause ;)] (which . . . Cause; 1678

Straitway she loaths her pleasant food
And with sad looks longs for the *Wood*. 30
The wood, the wood alone she loves !
And towards it she looks and moves :
And in sweet *notes* (though distant from,)
Sings to her first and happy home !

That *Plant*, which of it self doth grow
Upwards, if forc'd, will downwards bow ;
But give it freedom, and it will
Get up, and grow erectly still.

The *Sun*, which by his prone descent
Seems westward in the Evening bent, 40
Doth nightly by an unseen way
Haste to the *East*, and bring up day.

Thus all things long for their first State,
And gladly to't return, though late.
Nor is there here to any thing
A *Course* allow'd, but in a *Ring*;
Which, where it first *began*, must *end* :
And to that *Point* directly tend.

Metrum 6 Lib. 4.

Who would unclouded see the Laws
Of the supreme, eternal *Cause*,
Let him with careful thoughts and eyes
Observe the high and spatious Skyes.
There in one league of Love the *Stars*
Keep their old peace, and shew our wars.
The *Sun*, though flaming still and hot,
The cold, pale *Moon* annoyeth not.
Arcturus with his *Sons* (though they
See other stars go a far way, 10
And out of sight,) yet still are found
Near the *North-pole*, their noted bound.
Bright *Hesper* (at set times) delights
To usher in the dusky nights :
And in the *East* again attends
To warn us, when the day ascends,
So alternate *Love* supplys
Eternal Courses still, and vies
Mutual kindness ; that no Jars
Nor discord can disturb the Stars. 20

The same sweet *Concord* here below
Makes the fierce *Elements* to flow
And *Circle* without quarrel still,
Though temper'd diversly ; thus will
The *Hot* assist the *Cold* : the *Dry*
Is a friend to *Humidity*.
And by the *Law* of *kindness* they
The like relief to them repay.
The *fire*, which active is and bright,
Tends upward, and from thence gives light.   30
The *Earth* allows it all that space
And makes choice of the lower place ;
For things of weight hast to the Center
A fall to them is no adventure.
From these kind *turns* and *Circulation*
Seasons proceed and *Generation*.
This makes the *Spring* to yield us flow'rs,
And melts the Clouds to gentle show'rs.
The *Summer* thus matures all seeds
And ripens both the Corn and weeds.   40
This brings on *Autumn*, which recruits
Our old, spent store with new fresh fruits.
And the cold *Winters* blustring Season
Hath snow and storms for the same reason.
This *temper* and wise *mixture* breed
And bring forth ev'ry living *seed*.
And when their *strength* and *substance* spend
(For while they *live*, they drive and tend
Still to a *change*,) it takes them hence
And shifts their *dress* ; and to our sense   50
Their *Course* is over, as their *birth* :
And hid from us, they turn to Earth.
But all this while the *Prince* of life
Sits without *loss*, or *change*, or *strife* :
Holding the *Rains*, by which all move ;
(And those his *wisdom*, *power*, *Love*
And *Justice* are ;) And still what he
The *first life* bids, that needs must be,
And live on for a time ; that done
He calls it back, meerly to shun   60
The mischief, which his *creature* might
Run into by a further flight.

For if this dear and tender sense
Of his preventing providence
Did not restrain and call things back :
Both heav'n and earth would go to wrack.
And from their great *preserver* part,
As *blood* let out forsakes the *Heart*
And perisheth ; but what returns
With fresh and Brighter spirits burns.   70
  This is the *Cause* why ev'ry living
Creature affects an *endless being*.
A *grain* of this bright *love* each thing
Had giv'n at first by their great King ;
And still they creep (drawn on by this :)
And look back towards their *first bliss*.
For otherwise, it is most sure,
Nothing that liveth could *endure* :
Unless it's Love turn'd retrograde
Sought that *first life*, which all things made.   80

Metrum 3. Lib. 4

If old tradition hath not fail'd,
Ulysses, when from *Troy* he sail'd,
Was by a tempest forc'd to land
Where beauteous *Circe* did command.
Circe, the daughter of the Sun,
Which had with *Charms* and *Herbs* undone
Many poor strangers, and could then
Turn into Beasts, the bravest Men.
Such *Magic* in her potions lay
That whosoever past that way   10
And drank, his shape was quickly lost ;
Some into *Swine* she turn'd, but most
To *Lyons* arm'd with teeth and claws ;
Others like *Wolves*, with open Jaws
Did howl ; But some (more savage) took
The *Tiger's* dreadful shape and look.
  But wise *Ulysses* by the *Aid*
Of *Hermes*, had to him convey'd
A *Flow'r*, whose virtue did suppress
The force of charms, and their success.   20

While his *Mates* drank so deep, that they
Were turn'd to *Swine*, which fed all day
On *Mast*, and humane food had left ;
Of shape and voice at once bereft.
Only the *Mind* (above all charms,)
Unchang'd, did mourn those monstrous harms.
    O worthless *herbs*, and weaker *Arts*
To change their *Limbs*, but not their *Hearts*!
Mans *life and vigor* keep within,
Lodg'd in the *Center*, not the *Skin*.   30
Those piercing charms and poysons, which
His *inward parts* taint and bewitch,
More fatal are, than such, which can
Outwardly only spoile the man.
Those change his *shape* and make it foul ;
But these deform and kill his soul.

                Metrum 6. Lib. 3.

All *sorts* of men, that live on Earth,
Have one *beginning* and one *birth*.
For all things there is one *Father*,
Who *lays out* all, and all doth *gather*.
He the warm Sun with rays adorns,
And fils with brightness the Moon's horns.
The azur'd heav'ns with stars he burnish'd
And the round world with creatures furnish'd.
But *Men* (made to inherit all,)
His *own Sons* he was pleas'd to call,   10
And that they might be so indeed,
He gave them *Souls* of divine seed.
A noble *Offspring* surely then
Without distinction, are all men.
    O why so vainly do some boast
Their *Birth* and *Blood*, and a great *Hoste*
Of Ancestors, whose *Coats* and *Crests*
Are some rav'nous *Birds* or *Beasts* !
If *Extraction* they look for
And *God*, the great *Progenitor* :   20
No man, though of the meanest state
Is *base*, or can *degenerate* ;
Unless to *Vice* and *lewdness* bent
He leaves and *taints* his true *descent*

The old man of Verona out of Claudian.

Fælix, qui propriis ævum transegit in arvis,
Una domus puerum &c.

Most happy man! who in his own sweet *fields*
Spent all his time, to whom one *Cottage* yields
In *age* and *youth* a lodging : who grown *old*
Walks with his *staff* on the same *soil* and *mold*
Where he did creep an *infant,* and can tell
Many fair years spent in one quiet *Cell* !
No *toils* of fate made him from home far known,
Nor forreign *waters* drank, driv'n from his own.
No loss by *Sea,* no wild *lands* wastful war
Vex'd him ; not the brib'd *Coil* of *gowns* at bar.　　　10
Exempt from *cares,* in *Cities* never seen
The fresh *field-air* he loves, and rural *green.*
The years set *turns* by *fruits,* not *Consuls* knows ;
Autumn by apples : *May* by blossom'd boughs.
Within one hedg his *Sun* doth set and rise,
The world's wide day his short Demeasnes comprise.
Where he observes some known, concrescent *twig*
Now grown an *Oak,* and old, like him, and big.
Verona he doth for the *Indies* take,
And as the *red Sea* counts *Benacus* lake.　　　20
Yet are his *limbs* and *strength* untir'd, and he
A lusty *Grandsire* three *descents* doth see.
Travel and sail who will, search sea, or shore ;
This man hath *liv'd,* and that hath *wander'd* more.

The Sphere of Archimedes out of Claudian.

Jupiter *in parvo cum cerneret æthera vitro*
Risit, & ad superos &c.

When *Jove* a heav'n of small glass did behold,
He smil'd, and to the Gods these words he told.
Comes then the power of mans *Art* to this ?
In a fraile *Orbe* my work new acted is.
The *poles* decrees, the *fate* of things : *God's* laws
Down by his *Art* old *Archimedes* draws.

10 *gowns GC* : *growns 1678*

Spirits inclos'd the sev'ral *Stars* attend,
And orderly the *living work* they bend.
A feigned *Zodiac* measures out the year,
Ev'ry new *month* a false *Moon* doth appear.   10
And now bold *industry* is proud, it can
Wheel round its *world*, and rule the *Stars* by man.
Why at *Salmoneus* thunder do I stand?
Nature is rivall'd by a *single hand*.

The Phœnix *out of* Claudian.

Oceani summo circumfluus æquore lucus
Trans Indos, Eurumque viret &c,

A grove there grows round with the *Sea* confin'd
Beyond the *Indies*, and the *Eastern* wind.
Which, as the *Sun* breaks forth in his first beam,
Salutes his *steeds*, and hears him whip his *team*.
When with his dewy *Coach* the *Eastern* Bay
Crackles, whence blusheth the approaching day;
And blasted with his burnish'd *wheels*, the night
In a pale dress doth vanish from the light.
  This the blest *Phœnix* Empire is, here he
Alone exempted from mortality,   10
Enjoys a land, where no diseases raign;
And ne'r afflicted, like our world, with pain.
A *Bird* most equal to the Gods, which vies
For length of life and durance, with the skyes;
And with renewed limbs tires ev'ry age,
His appetite he never doth asswage
With common food.   Nor doth he use to drink
When thirsty, on some *River's* muddy brink.
A purer, vital *heat* shot from the Sun
Doth nourish him, and *airy sweets* that come   20
From *Tethis* lap, he tasteth at his need;
On such *abstracted Diet* doth he feed.
  A secret *Light* there streams from both his Eyes
A firy *hue* about his *cheeks* doth rise.
His *Crest* grows up into a glorious *Star*
Giv'n t' adorn his head, and shines so far,
That piercing through the bosom of the night
It rends the darkness with a gladsome light.
His thighs like *Tyrian* scarlet, and his wings
(More swift than *Winds* are,) have skie-colour'd *rings*   30

26 far,] far. *1678*

Flowry and rich : and round about inroll'd
Their utmost *borders* glister all with gold.
Hee's not conceiv'd, nor springs he from the Earth,
But is himself the *Parent*, and the *birth*.
None him begets ; his fruitful death reprieves
Old age, and by his funerals he lives.
For when the tedious *Summer*'s gone about
A thousand times : so many *Winters* out,
So many *Springs* : and *May* doth still restore
Those leaves, which *Autumn* had blown off before ; 40
Then prest with years his vigour doth decline
Foil'd with the number ; as a stately *Pine*
Tir'd out with storms, bends from the top & height
Of *Caucasus*, and falls with its own weight :
Whose part is torn with dayly *blasts*, with *Rain*
Part is consum'd, and part with *Age* again.
So now his Eyes grown dusky, fail to see
Far off, and drops of colder rheums there be
Fall'n slow and dreggy from them ; such in sight
The cloudy *Moon* is, having spent her light. 50
And now his *wings*, which used to contend
With *Tempests*, scarce from the low Earth ascend.
He knows his time is out ! and doth provide
New principles of life ; herbs he brings dried
From the hot hills, and with rich spices frames
A *Pile* shall burn, and *Hatch* him with its flames.
On this the *weakling* sits ; salutes the Sun
With pleasant noise, and prays and begs for some
Of his own fire, that quickly may restore
The youth and vigour, which he had before. 60
Whom soon as *Phœbus* spyes, stopping his rayns,
He makes a stand and thus allayes his pains.
O thou that buriest old age in thy grave,
And art by seeming funerals to have
A new return of life ! whose custom 'tis
To rise by ruin, and by death to miss
Ev'n death it self : a new beginning take,
And that thy wither'd body now forsake !
Better thy self by this thy change ! This sed,
He shakes his *locks*, and from his golden *head* 70

44 *Caucasus*] *Causacus 1678*

Shoots one bright *beam*, which smites with vital fire
The willing bird ; to burn is his desire,
That he may live again : he's proud in death,
And goes in haste to gain a better breath.
The spicie heap fir'd with cœlestial rays
Doth burn the aged *Phœnix*, when strait stays
The Chariot of th' amazed *Moon* ; the *pole*
Resists the wheeling, swift *Orbs*, and the whole
Fabric of *Nature* at a stand remains,
Till the old bird a new, young being gains.   80
All stop and charge the faithful flames, that they
Suffer not nature's glory to decay.
    By this time, *life* which in the ashes lurks
Hath fram'd the *Heart*, and taught new *bloud* new *works* ;
The whole *heap* stirs, and ev'ry *part* assumes
Due vigour ; th' *Embers* too are turn'd to *plumes*.
The parent in the Issue now revives,
But young and brisk ; the bounds of both these lives
With very little space between the same,
Were parted only by the middle flame.   90
    To *Nilus* straight he goes to consecrate
His parents ghoste ; his mind is to translate
His dust to *Egypt*. Now he hastes away
Into a distant land, and doth convey
The ashes in a turf. Birds do attend
His Journey without number, and defend
His pious flight like to a guard ; the sky
Is clouded with the Army, as they fly.
Nor is there one of all those thousands dares
Affront his leader : they with solomn cares   100
Attend the progress of their youthful king ;
Not the rude hawk, nor th' Eagle that doth bring
Arms up to *Jove*, fight now ; lest they displease ;
The miracle enacts a common peace.
So doth the *Parthian* lead from *Tigris* side
His barbarous troops, full of a lavish pride
In pearls and habit, he adorns his head
With royal tires : his steed with gold is lead.
His robes, for which the scarlet fish is sought,
With rare *Assyrian* needle work are wrought.   110
And proudly reigning o're his rascal bands,
He raves and triumphs in his large Commands.

A City of *Egypt* famous in all lands
For rites, adores the *Sun*, his temple stands
There on a hundred pillars by account
Dig'd from the quarries of the *Theban* mount.
Hcrc, as the Custom did require (they say,)
His happy parents dust down he doth lay ;
Then to the Image of his *Lord* he bends
And to the flames his burden strait commends.   120
Unto the *Altars* thus he destinates
His own Remains : the light doth gild the gates ;
Perfumes divine the *Censers* up do send :
While th' *Indian* odour doth it self extend
To the *Pelusian* fens, and filleth all
The men it meets with the sweet storm.   A gale
To which compar'd, *Nectar* it self is vile :
Fills the seav'n channels of the misty *Nile.*
   O happy bird ! sole heir to thy own dust !
Death, to whose force all other Creatures must   130
Submit, saves thee.   Thy ashes make thee rise ;
'Tis not thy nature, but thy age that dies.
Thou hast seen All ! and to the times that run
Thou art as great a witness, as the Sun.
Thou saw'st the *deluge*, when the sea outvied
The land, and drown'd the mountains with the tide.
What year the stragling *Phaeton* did fire
The world, thou know'st.   And no plagues can conspire
Against thy life ; alone thou do'st arise
Above mortality ; the Destinies   140
Spin not thy days out with their fatal Clue ;
They have no Law, to which thy life is due.

Pious thoughts and Ejaculations.

To his Books.

Bright books ! the *perspectives* to our weak sights :
The clear *projections* of discerning lights.
Burning and shining *Thoughts* ; man's posthume *day* :
The *track* of fled souls, and their *Milkie-way.*
The dead *alive* and *busie*, the still *voice*
Of inlarg'd Spirits, kind heav'ns white *Decoys.*

Who lives with you, lives like those knowing *flow'rs*,
Which in commerce with *light*, spend all their hours :
Which shut to *Clouds*, and *shadows* nicely shun ;
But with glad haste unveil to *kiss* the Sun.   10
Beneath you all is dark and a dead night ;
Which whoso lives in, wants both health and sight.
  By sucking you, the wise (like *Bees*) do grow
Healing and rich, though this they do most slow :
Because most choicely, for as great a store
Have we of *Books*, as Bees of *herbs*, or more.
And the great task to *try*, then know the good :
To discern *weeds*, and Judge of wholsome *Food*,
Is a rare, scant performance ; for *Man* dyes
Oft e're 'tis done, while the *bee* feeds and flyes.   20
But you were all choice *Flow'rs*, all set and drest
By old, sage *florists*, who well knew the best.
And I amidst you all am turn'd a *weed* !
Not wanting knowledge, but for want of heed.
Then thank thy self *wild fool*, that would'st not be
Content to know——what was to much for thee !

Looking back.

Fair, shining *Mountains* of my pilgrimage,
    And flow'ry *Vales*, whose flow'rs 'were stars :
The *days* and *nights* of my first, happy age ;
    An age without distast and warrs :
When I by thoughts ascend your *Sunny heads*,
    And mind those sacred, *midnight* Lights :
By which I walk'd, when curtain'd Rooms and Beds
    Confin'd, or seal'd up others sights :
        O then how bright
        And quick a light   10
Doth brush my heart and scatter night ;
        Chasing that shade
        Which my sins made,
    While I so *spring*, as if I could not *fade* !
How brave a prospect is a bright *Back-side* !
    Where flow'rs and palms refresh the Eye :
And days well spent like the glad *East* abide,
    Whose morning-glories cannot dye !

14 slow :] slow, *LGC*   18 *Food, LGC*: *Food*. 1678 : *Food, MS.*
alteration in Bodleian copy.

The Shower.

Waters above! eternal Springs!
The dew, that silvers the *Doves* wings!
O welcom, welcom to the sad :
Give dry dust drink ; drink that makes glad !
Many fair *Ev'nings*, many *Flow'rs*
Sweeten'd with rich and gentle showers
Have I enjoy'd, and down have run
Many a fine and shining *Sun* ;
But never till this happy hour
Was blest with such an *Evening-shower* !   10

Discipline.

Fair prince of life, lights living well !
Who hast the keys of death and hell !
If the mole man despise thy day,
Put chains of darkness in his way.
Teach him how deep, how various are
The Councels of thy love and care.
When Acts of grace and a long peace
Breed but rebellion and displease ;
Then give him his own way and will,
Where lawless he may run until   10
His own choice hurts him, and the sting
Of his foul sins full sorrows bring.
If Heav'n and Angels, hopes and mirth
Please not the *mole* so much as Earth :
Give him his *Mine* to dig, or dwell ;
And one sad *Scheme* of hideous hell.

The Ecclipse.

Whither, O whither did'st thou fly
When I did grieve thine holy Eye ?
When thou did'st mourn to see me lost,
And all thy Care and Councels crost.
O do not grieve where e'er thou art !
Thy grief is an undoing smart.
Which doth not only pain, but break
My heart, and makes me blush to speak.
Thy anger I could kiss, and will :
But (O !) thy grief, thy grief doth kill.   10

Discipline] 3 mole *GC* : mule *1678*

X X

Affliction.

O come, and welcom! Come, refine;
For *Moors* if wash'd by thee, will shine.
Man *blossoms* at thy touch; and he
When thou draw'st blood, is thy *Rose-tree.*
Crosses make strait his *crooked* ways,
And *Clouds* but cool his *dog-star* days.
Diseases too, when by thee blest,
Are both *restoratives* and *rest.*
  Flow'rs that in *Sun-shines* riot still,
Dye scorch'd and sapless; though *storms* kill.   10
The fall is fair ev'n to desire,
Where in their *sweetness* all expire.
O come, pour on! what *calms* can be
So fair as *storms*, that appease thee?

Retirement.

Fresh *fields* and *woods*! the Earth's fair *face*,
God's *foot-stool*, and mans *dwelling-place.*
I ask not why the first *Believer*
Did love to be a Country liver?
Who to secure pious content
Did pitch by *groves* and *wells* his tent;
Where he might view the boundless *skie*,
And all those glorious *lights* on high:
With flying *meteors*, *mists* and *show'rs*,
Subjected *hills, trees, meads* and *Flow'rs*:   10
And ev'ry minute bless the King
And wise Creatour of each thing.
  I ask not why he did remove
To happy *Mamre*'s holy grove,
Leaving the *Citie*'s of the plain
To *Lot* and his successless train?
All various Lusts in *Cities* still
Are found; they are the *Thrones* of Ill.
The dismal *Sinks*, where blood is spill'd,
Cages with much uncleanness fill'd.   20
But *rural shades* are the sweet fense
Of piety and innocence.

21 fense] sense *LGC*

They are the *Meek*'s calm region, where
Angels descend, and rule the sphere :
Where heav'n lyes *Leiguer*, and the *Dove*
Duely as *Dew*, comes from above.
If *Eden* be on Earth at all,
'Tis that, which we the *Country* call.

The Revival.

Unfold, unfold ! take in his light,
Who makes thy Cares more short than night.
The Joys, which with his *Day-star* rise,
He deals to all, but drowsy Eyes :
And what the men of this world miss,
Some *drops* and *dews* of future bliss.
  Hark ! how his *winds* have chang'd their *note*,
And with warm *whispers* call thee out.
The *frosts* are past, the *storms* are gone :
And backward *life* at last comes on.   10
The lofty *groves* in express Joyes
Reply unto the *Turtles* voice,
And here in *dust* and *dirt*, O here
The *Lilies* of his love appear !

The Day-spring.

Early, while yet the *dark* was gay,
And *gilt* with stars, more trim than day :
Heav'ns *Lily*, and the Earth's chast *Rose* : ⎱ *S. Mark*
The green, immortal B R A N C H arose ; ⎰ *c. 1. v. 35.*
And in a solitary place
Bow'd to his father his bless'd face.
  If this calm season pleas'd my *Prince*,
Whose *fullness* no need could evince,
Why should not I poor, silly sheep
His *hours*, as well as *practice* keep?   10
Not that his hand is tyed to these,
From whom *time* holds his transient *Lease :*
But *mornings*, new Creations are,
When men all night sav'd by his Care,
Are still reviv'd ; and well he may
Expect them grateful with the day.

So for that first *drawght* of his hand,
Which finish'd heav'n and sea and land, ⎫
The *Sons* of God their thanks did bring, ⎬ Job. *c.* 38.
And all the *Morning-stars* did sing. ⎭ *v.* 7.   20
Besides, as his part heretofore
The *firstlings* were of all, that bore :
So now each day from all he saves,
Their Soul's *first thoughts* and fruits he craves.
This makes him daily shed and shower
His graces at this early hour ;
Which both his Care and Kindness show,
Chearing the good : quickning the slow.
As holy friends mourn at delay,
And think each minute an hour's stay :   30
So his divine and loving *Dove*
With longing throws doth heave and move,
And soare about us, while we sleep :
Sometimes quite through that *lock* doth *peep*,
And shine ; but always without fail
Before the slow Sun can unveile,
In new *Compassions* breaks like light,
And *Morning-looks*, which scatter night.
   And wilt thou let thy *creature* be
When *thou* hast watch'd, asleep to thee ?   40
Why to unwellcome, loath'd surprises
Do'st leave him, having left his vices ?
Since these, if suffer'd, may again
Lead back the *living*, to the *slain*.
O change this *Scourge* ! or, if as yet
None less will my transgressions fit :
Dissolve, dissolve ! death cannot do
What I would not submit unto.

The Recovery.

Fair *Vessell* of our daily light, whose proud
And previous *glories* gild that blushing Cloud :
Whose lively *fires* in swift projections glance
From hill to hill, and by refracted chance
Burnish some neighbour-*rock*, or tree, and then
Fly off in coy and winged *flams* agen :
        If thou this day
        Hold on thy way,

Know, I have got a greater *light* than thine ;
A light, whose *shade* and *back-parts* make thee shine.   10
    Then get thee down : then get thee down ;
    I have a *Sun* now of my own.

II.

Those nicer livers, who without thy Rays
Stirr not abroad, those may thy lustre praise :
And wanting light (*light*, which no *wants* doth know !)
To thee (weak *shiner* !) like blind *Persians* bow ;
But where that *Sun*, which tramples on thy head,
From his own bright, eternal *Eye* doth shed
    One living *Ray*,
    There thy dead day   20
Is needless, and man to a *light* made free,
Which shews what thou can'st neither shew, nor see.
    Then get thee down, Then get thee down ;
    I have a *Sun* now of my own.

The Nativity.

Written in the year 1656.

Peace ? and to all the world ? sure, one
And he the prince of peace, hath none.
He travels to be born, and then
Is born to travel more agen.
Poor *Galile* ! thou can'st not be
The place for his Nativity.
His restless mother's call'd away,
And not deliver'd, till she pay.
   A *Tax* ? 'tis so still ! we can see
The Church thrive in her misery ,   10
And like her head at *Bethlem*, rise
When she opprest with troubles, lyes.
Rise ? should all fall, we cannot be
In more extremities than he.
Great *Type* of passions ! come what will,
Thy grief exceeds all *copies* still.
Thou cam'st from heav'n to earth, that we
Might go from Earth to Heav'n with thee.
And though thou found'st no welcom here,
Thou did'st provide us *mansions* there.   20

A *stable* was thy *Court*, and when
Men turn'd to *beasts* ; Beasts would be *Men*.
They were thy *Courtiers*, others none ;
And their poor *Manger* was thy *Throne*.
No swadling *silks* thy Limbs did fold,
Though thou could'st turn thy Rays to gold.
No *Rockers* waited on thy birth,
No *Cradles* stirr'd : nor songs of mirth ;
But her chast *Lap* and sacred *Brest*
Which lodg'd thee first, did give thee *rest*.   30
But stay : what light is that doth stream,
And drop here in a gilded beam ?
It is thy Star runs *page*, and brings
Thy tributary *Eastern* Kings.
Lord ! grant some *Light* to us, that we
May with them find the way to thee.
Behold what mists eclipse the day :
How dark it is ! shed down one *Ray*
To guide us out of this sad night,
And say once more, *Let there be Light*.   40

The true Christmas.

So stick up *Ivie* and the *Bays*,
And then restore the *heathen* ways.
Green will remind you of the spring,
Though this great day denies the thing.
And mortifies the Earth and all
But your wild *Revels*, and loose *Hall*.
Could you wear *Flow'rs*, and *Roses* strow
Blushing upon your breasts *warm Snow*,
That very *dress* your lightness will
Rebuke, and wither at the Ill.   10
The brightness of this day we owe
Not unto *Music*, *Masque* nor *Showe* :
Nor gallant *furniture*, nor *Plate* ;
But to the *Manger's* mean Estate.
His *life* while here, as well as *birth*,
Was but a check to *pomp* and *mirth* ;
And all mans *greatness* you may see
Condemn'd by his *humility*.

26 Rays] rags *LG* 16 check] check *1678* (*MS. alteration in Bodleian copy*)

Then leave your open *house* and *noise*,
To welcom him with *holy Joys*,   20
And the poor *Shepherd's* watchfulness :
Whom *light* and *hymns* from Heav'n did bless.
What you *abound* with, cast abroad
To those that *want*, and ease your loade.
Who empties thus, will bring more in ;
But riot is both *loss* and *Sin.*
Dress finely what comes not in sight,
And then you keep your *Christmas* right.

The Request.

O thou ! who did'st deny to me
This world's ador'd felicity,
And ev'ry big, imperious lust,
Which fools admire in sinful Dust ;
With those fine, subtile *twists*, that tye
Their *bundles* of foul gallantry :
Keep still my weak Eyes from the *shine*
Of those gay things, which are not thine,
And shut my Ears against the noise
Of wicked, though applauded *Joys.*   10
For thou in any land hast store
Of shades and Coverts for thy poor,
Where from the busie dust and heat,
As well as storms, they may retreat.
A Rock, or Bush are douny beds,
When thou art there crowning their heads
With secret blessings : or a *Tire*
Made of the *Comforter's* live-fire.
And when thy goodness in the *dress*
Of anger, will not seem to bless :   20
Yet do'st thou give them that rich *Rain,*
Which as it drops, clears all again.
    O ˙what kind *Visits* daily pass
'Twixt thy great self and such poor *grass,*
With what sweet looks doth thy love shine
On those low *Violets* of thine !
While the tall *Tulip* is accurst,
And *Crowns Imperial* dye with thirst.

O give me still those secret meals,
Those rare *Repasts*, which thy love deals!   30
Give me that Joy, which none can grieve,
And which in all griefs doth relieve.
This is the portion thy Child begs,
Not that of rust, and rags and dregs.

Jordanis.

Quid celebras auratam undam, Et combusta pyropis
   Flumina, vel Medio quæ serit æthra salo?
Æternùm refluis si pernoctaret in undis
   Phœbus, *& incertam sydera suda* Tethyn
Si colerent, tantæ gemmæ! nil cærula librem:
   Sorderet rubro in littore dives Eos.
Pactoli *mea lympha macras ditabit arenas,*
   Atq; Universum gutta minuta Tagum.
O charum caput! O cincinnos unda beatos
   Libata! O domini balnea Sancta mei!   10
Quod fortunatum voluit spectare Canalem,
   Hoc erat in laudes area parva tuas.
Jordanis *in medio perfusus flumine lavit,*
   Divinoq; tuas ore beavit aquas.
Ah! Solyma *infœlix rivis obsessa prophanis!*
   Amisit Genium *porta* Bethesda *suum.*
Hic Orientis *aquæ currunt, & apostata* Pharpar,
   Atq; Abana *immundo turbidus amne fluit.*
Ethnica te totam cum fœdavere fluenta,
   Mansit Christicolâ Jordanis *unus aqua.*   20

Servilii Fatum, *sive* Vindicta divina.

Et sic in cythara, *sic in* dulcedine *vitæ*
   Et facti & luctus regnat amarities.
Quàm subitò in fastum *extensos atq;* effera *vultus*
   Ultrici *oppressit* vilis *arena sinu!*
Si violæ, spiransque crocus: si lilium ἄεινον
   Non nisi Justorum nascitur è cinere:
Spinarum, tribuliq; atq; infœlicis avenæ
   Quantus in hoc tumulo & qualis acervus erit?

Dii superi ! damnosa piis sub sydera longum
Mansuris stabilem conciliate fidem ! 10
Sic olim in cœlum post nimbos clariùs ibunt,
Supremo occidui tot velut astra die.
Quippe ruunt horæ, qualisq; in Corpore vixit,
Talis it in tenebras bis moriturus homo.

De Salmone.

Ad virum optimum, & sibi familiariùs notum: D. *Thomam Poellum*
Cantrevensem : S. S. Theologiæ Doctorem.

Accipe prærapido Salmonem in gurgite captum,
Ex imo in summas cum penetrásset aquas.
Mentitæ culicis quem forma elusit inanis :
Picta coloratis plumea musca notis.
Dum captat, capitur ; vorat inscius, ipse vorandus ;
Fitq; cibi raptor grata rapina mali.
Alma quies ! miseræ merces ditissima vitæ,
Quàm tutò in tacitis hic latuisset aquis !
Qui dum spumosi fremitus & murmura rivi
Quæritat, hamato fit cita præda cibo. 10
Quam grave magnarum specimen dant ludicra rerum ?
Gurges est mundus : Salmo, homo : pluma, dolus.

The World.

Can any tell me what it is? can you,
   That wind your thoughts into a *Clue*
To guide out others, while your selves stay in,
              And hug the Sin?
  I, who so long have in it liv'd,
             That if I might,
  In truth I would not be repriev'd :
           Have neither sight,
        Nor sense that knows
          These *Ebbs* and *Flows.* 10
But since of all, all may be said,
And *likelines* doth but upbraid,
  And mock the *Truth*, which still is lost
In fine *Conceits*, like streams in a sharp frost :

The World] 12 upbraid,] upbraid. *1678*: upbraid *LGC*

I will not strive, nor the *Rule* break
Which doth give Loosers leave to speak.
Then false and foul World, and unknown
                    Ev'n to thy own:
Here I renounce thee, and resign
Whatever thou can'st say, is thine.   20
    Thou art not *Truth*; for he that tries
Shall find thee all deceit and lyes.
Thou art not *friendship*; for in thee
'Tis but the *bait* of policy.
Which, like a *Viper* lodg'd in *Flow'rs*,
Its venom through that sweetness pours.
And when not so, then always 'tis
A fadeing *paint*; the short-liv'd bliss
Of *air* and *Humour*: out and in
Like *Colours* in a *Dolphin*'s skin.   30
But must not live beyond *one day*,
Or *Convenience*; then away.
Thou art not *Riches*; for that *Trash*
Which one age hoords, the next doth wash
And so severely sweep away;
That few remember, where it lay.
So rapid *streams* the wealthy *land*
About them, have at their command:
And shifting *channels* here restore,
There break down, what they bank'd before.   40
Thou art not *Honour*; for those gay
Feathers will wear, and drop away;
And princes to some upstart *line*
Give new ones, that are full as fine.
Thou art not *pleasure*; for thy *Rose*
Upon a *thorn* doth still repose;
Which if not cropt, will quickly shed;
But soon as cropt, grows dull and dead.
    Thou art the *sand*, which fills one *glass*,
And then doth to another pass;   50
And could I put thee to a stay,
Thou art but *dust*! then go thy way,
And leave me *clean* and bright, though *poor*;
Who stops thee, doth but *dawb* his floor,

30 skin.] skin : *G* : skin ; *C*   32 Or *Convenience*] Or for *Convenience L*

And *Swallow*-like, when he hath done,
To *unknown dwellings* must be gone!
Welcom pure thoughts and peaceful hours
Inrich'd with *Sunshine* and with *show'rs*;
Welcom fair hopes and holy Cares,
The not to be repented *shares*   60
Of time and business : the sure *rode*
Unto my last and lov'd *Abode*!
                              O supreme *Bliss*!
The Circle, Center and Abyss
Of blessings, never let me miss
Nor leave that *Path*, which leads to thee :
Who art alone all things to me!
I hear, I see all the long day
The noise and pomp of the *broad way*;
I note their Course and proud approaches :   70
Their silks, perfumes and glittering Coaches.
But in the *narrow way* to thee
I observe only poverty,
And despis'd things : and all along
The ragged, mean and humble throng
Are still on foot, and as they go,
They sigh and say ; *Their Lord went so*!
   Give me my *staff* then, as it stood
When green and growing in the Wood.
(Those *stones*, which for the *Altar* serv'd,   80
Might not be smooth'd, nor finely carv'd :)
With this *poor stick* I'le pass the *Foord*
As *Jacob* did ; and thy dear *word*,
As thou hast dress'd it : not as *Witt*
And *deprav'd tastes* have poyson'd it :
Shall in the passage be my meat,
And none else will thy Servant eat.
Thus, thus and in no other sort
Will I set forth, though laugh'd at for't ;
And leaving the wise *World* their way,   90
Go through ; though Judg'd to go astray.

73 poverty,] poverty. *1678*   83 *word,*] *word. 1678*

The Bee.

From fruitful *beds* and flowry *borders*
Parcell'd to wastful Ranks and Orders,
Where *state* grasps more than plain *Truth* needs
And wholesome *Herbs* are starv'd by *Weeds* :
To the wild Woods I will be gone,
And the course Meals of great *Saint John*.
  When truth and piety are mist
Both in the Rulers and the Priest ;
When pity is not cold, but dead,
And the rich eat the Poor like bread ;   10
While factious heads with open Coile
And force first make, then share the spoile :
To *Horeb* then *Elias* goes,
And in the *Desart* grows the *Rose*.
    Hail Christal Fountains and fresh shades,
      Where no proud look invades.
No busie worldling hunts away
The sad Retirer all the day :
Haile happy harmless solitude,
Our Sanctuary from the rude   20
And scornful world : the calm recess
Of faith, and hope and holiness !
Here something still like *Eden* looks,
Hony in Woods, *Julips* in Brooks :
And *Flow'rs*, whose rich, unrifled *Sweets*
With a chast kiss the cool dew greets.
When the toyls of the Day are done
And the tir'd world sets with the Sun,
Here *flying* winds and *flowing* Wells
Are the wise, watchful Hermits *Bells* ;   30
Their buisie *murmurs* all the night
To *praise* or *prayer* do invite,
And with an awful sound arrest
And piously employ his breast.
    When in the *East* the Dawn doth blush,
Here cool, fresh *Spirits* the air brush ;

2 Orders,] Orders. *1678*   16 invades.] invades, *LGC*

Herbs (strait) get up, *Flow'rs* peep and spread :
Trees whisper praise, and bow the head.
Birds from the shades of night releast
Look round about, then quit the neast, 40
And with united gladness sing
The glory of the morning's King.
The *Hermit* hears, and with meek voice
Offers his own up, and their Joys :
Then prays, that all the world may be
Blest with as sweet an unity.
If sudden storms the day invade,
They flock about him to the shade :
Where wisely they expect the end,
Giving the tempest time to spend ; 50
And hard by shelters on some bough
Hilarion's servant, the sage *Crow*.
O purer years of light, and grace !
The *diff'rence* is great, as the *space*
'Twixt you and us : who blindly run
After *false-fires*, and leave the *Sun*.
Is not fair *Nature* of her self
Much richer than dull *paint*, or *pelf*?
And are not *streams* at the *Spring-head*
More sweet than in carv'd *Stone*, or *Lead*? 60
But *fancy* and some *Artist's* tools
Frame a Religion for fools.
The *truth*, which once was plainly taught,
With *thorns* and *briars* now is fraught.
Some part is with bold *Fables* spotted,
Some by strange *Comments* wildly blotted :
And *discord* (old Corruption's Crest,)
With *blood* and *blame* hath stain'd the rest.
So *Snow*, which in its first descents
A whiteness, like pure heav'n presents, 70
When touch'd by *Man* is quickly soil'd
And after trodden down, and spoil'd.
O lead me, where I may be free
In *truth* and *Spirit* to serve thee !
Where undisturb'd I may converse
With thy great self, and there rehearse
Thy gifts with thanks, and from thy store
Who art all blessings, beg much more !

Give me the Wisdom of the *Bee*,
And her unwearied Industry :   80
That from the *wild Gourds* of these days
I may extract Health and thy praise ;
Who can'st turn darkness into light,
And in my weakness shew thy might !
    Suffer me not in any want
To seek refreshment from a *Plant*,
Thou did'st not *set* ! since all must be
Pluck'd up, whose *growth* is not from thee.
'Tis not the *garden* and the *Bowrs*,
Nor *fense* and *forms* that give to flow'rs   90
Their *wholsomness* : but thy *good will*,
Which *truth* and *pureness* purchase still.
    Then since corrupt man hath driv'n hence
Thy kind and saving *Influence*,
And *Balm* is no more to be had
In all the Coasts of *Gilead* :
Go with me to the *shade* and *cell*,
Where thy best *Servants* once did dwell.
There let me know thy *Will*, and see
Exil'd *Religion* own'd by thee.   100
For thou can'st turn dark *Grots* to *Halls*,
And make *Hills* blossome like the *vales* :
Decking their untill'd *heads* with flow'rs
And fresh delights for all sad hours :
Till from them, like a laden *Bee*,
I may fly home, and *hive* with thee.

To Christian Religion.

Farewel thou true and tried Refection
Of the still poor and meek *Election* !
Farewel Souls *Joy*, the quickning *health*
Of Spirits, and their secret *wealth* !
Farewel my *Morning-star*, the bright
And dawning *looks* of the true Light !
O blessed *shiner* ! tell me whither
Thou will be gone, when night comes hither ?
A *Seer*, that observ'd thee in
Thy Course, and watch'd the growth of Sin,   10

86 *Plant*,] *Plant. 1678* : *plant LGC*

Hath giv'n his Judgment and foretold,
That *West-ward* hence thy *Course* will hold :
And when the day with us is done,
There fix, and shine a glorious Sun.
O hated *shades* and *darkness* ! when
You have got here the Sway agen,
And like unwholsome *fogs* withstood
The light, and blasted all that's good :
Who shall the happy *shepherds* be
To watch the next *Nativity*   20
Of Truth and brightness, and make way
For the returning, rising day ?
O ! what year will bring back our bliss,
Or who shall live, when God doth this ?
   Thou *Rock* of Ages, and the *Rest*
Of all, that for thee are opprest !
Send down the *Spirit* of thy truth,
That Spirit, which the tender *Youth*
And first *growths* of thy *Spouse* did spread
Through all the world, from one small *head* !   30
Then, if *to blood we must resist*
Let thy mild *Dove*, and our high *Priest*
Help us, when man proves false, or frowns,
To bear the *Cross*, and save our *Crowns* :
O ! honour those, that honour thee !
Make *Babes* to still the Enemy :
And teach an *Infant* of few days
To perfect by his death, thy praise !
Let none defile what thou did'st *wed*,
Nor tear the *garland* from her head :   40
But chast and chearful let her dye,
And pretious in the *Bridegrooms* Eye !
So to thy glory, and her praise
These last shall be her brightest dayes.

Revel. Chap. last, vers. 17.
The Spirit and the Bride say, Come.

DAPHNIS.

An Elegiac *Eclogue.*

The Interlocutors, *Damon, Menalcas.*

Da. What clouds, *Menalcas*, do oppress thy brow?
Flow'rs in a Sunshine never look so low.
Is *Nisa* still cold Flint? or have thy Lambs
Met with the Fox by straying from their Dams?

Men. Ah! *Damon*, no; my Lambs are safe, & she
Is kind, and much more white than they can be.
But what doth life, when most serene, afford
Without a worm, which gnaws her fairest gourd?
Our days of gladness are but short reliefs,
Giv'n to reserve us for enduring griefs.   10
So smiling Calms close Tempests breed, wch break
Like spoilers out, and kill our flocks, when weak.
    I heard last *May* (and *May* is still high Spring,)
The pleasant *Philomel* her Vespers sing.
The green wood glitter'd with the golden Sun
And all the West like Silver shin'd; not one
Black cloud, no rags, nor spots did stain
The Welkins beauty: nothing frown'd like rain;
But e're night came, that Scene of fine sights turn'd
To fierce dark showrs; the Air with lightnings burn'd;   20
The woods sweet Syren rudely thus opprest,
Gave to the Storm her weak and weary Breast.
I saw her next day on her last cold bed;
And *Daphnis* so, just so is *Daphnis* dead!

Da. So Violets, so doth the Primrose fall,
At once the Springs pride and its funeral.
Such easy sweets get off still in their prime,
And stay not here, to wear the soil of Time.
While courser Flow'rs (which none would miss, if past;)
To scorching Summers, and cold Autumns last.   30

Men. Souls need not time, the early forward things
Are always fledg'd, and gladly use their Wings,

17 cloud] cloud appeared *LG*   27 easy] early *LG*   29 past;)] past; *1678*

Or else great parts, when injur'd quit the Crowd,
To shine above still, not behind the Cloud.
And is't not just to leave those to the night,
That madly hate, and persecute the light?
Who doubly dark, all *Negroes* do exceed,
And inwardly are true black Moores indeed.
    Da. The punishment still manifests the Sin,
As outward signs shew the disease within,   40
While worth opprest mounts to a nobler height,
And Palm-like bravely overtops the weight.
    So where swift *Isca* from our lofty hills
With lowd farewels descends, and foming fills
A wider Channel, like some great port-vein,
With large rich streams to feed the humble plain :
I saw an Oak, whose stately height and shade
Projected far, a goodly shelter made,
And from the top with thick diffused Boughs
In distant rounds grew, like a Wood-nymphs house.   50
Here many Garlands won at Roundel-lays
Old shepheards hung up in those happy days,
With knots and girdles, the dear spoils and dress
Of such bright maids, as did true lovers bless.
And many times had old *Amphion* made
His beauteous Flock acquainted with this shade ;
A Flock, whose fleeces were as smooth and white
As those, the wellkin shews in Moonshine night.
Here, when the careless world did sleep, have I
In dark records and numbers noblie high   60
The visions of our black, but brightest Bard
From old *Amphion*'s mouth full often heard ;
With all those plagues poor shepheards since have known,
And Ridles more, which future times must own.
While on his pipe young *Hylas* plaid, and made
Musick as solemn as the song and shade.
But the curs'd owner from the trembling top
To the firm brink, did all those branches lop,
And in one hour what many years had bred,
The pride and beauty of the plain lay dead.   70
The undone Swains in sad songs mourn'd their loss,
While storms & cold winds did improve the Cross.

    39 *Da.*] *Da, 1678*

Y y

But Natuie, which (like vertue) scorns to yield
Brought new recruits and succours to the Field;
For by next Spring the check'd Sap wak'd from sleep
And upwards still to feel the Sun did creep,
Till at those wounds, the hated Hewer made,
There sprang a thicker and a fresher shade.

Men. So thrives afflicted Truth! and so the light,
When put out, gains a value from the Night.   80
How glad are we, when but one twinkling Star
Peeps betwixt clouds, more black than is our Tar?
And Providence was kind, that order'd this
To the brave Suff'rer should be solid bliss;
Nor is it so till this short life be done,
But goes hence with him, and is still his Sun.

Da. Come Shepherds then, and with your greenest Bays
Refresh his dust, who lov'd your learned Lays.
Bring here the florid glories of the Spring,
And as you strew them pious *Anthems* sing,   90
Which to your children and the years to come
May speak of *Daphnis*, and be never dumb.
While prostrate I drop on his quiet Urn
My Tears, not gifts; and like the poor, that mourn
With green, but humble Turfs; write o're his Hearse
For false, foul Prose-men this fair Truth in Verse.

" Here *Daphnis* sleeps! & while the great watch goes
" Of loud and restless Time, takes his repose.
" Fame is but noise, all Learning but a thought:
" Which one admires, another sets at nought.   100
" Nature mocks both, and Wit still keeps adoe;
" But Death brings knowledge and assurance too.

Men. Cast in your Garlands, strew on all the flow'rs
Which *May* with smiles, or *April* feeds with show'rs.
Let this days Rites as stedfast as the Sun
Keep pace with Time, and through all Ages run,
The publick character and famous Test
Of our long sorrows and his lasting rest;
And when we make procession on the plains,
Or yearly keep the Holyday of Swains,   110
Let *Daphnis* still be the recorded name
And solemn honour of our feasts and fame.

106 run,] run. *1678*   "

For though the *Isis* and the prouder *Thames*
Can shew his reliques lodg'd hard by their streams,
And must for ever to the honour'd name
Of Noble *Murrey* chiefly owe that fame :
Yet, here his Stars first saw him, and when fate
Beckon'd him hence, it knew no other date.
Nor will these vocal Woods and Valleys fail,
Nor *Isca*'s lowder Streams this to bewail,   120
But while Swains hope and Seasons change, will glide
With moving murmurs, because *Daphnis* di'd.

Da. A fatal sadness, such as still foregoes,
Then runs along with publick plagues and woes,
Lies heavy on us, and the very light
Turn'd Mourner too, hath the dull looks of Night.
Our vales like those of Death, a darkness shew
More sad than Cypress, or the gloomy Yew,
And on our hills, where health with height complied,
Thick drowsie Mists hang round and there reside.   130
Not one short parcel of the tedious year
In its old dress and beauty doth appear ;
Flowr's hate the Spring, and with a sullen bend
Thrust down their Heads, which to the Root still tend,
And though the Sun like a cold Lover, peeps
A little at them, still the Days-eye sleeps.
But when the Crab and Lion with acute
And active Fires their sluggish heat recruit,
Our grass straight russets, and each scorching day
Drinks up our Brooks as fast as dew in May.   140
Till the sad Heardsman with his Cattel faints,
And empty Channels ring with loud Complaints.

Men. Heaven's just displeasure & our unjust ways
Change Natures course, bring plagues dearth and decays.
This turns our lands to Dust, the skies to Brass,
Makes old kind blessings into curses pass.
And when we learn unknown and forraign Crimes,
Brings in the vengeance due unto those Climes.
The dregs and puddle of all ages now
Like Rivers near their fall, on us do flow.   150
Ah happy *Daphnis* ! who, while yet the streams
Ran clear & warm (though but with setting beams,)

117 Stars] Star *conj.* GM

Got through : and saw by that declining light
His toil's and journey's end before the Night.
   Da. A night, where darkness lays her chains and Bars,
And feral fires appear instead of Stars.
But he along with the last looks of day
Went hence, and setting (Sun-like) past away.
What future storms our present sins do hatch
Some in the dark discern, and others watch ;   160
Though foresight makes no Hurricane prove mild ;
Fury that's long fermenting, is most wild.
   But see, while thus our sorrows we discourse,
Phœbus hath finish't his diurnal course.
The shades prevail, each Bush seems bigger grown :
Darkness (like State,) makes small things swell and frown.
The Hills and Woods with Pipes and Sonnets round
And bleating sheep our Swains drive home, resound.

   Men. What voice from yonder Lawn tends hither ? heark
'Tis *Thyrsis* calls, I hear *Lycanthe* bark.   170
His Flocks left out so late, and weary grown
Are to the Thickets gone, and there laid down.

   Da. Menalcas, haste to look them out, poor sheep
When day is done, go willingly to sleep.
And could bad Man his time spend, as they do,
He might go sleep, or die, as willing too.

   Men. Farewel kind *Damon* ! now the Shepheards Star
With beauteous looks smiles on us, though from far.
All creatures that were favourites of day
Are with the Sun retir'd and gone away.   180
While feral Birds send forth unpleasant notes,
And night (the Nurse of thoughts,) sad thoughts promotes.
But Joy will yet come with the morning-light,
Though sadly now we bid good night ! *Da.* good night !

ADDITIONAL POEMS.

(1) From Dr. Thomas Powell's *Humane Industry: Or, A History Of most Manual Arts, Deducing the Original, Progress, and Improvement of them. Furnished with variety of Instances and Examples, shewing forth the excellency of Humane Wit* . . . (1661.)

CAP. I. 'ΩΡΟΛΟΓΙΚΗ`: Or The Invention of *Dyals, Clocks, Watches,* and other *Time-tellers.* Page 11.

Of a portable Clock or Watch, take this ensuing Epigram of our Countryman *Thomas Campian, de Horologio Portabili.*

> *Temporis interpres parvum congestus in orbem.*
> *Qui memores repetis nocte die& sonos.*
> *Ut semel instructus jucundè sex quater horas*
> *Mobilibus rotulis irrequietus agis.*
> *Nec mecum (quocun& feror) comes ire gravaris*
> *Annumerans vitæ damna, levans& meæ :*

Translated
H. V.
> Times-Teller wrought into a little round,
> Which count'st the days and nights with watchful sound ;
> How (when. once fixt) with busie Wheels dost thou
> The twice twelve useful hours drive on and show.
> And where I go, go'st with me without strife,
> The Monitor and Ease of fleeting life.

CAP. II. ΣΦΑΙΡΟ-ΠΟΙΗΤΙΚΗ' : or, Some curious Spheares and Representations of the World. Page 20.

Of this Microcosme or Representation of the World which we now mentioned, the excellent *Grotius* hath framed this Epigram following.

> *In organum motus perpetui quod est penes*
> *Maximum* Britanniacum *Regem* Jacobum.

> *Perpetui motus indelassata potestas*
> *Absğ quiete quies, absğ labore labor,*
> *Contigerant cœlo, tunc cùm Natura caducis,*
> *Et solidis unum noluit esse locum.*
> *Et geminas partes Lunæ dispescuit orbe,*
> *In varias damnans inferiora vices.*
> *Sed quod nunc Natura suis è legibus exit*
> *Dans terris semper quod moveatur opus ?*

Mira quidem res est sed non nova (maxime Regum)
Hoc fieri docuit mens tua posse prius.
Mens tua quæ semper tranquilla & torpida nunquam,
Tramite constanti per sua regna meat.
Ut tua mens ergò motûs cœlestis Imago :
Machina sic hæc est mentis Imago tuæ.

Translated thus.

The untired strength of never-ceasing motion,
A restless rest a toyl-less operation,
Heaven then had given it, when wise Nature did   H. V.
To frail & solid things one place forbid ;
And parting both, made the Moons Orb their bound,
Damning to various change this lower ground.
But now what Nature hath those Laws transgrest,
Giving to earth a work that ne're will rest ?
Though 'tis most strange, yet (great King) 'tis not new ;
This Work was seen and found before in You.   10
In You, whose minde (though still calm) never sleeps,
But through your Realms one constant motion keeps :
As your minde (then) was Heavens type first, so this
But the taught *Anti-type* of your mind is.

De AQUATICIS MACHINIS, Of WATER
MOTIONS.

(Sub-division of CAP. III. ΑΥΤΟΜΑΤΟ-ΠΟΙΗΤΙΚΗ`, *Of*
sundry Machins, and Artificial Motions.)   p. 39.

There were Amphitheaters both at *Rome* and *Verona*, and
elsewhere, which were *prodigious piles*, both for magnificence of
cost, and inventions of Art ; whole groves of great Trees (with
green branches) were brought and planted upon the sandy
Theater, and therein a thousand Estridges, a thousand wilde
Boars, and a thousand Stags put in for the people to hunt.
This Forrest being removed, they would on a sudden overflow all
with a deep Sea, fraught with Sea monsters, and strange Fishes ;
then might you see a Fleet of tall Ships ready rigged and
appointed, to represent a Sea-fight : then all the water was let out
again, and Gladiators or Fencers fight, where the Gallies stood but

5 bound,] bound. *1661*   9 King)] King *1661*

even now ; which things are expressed in verse by *Juvenal* in his third *Satyr* thus :

> —— *Quoties nos descendentis Arenæ*
> *Vidimus in partes, ruptâ& voragine terræ*
> *Emersisse feras & iisdem sæpe latebris*
> *Aurea cum Croceo creverunt Arbuta libro ?*
> *Nec solum nobis Sylvestria cernere monstra*
> *Contigit, Æquoreos ego cum cortantibus Ursis*
> *Spectavi vitulos & equorum nomine dignum*
> *Sed deforme pecus——*

Translated by *H. V.*

How oft have we beheld wilde Beasts appear
From broken gulfs of earth, upon some part
Of sand that did not sink ? How often there
And thence did golden boughs ore saffron'd start ?
Nor only saw we monsters of the wood,
But I have seen Sea-Calves whom Bears withstood ;
And such a kinde of Beast as might be named
A horse, but in most foul proportion framed.

CAP. XI. 'HMEPΩTIKH' : Or, *The Art of Cicuration
and Taming wilde Beasts.* p. 174.

Many of these examples that I have produced to make good the Title of this Chapter, and the Apostles saying above-mentioned, are briefly sum'd up by *Martial* in his Book of Shows, the 105th *Epigr.* which I have here annexed, with the Translation of M. *Hen. Vaughan Silurist,* whose excellent Poems are publique.

> *Picto quod juga delicata collo*
> *Pardus sustinet, improbæ& Tygres*
> *Indulgent patientiam flagello,*
> *Mordent aurea quod lupata Cervi ;*
> *Quod Frænis Lybici domantur Ursi,*
> *Et quantum* Caledon *tulisse fertur*
> *Paret purpureis Aper Capistris.*
> *Turpes* a *esseda quod trahunt Bisontes* b,
> *Et molles dare jussa quod choreas :*
> *Nigro* c *Bellua* d *nil negat Magistro,*
> *Quis spectacula non putet Deorum ?*
> *Hæc transit tamen ut minora, quisquis*
> *Venatus humiles videt Leonum,* &c.

a Brittish Chariots.
b Wild Oxen in the *Hercynian* Forrest called Buffles.
c The Negro or Black-Moor, that rides him.
d The Elephant.

That the fierce Pard doth at a beck
Yield to the Yoke his spotted neck,
And the untoward Tyger bear
The whip with a submissive fear ;
That Stags do foam with golden bits
And the rough Lybic bear submits
Unto the Ring ; that a wild Boar
Like that which *Caledon* of Yore
Brought forth, doth mildly put his head
In purple Muzzles to be lead :   10
That the vast strong-limb'd Buffles draw
The *Brittish* Chariots with taught awe.
And the Elephant with Courtship falls
To any dance the *Negro* calls :
Would not you think such sports as those
Were shews which the Gods did expose ;
But these are nothing, when we see
That Hares by Lions hunted be, &c.

(2) From Ezekiel Polsted's Καλῶς Τελωνήσανται *Or*, *The Excise=Man. . . . London . . .* 1697, f. a4ᵛ :

ALIUD,

TO THE

Officers *of the* Excise.

We own'd your Power, *and the* Pleasures *too*
That, as their Center, *ever meet in you ;*
But your monopolizing Sense, *affords*
A Ravishment, beyond the Pow'r *of Words :*
To Silence *thus* confin'd, *I must obey,*
And only freely say, *that I can* nothing say.

Henry Vaughan Silurist.

APPENDIX I.

DUBIA.

(1) From *Eucharistica Oxoniensia. In Exoptatissimum &*
Auspicatissimum Caroli . . . *E Scotia Reditum Gratulatoriu.*
Oxoniæ . . . *1641.*

As Kings *doe rule like th'* Heavens, *who dispense*
To parts remote *and neare their* influence,
So doth our CHARLES *Move also ; while he posts*
From South *to* North, *and back to* Southerne *coasts.*
Like to the Starry Orbe, *which in it's round*
Move's to those very Poynts *; But while 'tis bound*
For North, *there is (some guesse) a* Trembling *fitt*
And shivering in the part *that's* opposite.
What were our feares *and* Pantings, *what dire* fame
Hear'd we of Irish Tumults, *sword, and flame !*   10
Which now we thinke but Blessings, *as being sent*
Only as Matter, whereupon 'twas mean't
The Brittish *thus* united *might expresse,*
The strength of joyned Powers *to suppresse,*
Or conquer *Foes ; This is great* Brittaines *blisse ;*
The Island *in it selfe a just World is.*
Here no commotion shall we find or feare,
But of the Courts removeall, *no sad teare*
Or clowdy Brow, *but when You leave Vs, then*
Discord *is loyalty professed, when*   20
Nations *doe strive, which shall the happier bee*
T'enjoy your bounteous ray's *of* Majestie.
Which yet you throw in undivided *Dart,*
For Things divine *allow no* share *or* part.
The same Kind vertue doth at once disclose,
The Beauty of their Thistle, *and our* Rose.
Thus You doe mingle Soules *and firmely knitt*
What were but joyn'd before ; You Scots-men *fitt*
Closely with Vs, *and Reuniter prove,*
You fetch'd the Crowne *before, and now their* Love.   30

H. VAUGHAN. Ies. Col.

(2) From Dr. Thomas Powell's *Cerbyd Jechydwriaeth*, 1657,
p. 39.

> *Y Pader, pan trier, Duw-tri a'i dododd*
> *O'i dadol ddaioni,*
> *Yn faen-gwaddan i bob gweddi,*
> *Ac athrawiaeth a wnaeth i ni.*

Ol. Vaughan.

(3) Epitaph on a tombstone in Llansantfraed Church.

In Memory of
Games Jones late of
Grays-Inn Esq. & Recorder of
Brecknock, who dyed in ye 31th year
Of His Age May the 18th 1681.

Stay Passenger
And know who lyes beneath this Stone
One who was no mans Foe, no not his owne
Who liv'd as Adam did before he fell
But yt no Rib of his conspir'd with Hell
Who Arts & Manners Townes and Men survey'd
But beyond vertue & himself nere Stray'd
Soe farr above our scantling yt we knew
What he was then no more then wt he's now
The craggy fortress of the knotty Law
10 Like Caesar he did conquer as he saw
Learning & parts wch seldom met elswhere
Ev'n wth the strictest tyes were Marry'd here
And yet his parts ne'er grew so nicely high
As wth them him that gave them to defy
Nor was his curious Learning e'er employ'd
In making of its own great Charter voyd
He dy'd too soon but not too young who
in his own could shew
The Age of Sixteen Hundred years agoe.
In short here lyes a Brother Freind & Son
20 (Of Vertues a Community in one)
Of each ye best, now passenger be gone.

APPENDIX II.

LETTERS.

A. TO JOHN AUBREY AND ANTHONY WOOD.

(*Bodleian Library*)

I. MS. *Wood F* 39, fol. 216. To Aubrey.

Honoured Cousin

Yours of the 10th of June I received att Breckon, where I am still attendinge our Bishops Lady in a tertian feaver, & cannot as yet have the leasure to step home. butt lest my delayinge of tyme heere should bringe the account (you expect,) too late into your hands : I shall now in part give you the best I can, & be more exact in my next.

My brother and I were borne att *Newton in the parish of St Brigets in the yeare 1621. I stayed not att Oxford to take any degree, butt was sent to London, beinge then designed by my father for 10 the study of the Law, wch the sudden eruption of our late civil warres wholie frustrated. my brother continued there for ten or 12 years, and (I thinke) he could be noe lesse than Mr of Arts. he died (vpon an imployment for his majesty,) within 5 or 6 miles of Oxford, in the yeare that the last great plague visited London. He was buried by Sr Robert Murrey (his great friend,) & then Secretary of Estate for the kingdome of Scotland : to whome he gave all his bookes & manuscripts. The several Tractates, which he published in his life-tyme, were these followinge :

Anthroposophia Theo-magica.   20

Magia Adamica.

Lumen dè Lumine : all printed by Mr Humphrey Blunden att the Castle in Corn-hill.

* In Brecknockshire (*marginal note by Vaughan*).

Aula Lucis, a short discourse printed for William Leak att
the Crowne betwixt the two temple-gates in fleet street.

The Historie of the fraternitie of the Rosie Crosse : with his
animadversions & Judgement of them.   printed for Giles Cal-
vert att the west end of Paules.   These are all that came to my
cognisance.

30 What past into the presse from me, this short Catalogue comprehends ;

Silex Scintillans : Sacred poems & private Ejaculations in
two bookes :

The Mount of Olives : or solitarie Devotions.

Olor Iscanus : A Collection of some poems & translations :
printed for Mr Humphrey Moseley.

Flores Solitudinis : A translation of some choice peeces out
of the Latine, With the life of Paulinus Bishop of Nola, collected
out of his owne writinges, and other primitive Authours.

40 Nollius his Systema medicinæ Hermeticum, & his discourse
dè generatione done into English.   To these you may adde
(if you thinke it fitt,)

Thalia Rediviva, a peece now ready for the presse, with the
Remaines of my brothers Latine Poems (for many of them are
lost,) never published before : butt (I believe) wilbe very wellcome, & prove inferiour to none of that kind, that is yet extant.

Dr Powell of Cantre I can give you an exact account of, as soone
as I have Conference with his brother, whoe is my nighbour : you
shall have it in my next.   The other persons mentioned in yor lre,
50 were Northwales gent & vnknowne to any in these parts.   If tyme
will permitt, I advise you to Consult (by lre,) with Dr. Thomas
Ellis sometymes of Jesus College, butt livinge now att Dole y
gellie in ye County of Merionith.

He hath bine many yeares busied in makinge vp a supplement to
Dr Powells Chronicle, & knowes more of him than any man else
doth, and (I believe) of all the rest.   He is a person of excellent
accomplishments, & very solid learninge.   My brothers imploym^t
was in physic & Chymistrie.   he was ordayned minister by bishop
Mainwaringe & presented to the Rectorie of St Brigets by his
60 kinsman Sr George Vaughan.

My profession allso is physic, wch I have practised now for many
years with good successe (I thank god !) & a repute big enough
for a person of greater parts than my selfe.

Deare S^r I am highly obliged to you that you would be pleased to remember, & reflect vpon such low & forgotten thinges, as my brother and my selfe : I shalbe ever ready to acknowledge the honour you have done vs, & if you have any Concerne in these parts that I may be serviceable in : I humblie beg, that you would call upon & Command

	Honour'd Cousin	70
Breckon June the 15th	Yo^r most affectionate	
—73	& most faithfull, humble	
	servant	
	H: Vaughan	

My Cousin Walbeoffe is exceedinge glad to heare of yor health & p^rsents you with her true love & respects. her sonne is long since dead without yssue, & left the estate (after his mother's decease,) amongst his fathers nearest relations.

> To his ever honoured & obliginge
> Kinsman John Awbrey Esq   80
> most humblie these

> Leave this letter with Mr Henry
> Coley in Rose & Crowne Court in
> Grayes Inne Lane to be de-
> -livered as above directed
> London

75-78 *Written down the left-hand margin of the letter.*
79-86 *On outer leaf.*

II. MS. *Wood F* 39, fol. 227.   To Aubrey.

Honoured Cousin

In my last (wch I hope, is come to yor hands,) I gave you an account of my brother & my selfe : & what bookes we had written. I have nothinge to add butt this; that he died in the seaven & fortieth year of his age, upon the 27th of februarie, in the yeare 1666. & was buried upon the first of March.

Thomas Powell of Cantre was since the kinge came in made D^r of divinity att Oxford, by a mandamus, as I have heard. He was borne att Cantre within the County of Brechon in the year 1608.

10 he dyed att London vpon the last day of December in the year 1660 in the two and fiftieth yeare of his age & lyes buried in S. Dunstans church in fleetstreet.

His printed bookes are these.

Elementa Opticæ.

Recveil de Nowelles Lettres de Monsieur de Balzac, translated into English.

Stoa Triumphans: two lr̄es of ye noble & learned Marquesse Virgilio malvezzi, to the illustrious Signior John Vincent Imperiale : translated out of Italian into English.

20   Quadriga Salutis: or the 4 general heads of Christian Religion surveyd & explained.

Humane Industrie: Or a short account of most manual Arts: their original, progress & improvement &c

Manuscripts left in my Custodie, & not yet printed.

The Insubrian historie: Conteyninge an exact account of the various fates, Civil commotions, battells & sieges acted vpon the theater of Lumbardie, & the adiacent parts of Italie from the first Irruptions & Conquests of the Goths to their final expulsion by the Emperour Justinian. Written originalie in the

30 Latine by the Learned Puteanus & now done into English.

The Christian-politic Favourite : or A vindication of the politic transactions of Count-duke de S. Lucar: that great minister of state & favourite Counsellour to Philip the 4th of Spaine. written originalie by Virgilio Malvezzi & now (not tra=duced (as one hath done) butt faithfully translated into English.

Fragmenta de rebus Brittannicis :

A short account of the lives, manners & religion of the Brittish Druids and the Bards &c.

S^r this is all the account I can give you of any writers of
Jesus College. The name of the place, where my brother lyes 40
buried, I doe not know ; butt tis a village upon the Thames side
within 5 or 6 miles of Oxford, & without doubt well knowne to
the Vniversity. My Cousin Walbeoffe p^rsents you with her real
affections & respects, & would be very glad to see you in these
parts. S^{ir} John with his Son & Lady are come well home from
London. I begge y^{or} pardon for all this trouble & remaine
with all integritie

Honoured Cousin,

Y^{or} most affectionate and
faithfull servant   50

Newton Julie 7th

—73   H Vaughan.

> To his ever honoured & deservinge
> friende : John Awbrey,
> Esq :
>
> Humblie these.
>
> Leave this l<del>r</del>e with Mr Henrie
> Coley in Rose & Crowne Court
> in Gray's Inne Lane to be
> deluᵗed accordinge to the   60
> Directions above written.
> London.

III. MS. *Aubrey* 13, fol. 337. To Aubrey.

Brechon Decemb: 9th
—75.

Honoured Cousin.

    Your l<del>r</del>e of the 27th of November I received butt the last week.
my occasions in Glamorganshire having detained me there the
best part of the month : how wellcom it was to me (after your
long silence) I will not goe about to express : butt assure you,
that noe papyrs (wch I have the honour somtymes to receive
from very worthie persons,) refresh me soe much, nor have soe
dear an entertainment as yours.   10

II. 53–62 *On outer leaf.*

That my dear brothers name (& mine) are revived, & shine
in the Historie of the Vniversitie ; is an honour we owe vnto your
Care & kindnes : & realie (dear Cousin !) I am verie sensible of
it, & have gratefull reflections vpon an Act of so much love, and
a descendinge from yor great acquaintance & Converse to pick vs
vp, that lay so much below you.

'Tis a noble & excellent Designe that yor learned friend Dr Plott
hath now in hand, & I returne you my humble & hearty thanks
for Communicatinge it with me.   I shall take Care to assist him
20 with a short account of natures Dispensatorie heer, & in order to
it, I beg you would acquaint me with the method of his writinge :

I am in great haste & beg yor pardon for this short & rude returne
to yor kind letter : butt (dear S^r !) accept of my love & all the
effects it can produce in a gratefull Heart, which nowe hath

More than

Honoured Cousin,

Your most obliged, affectionate

friend & servant

H: Vaughan.

IV.   MS. *Aubrey* 13, fol. 338.   To Aubrey.

Brechon June 28th

—68o.

Most honoured Cousin.

Yours of the 17th of May, came not to Brechon, till June was
pretty far in ; & then was I a great way from home.   Last week
calling there in my return, I joyfullie received yours, & shall
endeavour withall possible speed to perform yor desire.   I shall not
omitt the most curious search, that can be made into such distant
& obscure nativities : wch none then tooke care to record, & few
are now alive that have them in memorie.   If in my attendance
vpon (rather than speculations into) Nature, I can meet with any
10 thing that may deserve the notice of that learned & Honourable
Societie : I shall humblie present you with it, & leave it wholie to
your Censure and disposal.

That the most serious of our profession have not only an vnkind-
nes for, butt are persecutors of Astrologie : I haue more than once

admired : butt I find not this ill humour amongst the Antients, so much as the modern physicians : nor amongst them all neither. I suppose they had not travelled so far, & having once enterd upon the practise, they were loath to leave off, and learn to be acquainted with another world. for my owne part (though I could never ascend higher,) I had butt litle affection to the skirts 20 & lower parts of learning ; where every hand is graspinge & so litle to be had. butt neither nature, nor fortune favoured my ambition. I am only happy in yor Condescensions, whoe cease not to oblige me in the highest maner, that the most deserving and eminent persons could expect. I never was of such a magnitude as could invite you to take notice of me, & therfore I must owe all these favours to the generous measures of yor owne free & excellent spirit.

S^r I can make noe Returns proportionable to such matchles affections & merits ; butt this I dare assure you, that if any thing 30 happens wherin I may serve you : then I will (without reserves or exceptions) lett you see, that nothing hath bine heer written, butt what was first sincerely resolved vpon by

Honoured S^r

Your most obliged, most affectionate
& most faithfull servant

H: Vaughan.

Expect the best account I can give you, within this fortnight.

To his worthily honoured Cousin,
    John Aubrey Esq$_3$ att   40
    Mr Hookes lodgings
        in Gresham College
London.

Humblie these

39–44 *On outer leaf.*

V. MS. *Wood F* 45, fol. 68.   To Wood.

Worthy S^r

   I received your leter in the declination of a tedious and severe
sickness with a very slow recovery ; butt as soon as I can gett
abroad, I will contribute all I can to give satisfaction to yor
Inquiries ; especialy about the learned Dr John David Rhesus :
a person of great & curious learning ; butt had the vnhappines
to sojourn heer in an age that vnderstood him not. for the
Stradlings I shall imploy a learned friend I have in Glamorganshire, to pick vp what memorials remain of them in those parts.

10 I received a leter in the beginning of my sicknes from my Cousin
John Awbrey about these inquiries you make now, & writt by
him in yor behalf ; butt it was my misfortune to continue so
very weak and such a forlorn Clinic, that I could not to this
day return him an answer. If you intend a second Edition of
the Oxford-historie, I must give you a better account of my brothers
books & mine ; wch are in the first much mistaken, and many
omitted. I shallbe very carefull of what you have recommended
to my trust : & shall (in any thing els) with much chearfullnes &
fidelity pay you the respects & service due to a person of such
20 public & obliging deserts.   I am sincerely

S^r

Yo^r most affectionate
& very willing servant

Newton-St Brigets, within
three miles of Brechon :
March 25th 1689.

Hen: Vaughan.

To the reverend, his honoured
friend : Mr Antonie
Wood att his lodgings
in Merton-College
30   in Oxford :
Present this

26–31 *On verso of letter.*

VI. MS. *Autog.* c. 9, fol. 81. To Wood.

April 25th
— — 89.

Worthy S^r

I received yours by our Carrier & in order to give som satisfaction to yor Quaeres about the Stradlings : I have sent a leter to my learned friend Mr John Williams (somtimes of Jesus College :) now Archdeacon of Cardigan, from whom I expect a good account As for John David Rhesus, I find by yor last leter that you are like to run into a great mistake, when you take him for the Authour of the welch Dictionarie : wch he was not. Our Doctour John David Rhesus was not a Divine, butt a physician, & of the Roman communion. He took his degree att the vniversity of 10 Siena in Italy, where he had his Education, & was a person of great parts & curious learning. This much for the p^rsent ; you will have more heerafter. He wrott (indeed) the welch grammer, & an Italian one dedicated to a Venetian Senatour, with som other rare Tractates, wch are all lost. butt the Authour of the welch Dictionary lived a great while after him & was of the same Communion with vs & a Dignitarie of this Church of England, as you have righ[t]ly recorded.

I doubt not butt my Cousen Awbreys leter from me, gave (then) a true account of what I, or my brother had written & published. 20 butt in the Latin Edition of the history of Oxford, I doe assure you, it is quite otherwise ; butt I shall redress that.

with my hearty respects I shall remain

S^r

To the Reverend,   Your very ready Servant
Mr Antonie Wood att   Hen. Vaughan.
his lodgings near to
Merton College in
Oxford :
Present this   30

25–30 *Address on verso of letter.*

VII. MS. *Aubrey* 13, fol. 340. To Aubrey.

Octob: 9th –94.

Honoured Cousin.

I received yours & should have gladly served you, had it bine
in my power. butt all my search & consultations with those few
that I could suspect to have any knowledge of Antiquitie, came to
nothing; for the antient Bards (though by the testimonie of their
Enemies, the Romans;) a very learned societie: yet (like the
Druids) they communicated nothing of their knowledge, butt by
way of tradition: wch I suppose to be the reason that we have no
account left vs: nor any sort of remains, or other monuments of ·
10 their learning, or way of living.

As to the later Bards, who were no such men, butt had a societie
& some rules & orders among themselves: & several sorts of
measures & a kind of Lyric poetrie: wch are all sett down exactly
In the learned John David Rhees, or Rhesus his welch, or British
grammer: you shall have there (in the later end of his book) a most
curious Account of them. This vein of poetrie they called Awen,
which in their language signifies as much as Raptus, or a poetic
furor; & (in truth) as many of them as I have conversed with are
(as I may say) gifted or inspired with it. I was told by a very sober
20 & knowing person (now dead) that in his time, there was a young
lad father & motherless, & soe very poor that he was forced to beg;
butt att last was taken vp by a rich man, that kept a great stock
of sheep vpon the mountains not far from the place where I now
dwell. who cloathed him & sent him into the mountains to keep
his sheep. There in Summer time following the sheep & looking
to their lambs, he fell into a deep sleep; In wch he dreamt, that
he saw a beautifull young man with a garland of green leafs vpon
his head, & an hawk vpon his fist: with a quiver full of Arrows att
his back, coming towards him (whistling several measures or tunes
30 all the way) & att last lett the hawk fly att him, w^{ch} (he dreamt)
gott into his mouth & inward parts, & suddenly awaked in a great
fear & consternation: butt possessed with such a vein, or gift of
poetrie, that he left the sheep & went about the Countrey, making
songs vpon all occasions, and came to be the most famous Bard in
all the Countrey in his time.

Dear Cousin I should & would be very ready to serve you in any thing wherein I may be usefull, or qualified to doe it, & I give you my heartie thanks for yor continued affections & kind remembrances of

S^r 40

Yo^r most obliged & faithfull

Servant,

Hen: Vaughan

To his honoured friend & kinsman
    John Awbrey, Esq₃ :
       present this.

> Leave this letter with the truly
> honoured & most nobly accomplished
> Dr Thomas Gale in S.
> Pauls schoole.   50
>   London.

44–51 *On outer leaf.*

B. TO OTHER CORRESPONDENTS.

I. Lambeth Palace Library.   Sequestered Livings 1650–62. MS. 1027, County of Brecon, fol. 36 b.   Endorsed 1662.

To the honored gentlemen : the Commissioners sittinge at New Radnor : present this.

Gentlemen

Some few dayes since there was a processe left att my house (in my absence) without any account, either from whome it came, or for what cause, butt havinge learnt since, that it was sent hither by yor Commande, I resolved to make my Addresse accordinglie. And (in truth) I had not fayled to wayt upon you my selfe, if weaknes, & other violent effects of a late feaver, had not resisted my real intentions.

The Cause of this service I coniecture to be about one years profits of Lansanfred Church. wch were granted to my father & to 10 Mr William Jones of Buckland Jointenants for them, & both deceased. My father, whoe had some reason to looke after the

profits of this Church, they being (by right) my brothers (whoe for
his loyalty to his late Majesty was sequesterd & persecuted for his
life,) had often petitiond the Committees then in being, to allow
him the profits of the Church towards the paym^t of a considerable
summe of money, wch was well knowne, to be due to him from my
brother, butt this he could never effect, the persons then in power
being all his adversaries. Att last in the year –56, (as I suppose,)
20 it was graunted to him ; butt Mr Jones was made Joint-tenant with
him. And att the years end my father insisting still for allowance
& delayinge the paym^t the Committees sent their Agent Thomas
Williams, whoe with some foote-souldiers tooke my father prisoner
& carryed him to Brechon goale, where he remayned till the rent
was payed, wch by the graunt were thirtie pounds. The bearer
heerof payd twenty pounds of it att the Hay unto Thomas Williams
the agent & the other ten were paid unto the said Williams att
Brechon, & the bearer (as he saith) upon the payment received an
Acquittance, & gave it my father, butt I cannot find it amongst
30 all his papyrs, wch are still in my Custodie. butt the bearer is
ready to make oath of the paym^t if you please to receive it.
Gentlemen, this is all that I know off, or am concernd in this
matter ; & how litle this will amount unto, I referre unto yor
Judgements. The processe I have sent by the bearer, with a civil
confidence, that you will take it up. butt if you see any cause to
doe otherwise, I shall observe ye Commands of that honorable
Court I am serv'd into, & remayne

Gentlemen !

Yo^r very humble servant

Henry Vaughan

40

II. National Library of Wales.   Brecknockshire Sessions,
2nd Session of 1693 : Welsh Papers, Bundle 178.

Honoured Syr !

That I am accused by adversaries of all sorts & renderd to your
Lordship as a person guiltie of all they can devise & declare
against me : I doe not at all doubt ; but I hope that you will give
ear to what I allso have to say & shall make good.

According to the promise & agreement made to & with your
Lordship, I payed & tenderd half a crown weekly to the petitioner,

butt she refused it. butt of thirty shillings to be payd her att one tyme, I know nothing & never made any such promise.

Bysides all this, your Lordship will give me leave to tell you that among heathens noe parents were ever compelld to maintain or relieve disobedient & rebellious children, that both despise & vilifie their parents, & publickly give out most scandalous & reproachfull lyes concerning them : which this pious petitioner hath done, & still doth. How far this may enter into your Lordships brest, or whither it willbe of any weight, or value with your Lordship, I am vncertain : butt I am sure that among Christians & in all civil governments it is, or should be looked vpon as a practise directly against his precepts & commands, who is the great Judge of all our actions.

My Lord,

What ever your Lordship intends, or will resolve to doe : I shall with such respects & civilities as are due to your person & the place you sitt in : receive & digest them. butt must not prostrate my self to the designs or devices of vnreasonable adversaries, or informers. I had wayted vpon your Lordship, butt my present engagement with Mr. Serjeant Le Hunts Lady, who is most dangerously sick in a putrid fever with most malignant symptoms detein me heer : & will (I hope) obtein your pardon : which shallbe thankfully acknowledged by

Your Lordships most
humble servant
Henry Vaughan.

Crickowel :
Septemb: 14th 93.

COMMENTARY.

POEMS, WITH THE TENTH SATYRE OF IUVENAL ENGLISHED.

1 (*title-page*). *Tam nil, &c.* Persius, i. 122–3.

3 (*heading*). *R. W.* Possibly though not surely the same as the 'Mr. R. W. slain at Routon Heath' (see p. 49, and note; also *Life*, 61, footnote). Miss Guiney thought this an Oxford poem (see *Academy*, 15, 22, and 29 April 1911), but some of the references suggest London rather, and the first edition of Randolph's works to contain everything mentioned in ll. 33–5 was that of 1640, the year in which Vaughan is supposed to have gone to London. (*Life*, 39.)

3. 8. *Moone, or Starre.* Cf. 11. 25–8 and see note.

3. 13. *the Maze.* Probably in the sense of dissipation, *O.E.D.* art. Maze, 1 b.

3. 28. *More . . . mind.* Sc. others resembling you in genius and approved by me (to my mind).

3. 34. *His Lovers, &c.* See note to 3 (heading). *The Jealous Lovers* is not in all copies of Randolph's *Poems* as published in 1640. In the following notes I refer to G. Thorn-Drury's edition of the *Poems* (1929).

4. 53–4. *And now, &c.* An obscure couplet, which may mean that the inconstant sex (l. 49), left on earth, will now get the last thoughts they will ever have from ('of') us or from any others here.

4. 57–8. A reminiscence of Habington, *Castara*, 'To Castara', ll. 31–3 (*Poems*, ed. Allott, 1948, p. 15):

> So they whose wisdome did discusse
> Of these as fictions : shall in us
> Finde, they were more then fabulous.

5. 17. *influxe.* Influence in the quasi-astrological sense. (*O.E.D.* 2 b.)

5. 27. *the first, &c.* Sc. *showing* a shaft withstood.

5. 28. A forecast of the emblem preceding the title-page of *Silex Scintillans*, 1650.

5. *To Amoret.* For arguments identifying her with Catherine Wise, Vaughan's first wife, see *Life*, 50–4. 597. 9–10 suggests that Amoret was not imaginary.

5. 1. Cf. *Castara*, 'To Cupid', l. 1 (ed. cit. p. 24) : 'Nimble boy in thy warme flight'.

6. *To his Friend, &c.* 'me' in l. 13 suggests either that the whole poem is supposedly spoken by the friend, or that ll. 13–18 are the friend's answer to the address in ll. 1–12.

6. 7. *Witty to.* Clever in exercising. 'tyranny' may, however, be a verb, to tyrannize.

8 (*continuation*). 20. *sight.* Sc. mere sight or physical appearance. Cf. 12. 15–19.

8 (*continuation*). 23. *start.* Loosen. *decline.* Weaken.

8 (*To Amoret gone from him*). 19–20. *no sence . . . influence.* Cf.
432. 1–2. Influence, like 'influxe' in 5. 17, has the quasi-astrological
meaning. (*O.E.D.* 2 b.)

8. 22. *Those . . . love.* The concrete things that give their love what
substance it has. Cf. Donne, 'A Valediction : forbidding mourning ',
15–16, quoted below, on 12. 15–28.

9. 23–4. *had from above, &c.* Cf. Habington, ' To Castara, Inquiring
why I loved her ', ll. 28–9 (ed. cit. p. 18) :

> But there was something from above,
> Shot without reasons guide, this fire.

and ' Loves Aniversarie ', l. 14 (ed. cit. p. 78) :

> But vertuous love is one sweet endlesse fire. (GM.)

9 (*Elegy*). 5. *love.* ? Misprint for ' live '. (GM.)

10 (*continuation*). 25. *Oh! jam satis.* Cf. Martial, iv. 91. 1 : ' Ohe,
jam satis est, ohe, libelle ', and Horace, *Sat.* ii. 5. 96. (GM.)

10. *A Rhapsodie.* ' Rhapsodis ' in *1646.* There is no etymological
reason for a final ' s ', but ' e ' in one of its manuscript forms was
much like one form of final ' s '. A meaning of ' rhapsody ', now
obsolete, was a miscellaneous collection or medley, which may have
some bearing on the general incoherence of this poem. As pointed
out by GM, the Globe was probably the tavern in Fleet Street so
named (marked in Hollar's map of 1647), not the Globe Tavern at
Southwark.

10. 14. *one great Star.* Possibly a painted star representing the name
of the room. See 3. 8 and 11. 25–8.

10. 22. *Lycoris.* Virg. *Ecl.* x. 22. 42. (GM.)

11. 25–8. *Moone.* See 3. 8 and 10. 14, with note thereto.

11. 31–4. The dismissal of the painter ' is decidedly unexpected after
the sympathetic interpretation of his decorative scene ' (GM).
' Boxe ' may refer punningly to the painter's coffin, as l. 34 probably
to his funeral.

11. 44. *Tower-wharfe, &c.* From east to west of the city. Statues of
the 'early kings' were placed on Ludgate in 1260, and when Ludgate
was rebuilt in 1586 the statues were renewed. (See Stow, *Survey
of London*, ed. Kingsford, 1908, i, pp. 38–9.)

11. 46–57. According to GM, Vaughan, under cover of the toasts
proposed, alludes to the political situation in London while he was
there. See *Life*, 43–4.

11. 48. *made his horse a Senatour.* Sc. Caligula.

11. 61–2. *sent . . . plate.* There may be an allusion here to the Parlia-
mentary order of 10 June 1642, for raising equipments, ammunition,
money, and plate. May, *History of the Parliament of England*,
1647, ii, ch. v, pp. 83–4. (GM.)

12. 67. *influxe.* Influence in the astrological sense. (*O.E.D.* 2 a.)

12. *To Amoret, &c.* 1–14. It has been suggested that the imagery is
from sunset colours in the sky, but it seems more likely that Vaughan
had in mind the *ignis fatuus.* He refers to this also in 445. 31 sqq.
(Cf. 339. 30 and 673. 55–6.) See note on 445. 31 sqq.

12. 15–16. *Just so, &c.* Just as the will o' the wisp is engendered in
slime and earth (l. 5).

12. 17–21. They will make themselves agreeable while they are attracted by some pleasing physical feature, but when that is removed they will soon depart, revealing their deception and hypocrisy.

12–13. 15–28. This, as Beeching observed, is clearly influenced by Donne's 'A Valediction : forbidding mourning', ll. 13–20 :

> Dull sublunary lovers love
> (Whose soule is sense) cannot admit
> Absence, because it doth remove
> Those things which elemented it.
>
> But we by a love, so much refin'd,
> That our selves know not what it is,
> Inter-assured of the mind,
> Care lesse, eyes, lips, and hands to misse.

See Habington, 'To the World, &c.', ll. 28–30, and 'The harmony of Love', ll. 15–16 (*Poems*, ed. cit. pp. 49 and 92). GM also compares Habington, 'A Dialogue betweene Araphill and Castara', ll. 23–4 (*Poems*, ed. cit. p. 70) :

> For then wee'd like two Angels love,
> Without a sense ; imbrace each others mind.

13. *To Amoret Weeping.* See note on 5, 'To Amoret'.

13. 13. *their.* Of Fate and its Book (l. 9).

14. 27–8. *eate Orphans, &c.* Cf. Randolph, 'On the Inestimable Content he Injoyes in the Muses' (*Poems*, ed. cit. p. 25) :

> Noe widdowes curse caters a dish of mine,
> I drinke no teares of Orphans in my wine.

14. 33. *Geld.* Weaken (by adulteration).

14. 42. Cf. Traherne, 'The Person' (*Poems of Felicity*, ed. Bell, p. 94) :

> Nor *paint*, nor *cloath*, nor *crown*, nor add a *Ray*,
> But glorify by taking all away.

14. 57. *vye.* Practise, display, in mutual competition.

15 *(heading).* *Priorie Grove.* Belonging to Brecon Priory, the home of Colonel Herbert Price. See *Life*, 52–3, &c.

15. 3–4. According to *Life* (following GM), 52, 'Evidently it was while he lay on the "soft bosome" of the Priory Grove lawns that his future wife's "faire steps" approached him unawares'; but this is difficult to reconcile with 'I first betrayd', which probably means rather 'I first made known'; 'my loves faire steps' would then mean the development of my love for her. Cf., for the expression, 412. 28 : 'one faire step'.

15–16. 29–36. Cf. Randolph, 'On the Death of a Nightingale', ll. 9–14 (ed. cit. p. 93) :

> That soule is fled, and to *Elisium* gone ;
> Thou a poore desert left ; goe then and runne,
> Begge there to stand a grove, and if shee please
> To sing againe beneath thy shadowy Trees ;
> The soules of happy Lovers crown'd with blisses
> Shall flock about thee, and keepe time with kisses.

16. 32. *growth and birth.* Sc. of our affection ? GM suggests that Vaughan knew Cartwright's 'To Chloe who wish'd her self young enough for me' (*Poems*, 1651, p. 244) :

> There are two Births: the one when Light
> First strikes the new-awak'ned sense;
> The Other when two Souls unite;
> And we must count our life from thence:
> When you lov'd me, and I lov'd you,
> Then both of us were born anew.

Vaughan's metaphor of 'growth' is possibly related to Cartwright's succeeding lines:

> Love then to us did new Souls give,
> And in those Souls did plant new pow'rs.

17. *Ivvenals Tenth Satyre.* See *Life*, pp. 42–3, on the connexion which, according to GM, Vaughan may have seen between Juvenal x and the events of the early 1640's, especially the execution of Strafford.

17. *Nèc verbum, &c.* Horace, *Ars Poetica*, 133 ('curabis'). The quotation is an understatement of Vaughan's freedom in translating.

18. 36. *the Souldier.* Vaughan's addition. (GM.)

19. 69–73. *Had he ... ours.* Vaughan's addition

20. 117–18. *the least ... Favourite.* Vaughan's addition.

21. 141–3. *since ... name.* Vaughan's addition. (GM.)

21–2. 159–65. *So fals ... Sejanus.* Vaughan's addition. (GM.)

22. 173–4. *But O ... bloud.* Vaughan's addition. (GM.)

29. 452. *And why reprov'd.* Juvenal, 291–2: 'Cur tamen,' inquit, 'Corripias?'

29. 454–9. Appropriated from Felltham, *Resolves*, i. 37, 'Of Natures recompencing wrongs' (5th ed., 1634, p. 123):

> *Lucretia's* fate warnes us to wish no *face*
> Like hers; *Virginia* would beneath [read 'bequeath'] her grace
> To Lute-backt *Rutilæ*, in exchange: for till [read 'still'],
> The fairest Children doe their Parents fill
> With greatest care; so seldome *modesty*
> Is found to dwell with *Beauty.*

30. 485. *Is of any race.* 'Is' is probably the form of 'Yes' used again by Vaughan at 446. 46; it contradicts the supposition in the preceding sentence. Juvenal, 318–19:

> Sed tuus Endymion dilectae fiet adulter
> Matronae; mox quum dederit Servilia nummos ...

30. 489. *Ring* (*King 1646*). Juvenal, 300 1: 'exuct omnem Corporis ornatum'.

30. 514–17. Juvenal, 340–2:

> Si scelus admittas, dabitur mora parvula, dum res
> Nota urbi et populo contingit principis aurem.
> Dedecus ille domus sciet ultimus.

OLOR ISCANUS.

For the circumstances in which this volume was published see Introduction, p. xviii, and *Life*, 73–88; also note below on 33 (title-page).

32. 6. *Herbertus.* Matthew Herbert, Rector of Llangattock 1621–46; see p. 93, and *Life*, 27–9, 109–10, 201–2.

32. 19–26. *partem . . . atra fuit.* This passage, especially ll. 19–20, '*partem Me nullam in tantâ* strage *fuisse*', has been interpreted as meaning that Vaughan took no part in the Civil War; but elsewhere (e.g. 52. 19–22, 54. 85–6) he seems to imply the contrary. See *Life*, 55 sqq. Some of the Latin phrases are doubtless vague by intention; but what Vaughan probably wished chiefly to convey was that he was not on the side which, in his view, was guilty of bringing about the Civil War and its consequences.

Facing **32** (*engraved title-page*). GM notes that Isca was already associated with swans in W. Browne's *Britannia's Pastorals*, ii. 3. 771–2. '*R: Vaughan sculp:*'. Robert Vaughan, q.v. in *Bryan's Dictionary of Painters and Engravers*. He is not known to have been related to the poet.

33 (*title-page*). *Published by a Friend.* This was probably Thomas Powell, 1608–60, Rector of Cantref since 1635, and Fellow of Jesus College, Oxford. See *Life*, 75, &c. As was first pointed out by W. R. Parker, 'Henry Vaughan and his Publishers', *Library*, 4th ser., xx, 1940, pp. 401–11, *Olor Iscanus* and Powell's *Stoa Triumphans* were both entered by Humphrey Moseley at Stationers' Hall on the same day, 28 April 1651. Vaughan's own account of Powell is on p. 690, below. See also pp. 36 (*foot*), 60, 93, 618, 623, 634, 669, 681, 686, and 688.

33. *Flumina amo, &c.* Virg. *Georg.* ii. 486 ('amem').

34. *O quis me, &c.* Virg. ibid. 488–9:
> O qui me gelidis convallibus Haemi
> Sistat . . .

35 (*heading*). *Lord Kildare Digby.* Son of Robert, Lord Digby, and Sara, daughter of Richard, Earl of Cork; grandson of Sir Robert Digby and Lettice, Baroness Offaley (q.v. *D.N.B.*). Born, according to *Complete Peerage*, iv, 1916, p. 353, about 1631. Hutchinson, *Life*, 72, supposes however that he may have been twenty by the end of 1647. The Digbys had a home at Coleshill, Warwickshire, whence Vaughan's wife, Catherine Wise, came. (*Life*, 73.)

36. *The Publisher to the Reader.* Probably written by Moseley, not by Powell. (*Life*, 76.)

37. 1. *I call'd.* Here and in other places where the original texts print 'I' or 'O' outside the line, the second word acquires an initial capital by position. This has been discarded save where the capital may have an emphasizing value as on p. 646.1 : 'O Subtile Love!'

37. 5. *breath'd it.* Gave it a breathing-time, kept it fresh.

37 (*signature*). *I. Rowlandson Oxoniensis.* Probably either John or James Rowlandson, both of Queen's College between 1630 and 1640. See *Alumni Oxon.*

37 (*second poem*). 4. *rise.* Raise. (*O.E.D.* Rise, *v.* 28.)

37. 12–14. The allusion is probably to a hospital for disabled soldiers.

38. 28. *Desamour to Poetrie.* Cf. 2. 4–5.

38. 33. *Eugenius Philalethes.* Thomas Vaughan, Henry's twin brother. See Introduction, pp. xviii–xix; also 687. 8 sqq. and *Life*, 141 sqq.

39. 5–8. Cf. Habington, 'His Muse speakes to him', ll. 6–8 (ed. cit. p. 73):

> and to *Arn* is knowne
> But *Petrarchs Laura*; while our famous Thames
> Doth murmur *Sydneyes Stella* to her streames.

39. 10. *Sabrin's tears.* See Spenser, *The Faerie Queene*, ii. 10. 19.

40. 48. *Sun-shine dayes.* Cf. 411 (*Mans fall*). 10. (GM.)

40. 51–6. G. Goodwin (in *Vaughan*, ed. Chambers) compares W. Browne, *Britannia's Pastorals*, i, Song 2 (1616, p. 28):

> May neuer *Euet*, nor the *Toade*,
> Within thy Bankes make their abode!
> Taking thy iourney from the Sea,
> Maist thou ne'er happen in thy way
> On Niter or on Brimstone Myne.

40. 65–6. Chambers compares 'A Dialogue betweene Sr Henry Wotton and Mr Donne' (attributed to Donne, but see *Donne*, ed. Grierson, i, pp. 430 and 432):

> Nor roast in fiery eyes, which alwayes are
> Canicular.

Moore Smith, in *Mod. Lang. Rev.* xi, 1916, p. 246, cites Horace, *Odes* iii. 13. 9–10:

> Te flagrantis atrox hora Caniculae
> Nescit tangere.

41. 2. *Kelder.* Womb, from Dutch = cellar. *Mists.* Cf. Habington, 'Elegie 8 to Talbot', l. 16 (ed. cit. p. 110): 'the thicke mists about thy Tombe'.

41. 2. *a second Fiats care.* Chambers compares Donne, 'The Storme', ll. 70–2:

> Since all formes, uniforme deformity
> Doth cover, so that wee, except God say
> Another *Fiat*, shall have no more day.

41. 8. *Exchequer.* Treasury. Cf. Habington, 'Elegie 8 to Talbot', ll. 5–6 (ed. cit. p. 110):

> Here is th' Epitome of wealth, this chest
> Is Natures chief Exchequer . . .

41. 11. *Torpedo.* Cf. 185. 18.

41. 13. *Eloquent silence.* Cf. Habington, 'To a Tombe', l. 4 (ed. cit. p. 71): 'silent eloquence'.

41. 21. *Chameleons.* Feeding on air. See M. P. Tilley, *The Proverbs in England*, M 226: 'A Man cannot live on air like a chameleon.'

41. 21. *Aire-monging.* Cf. Felltham, *Resolves*, i. 15, 'Of Fame' (1634, p. 49): '*Checke* thy selfe, thou *Ayremonger*.'

41. 24. *loath'd nothing.* Cf. Habington, 'Elegie 8 to Talbot', l. 36 (ed. cit. p. 111): 'To a loath'd nothing in our Funerall'; and Habington, 'Qui quasi flos', 23 (ed. cit. p. 133): 'How loath'd a nothing it must be.' (GM.)

42. 35–6. E. Bensly in *Mod. Lang. Rev.* xiv, 1919, pp. 103–4, refers to Plutarch, *Life of Alexander*, 69, and quotes Felltham, *Resolves*, i. 13 (1634, p. 40): 'Into what a *dumpe*, did the sight of *Cyrus* Tombe, strike the most noble *Alexander?*' With l. 36 cf. Juvenal x. 168: 'unus Pellaeo iuveni non sufficit orbis.'

42. 43. *th' Ostrich-man.* Sc. the soldier. Cf. 217. 8–9.

42. 46. *As if . . . Buffe.* Alluding to the soldier's coat of buff leather.

43. *In Amicum fœneratorem.* GM connects this poem and the next
' To his friend —— ' with Randolph's ' On the Inestimable Content
he Injoyes in the Muses ' and his ' parley with his empty Purse ' (ed.
cit. pp. 23 and 127). See 637. 105.

43. 16. *gold's . . . wit.* H compares G. Herbert, ' To all Angels and
Saints ', ll. 11–13 (*Works*, p. 78) :

> the gold,
> The great restorative for all decay
> In young and old.

43. 19. *Og.* GM observes that Cleveland uses this name in ' A Dialogue between two Zealots ' and ' The Author's Hermaphrodite '.
See Saintsbury, *Caroline Poets*, iii, p. 31, l. 35 (with note) and p. 45,
l. 47. But this does not explain Vaughan's allusion.

43. 32. Cf. Cartwright, ' On Mr Stokes his Book on the Art of
Vaulting ' (*Poems*, 1651, p. 211) :

> Then for the *Pegasus* he 'l do 't
> And strike a Fountain with his foot.

44. 41-2. Cf. Randolph, ' In anguem, &c.' (*Poems*, ed. cit. p. 32) :

> Hence he slides
> Up to her lockes, and through her tresses glides,
> Her yellow tresses ; dazel'd to behold
> A glistring grove, an intire wood of Gold ;

and Edward Herbert, ' A Vision. A lady combing her hair ', l. 1
(*Poems*, ed. Moore Smith, p. 24).

45. 63-4. *that starre, &c.* Saturn.

45. 65. *angel'd, &c.* (?) Governed by angels from Saturn.

46. *To his retired friend.* See *Life*, 82–3, where the poem is dated
March 1648/9. See l. 48. ' War ' in l. 76 may be used in a general
sense, not referring specifically to the Civil War. GM suggests that
Vaughan may have thought ' *Charles* his raign ' over in 1646, when
the King was in Parliamentarian hands.

46. 7-8. *Or taught, &c.* Sc. taught fasting. Pythagoras persuaded
an ox at Tarentum to abstain from eating beans in the field. Iambli-
chus, *De Vita Pythagorae*, 13. 61.

46. 13. *foule, polluted walls.* The walls of Brecon were pulled down
to make it an open city. See *Life*, 64, and Grose, *Antiquities of
England and Wales*, vii, 1797, p. 10.

46. 16. *blew Aprons.* Tradesmen.

46. 19-20. There seems to be an allusion to Walter Rumsey, formerly
Puisne Justice of the Brecon circuit, and thus a colleague of Sir
Marmaduke Lloyd, to whom Vaughan had been secretary. See
W. R. Williams, *The History of the Great Sessions in Wales*, 1899,
p. 133. Rumsey, who suffered from phlegm, invented the probang,
or provang, an instrument for the treatment of throat affections. See
his *Organon Salutis*, 1657. Eltonhead, who replaced Lloyd in 1647,
may have been the ' old Saxon Fox '. See *Life*, 83.

46. 31-2. *the Greek, &c.* Alluding to the story of Hercules and
Omphale.

46. 36. Suetonius, *Domitian*, 3.

47. 65–6. In some manuscript versions of Herrick's 'Welcome to Sack' (O.E.T., p. 77) there are additional lines after l. 48 wherein the poet says of sack that

'tis the principall
Fire to all my functions, gives me blood,
An active spiritt, full marrow, and what 's good.

48. *Monsieur Gombauld. Endymion,* a prose romance by Jean Ogier de Gombauld (1570?–1666), appeared in 1624. An English translation was published in 1639: *Endimion. An Excellent Fancy . . . now Elegantly Interpreted, by Richard Hurst Gentleman.* The dedication of this volume begins with the same four words as Vaughan's dedication of *Olor Iscanus,* p. 35: 'It is a position'. The translator was probably the Richard Hurst who matriculated from Christ Church in 1615, aged 19. (*Alumni Oxon.*)

48. 17–18. Cf. Habington, *Castara,* 'To . . . R. B. Esquire', ll. 29–30 (ed. cit. p. 17):

But should she scorne my suite, I'le tread that path
Which none but some sad Fairy beaten hath.

49. 48. *that commended mixture.* 'utile dulci'. Horace, *Ars Poetica,* 343.

49. 51–2. This resembles a sentence on p. 202 of Hurst's translation (the Moon addresses Endimion): 'as long as there shall be any speech of the *Moone,* or that shee shall shine in the Heavens, thy name shall remaine in the mouths and memory of men.' (GM.)

49 (*heading*). *Mr. R. W.* See note to 3 (heading) and *Life,* 60–2.

49–50. 9–18. Cf. Virgil, *Aen.* ii. 79–82. (GM.)

50. 25–32. *time . . . skull.* Cf. Habington, *Castara,* 'An Elegy upon the Honourable Henry Cambell', ll. 1–10 (ed. cit. p. 87):

Its false Arithmaticke to say thy breath
Expir'd to soone, or irreligious death
Prophan'd thy holy youth. For if thy yeares
Be number'd by thy vertues or our teares,
Thou didst the old *Methusalem* out-live.
Though Time, but twenty yeares account can give
Of thy abode on earth, yet every houre
Of thy brave youth by vertues wondrous powre
Was lengthen'd to a yeare. Each well-spent day
Keepes young the body, but the soule makes gray. (GM.)

50. 30. *outgone . . . Arithmetick.* Become prematurely old. Cf. (?) F. Beaumont, 'An Elegie on the Death of the Lady Rutland' in later editions of *Sir Thomas Overbury His Wife'&c.,* e.g. tenth impression, 1618, sig. A6ʳ:

Mankinde is sent to sorrow; and thou hast
More of the busines which thou cam'st for past,
Then all those aged Women which yet quicke
Haue quite out-liu'd their own Arithmeticke. (GM.)

50. 32. *a solid skull.* A fully-developed intelligence, with no implication of dullness. Hutchinson, *Life,* 61 (footnote), makes the phrase a point of contrast with the R. W. addressed as a 'deare wit', 3. 18 above; but this seems unconvincing as an argument against the identity of the two R. W.'s.

50. 38. Cf. *Hamlet*, III. ii. 77–8 :

> I will wear him
> In my heart's core, ay, in my heart of heart.

50. 50–51. 61. See *Life*, 62. Vaughan may have been in the battle or, as Chambers suggested, among the garrison in Beeston Castle.

51. 68. *Civill.* Non-military. *Common.* Ordinary (in war).

51. 70. *Fail'd in.* Failed to do justice to.

51. 93–4. Cf. Robert Randolph, 'To the Memory of his deare brother . . .' in T. R.'s *Poems* (ed. cit. p. 2) :

> And like Sun-dialls to a day that 's gone,
> Though poore in use, can tell there was a Sunne.

51. 99–100. *Nomen, &c.* Virgil, *Aen.* vi. 507–8.

52 (*heading*). *J. Ridsley.* Unidentified.

52. 2. *Courtship.* Courtesy. (*O.E.D.* Courtship, 1. b.)

52. 10. *for.* Before, on the front of. (*O.E.D.* Before, A. *prep.* I. 1.)

52. 18. *shag.* Nap ; it was not cut even.

52. 19–20. See *Life*, 65. The garrison of Beeston Castle, having surrendered, was allowed to march out on 16 Nov. 1645.

52. 39–40. The reference is to *Adamite* (= naked) in l. 41 and to the saying attributed to Bias of Priene by Cicero, *Paradoxa*, i. 8 : 'Omnia mecum porto mea.' (EB.)

53. 44. *Micro-cosmo-graphie.* He was marked with lines, as in a map.

53. 46. *seven pillars.* Prov. ix. 1. But 'before the floud' suggests rather the *two* inscribed pillars attributed to Seth and supposed to have survived the flood. See Josephus, *Antiq. Jud.* I. ii. 3.

53. 49. *Cere-cloth.* Surgical plaster.

53. 52. *Speeds old Britans.* See the illustrations on p. 180 of Speed's *History of Great Britaine*, 1611.

53. 60. *statue of Fetter-lane.* Edward Marshall 1578–1675, master mason, resided as a 'stonecutter' at Fetter Lane. See *D.N.B.* (GM.)

53. 64. *Herball.* Referring to plant-illustrations showing branches, &c.

53. 70–1. GM conjectures that two lines are missing after this, but this is hardly necessary. There should perhaps be a full stop after 'showre'. 'It shall performe' can mean 'It will do this job', referring to ll. 68–70.

53. 76. *Mouthes.* Sc. jaw-bones.

53. 77. *In a wet day.* Making roads dangerous.

54. 90. *Lapland-lease.* No explanation of this has been found.

54 (*heading*). *Mr. Fletchers Playes.* Vaughan's tribute was not published with the many others in the folio edition of 1647.

54. 2. *remonstrative.* Exhibitive, demonstrative.

54. 4. *Lent before a Christmasse.* Hutchinson, *Life*, 79, observes that Advent was early known as Quadragesima Sancti Martini.

54. 6. *from . . . date.* Beg permanence from being associated with your work.

54. 7. *dub the Coppy.* By putting a title before my own name.

54. 8. *reare.* Conclusion.

54. 13. *adopt.* Stand sponsor for.

55. 33. *the Eares.* Referring to the appearance of the close-cropped Roundheads.

55. 38. *Swansteed.* Eliard Swanston.

55. 42. *Bayle.* Presumably meaning defence. See *O.E.D.* Bail *sb.*[3]

55 (*heading*). *Upon the Poems, &c.* This is printed among the commendatory poems in the volume of Cartwright's *Comedies, &c.*, 1651, and is signed HENRY VAUGHAN, *Silurist.*

55. 2. *Remonstrances.* See note on 54. 2.

56. 29. *.thy Slave.* Hutchinson, *Life*, 44, observes that *The Royall Slave*, performed at Oxford in 1636, was twice issued during Vaughan's 'Oxford years' (1639 and 1640).

56. 40. *so exprest.* See *D.N.B.* art. Cartwright, on the wearing of mourning by the King on the day of Cartwright's funeral.

57 (*heading*). The 'most accomplish'd Couple' may have been James Philips, of Cardigan, and Katherine Fowler ('the matchless Orinda'), married August 1648. Cf. second heading on p. 61. See *Life*, 81-2.

57. 13. *Soft as your selves.* Cf. 62. 10. (GM.)

57. 18. *silent as his feet.* Cf. 61 (*To Mrs. Philips*). 5-6. (GM.)

58 (*heading*). *Mr. R. Hall.* For a likely identification with 'Dr. Hall, a Clergyman', see *Life*, 61.

58. 3-7. There is some borrowing from Robert Randolph's elegy on his brother Thomas. See T. R.'s *Poems*, ed. Thorn-Drury, p. 2 :

> Yet flow these teares not that thy Reliques sit
> Fix'd to their cell a constant Anchorit . . .
> such distempers flow . . . (GM.)

58. 36. *Church'd.* Re-consecrated (sc. 'after the Puritan occupation had "Prophan'd" it'). (H in GM.)

59. 57-8. Cf. Suckling, verses to Hales, ll. 41-2 (*Works*, ed. Thompson, p. 28). (GM.)

59. 63-4. *West.* Cf. 169. 26 and Donne, 'Hymn to God my God, in my sicknesse', ll. 11-15 (*Poems*, ed. Grierson, i, p. 368) ; also Donne, 'Goodfriday, 1613. Riding Westward' (ibid. p. 336).

59. 75-6. *Salve, &c.* Virgil, *Aen.* xi. 97-8.

60 (*heading*). See 690. 31-5 and note on 34-5. Malvezzi's book was published at Bologna in 1635 and at Antwerp in 1641. For Powell, see note on 33 (*title-page*), and *Life*, 75, &c.

60. 9-10. Cf. Feltham, *Resolves*, i. 12 (ed. cit. p. 37) : 'Every *good man* is a Leiger here for Heaven', see also 440. 25 and note.

61 (*first heading*). *Master T. Lewes.* Rector of Llanfigan, near Newton. Evicted under the Act for the Propagation of the Gospel in Wales (1650). Hutchinson, in *Life*, 81, following GM, observes that the meeting would be easier while the Usk, which separated Newton and Llanfigan, was frozen over (see ll. 5-6).

61. 1-4, 13 sqq. Based on Horace, *Odes*, i. 9. 1-4, 'Vides ut alta stet nive candidum', &c., and 13-14 :

> Quid sit futurum cras, fuge quaerere et
> Quem fors . . .

61. 17-18. From G. Herbert, 'The Discharge', ll. 38-40 and 45 (*Works*, p. 145). Vaughan in ll. 11-16 is also following the thought in Herbert's poem. (GM.)

3 A

61. 20. *bottome.* Skein of thread. See *O.E.D.* Cf. G. Herbert, 'The Discharge', l. 45 : 'And draw the bottome out an end'. (H.)

61 (*second heading*). *Mrs. K. Philips.* See note to 57 (heading) and *Life,* 81–2. Neither these verses nor those on pp. 641–2 are found in the editions of her poems published in 1664 and after. For her poem on Vaughan see pp. 617–18.

62. 15–16. Cf. I.T.A.M., commendatory poem, ll. 1–2, in Randolph's *Poems* (ed. cit. p. 5) :

> Blest Spirit, when I first did see
> The Genius of thy Poetrie . . .

and Randolph, 'An Elegie on . . . Sir Rowland Cotton', l. 4 (ed. cit. p. 89) :

> A new strange miracle, wealth in Poetrie.

62. 29. *A Persian Votarie.* Alluding to the three wise men.

62. 30. Cf. 645. 46. (GM.)

63. *The Lady Elizabeth.* 1635–1650 (8 Sept.). See *D.N.B.* and *Life,* 80.

63. 2. Cf. 401. 12.

63. 7–8. Cf. (?) F. Beaumont, 'An Elegie on . . . Lady Rutland' (see note to 50. 30) :

> As soone as thou couldst apprehend a griefe
> There were enough to meet thee . . .
> . . . .
> But thou hadst ere thou knewst the vse of teares
> Sorrow layd vp against thou com'st to yeares.

63. 13–14. Hutchinson compares 453. 1 and G. Herbert, 'The Familie', ll. 17–20 (*Works,* pp. 137 and 525) :

> Joyes oft are there, and griefs as oft as joyes ;
> But griefs without a noise :
> Yet speak they louder then distemper'd fears.
> What is so shrill as silent tears ?

63. 21. *as Rhumes.* Sc. fall on. Cf. G. Herbert, 'Confession', l. 12 (*Works,* p. 126) : 'And fall, like rheumes, upon the tendrest parts'; and *Outlandish Proverbs,* No. 475 (*Works,* p. 337).

63. 23. *gently spend.* See note on 509. 11.

63. 32. *Influxe.* See note to 12. 67.

63. 34. *back-side.* Reverse side. Apparently some lines were excised after this one.

63. 36–7. *As by . . . reads.* This passage might have been clearer in the light of the lines which seem to have been removed, but there may be some reference to Ezek. ii. 9–iii. 3 : 'an hand was sent unto me . . .'.

64 (*heading*). *Gondibert.* Published in 1651.

64. 13–24. Davenant is similarly praised by Cowley and Waller in their commendatory verses accompanying *Gondibert.*

64. 27–30. Part of the difficulty in these lines would disappear if 'his sight' in l. 30 could be replaced by 'thy sight': Davenant *sees,* whereas his forebear had only imagined. (The printer might have caught 'his' from l. 32, 'his *bayes*'.) But as 'his' is the reading it must be taken into account in any explanation of the passage. With either 'his' or 'thy' the identity of 'thy aged *Sire*' is uncertain.

Three possibilities have been put forward, none of them entirely convincing :

1. Homer. See H. F. B. Brett-Smith in *Mod. Lang. Rev.* xi, 1916, pp. 76-8. Line 30 is supposed to refer to Homer's physical blindness. It is also pointed out that Homer is much alluded to in Davenant's Preface to *Gondibert* and in Hobbes's *Answer*. Davenant as the reformer of heroic poetry is metaphorically the son of Homer, whose writings, by comparison with *Gondibert*, appear even darker (i.e. less revealing) than his own eyesight.

2. Jonson. Davenant succeeded Jonson as Poet Laureate. The meaning of l. 30 might be that Jonson's imaginative works are inferior to Davenant's writings in perceptive value.

3. Shakespeare. This was tentatively suggested by Chambers (ii, p. 341). See Spence, *Anecdotes* (1820, p. 82): ' That notion of Sir William D'Avenant being more than a poetical child only of Shakspeare was common in town, and Sir William himself seemed fond of having it taken for truth.—[*Mr. Pope.*]' Cf. Spence's following anecdote. The story is first explicitly told by Vaughan's relative, Aubrey (*Brief Lives*, i, p. 204), but see the lines of 1655 quoted in *D.N.B.* art. D'Avenant. On this identification Vaughan's l. 30 could mean that what Shakespeare did in the realm of 'fancy' was less glorious than the practical achievement of begetting so illustrious a son.

With ll. 28-9 cf. Randolph, *The Jealous Lovers*, II. ii :

    And must her lust break into open flames,
    To lend the world a light to view her shames ?

64. 31. *bars and length of dayes.* ' The obstacles caused by or incident to length of days ' (see *Mod. Lang. Rev.* loc. cit., footnote to p. 76) ; ' bars and length ' is then a hendiadys for bars of (caused by) length.

64. 33. Alluding to Davenant's imprisonment at Cowes in 1650.

65. 46. *Emrauld.* See *Gondibert*, III. iv. 45 sqq.

66 (*heading*). *Lib. 3⁰.* iii. 7.   *after . . . releasement.* Vaughan's addition. (GM.)

67. 29-30. Cf. 664. 47-8. (GM.)

68. 47-8. *with many . . . Groves.* A characteristic interpolation. Ovid, ll. 33-4 :

    Torqueor en gravius, repetitaque forma locorum
    Exsilium renovat triste, recensque facit.

68 (*heading*). *translated . . . Age.* Vaughan's addition. (GM.) *Judases.* Cf. 348. ? (H.)

69. 53-8. Jean Robertson, in *Mod. Lang. Rev.* 1944, pp. 108-9, ' The use made of Felltham's *Resolves* ', points out Vaughan's indebtedness to Felltham at this point. With ll. 53-4 cf. *Resolves*, i. 49, ' That all things have a like progression and fall ' (ed. cit. p. 154):

    All that *Man* holds, hangs but by slender twine,
    By sudden chance the strongest things decline.

and with ll. 55-8 cf. *Resolves*, i. 46, ' Of the waste and change of Time ' (ed. cit. p. 146) :

    Who has not heard of *Crœsus* heapes of Gold,
    Yet knowes his Foe did him a prisoner hold ?
    He that once aw'd *Sycilia's* proud extent,
    By a poore *Art*, could *Famine* scarce prevent.

71. 49–50. Ovid, ll. 45–6. Vaughan omits Ovid, ll. 67–8.

71. 68. *as Pythagoras believes.* Vaughan's addition. (GM.)

72. 77. *the . . . Love.* 'tenerorum lusor amorum.'

72. *Ausonii Cupido.* The translation of 'Cupido Cruciatur' is very free. Lines 67–72, for instance ('As in a dream . . . shout'), and ll. 135–8 are additional.

74. 89–92. *As a thiefe, &c.* Chambers points out that this is partly from Donne, *Elegies*, iv. 3–4:

> And as a thiefe at barre, is question'd there
> By all the men, that have beene rob'd that yeare . . .

75. 112. *Sconce.* A protective screen or shelter (*O.E.D.* sb.^{3}).

76 (*continuation*). 135–8. Vaughan's addition.

77. 33. *And . . . birth.* Vaughan's addition. (GM.)

77. 3–4. Cf. 629. 25–6. (GM.)

80 (*Metr.* 7). 21. *inlightned Rayes.* Cf. 402. 55. (GM.)

80 (*second poem*). 5–6. 'Humilemque victi sublevat fallax vultum.'

81 (*second poem*). 7. *Etesian.* Not in Boethius.

82. 3. *stov'd in silence.* Cf. 121. 11 and Felltham, *Resolves*, i. 18 (1634, p. 59): 'while the *rich* lie stoved in *secure reposes*'.

83. 15–16. Hutchinson, referring to Vaughan's love of trees (*Life*, 22), observes that these two lines are Vaughan's addition to his original.

84 (*headings*). *Metra* 6 and 7 should be *Metra* 7 and 8.

84. 1–6. Appropriated from Felltham, *Resolves*, i. xv (ed. cit. p. 50):

> He that thirsts for Glories prize ;
> Thinking that, the top of all :
> Let him view th' expansed skies,
> And the Earth's contracted Ball.
> Hee 'l be ashamed then, that the name he wanne,
> Fils not the short walke, of one healthfull man.

84. 24. *a second death.* In a sense different from that intended in 456. 8. See note thereto.

84–5. 1–15. Appropriated from Felltham, *Resolves*, i. lxxxvi (ed. cit. p. 269):

> That the *World* in constant force,
> Varies his concordant course :
> That seeds iarring, *hot* and *cold*,
> Doe the *Breed* perpetuall hold :
> That the Sunne in 's golden *Car*
> Does the *Rosie Day* still rere.
> That the *Moone* swayes all those *lights*,
> *Hesper* ushers to *darke nights*.
> That *alternate Tydes* be found,
> *Seas* high-prided *waves* to bound,
> Lest his *fluid* waters Mace,
> Creeke broad Earths invallyed face.
> All the *Frame* of things that be,
> *Love* (which rules *Heaven*, *Land*, and *Sea*)
> Chaines, keepes, orders, as you see.

85. 16. *This.* Sc. Love. Cf. ll. 22 and 26.

85 (*heading*). *Casimirus.* Another translation had appeared in 1646 :

The Odes of Casimir Translated by G. H. [Hils.] See an article, 'Casimire Sarbiewski and the English Ode', by Maren-Sofie Röstvig (*Studies in Philology*, li, 1954, pp. 443-60).

86 (*continuation*). 22. *At rest, &c.* Vaughan's addition.

86 (*heading*). *Ode* 8. Ode 7 in the edition of Casimir's *Odes* of 1647.

89 (*second poem*). 1-4. Mostly Vaughan's addition.

90. 27. The reference to the Virgin Mary in Casimir is omitted by Vaughan. (GM.)

91. 77. *Quitst.* Ring-dove. See *O.E.D.* s.v. Queest. Cf. 132. 4.

93 (*first heading*). *Mathæo Herbert.* See 32. 6 and note.

93 (*second heading*). *Thomæ Poëllo.* See note to 33 (*title-page*). Powell's work referred to is *Elementa Opticæ: Novâ, Facili, & Compendiosâ Methodo Explicata . . . Londini.* 1651. [Dedication signed T. P.] Vaughan's verses are on A6ᵛ. They are there headed Eximio Viro, Et Amicorum longè optimo, *T. P.* In hunc suum de Elementis Opticæ libellum. They are signed Hen: Vaughan *Siluris.*

95 (*title-page*). *translated . . . I. Reynolds.* The Latin versions are in *D. Iohannis Rainoldi . . . Orationes 5. cum aliis quibusdam opusculis . . . Oxoniæ . . .* 1613. There was another edition in 1619.

> *Dolus, an, &c.* Virgil, *Aen.* ii. 390.
> *fas est, &c.* Ovid, *Met.* iv. 428.

103. 31 sqq. The note is Vaughan's addition. The Juvenal reference is to *Satires*, ix. 131-3.

109 (*title-page*). *Omnia, &c.* Ovid, *Tristia*, ii. 301 : 'Omnia perversas possunt (*or* poterunt) corrumpere mentes.' (EB.)

117. 1-5. E. Bensly, in *Mod. Lang. Rev.* xiv, Jan. 1919, p. 105, observes that 'by some unknowne Poet' in l. 1 is an addition to the statement of Maximus Tyrius. The addition is presumably Vaughan's, as there is no corresponding remark in Reynolds's Latin. Bensly shows that the quotation (ll. 3-5) 'is the beginning of the Paean to Hygieia written by Ariphron of Sicyon '; Bensly refers also to Athenaeus, xv. 701-2.

123 (*title-page*). *Written Originally in Spanish.* A Latin version was published in 1578, and another in 1633 with *Oblectatio Vitæ Rusticæ Egidii vander Myle.* In that volume *Vitæ Rusticæ Encomium Dn. Antonii de Guevara* begins at p. 321.

> *O fortunatos, &c.* Virgil, *Georg.* ii. 458.

131. 1-2. *that are   spirit.* 'quos supina sapientia inflat'.

131. 16-18. *and every . . . Lord.* Vaughan's addition.

131. 34-5. *But let us . . . Country.* Vaughan's addition.

133. 15-18. Cf. Guevara : 'Non alienos talis heredes, non fiscum, aut bonorum translationes formidat'; and *The Mount of Olives*, 167. 1-4.

135. 26-7. *that claps . . . back.* Cf. Marlowe, *Edward II*, I. iv. 408 : 'He weares a lords reuenewe on his back '; and *2 Henry VI*, I. iii. 83. Miss E. Holmes observes that Thomas Vaughan has the same expression in his *Cœlum Terræ*, 165 p. 92 : 'Some *Cockney* claps his *Revenues* on his *backe* '.

THE MOUNT OF OLIVES.

138 (*heading*). *S*ʳ· *Charles Egerton.* Brother of Lucy, who married Richard Wise. These were the parents of Catherine and Elizabeth Wise, whom Vaughan married successively. See *Life*, 53, 73, &c.

138. 3. *my dearest friend.* Probably Catherine Vaughan. See preceding note and *Life*, 195–6.

138. 11–12. *Cœlo dignus, &c.* Marcus Aurelianus Nemesianus, *Eclogues*, i. 50 ('concilio'). (EB.)

140. 32–4. Vaughan alludes to 'Rules and Lessons', 436–9.

141. 6–7. *If . . . blinde them.* See note to 413. 29–30.

141. 13–15. See 183. 18–31, 33–9 and note.

143. 1–4. See 187. 14–17 and note; also Chrysostom, *Hom. in Epist. Hebr.* xiv (*Opera*, Migne, xii, col. 116). (Miss Guiney in her edition.)

143. 7–8. *Contemplate . . . Stars.* See note on 469. 1 sqq.

143. 20–5. Cf. 436. 1–10.

144. 9. *Ray . . . soul.* Cf. 408. 8, and Felltham, *Resolves*, 'Deo Authoris Votum' (ed. cit. Ggʳ and Ggᵛ): '*streame thy* selfe *into my* soule' . . . 'ray *thy selfe into my* Soule'. (GM.)

147. 23–8. G. Herbert, 'The Church-Porch', st. 71 (*Works*, p. 23).

148. 29. *Cave of Macpelah.* Gen. xxiii. 9 sqq.

149. 2. *Hin.* A measure of just over a gallon. Exod. xxix. 40, &c.

156. 14–15. From G. Herbert, 'The Priesthood', ll. 29–30 (*Works*, p. 161):

> O what pure things, most pure must those things be,
> Who bring my God to me! (H.)

161. 9. *O Rose of Sharon.* Song of Sol. ii. 1. Cf. 410. 21–2 and 458. 49–50.

161. 14–16. *Thou that feedest . . . flee.* Song of Sol. ii. 16–17.

162. 10–14. See 518, 'The Ass', and note.

163. 35 (*note*). *Cyprian de cœnâ.* The work is *attributed* to Cyprian. See *Opera* (Oxford, 1682), sig. Ffffff, p. 41.

166. 10–19. See *Life*, 113–14. (Hutchinson there observes that Vaughan is quoting Lamentations i. 4 and Song of Sol. ii. 12.) Cf. 131. 15.

166. 13–15. *Thy Ministers . . . place.* Cf. 171. 1–4.

168. 17. Miss Guiney compares 86 (Ode 8). 19–20; but the line is borrowed from G. Herbert, 'Vanitie' (II), ll. 9–10 (*Works*, p. 111).

169. 2 (*note*). Miss Guiney refers to *Select Italian Proverbs; The most significant, very usefull for Travellers, and such as desire that Language . . .* By Gio. Torriano . . . 1649 (p. 67). See also G. Herbert, *Outlandish Proverbs*, No. 746 in *Works*, p. 346: 'Night is the mother of Councels.'

169. 15. *Cremationem, &c.* Gregory, *Moralia*, ix. 56 (*Opera*, Migne, i, col. 912).

169. 18–19. Cf. 522. 12.

169. 22. *the portion preceding it.* Cf. 419. 4.

169. 24. *an apparition.* See 174. 2 and note; also 214. 25.

169. 26. *Westward.* Cf. 59. 63–4 and note; also 213. 6 and 296. 20.

169. 27-8. *Pilgrim . . . Countrey.* Cf. Chaucer, 'Truth', ll. 18-19
(*Works*, ed. Skeat, i, pp. 390-1):
> Forth, pilgrim, forth! Forth, beste, out of thy stal!
> Know thy contree, look up, thank God of al.

169. 29-31. *like holy Macarius, &c.* Macarius Aegyptius, *Apo-
phthegmata (Opera*, Migne, col. 258): 'Iter agens aliquando per
eremum, inveni calvariam mortui', &c. H compares 493 (continuation). 26: 'I met with a dead man'.

169. 38. *They put farre away.* The quotation from Amos vi. 3-6,
ending 170. 1, begins here.

171 (*first note*). The author of *Speculum naturalis cœlestis & pro-
pheticæ visionis* was Josephus Grünbeck.

171. 3-4. *light or perfection.* Cf. G. Herbert, 'Aaron', l. 22 (*Works*,
p. 174): 'Perfect and light in my deare breast'.

171. 4-8. E. Bensly, in *Mod. Lang. Rev.* xiv, Jan. 1919, p. 10, traces
this to Isaac Casaubon's Preface to his *Polybius* (1609), sig. ã ij
verso, ll. 24 sqq.: 'dies, hora, momentum, euertendis dominationibus
sufficit, quae adamantinis credebantur radicibus esse fundatæ.' But
Vaughan found the Latin passage in the Preface to Ralegh's *History
of the World* (1628, A3 verso), from which he quotes again a few
lines farther on.

171. 14-15. Grosart cites Ralegh, Preface to *History of the World*
(1628, A2 verso): '*Others, That the diuine prouidence (which
Cratippus obiected to* Pompey) *hath set downe the date and period of
euery Estate, before their first foundation and erection.*'

171 (*second note*). Nonius Marcellus, *De Compendiosa Doctrina*, xii;
ed. Lindsay, p. 846, 30-32.

171 (*third note*). 1-4. *Non est, &c. Anthol. Lat.* (ed. Buecheler and
Riese), I. i, p. 333, No. 444. 5-8. *Qui vultus, &c.* Seneca, *Agamemnon*, 607-10.

172. 5-9. *Anacreon, &c.* Cf. Stobaeus, *Florilegium*, iii. 93. 25 (ed.
Gaisford, p. 235).

172. 10. *parentage is low.* Cf. G. Herbert, 'Avarice', l. 3 (*Works*,
p. 77):
> I know thy parentage is base and low.

172. 22-173. 4. *But if . . . desolation.* Roughly translated from Petrarch,
De Otio Religiosorum, ii (*Opera* . . . 1554, p. 355): 'sed subsiste,
obsecro . . . in nihilum abiere.'

172. 30 (*note*). *Ingeniosa, &c.* Petronius, *Saturae,* ed. Buecheler, 119.
33-8.

173. 4-5. *bones . . . pit.* Psalm cxli. 7.

173. 5-7. *instead . . . beauty.* Is. iii. 24.

173 (*first note*). *mors sola, &c.* Juvenal x. 172-3. Quoted by Petrarch
in *De Contemptu Mundi*, Dial. ii (ed. cit. p. 384).

173. 7-22. *and (O blessed Jesus!), &c.* Partly a reminiscence of
Petrarch, *De Otio*, ii (ed. cit. pp. 355-6): '& ô bone *IESV* . . . dabis
iocos.'

173. 31-2. *tears . . . heart of flint.* Cf. the emblem on the title of *Silex
Scintillans*, 1650.

173. 35 (*second note*). See Jerome, *Vita Hilarionis* (*Opera*, Migne, ii,
col. 52).

174. 1-2. *Our present life, &c.* Chrysostom, *Hom. in Matt.* xii (*Opera*, Migne, vii, col. 206): 'praesentia omnia umbram et somnium esse putemus.' Cf. 169. 23-4.

174. 4-11. *Natural histories, &c.* Miss Guiney notes that this is probably a reminiscence (it is not a direct translation) of Drexelius, *Æternitatis Prodromus*, i. 6 (*Opera*, 1647, i, p. 34): 'Sed & volucris', &c. Cf. Pliny, *Hist. Nat.* xi. 36 (43).

174. 14. *have their rootes, &c.* Cf. G. Herbert, 'Vertue', l. 7 (*Works*, p. 87):

> Thy root is ever in its grave.

174. 23-30. *Nam mihi, &c.* Cf. Vaughan's translation, 383. 33-8, where the lines are attributed to Paulinus. Petrarch, *De Otio* (ed. cit. p. 354), quotes them and attributes them to Prosper.

174. 35. *flowers . . . keep house . . .* Miss E. Holmes compares G. Herbert, 'The Flower', ll. 10-14 (*Works*, p. 166).

175. 1-3. *Mis mawrddh, &c.* These lines (attributed to Aneurin) are printed again in *The Myvyrian Archaiology* (2nd ed., 1870, p. 21), where they form ll. 1, 7, and 8 of the *Englyns of the months*, st. 3:

> Mis MAWRTH, mawr ryfig adar
> . . . . . .
> Pob peth a ddaw trwy'r ddaer
> Ond y Marw, mawr ei Garchar!

175. 10-11. *he shall not . . . more.* Job xiv. 12.

176. 16-24. *A great Philosopher, &c.* Miss Guiney compares Cornelius Agrippa, *De Occulta Philosophia*, i. 58. Three books (of the four) were translated in 1651 by J. F. In the translation the passage referred to is on p. 129: 'And I have often seen a Dor-mouse dissected, and continue immovable, as if she were dead, untill she was boyled, and then presently in boyling the water the dissected members did shew life.'

176. 29 (*note*). Marcellus Palingenius, *Zodiacus Vitae*, ix. 180-1, xi. 658-60, viii. 249-51.

177. 4. *Sic nostros, &c.* Manilius, *Astronomicon*, ii. 261. (EB.)

177. 8 and 24. Cf. 400. 5 sqq.

178. 4-6. *Sunt qui, &c.* Juvenal xiii. 86:

> Sunt in fortunae qui casibus omnia ponant
> Et nullo credant, &c.

178. 16. *Ex hoc momento, &c.* A favourite thought of Drexelius, e.g. *De Damnatorum Rogo*, xi. 2 (*Opera*, ed. cit. i, p. 172): 'pendet ab hoc momento æternitas.'

178. 19-33. Miss Guiney compares Drexelius, *De Damnatorum Rogo* (*Opera*, ed. cit. i, p. 146): 'Memini legere, nec sine admiratione', &c.

178. 34-41. Miss Guiney compares Drexelius, *Considerationes de Æternitate* (ed. cit. i, p. 11), noting that Vaughan's 'a little Wren' corresponds to the phrase 'ab angelo'. Drexelius, as he acknowledges in a marginal note, is here indebted to Cornelius a Lapide, *Comm. in Pentateuch.*, on Exodus xv. 18.

179. 1-22. Cf. Drexelius, op. cit. Consideratio ix, Conclusio v (*Opera*, ed. cit. I, p. 25): 'Nam hoc habet Æternitas, integra est quidquid inde demas: demantur tot anni quot sunt stellæ cæli, guttæ maris, arenæ granula, folia arborum, terræ gramina; adhuc tota est: addantur tot, non erit maior; quamdiu Deus erit, tamdiu damnatos puniet.' The authorship of the verses is still unknown. Miss Guiney was mistaken in attributing them to St. Hildebert.

180. 38. *closet-sins, bosome-councels.* Cf. G. Herbert, 'Sinne' (1), l. 14 (*Works*, p. 46): 'One cunning bosome-sin'.

181 (*first note*). Seneca, *Hippolytus*, 162-4. (E.B.)

181. 22-37. The passage consists of several extracts from *Prologus sancti Hieronymi . . . in libros Vitaspatrum* (wrongly attributed to Jerome).

183. 2-4. See *Shakspere's Holinshed*, p. 158 (*Hol.* iii. 541/1/22).

183. 9 (*first note*). Cf. *Outlandish Proverbs*, 1640 (G. Herbert, *Works*, p. 352, no. 942): 'Sinnes are not knowne till they bee acted.'

183. 18-31, 33-9. Cf. 141. 13-15 and see Jerome, *Vita S. Pauli Primi Eremitae* (*Opera*, Migne, ii, cols. 28-30).

183. 27-40 (*first note*). *Cœlo, &c.* Lucan, vii. 819.

(*second note*). *Jam ruet, &c.* Quoted by Petrarch, *De Contemptu Mundi*, Dial. iii (ed. cit. p. 413), from his own *Africa*, ii. 431 and 464 ('Mox ruet', and 'libris' for 'tumulis').

(*fourth note*). Seneca, *Thyestes*, 449-51 ('capere' and 'jacentem').

184. 1-2. *Cleopatra's banquets of dissolved pearles.* Pliny, *Hist. Nat.* ix. 120.

184. 2. *Hilarion's Crow.* Cf. 673. 52. Jerome's story of the crow which brought bread to the anchorite is told of his St. Paul. See *Vita S. Pauli* (*Opera*, Migne, ii, cols. 25-26).

184. 41-185. 13. *in the life of Antonius.* The story is told about Antonius in the *Life* of Hilarion, chs. 3 and 31 (Jerome, *Opera*, Migne, ii, cols. 31 and 46-7).

185. 18. *Torpedo.* Cf. 41. 11.

185 (*first note*). *Arcanas hyemes, &c.* Baudouin Cabilliau of Ypres (1568-1652), *Epigrammata Selecta* (Antv. 1620), p. 7, no. 29. (E.B.)

(*second note*). *Qui jacet, &c.* Alanus de Insulis, *Liber Parabolarum*, ii (*Opera*, Migne, col. 584). See also Tilley, *Proverbs in England*, G464, 'He that lies upon the Ground . . .'.

185. 38-9. *a deaths-head, &c.* See 491. 6 and note.

186. 1-2. *no pleasures, &c.* Hutchinson observes that this is a reminiscence of G. Herbert, ' The Rose ', ll. 5-8 (*Works*, p. 177):

First, there is no pleasure here :
  Colour'd griefs indeed there are,
  Blushing woes, that look as cleare
As if they could beautie spare.

186 (*first note*). *Omnem crede, &c.* Horace, *Ep.* i. 4. 13. Quoted by Petrarch, *De Contemptu Mundi*, Dial. iii (ed. cit. p. 409).

186. 7-8. *Soles occidere, &c.* Catullus, v. 4.

186 (*second note*). *The Church militant.* See note to 674. 9-675. 14.

186. 21-38. G. Herbert, 'Life' (*Works*, p. 94).

187. 1-41. Translated, sometimes roughly, from Petrarch, *De Contemptu Mundi*, Dial. iii (ed. cit. pp. 414-15) : 'Quotiens igitur . . . nepotibus umbra.'

187. 3 (*note*). *Immortalia, &c.* Horace, *Odes* iv. 7. 7–12. Not in Petrarch.

187. 11–17. Cf. 143. 1–4, 436. 7, 439. 127–38, and 522. 25–30.

187. 20–1. Virgil, *Aen.* iii. 515.

187. 41. Virgil, *Georg.* ii. 58. H compares G. Herbert, *Outlandish Proverbs*, No. 198 (*Works*, p. 327): 'The tree that growes slowly, keepes it selfe for another.'

188. 14. *God . . . bell.* In G. Herbert, *Outlandish Proverbs*, No. 384: 'God comes to see without a bell' (*Works*, p. 334).

188. 26–9. *We can go die, &c.* G. Herbert, 'Death', ll. 21–4 (*Works*, p. 186).

190. 12–13. *Glory . . . men.* Hutchinson (G. Herbert, *Works*, p. 189, footnote) points out that Herbert ends *The Temple* with this quotation, and that Vaughan's following words, 'Blessed . . . one', are those with which Herbert closes 'L'Envoy' after 'The Church Militant'.

192. 19. *Eadinerus.* See note to ll. 22–3.

192. 21. *De Similitud.* Both *De Similitudinibus* and the 'genuine discourse' (l. 22) are works *attributed* to Anselm.

192. 22–3. *made publick at Paris. S. Anselmi . . . De Felicitate Sanctorum Dissertatio. Exscriptore Eadinero* [read '*Eadmero*'] *Anglo Canonico Regulari . . . Parisiis, . . . M. DC. XXXIX.*

193. 5. *that little hand.* I Kings xviii. 44–5.

FLORES SOLITUDINIS.

211 (*title-page*). *Tantus Amor, &c.* Virgil, *Georg.* iv. 205.

213 (*heading*). Sir Charles Egerton. See note on 138 (*heading*).

213. 6. *in Occidentem.* Cf. 169. 26.

213. 22–3. *Puella tota, &c.* Bisselius, *Icaria* (Ingolstadii, 1637, pp. 215–16). (EB.)

213. 33. *the Canker-Rose in the mouth of the fox.* Cf. L. Hervieux, *Les fabulistes latins*, ii, p. 315, No. xlv: 'Vulpes dedit Lupo rosorium involutum sanguine, et cum glutiret et optimum diceret, dixit ei Vulpis: In exitu sencies, cum te scindet.' (EB.)

214. 13–14. *Nescio, &c.* Cf. Chytraeus, *Deliciae*, ed. 3, 1606, p. 20, under 'Romana': 'Athei. Vixi. & ultra vitam nil credidi. quó vadam nescio. invitus morior. Valete posteri.' (EB in H.)

214. 22. *Amæna, Petre, &c.* Augurellus, *Geronticon*, i, *Ad Petrum Lipomanum in obitu Claræ sororis* (Antv. 1582, p. 92). (EB.)

216. 1. E. Bensly, in *Mod. Lang. Rev.* xiv, 1919, p. 104, identifies 'the Poet' with St. Paulinus of Nola and refers to his *Natales Sancti Felicis*, Natalis viii, l. 332 (for all the words quoted by Vaughan except 'est').

216. 30–7. *Whose gentle measure, &c.* G. Herbert, 'Content', ll. 13–20 (*Works*, p. 69). Herbert has 'cloisters' in l. 16.

217. 3–5. *Mounsier Mathieu.* Pierre Matthieu, *Unhappy Prosperity. Expressed in the History of Ælius Seianus And Philippa the Catanian . . . Translated by S^r. T. H.* (2nd ed. 1639, p. 313): 'they would have married him to the Princesse of Majorica, he left Roses to make a conserve of Thornes'. This was Ludovico, eldest son of Charles II, King of Naples. Ludovico became a Franciscan and was later canonized.

217. 5–6. *Saint Pauls content.* Phil. iv. 11 and Heb. xiii. 5.

217. 33. *propagation.* Vaughan refers to the Act for the Propagation of the Gospel in Wales (1649/50), under which his brother Thomas and his friend Thomas Powell were evicted from their livings. See 346. 8 and 166. 13–15; also *Life*, 111 and John Walker, *Sufferings of the Clergy*, 1714, Part I, pp. 147–70.

218. This poem was also included in the second part of *Silex Scintillans*, with the title 'Begging'. For variants see p. 500.

219 (*title-page*). Editions of the work translated (*Ioannis Eusebii Nierembergii Ex Societate Iesu, De Arte Voluntatis, Libri Sex*) were published in 1631, 1639, and 1649. References in these notes are to that of 1639.

220. *Of Temperance and Patience.* Op. cit. Lib. II, Appendix I, 'Tolerantia, & temperantia rerum'. Beginning on p. 105, Vaughan goes from 'Breuis est' to p. 161 (end of Appendix III), corresponding to 267. 2 in the present volume. He then goes back to p. 93 (Epistasis to Lib. I).

225. 12. *that troublesome Tympany.* Vaughan's addition.

226. 11. *as the heart with Dittany.* 'quo velut dictamo expellimus aciem' (op. cit., p. 113). See *O.E.D.* s.v. Dittany. 'heart' is for 'hart'.

227. 30. *his relatives.* 'quod nostra refert' (op. cit. p. 115). Cf. 295. 4.

231. 16. *at sharpe.* With unbated sword.

231. 32 (*note*). See on 233. 40.

233. 40 (*note*). *Volater.* Raphael [Maffejus] Volaterranus, *Commentarii* (Basileae, 1559, pp. 356–7). The last sentence of the note, 'And so,' &c., is Vaughan's. Most of the material in the preceding note (p. 231) is also in Volaterranus (p. 140).

236. 4. *Comethe.* For 'Cometho'; but it is 'Comethe' also in Nieremberg.

243. 7–8. *for God . . . Divell.* V's addition, from Wisd. of Sol. ii. 24 : 'through envy of the devil came death into the world.'

253. 17 (*note*). Volaterranus, op. cit. p. 45 : 'Pelusium nunc Damiatam in Aegypto'.

253. 41 254. 2. *The brest, &c.* 'inque ipso peccaturi pectore dum concipitur malignitas, iam grauida est, imò puerpera suæ pœnæ' (op. cit. p. 145).

254. 4–12. *Conscience, &c.* 'Quin ipsius culpæ ipsa est maxima, & prima pœna : nullum non capitale scelus cuique apud se est, etiam post indulgentiam omnium' (loc. cit.).

255. 32–4. *or if she doth . . . hurt him.* V's addition.

255. 40. *after-games.* 'A second game played in order to reverse or improve the issues of the first.' (*O.E.D.*)

255. 42–256. 18. *In the affaires . . . they might.* 'namque tristitia, quam fors ardua immisit, potest in se eleuari ; quam verò dimisit culpa, non dimissa, non debet, etiamsi possit' (op. cit. p. 147).

256. 37–40. *he that dryes . . . precaution.* V's addition, replacing five lines of original (loc. cit.). From this point Vaughan omits longer passages of Nieremberg.

259. 10–11. *Indiscretion . . . importance.* V's addition.

259. 24. *the crown of life.* Nieremberg gives the Latin of Juvenal (viii. 84) correctly : ' Et propter vitam vivendi perdere *causas.*'

262. 23. *proventions.* Returns, produce. Not in *O.E.D.*, but see s.v. ' Provent '.

263. 23–30. *Care thou, &c.* ' Cura, quæ tibi transire modò putas, actiones, vt rectæ sint : hæc manebunt' (op. cit. p. 157).

263. 40–1. *though . . . immortality.* ' liberum immortalitati post mortem ius relinquit' (loc. cit.).

264. 4–5. *Gold . . . unrighteousnesse.* V's addition.

264. 14–17. *and her perswasions . . . corruption.* V's addition.

264. 36–7. *Knowledge . . . dead.* V's addition.

265. 25–32. *Christians . . . Humility.* V's addition.

266. 3–4. *He . . . hastie.* V's addition.

266. 12–14. *Rivers . . . sterility.* V's addition.

266. 37–**267.** 6. *Nothing . . . Calamities.* V's addition.

269. 2. *No man can take up a Child.* ' Nullus iacentem suscitabit' (op. cit. p. 96). Vaughan supplies the ' Child '.

270. 2–3 and 31–2. *yea . . . men. which . . . private.* V's additions.

271. 22–6. *All . . . himself.* ' Currunt & simulatæ : compar his fiet, qui saltem se dissimulat' (op. cit. p. 98).

271. 29–30. *nor . . . hope.* V's addition.

272. 22–4. *He saw . . . Veyle.* V's addition.

272. 41–**273.** 3. *They are . . . within.* ' Quò? rogabis. Meta, nihilum est : euanent, non sinunt, vt fumus è camino' (op. cit. p. 100).

273. 15–20. *but the Soul . . . Soul.* V's addition.

273. 24–37. A very free paraphrase. See Nieremberg, op. cit. p. 101.

274. 8 and 10. *these . . . peace. What . . . them!* V's additions.

274. 39–**275.** 2. *which tears . . . planted.* ' quominùs fortunam ibi radicatam, non videremus reuulsam' (op. cit. p. 103).

275. 16–17. *Seeing . . . earnest.* V's addition.

275. 21–8. *Why . . . Cap.* ' Quia nemo alienis rebus afficitur, qui vixerit alienam vitam sine affectu, id est, suus erit : omnia, vt histrio, fabulam putabit' (op. cit. p. 103).

276. 10–14. *In all, &c.* V's addition.

277. *Of Life and Death.* See notes on 219 (*title-page*) and 220. Vaughan now begins to translate ' Ex comparatione vitæ, & mortis ', op. cit. Lib. VI, Diorismus V.

277. 23 (*note*). Cf. Volaterranus, op. cit. p. 325 (see note to 233. 40). *who feeling . . . therein.* ' ex animi sententia nullo cogente secundum ritum . . . ardentem conscendit rogum.'

277. 23–6. *hee . . . her.* V's addition.

278. 3–5 and 17–26. *Whose . . . blockish. and washing . . . Conscience.* V's additions.

279. 28. *in his Recreations.* V's addition.

281. 16–17. *and glorifies . . . cause.* V's addition.

281. 19–22. *It . . . sorrows.* 'omnium malorum remedium est, quo desinunt omnia' (op. cit. p. 477).

283. 15. *like . . . fall.* V's addition.

283. 23. *The Rod . . . joyes.* 'Terret pueros flagellum' (op. cit. p. 478).

284. 2–9. Largely V's addition.

284. 40. *It . . . troubles.* V's addition.

285. 2–5. *that . . . them.* 'quò procedant iam placidius per decliuia & plana' (op. cit. p. 481).

285. 21. *in the shade.* 22. *the shadow of death.* 33. *in its shadow and projection.* V's additions.

286. 15–16 and 29–32. *and make . . . fairest faces. Thou mayst . . . sleepes.* V's additions.

286. 41–287. 1. *the Nurse . . . to it.* V's addition.

287. 19–22. *by which . . . world.* V's addition.

287. 35–6. *impieties . . . sacriledge.* 'malitia' (op. cit. p. 483).

288. 5–12. *It becomes . . . made them for.* 'Vindicatur tunc natura rerum ordine, temperieque constans, consonans, sed violata ab homine quàm intemperatissimo euersore totiùs ordinis' (op. cit. pp. 483–4).

288. 18–21. *They plot . . . prevail.* 35–6. *by turning . . . out.* 38–9. *Before . . . veile.* V's additions.

288. 41–289. 10. *It was . . . Christ.* 'fauor fuit non properare illò, vbi nec meritum, nec præmium futurum erat. Nunc, quia Cælum nos expectat, mora mortis non promittitur, potiùs commendatur intempestiua & violenta, beatitudinis exaggerata titulo, quia illuc conuehat morientes pro Christo' (op. cit. p. 484).

289. 30–1. *which cannot . . . sorrowes.* V's addition.

290. 15–17. *the blessed Jesus.* 'Jesus frater'. *the mild . . . for us.* V's addition.

291. 14–15. *lest . . . Archiplast.* 'ne aegre tulissent carcerem'. 'Archiplast' is not in *O.E.D.*

291. 36–7. *Rom. . . . Sinne.* V adds the quotation.

292. 4–8. *Life . . . intimations.* 'feriata mens sensibus idoneè diuina excipit' (op. cit. p. 487).

292. 16. *Primrose.* 'flos' (loc. cit.).

294. 15–16. *That humble . . . mouth.* 'nemini non honorificus defunctus est' (op. cit. p. 490).

294. 18–19. *He saw . . . downe.* V's addition.

295. 1–2. *and discerning . . . humanity.* 11–12. *and the Depositum . . . Restauratour.* 32–3. *whose . . . any.* V's additions.

296. 6–7. *in that . . . day.* 'post mortem' (op. cit. p. 491).

296. 31–9. *God . . . body.* V's addition.

297. 37–40. *He quarrelled . . . Almighty.* V's addition. Cf. 417. 21–8.

298. 13–17. *The ignorance . . . so well.* V's addition.

299. 10–12. *though . . . believers.* 'omnibus mutatis' (op. cit. p. 494).

299. 23–4. *Life . . . out.* V's addition. See Tilley, *Proverbs in England*, D140, 'Death has a thousand doors to let out life'.

299. 30–3. *therefore . . . protractions.* 'protractius protelat. Mors optima est, ideo sine lege moræ' (op. cit. p. 495).

300. 26-8. *it is . . . weather.* 'Caduca possessio vita est' (ed. cit. p. 496).

301. 5-6. *Good . . . bolts.* V's addition.

301. 32-5. *and by . . . feet.* 'infantiam per compendium maturat, ianuam Cæli gratis aperiens, viâ rectâ, & sine obice dirigens' (op. cit. p. 497).

301. 37-9. *Death . . . divinity.* 'fuisse argumentum Diuinitatis' (loc. cit.).

301. 40-302. 6. *The Divell . . . daies.* 'Æmulus Diabolus cultum falsum beneficio mortis fulciit, petentibus magnum domum, exiguam vitam concedens' (loc. cit.).

302. 15-24. *What . . . shed.* 'Quid felicius Pompeio accidisset, quàm antè, aut in sua felicitate perire, cùm sui desiderium relinqueret, si non expecteret fastidium fortunæ' (op. cit. p. 497).

303. 9-13. *For those . . . morning.* V's addition, replacing five lines of original (p. 498).

303. 14-19. *but he . . . dissolution.* 'sed casum putares, intempesti- uam mortem, non consilium Dei, non donum' (op. cit. p. 498).

304. 27-32. *Life . . . dust.* V's addition.

304. 32-42. *Sleepe . . . cares.* 'Somnus quædam effigies mortis, & prælibatio est : somnum appetimus, somno recreamur, somnus requies laborum est, reparatio hominis, depositio curarum' (op. cit. p. 500).

305. 19-25. *Paracelsus . . . flesh.* V's addition. Cf. Paracelsus, 'De Meteoricis Expressionibus' (*Philosophiæ et Medicinæ . . . Compendium*, 1568, p. 34) : 'Non est spiritui tamen sabathi requies imposita, sed corpori solùm hominis, vt aliorum animalium auxiliantium illi. Spiritus verò semper & in assiduo labore positus est, vt neque nox, neque sabathum ad requiem eum compescat, in omnibus etiam creaturis.' With l. 21 cf. 522. 27.

305. 32 and 38-41. *like the Phœnix.* (*more*) *then . . . joyes.* V's additions.

306. 33-4. *imitation . . . World.* V's addition.

307. 31-2. *and not . . . fellow.* V's addition.

307. 35-9. *That death . . . head.* 'quæ suffragio pereuntis expectatur, quâ crescit illæsus etiam minutus capite' (op. cit. p. 503).

307. 41-308. 1. *Whose . . . joy.* V's addition.

308. 16-17. *the Elixir . . . immortal.* V supplies the alchemical metaphor.

308. 27. *politick, irreligious Tyrants.* 'instantem tyrannum' (op. cit. p. 504).

309. 1. *they . . . of it.* 5-7. *Death . . . hands.* 13-14. *Sickness . . . wings.* V's additions.

312. 1. *published this peece at Antwerp.* Vaughan refers to *D. Eucherii Episcopi Lugdunensis De Contemptu Mundi Epistola parænetica ad Valerianum cognatum. Accedit Vita D. Paulini Nolani Veri Mundi Contemptoris. Antverpiæ . . . M.D.XXI.*

312. 2. *Gennadius cap. 63.* Migne, *Patr. Lat.*, lviii, col. 1096.

312. 3. *and Erasmus, &c.* *Epistola Parænetica . . . Cum Scholijs D. Erasmi Roterodami . . . M.D.XXXI.*

312. 9. *placed by Helvicus.* *Theatrum Historicum* (5th ed., Oxford 1651, p. 100).

312. 15–19. *Some will have, &c.* The conjectures are taken from a note on p. 185 of Vaughan's original.

315. 14–15. *Soul the Mistris.* Cf. 552. 33–34. (H.) But in each place the thought is in V's original.

318 (*note*). *An excellent Dilemma.* The note is in V's original.

318. 42. *this rope of sands.* V's addition. See Tilley, *Proverbs in England*, R174. G. Herbert uses the expression in 'The Collar', l. 22 (*Works*, p. 153).

320. 2–4. *and in the custody ... goods.* 'proscriptionesque ipsas quodammodò ostentant & inuitant?' (op. cit. p. 13.)

325. 25–6. *What Covert ... things?* V's addition.

325. 37–40. V adds these last two verses.

329. 8–9. *from the farthest ... Christ.* 'ab Aquilone & mari Christum resonat' (op. cit. pp. 28–9).

330. 28–31. *Hence ... heaven.* 'Hinc sæpè illa cæli cernuntur signa' (op. cit. p. 31).

333. 12–14. *the disputers ... wisedome.* V's addition.

336. 34. V's addition.

337 (*title-page*). *Collected out of his own Works ... by Henry Vaughan.* The title of the work following Eucherius's *Epistola* in the 1621 edition (see note to 312. 1) is as follows : *Vita Diui Paulini Episc. Nolani ex scriptis eius, & veterum de eo Elogiis concinnata.* The Preface by Heribertus Rosweydus begins : 'Vti Româ hanc Vitam ab amico Socio concinnatam accepi, ita tecum communico.' In 1622 Rosweydus and Ducæus brought out an edition (with notes and a reprint of the *Vita*) of the Works of Paulinus. Vaughan draws upon the Works and the notes, and since he translated the *Epistola* of Eucherius presumably had both publications (i.e. those of 1621 and of 1622). Although Vaughan does not here acknowledge that his Life of Paulinus is largely a translation of the *Vita*, the entry of *Flores Solitudinis* in the Stationers' Register states that its contents are 'all translated by Henry Vaughan'.

338. 10. *Gourd.* See note to 449. 71–2.

338. 15–20. *Desine, &c. Ioh: Baptistæ Ferrarii Senensis, S.I., Flora, seu De Florum Cultura Lib. IV.* (Ed. nova, 1646, Lib. I, i, p. 3.) Cf. 493. 33–6.

339. 8–21. Ecclus. l. 6–11.

340. 4–5. *Which silently, &c.* Miss Guiney compares Horace, *Odes*, i. 12. 45 6:
>Crescit occulto velut arbor ævo
>Fama Marcelli.

340. 7–15. *And this ... account.* Here Vaughan begins his series of derivations from the *Vita*. See note to 337.

340. 25–30. *In a Golden Age ... others.* 'Sæculo aureo ... multiplicandæ suæ' (*Vita*, p. 51).

340. 30–41. *It was ... day.* 'Quippe ea tempestate ... gloriantur' (*Vita*, p. 49).

341. 2–16. *His Patrimonies ... unknown.* 'Patrimonium ... fleamus' (*Vita*, pp. 50–1).

341. 19–30. *Ergo ... future.* 'Ergo nihil ... negligamus' (*Vita*, p. 47).

341. 31–6. *He had conferred . . . disposition.* 'Humanae vitae ornamenta . . . suavissimis' (*Vita*, pp. 46–7).

341. 36–**342.** 2. *To bring . . . plant.* 'Ita factum est . . . formaritque' (*Vita*, pp. 51–2).

341. 39–40. *who . . . Burdeaux.* 'Burdigalæ . . . rexit' (*Vita*, p. 60).

342. 3–26. For the origin of this passage, including the note (four lines from Ausonius, *Ep.* xx), see *Vita*, pp. 51, 52, 55, 56, 57, 60.

342. 9 sqq. (*note*). *Cedimus, &c.* Ausonius, *Ep.* xx. 11–12, 3–4.

342. 41–**343.** 5. *In these . . . unknown.* 'Quos inter errores . . . norint' (*Vita*, p. 60).

343. 12–14. *associating . . . Tours.* Cf. *Vita*, p. 63.

343. 15–25. *That . . . Lord.* 31–4. *So . . . age.* Cf. *Vita*, pp. 65–6.

343. 40. *calling, &c.* 'Tanaquilem . . . imperitaretque viro' (*Vita*, p. 63).

344. 2. *Thus . . . barks at him.* 'Sic enim latrat' (*Vita*, p. 63).

344. 3–14. *Undè istam, &c.* Ausonius, *Epist.* xxix. 5–9, 17, 14; and xxviii. 30–1 (ed. White, Loeb ed. ii. 112–14). These two lines are also in *Vita*, p. 63.

344. 17–33. *Continuata, &c.* Paulinus, *Carm.* xi. 1–5 and x. 189–92 (*Corpus Script. Eccl. Lat.* xxx, pp. 39 and 32).

345. 3–23. *Hoc pignus, &c.* Paulinus, *Carm.* xxxi (ed. cit. pp. 328–9), 581–2, 585–90, 601–2, 607–8, 615–16, 624, 626; ll. 20–1 are almost completely V's addition.

345. 39–41 (*with note*). The first step . . . men. Cf. *Vita*, p. 78.

346. 2. *Superstitie.* Apparently a coinage, meaning power of survival.

346. 11–22 and 23–5. *Utinam . . . Christ.* Cf. *Vita*, p. 80.

346. 34–**347.** 34. *Four yeares . . . called.* Cf. *Vita*, 'Porrò . . . expaui' (p. 86); 'Data . . . vocauit' (p. 88).

348. 41–**350.** 6. *Revocandum, &c.* Paulinus, *Carm.* x. 110–13, 131–3, 137, 283–331 (ed. cit. pp. 29–39).

350. 19–28. *And here . . . himself.* 'Hic (vt loquitur Vranius) . . . restituens' (*Vita*, pp. 89–90).

350. 30–**351.** 1. *Paulinum . . . holinesse.* 'Paulinus . . . diuitiis' (*Vita*, pp. 72–3).

351. 2–5, 20–38, 38–**352.** 15. *Saint Augustine, &c.* Cf. *Vita*, pp. 124–31.

352. 35–9. *for he onely is a stranger, &c.* See 440. 9 sqq. and notes to that poem.

353. 23–6. *His Estate . . . Sea.* 'Rebus in Gallia . . . accessit' (*Vita*, p. 90).

353. 30. *Flyes . . . Sun-shine.* Cf. G. Herbert, 'The Answer', l. 5 (*Works*, p. 169): 'Flyes of estates and sunne-shine'. (H.)

353. 40–**354.** 9. *From Millaine . . . edicts.* Cf. *Vita*, pp. 90–1.

354. 11–12. *boars . . . Vineyard.* See note to 410. 21–22.

354. 18. *Church-rents.* Cf. the title of G. Herbert's poem, 'Church-rents and schismes' (*Works*, p. 140). (H.)

354. 23–4. *In a pleasant . . . Felix.* 'Amoeno in agro', &c. (*Vita*, p. 92).

354. 31–**355.** 11. Part of a note to the edition of Paulinus' works published in 1622 (p. 847 : 'Constantinus in templo . . . *requiescere terrâ*'). See note on 337.

355 (*note*). Cf. Paulinus, *Carm.* xii. 9 (ed. cit. p. 43): 'sine sanguine martyr'.

355. 25-30. *This Felix, &c.* Cf. Paulinus, *Carm.* xv. 72-80 (ed. cit. p. 54).

355. 32-**356.** 4. *Saint Augustine . . . them.* 'S. Augustinus . . . propalatum' (*Vita*, p. 97).

355. 39. *peragrent.* 'pergerent' in *Vita*.

356. 5-6. *Paulinus . . . sicknesse.* 'Verùm non multis', &c. (*Vita*, p. 98).

356 (*note*). Cf. Paulinus, *Epist.* xl. 6 (*Corpus Script. Eccl.* xxix. 346-7).

356. 38-**357.** 9. *viderunt . . . comfort me.* Cf. *Vita*, pp. 98-9.

357. 13-16, 22-**360.** 23. *As touching, &c.* Cf. *Vita*, pp. 99-103.

360. 40-**361.** 22. *Librum tuum . . . Martyrs.* Cf. *Vita*, pp. 105-6, 172, 171.

361. 23-**362.** 22. *Much about . . . Burdeaux.* Cf. *Vita*, pp. 106-15.

362. 32-**363.** 1. *Potiore . . . ashamed of me.* See Paulinus, *Epist.* xi. 3 (ed. cit. pp. 61-2).

363. 2-7. *If I shall . . . debtor, &c.* 'Prætereà peto . . . debitores' (*Vita*, p. 116).

363. 13-17. *The Ape, &c.* See *Locmani Sapientis Fabulæ* (Leidæ, 1615, p. 15), 'Lepus & Leaena'.

363. 21. *Raymond Cabanes.* Saracen favourite of Charles II, King of Naples. The story of his marriage to Philippa the Catanian, and of their rise and fall, is told in Matthieu's *Unhappy Prosperity*, from which Vaughan has quoted previously. See note to 217. 3-5. The story is also in Boccaccio, *De Casibus Virorum Illustrium*, ix. 26, 'De Philippa Catanensi'. *Massinello.* Tommaso Aniello (abbreviated to Masaniello), born in 1622, and killed at Naples in 1647, a few days after his successful revolt against the oppressions of the Spanish vice-regal government.

363. 29-35. *Apologues, &c.* Cf. Locmannus, *Fabulæ* (ed. cit. p. 38), 'Faber et Canis'.

364. 1-33 (*with note*). *And on . . . am not.* 'At laudes . . . quod non sum' (*Vita*, pp. 116-19).

364. 38-**365.** 10. *Abluitis . . . blisse.* Cf. Paulinus, *Epist.* xxxii. 3 (ed. cit. p. 277).

365. 12-25. *Hic reparandarum . . . sway.* Cf. Paulinus, *Epist.* xxxii. 5 (ed. cit. p. 279).

365. 26-43. *all his Garments . . . vessells.* Cf. *Vita*, p. 123.

365. 31. *Righteousnesse . . . poor.* V's addition.

366 (*note*). See Paulinus, *Epist.* xl. 8 (ed. cit. pp. 349-50).

366. 31. Tὸ πτωχὸν, *&c.* Georgius Pisida, Εἰς τὸν μάταιον βίον, l. 237 (*Opera*, Migne, col. 1598).

366. 35-**367.** 25. *In the four hundred . . . poore man.* 'Namque sub annum', &c. (*Vita*, p. 127).

367. 26-9. *In his own . . . glory.* 'Quæ extant', &c. (*Vita*, pp. 144-5).

367. 38–**368.** 33. *Cum autem . . . falshood.* ' Cùm autem ', &c. (*Vita*, pp. 148–50).

368. 34–40. *Nola . . . honour him.* ' per id tempus ', &c. (*Vita*, p. 151).

368. 42–**369.** 9. *Prosper . . . them.* ' vt inde ostendat ', &c. (*Vita*, p. 152).

369. 16. *one of his Epistles. Epist.* iii. 4 (ed. cit. p. 17).

369. 29–39. *Victor . . . hands.* ' Immensis ', &c. (*Vita*, pp. 121–2).

369. 39–**370.** 3. Miss Guiney refers to the similar story told of Pope Sixtus V. See *Storia della Vita . . . di Sisto Quinto . . . scritta dal P. M. Casimiro Tempesti . . .* Rome, 1866, i, p. 185.

370. 8–**371.** 30. *In the year . . . long for.* ' docet epistola ', &c. (*Vita*, p. 152).

372. 5–**374.** 5 (*except note on p. 373*). *Whose . . . fire.* ' Sed misericordia ', &c. (*Vita*, pp. 154–8).

372. 6–7. *This iron age . . . mercy.* V's addition.

374. 40–**375.** 2. *He repaired . . . Christ.* Cf. Paulinus, *Epist.* xxxii. 10 (ed. cit. p. 286).

375. 9–13. *Cælestes, &c.* Cf. Paulinus, *Epist.* xxxii. 12 (ed. cit. p. 288).

375. 24–8. *Ardua, &c.* Cf. Paulinus, loc. cit. p. 289.

375. 41. *his twelfth Epistle. Epist.* xxxii. 10–16 (ed. cit. pp. 286–91).

376. 1–16. *his ninth Natalis. Carm.* xxvii. 387–92 (ed. cit. p. 279).

376. 17–45. *Having finished . . . light.* Cf. Paulinus, *Epist.* xxxii. 17 (ed. cit. pp. 291–2).

376. 43–5. *The spotted, &c.* Miss Guiney notes the differences from the original :

> Laevos avertitur haedos
> Pastor, et emeritos dextra complectitur agnos.

377. 3–4. *Mr. Herbert . . . nothing.* Cf. *The Temple*, ' The Printers to the Reader ' (*Works*, p. 4) : ' when a friend went about to comfort him on his deathbed, he made answer, *It is a good work, if it be sprinkled with the bloud of Christ :* otherwise then in this respect he could find nothing to glorie or comfort himself with, neither in this, nor in any other thing '.

377. 6–14. *Nisi . . . hands.* Cf. Paulinus, *Epist.* xxxii. 22–3 (ed. cit. p. 297).

377. 16–17. *Cum suis, &c.* ' ut tunc ibi locupletemur ' (loc. cit. p. 295).

377. 39–**378.** 28. *hos per longa . . . mortis.* Paulinus, *Carm.* xxvii. 3–11, 107–16, 119–23, 127–34 (ed. cit. pp. 262–8).

379. 32–3. *These two . . . away.* See 443. 15–18.

379. 40–2. *the forerunners . . . years.* Cf. G. Herbert, ' The Forerunners ', ll. 1–2 (*Works*, p. 176) :

> The harbingers are come. See, see their mark ;
> White is their colour, and behold my head.

380. 7–**381.** 29. *Three daies . . . Master.* ' Ante triduum ', &c. (*Vita*, pp. 161–4).

381. 32–3. *Gregory, &c. Vita*, loc. cit.

381. 35–**382.** 4. *Three daies . . . Church.* ' Ante diem ', &c. (*Vita*, pp. 166–7).

382. 8–10, 12–13. *Blessed . . . Tombe.* ' Decessit ', &c. (*Vita*, pp. 167–8).

382-5. *Poem.* Attributed to Paulinus and given in the edition of 1622. See note on 174. 23, and Appendix to *Carmina*, ed. cit. pp. 344–8.

SILEX SCINTILLANS.

386. *Authoris (de se) Emblema.* 1–4. Cf. 189. 1–3. (H.)

386. 5–12. *Silex, &c.* Cf. Nieremberg, *De Arte Voluntatis*, ed. cit. p. 139: 'Subsiliunt è plagis quædam animo diuinæ luces, velut scintillæ è silice afflicto', translated 249. 10–11 above, 'Certain Divine Raies', &c. See also 169. 3, 173. 31–2, and 462. 58–60. Thomas Vaughan applies the image similarly in *Anthroposophia Theomagica*, 1650, p. 28. H compares also G. Herbert, 'Discipline', ll. 19–20 (*Works*, p. 179):

> For with love
> Stonie hearts will bleed.

See Tilley, *Proverbs in England*, F371, 'In the coldest Flint there is hot fire.'

386. 10. See 403. 41 and note.

388. 8. *a Predecessor . . . Parricides.* Grosart compares Greene, *Groats-worth of Wit* (1596, f. E1ᵛ): 'looke not I should (as I was wont) delight you with vaine fantasies, but gather my follies altogether, and as you would deale with so many parricides, cast them into the fire: call them *Telegones*, for now they kill their father, and euerie lewd line in them written, is a deep piercing wound to my heart; euery idle houre spent in reading them, brings a million of sorrowes to my soule'.

388. 26–30. *Os dignum, &c.* Prudentius, *Contra Symmachum*, i. 636–40 (reading 'tentat' or 'tentet').

389. 29–30. *if that . . . Ivy-bush.* Unless it is a mere pretence to call such people persons of honour.

390. 3–13. *That he would read . . . life.* From Felltham, *Resolves*, ii. 1, 'Of Idle Bookes', ed. cit. pp. 323–4. Not quoted exactly. H notes a parallel in Donne, *L Sermons*, 1649, Sermon xlvii, p. 445: 'they that write wanton books, or make wanton pictures, have additions of torment, as often as other men are corrupted with their books, or their pictures'.

390. 37. *Relatives.* ? Attributes. Meaning not in *O.E.D.* See 227. 30 (with note) and 295. 4.

391. 26. *a most flourishing and admired wit of his time.* Chambers suggested Donne, though noting the difficulty of Herbert's age. The reference may be to Robert Herrick, some of whose poems were much admired during the 1620's, and whose *Noble Numbers*, published with *Hesperides* in 1648, occasionally seem to show the influence of Herbert. See Herrick, *Works* (O.E.T., sec. ed., 1956), p. xviii, footnote 3.

391. 31–2. *frequent . . . pages.* Possibly, as suggested by Chambers, the reference is to Francis Quarles.

392. 8. *Hierotheus.* A mythical first-century bishop of Athens, apparently invented by Dionysius the pseudo-Areopagite, who in *De divinis nominibus*, ch. iv, speaks of Hierotheus as his teacher and as a writer of hymns.

392. 9. *A true Hymn.* Herbert uses this title in *The Temple* (*Works*, p. 168). (H.)

393. The verses are chiefly from Isa. xxxviii, Jonah ii, Jer. xvii, and Ps. v, xlii, and xliii. (H.)

395. 28. *The Candle . . . heads.* Job xxix. 3 : 'When his candle shined upon my head'. (H.)

397. *Regeneration.* Perhaps influenced by G. Herbert's 'The Pilgrimage' (*Works*, pp. 141–2).

397. 1–16. Cf. Thomas Vaughan, *Lumen de Lumine : Or a new Magicall Light discovered, and Communicated to the World By Eugenius Philalethes . . . London . . .* 1651, pp. 1–2 : 'It was about the *Dawning* or Day-breake, when tyr'd with a tedious *solitude,* and those *pensive Thoughts* which *attend it,* after much *Losse* and more *Labour,* I suddainly fell *a sleep.* Here then the *Day* was no sooner *borne,* but *strangled*; I was reduc'd to a *night* of a more deep *tincture* than that which I had *formerly spent.* My *fansie* placed me in a *Region* of inexpressible *Obscuritie,* and as I thought more than *Naturall*; but without any *Terrors* . . . I moved every way for *Discoveries,* but was still intertained with *Darknesse* and *silence,* and I thought my self translated to the *Land* of *Desolation.*'

397. 3–4. *and all, &c.* Cf. op. cit. p. 6 : 'Her *walk* was *green* . . . and purl'd all the Way with *Daysies* and *Primrose.*'

397. 32. *Prophets, and friends of God.* Cf. Wisd. of Sol. vii. 27.

398. 33–48. *Here, I repos'd, &c.* Cf. T. V., op. cit. p. 2 : 'Being thus troubled to no purpose, and wearied with long Indeavours, I resolved to rest my self, and seeing I could find nothing, I expected if any thing could find me. I had not long continued in this humor, but I could heare the *whispers* of a *soft wind,* that travail'd towards me, and suddainly it was in the *Leaves* of the *Trees,* so that I concluded my self to be in some *Wood,* or *Wildernesse.* With this gentle *Breath* came a most *heavenly, odorous Ayre,* much like that of *sweet Briars,* but not so *rank,* and *full.*'

398. 44. *Checqur'd.* Cf. op. cit. p. 4 : 'The *Ground* . . . presented a *pleasing* kind of *Checquer.*'

398. 49–52. *Only . . . teares.* Cf. Habington, *Castara,* 'To the . . . Earle of SHREWES.', ll. 3–4 (*Poems,* ed. K. Allott, p. 31) :

> your eares
> Delighted in the musicke of her teares. (GM.)

399. 65–80. *It was, &c.* Cf. *Lumen de Lumine,* p. 15 : 'Now verily was I much troubled, and somewhat disordered, but composing my self as well as I could, I came to a *Cop* of *Myrtles,* where resting my self on a *Flowrie Bank,* I began to consider those Things which I had seen.'

399. 70. *A rushing wind.* See note on 398. 33–48.

399. 75. *if any leafe.* See note on 398. 33–48.

399. 83. *Cant. Cap. 5.* For 5 read 4.

400. 1–401. 18. *Oft have I seen, &c.* Cf. 177. 7–31 : 'Do not we see', &c.

400. 5. *silk-worme.* Cf. 177. 8.

401. 9–14. *Untill at last, &c.* Cf. Felltham, *Resolves,* i. 47, 'Of Death' (ed. cit. p. 149) : 'That grosse object which is left to the spectators eyes, is now onely a composure but of two *baser Elements, Water,* and *Earth* : that now it is these two onely, that seeme to make the *body,* while the two purer, *Fire* and *Ayre,* are wing'd away, as being more fit for the compact of an *elementall* and *ascentive Soule.*' Vaughan's butterfly reckons earth and water as contemptible ('mean', 'vaine things') and limited (extending no more than a span).

401–2. 19–70. Sections 2 and 3 of this poem are influenced, directly or indirectly, by the Hermetic writings, on which see the edition of *Hermetica* by W. Scott, 4 vols., Clarendon Press, 1924. See also Elizabeth Holmes, *Henry Vaughan and the Hermetic Philosophy*, 1932, and L. C. Martin, 'Henry Vaughan and Hermes Trismegistus', *R.E.S.*, July 1942. The following passages (in W. Scott's translation) are arranged in two groups according as they are relevant to section 2 or 3 of the poem:

Section 2 (ll. 19–50):

(*a*) 'The word "death" is a mere name, without any corresponding fact. For death means destruction; and nothing in the Kosmos is destroyed.' (Libellus viii. 1 b, ed. cit. i, p. 175.)

(*b*) 'The Kosmos produces life in all things by its movement; and decomposing them, it renews the things that have been decomposed.' (Lib. ix. 6; p. 183.) Cf. Thomas Vaughan, *Anthroposophia Theomagica*, 1650, p. 56: 'For God *breathes continually*, and passeth through all things like an *Aire* that refresheth.'

(*c*) 'But men call the change "death", because, when it takes place, the body is decomposed, and the life departs and is no longer seen.' (Lib. xi. 15 b; pp. 218–19.)

(*d*) 'Now this whole Kosmos . . . is one mass of life. . . . There is not, and has never been, and never will be in the Kosmos anything that is dead. . . . Dissolution is not death; it is only the separation of things which were combined; and they undergo dissolution, not to perish, but to be made new.' (Lib. xii. 15 b, 16; pp. 233–5.) Cf. Thomas Vaughan, op. cit., The Author to the Reader, f. B1ᵛ: 'Ignorance gave this *release* the Name of *Death*, but properly it is the *Soules Birth*, and a *Charter* that makes for her *Liberty.*'

(*e*) '[The Sun] puts life into the things in this region of the Kosmos, and stirs them up to birth, and by successive changes remakes the living creatures and transforms them. . . . For the permanence of every kind of body is maintained by change.' (Lib. xvi. 8, 9; pp. 267–9.)

Section 3 (ll. 51–70):

(*a*) '. . . we men see, as through dark mist, the things of heaven.' (Asclepius iii. 32 b; p. 357).

(*b*) '. . . in this life we are still too weak to see that sight; we have not strength to open our mental eyes, and to behold the beauty of the Good, that incorruptible beauty which no tongue can tell.' (Lib. x. 5, 6; p. 191.)

(*c*) 'Bid your soul travel to any land you choose, and sooner than you can bid it go, it will be there. Bid it pass on from land to ocean, and it will be there no less quickly. . . . Bid it fly up to heaven, and it will have no need of wings. . . . Leap clear of all that is corporeal . . . rise above all time, and become eternal; then you will apprehend God.' (Lib. xi (ii), 18, 20 b; p. 221.) Cf. Thomas Vaughan, op. cit. pp. 47–48.

(*d*) 'None of the gods of heaven will ever quit heaven . . . and come down to earth ; but man ascends even to heaven, and measures it.' (Lib. x. 25 ; p. 205.)

(e) 'Would it were possible for you to grow wings, and soar into the air ! Poised between earth and heaven, you might see the solid earth, the fluid sea . . . What happiness were that, my son, to see all these . . . and to behold Him who is unmoved moving in all that moves, and Him who is hidden made manifest through his works !' (Lib. v. 5 ; p. 161.)

401. 25. *For . . . fall.* Cf. Donne, 'The broken heart', l. 25 (*Poems*, ed. Grierson, i. 49) : ' Yet nothing can to nothing fall.'

402. 45. *Cottage.* Cf. 381. 21 and 417. 15. (GM.)

402. 55. *Inlightned Rayes.* Cf. 80. 21. (H.)

402. 59. *To reade some Starre.* See 692 (IV). 13 sqq.

402. 68. Deut. xxviii. 67. (GM.)

403. 41. *Heart of flesh.* Ezek. xi. 19. (GM.) Cf. 386. 10.

404. *Religion.* Cf. ' Corruption ', p. 440. (GM.) Cf. also G. Herbert, 'Decay' (*Works*, p. 99).

404. 4–5. *An Angell . . . Juniper.* Cf. 499. 4–7, and 1 Kings xix. 5.

404. 5–8. Cf. G. Herbert, ' Decay ', ll. 6–7 (*Works*, p. 99):

One might have sought and found thee presently
At some fair oak, or bush, or cave, or well.

404. 7. Cf. Judges vi. 11–12.

404. 14. *O how familiar, &c.* Cf. Thomas Vaughan, *Anthroposophia Theomagica*, 1650, p. 49 : ' in *Paradise* how familiar is he . . .'.

405. 46. *Samaritans . . . Well.* John iv. 7–15.

405 (*The Search*). 17–20. See 439. 134 and note.

406. 43. Cf. Fortunatus, ' Pange lingua gloriosi ', l. 23 : ' Silva talem nulla profert fronde, flore, germine '. (GM.)

406. 60. *flaming ministrie.* Ps. civ. 4. (GM.)

407. 63–4. Rev. xii. 6. (GM.)

407. 70. *Wells.* See 484. 23 and note.

407. 74. *Me thought . . . singing.* Cf. G. Herbert, 'The Collar', l. 35 (*Works*, p. 154) : ' Me thoughts I heard one calling, *Child!* '

407. 95. *Search well another world.* Cf. 693. 18–19.

408. 8. *Ray'd into thee.* See note on 144. 9.

410 (*The Brittish Church*). 4. *hills of Mirrhe.* Cf. 447 (*Son-dayes*). 14 and 475. 11. (GM.)

410. 6–10. *The Souldiers, &c.* See *Life*, 122.

410. 21–2. *O Rosa, &c.* See 161. 9–10 and note. Hutchinson, *Life*, 122 (footnote), observes that ' Rosa ' is from Tremellius's Latin Bible, where the Vulgate has ' flos '. For the rest see Ps. lxxx. 13 ; Ezek. xxix. 5, xxxiv. 5, and xxxix. 4 ; also 1 Sam. xvii. 44–6.

411. *Mans fall, and Recovery.* GM points out the relationship of this poem to Rom. v–vii.

412 (*continuation*). Rom. Cap. 18. For 18 read 5.

412. *The Showre.* See note on 445. 31–7.

412. 1. *That drowsie Lake.* Llangorse Pool, about two miles from Newton, may have been in Vaughan's mind (see *Life*, 23).

412. 9. *quick accesse.* Cf. G. Herbert, 'Prayer' (II), l. 1 (*Works*, p. 103): 'Of what an easie quick accesse . . .'.

412. 12. *smoke.* H compares Lucretius, v. 464.

413. 6. *starre, &c.* Miss E. Holmes compares G. Herbert, 'Mattens', ll. 5–8 (*Works*, p. 62):

> My God, what is a heart?
> Silver, or gold, or precious stone,
> Or starre, or rainbow . . .

413. 12–13. *Man . . . each.* Miss E. Holmes compares G. Herbert, 'Dooms-day', ll. 27–8 (*Works*, p. 187):

> Man is out of order hurl'd,
> Parcel'd out to all the world.

413. 29–30. *keepe . . . sight.* Miss E. Holmes compares 141. 6–7 and G. Herbert, 'Frailtie', ll. 15–16 (*Works*, p. 71):

> That which was dust before, doth quickly rise,
> And prick mine eyes.

414. *The Pursuite.* Cf. 'Man', p. 477, and G. Herbert, 'The Pulley' (*Works*, p. 159).

414. 1–2. Cf. G. Herbert, 'Giddinesse', ll. 1–2 (*Works*, p. 127): 'Oh, what a thing is man!' &c. (H.)

414 (*Mount of Olives*). 4. *shade, or grove.* Perhaps with some reference to the earlier poem 'Upon the Priorie Grove' (p. 15).

414. 9. *Cotswold, and Coopers.* See *Annalia Dubrensia. Vpon the yeerely celebration of M*^r· *Robert Dovers Olimpick Games vpon Cotswold-Hills . . .* 1636. But Vaughan was perhaps thinking of one poem only, Randolph (ed. cit. p. 118), 'An Eclogue on the noble Assemblies revived on Cotswold Hills, by M. Robert Dover'.

415 (*continuation*). 32. *Chaire.* It has been suggested that Vaughan was influenced by the appellation 'Cader', meaning 'chair', applied to certain Welsh mountains (see *Life*, 23 and E. W. Williamson, *Henry Vaughan* (B.B.C. lecture, 1953), p. 38).

415. 1–6. See 157. 36–9 and 161. 41–2. Cf. G. Herbert, 'The Bag', ll. 9–12 (*Works*, p. 151):

> The God of power, as he did ride
> In his majestick robes of glorie,
> Resolv'd to light; and so one day
> He did descend, undressing all the way. (H.)

416 (*The Call*). 4. *Some twenty years.* Hutchinson (*Life*, 108, footnote), following GM, suggests that Vaughan is reckoning from the time when he was about seven years old, the age of innocence then over. This would date the poem about 1649.

416 (*second poem*). *Thou that know'st, &c.* He mourns the death of his brother William in 1648. See also 420 ('Come, come, what doe I here?'), 426. 27–8, 479. 61, and *Life*, 104–5. Cf. Thomas Vaughan, *Anthroposophia Theomagica*, 1650, p. 65: 'this *Piece* was compos'd in *Haste*, and in my *Dayes* of *Mourning*, on the sad *Occurence* of a *Brother's Death*.'

417. 21–4. *Yet . . . excell.* Cf. 297. 37–40.

417. 36. *The wise-mans-madnes Laughter.* Eccles. ii. 2: 'I said of laughter, It is mad.'

418 (*continuation*). 49–50. *A silent teare, &c.* Cf. G. Herbert, 'The Familie', ll. 17–20 (*Works*, p. 137):

> Joyes oft are there, and griefs as oft as joyes;
> But griefs without a noise:
> Yet speak they louder then distemper'd fears.
> What is so shrill as silent tears?

also 'Sion', l. 21 (*Works*, p. 107): 'But grones are quick, and full of wings.' (H.)

418. 51–2. *And sweeter . . . string.* Cf. G. Herbert, 'Sion', ll. 17–18 (*Works*, p. 106):

> All Solomons sea of brasse and world of stone
> Is not so deare to thee as one good grone;

and Herbert's 'Gratefulnesse', st. 6 (*Works*, p. 124). Vaughan has 'arted' also in 177. 27.

418. 62. *pure, and steddy.* Cf. 534. 3.

418 (*Vanity of Spirit*). 3 sqq. *gron'd to know, &c.* Cf. *Hermetica*, Libellus v. 3 (ed. W. Scott, i, p. 159): 'If you wish to see Him, think on the Sun . . . Moon . . . stars. . . . Each of these stars too is confined by measured limits . . .'.

418. 5–6. *circled . . . Ring.* Cf. 466. 2. (H.)

418. 9–10. Cf. Joseph Hall, 'To Mr Iosuah Syluester', ll. 11–12 (*Poems*, ed. Davenport, p. 144):

> Thence, rushing down, through *Nature's* Closet-dore,
> She ransacks all her Grandame's secret store.

See also 549. 28–9 and 580. 28–9.

418. 10. *Broke . . . seales.* Cf. Thomas Vaughan, *Cœlum Terrae*, 1650, p. 53: 'But one thinks Nature complains of a prostitution, that I goe about to diminish her majesty, having almost broken her seall, & exposed her naked to the world.' See also 520. 7–14.

418. 19–20. *Weake beames . . . night.* Cf. 402. 51–4 and Thomas Vaughan, *Lumen de Lumine*, 1651, p. 3: 'I could discover a white weake *Light*, not so *cleare* as that of a *Candle*, but *mystie*, and much resembling an *Atmospheare*.' The writer goes to the Mountains of the Moon, and is conducted by Nature, whose garment '*smelt*' like the *East*'. (Miss E. Holmes.)

419 (*continuation*). 22–4. *A peece . . . remembred.* It may be that, as suggested in *Life*, 24, the imagery is partly drawn from the cromlech Ty Illtyd, near Newton.

419. *The Retreate.* For some anticipations and analogues see 'Henry Vaughan and the Theme of Infancy', by L. C. Martin, in *Seventeenth Century Studies presented to Sir Herbert Grierson*, 1938, pp. 243–55, and M. Y. Hughes, 'The Theme of Pre-existence and Infancy in *The Retreate*', *Philological Quarterly*, xx, 1941, pp. 484–500. The essence of Vaughan's thought is set forth in the *Hermetica*, Libellus x. 15 b (ed. W. Scott, i. 197): 'Look at the soul of a child, my son, a soul that has not yet come to accept its separation from its source; for its body is still small, and has not yet grown to its full bulk. How beautiful throughout is such a soul as that! It is not yet fouled by the bodily passions; it is still hardly detached from the soul of the Kosmos. But when the body has increased in bulk, and has drawn the soul down into its material mass, it generates oblivion; and so the soul separates itself from the Beautiful and Good, and no longer

partakes of that ; and through this oblivion the soul becomes evil.'
The Platonic relationship is evident (cf. 282. 19–21 and 284. 8) ;
the distinguishing feature is the blending of the Platonic doctrine
with a belief in the special innocence of children, as suggested in
Mark x. 14–15. Vaughan's poem (cf. 520 and 660) is foreshadowed
in G. Herbert's 'H. Baptisme' (II), ll. 6–15 (*Works*, p. 44), and
(more lightly) in Earle's Character of a Child (*Micro-cosmographie*,
1628, No. 1) : '*A Child* is a Man in a small Letter, yet the best Copie
of *Adam* before hee tasted of *Eue*, or the Apple. . . . Hee is natures
fresh picture newly drawne in Oyle, which time and much handling
dimmes and defaces. . . . His father . . . sighes to see what innocence
he ha's out-liu'd. The elder he growes, he is a stayre lower from God ;
and like his first father, much worse in his breeches.   He is the
Christians example, and the old man's relapse : The one imitates
his purenesse, and the other falls into his simplicitie. . . .'

GM quotes Cartwright, 'Consideration' (*Comedies &c.*, 1651,
p. 259) :

> Off then thou Old Man, and give place unto
> The Ancient of daies ; Let him renew
> My breast with Innocence, That he whom Thou
> Hast made a man of sin, and subt'ly sworn
> A Vassall to thy Tyranny, may turn
> Infant again, and having all of Child,
> Want wit hereafter to be so beguild . . .

and compares lines by Cartwright on pp. 293 and 300 of the same
volume.

419. 4. *my second race.* Cf. 169. 21–3 : 'and [when I] compare my
appointed time here with the *portion* preceding it . . .'.

419. 8. *my first love.* Cf. 355. 24, 440. 7, 470. 48, 510. 5, 653. 72–80,
and Rev. ii. 4. (GM.)

419. 20. *Bright shootes of everlastingnesse.* Cf. Felltham, *Resolves*,
i. 64, ' Of the Soule' (ed. cit. p. 197) : 'The *Conscience*, the *Caracter*
of a *God* stampt in it, and the apprehension of *Eternity*, doe all prove
it a *shoot of everlastingnesse*.' Cf. also 447. 1 : '*shoots* of blisse'
and 424. 2 : ' shoots of glory'.

419. 26. *City of Palme trees.* Jericho is so designated in Deut. xxxiv.
3, &c. (GM.)

420. 2. *he is gone.* See note on 416 (*second poem*).

421. 4. *The starres shine in their watches.* Baruch, iii. 34. (H.)

421. 7. *work, and wind.* See note to 489. 3–4.

422. *Joy of my life.* See *Life*, 195, on the possibility that this poem
was written in memory of Vaughan's first wife, Catherine.

423. 1. *I see the use.* Miss Guiney was for some time inclined to
believe that ' use' was a printer's error for ' Usk', an emendation
proposed independently by Sir Edward Marsh in *T.L.S.*, 19 July
1947. Miss Morgan, supporting her friend's conjecture, wrote to her
on 29 July 1907, with reference to 'red' in l. 4, 'There have been
the reddest of red floods in the Usk : I never saw him redder. . . . In
Welsh rivers are masculine.' ' use', however, makes good sense with
the obsolete meaning of a moral or application. See *O.E.D.* s.v.
16 d, quoting South, *Serm.* 43 : 'I proceed now to the Uses which
may be drawn . . . .' Vaughan may have been impressed by the sight
of a storm at sea under a reddish sky, and moralizes thereon.   But

˙the germ of the poem may be the following, from Felltham, *Resolves*, i. 62, ed. cit. p. 190: 'Every *Man* is a vast and *spacious Sea*: his *passions* are the *winds*, that swell him in *disturbant waves*: How he *tumbles*, and *roares*, and *fomes*, when they in their fury trouble him!...' Cf. 468. 6–12.

424 (*continuation*). 21–4. *So shall, &c.* Cf. G. Herbert, 'The Storm', ll. 17–18 (*Works*, p. 132):

> Poets have wrong'd poore storms: such days are best;
> They purge the aire without, within the breast.

424 (*The Morning-watch*). 1. Cf. G. Herbert, 'The H. Scriptures. I.', l. 1 (*Works*, p. 58):

> Oh Book! infinite sweetnesse!

424. 13. *falling springs.* Cf. G. Herbert, 'Providence', l. 16 (*Works*, p. 117): 'as springs that fall'.

424. 18–19. *Prayer...tune.* Cf. G. Herbert, 'Prayer' (I), l. 8 (*Works*, p. 51):

> A kinde of tune, which all things heare and fear.

425. 33–4. See 439. 134 and note.

425 (*Silence, and stealth of dayes*). 3. *Twelve hundred houres.* Fifty days. As William Vaughan died on or about 14 July 1648 (see *Life*, 95–6), the poem can be dated 1 or 2 Sept. in that year.

426. 25. *O could I track them!* Cf. Habington, 'Elegie 3 to Talbot', ll. 2–3 (ed. cit. p. 103):

> I cannot tracke the way, which thou didst goe
> In thy cœlestiall journey.

426 (*Church-Service*). 3 sqq. Cf. Rom. viii. 26, &c. (GM.)

428. 25–6. *I stray In blasts.* Hutchinson compares G. Herbert, 'Dooms-day', l. 21 (*Works*, p. 187): 'Some to windes their bodie lend.'

428. 27. *Exhalations.* See 561. 36 sqq.

428. 33–5. *Tyme, &c.* Cf. 171. 11–12.

428 (*Chearfulness*). 11. *If thou be in't.* Cf. G. Herbert, 'Affliction' (III), l. 2 (*Works*, p. 73): 'But that I knew that thou wast in the grief'. (H.)

429. 1. *Sure...Bodyes.* Cf. Felltham, *Resolves*, i. 82, 'That sufferance causeth Love' (ed. cit. p. 253): 'Nothing surer tyes a friend ... Sure, there is a *Sympathy of soules.*'

429. 5. *Center'd.* Fixed in one place; brought to rest.

429. 5–6. *without ... Contaction.* Lacking radiation (see note to 492. 7–8) and movement, they can neither make nor feel any contacts.

429. 9. Cf. 469. 12, 483. 20, and 497. 9; 'within the Line' may mean 'within the boundaries of life'; persons absent from one another, though not dead, feel a mutual sympathy.

429. 15–16. *And wrap ... grave.* Involve us in false imaginings far removed from religious ideas about death.

429. 17. *Lazarus... town.* To make it easier to forget him.

430. *Peace.* Cf. 475. 11–16, and see notes thereto.

430. 3–4. The Archangel Michael. Rev. xii. 7. (GM.)

430. 15-20. Cf. 338. 15-20. With l. 15 H compares G. Herbert, 'The Flower', l. 23 (*Works*, p. 166):

> Fast in thy Paradise, where no flower can wither.

431. 15-18. Cf. G. Herbert, 'The Agonie', ll. 17-18 (*Works*, p. 37):

> Love is that liquour sweet and most divine,
> Which my God feels as bloud; but I, as wine.

432 (*heading*). *Etenim, &c.* Hutchinson, *Life*, 174, observes that Vaughan quotes Beza's version, which has 'exerto capite'. Cf. l. 3.

432. 1 sqq. Cf. 436. 13-16, 497 (*continuation*). 13-16, 501. 11-12, 515. 18-36, 531. 15-16. See also 401. 19 sqq. and note.

432. 1-2. *have they ... Influence?* Do they feel anything but a sense of obedience to celestial control? Cf. 8. 19-20.

432. 5-14. Miss E. Holmes compares G. Herbert, 'Affliction' (I), ll. 55-60 (*Works*, p. 48):

> Now I am here, what thou wilt do with me
>   None of my books will show:
> I reade, and sigh, and wish I were a tree;
>   For sure then I should grow
> To fruit or shade: at least some bird would trust
> Her houshold to me, and I should be just.

432. 11-16. Cf. G. Herbert, 'Employment' (II), ll. 21-5 (*Works*, p. 79):

> Oh that I were an Orenge-tree,
>   That busie plant!
> Then should I ever laden be,
>   And never want
> Some fruit for him that dressed me.

H compares also 'Affliction' (I), ll. 57-60 (*Works*, p. 48).

433 (*continuation*). 39. *Sure ... see.* Cf. G. Herbert, 'The Starre', l. 29 (*Works*, p. 74):

> Sure thou wilt joy, by gaining me ...

433. 11. Cf. G. Herbert, 'The Thanksgiving', l. 34 (*Works*, p. 36): 'But mend mine own without delayes.' (H.)

433. 9-12. Cf. G. Herbert, 'Discipline', ll. 1-4 (*Works*, p. 178):

> Throw away thy rod,
> Throw away thy wrath:
>   O my God,
> Take the gentle path.

433. 13-14. Cf. G. Herbert, 'Sighs and Grones', ll. 14-15 (*Works*, p. 83):

> I have deserv'd that an Egyptian night
> Should thicken all my powers. (H.)

434. 1. *I have, &c.* This is also the first line of G. Herbert's 'The Reprisall' (*Works*, p. 36).

434. 11-28. These lines were printed in the 1650 edition of *Witt's Recreations*, final leaf, and also in the editions of 1654, 1663, and 1667. They form a conclusion to the volume: 'Having now fed thy youthfull frencies, with these Juvenilian Fancies; let me invite thee (with my selfe) to sing *Altiora peto*. And then to meet with this thy noble resolution; I would commend to thy sharpest view and serious consideration; The Sweet Cælestiall sacred Poems by Mr. *Henry Vaughan*, intituled *Silex Scintillans*.

> There plumes from Angels wings, he'l lend thee,
> Which every day to heaven will send thee.
> (*Heare him thus invite thee home*.)'

The two lines 'There plumes', &c. are from Crashaw's lines 'On Mr. G. Herberts . . . the Temple . . .' (*Poems*, O.E.T., p. 130).

434. 10. *Catch at the place*. Cf. G. Herbert, 'Affliction' (I), l. 17 (*Works*, p. 46): 'my sudden soul caught at the place'. (H.)

434. 19-20. *before . . . night*. Cf. Benlowes, *Theophila*, 1652, ii. 48. 1 (Saintsbury, *Caroline Poets*, i. 349):

> Before the sun's long shadows span up night.

434. 23-4. *All strewed, &c.* Cf. G. Herbert, 'Affliction' (I), ll. 21-2 (*Works*, p. 47):

> My dayes were straw'd with flow'rs and happinesse;
> There was no moneth but May;

also 'The Flower', ll. 6-7 (ibid. p. 165).

434. *The Match*. In the sense of a compact or bargain. Cf. 446. 7. (GM.)

434 (*The Match*). 1-6. Cf. 391. 22-6.

435 (*continuation*). 7-8. As pointed out by Miss E. Holmes (*H. V. and the Hermetic Philosophy*, pp. 12-13) and by GM, Vaughan here takes up the proffer made by G. Herbert in 'Obedience', ll. 36-43 (*Works*, p. 105):

> He that will passe his land,
> As I have mine, may set his hand
> And heart unto this Deed, when he hath read:
>
> .   .   .   .
> How happie were my part,
> If some kinde man would thrust his heart
> Into these lines . . .

435. 10-12. Cf. G. Herbert, loc. cit. ll. 11-15. (H.)

435. ii. 7-12. *Two Lifes, &c.* Cf. G. Herbert, 'Love unknown', ll. 3-5 (*Works*, p. 129):

> A Lord I had,
> And have, of whom some grounds, which may improve,
> I hold for two lives, and both lives in me.

435. 19-22. Cf. G. Herbert, 'Longing', ll. 29-36 (*Works*, p. 149). (H.)

436. *Rules and Lessons*. See 140. 28-34. Cf. (for the form) G. Herbert, 'The Church-porch' (*Works*, pp. 6 sqq.).

436. 7. Cf. 143. 2, and see note on 187. 11-17.

436. 11. *Rise to prevent the Sun*. Wisd. of Sol. xvi. 28: 'we must prevent the sun'. Cf. 143. 21. (H.)

436. 13-16. See note on 432. 1 sqq. and note on 401-2, 19-70, section 2 (*d*). Cf. Thomas Vaughan, *Anima Magica Abscondita*, 1650, p. 52: 'In the *Summer* translate thy self to the Fields, where all are green with the Breath of God, and fresh with the Powers of Heaven. Learn to refer all Naturals to their Spirituals, *per viam Secretioris Analogiæ*.'

436. 28. *stone, and hidden food*. Rev. ii. 17. (H.) Quoted by Vaughan, 469.

437. 45. *a Judas Jew.* Cf. G. Herbert, 'Self-condemnation', ll. 17–18 (*Works*, p. 171):

> For he hath sold for money his deare Lord,
> And is a Judas-Jew.

437. 52 *lag behind.* Cf. G. Herbert, 'Constancie', l. 10 (*Works*, p. 72). (H.)

437. 54. *lines.* Reaches, as with a measuring-line. (*O.E.D. v.*² 2.)

437. 63–4. *Thou mai'st . . . a Curse.* Hutchinson compares G. Herbert, 'An Offering', ll. 11–12 (*Works*, p. 147, note p. 529).

> In publick judgements one may be a nation,
> And fence a plague . . .

i.e. one, a ruler or sovereign, can represent a nation and ward off a disaster by his intercession.

438. 81–94. Cf. Lucretius, v. 1191–3: 'noctivagaeque faces caeli flammaeque volantes, &c.' (GM.)

439. 118. Cf. G. Herbert, 'Sunday', ll. 29–30 (*Works*, p. 76):

> The Sundaies of mans life,
> Thredded together on times string . . .

439. 121–6. Cf. G. Herbert, 'Church-monuments' (*Works*, pp. 64–5). (H.)

439. 134. Cf. Felltham, *Resolves*, i. 47, 'Of Death' (ed. cit. p. 149): 'when thou shalt see the *body* put on *Deaths* sad and ashy *countenance*, in the dead age of *night*'. Cf. 522. 14. GM, approving of Grosart's emendation 'ash' for 'age', refers to the Welsh custom of covering the live embers in ashes at night for kindling the next day's fire. (F. Seebohm, *The Tribal System in Wales*, 1904, pp. 82–6.) Cf. 405. 17–20 and 425. 33–4.

439. 139. *Doe . . . unto.* G. Herbert arranges the words of the quotation thus in 'Divinitie', l. 18 (*Works*, p. 135). (H.)

440. *Corruption.* See 'Religion', 404–5 and note. Cf. 352. 35–9; also Thomas Vaughan, *Magia Adamica*, 1650, p. 17: 'He was excluded from a *glorious Paradyse*, and confin'd to a *base world*, whose *sickly infected Elements* conspiring with his *own Nature*, did assist and hasten that *Death*, which already began to reign in his *Body*. Heaven did mourn over him, The Earth, and all her Generations about him. He look'd upon himself as a *Felon*, and a *Murtherer*, being *guilty* of that *Curse* and *Corruption*, which succeeded in the *world* because of his fall . . .'

440. 9. Cf. T. Vaughan, op. cit. p. 18: 'He was a meer stranger in this World.'

440. 19. Cf. T. Vaughan, op. cit. p. 18: 'He heard indeed sometimes of a *Tree* of *Life* in Eden.'

440. 25. *Leiger here.* See 60. 10 and note. Cf. G. Herbert, 'The H. Scriptures. I.', l. 11 (*Works*, p. 58): 'thou art heav'ns Lidger here.'

440. 25–7. See note on 404. 5–8.

440. 40. *Thrust in thy sickle.* Rev. xiv. 14–18.

441 (*H. Scriptures*). **3–4.** Cf. 446. 47 and G. Herbert, 'Whitsunday', ll. 14 (*Works*, p. 59):

Listen sweet Dove unto my song,
And spread thy golden wings in me ;
Hatching my tender heart so long,
Till it get wing, and flie away with thee.

441. 9-12. Miss E. Holmes compares G. Herbert, 'The Altar', ll. 5–12 (*Works*, p. 26) :

A HEART alone
Is such a stone,
As nothing but
Thy pow'r doth cut.
Wherefore each part
Of my hard heart
Meets in this frame,
To praise thy Name.

441. 13. *my faults are thine.* G. Herbert, 'Judgement', l. 15 (*Works*, p. 188). (H.)

441. *Unprofitableness.* Cf. 476, 'Mount of Olives'; also G. Herbert, 'The Flower' and 'The Glance' (*Works*, pp. 165 and 171). (Miss E. Holmes.)

441 1. *How rich, &c.* Cf. G. Herbert, 'The 'Flower', ll. 1–2 :

How fresh, O Lord, how sweet and clean
Are thy returns !

442. 7. Cf. G. Herbert, 'Mans medley', ll. 1–2 (*Works*, p. 131):

Heark, how the birds do sing,
And woods do ring.

442. 11–12. Cf. G. Herbert, 'Providence', ll. 13–14 (*Works*, p. 117):

Man is the worlds high Priest : he doth present
The sacrifice for all.

442. 18. *Shining, or singing.* Cf. G. Herbert, 'Christmas', ll. 31–4 (*Works*, p. 81) :

Then we will sing, and shine all our own day

. . . . . .

Till ev'n his beams sing, and my musick shine.

443. 9–18. Cf. 379. 30–3. GM refers to Act of Parliament, 23 Dec. 1644, abolishing observance of Christmas and Good Friday.

443 (*The Check*). **2–6.** Cf. G. Herbert, 'Death', ll. 5–8 (*Works*, p. 186) :

For we consider'd thee as at some six
Or ten yeares hence,
After the losse of life and sense,
Flesh being turn'd to dust, and bones to sticks.

Also Herbert's 'Church-monuments' (ibid., pp. 64–5). (GM.)

443 11. *dear flesh.* The same apostrophe is in Herbert's 'Church-monuments', l. 17 (*Works*, p. 65). (GM.)

444. 44–5. *wher's now . . . Thy Lines.* Cf. G. Herbert, 'Dulnesse', l. 17 (*Works*, p. 116) :

Where are my lines then ? . . . (GM.)

445. 31 sqq. Cf. 12. 1–21 and G. Herbert, 'The Answer', ll. 8–12 (*Works*, p. 169) :

> As a young exhalation, newly waking,
> Scorns his first bed of dirt, and means the sky ;
> But cooling by the way, grows pursie and slow,
> And setling to a cloud, doth live and die
> In that dark state of tears . . .

The account of the phenomenon in *Stobaei Hermetica* (Excerpt vi. 15) is translated as follows by W. Scott, *Hermetica*, i. 417 : ' And below the moon are stars of another sort, perishable and inert, which are so composed as to last but for a little time, rising as exhalations from the earth itself into the air above the earth ; and we can see their dissolution with our own eyes. . . . [They] do not attain to the region of heaven . . . they are dragged down by their own matter, and are quickly dissipated, and being broken up, they fall down again to earth, having effected nothing except a troubling of the air above the earth.'

446. 46. *O, is!* See note on 30. 485, and *O.E.D.* s.v. Yes.

446. 46-8. *give wings . . . art.* Cf. G. Herbert, ' Whitsunday ', ll. 1–4 (*Works*, p. 59). (H.)

446. 59-60. *tune . . . verse.* See 460. 37–40 and note.

446. *Idle Verse.* Cf. 390. 4 sqq.

447 (*continuation*). **16.** Cf. G. Herbert, ' Love I.', ll. 13–14 (*Works*, p. 54) :

> Who sings thy praise? onely a skarf or glove
> Doth warm our hands, and make them write of love.

447. 18. *Simper'd, and shin'd.* Cf. G. Herbert, ' The Search ', ll. 13–14 (*Works*, p. 162) :

> Yet can I mark how starres above
>   Simper and shine. (Miss E. Holmes.)

447. *Son-dayes.* Cf. G. Herbert, ' Prayer ' (I), for the form (on which see *Life*, p. 163) and some of the images ; and for other images ' Sunday ' (*Works*, pp. 51 and 75).

447. 1. *shoots of blisse.* Cf. 419. 20.

447. 9. *The Pulleys.* Cf. G. Herbert's title ' The Pulley ' (*Works*, p. 159).

448. 5-9. There are several correspondences with G. Herbert, ' H. Baptisme ' (II) (*Works*, p. 44). (H.)

448. 9. *He.* Sc. my flesh (l. 5).

449. 41. *signature.* See 583. 11–13.

449. 55-6. Cf. 535. 31–3. (GM.)

449. 71-2. *gourd . . . morrow.* Jonah iv. 6, 7, 10. (GM.) Cf. 338. 10.

449. 75-6. Cf. G. Herbert, ' Aaron ', ll. 6–7 (*Works*, p. 174) :

> Prophanenesse in my head,
> Defects and darknesse in my breast.

451. 34. Cf. 461. 32–3, and G. Herbert, ' The Starre ', ll. 17–18 (*Works*, p. 74) : ' our trinitie of light, Motion, and heat.' (H.)

452. 27. *the Van.* The Rev. W. M. Merchant suggests that in addition to the obvious meaning, advance-guard, Vaughan may have intended a reference to the Welsh word Ban, a peak, which as a feminine noun undergoes mutation with the definite article to Fan. This was frequently spelt as pronounced in the seventeenth century, Van or

Vann. Vaughan could see mountains in the east from his home. This kind of punning would be in accordance with Welsh poetic tradition.

453. 1. *How . . . tears.* See note on 63. 13–14 ; also 418. 49–50.

453. 3. *my stock lay dead.* Cf. G. Herbert, 'Grace', l. 1 (*Works*, p. 60) : ' My stock lies dead.'

453. 5-6. *for Marble sweats, &c.* Cf. G. Herbert, 'The Church-floore', l. 15 (*Works*, p. 67) :

But all is cleansed when the marble weeps.

453. 9–10. Cf. **455.** 52 and G. Herbert, 'Gratefulnesse', ll. 3–4 (*Works*, p. 123) :

See how thy beggar works on thee
                    By art. (Miss E. Holmes.)

453. 13–14. Cf. G. Herbert, 'The Pearl', l. 35 (*Works*, p. 89). (H.)

453. 17. *Wee are . . thee.* Cf. G. Herbert, 'Longing', ll. 14–17 (*Works*, p. 148) :

Mothers are kinde . . .
    .   .   .   .
Their infants, them ; and they suck thee.

453. 25-6. Cf. G. Herbert, 'Gratefulnesse', ll. 2 and 25–32 (*Works*, pp. 123–4). (Miss E. Holmes.)

454. *Praise.* For the metre of ll. 1–32 cf. G. Herbert, 'Praise' (II) (*Works*, p. 146).

455 (*Dressing*). 4–5. *thy secret key . . . rooms.* Cf. G. Herbert, 'The H. Communion', ll. 21–2 (*Works*, p. 52) :

And hath the privie key,
Op'ning the souls most subtile rooms. (H.)

455. 6–7. *refine . . . Confusions.* Cf. G. Herbert, 'The Starre', ll. 9–12 (*Works*, p. 74). (H.)

456 (*continuation*). 23–4. *Whatever, &c.* Cf. G. Herbert, 'Divinitie', ll. 21–4 (*Works*, p. 135) :

But he doth bid us take his bloud for wine.
    Bid what he please ; yet I am sure,
To take and taste what he doth there designe,
    Is all that saves, and not obscure. (GM.)

456. *Easter-day.* For the metre cf. G. Herbert, 'The Dawning' (*Works*, p. 112).

456. 8. *two deaths.* Hutchinson, following GM, cites this with reference to G. Herbert's 'Businesse', l. 22 ('And two deaths had been thy fee '), *Works*, p. 113, and note, p. 517 ; explaining that the second death (Rev. xx. 6, 14 ; xxi. 8) is 'eternal death, the condemnation of the lost soul after the Judgement '. Cf. **475.** 22.

457. *The Holy Communion.* Cf. G. Herbert, 'The Banquet', ll. 1–2 (*Works*, p. 181) :

Welcome sweet and sacred cheer,
            Welcome deare. (GM.)

457. 11–16. See pp. 459–60, 'Affliction', and note.

458. 52. *both food, and Shepheard.* Cf. 'Bone pastor, panis vere', l. 89 in St. Thomas's 'Lauda Sion'. (GM.)

458 (*Psalm 121*). 3–4. *who fils* (*Unseen*). 'which made', A.V.; 'who hath made', B.C.P. Cf. 479. 54.

459–60. *Affliction.* Cf. 457. 11–16 and Felltham, *Resolves*, i. 41, 'That all things are restrained' (ed. cit. pp. 130–3): ' The whole *world* is kept in order by *discord,* and every part of it, is but a more particular *composed jarre*. . . . Every string has his *use*, and his *tune*, and his *turne*. When the *Assyrians* fell, the *Persians* rose. . . . The losse of one *Man*, is the gaine of another. 'Tis *vicissitude* that maintaines the *World*' (see 460. 29). Cf. also *Hermetica*, Libellus xvi. 9 (ed. cit. p. 269): ' For the permanence of every kind of body is maintained by change.'

459. 9–10. *greater . . . lesser.* Cf. 561. 36 and 562. 4. (H.)

460. 37–40. *Tuning, &c.* Cf. G. Herbert, 'The Temper' (I), ll. 21–4 (*Works*, p. 55):

> Yet take thy way; for sure thy way is best:
>   Stretch or contract me, thy poore debter:
>   This is but tuning of my breast,
>   To make the musick better.

460. *The Tempest.* Influenced by G. Herbert's 'Miserie' (*Works*, pp. 100–2), especially in ll. 37–40, 45–8, 53–6 (cf. 'Miserie', ll. 43–66).

460. 1. *parcell'd out.* See note on 413. 12–13.

460. 5–16. An insertion or postscript. Line 17 follows on l. 4.

461. 17. *do so.* Sc. 'see' (l. 2).

461. 23–4. *snares, &c.* Cf. G. Herbert, 'Sinne' (I), ll. 7–8 (*Works*, p. 45):

> Fine nets and stratagems to catch us in,
> Bibles laid open, millions of surprises. (GM.)

461. 25–40. Cf. G. Herbert, ' Man', ll. 25–42 (*Works*, pp. 91–2).

461. 30. *Issachar.* Gen. xlix. 14–15.

461. 31 (*note*). Cf. 451. 34.

461. 37. *keyes.* Scales, as in music; ordered sequences.

461. 37–9. *but man . . . Sleeps.* Cf. G. Herbert, ' Miserie ', ll. 59–62 (*Works*, pp. 101–2):

> But Man doth know
> The spring, whence all things flow:
>
> And yet, as though he knew it not,
> His knowledge winks, and lets his humours reigne.

461. 45. *Yet . . . durt.* Cf. G. Herbert, 'Miserie', ll. 45–6:

> He doth not like this vertue, no ;
> Give him his dirt to wallow in all night.'

461. 48. *money, &c.* Cf. G. Herbert, 'The Quip', ll. 9–12 (*Works*, p. 110).

461. 49. *Life's . . . knows it.* Cf. G. Herbert, ' Miserie ', ll. 5–6 :

> *Man is but grasse,*
> *He knows it, fill the glasse.*

461. 51–2. Cf. G. Herbert, 'The Collar', ll. 13–15 (*Works*, p. 153):

> Is the yeare onely lost to me ?
>   Have I no bayes to crown it ?
> No flowers, no garlands gay ?

462 (*continuation*). 53. *O foolish*, &c. Cf. G. Herbert, 'Miserie', ll. 49–50:

> Oh foolish man ! where are thine eyes?
> How hast thou lost them in a croud of cares?

462. 56. *flesh no softness*. Cf. 386. 10.

462. 58–60. *flints*, &c. Cf. the title of *Silex Scintillans* and see note on 386.5–12.

462. 22. *My love-twist*, &c. Cf. G. Herbert, 'The Pearl', ll. 38–9 (*Works*, p. 89):

> But thy silk twist let down from heav'n to me,
> Did both conduct and teach me . . .

462. 23–4. *I have fram'd*, &c. Cf. Wisd. of Sol. xi. 24. (GM.)

463. 40. *I make all new*. Cf. 531. 46, 540. 27, and Rev. xxi. 5. (GM.)

463. 45–8. *A faithful . . . descent*. Cf. G. Herbert, 'Church-monuments', ll. 6–9 (*Works*, pp. 64–5):

> Therefore I gladly trust
>
> My bodie to this school, that it may learn
> To spell his elements, and finde his birth
> Written in dustie heraldrie and lines.

464 (*continuation*). 11. *The frosts*, &c. Cf. G. Herbert, 'Mans medley', l. 28, and 'Employment' (I), ll. 3–4 (*Works*, pp. 131 and 57).

464. 17–18. *tears . . . Ears*. Cf. G. Herbert, 'Hope', ll. 5–6 (*Works*, p. 121):

> With that I gave a viall full of tears :
> But he a few green eares.

464 (*The Pilgrimage*). 17–20. Cf. 650. 21 sqq. (GM.)

465 (*continuation*). 28. *thy Mount*. 1 Kings xix. 8. (GM.)

466. *The World*. In the article by M.-S. Röstvig mentioned in the note above on 85 (*heading*) it is suggested that this poem, like 'The importunate Fortune' (634–7), is influenced by *Hermetica*, Libellus i (ed. W. Scott, p. 129), where the seven different zones or spheres are described ; and that Vaughan may have been partly indebted also to Casimir's adaptation of the same Hermetic passage (Casimir, *Odes*, ii. 5). Felltham, *Resolves*, i. 9, ' Of Time's continuall speede' (ed. cit. pp. 24–5), describes Virtue and Vice with their various attendants travelling through the world and competing for the soul of man: 'And behinde all these, came *Eternity*, casting a *Ring* about them, which like a strong *inchantment*, made them for ever the same.'

466. 1–6. *Eternity . . . calm . . . Time . . . mov'd*. H compares Plato, *Timaeus*, 37d (Jowett, 1892, iii, p. 456).

466. 2. *Ring*. Cf. 7. 7 and 418. 5–6. (H.)

466. 8. Cf. G. Herbert, 'Dulnesse', l. 5 (*Works*, p. 115):

> The wanton lover in a curious strain . . .

466. 23–5. *Mole . . . prey*. Cf. G. Herbert, 'Confession', ll. 14–15 (*Works*, p. 126):

> Like moles within us, heave, and cast about :
> And till they foot and clutch their prey . . . (H.)

467. 44–5. Cf. G. Herbert, 'The Church Militant', l. 190 (*Works*, p. 195):

> While Truth sat by, counting his victories. (GM.)

467. 59–60. Cf. 539 (*The Queer*). 3–4.

468. *The Mutinie.* The imagery is chiefly from the story of Israel's bondage in Egypt, 'in morter and in brick', as told in Exodus i and v.

468. 11–12. *who made . . . waves.* Cf. G. Herbert, 'Providence', ll. 47–8 (*Works*, p. 118):

> Thou hast made poore sand
> Check the proud sea, ev'n when it swells and gathers.

See note on 423. 1.

469. 1 sqq. *Fair, order'd lights, &c.* Cf. *Hermetica*, Libellus viii. 4 (ed. W. Scott, i. 177): 'The bodies of the celestial gods keep without change that order which has been assigned to them by the Father in the beginning.' Cf. Libellus v. 3, 'think on the order of the stars', and Libellus xii (ii). 21 (ed. cit. pp. 159 and 237). See 143. 7–8, above. Cf. also 1 Enoch ii. 1 (ed. Charles, 1912, pp. 8–9).

469. 14. *wind the Clue.* Cf. 448 (*continuation*). 21–2 and 669. 2.

469. 21. *Musick and mirth.* Cf. G. Herbert, 'The Pearl', l. 24 (*Works*, p. 89). (H.)

469. 28. *when th' herb . . . more.* Miss E. Holmes compares G. Herbert, 'Man', ll. 43–5 (*Works*, p. 92):

> More servants wait on Man,
> Then he'll take notice of: in ev'ry path
> He treads down that which doth befriend him.

470. 31. *the glory differ . . . star.* 1 Cor. xv. 41. (GM.)

470. 36. *in your Courses fought.* Judges v. 20. (H.)

470. 43. *Lamb . . . Dragons voice.* Rev. xiii. 11.

470. *The Shepheards.* This poem is quoted in *A Breife Epistle to the Learned Manasseh Ben Israel. In Answer to his. Dedicated to the Parliament*, by E. S., pp. 23–5. The quotation follows a passage on the virgin birth, and is immediately preceded by the direction 'See *Sylex scintillans*, 97. pag.' and eight lines of verse apparently not by Vaughan. The book bears the date 1650 with Imprimatur September 6.

470. 1. *livers.* The emendation, necessary on metrical grounds, is further justified by Vaughan's use elsewhere of the word 'liver' in this sense. See, for example, 662 (*Retirement*). 4.

471. 45. *souls great shepheard.* The same expression occurs in Cotton's Hymn 'On Christmas-Day', st. ii (ed. Beresford, 1923, p. 104):

> Rise Shepherds, leave your flocks, and run,
> The soul's great Shepherd now is come. (GM.)

472. 5. *wind . . . fist.* Prov. xxx. 4. (H.)

472. 23. *fig-leafs, &c.* Cf. G. Herbert, 'Sighs and Grones', ll. 15–16 (*Works*, p. 83). (H.)

473. 35–6. *who . . . Court.* Cf. G. Herbert, 'The Glimpse', ll. 29–30 (*Works*, p. 155):

> O make me not their sport,
> Who by thy coming may be made a court!

473. 57–8. *I School . . . Cel.* Cf. G. Herbert, 'Mortification', ll. 20–2 (*Works*, p. 98):

Getting a house and home, where he may move
Within the circle of his breath,
Schooling his eyes. (GM.)

473. 65–74. Cf. G. Herbert, 'Giddinesse', ll. 9–11 (*Works*, p. 127):

Now he will fight it out, and to the warres;
Now eat his bread in peace,
And snudge in quiet.

474. 74. Cf. G. Herbert, 'Nature', ll. 1–2 (*Works*, p. 45):

Full of rebellion, I would die,
Or fight, or travell . . . (H.)

474. 77–8. *flames . . . wind.* Cf. G. Herbert, 'Jordan' (II), ll. 13–15 (*Works*, p. 103): 'As flames do work and winde'. (H.)

474. 81. *wilded . . . heart.* Miss E. Holmes compares G. Herbert, 'Sion', l. 13 (*Works*, p. 106):

There thou art struggling with a peevish heart.

474. 96. *To look him, &c.* Cf. G. Herbert, 'The Glance', l. 21 (*Works*, p. 172):

When thou shalt look us out of pain.

475. *The Sap.* Apart from the particular instances given below, there is a general relationship between this poem and G. Herbert's 'Peace' (*Works*, pp. 124–5). (GM.)

475. 4. *cal . . . dew.* Cf. G. Herbert, 'Grace', l. 11 (*Works*, p. 60): 'The dew, for which grasse cannot call'. (H.)

475. 7–8. *Thy root, &c.* Miss E. Holmes compares G. Herbert, 'Peace', ll. 17–18 (*Works*, p. 125):

But when I digg'd, I saw a worm devoure
What show'd so well.

475. 11, 15. *beyond the Stars . . . thy Country.* Cf. 430 (*Peace*). 1–2.

475. 13. *Prince of Salem.* Cf. G. Herbert, 'Peace', ll. 22–3:

There was a Prince of old
At Salem dwelt.

As Hutchinson, in a note on Herbert's poem, observes, 'Melchisedec, "king of Salem, which is, king of peace" (Heb. vii. 2), who "brought forth bread and wine" (Gen. xiv. 18), prefigures Christ.'

475. 14. *thy secret meals.* Cf. G. Herbert, 'Peace', ll. 27–39.

475. 16. *the key.* See note to 455. 4–5.

475. 22. *Two deaths had bin thy due.* Cf. 456. 8 and see note thereto.

475. 26–7. *bloud . . . Cordial.* Cf. G. Herbert, 'The Sacrifice', l. 159 (*Works*, p. 31).

476. *Mount of Olives.* Related to G. Herbert's 'The Flower' (*Works*, pp. 165–7).

476. 14. *And was . . . wind.* Almost verbatim from G. Herbert, 'Affliction', l. 36 (*Works*, p. 47). (H.)

477. 5. *home and hive.* Cf. G. Herbert, 'The Starre', ll. 30–1 (*Works*, p. 74). (GM.)

477. 15 sqq. Cf. G. Herbert, 'Giddinesse' (*Works*, p. 127). (H.)

477. 28. *ordain'd no rest.* Cf. G. Herbert, 'The Pulley', ll. 16–20 (*Works*, p. 160).

478. 1–4. Cf. G. Herbert, 'Peace', ll. 13–14 (*Works*, p. 125):
> Then went I to a garden, and did spy
> A gallant flower,
> The Crown Imperiall.

478. 19–21. Cf. 511. 25–6 and G. Herbert, 'The Flower', ll. 8–14 (*Works*, p. 166); also Donne, 'A Hymne to Christ', ll. 13–16. (GM.)

479. 50. *Masques and shadows.* Cf. 214. 17–20 and 37–41. (GM.)

479. 54. See 458. 3–4 and note.

479. 59. *Light, Joy, Leisure.* Cf. G. Herbert, 'Heaven', l. 19 (*Works*, p. 188). (H.)

480. 13–16. *O it is, &c.* Cf. G. Herbert, 'Nature', ll. 4–6 (*Works*, p. 45):
> O tame my heart;
> It is thy highest art
> To captivate strong holds to thee.

481. 22. *Primros'd-fields.* Hutchinson notes in GM that in 1654 Ascension Day fell on 4 May, the earliest day possible but one.

481. 23. *the.* Probably for 'thee'. *light . . . deceast.* Cf. 90. 33.

482. 47. *dissolv'd Pearls.* Cf. 184. 1–2.

482. 60. *answer . . . Jew.* John viii. 17.

482 (*Ascension-Hymn*). 6. *ascend . . . undrest.* See note on 415. 1–6.

483. 20. *Within the line.* See 429. 9 and note.

483. 33–6. *Made his cloathes . . . snow.* Mark ix. 3. (GM.)

483. 39. *bone to bone.* Ezek. xxxvii. 7. (H.)

483. 39–42. Phil. iii. 21. (GM.)

484. 9. *walking in an Air of glory.* Cf. *Hermetica*, Asclepius iii. 33 b (ed. W. Scott, pp. 369–71): 'and others [daemons] again, whose abode is in the purest part of the air, where no mist or cloud can be, and where no disturbance is caused by the motion of any of the heavenly bodies'.

484. 11. *My days, &c.* Cf. 170. 4–5.

484. 12. *glimering and decays.* See note on 479. 50 and cf. *Hermetica*, Libellus vi. 4b (ed. cit. p. 169): 'For all things which the eye can see are mere phantoms, and unsubstantial outlines; but the things which the eye cannot see are the realities . . .'

484. 23. *Well.* The neighbourhood of a well or fountain. See 404. 5–8, 407. 70, and cf. 511. 21–4.

484. 35–6. Rom. viii. 21. (GM.)

484. 39–40. *Or else, &c.* Cf. G. Herbert, 'Grace', ll. 22–4 (*Works*, p. 61):
> Or if to me thou wilt not move,
> Remove me; where I need not say,
> *Drop from above.*

485. 9. *new lights.* See *O.E.D.* s.v. Light, sb. 6 d.

485. 16. *His candle . . . heads.* See note to 395. 28.

485. 28. *These last . . . worst.* 2 Tim. iii. 13: 'evil men and seducers shall wax worse and worse.'

485. 30–32. *pens . . . set down . . . Crimes.* Cf. G. Herbert, 'The Bunch of Grapes', ll. 11 and 14 (*Works*, p. 128): 'Their storie pennes and sets us down' . . . 'His ancient justice overflows our crimes.' (H.)

485. 33. *if worst.* Referring back to l. 28. The rest of this line, with the following line, 'and worst . . . admits', is parenthetical.

486. 55–6. *to destroy The knots, &c.* Cf. G. Herbert, 'Prayer' (II), ll. 17–18 (*Works*, p. 103):

> That by destroying that which ty'd thy purse,
> Thou mightst make way for liberalitie! (H.)

486. 63. *Balaams hire.* Numb. xxii. 17–18.

486. *The Proffer.* See *Life*, 124–5, where it is suggested that Vaughan is likely to have received offers of place under the Commonwealth.

486. 5. Hutchinson (note in GM) suggests that Vaughan may allude here to recovery from an illness or, more probably, to an improvement in his fortunes, owing perhaps to inheritance after his first wife's death.

487. 11. *husbands.* Husbandmen.

487. 18. *I've read, &c.* Exod. viii. 31. (GM.)

487. 25–7. *Shall my, &c.* Cf. G. Herbert, 'Complaining', ll. 16–18 (*Works*, p. 144):

> Let not thy wrathfull power
> Afflict my houre,
> My inch of life. (GM.)

488 (*continuation*). 44–5. *Spit . . . home.* Cf. G. Herbert, 'The Church-Porch', l. 92 (*Works*, p. 10): 'Spit out thy flegme, and fill thy brest with glorie.' (H.)

488. 45–8. *think on thy dream, &c.* Cf. G. Herbert, 'The Size', ll. 44–7 (*Works*, p. 138):

> Call to minde thy dream,
> An earthly globe,
> On whose meridian was engraven,
> *These seas are tears, and heav'n the haven.*

488. *Cock-crowing.* See E. Holmes, op. cit. pp. 36–8, and Don Cameron Allen, 'Vaughan's "Cock-crowing" and the Tradition', *ELH*, June 1954, pp. 94–106.

488. 1. *Father of lights.* James i. 17.

488. 1–3, 7–9 *and* **489.** 41. Miss Holmes compares Thomas Vaughan, *Anima Magica Abscondita*, 1650, p. 13: 'For she [the Anima] is guided in her Operations by a *Spirituall Metaphysicall Graine*, a Seed or Glance of *Light*, simple, and without any Mixture, descending from the *first Father of Lights*. For though his *full-ey'd* Love shines on nothing but *Man*, yet every thing in the World is in some measure directed for his Preservation by a *Spice* or *touch* of the *first Intellect.*' 'full-ey'd Love' is from G. Herbert, 'The Glance', l. 20 (*Works*, p. 172).

488. 10. *house of light.* Cf. the title of Thomas Vaughan's treatise, *Aula Lucis, Or, The House of Light*, 1652.

488. 11–12. *their candle, &c.* Cf. Thomas Vaughan, *Lumen de Lumine*, 1651, p. 41: 'This is the *secret candle* of God, which he hath *tinn'd* in the *Elements*.' (Miss E. Holmes.)

488. 20–2. Cf. Rom. i. 20–1. (GM.)

488. 29. *dark, Ægyptian border.* Exod. x. 21–2.

489. 37-41. *this Veyle, &c.* See 2 Cor. iii. 13-16. (GM.)

489. 41. *thy full-ey'd love.* See note above on 488. 1-3, &c.

489. 48. *no Lilie.* Referring to Song of Sol. ii. 16, quoted by Vaughan, *Mount of Olives*, 161. 15 above.

489-90. *The Starre.* Cf. Thomas Vaughan, *Magia Adamica*, 1650, 'To the Reader': 'Look up then to *Heaven*, and when thou seest the Cœlestiall fires move in their swift and glorious *Circles*, think also there are *below* some *cold Natures*, which they *over-look*, and about which they *move* incessantly to *heat*, and *concoct* them.' Ibid. p. 68: 'To speak plainly, *Heaven* it self was *originally extracted* from *Inferiors*, yet not so *intirely*, but some *portion* of the *Heavenly Natures* remained still *below*, and are the *very same* in *Essence* and *Substance* with the *separated starrs* and skies.'

489. 3-4. *And winde and curle, &c.* Cf. G. Herbert, 'The Starre', ll. 25-6 (*Works*, p. 74):

> That so among the rest I may
> Glitter, and curle, and winde as they.

489. 17-20. Cf. 492 (*The Favour*). 7-8, and see note.

490 (*continuation*). **27-8.** *There God, &c.* Cf. Thomas Vaughan (on Cornelius Agrippa), *Anthroposophia Theomagica*, 1650, p. 54:

> *Heav'n* states a *Commerce* here with *Man*. (Miss E. Holmes.)

490 (*The Palm-tree*). **1.** *Deare friend sit down.* The opening words of G. Herbert's 'Love unknown' (*Works*, p. 129).

490. 3, 7-9. See M. P. Tilley, *Proverbs in England*, P37, 'The straighter grows the Palm the heavier the weight it bears.' Also 502. 39.

490. 11. *By flowers, &c.* Cf. G. Herbert, 'Sion', ll. 4-5 (*Works*, p. 106):

> The wood was all embellished
> With flowers and carvings, mysticall and rare.

491 (*continuation*). **21.** *patience of the Saints.* Rev. xiii. 10, xiv. 12. (GM.)

491 (*Joy*). **6.** *a Deaths-head . . . Roses.* Cf. 185. 38-9 and Wisd. of Sol. ii. 8: 'Let us crown ourselves with rosebuds.'

491. 8. *a winde or wave.* Cf. G. Herbert, 'The Glimpse', l. 8 (*Works*, p. 154):

> Wert thou a winde or wave.

491. 12. *More . . . stars.* More eyes (for weeping) than there are stars.

491. 28. *solitary years.* 'The allusion may be to the interval between his first wife's death and his second marriage' (*Life*, 197).

491. 30. *shaking fastens thee.* Cf. G. Herbert, 'Affliction' (V), l. 20 (*Works*, p. 97):

> We are the trees, whom shaking fastens more.

492 (*The Favour*). **1-2.** Cf. G. Herbert, 'The Glance', ll. 17-18 (*Works*, p. 172):

> If thy first glance so powerfull be,
> A mirth but open'd and seal'd up again. (GM.)

492. 7-8. *Some kinde herbs, &c.* Cf. Thomas Vaughan, *Lumen de Lumine*, p. 88: 'There is not an *Herb* here *below*, but he hath a *star* in *Heaven above,* and the *star* strikes him with her *Beame,* and sayes to him, *Grow.'* See 'The Starre', p. 489, and notes thereto.

492 (*The Garland*). 9-10. *I flung ... affections.* Cf. G. Herbert, 'Christmas', ll. 1-3 (*Works,* p. 80):

> All after pleasures as I rid one day,
> My horse and I, both tir'd, bodie and minde,
> With full crie of affections. (GM.)

493. 33-6. Cf. 338. 19-20.

493 (*Love-sick*). On the technique of linked phrases employed here see note on 'The Wreath' (p. 539).

493. *Trinity-Sunday.* This follows the form of Herbert's poem with the same title (*Works,* p. 68). GM notes that Jonson and Drummond wrote poems in triads on this theme.

494. 26. *though but sand, &c.* See note to 468. 11-12. (H.)

495. 37. *upper Springs above.* Cf. 498. 49. (GM.)

495. 38. *Heav'ns large bottles.* Job xxxviii. 37. (H.)

496. 91. *That gift of thine.* Cf. 395. 44. (GM.)

497 (*continuation*). 13-16. Cf. 432. 1-10.

498. 48. *fill my bottle, &c.* See note on 500. 12.

498. 50. *Begetting Virgins.* Cf. 407. 70: 'Faire, virgin-flowers'; 92. 1: 'Isca *parens florum*'; and 661 (*The Shower*). 1-7. GM adduces Zech. ix. 17 (Vulg.): 'vinum germinans virgines', explained in the Douay Bible, 'maketh virgins to bud, or spring forth ... like flowers among thorns'.

499. 4-7. See 404. 1-8 and notes.

500. 37. *veil.* See note on 489. 37-41.

500. *Begging.* First published in *Flores Solitudinis,* 1654. See 218.

500. 12. *the weeping Lad.* Sc. Ishmael. Gen. xxi. 9-21. Cf. 498. 48, 505. 1-6, and 511. 16. (GM.)

501. 3. *green and gay.* Cf. 174. 37. (H.)

501. 4. *King of grief.* Cf. G. Herbert, 'The Thanksgiving', l. 1 (*Works,* p. 35):

> Oh King of grief! (a title strange, yet true). (H.)

501. 12. *expect with groans.* Cf. 432. 3-4.

501. 13. *which all at once.* Sir Edward Marsh's emendation (*T.L.S.* 19 July 1947), 'all atones', is tempting. The 1655 reading is possible if ll. 11-14 are taken as carrying on the construction of ll. 8-10. 'Once' rhymes with 'stones' again, at 515. 39. But cf. also 623. 7-8.

502. 35-6. *I'le get me up, &c.* Cf. G. Herbert, 'Easter', ll. 19-20 (*Works,* p. 42):

> I got me flowers to straw thy way;
> I got me boughs off many a tree.

502. 39. *like the Palm, &c.* 'wrong' = bent (*O.E.D.* s.v. A. 1). See 490. 3, 7-9 and note.

503. 6-8. *to his sins ... lust.* Cf. 390. 17. (H.)

503. 9-10. *the Ice, &c. (with Vaughan's note).* D. C. Allen, in *Philological Quarterly,* Jan. 1944, pp. 84-5, gives the story as told by Nicephorus Callistus.

504. 9. *Groans of the Dove.* Rom. viii. 26. (GM.)

505. 18. *no moneth but May.* See note on 434. 23-4.

506. 37-40. Cf. 167. 1-5. (GM.)

506. 46-7. *like Pontick sheep, &c.* Pliny, *Nat. Hist.* xxvii. 28 : 'Absinthi genera plura sunt : . . . Ponticum e Ponto, ubi pecora pinguescunt illo et ob id sine felle reperiuntur.' 'their wormwood diet' means 'a wormwood diet like theirs'.

506. *The Knot.* The Virgin Mary is addressed as 'pacis vinculum' in l. 65 of the hymn (no. 512) beginning 'Ave decus virginum' in *Lateinische Hymnen des Mittelalters*, ed. F. J. Mone, 1853, ii, p. 291). Cf. also no. 511, l. 20, where she is addressed as 'vinculum amoris'. (E. Bensly in GM.)

507. 16. *the sheep-keeping Syrian Maid.* Rachel. Gen. xxix. 9 and 17. See 408-9. 30-42, where Rebekah is praised in similar terms.

508. 13. *Magdal-castle.* Chambers quotes Donne, 'To the Lady Magdalen Herbert : of St. Mary Magdalen' (ed. Grierson, i, p. 317) :

> Her of your name, whose fair inheritance
> Bethina was, and jointure Magdalo :

and Jacobus de Voragine, *Legenda Aurea*, ch. 96 (90), ed. Graesse, 1846, p. 408 : 'Maria Magdalena a Magdalo castro cognominata'.

508. 21. *Pistic Nard.* John xii. 3 : ἡ οὖν Μαριὰμ λαβοῦσα λίτραν μύρου νάρδου πιστικῆς . . . . See *O.E.D.* s.v. Pistic, *a.*

508. 27. *Dear . . . knew'st.* Cf. G. Herbert, 'Marie Magdalene', l. 13 (*Works*, p. 173) : 'Deare soul, she knew . . .' (H.)

508. 49. *Art of love.* Cf. G. Herbert, 'The Thanksgiving', l. 47 (*Works*, p. 36). (GM.)

509. 54. *Heaven . . . came.* Cf. G. Herbert, 'Divinitie', l. 14 (*Works*, p. 135) : '[the doctrine] Was cleare as heav'n, from whence it came.' (H.)

509. 59. *now are fixed stars.* Cf. Crashaw, 'The Weeper', sts. 2-3 (*Poems*, O.E.T., p. 79).

509. 61. *Pharisee.* Luke vii. 36-50. Identified by Vaughan with Simon the leper. See l. 69.

509. 69. *Leper.* Matt. xxvi. 6 ; Mark xiv. 3.

509. 70. *like a childes.* 2 Kings v. 14.

509. 71-2. Cf. 180. 20-1, 181. 14-15, 182. 21-7 (GM.) Cf. also 517. 9 sqq.

509 (*The Rain-bow*). 3. *Shem.* Gen. ix. 18. (GM.)

509. 11. *Rain, &c.* Cf. G. Herbert, 'Providence', ll. 117-18 (*Works*, p. 120) :

> Rain, do not hurt my flowers ; but gently spend
> Your hony drops.

510 18. *All and One.* Gen. ix. 16. (H.)

510. 41-2. Miss E. Holmes, observing the general resemblance of this poem to G. Herbert's 'Decay' (*Works*, p. 99), points out a particular correspondence between these two lines and Herbert's ll. 16-20.

510 (*The Seed*). 5. *my early love.* Cf. 419. 8.

511. 16. See note to 500. 12.

511. 25-6. *Greenness, &c.* See note to 478. 19-21.

511. 40. *thriving vice.* Cf. 517. 16 and 518. 26. (GM.)

511. 48. *the white winged Reapers.* See 440. 40 and note.

512. 29. *recruits.* Supplies.

513. 1. *Fair and yong light.* In *Life*, 107-8, the question is raised whether this poem commemorates the death of Vaughan's first wife.

514. 46. *he that's dead, &c.* Rom. vi. 7.

514. 50. *spicy mountains.* Song of Sol. viii. 14.

514 (*The Stone*) (*heading*). Josh. xxiv. 27 : 'And Joshua said unto all the people, Behold, this stone shall be a witness unto us ; for it hath heard all the words of the Lord which he spake unto us : it shall be therefore a witness unto you, lest ye deny your God.'

515. 14-15. See Hazlitt, *English Proverbs*, 1907, p. 227.

518. *The Ass.* See 162. 10-14. As A. C. Judson observes (*M.L.N.* xli. 178-81), Vaughan may have had in mind 'Ad Encomium Asini Digressio' in Cornelius Agrippa's *De Incertitudine et Vanitate Omnium Scientiarum et Artium,* where the Ass symbolizes humility and patience. D. C. Allen (*M.L.N.* lviii. 612-14) gives other instances and suggests that Vaughan was probably indebted more to common tradition than to any particular author.

518. 21-2. *wise...mysteries.* Cf. Erasmus, *Adagia*, 2204 : 'Asinus mysteria portans'; also Aesop, ed. Chambry, No. 266, and Joseph Hall, *Meditations*, iii. 63 : 'the ass that carried the Egyptian Goddess, had many bowed knees; yet not to the beast, but to the burthen.'

519. 57-8. *the Ass is free, &c.* Cf. Job xxxix. 5-8. (H.)

519-20 (*The hidden Treasure*). 1-14. Cf. 418 (*Vanity of Spirit*), 461. 40, and 693. 19-22.

520. 12. *Paths, &c.* Job xxviii. 7.

520. *Childe-hood.* See note on 419 (*The Retreate*).

521. 14-16. *But flowers, &c.* Cf. G. Herbert, 'Life', ll. 13-15 (*Works*, p. 94) :

> Farewell deare flowers, sweetly your time ye spent,
> Fit, while ye liv'd, for smell or ornament,
>   And after death for cures.

521. 36. *Must...see.* Mark x. 15. (H.)

522 (*heading*). *John* 2. 3. Read 3. 2.

522. 9-10. *healing wings, &c.* Malachi iv. 2. Cf. 151. 31. (H.)

522. 23-4. *trees, &c.* Cf. 432 ('And do they so ?'), 514 (*The Stone*), &c.

522. 25-6. See 143. 1-4, 187. 11-17, 305. 19-24 and notes. For a similar accumulation of comparisons see 447, 'Son-dayes', and note.

522. 32-3. Cf. Song of Sol. v. 2.

523. 35. *His knocking time.* Rev. iii. 20. (GM.)

523. 50. *A deep, but dazling darkness.* Cf. St. Dionysius Areop., *Epist.* v, Dorotheo Ministro (*Opera*, Migne, i, cols. 1073-4) : 'Divina caligo lux est inaccessa, quam inhabitare Deus perhibetur ... inaspectabilis, propter exuberantem supernaturalis luminis effusionem ...'

524. 33-5. *I, may that flood, &c.* Cf. Cleveland, Epitaph on Strafford, ll. 13-14 :

> Here lies blood ! and let it lie
> Speechless still and never cry. (GM.)

524. 40. *speak better things.* Heb. xii. 24. (H.)

524. *Righteousness.* Cf. Ps. xv and G. Herbert, 'Constancie' (*Works*, pp. 72–3).

526 (*Anguish*). 13–16. Cf. G. Herbert, 'Praise' (I) and 'A true Hymne' (*Works*, pp. 61 and 168). (H.)

527 (*continuation*). 11. *thy poor Ass.* Cf. 518. 21.

527. 3. Cf. G. Herbert, 'To all Angels and Saints', l. 2 (*Works*, p. 77): 'See the smooth face of God without a frown.' (H.)

531. 16. *stones, &c.* Cf 497 (*The Bird*). 14–16, 514 (*The Stone*), and see note to 432. 1 sqq.

531. 44. *Thy arm doth sleep.* Isa. li. 9: 'Awake . . . O arm of the Lord.' (H.)

532. 37–8. *unseen, &c.* Cf. 478. 19–21.

533 (*The Throne*). 5–6. *kneeling, &c.* Cf. 456. 37–42.

534. 21–5. See note on 521. 14–16.

534 (*The Feast*). 1–2. Cf. G. Herbert, 'Dooms-day', ll. 1–2 (*Works*, p. 186):

> Come away,
> Make no delay. (GM.)

534. 12. *inherit.* Sc. prematurely. (GM.)

535. 40. *veyls.* Cf. S. Thomas, 'Adoro te', l. 25: 'Jesu quem velatum nunc aspicio'. (GM.)

535. 42. *Present . . . seeing.* Cf. S. Thomas, 'Pange lingua', ll. 29–30: 'Praestet fides supplementum sensuum defectui.' (GM.)

536. 61–9. *O thorny crown, &c.* Cf. G. Herbert, 'The Thanksgiving', ll. 13–14 (*Works*, p. 35):

> Shall thy strokes be my stroking? thorns, my flower?
> Thy rod, my posie? crosse, my bower?

537. 25–8. *those Kerchiefs, &c.* Miss E. Holmes compares G. Herbert, 'The Dawning', ll. 15–16 (*Works*, p. 112):

> Christ left his grave-clothes, that we might, when grief
> Draws tears, or bloud, not want a handkerchief;

and also Drexelius, *Aeternitatis Prodromus*, ii. 23 (*Opera*, 1647, i, p. 53): 'Christus sudarium tibi quoque mittit . . .'

537 (*The Water-fall*). 17–18. Cf. 282. 18–24 and 284. 6–9.

538. 38. Rom. viii. 21. (GM.)

539 (*The Wreath*). 9 sqq. *praise, &c.* For the linked phrasing cf. 493 (*Love-sick*) and G. Herbert, 'A Wreath' (*Works*, p. 185).

539. *The Queer.* 'Quere' in Index. The meaning is 'Query'. 'Queer' in this sense is not recorded in *O.E.D.*

539. 3. *ring.* Cf. 467. 59–60.

539. 9. *thee.* Sc. joy.

541. 23. *art of love.* See note to 508. 49.

541. 38–9. See note to 190. 12–15.

542. 21–2. See 432. 1 sqq. and note.

542. 41–2. *words . . . swords.* Ps. lv. 21. (H.)

543. 63–5. *S. Clemens apud Basil.* Basilius, *Liber de Spiritu Sancto*, xxix (*Opera*, Migne, iv, col. 201).

HERMETICAL PHYSICK.

547 (*title-page*). *Hermetical . . . Nollius.* The work which Vaughan translates is not, as stated by Grosart, *Naturae Sanctuarium : quod est Physica Hermetica*, but *Systema* Medicinae Hermeticæ Generale, In quo

I. Medicinae veræ fundamentum.　⎫ Methodo dilucidissima
II. Sanitatis conseruatio.　　　　⎬ generaliter explicantur
III. Morborum cognitio, & Curatio.⎭

Ab Henrico Nollio Philo-chymiatro . . . In nobilis Francoforti Paltheniana. 1613.

Vaughan begins to translate at p. 60, where the *Systema* begins after *Prodromus Medicus*, pp. 7–60.

548. 4–5. *all . . . but.* All except.

548. 6. *twice . . . Colworts.* See Tilley, *Proverbs in England*, C 511 : 'Coleworts twice sodden'.

548. 10. *Veritatem tempus manu-ducit.* Cf. Menander, Monosticha 11 : ἄγει δὲ πρὸς φῶς τὴν ἀλήθειαν χρόνος (Otto, *Die Sprichwörter der Römer*, p. 343), and Seneca, *De Ira*, ii. 22. 3 : 'Dandum semper est tempus: veritatem dies aperit.' (EB.) See also Tilley, *Proverbs in England*, T 324 : 'Time brings the truth to light.'

548. 26–9. *Plautus.* E. Bensly in *Mod. Lang. Rev.* xiv, Jan. 1919, pp. 104–5, notes that Vaughan is quoting from the spurious part of the Prologue to *Pseudolus*. E. Bensly gives the words as they appear in the edition of Lambinus :

> Studete hodiè mihi, bona in scenam affero.
> Nam bona bonis ferri, reor aequom maxume,
> Ut mala malis, ut qui mali sunt, habeant mala :
> Bona, qui boni.   bonos quod oderint mali,
> Sunt mali : malos quod oderint boni, bonos
> Esse oportet.

550. 10–14. *Now all . . . leader.* V's addition.

553. 16. *Gods.* See footnote. The plural, correctly, is in the Latin.

553. 36. *bark before he bites.* See footnote. '*latrat . . .* antequam mordeat' (Nollius, p. 66).

554. 18. *our Saints of Europe.* 'Europæi nostri'. (Nollius, p. 66.)

554. 22. *us Saints.* 'nos homines'.

554. 27–9. *for they . . . deliver them.* V's addition.

558. 1–2. *The dose, &c.* Out of its original place ; p. 115 in Nollius.

558, 560, 561. The notes, as usual, are V's additions.

561. 20–1. *Treatise of Meteors.* Apparently not finished, or not published. See *Life*, 212, footnote.

567. 22–9. *I mean . . . Law.* Shorter in original.

567. 29–568. 1. *For thus . . . possessest.* V's addition.

568. 2–9. *The Lord . . . Deuteron.* 28. Shorter in original. 9. For 29. 16 read 26. 15–16.

569. 8. ἀπνευστί. In Nollius the word is printed ἀπνόϛϛῆ. The first contraction, apparently, was mistaken for *a*. See footnote.

572. 4. *Bergkranckheiten.* The mistake in the text of 1655 seems to be due to a misreading of the German '**ł**'; see Nollius, p. 91, and cf. 588. 19.

576. 25–6. *Eucherius, &c.* Cf. Nollius, p. 97 : 'Eucharius Rosenbader ex Weissenburg, Noricorum oppido, ac Ioannes ab Ettenstet chirurgi'.

577. 7. *seven Sections.* Cf. Nollius, p. 97 : 'sectiones ... octo', and p. 98 : '8. Quid sit vniversalis medicina ; ex qua materia fiat, & quis eius legitimus vsus.' See note to 592. 26–41.

581. 12. *And after all ... Doctors.* V's addition.

583. 11–13. *That is to say, &c.* V's addition.

584. 29. *a Pythagorical Metempsuchosis, or.* V's addition.

584. 31–2. *as an old womans Recipe.* V's addition.

585. 5–6. *by those ... mankind.* V's addition.

585. 17–19. *and the success ... impostors.* Cf. Nollius, p. 108 : 'aut salus nocentibus adscribatur'.

585. 20. *Medicasters.* 'medicorum'.

585. 25. *who suffer most by them.* V's addition.

585. 31–2. *that is to say ... diseases.* V's addition.

586. 22. *but for a bad one, &c.* V's addition.

587. 5–6. *in imitation ... Sonne.* V's addition.

588. 13–14. *not omitting his own observations.* V's addition.

588. 19. *Arzt* printed '*Arkt*'. See note on 572. 4.

589. 12–15. *and he ... heaven.* Cf. Nollius, p. 113 : 'eosque instruere non erubuerit'.

590. 39–**591.** 3. *Let him, &c.* Cf. Nollius, p. 115 : 'Deum sibi reconciliato poenitentia vera, ac deinceps Deum adorato, vt auxilietur.'

592. 26–41. Shorter in original. After this Nollius goes on to his 'Sectio viii. Quid sit universalis medicina', &c. (pp. 118–26) and *Epilogus* (pp. 126–7). Then (after a blank page) *De Generatione*, &c., the original of *The Chymists Key.* See 688. 40–1.

THE CHYMISTS KEY.

593 *(title-page).* *By ... Henry Nollius.* See note on 592. 26–41. The full title of the work (on p. 129) is: De Generatione Rerum Naturalium Liber *Ex Vero Natvrae lumine in gratiam sincerioris philosophiæ studiosorum conformatus Ab* Henrico Nollio. Christus Iesus Dominus noster: *Facilius est Camelum per foramen acus transire, quam diuitem participem fieri regni Cælorum.* [Device] Francoforti, E Collegio Musarum Paltheniano. Anno M. DC. XV. Page 130 is blank. The text of *De Generatione* occupies pp. 131–52 of the volume, which begins with *Systema Medicinae Hermeticæ Generale* (1613), the source of *Hermetical Physick.*

593. *Rob. Flud.* The quotation is from his *Utriusque Cosmi ... Historia,* 1617, I. vi. 2, p. 171 ('appetit' and 'formam').

593. *Published by Eugenius Philalethes.* This phrase probably accounts for Wood's ascription of *The Chymists Key* to Thomas Vaughan, who adopted 'Eugenius Philalethes' as his *nom de plume,* and signs the address To the Reader thus (p. 596). In the second paragraph of that address, however, he clearly distinguishes the translator from himself. Henry Vaughan claims the translation in his letter to Aubrey of 15 June 1673 (see p. 688).

594. 7–8. *Menelaus ... not invited.* *Iliad,* ii. 408.

595. 9. *D. Espagnet.* The reference here and in ll. 19–20 and 26 is to Jean d'Espagnet's *Enchiridion Physicæ Restitutæ,* of which a third edition was published in 1642.

595. 17. *Hali-Caly.* 'that *subject,* which the *Arabians* call *Halicali,* from *Hali summum* and *Calop Bonum:* but the Latine *Authors* corruptly write it *Sal Alkali.*' Thomas Vaughan, *Lumen de Lumine,* 1651, p. 42.

595. 22–3. *what thou hast attained to.* 'summum vitæ humanæ subsidium ac pretiosissimam panaceam' (d'Espagnet).

597. 17–19. *did nothing like ... wide.* 'simplex visa fuerit' (Nollius, p. 132).

597. 22–3. *which in our ... come by.* 'quorum in nostra philosophia usus est' (p. 132).

597. 27. *noble and matchlesse.* 'nobilissimam' (p. 132).

597. 29–30. *most covetous, chargeable and fruitlesse processes.* 'scriptis processibus' (p. 132). Expansions of this kind occur fairly frequently and are not as a rule noted here.

597. 30. *into their silly readers.* V's addition.

598. 2. *obstructing, discordant impurities.* 'peregrinas naturas' (p. 132).

598. 3. *the Philosophers doe know very well.* After this Vaughan omits 'ignorant contra artem, qua sola aurum fieri queat' (p. 132).

598. 11–12. *after ... performed.* V's addition.

598. 13. *subsistence and health.* 'salutem' (p. 133).

598. 28. (*without ... Ciborum*). V's addition.

598. 33–4. *this ... assistance.* 'hac ratione' (p. 134).

599. 2. *Chymistry.* 'vere philosophica Alchymia' (p. 134).

599. 13. *Augurellus.* The passage is quoted by Nollius as follows:

> Hanc non impuris manibus fraudator auarus
> Attingat, decoctor item, quisquisue fabrili
> Arte valet, mollisue etiam cum perdita cordi
> Otia Mercatorque vagus, &c.
> *Et paulo post:*
> Ast sapiens superos inprimis qui colat, & qui
> Noscendis penitus causis modo gaudeat; huc se
> Conferat & totis sectetur viribus artem.
> Tunc Comes hærebit grauis exploratio rerum
> Intima naturæ passim vestigia seruant.
> Tunc mora sollicitos cursus remorata sequetur,
> Et visura olim stabilis patientia finem.

599. 37–8. *hath its ... grounds ... down.* 'robur suum trahit' (p. 135).

600. 6–7. *decayed ... radical.* V's addition.

600. 7–10. *and excite ... expelled.* 'eumque ad morbos propulsandos confortare' (p. 135).

600. 12–14. *those extrarious ... man.* 'naturae peregrinae molestiam & morbum nobis invehentes' (p. 135).

600. 17. *in the greater world.* V's addition.

600. 18. *Microcosmic.* V's addition.

600. 21–4. *It is a noble ... man.* 'Tutius est vires medicamentorum in rebus macrocosmicis primum experiri, quam in microcosmo' (p. 136).

600. 31–3. *really ... Diseases.* 'certissimam antidotum' (p. 136).

602. 3–7. *(he meanes ... Athens,).* V's addition.

602. 9. *(like a Plagiary).* V's addition.

602. 15–30. *for while ... opposition.* 'siquidem dum de rerum natura disputant, alter alterius non sine magna arrogantia, qua quisque sibi sophiam arrogat, opinionem insectari & refellere annititur: Atque hinc à vero fundamento discedunt & in inextricabilem labyrinthum fictis principiis munitum dilabuntur, vt quis alius irretitus se ex eiusmodi tricis difficulter expedire queat' (pp. 138–9).

602. 30–1. *these lewd ... verbosity.* 'his nugis' (p. 139).

603. 5. *owne fraile.* V's addition.

603. 10. *carelesse and transient eyes.* 'limis oculis & obiter' (p. 139).

603. 14. *of the secret generation.* V's addition.

603. 15–16. *that rich ... metals.* 'metallicae medicinae' (p. 140).

603. 17. *Of the Generation ... things.* 'Liber De Generatione Vnus.' (p. 141.)

603. 24–5. *dung and putrefaction.* 'fimo' (p. 141).

603. 25–6. *in the Schooles.* 'alias' (p. 141).

603. 35. *The Commentarie or Illustration.* V's addition, as also '*The Commentary*' in corresponding places later.

603. 36. *or subtile.* V's addition.

604. 6. *some perfect.* V's addition.

604. 13. *That Matrix.* New sentence in the Latin (p. 142).

604. 13–15. *That Matrix ... regiment.* 'Matrix debita est, quae cuique semine in suo regno respondet' (p. 142).

604. 16. *animal Matrix.* After this Vaughan omits 'Matrices hae probe discernendæ sunt, ne in grandem errorem prolabamur'.

604. 24. *Believe our Saviour.* V's addition.

604. 28. *Raymond Lullie.* Here and elsewhere Vaughan omits more precise references given by Nollius.

604. 31. *centrall.* V's addition.

605. 21–23. *therefore ... lyonesse, &c.* Abbreviated.

605. 26 7. *by his dissolving ... nature.* 'soluens' (p. 144).

605. 37–8. *by reason ... betwixt them.* 'ratione similitudinis' (p. 144).

606. 3. *(as the Proverb hath it).* V's addition.

606. 32. *(which ... body).* V's addition.

606. 33–4. *(the spirit attracting it).* V's addition.

607. 2. *Let us, &c.* The Latin begins a new sentence.

609. 11. *frequent and wearisome.* 'nimia' (p. 148).

609. 16–17. *not be laved ... from it.* 'haud recedat' (p. 149).

609. 28–9. *Thou that aimest ... medicine.* V's addition.

610. 9. *weak ... uselesse.* 'fragilem' (p. 150).

610. 34. *effectuall medicine.* Section vii in the Latin ends: 'Confer *Lull. c. 26. theor. test. mihi. p. 50.*'

611. 5–8. *so the husbandmen ... seed.* 'Sic agros induratos arando, occando, & glebas discutiendo renouamus & rarefacimus, vt frumenti semen facilius ab agro admittatur.' (p. 151.)

611. 23–4. *dryed up by ... waters.* 'per aquas fortes euerso'.

611. 24. *contagious incurable disease.* 'grauibus morbis' (p. 151).

611. 28. *dry trees and lopt branches.* 'arboribus amputatis' (p. 151).

611. 29. *green and living.* 'viridibus'.

611. 33–4. *yeilds ... seed.* 'constantius semen emittit'.

612. 19. *only those envious ignorants.* 'tantum de iis' (p. 152).

612. 23. *great and manifest.* V's addition.

612. 24. *evident.* V's addition.

612. 28. *wretched ... call them.* 'misellis ratiunculis' (p. 152).

THALIA REDIVIVA.

613 *(title-page).* For the choice of title see *Life*, 214.
Nec erubuit, &c. Virgil, *Ecl.* vi. 2.

614 *(heading). Earl of Worcester.* Henry Somerset, third Marquess and seventh Earl, distantly related to Vaughan. See *Life*, 6, 215–16, 243–4.

615 *(signature). J. W.* Probably John Williams, made Prebendary of St. David's in 1678, when he was in his thirtieth year, and Archdeacon of Cardigan in 1680. The same, presumably, as 'I. W.' on pp. 616 and 622. See *Life*, 215.

617–18. *Commendation by Orinda (Katherine Philips).* This is included in the editions of Orinda's poems of 1664, 1667, 1678, and 1710. Only the more important variants are given in the footnotes. For Orinda herself see *Life*, 81–2.

617. 9–10. This implies that Amoret was a real person, presumably Catherine Wise, Vaughan's first wife. See *Life*, 50–4.

617. 11–12. 'the best of Unions' is that between 'Truth' and 'Love'. Hutchinson suggests, not convincingly, that the phrase alludes to the marriage of Henry and Catherine Vaughan.

618 *(second signature). Tho. Powel.* See note on 33 (title-page). These verses were presumably written during the Civil War and with reference to war-poems by Vaughan, probably others besides the two or three included in *Olor Iscanus.* See *Life*, 60–4. There are no such poems in *Thalia Rediviva.*

618. 15–16. Hutchinson, *Life*, 51–2, following GM, is inclined to identify 'Etesia' with 'Amoret'. But it does not seem quite certain that 'Timander', in l. 16, is Vaughan. See 643 (heading).

620 *(signature). N. W.* Presumably Nathaniel, brother of John Williams (see note to 615). Nathaniel matriculated in 1672.

621. 37–8. These lines do not well describe any of the poems actually included in *Thalia Rediviva.*

623 *(heading). his Learned Friend, &c.* See note on 33 (title-page). It is not clear in what sense Powel is addressed as Vaughan's 'Loyal Fellow-Prisoner'. Hutchinson, *Life*, 69, takes the phrase literally and this may be right; the poem, however, speaks as if it would not be physically difficult for the two friends to meet (ll. 3–5 and 43–8), and possibly 'Prisoner' refers to nothing more than a privacy self-imposed when the Parliamentarians entered Breconshire in 1645.

624. 48. *two Ev'ls, &c.* I see you with my mind's eye (which is not enough) and cannot see you physically; or, I see much that I dislike seeing and do not see you.

625. *The King Disguis'd.* Presumably written soon after 27 April 1646, when Charles left Oxford dressed as a gentleman's servant. See *Life*, 69–70.

625. 2. *into his Coffin.* The idea is paralleled in the 1677 version of Cleveland's 'The King's Disguise':

And why so coffin'd in this vile Disguise . . . ?

In 1647 and 1653 the passage runs:

And why a Tenant to this vile disguise . . . ?

625. 8. *sheep-skin.* Hutchinson (addition to GM) compares Heb. xi. 37.

625. 13. *Thou flying Roll, &c.* A combination of Ezek. ii. 9 and Zech. v. 1–2. (GM.)

625. 21–2. *Purim . . . Wilderness.* GM suggests that Vaughan means not the feast of Purim (Esther iii. 7, &c.) but the day of Atonement, when the scapegoat is driven into the wilderness (Lev. xvi. 8 sqq.).

625. 31. *Zeal.* Cf. 470. 40.

626. *The Eagle.* See *Life*, 87.

628. *To Mr. M. L., &c.* Probably not Matthew Locke, whose setting of the Psalms to music was not published. 'Method' may signify metre rather than a musical setting. See *Life*, 217.

629 (*heading*). *C. W. Esquire.* Vaughan's cousin and neighbour, Charles Walbeoffe. See *Life*, 124–5, 255, &c.

629. 12. *As Gloworms, &c.* Cf. 642. 16. (GM.)

629. 21. *my sad retirements.* Hutchinson, *Life* 197, suggests that Vaughan may refer to 'a period of mourning after his first wife's death, but . . . more probably . . . to his sickness'. Cf. title-page of *Flores Solitudinis*, 1654 (211 above).

630. 59–60. *Key, &c.* See note to 455. 4–5. (H.)

631. 79. *yield.* Consent.

631. 85–6. *thick, black night, &c.* Cf. 217. 34–6. *Forlorn.* Vanguard.

631. *In Zodiacum, &c.* The *Zodiacus Vitae*, first published in ?1531, is quoted by Vaughan in his note on 176 above.

632. *To Lysimachus.* Chambers (ll. 340–1) suggests that this may have been one of the pseudonyms adopted by members of Orinda's coterie. See note to 57 (heading). The name reappears in the heading of the poem beginning on p. 638.

632. 21–2. *one could tell, &c.* Cf. Jonson, *Underwoods*, liii, Epigram to the Earl of Newcastle, ll. 9–10:

Or what we heare our home-borne Legend tell,
Of bold Sir *Bevis*, and his *Arundell*. (GM.)

633. 23. *Lucilius.* The younger, to whom some of Seneca's works were addressed.

634. 44. *Walsam.* Walsingham, as a place of pilgrimage.

634. 52. *one Letter of thy name.* Sc. T, the shape of the Library when the Arts End was added to Duke Humphrey's Library. The T

became an H in 1640 when the Selden End was added. This reference to the earlier shape, together with the apparent reminiscences
in ll. 39 and 53–4, may indicate that the poem was written while
Vaughan was a student. See *Life*, 31.

634. *The importunate Fortune.* Cf. ' In Amicum fœneratorem' and
' To his friend' (pp. 43–5). 'Fortune' (which the poet addresses)
here = wealth. Cf. Randolph ' On the Inestimable Content he
injoyes in the Muses' (ed. cit. pp. 23–8).

635. 35. *Stamps.* Coins.

635. 39–40. *those three . . . Stories.* Accepted theory divided the air
into three portions.

635. 41. *in Capite.* Direct from the King.

636. 57–77. This passage appears to be based on one in Libellus i.
24–26 a, of the *Hermetica* (ed. W. Scott, i. 129): 'And thereupon [at
the dissolution of the material body] the man mounts upward through
the structure of the heavens. And to the first zone of heaven he
gives up the force which works increase and . . . decrease; to the
second zone, the machinations of evil cunning; to the third zone,
the lust whereby men are deceived; to the fourth zone, domineering
arrogance; to the fifth zone, unholy daring and rash audacity; to
the sixth zone, evil strivings after wealth; and to the seventh zone,
the falsehood which lies in wait to work harm. And thereupon,
having been stripped of all that was wrought upon him by the structure of the heavens, he ascends to the substance of the eighth sphere,
being now possessed of his own proper power . . .'

636. 75–90. See note on 401–2. 19–70, section 3 (*c*) and (*e*).

636. 80. *the Emanations of the Deitie.* Cf. *Hermetica*, Libellus x. 22 b
(ed. W. Scott, i. 203): 'The divine forces are . . . radiations emitted
by God; the forces that work birth [see Vaughan's l. 86] and growth
are radiations emitted by the Kosmos . . .'

637. 105. *My purse as Randolph's was.* See Randolph, 'A parley
with his empty Purse' (ed. cit. p. 127).

637. 106. *to.* Compared to.

637. *l. Morgan of White-Hall.* John Morgan of Wenallt (or White
Hill), a neighbour and kinsman of Vaughan. See *Life*, 217, &c.;
also, for pedigree, Chambers, ii. 349.

638. 27–8. Cf. 40. 60.

638. *Fida.* The name occurs in Browne's *Britannia's Pastorals*, i. 3,
&c. (GM.)

638. 3. *A face, &c.* Cf. 7. 22. (GM.)

641 (*Fida forsaken*). **14.** *descri'd.* Emendation suggested by GM.

641. *the matchless Orinda.* Mrs. Katherine Philips. See note on 61
(second heading).

642. *Judge Trevers.* Arthur Trevor, Puisne Judge of the Brecon
circuit 1661–1666/7. See *Life*, 217–18.

643 (*heading*). *To Etesia.* See 6:8. 15–16 and note. 'Etesia' is from
ἐτησίαι (sc. ἄνεμοι), the winds that blow during the dog-days; hence
summer-like. GM observes that W. Browne uses the name in
Britannia's Pastorals, ii. 3. 1168. See also 81 (second poem). 7 and
note.

644. 19–20. Cf. 7 (*To Amoret*). 14–15.

645. 44. *to.* To the point of.

645. 46. Cf. 62. 30. (H.)

649. 35-48. Enlarged from Boethius, iii, *Met.* xii, ll. 27-30 :

> Et dulci ueniam prece
> Umbrarum dominos rogat.
> Stupet tergeminus novo
> Captus carmine ianitor . . .

651. 6. *and shew our wars.* Vaughan's addition.

650. 33 4. *For things of weight, &c.* Vaughan's amplification.

652. 43-9. V's amplification. Cf. 401. 35-50.

653. 68-70. V's addition, possibly with reference to Harvey's doctrine.

653. 79-80. Cf. Boethius, iv, *Met.* vi. 47-8 :

> Nisi converso rursus amore
> Refluant causae, quae dedit esse.

654 (*Metr.* 6). 15-24. Much amplified from Boethius.

655. 13-24. *by fruits, not Consuls, &c.* Vaughan is indebted to Randolph's translation of the same poem : '*De Sene* Veronensi. *Ex* Claudiano' (*Poems*, ed. cit. p. 49) :

> From fruits, not Consuls, computation brings,
> By Apples, Autumnes knows, by flowers the Springs.
> Thus he the day by his owne orbe doth prize ;
> In the same feild his Sunne doth set and rise.
> That knew an oake a twigge, and walking thither
> Beholds a wood and he grown up together.
> Neighbou'ring *Veron* he may for *India* take,
> And thinke the *Red Sea* is *Benacus* lake.
> Yet is his strength untam'd, and firme his knees,
> Him the third age a lusty Grandsire sees.
> Goe seeke who s' will the farre *Iberian* shore,
> This man hath liv'd, though that hath travel'd more.

655-6. 1-14. *When Jove, &c.* Vaughan is indebted to Randolph's translation of the same poem : '*In Archimedis Sphæram ex Claudiano*' (ed. cit. p. 46) :

> Jove saw the Heavens fram'd in a little glasse,
> And laughing, to the Gods these words did passe ;
> Comes then the power of mortall cares so farre?
> In brittle Orbes my labours acted are.
> The statutes of the Poles, the faith of things,
> The Laws of Gods this *Syracusian* brings
> Hither by art : Spirits inclos'd attend
> Their severall spheares, and with set motions bend
> The living worke : Each yeare the faigned Sun,
> Each Month returnes the counterfeited Moon ;
> And viewing now her world, bold Industrie
> Grows proud, to know the heavens her subjects bee.
> Beleive *Salmonius* hath false thunders thrown,
> For a poore hand is Natures rivall grown.

660. 5-8. *When I by thoughts, &c.* Cf. 421. 1-4.

661 (*The Shower*). 1. *Waters above, &c.* Cf. 498. 49, and 511. 21. (GM.)

661 (*Discipline*). 3. Cf. l. 14 ; but 'moule' and 'mulle' are spellings recorded in *O.E.D.*

661 (*Discipline*). 4. *chains of darkness*. 2 Pet. ii. 4. (H.)

661. 15. *Give him, &c.* Cf. G. Herbert, 'Miserie', l. 46 (*Works*, p. 101):
> Give him his dirt to wallow in all night.

661 (*The Ecclipse*). The beginning is like that of Herbert's 'The Search' (*Works*, p. 162), and there are also resemblances to Herbert's 'Ephes. 4. 30.', 'And art thou grieved' (*Works*, p. 135). (GM.)

661. 7-8. *break my heart*. Cf. G. Herbert, 'Dialogue', l. 32 (*Works*, p. 115).

663. 25. *heav'n lyes Leiguer*. See note to 440. 25.

663 (*The Revival*). 7-14. Cf. Song of Sol. ii. 11-12 and vi. 2-3.

664. 47-8. Cf. 67. 29-30. (H.)

665 (*The Recovery*). 10. *back-parts*. Exod. xxxiii. 23. (GM.)

665. 17. *that Sun, &c.* Cf. G. Herbert, 'Jordan' (II), ll. 11-12 (*Works*, p. 102):
> Nothing could seem too rich to clothe the sunne,
> Much lesse those joyes which trample on his head. (H.)

665 (*The Nativity*). 9. *A Tax? 'tis so still.* Vaughan probably refers to the Decimation Tax imposed on Royalists in 1655. The tax was extended at the end of 1656 so as to fall on lower incomes. (Gardiner, *Commonwealth and Protectorate*, Supplement, p. 1.)

666. *The true Christmas.* Probably written near the time of the preceding poem. See *Life*, 218.

667 (*The Request*). 7-8. *Keep still, &c.* Cf. Ps. cxix. 37. (H.)

667. 24. *thy great self.* Cf. 673. 76. (H.)

667. 28. *Crowns Imperial.* See note to 478. 1-4.

668. *Servilii Fatum.* Chambers suggested that Vaughan alludes to P. Servilius Casca, and through him to one of the regicides, Bradshaw or Ireton. See *Life*, 218-19. EB thought that Vaughan may also have had in mind Pliny, *Nat. Hist.* vii. 53 (54). 182, where among examples of people who 'nullis evidentibus causis obiere' mention is made of 'C. Servilius Pansa, cum staret in foro ad tabernam hora diei secunda in P. fratrem innixus'—although among 'felicia exempla'.

669. 14. *bis moriturus.* Cf. Boethius, *Met.* ii. 7 (6 in Vaughan's translation, p. 84, l. 24 above). See also 456. 8 and note.

670. 16. *give Loosers leave to speak.* Sc. after judgement. Cf. G. Herbert, 'A Dialogue-Antheme', l. 7 (*Works*, p. 169): 'Let losers talk.' (GM.) See also Tilley, *Proverbs in England*, L458, 'Give Losers leave to speak.'

670. 21, 23, 33, 41, 45. *Thou art not Truth, &c.* GM compares *Measure for Measure*, III. 1. 13 sqq. Hutchinson notes also the resemblance to Herbert's 'The Pearl' (*Works*, p. 88).

670. 29-30. *out and in . . . skin.* GM compares G. Herbert, 'Giddinesse', ll. 17-20 (*Works*, p. 127):
> O what a sight were Man, if his attires
> Did alter with his minde;
> And like a Dolphins skinne, his clothes combin'd
> With his desires!

671. 84–5. *not as Witt, &c.* Cf. 673. 63–8. (GM.)

672. 1. *From fruitful beds, &c.* Cf. G. Herbert, 'Sunday', ll. 26–7 (*Works*, p. 75):

> They are the fruitfull beds and borders
> In Gods rich garden.

673. 52. *Hilarion's servant.* See note to 184. 2.

673. 65–6. Cf. 531. 35–6. (H.)

674. 90. *forms.* Parterres.

674. 105–6. *like a laden Bee, &c.* Hutchinson compares to G. Herbert, 'The Starre', ll. 30–1 (*Works*, p. 74):

> To flie home like a laden bee
> Unto that hive of beams.

674–5. 9–14. *A Seer, &c.* Hutchinson points out that Vaughan here summarizes G. Herbert's 'The Church Militant' (*Works*, pp. 190–8). Vaughan mentions the poem in his second note on p. 186 above.

676–80. *Daphnis.* It is possible, as Hutchinson suggests (*Life*, 220–2), that this poem was first written for the death of William Vaughan in 1648 and adapted for the death in 1666 of Thomas Vaughan, who is clearly referred to in ll. 113–16. See also note to ll. 37–8. Vaughan emphasizes youth in ll. 25 sqq.

676. 25. *Primrose.* Cf. 417. 10 (in a poem apparently on the death of William Vaughan).

677. 37–8. *Who doubly dark, &c.* Evidently with reference to Dr. Henry More's criticisms of Thomas Vaughan's works. Henry Vaughan was not the first to make the pun in l. 38. Cf. Thomas's pamphlet, *The Second Wash: Or the Moore Scour'd once more* ... 1651, answering More's *The Second Lash of Alazonomastix.*

677. 42. *Palm-like, &c.* See note on 490. 7–9.

677. 45. *port-vein.* 'called the port-veine, because it is as it were the doore of the liuer out of which it proceedeth': La Primaudaye, *Fr. Acad.*, 1594, ii. 356 (cited in *O.E.D.*).

677. 47–50. *I saw an Oak, &c.* See *Life*, 20–21.

677. 55 and 62. *Amphion.* Perhaps Matthew Herbert, as Chambers suggested. See 32. 6 and note.

677. 61. *our black, but brightest Bard.* Miss Guiney, in *Quarterly Rev.*, April 1914, p. 356, suggests that this is Myrddin Emrys (Merlin Ambrosius), and mentions Thomas Heywood's *The Life of Merlin ... His Prophesies, and Predictions Interpreted* ... 1641. Cf. title of *The Mad-merry Merlin, or the Black Almanack*, 1653.

678. 77–8. Cf. 248. 32–5. (GM.)

678. 79–82. *light ... clouds.* Cf. 217. 36–7, 'light ... darknes'.

679. 113–16. *For though, &c.* See Vaughan's letters to Aubrey of 15 June and 7 July 1673 (viz. pp. 687–8 and 691). Aubrey annotated the first of these two letters on 8 July: 'As to my cosen Tho: Vaughan he [sc. Sir Robert Moray] told me he buryed him at Albury neer Ricot within three miles of Oxon. he dyed at Mr. Kem's house, the Minister.' Hutchinson, *Life*, 145, notes that 'the Thames, known in its Oxford reaches as the Isis, is not near Albury, but the Thame flows half a mile from the church and eventually joins the Thames at the Oxfordshire Dorchester'. For more on the circumstances of Thomas's death see *Life*, 144–6. On Sir Robert Moray see ibid. 144 and Vaughan's letter, p. 687 above, ll. 16–17.

679. 137-42. Cf. 460. 5-16.

680. 170. *Lycanthe.* Apparently not a classical name. It occurs, however, in Gombauld's *Endimion*, praised by Vaughan (pp. 48-9 above), Hurst's translation, 1639, book ii, p. 65 : ' I heard a Nymph, who calling aloud for her Dogge, cryed sundry times, *Licanthe, Licanthe.*'

HUMANE INDUSTRY (THOMAS POWELL).

In this volume there are many fragmentary translations besides those given here ; but they are not specially assigned to Vaughan. One is by Thomas May ; the rest may be by Powell himself. For Powell see p. 690 and note on 33 (title-page).

683. (*Cap. xi*). 2. *the Apostles saying.* James iii. 7.

684. 18. *Hares by Lions.* This may be a misprint for ' Lions by Hares', though it is possible that Vaughan misunderstood his text, if he had no more than is given on p. 683.

THE EXCISE-MAN (EZEKIEL POLSTED).

684. These verses are printed immediately after a commendatory poem by ' John Morgan senior de Wenallt in Com. Brecon'. Cf. heading of poem on p. 637 above. Hutchinson first reprinted the verses in *Life*, 222. The verses are in the satirical spirit which governs Polsted's volume throughout.

APPENDIX I. DUBIA.

685-6. (1) The signature to the lines in *Eucharistica Oxoniensia,* as pointed out by Chambers (ii, p. xxviii), might equally well be that of Henry Vaughan, M.A., Fellow of Jesus College at the time, or of Herbert Vaughan, who was a Gentleman-Commoner in 1641. Neither of these, however, seems to be known otherwise as an English poet. ' Hen. Vaugh. *Ies. Soc.*' has Latin verses in *Eucharistica Oxoniensia,* and both he and Herbert Vaughan contributed verses to ΠΡΟΤΕΛΕΙΑ *Anglo-Batava . . . Oxoniæ . . .* 1641.

686. (2) These lines have sometimes been ascribed to Vaughan because of his friendship with the author of the book and because the signature can be interpreted to mean ' Olor Vaughan '. But Vaughan would probably not have abbreviated the distinctive word ; he would rather have given the complete title ' Olor Iscanus'. The lines are printed, from an eighteenth-century Welsh manuscript, in *Y Cymmrodor*, xi, part 2, p. 223, with variants. They are not there ascribed to Vaughan. See Hutchinson, *Life*, 157.

686. (3) The text of the epitaph, first printed by Theo. Jones, *Hist. Breck.*, 1809, ii, p. 532, is as it is given by W. F. Stead in *T.L.S.* 8 Feb. 1952 (p. 116) under heading ' Some unknown verses by Vaughan ? ' Miss G. E. F. Morgan was inclined to attribute the verses to Vaughan, and Mr. Stead points to the connexions between the Vaughan and Jones families as favouring this attribution. In l. 17 the phrase ' but not too young ', which makes the verse irregular, was perhaps written into the manuscript by someone other than the poet. The touch of primitivism in l. 18 suggests Vaughan's authorship, though not at all conclusively.

APPENDIX II. LETTERS.

The proper names in the letters might often have been printed in italics to correspond with the larger hand in which they are written, and in accordance with contemporary usage. But as they are not always made sufficiently distinct, roman type has been used throughout. 'D^r', 'w^{ch}', &c. are, in the MSS., usually accompanied by a dot under or after the raised letters. The lists of works on pp. 687–8 and 690 are inset in narrow columns.

687. 3. *our Bishops Lady.* Martha, wife of William Lucy, Bishop of St. Davids, residing at Christ College, Brecon. See *Life*, 194.

The biographical material given here was used as a basis for the lives of Henry and Thomas Vaughan in *Historia et Antiquitates Universitatis Oxoniensis*, 1674, and in *Athenae Oxonienses*.

687. 9. *I stayed not att Oxford.* See Introduction, p. xvii.

687. 16. *Sr Robert Murrey.* See *Life*, 144.

688. 40–1 *his discourse de genèratione.* Translated as *The Chymists Key.* See p. 593.

688. 44–5. *many . . . lost.* Cf. *Thalia Rediviva*, 1678, p. 93, at end of Thomas Vaughan's *Choice Poems*: 'Desiderantur *Alcippus* & *Jacintha* (Poema Heroicum absolutissimum,) cum multis aliis Oxonii ab Authore relictis.'

688. 47. *Dr Powell.* See p. 690 and note on 33 (title-page).

688. 51–2. *Dr. Thomas Ellis.* See *D.N.B.*

688. 58–60. *ordayned . . . Vaughan.* See *Life*, 91–4.

689. 75. *My Cousin Walbeoffe.* See *Life*, 124–5 and 206–7.

689. 79–86. Aubrey notes 'I p^d 3^d for y^s'.

690. 15. *Recveil, &c.* The letters of Jean Louis Guez, seigneur de Balzac, were several times translated in the seventeenth century, but no translation bears Powell's name. That of 1654 was by Sir R. Baker 'and others'. That of 1658 was anonymous.

690. 24. *& not yet printed.* Apparently never printed.

690. 34–5. *not traduced (as one hath done).* Presumably the version published in 1647, without translator's name.

691. 45. *S^{ir} John.* Sc. Aubrey. See *Life*, 207.

692. 17. *Dr Plott.* See *D.N.B.* art. Plot, Robert. Cf. Aubrey's letter to Wood of 19 March 1680/1 (Bodl. MS. Ballard xiv, f. 80): 'When you see Dr. Plott, mind him to send me halfe a dozen printed Queres, wch I would send to my Cosen Hen: Vaughan in Breck[nock?]shire, whom I have engaged to follow his method. he has great & steady practise there, & may unâ fidelia duos dealbare parietes. He is very fitt for † †.'

693. 41. *Mr Hookes lodgings.* See *D.N.B.* art. Hooke, Robert (1635–1703).

694. 5. *Dr John David Rhesus.* See *D.N.B.* art. Rhys, Ioan Dafydd; also 695. 6–12 and Aubrey's life (Bodl. MS. Aubrey 8, f. 11): 'he wrote a Compendium of Aristotles Metaphysiques in the British Language, mentioned in his Eple [to S^r ... Stradling] before his Welsh Gramēr. 'Twas in Jesus-coll. library Oxd. & my cos. Henry Vaughan [Olor Iscans] had it in his custody ... I have [sent ?] to H. Vaughan for it.' Wood (ed. Bliss, ii. 62) observes : 'He hath written other excellent things, but are lost, as I have been assured by OLOR ISCANUS.'

694. 7-8. *the Stradlings.* Sir Edward (1529-1609) and Sir John (1563-1637), q.v. *D.N.B.*

694. 8. *a learned friend.* See 695. 3 and note to 615 (signature).

695. Letter VI was presented to the Bodleian Library in 1910 by Mr. Aleck Abrahams and first printed in *Life*, 210.

695. 8. *Authour of the welch Dictionarie.* Wood writes in the margin 'I said no such thing'. The author was John Davies, D.D. (1570 ?- 1644), q.v. in *D.N.B.* His *Antiquæ linguæ Britannicæ Dictionarium duplex* was published in 1632.

696. 25-35. Aubrey writes in the margin : 'In Michael Psellus de Daemonibus is a story parallell to this, of one that dreamt a Crow flew into his mouth & entrails, whereby he had the gift of Prophesie ...' See *M. Pselli De Operatione dæmonum Dialogus* (edition of 1615, pp. 62-3).

697. 49. *Dr Thomas Gale.* 1635 ?-1702. High Master of St. Paul's School 1672-97. See *D.N.B.*

697-9. *Letters. B. I and II.* For accounts of the circumstances in which these two letters were written see *Life*, 199-200 and 231-7.

ADDITIONAL NOTES

401. 35-37. *Nor ... all.* Cf. Browne, *Rel. Med.* i. 48 : 'the formes ... perish not ;' (ed. Martin, p. 46, 6-8 ; see notes on pp. 265 and 307). Also Ovid, *Met.* xv. 252-8, and Macrobius, *In Somnium Scipionis*, ii. 12 : '... nihil intra mundum perire,' &c.

452. 18. *thy shadow ... the light.* Cf. Ralegh, *History of the World*, I. i. 11, 'Of Fate' (1614, p. 15): *Lumen est Vmbra Dei*'; and Browne, *Rel. Med.* i. 10 (ed. Martin, p. 10, 19-20 ; see note on p. 291).

505. 15. *A fish ... pay.* Matt. xvii. 27.

528. 33. *Tithes.* Gen. xxviii. 22.

533 (*Death*). **3.** *six thousand years.* A commonly accepted estimate for the duration of the world. Cf. Browne, *Religio Medici*, i. 46.

625. 12. *Esdras books.* 2 Esdras xiv. 26, 44-46.

INDEX OF FIRST LINES.

The poems marked * are fragments and translations to be found among the prose works. Those marked † are commendatory poems addressed to Vaughan.

DATE DUE

APR 7 1976			

GAYLORD   PRINTED IN U.S.A.